THE

YAKUZA

MOVIE

BOOK

THE YAKUZA MOVIE BOOK

A GUIDE TO JAPANESE GANGSTER FILMS

MARK SCHILLING

STONE BRIDGE PRESS • BERKELEY, CALIFORNIA

Published by
Stone Bridge Press, P.O. Box 8208, Berkeley, CA 94707
TEL 510-524-8732 • sbp@stonebridge.com • www.stonebridge.com

Every effort has been made to contact the copyright owners of the images reproduced in this book. Omissions brought to our attention will be corrected in subsequent editions. We gratefully acknowledge the following for granting permission to use their material in this book: Excellent Films, Film Partners, For Life Music Entertainment, Inc., Gaga Communications Inc., Image Factory IM, Teruo Ishii, KSS, Inc., Kadokawa-Daiei Pictures, Inc., Mamiko Kawamoto, Little More Co., Ltd., Miura Photo, New Wave, Nikkatsu Corporation, Office Kitano, Ogura Jimusho, Pony Canyon, Production Ryuji, Scorpion, Shochiku, Toei Company, Ltd., Toei Video, Tsukumo Shobo, and York Entertainment (USA).

Book design and layout by Linda Ronan. Image on front cover used by permission of Toei Company, Ltd.

Printed in the United States of America.
10 9 8 7 6 5 4 3 2 1   2008 2007 2006 2005 2004 2003

LIBRARY OF CONGRESS CATALOGING-IN-PUBLICATION DATA
Schilling, Mark.
  The yakuza movie book: a guide to Japanese gangster films / Mark Schilling.
    p. cm.
  ISBN 1-880656-76-0
    1. Gangster films—Japan—History and criticism. I. Title.
PN1995.9.G3 S33 2003
791.43'655—dc21
                        2003003855

To Mark Schreiber, my partner in crime

CONTENTS

11   *Foreword*

INTRODUCTION

19   A Brief History of Japanese Yakuza Films

DIRECTOR PROFILES & INTERVIEWS

43   Kinji Fukasaku (1930–2003)
Kinji Fukasaku Interview 46

55   Teruo Ishii (1924–)
Teruo Ishii Interview 57

70   Tai Kato (1916–85)

73   Takeshi Kitano ("Beat" Takeshi; 1947–)

76   Takashi Miike (1960–)
Takashi Miike Interview 78

85   Rokuro Mochizuki (1957–)
Rokuro Mochizuki Interview 87

95   Seijun Suzuki (1923–)
Seijun Suzuki Interview 98

ACTOR PROFILES & INTERVIEWS

109   Show Aikawa (1961–)
Show Aikawa Interview 110

119   Noboru Ando (1926–)
Noboru Ando Interview 121

123   Junko Fuji (1945–)

125   Shintaro Katsu (1931–97)

126   Akira Kobayashi (1937–)

127   Hiroki Matsukata (1942–)

128   Jo Shishido (1933–)

130   Bunta Sugawara (1933–)
Bunta Sugawara Interview 132

143   Ken Takakura (1931–)

145   Riki Takeuchi (1964–)

146   Koji Tsuruta (1924–87)

148   Tatsuo Umemiya (1938–)

149   Tomisaburo Wakayama (1929–92)

150   Tetsuya Watari (1941–)

FILM REVIEWS

155   *A Homansu* (1986)

156   *Abashiri Bangaichi* (A Man from Abashiri Prison, 1965)

156   *Abashiri Bangaichi: Bokyohen* (A Man from Abashiri Prison: Going Home, 1965)

157   *Adrenaline Drive* (1999)

158   *Akumyo* (Tough Guy, 1961)

159   *American Yakuza* (1994)

160   *Ankokugai no Kaoyaku* (The Big Boss, 1959)

161   *Asu Naki Machikado* (End of Our Own Real, 1997)

162 *Bakuchiuchi Socho Tobaku* (Big Gambling Ceremony, 1968)

164 *Bakuto Gaijin Butai* (Sympathy for the Underdog, 1971)

167 *Bakuto Kaisanshiki* (Gambler's Dispersion, 1968)

168 *Blood* (1998)

169 *Bo no Kanashimi* (Hard-Head Fool, 1994)

170 *Brother* (2000)

172 *Burai Yori Daikanbu* (Gangster VIP, 1968)

173 *Chinpira* (1996)

174 *Chinpira* (Chinpira/Two Punks, 2000)

176 *Choeki Juhachinen* (Sentence: Eighteen Years, 1967)

178 *Chuji Tabi Nikki* (Diary of Chuji's Travels, 1927)

179 *Dead or Alive: Hanzaisha* (Dead or Alive, 1999)

180 *Don e no Michi* (The Road to Bossdom, 2003)

182 *Don o Totta Otoko* (The Man Who Shot the Don, 1994)

183 *Freeze Me* (2000)

183 *Fukushu: Kienai Kizu Ato* (The Revenge: The Scar that Never Fades, 1997)

184 *Full Metal Gokudo* (Full Metal Yakuza, 1997)

186 *Fuyajo* (Sleepless Town, 1998)

187 *Gang tai G-men* (Gang versus G-men, 1962)

188 *Gedo* (The Outer Way, 1998)

190 *Gendai Yakuza: Hitokiri Yota* (Street Mobster, 1972)

191 *Gokudo Kuro Shakai Rainy Dog* (Rainy Dog, 1997)

193 *Gokudo no Ane: Reiko* (Gang Lady: Reiko, 1994)

193 *Gokudo no Onnatachi* (Gang Wives, 1986)

197 *Gokudo no Onnatachi: Kejime* (Gang Wives: Decision, 1998)

198 *Gokudo Sengokushi Fudo* (Fudoh: The New Generation, 1996)

200 *Gonin* (1995)

201 *Gorotsuki* (Tough Guys, 1992)

202 *Hana to Arashi to Gang* (Flower and Storm and Gang, 1961)

203 *Hana to Doto* (Flower and the Angry Waves, 1964)

206 *Harukana Jidai no Kaidan o* (The Stairway to the Distant Past, 1994)

207 *Heitai Yakuza* (Hoodlum Soldier, 1965)

208 *Hibotan Bakuto: Hanafuda Shobu* (Red Peony Gambler: Flower Cards Match, 1969)

210 *Hibotan Bakuto: Oinochi Itadakimasu* (Red Peony Gambler: Death to the Wicked, 1971)

211 *Irezumi Ichidai* (One Generation of Tattoos, 1965)

212 *Jingi Naki Tatakai* (Battles without Honor and Humanity, 1973)

214 *Jingi Naki Tatakai: Hiroshima Shitohen* (Battles without Honor and Humanity 2: Fight to the Death at Hiroshima, 1973)

216 *Jingi Naki Tatakai: Dairi Senso* (Battles without Honor and Humanity 3: Proxy War, 1973)

217 *Jingi Naki Tatakai: Chojo Sakusen* (Battles without Honor and Humanity 4: High Tactics, 1974)

218 *Jingi Naki Tatakai: Kanketsuhen* (Battles without Honor and Humanity 5: The Final Episode, 1974)

219 *Jingi no Hakaba* (Graveyard of Honor, 1975)

221 *Jinsei Gekijo: Hishakaku* (Theater of Life:

Hishakaku, 1963)

222 *Jinsei Gekijo: Hishakaku to Kiratsune* (Theater of Life: Hishakaku and Kiratsune, 1968)

224 *Jitsuroku Ando Gumi Gaiden: Garo no Okite* (The True History of the Ando Gang: Rules of the Starving Wolf, 2002)

226 *Jitsuroku Ando Noboru Outlaw-den: Rekka* (Deadly Outlaw: Rekka, 2002)

227 *Juichinin no Gang* (Eleven Gangsters, 1963)

228 *Kamikaze Taxi* (1995)

229 *Kanto Mushuku* (Kanto Wanderer, 1963)

231 *Kaoyaku* (Boss, 1965)

232 *Karakkaza Yaro* (Afraid to Die, 1960)

233 *Katte ni Shiyagare!! Godatsu Keikaku* (Suit Yourself or Shoot Yourself: Extortion Plot 1, 1995)

235 *Kawaita Hana* (Pale Flower, 1964)

236 *Keisho Sakazuki* (Succession Ceremony, 1992)

237 *Kids Return* (1996)

238 *Kishiwada Shonen Gurentai* (Boys, Be Ambitious, 1996)

239 *Kizuna* (Ties, 1998)

240 *Koroshiya Ichi* (Ichi the Killer, 2001)

241 *Kunisada Chuji* (1958)

242 *Kurenai no Nagareboshi* (The Velvet Hustler, 1967)

243 *Kuro no Tenshi, Vol. 1* (Black Angel, Vol. 1, 1998)

245 *Kutsukake Tokijiro* (1929)

246 *Kyohansha* (Partners in Crime, 1999)

247 *Level* (1994)

249 *Matatabi* (The Wanderers, 1973)

250 *Meiji Kyokakuden: Sandai Shumei* (Blood of Revenge, 1965)

251 *Minazuki* (Everyone's a Moon, 1999)

252 *Minbo no Onna* (The Gentle Art of Japanese Extortion, 1992)

253 *Mukokuseki no Otoko: Chi no Shukaku* (Pinocchio: A Man without Nationality, 1997)

254 *Narazumono* (The Untamed, 1964)

255 *Nihon Kuroshakai Ley Lines* (1999)

257 *Nihon Kyokakuden: Naniwahen* (1965)

258 *Nihon Kyokakuden: Shiraha no Sakazuki* (1967)

259 *Nihon Boryokudan: Kumicho* (Japan Organized Crime Boss, 1969)

260 *No Way Back: Toso Yugi* (No Way Back, 1995)

261 *Nobody* (1994)

263 *Oedo Gonin Otoko* (Five Men from Edo, 1951)

264 *Onibi* (The Fire Within, 1997)

265 *Otoko no Monsho* (Symbol of a Man, 1963)

268 *Otokotachi no Kaita E* (The Man with Two Hearts, 1996)

269 *PornoStar* (1999)

271 *Ryuji* (1983)

272 *Shiawase ni Naro ne* (Let's Get Happy, 1998)

274 *Shin Jingi Naki Tatakai* (Another Battle, 2000)

276 *Shin Jingi Naki Tatakai: Bosatsu* (Another Battle: Conspiracy, 2003)

277 *Shin Jingi no Hakaba* (Graveyard of Honor, 2002)

278 *Shin Kanashiki Hitman* (Another Lonely Hitman, 1995)

280 *Shinjuku Kuro Shakai China Mafia Senso* (Shinjuku Triad Society, 1995)

281 *Shinjuku Yokubo Tantei* (The Hungry Shinjuku Detective, 1994)

283 *Showa Zankyoden: Shinde Moraimasu* (Remnants of Chivalry in the Showa Era: I Want You to Die, 1970)

284 *Shuraba ga Yuku* (The Carnage Comes, 1995)

286 *Shuraba no Gokudo: Hebi no Michi* (Serpent's Path, 1997)

287 *Shuraba no Ningengaku* (The Anthropology of a Fight Scene, 1993)

288 *Shuraba no Okami: Kumo no Hitomi* (Eyes of the Spider, 1997)

289 *Sonatine* (1993)

291 *3–4 X Jugatsu* (Boiling Point, 1990)

292 *Tokyo Gang tai Hong Kong Gang* (Tokyo Gang versus Hong Kong Gang, 1964)

293 *Tokyo Mafia: Yakuza Wars* (1995)

295 *Tokyo Nagaremono* (Tokyo Drifter, 1966)

295 *Unlucky Monkey* (1998)

297 *Waga Jinsei Saiaku no Toki* (The Most Terrible Time in My Life, 1993)

299 *Waka Oyabun* (Young Boss, 1965)

300 *Wakaki Hi no Jirocho* (The Young Days of Jirocho, 1962)

301 *Watashi no Grandpa* (My Grandpa, 2003)

303 *Wild Life* (1997)

303 *Yaju no Seishun* (Youth of the Beast, 1963)

305 *Yaju Shisubeshi: Fukushuhen* (The Beast Must Die: Revenge, 1997)

306 *Yakuza, The* (1975)

308 *Yakuza Keibatsushi: Lynch!* (A History of Yakuza Punishments: Lynch!, 1969)

309 *Yakuza no Hakaba: Kuchinashi no Hana* (Yakuza Burial: Jasmine Flower, 1976)

310 *Yakuza Way, The* (1998)

311 *Yamaguchi Gaiden Kyushu Shinko Sakusen* (The Tattooed Hitman, 1974)

313 *Yoidore Tenshi* (Drunken Angel, 1948)

314 *Yurusarezaru Mono* (The Man in White, 2003)

315 *Zankyo* (Remnants of Chivalry, 1999)

318 *Zatoichi Monogatari* (The Tale of Zatoichi, 1962)

323 *Glossary*

325 *Bibliography*

326 *Video & DVD Sources*

328 *Finding Guides*

FOREWORD

Why a book about Japanese gangster movies? Aren't there more worthy topics than a disreputable genre whose real-life models are mainly thugs with retrograde ideas about women, minorities, the emperor, and nearly everything under the sun? And whose fans are mainly men blowing off work in seedy theaters or watching videos alone in rented rooms? Yes, more worthy topics may exist, but there are also reasons for examining the genre at length. One is the sheer number—thousands of movies have been produced over a period of eight decades, with dozens more released every year. If one counts all the films in which yakuza, Japan's home-grown gangsters, play an important role—everything from villains to comic foils—the total soars far higher.

The samurai drama was once the Japanese film industry's single most dominant genre, from the silent period onward. But since the beginning of the television era, four decades ago, the genre has largely retreated to the small screen. Meanwhile, the yakuza film, cheaper and easier to produce, superseded it in the theaters, then on the video shelves, supported by a large, if almost entirely male, audience.

The films themselves long got little respect from critics and scholars, whose attitudes ranged from the dismissive to the condescending. But just as once lightly regarded makers of Hollywood studio product—from Howard Hawks to John Ford—rose in critical esteem, so have directors of Japanese gangster films. Tai Kato, Seijun Suzuki, Kinji Fukasaku, and Takeshi Kitano now receive the sort of attention, from retrospectives to book-length studies, once accorded the most impeccably high-minded of auteurs. Meanwhile, movie geeks who once worshipped Hong Kong cult icons like Tsui Hark or John Woo are now celebrating the latest cinematic outrage by Takashi Miike, the new outlaw master of the yakuza genre. Some of this attention is critical front running or fan-boy raving, but some of it is justified. Within all the formula product that is out there, assembled like so many box lunches on an assembly line, gems do exist; many are all but unknown abroad.

One often-heard slam against the yakuza film is its repetitiveness—the endless variations on the theme of revenge. But directors of the genre's Golden Age, including Kato, Suzuki, and Fukasaku, injected their own styles and concerns into these often-told stories. While filling studio schedules, they were able to perfect their craft in ways now impossible with the dismantling of the studio system. Like Ford and Hawks, these directors learned to dance in their chains—or discard them altogether.

Today, Miike is still turning out gang films at a ferocious pace but doing so with relatively fewer resources than were available to Golden Age studio filmmakers, particularly for the straight-to-video product that accounts for most of his work. Even so, he has more freedom than his elders—and uses it to create some of the wilder imaginative flights in contemporary Japanese cinema. Meanwhile, others of his generation, including Shinji Aoyama, Junji Sakamoto, and Kiyoshi Kurosawa, are also reinventing the genre in films that, far from being slumming expeditions, rank among the best of their work.

Gangsters are not nice people, really. Yet, movies have a way of romanticizing them, making them seem, if not always noble, then larger than life. From *Public Enemy* to *The Godfather* to *Goodfellas*, Hollywood movie gangsters have not only shocked audiences with their crimes but impressed them with their toughness, cool, and, in the case of Don Vito Corleone and his successors, values.

Hollywood, however, has never made gangster movies the way it once made Westerns or now makes action movies, in large quantities, as a bread-and-butter genre. In the early days, censors frowned on the gangster films, fretting that George Raft, James Cagney, and Edward G. Robinson were a bad influence on the nation's youth (although the "bad influence" was usually limited to bad impressions of Raft, Cagney, and Robinson by said youth).

After the success of *The Godfather* (1972), gangster movies became hot again as studios competed to make meditations on gangsters as the most violent of American dreamers, with a requisite high body count. But gangster movies posed problems that became apparent as the boom passed. First, only people with names like

Coppola, Scorsese, De Palma, and Leone seemed able to make them well. Second, the American mass audience preferred its movie heroes, even the anti-variety, to be on the right side of the law. The studios could make more money more consistently from films about cops than gangsters. *Dirty Harry*'s Harry Callahan and his successors were better box office, finally, than *The Godfather*'s Michael Corleone.

In Japan, however, the history of its yakuza, or gangster, movies has been very different. In the silent era, these films remained a subset of the samurai period drama, which was then the most popular domestic genre. Their heroes were usually Robin Hood types from the feudal past who may have made their living from gambling but fought selflessly for the powerless. Instead of growing rich from their winnings, these men often wandered the countryside, poor and lonely, but faithful to the gangster's code.

In the upheavals that followed Japan's defeat in World War Two, the gang films changed. With old values discredited and new Western influences flooding in, audiences demanded fresh cultural affirmations of Japanese identity. Period dramas, including those with gambler heroes, supplied this demand; but, being set in the pre-modern past, they could comment only indirectly on the conditions of contemporary life.

The zeitgeist had shifted. Gangsters no longer were romantic figures from a distant past but a present-day reality in every black market or entertainment district. Ruthless and dangerous, they swaggered where others cowered, flourished where others starved. These men attracted a new kind of admiration, not for their virtue, like the old-time gamblers of story and song, but rather their power and élan. Films thus began to appear about these postwar gangsters in the hard-boiled style of Hollywood noir. But the gang film didn't rise to true popularity until a new subgenre arose, following the box office success of Tadashi Sawashima's *Jinsei Gekijo: Hishakaku* (Theater of Life: Hishakaku) in 1963. Set in the seventy-year period from the end of the shogunate to the beginning of World War Two, these films came to be called *ninkyo eiga* (chivalry films).

The heroes of this genre were the spiritual descendants of the silent-era gamblers who had upheld traditional values while slicing through crowds of opponents with swift, deadly swords. Their enemies, however, were not only the usual bad gangsters who flouted the gang code but also their corrupt allies in business, government, and the military. These heroes defended not only the gang boss or the occasional helpless widow but also the exploited workers of Japan's belated Industrial Revolution.

The closest Hollywood parallel to this were the Westerns that dealt with the closing of the open range and the coming of the railroad—i.e., the march of civilization spelling the end of the Old West. But where Westerns were usually content to lament the passing of an era, *ninkyo eiga* had a more conflicted relationship with the past, celebrating the building of a stronger, wealthier country while criticizing the forces that manipulated such rebirth to their own advantage.

In the more realistic yakuza films of the 1970s, the focus shifted to the postwar period itself, discarding much of the mythological baggage of the past. Now, the approach was that of the news cameraman, recording the carnage but refraining from judgment. A new hero appeared, whose loyalty was conditional and who lived for himself—and to hell with the consequences. In the most extreme form, such as Tetsuya Watari's Rikio Ishikawa in *Jingi no Hakaba* (Graveyard of Honor, 1975), the hero was no longer a romantic lone wolf but a self-destructive loner in rebellion against the human race.

The genre went into retreat in the 1980s but returned with a bang in the 1990s, flooding the video shelves. The gangster heroes of these straight-to-video films were often more sophisticated and stylish than their predecessors: Aloha shirts were out; Armani was in. The films themselves became more diverse, with some trying to revive the glories of the 1960s Golden Age, while others reflected current-day realities of the meaner Tokyo streets—or their young makers' own *manga*- and *anime*-fed fantasies. Directors like Takashi Ishii and Rokuro Mochizuki commented on economic post-bubble issues, particularly the dissolution of the social contract. No comparisons with cowboys possible here.

In short, the genre adapted and thrived in ways that the Western and samurai period drama did not, although the latter has made something of a comeback in recent years with both young and veteran directors contributing.

But having said that gang films matter, I have to admit that many of them have few redeeming qualities, aesthetic or otherwise. They are violent fantasies whose ideology—if it can be called that—ranges from the feudalistic to the proto-fascist. Even the films of a more innocent day in which purely Japanese "white" struggles against Westernized "black" share this tendency. Viewers are asked to identify with the "good" gang, all of whose members are upstanding sorts, even though, as film critic Tadao Sato astutely noted, the very idea of a yakuza gang with no rotten eggs is absurd. The value derives from the same groupist ethic that once caused millions of Japanese to wage war, with the noble, upstanding aim of freeing Asia from Western domination.

That said, yakuza movies remain a great guilty pleasure—even ones with all the subtlety of a knee to the groin. For this outlander, they offer a glimpse inside a closed world in which all the bad qualities of the Japanese, as well as some of the good ones, are on naked display, and with few of the false fronts that official Japan presents to the world. Of course, even the "true story" films are often hyped to the skies, dramatizing the sort of brawls and gun battles that rarely if ever occur in real life. But lies can tell more than facts, can't they?

A word about the structure of the book. Several of the reviews first appeared in the *Japan Times* and are found here in revised form. Most of them, however, are originals, divided into two sections: story and critique. The former is intended to help readers whose Japanese is less than perfect to understand films that are neither subbed or dubbed, i.e., the great majority. To make the story summaries coherent, I had to add spoilers, though I have tried to limit them as much as possible.

I could have included far more reviews, profiles, and interviews but space limitations intervened. I have instead tried to be representative, covering the most important directors, stars, and films. If I have left out your favorites—see the next edition, perhaps. I have used Western name order and converted katakana titles to English to make the book more accessible for general readers. Purists may mentally convert "bloody" to *burodi* if they wish.

I would like to thank all who helped me with this project, beginning with my ever-patient publisher, Peter Goodman, and my editors, Bonnie Dehler and Barry Harris. Babu Sato, Ray Schilling, Lisa Schilling, and Yuko Schilling provided invaluable transcription assistance, while Mamiko Kawamoto supplied photos and translations. I would also like to thank Mark Schreiber and Tom Mes for their suggestions and my editors at the *Japan Times*, particularly Mark Thompson, for continued support. A special thanks to Teddy Stratton for digging up that Paul Schrader essay and to Louise Tutt for sending that Takashi Miike photo. *Arigato gozaimasu.*

INTRODUCTION

A BRIEF HISTORY OF JAPANESE YAKUZA FILMS

Film genres rise, fall, but never die (become comatose, yes, die, no). One example is films about Japan's native gangsters, the yakuza, which got their start in the silent days, became huge in the 1960s and 1970s, declined in the 1980s, but returned in force in the 1990s, flooding the video store shelves. In the process, the genre went through a radical metamorphosis, much as Hollywood gang films did en route from *Little Caesar* to *The Godfather*.

The modern-day gangsters played by Takeshi Kitano in *Sonatine* and *Brother* kill with all the emotion of roach exterminators and live according to their own Social Darwinian law: do unto others before others do unto you. Their characters are a far cry indeed from the noble stoics of 1960s icon Ken Takakura, who resorted to violence only after repeated provocation, while following the traditional gangster code of repaying one's moral obligations no matter what the personal sacrifice.

Kitano scorns the old gang films as unrealistic and says that his own, darker view of the gangs lies closer to the truth. Real gangsters, he told me in a 1998 interview, "could [never] take on a whole rival gang with a wooden sword," as Takakura did in film after film. "Stories like that were made into comics," he reminisced. "At the end, Takakura Ken says, 'I'll go alone.' The other guys in the gang say, 'Go ahead, we're not stopping you'" (Schilling, *Contemporary Japanese Film*, p. 93).

There are parallels, however, between Kitano's dirty heroes and Takakura's clean-cut ones: Both are contemptuous of death in the best samurai tradition and both define macho cool for their respective generations. Also, as removed from reality as the 1960s Golden Age films could be, their makers included quirky surrealists like Seijun Suzuki and cinema verité stylists like Kinji Fukasaku. They made defiantly individual statements—and provided creative inspiration for 1990s gang-movie directors such as Takashi Miike, Rokuro Mochizuki, and (despite his denials) Kitano himself.

THE HISTORY OF JAPANESE YAKUZA

Japanese gangs are ancient in origin. Early in the Tokugawa Period (1600–1867), roving samurai called *hatamono-yakko*, who had been left unemployed by the end of the previous era's incessant wars, turned to looting and banditry. Today's gangsters trace their beginnings to the bands of young townsmen, called *machi-yakko*, who organized to oppose the *hatamono-yakko*. Living on the fringes of the law themselves, the *machi-yakko* became folk heroes, with songs, stories, and plays retelling their exploits.

By the middle of the eighteenth century, Japan's criminal society began to assume its modern form, as the spiritual descendants of the *machi-yakko* evolved into two distinct groups: the *bakuto* (gamblers) and *tekiya* (peddlers), both of whom plied their trade on the famed Tokaido highway between Edo (present-day Tokyo) and Kyoto. The *bakuto* came to be called *yakuza*, or "eight, nine, three"— a losing hand in a traditional card game. Later, the term applied not only to *bakuto* but to *tekiya* and other outlaw groups. Both *bakuto* and *tekiya* were organized into hierarchies, with an *oyabun* (boss or, literally, "father") administering to the needs of his *kobun* (subordinates or, literally, "children") in return for their unswerving loyalty. This relationship, considered superior to blood ties, was cemented with elaborate ritual and, if necessary, honored with the ultimate personal sacrifice: death.

Though not all yakuza, even in the good old days, willingly threw their lives away at the whim of their *oyabun*, they did adhere to a certain code, called *jingi* (chivalry), that set them apart from straight society. Non-yakuza, for example, did not chop off a pinkie joint as a gesture of contrition to their superiors for a misdeed. In the popular imagination, certain exemplars of the *jingi* code achieved a romantic outlaw status as friends of the weak, enemies of the strong.

The *jingi* code prohibited yakuza from drawing ordinary citizens into their quarrels. Instead, the gangsters constituted a tightly knit guild that resembled other similar occupational groups in feudal Japan, from firemen to carpenters. Like them, the yakuza made no secret of their affiliation and were in fact often swaggeringly proud of it. (Postwar gangsters followed this tradition, affixing their gang name and logo on office signs, name cards, and even lapel pins.) They may not have been anyone's idea of a role model—few parents raised their sons to be yakuza—but these men had their uses and place. Thus developed the traditional Japanese tolerance of and sympathy for native gangsters, who have long been regarded less as predatory outsiders than errant members of the same cultural and racial family.

By the time films were introduced to Japan, the yakuza had already put down deep, enduring roots in society. No festival was complete without the stalls of the *tekiya*, no urban amusement district without the gambling dens of the *bakuto*. The latter, in particular, offered a rich source of material for early filmmakers.

Prewar yakuza films were usually set in the premodern past and based on historical figures who had acquired a heavy accretion of legend through centuries of oral and literary traditions. One favorite was Kunisada Chuji (1810–50), who as a young man became enraged by the injustices that a wicked magistrate perpetrated against the poor. Deciding to live outside the law rather than be crushed within it, Chuji joined a gang of *bakuto* and became its leader. In opposing corrupt authority, he emerged as a much-beloved champion of justice. Starting in the silent era, director after director made films about this Robin Hood-like hero, notably Daisuke Ito with his 1927 *Chuji Tabi Nikki* (Chuji's Travel Diary)—a three-part film depicting Chuji alone and on the run but still living strictly according to the *jingi* code, even though doing so endangers himself. Ito's aim was pathos, not simply thrills, and one he achieved well enough to make *Chuji Tabi Nikki* an influential hit.

Though not all versions of the Kunisada Chuji story emphasized his decline, prewar gang films tended to portray their vagabond heroes as sympathetic but lonely figures, forced to live an outlaw existence and longing, however hopelessly, to return to straight society. These characters had little in common with the strutting, wisecracking, bullet-spraying heroes of 1930s Hollywood gang films.

But as noble spirited as Chuji and his fictional fellow *bakuto* may have been, they were deemed not fit as heroes for wartime propaganda films. After the war, Occupation authorities took a dim view of feudalistic themes, forcing makers of period films to radically redefine the genre and severely limiting the types of stories they could put on the screen. The *giri-ninjo* (duty versus human feelings) dramas of the typical gangster film did not make the cut. When the Occupation ended in 1952, period dramas of all types, including ones about feudal-era gangsters, quickly returned to their place of prewar dominance. The old-style *bakuto*—that brave-but-pathetic hero trailing a cloud of doom—did not. In his place arose a new breed more in keeping with the optimistic, get-ahead spirit of the postwar boom.

One of its members was the title character of Masahiro Makino's Jirocho Sangokushi (Adventures of Jirocho), a hit, nine-part series that ran from 1952 to 1954 and inspired several spinoffs. Once again, inspiration came from a real-life source, the legendary gangster Shimizu no Jirocho, born in 1820 in Shimizu, a town halfway between today's Tokyo and Yokohama. After the death of his adoptive father, a rice merchant, Jirocho inherited the business; but four years later, at the age of twenty, he took to the road and became a gambler. A natural leader, Jirocho formed his own gang and had as many as six hundred men under his command. During the political upheavals of the 1860s that pitted the followers of the emperor against those of the shogun, Jirocho allied himself with the former and ended up on the winning side. When he died in 1893, at the age of seventy-three, Jirocho had become a pillar of the community, a man who may have run gambling games but also had actively contributed to the modernization of Shimizu and even founded one of the country's first English schools. Makino's films, understandably, focused on the early, more cinematic part of Jirocho's career, portraying him as a successful boss who looks out for his men's welfare and punishes the bad yakuza who stray from the *jingi* code.

Along with films about Tokugawa Era outlaws, Toei and other studios began making gang films set in modern-day Japan and influenced by Hollywood models. Among the more notable was Teruo Ishii's *Hana to Arashi to Gang* (Flower and Storm and Gang, 1961), starring a young Ken Takakura as a wild and wacky hood who gets involved in a bank heist that goes wrong, to wry comic effect. Takakura's character, cocky and arrogant, if not terribly bright, was a far cry from the stoic tough guys he later portrayed.

The film, however, was a hit that revived Takakura's flagging career and launched him toward stardom. It was also the first of an eleven-part series that ran until 1967, six of which were directed by Ishii and two by a promising new-comer, Kinji Fukasaku. In depicting contemporary gang life, including gang war-fare, semi-realistically, the series was a forerunner to the critically acclaimed *jitsuroku* (true story) gang films that Fukasaku shot in the early 1970s and which subsequently made his international reputation.

THE GOLDEN AGE OF JAPANESE YAKUZA FILMS

The genre's real Golden Age, however, was the 1960s. The films that drove and sustained it came from a specialized variety called *ninkyo eiga*—"chivalry films." Influenced more by the conventions of the samurai period drama and the culture of Japanese gangdom than Hollywood, *ninkyo eiga* were usually set in the seventy-year period from the end of feudalism to the beginning of World War Two. These films may have had a traditional appeal—with the good-guy gangsters being essentially good-guy samurai with tattoos—but they also dealt with relevant issues, such as the social and economic impact of Westernization, which was of interest to their contemporary audiences. The *ninkyo eiga* vogue lasted for more than a decade and generated stars, including Ken Takakura, Koji Tsuruta, and Junko Fuji, who became gangster archetypes for a generation, much as James Cagney and Edward G. Robinson did in 1930s America.

The genre's plots usually revolved around the age-old theme of *giri-ninjo*—the dilemma of the hero forced to choose between his own interests and an obligation that may cost him his life. The hero typically finds himself on the side of a gang that seeks to uphold tradition, against stronger, ruthless rivals who have been cor-rupted by materialism, individualism, and other Western values (or are just plain bad characters). The hero is usually a forbearing type who seeks a peaceful reso-lution to the struggle between the film's good and bad gangsters until being dri-ven to action by the repeated outrages of the latter.

Despite countless variations depicting this core narrative, the genre's climax usually featured a showdown between the hero, perhaps accompanied by an ally or two, and the bad guys. The resulting one-against-all fight, with the hero wield-ing a Japanese sword (never an automatic weapon) to deadly effect, was also a standard trope of period drama films (and before that, of period drama plays), one the audience never tired of. *Ninkyo eiga* drew millions of primarily young male fans and accounted for some of the biggest box office hits of the period. What was the reason for their popularity? For one thing, these films gave audiences a charge of violence that was unavailable from the then-tame medium of television. By the contemporary standards of Clint Eastwood, spaghetti Westerns, and *Bonnie and Clyde*, however, the bloodlettings were less than realistic, although body counts usually ran high.

More than in-your-face blood and gore, the *ninkyo* films relied on other elements for their appeal. First, their stories of the weak confronting the strong for the sake of honor drew heavily from older, enduringly popular forms. One was the *gamangeki* (forbearance drama), whose most famous representative is *Chushingura*. Based on a real incident, this story of forty-seven *ronin* (masterless samurai) seeking revenge for their unjustly disgraced lord, has enthralled Japanese audiences for three centuries in plays, novels, and films.

Second was the audience's identification with the heroes. Not that the fans of gang films wanted to become gangsters themselves, but they could relate to the loner hero—defending traditional values against weasely, often Westernized betrayers of same, while wearing Japanese clothes (symbolizing his all-Japanese virtue)—in a way they could not to Clint Eastwood.

Third was the social and political zeitgeist. Many fans of *ninkyo* films were young males who had moved from the countryside to the raw, sprawling cities in search of education or jobs. While the Japanese economy may have been booming, these young men subsisted at the bottom of the economic and social heap. In cramped offices and noisy factories, they slaved away for long hours for low pay, tightly bound by rules, written and unwritten. They often lived alone in company dorms and rooming houses—and were starved for entertainment.

Male students at elite universities may have had more personal freedom but were swept along by the same generational currents as their counterparts in the West. They were in rebellion against everything from hidebound university administrators to the right-wing Liberal Democratic Party bosses, who had signed the Japan-U.S. Security Treaty and were supporting the U.S. war effort in Vietnam.

These young men, note Tsukasa Shiba and Sakae Aoyama in their book *Yakuza Eiga to Sono Jidai* (Yakuza Film and Their Times, Chikuma Shinsho, 1998), "were isolated in an era of high economic growth and tight social strictures" and "felt a strong attraction to the standard [*ninkyo eiga*] motifs of male comrades banding together to battle the power structure" (ibid., p. 17). Also, with their stories of anti-establishment good guys struggling against establishment bad guys, *ninkyo eiga* "reflected the situation of the period" (ibid., p. 16).

The film igniting the *ninkyo eiga* boom was Tadashi Sawashima's *Jinsei Gekijo: Hishakaku*, mentioned above. Koji Tsuruta plays Hishakaku, a gangster on the run with Otoyo (Yoshiko Sakuma), a Yokohama courtesan. With the help of a friendly *oyabun* (Ryunosuke Tsukigata), the two hole up in a Tokyo amusement quarter; but Hishakaku finally turns himself in to repay an obligation. While he is in prison, Otoyo takes up with Miyagawa (Ken Takakura), a studly young gangster. The film's early-twentieth-century setting and love triangle story may not have broken new ground, but Tsuruta and Takakura brought a stylish dynamism to their roles, while exemplifying the *jingi* code. They made the sword and kimono cool again for fans who had been turning to the small screen for their period drama entertainment.

After the box office success of *Jinsei Gekijo: Hishakaku*, Toei quickly ramped up gang film production, releasing as many as thirty-seven in 1967 out of the fifty-five films in its lineup. Formed in 1951 from a merger of two small film companies, with backing from the Toyoko Railway Company, Toei had begun life as a maker of low-budget period dramas. Under the leadership of its first president, Hiroshi Okawa, the company developed a system for turning its more popular films into series and then block booking them in double bills throughout Japan. By 1954, only three years after its launch, Toei was releasing a new double bill every week, for a production pace of 104 films annually.

By the early 1960s, however, the period drama audience was migrating en masse to television, and Toei was in trouble. The success of *Jinsei Gekijo: Hishakaku* and the *ninkyo eiga* that followed it saved the company. Toei was fortunately able to change production gears from samurai swashbuckers to *ninkyo eiga* with relative ease, using the same sets, staff, and even fight choreography. Toei director Masahiro Makino, who had been directing since 1928 and whose father had been a pioneering director in the early years of the century, was soon turning out *ninkyo eiga* with his usual brisk efficiency.

As in Golden Age Hollywood, Toei's production system was the sum of many parts. Among its most important were its president Okawa, who knew nothing of filmmaking but was willing to trust those who did, and stars such as Takakura and Tsuruta, who could express traditional values with authority and conviction, while injecting their performances with a distinctly postwar sensibility and star charisma.

The catalyst behind Toei's success, however, was one producer, Koji Shundo, who supervised the studio's yakuza movie output throughout its peak years, taking a key role in nurturing its talent and defining the genre's style. Although ranking high in the Toei hierarchy just under the head of production, Shigeru Okada, Shundo was a hands-on type, who worked closely with staff and cast from the script stage on. *Ninkyo eiga* may have succeeded without him—he was not the producer of the first one, *Jinsei Gekijo: Hishakaku*—but Shundo was responsible for many of the genre's most popular films and enduring series.

Born in Kobe in 1916, he had been drafted into the Japanese Army in 1937 but was later discharged with a diagnosis of tuberculosis. Joining a company that processed magnesium for the military, Shundo spent the war years working in the Kansai—an area in western Japan that included Osaka, Kyoto, and Kobe. He also was a regular at a gambling den run by the Goshima-gumi gang and became an intimate acquaintance of its boss, Fukujiro Ono. Through these connections, Shundo came to know gang life from the inside, though he later claimed, despite rumors to the contrary, that he never became a gangster himself. During the war years, Shundo also married his second wife—he had divorced his first after a brief marriage that produced one child—and had three children with her: one boy and two girls. The younger daughter, Junko, would later become the biggest female star on the Toei lot.

After the war, Shundo dabbled in film production with veteran period drama director Masahiro Makino, ran a popular Kyoto bar with an ex-geisha, and acted as a fixer for his film-industry acquaintances. In 1960 Shundo helped Toei to sign megastar Koji Tsuruta and negotiated a deal that brought star baseball manager Shigeru Mizuhara from the Yomiuri Giants to the Toei Flyers, a team associated with the Toei Studio. These services won Shundo the trust of Toei president Okawa—who gave him carte blanche when he joined the company as a producer in 1962. Shundo soon justified this trust by turning out a string of hits. One of his early successes, the 1963 period drama *Jirocho Sangokushi* (Jirocho's Tale of the Three Kingdoms), became a four-part series that laid the groundwork for the *ninkyo eiga* he would later produce.

However far-fetched the story, Shundo insisted on accuracy of atmosphere and detail. For his first *ninkyo* film, *Bakuto* (The Gambler, 1964), he and director Shigehiro Ozawa investigated real gambling dens and invited real gamblers to the set as advisors. Shundo even cast a former gang boss, Noboru Ando, in leading roles in several films. He later insisted that these and other relationships he developed with the yakuza were strictly professional. "[Getting mixed up with the yakuza] is not the way to make good movies," Shundo told one interviewer (Shundo and Yamane, *Ninkyo Eiga-den* [The Story of the Ninkyo Film], 1999, p. 68).

Shundo also had a knack for generating hit series from successful films. Among the most successful were Nihon Kyokakuden (An Account of the Chivalrous Commoners of Japan, 1964–71, eleven entries); Showa Zankyoden (Tales of Chivalry in the Showa Era, 1965–72, nine entries); Abashiri Bangaichi (A Man from Abashiri Prison, 1965–73, eighteen entries); Bakuchiuchi (The Gambler, 1967–72, ten entries); and Hibotan Bakuto (Red Peony Gambler, 1968–72, eight entries). These series became brands that enabled Toei to attract a large and loyal following for its films and build an insurmountable box office lead over its rivals.

Also faced with the task of feeding the Toei assembly line with product, Shundo assembled a core unit of scriptwriters, directors, and stars and worked them (and himself) as hard as humanly possible. In his peak year with Toei, 1967, he produced thirty films, of which Koji Tsuruta starred in fourteen and Ken Takakura in six. Among the lesser stars in Shundo's firmament were Tomisaburo Wakayama, Tetsuro Tanba, Shin'ichi "Sonny" Chiba, Noboru Ando, Saburo Kitajima, Tatsuo Umemiya, Kyosuke Machida, Ryo Ikebe, and Shingo Yamashiro. To keep his stars, particularly the workaholic Tsuruta, busy and boost the marquee value of his product, Shundo often had them appear as featured players in films for the bottom half of the double bill. He would give lead roles to less prominent but promising actors. His biggest casting coup, however, was Ken Takakura, who created a new image of macho stardom and would later become an enduring icon personifying the Japanese male ideal for millions. Think John Wayne with a sword.

Born in Fukuoka in 1931 and educated at the elite Meiji University, Takakura passed a Toei "new face" film audition and made his film debut in 1956 in *Denko Karate Uchi* (Lightening Karate Blow). He didn't hit his box office stride, however, until he evolved from his early punkish on-screen persona into a stoic loner who could spend scene after scene in slow-burn mode before erupting into displays of kinetic violence. His launching pad to superstardom was Teruo Ishii's *Abashiri Bangaichi* (A Man from Abashiri Prison). Takakura played a convict who escapes from the notorious Abashiri Prison on Hokkaido, the northernmost island that has long been Japan's Siberia. Inspired by Stanley Kramer's *The Defiant Ones*, the film featured a breath-taking escape sequence in which Takakura and a fellow prisoner flee their pursuers while on a handcar, hurling down a Hokkaido mountainside in mid-winter; Takakura's husky rendition of the film's theme song, based on a prison folk tune, became a chart-topping hit.

Toei's other superstar, Koji Tsuruta, had already had a long run as a matinee idol before joining the studio in 1960. Typed as a romantic leading man at the start of his career in the early 1950s, Tsuruta had broadened his range, appearing in war movies, period dramas, and gang pictures for every major studio but Nikkatsu. He also launched his own short-lived production company; its first release, Masahiro Makino's period gangster film *Yataro Gasa* (Yataro's Bamboo Hat), became a hit in 1952.

Born in 1924 and raised by his grandmother after his parent's divorce, Tsuruta grew up tough in Osaka, running with a street gang. In an incident seemingly inspired by one of his movies, he once fought a dozen opponents single-handedly (though he lost and was beaten with his own *geta* [wooden clogs], an indignity he never suffered on the screen). Trained as an Imperial Navy pilot during World War Two, Tsuruta watched many of his comrades fly off to their deaths and, long afterward, suffered from survivor's guilt. He also carried psychic scars from a torrid love affair with actress Keiko Kishi, his costar in the 1953 *Hawaii no Yoru* (Hawaiian Nights), that his studio, Shochiku, forced him to end. In short, his romantic-gangster credentials were in order in a way that the younger, college-educated Takakura's were not.

By the mid-1960s, at the height of his popularity, Tsuruta was portraying middle-aged gangsters who may have been models of proper *jingi* behavior but cut a wearier, more tragic figure than the younger, more athletic Takakura. On screen Tsuruta was often a tough guy but exuded a deep inner dignity and decency, as well as an air of loneliness. If Takakura was the quintessential *tateyaku*, a player of many roles who was shy with the ladies but fearless with a sword, Tsuruta was the master of *gaman* (stoic endurance), who could be counted on to always do the right *jingi* thing but was also capable of falling passionately, even desperately, in love.

Shundo's biggest find, after Tsuruta and Takakura, was his own daughter, who took the professional name Junko Fuji. Shundo initially opposed her desire to enter show business. ("The reason was simple," he told Yamane, ". . . I wanted her to find a good husband and marry in the normal way" [*Ninkyo Eiga-den*, p. 150].) But when Makino expressed interest in casting her in his 1958 *Otoko no Sakazuki* (A Man's Sake Cup), Shundo reluctantly agreed; better Toei than rival Shochiku, which had also scouted the almond-eyed teenager. Fuji made an impression and was soon a rising star on the Toei lot. Often appearing opposite Takakura, she quickly became a favorite of fans, playing passionate, strong-willed women who are nonetheless models of *jingi* propriety. In 1968, Fuji starred in Kosaku Yamashita's *Hibotan Bakuto* (Red Peony Gambler) in which she portrayed a wandering gambler who seeks revenge for the murder of her *oyabun* father and finds it with the aid of a lone gangster, played by Takakura.

In the eight Hibotan installments, Fuji was convincingly the equal—mentally and physically—of any yakuza tough guy. She was skilled not only at cards but martial arts, tossing her loutish male foes with perfectly timed throws or slicing them with her short sword. With her steely glare and low, penetrating voice, the actress could dominate the room; but she also looked stunning in kimono, with a poised, undeniably feminine presence. Whether facing down a crowd of armed men or crying at the deathbed of a yakuza boss, her performance was all of a piece, her embodiment of the gang code was as powerful as her male costars'— but in her modesty, politeness, and essential gentleness she was also the ideal *yamato nadeshiko*, that is, a woman who exemplified traditional Japanese female virtues.

As the supervisor of a relentless assembly line, Shundo also needed directors who could both fit into the system and make hit products. He found them not only in Makino but Kiyoshi Saeki, Kosaku Yamashita, Sadao Nakajima, Junya Sato, Shigehiro Ozawa, Yasuo Furuhata, Norifumi Suzuki, and Takashi Harada. Shundo also tolerated types who departed from the norm—as long as they could deliver box office winners. One of these was Teruo Ishii, who specialized in films about modern gangsters and made them with a speed, stylishness, and quirky inventiveness that was the opposite of the *ninkyo eiga* aesthetic. Critics detected a strong "butter" (i.e., Western) flavor in his films, but Ishii was also a hitmaker who was responsible for the long-running Gang and Abashiri Bangaichi series.

Still another standout was Tai Kato, a period drama veteran. Best known for his low camera angles—Kato would have his crew dig holes to get the camera low enough—Kato developed an instantly recognizable style that brought a visceral excitement to action scenes but also expressed humanistic concerns, at times with a leftist slant. It contrasted sharply with that of the typical Toei *ninkyo eiga* director, who preferred a statelier pace and less advocatory view.

With his extreme closeups, often shot from below, Kato had a way of making his actors look larger than life—living icons in kimono—but usually wasted few words in his dealings with them. This tactic drove Koji Tsuruta up the wall when he was making *Meiji Kyokakuden: Sandai Shumei* (Blood of Revenge, 1965). After hearing "Sorry, that won't do," with no explanation for the umpteenth time, a fuming Tsuruta exploded on the set, retreating to his dressing room. Shundo rushed to calm his star while urging Kato to explain himself. The shooting resumed, the film became a hit—and Tsuruta's performance in it was one of his best. Kato continued to work for Shundo and Toei.

NIKKATSU AND DAIEI STUDIOS

The success of Toei's gang films soon had other studios gearing up their yakuza factories. The most serious challenger was Nikkatsu, a studio founded in 1912 that dominated the industry in the early decades of Japanese cinema. During the war years, Nikkatsu suspended production and did not resume until 1954, in a new studio complex built in western Tokyo. The company soon began nurturing its own stable of stars, including Yujiro Ishihara, a long-legged heartthrob who was Japan's answer to Elvis Presley and James Dean.

In contrast to Toei's *ninkyo eiga*, with their home-grown themes and values, Nikkatsu's *mukokuseki* action (borderless action) films borrowed more blatantly from Hollywood. The purest examples could be found in the Wataridori (Bird of Passage) series, starring Akira Kobayashi, and running for nine installments from 1959 to 1962. A boyishly handsome, ruggedly built man with a relaxed manner and crooked smile, Kobayashi played a guitar-strumming, horse-riding hero ranging on the wide-open spaces of Japan's north country. He moseys into town, finds gangsters or other evil characters harassing innocent folk, defeats them with the aid of an enemy-turned-ally (played in the first six installments by Jo Shishi-do), while winning and finally spurning the love of a pure-hearted maiden (played in all but the last installment by Ruriko Asaoka).

Kei'ichiro "Tony" Akagi, another top Nikkatsu star, launched a popular *mukokuseki* action series with *Kenju Buraicho: Nukiuchi no Ryu* (Pistol Rap Sheet: Fast Draw Ryu, 1960). Akagi played a gang gunman with the fastest draw in Japan, who nicks his opponents instead of killing them. Once again, Jo Shishido played the role of the rival, though in the course of the four-series installments his character and Akagi's developed a wise-cracking friendship. The series abruptly ended, however, when Akagi was killed in a go-cart accident in 1961.

But as successful as these and other *mukokuseki* action films were, Nikkatsu was struggling at the box office when Toei's *ninkyo eiga* began to fill theaters—and the studio strove to play catchup. In 1963, Nikkatsu released its first *ninkyo eiga*, Aki-nori Matsuo's *Otoko no Monsho* (Symbol of a Man), a drama about a gang boss's son who becomes a doctor but is forced to take over as *oyabun* when his father is killed by a rival gang. Starring Hideki Takahashi as the son, *Otoko no Monsho* launched a ten-part series that ran until 1966.

Ironically, Nikkatsu's best-known gang films today, both in Japan and abroad, were made by a director that the studio later fired: Seijun Suzuki. Entering Nikkatsu as an assistant director in 1954, Suzuki made his directorial debut in 1956 with *Minato no Kanpai: Shori o Wagate ni* (Toast of the Harbor: Victory Is in Our Grasp), a melodrama whose sailor hero helps his jockey brother fight a charge of fixing races.

Throughout much of the next decade Suzuki toiled away on the Nikkatsu assembly line, grinding out B programers in various genres. A spiritual anarchist with a love of theater and disdain for convention, he began, with the 1963 rogue-cop-on-a-mission film *Yaju no Seishun* (Youth of the Beast), to inject touches into his films that ranged from the gorgeously Kabukiesque to the mind-blowingly surreal. The culmination was the 1967 *Koroshi no Rakuin* (Branded to Kill), whose hitman hero, played by Jo Shishido, botches a job because a butterfly lands on the scope of his sniper rifle and whose femme fatale client decorates the rearview mirror of her sports car with a dead bird. Nikkatsu president Kyusaku Hori found the film incomprehensible, film fans stayed away (save for the small band of Suzu-ki loyalists)—and the director found himself without a job. *Koroshi no Rakuin* later became a cult favorite, endlessly revived and borrowed from (Jim Jarmusch used the famous bullet-through-the-water pipe shot in *Ghost Dog: The Way of the Samurai*).

Also revving up its yakuza production line was the Daiei Studio, beginning with *Akumyo* (Tough Guy, 1961). Shintaro Katsu, the younger brother of Toei star Tomisaburo Wakayama, played a poor farmer's son with a short temper who gets into a fight with a yakuza (Jiro Tamiya) at a brothel, beating him to a pulp. The yakuza becomes his follower and together they set out to rescue a young woman who has been sold into prostitution on the island of Innoshima. Made with a light comic touch and plenty of rough-and-tumble action, *Akumyo* shot both Katsu and Tamiya to stardom and generated a sixteen-part series that continued until 1974.

Another Daiei stalwart, Raizo Ichikawa, had already become enormously popular for his samurai period dramas when he starred in *Waka Oyabun* (Young Boss, 1965). Ichikawa played a young naval officer whose career is on the ascendant following Japan's victory in the Russo-Japanese War (1904–5). Then, his *oyabun* father is murdered by a rival gang and he becomes the gang's new boss, determined to get revenge. A clean-cut, classically handsome youth, whose pale skin made him a favorite with female fans, Ichikawa had a charismatic screen presence that helped make the film a hit. He appeared in all eight installments of the Waka Oyabun series, which ran until 1967, two years before Ichikawa's premature death in 1969.

Still another popular Daiei series was Onna Tobakuchi (Woman Gambler), whose seventeen installments were released from 1966 to 1971. Star Kyoko Enami was Daiei's answer to Junko Fuji. Enami plays a cool, calculating gambler whose dealer father commits suicide after being accused of cheating. She sets out to clear his name and get revenge. Enami, however, proved no match at the box office for Fuji, just as Daiei failed to stay the pace with Toei.

"PINKY VIOLENCE" AND JITSUROKU EIGA

Toei, which had been quicker than its rivals in cranking up gang movie production, was also quicker to switch strategies when the vogue for the genre began to wane. In 1967, Toei production chief Okada Shigeru started replacing poor-performing *ninkyo eiga* in the lower half of double bills with so-called "pinky violence" (*koshoku rosen*) films. While featuring girl gangsters, such series as Sukeban Burusu (Girl Boss Blues, 1971–77) were less interested in righting the gender balance with the top half of the bill than on simply selling sex, often with rape, torture, and bondage in attendance.

But as popular as some of the "pinky violence" films became, they could not stop the box office slide of *ninkyo* films in the early 1970s. The crowning blow came in 1972 when Junko Fuji quit Toei at the height of her popularity to marry Kabuki actor Kikunosuke Onoe. The loss was so great that Japanese critics commonly date the decline of *ninkyo eiga* from her retirement.

Ironically, the one who revived the genre and reversed Toei's eroding fortunes was Kinji Fukasaku, whose early films Shundo disliked—"He was making them for himself alone," he complained to Yamane (*Ninkyo Eiga-den*, p. 220). Shundo changed his mind about Fukasaku, however, after seeing *Gendai Yakuza: Hitokiri Yota* (Street Mobster, 1972)—an explosively violent, starkly nihilistic film about a wild-at-heart gangster, played by Bunta Sugawara, who wages a suicidal one-man war against a powerful gang. Though too dark to be a mass audience hit, the film had a raw vitality missing in formulaic gang films. Over strong opposition, Shundo brought Fukasaku to Toei's Kyoto Studio to make *Jingi Naki Tatakai* (Battles without Honor and Humanity)—a studio-saving success.

Released in 1973, *Jingi Naki Tatakai* tells the story of gang wars in early postwar Kure, a port town in Hiroshima Prefecture, with the characters based on real-life gangsters and the story, on actual events. Bunta Sugawara stars as an ex-con named Hirono, sent to the slammer for killing a rival punk in a street fight. Inside, he becomes close to Wakasugi (Tatsuo Umemiya), a lieutenant of the Doigumi gang. Back on the streets again, Hirono is recruited by the rival Yamamori-gumi, whose boss (Nobuo Kaneko) likes his take-no-prisoners style. The two gangs maintain an uneasy balance of power until their involvement in a city council election brings them head to head—and a war erupts, with Hirono caught in the middle. Beatings, murders, and betrayals follow in quick succession as the conflict escalates—and the gangster *jingi* code is revealed as a monstrous sham.

Though reminiscent of *The Godfather*, which had been a critical and popular success in Japan, *Jingi* is a far more crowded and chaotic film, shot in a cinema verité style that recalled TV news footage of the era's bloodier revolutions and coups. Sugawara became a star for his all-out performance, though the film also featured the cream of the studio's young acting talent, including Nobuo Kaneko, Tatsuo Umemiya, and Hiroki Matsukata.

Following the success of *Jingi Naki Tatakai*, Toei president Okada told Shundo that he was giving Takakura and Tsuruta a permanent "rest" from their yakuza labors, now that their films were faltering at the box office. Shundo objected strongly, arguing that both stars had carried the studio for years and deserved better treatment. "The past is the past, now is now," said Okada (*Ninkyo Eiga Den*, p. 220), refusing to budge. Shundo submitted his resignation from Toei soon after —though he later returned.

Both Shundo and Toei kept making films but Takakura and Tsuruta never recovered their popularity as gangster icons. Takakura put his sword and bellyband in storage and went on the straight and narrow as an ex-con (*Kofuku no Kiroi Handkerchief* [The Yellow Handkerchief], 1977); detective (Station, 1981); and baseball manager (Mr. Baseball, 1993). Tsuruta continued to play gang bosses, but roles became few and far between—the actor made only three films in the five years before his death in 1987.

Toei quickly cranked out five *Jingi* sequels before Fukasaku brought the story to a conclusion in 1974. Unwilling to let a profitable franchise die, the studio persuaded the director to return for a new series based on the original story and characters (though many of the principals in the first series had since met violent ends). He produced three highly fictionalized entries before signing off for good in 1976.

But while thrilling younger filmgoers impatient with stale *ninkyo eiga* conventions and in love with the realism of New Hollywood, *Jingi Naki Tatakai* was hardly an easy film to make or, just as importantly for bottom-line-minded Toei executives, to spin into sequels. The original material was based on a series of magazine articles on the life and times of Kozo Mino, a gang boss who had fought in the Kure war and became the model for the Hirono character. Producer Goro Kusakabe and scriptwriter Kazuo Kasahara went to Hiroshima to ask Mino's permission to make a movie and got a blunt "no." Shunned as a snitch by fellow gangsters for his revelations about the gang's inner workings, Mino didn't want any more trouble.

After weeks of patient persuasion by Kusakabe and Kasahara, Mino's desire to see his story on the screen finally overcame his scruples. He wasn't the only star-struck local gangster as it turned out. When Fukasaku started shooting in Kure—

using locations that had figured in the gang war—gangsters, including models for characters in the film, swarmed on the set, giving advice to the director and cast and performing in front of the camera. "I feel sorry for actors playing yakuza now—they don't have the chance to get to know real yakuza the way we did," said Tatsuo Umemiya in an interview with Taro Sugisaku and Takeshi Uechi for their book dedicated to the series, *Jingi Naki Tatakai: Roman Album* (Battles without Honor and Humanity: Romantic Album, Tokuma Shoten, 1998, p. 178).

The popularity of *jitsuroku* films about the gangs was brief, however. One reason was the steady decline of Japanese films in terms of both box office numbers and market share with the Hollywood competition. This was a tide that all studios, including Toei and its two main rivals—Daiei and Nikkatsu—had to fight against, some more successfully than others. Daiei went bankrupt in 1971, while Nikkatsu switched production to soft porn in 1972. Also, in spinning out the *Jingi Naki Tatakai* story over eight installments, Fukasaku and his scriptwriters departed farther and father from the semidocumentary realism that had made the first film so fresh. As in the case of *ninkyo* films, the makers of *jitsuroku* films (including a ninth "Jingi" installment in 1979) went to the well too often, and fans began to tire of the taste.

The late 1970s was a time of retrenchment for gang films, as what had once been a top box office genre became a specialty item for an ever-diminishing audience. In the 1980s, the home VCR market drew away more of the single males who had been the genre's biggest fans; they now opted to watch videos in the privacy of their six-mat rooms rather than pay three times as much to see the same films in Toei's decaying downtown theaters.

One exception to this downward trend was the Gokudo no Onnatachi (Gang Wives) series, which debuted in 1986. Based on a best-selling, nonfiction book of interviews with wives and girlfriends of gangsters by freelance journalist Shoko Ieda, the first film in the series was an immediate hit. Staying faithful to the outlines of the book, director Hideo Gosha gave the film his usual gloss of sensuality, while Shima Iwashita and Rina Katase played two strong-willed sisters—Iwashita's was married to a gang boss—with imposing diva dynamism. One memorable scene was a knock-down, drag-out fight between the two women that recalled the epic brawl between Marlene Dietrich and Una Merkel in *Destry Rides Again*.

Iwashita played the lead, although not a continuing character, in eight of the series' ten installments, until the last, *Gokudo no Onnatachi: Kejime* (Gang Wives: Decision), in 1998. She became indelibly identified with her commanding *Gokudo* persona—a vision of perfection in kimono, but hell to cross. After her departure, Toei released the first film of a new Gokudo series, starring Reiko Takashima, but it made a quick exit from the theaters.

Though the *Gokudo* films turned profits, Toei's gang films with male stars failed to fill seats. Finally, in 1994, the studio announced that it was making its "last yakuza movie," *Don o Totta Otoko* (The Man Who Shot the Don), starring Hiroki Matsukata. There was one proviso, however: if the film earned more than 4 billion yen ($4 million) in rentals, Toei execs said, they would grant the genre a reprieve.

Few fans turned out for this tired recycling of genre clichés, however, and Toei announced the closing of its yakuza shop. However, it later reopened for the so-called "new" *ninkyo* films, such as *Gendai Ninkyoden* (A Story of Modern Chivalry, 1997) and *Zankyo* (Remnants of Chivalry, 1999). Both, like *Don o Totta Otoko*, were retro in story and style and offered nothing to young audiences that their fathers hadn't seen a hundred times before. Neither impressed at the box office.

But while Toei was fighting a rearguard action in the theaters, it found a new market for its gang films in the video shops that, in the mid-1980s, were springing up like proverbial bamboo shoots after a rainstorm. In 1990 its group company, Toei Video, began making what it called its V Cinema series—straight-to-video films, or as they came to be called in Japan, "original videos" or simply OV. One was *Neo Chinpira: Teppodama Pyu* (Neo Punk: Bang Goes the Bullet), starring Show Aikawa and directed by Banmei Takahashi, a maker of so-called *pinku* films (soft porn). With his puffy choir boy's face, sandpapery voice, and meticulously sculpted pompadour, Aikawa was a 1950s *American Graffiti* punk transported to 1990s Japan—not the traditional image of *ninkyo* masculinity. But his contemporary brand of cool and the film's semi-comic Yakuza Lite approach appealed to the video shop crowd. Neo Chinpira and other V Cinema films became money-spinning hits.

Soon rival companies were grinding out low-budget OVs of their own in various action genres, but Toei Video remained the leader and the gang film, its mainstay. Far cheaper to make than a standard theatrical feature—$70,000 was an average budget—OVs were often shot on 16mm, blown up to 35mm prints, and given brief runs in second-run theaters before being relegated to the video bins. As in the 1960s heyday of the *ninkyo eiga*, many were slapdash collections of clichés, but others gave promising young directors and stars chances to push the genre envelope.

One was Rokuro Mochizuki, an adult film veteran who brought a dry-eyed, if downbeat, authenticity to his portraits of underworld life, beginning with *Gokudo Kisha* (The Wicked Reporter, 1993). Eiji Okuda plays a scruffy, bull-headed reporter for a race track tip sheet whose gambling addiction gets him in trouble with the yakuza. Think a Japanese Elmore Leonard hero.

Mochizuki's break-through film, however, was *Onibi* (The Fire Within, 1997), whose middle-aged hitman hero (Yoshio Harada) tries to go straight with a new young lover after serving time for a murder rap. He finds himself drawn back into his old trade, however, first by his old boss and then his girlfriend, who hires him for a hit. The narrative arc may be that of countless other yakuza movies, but *Onibi* is a freshly imagined, closely observed take on a familiar theme, with a powerfully understated performance by Yoshio Harada as a gangster willing to die for love.

Mochizuki's most volatile mix of Eros and violence is *Minazuki* (Everyone's a Moon, 1999) in which a sad-sack salaryman, played by Eiji Okuda, returns home one night to find his wife gone, along with all his money. During the course of his long search for her, the salaryman enlists the help of his psychopathic yakuza brother-in-law and falls in love with a prostitute who more than matches him in loneliness, desperation, and sexual hunger. A disturbing film, steeped in rough sex and raw violence, *Minazuki* is at the same time perceptive, not only exposing the inner demons of its characters but also revealing their capacity for tenderness.

The OV gang film maker who has attracted the most international attention, however, is Takashi Miike. Since making his first theatrical feature, *Daisan no Gokudo* (The Third Gangster) in 1995, Miike has continued to work in the gang genre for the video market, with a freedom, imagination, and energy that some have called manic and others praised as the mark of a world-beating talent. Not content to stay within genre confines, or even within the borders of Japan, Miike finds inspiration in the stranger reaches of *manga* and animation, while ranging over much of Asia. His films are truly borderless, with few limits of any kind, cinematic, cultural, or moral. "Basically, I am not the kind of person interested in making films that are just well done," he told Julien Fonfrede in an interview for Fantasiafest 2000. "If you make a genre film the way it's supposed to be done, there are always others who've done it better than you."

One of Miike's early adventures in cross-border filmmaking is the 1997 *Gokudo Kuro Shakai Rainy Dog* (Rainy Dog), whose hitman hero, played by Show Aikawa, lives alone in Taiwan working for a local gang—until his ex-girlfriend leaves him with a boy she claims is his son. Rejecting the standard plot trajectory (comic confusion, sentimental father-son bonding), the film stays cool and dark in tone as the hitman goes stolidly about his business, treating the boy with all the consideration of a stray dog. In the end, however, it is the hitman who is abandoned —a hunted stranger in a death-haunted land. Though saturated with macho romanticism, the film does not caricaturize or demonize its Taiwanese characters or milieu. Miike assumes, rightly, that we can understand both without the usual filters.

More typical of his recent work, and certainly getting more attention abroad, is *Dead or Alive* (1999), featuring Show Aikawa as a street-savvy Shinjuku detective who investigates a war between the yakuza and the Chinese Mafia and finds an unlikely ally in the gangster grandson of a Chinese "war orphan," played with snarling bravado by Riki Takeuchi. In the opening sequence—a cartoony, speed-crazed montage that presents the Tokyo underworld in all its grossness and glamour, feral violence and frantic sex—Miike creates moments of sheer visceral excitement, while jump-starting the story with minimum wasted motion and maximum cool. The film soon settles into a standard thriller groove, but Miike keeps interjecting similarly manic touches, right up to an ending that is straight out of a worlds-colliding Dragonball *anime*.

The OV mills have not only accounted for the great majority of the genre output in the past decade but served as a training ground for several directors who are now regulars on the international festival circuit, including Shinji Aoyama (*Chinpira*, 1996) and Kiyoshi Kurosawa (six films in the Katte ni Shiyagare!! [Suit Yourself or Shoot Yourself] series, 1995–96). Directors from non-OV backgrounds have also taken gangsters and gangs for their subjects in the past decade, from celebrated masters like Shohei Imamura, who hired Aikawa to play a hood in his Cannes Palme d'Or-winning film *Unagi* (The Eel, 1997), to indie film upstarts like Kazuhito Ishii, a TV commercial wunderkind. The latter's 1999 debut feature, *Samehada Otoko & Momojiri Onna* (Shark Skin Man & Peach Hip Girl), was a Tarantinoesque exercise in genre bending about a cool-dude thief, played by Tadanobu Asano, being pursued by a gang of cartoonish hitmen. Impeccably fashionable and deeply influenced by *manga* and *anime*, *Samehada* is less a yakuza *eiga* (movie) than an *eiga gokko* (movie game).

The most internationally honored director now working in the genre, in fact, paid no OV dues whatsoever. A stand-up comedian turned TV personality and actor, Takeshi Kitano had never directed anything when he filled in for Kinji Fukasaku on *Sono Otoko Kyobo ni Tsuki* (Violent Cop, 1989) after Fukasaku left the film because of a scheduling conflict. In this and subsequent films, including *3–4 X Jugatsu* (Boiling Point, 1990), *Sonatine* (1993), and *Brother* (2000), Kitano rejected both the rigidly structured romanticism of the *ninkyo eiga* and the chaotic semi-documentary realism of the *jitsuroku eiga*. Instead, he developed his own instantly identifiable style—a quirky mix of frontal compositions and elliptic editing, minimalist dialogue, and uninflected acting, brutal violence, and pawky comedy. At the same time, the outlaw heroes in these films, played by Kitano himself, share something of the traditional *ninkyo* stoicism and fatalism, facing death (or dealing it) with barely a flicker of emotion. Also, though Kitano insisted that his portrayal of gang violence was authentic—he had seen plenty of yakuza while growing up tough and poor in Tokyo's Asakusa amusement district—he staged many of his shoot-out and punch-up scenes with a stylization more reminiscent of Kabuki or, at times, stand-up comedy than the free-for-all brawls of Kinji Fukasaku. Kitano has exerted a strong influence on many younger Japanese filmmakers, after an international rise to prominence that began with *Sonatine* and culminated with a Venice Golden Lion for *Hana-Bi* (Fireworks) in 1997. But he is less a gang-genre director than a sui generis talent, who happens to find gangsters convenient vehicles for his existential meditations on life and death.

Largely dismissed or ignored by foreign critics when first released, gang films from the 1960s and 1970s have since attracted growing overseas interest, with the genre's most atypical director, Seijun Suzuki, becoming its first subject of retrospectives and serious critical attention abroad. Tai Kato and Kinji Fukasaku have also had their moments in the international spotlight in recent years (too late for Kato, who died in 1985). And Teruo Ishii has become known to non-Japanese audiences less for his gang films than his martial arts action and erotic cult items.

Meanwhile, films by less-celebrated Golden Age directors that Japanese critics and fans regard as genre masterpieces remain little known abroad. One is Kosaku Yamashita's *Bakuchiuchi Socho Tobaku* (Big Gambling Ceremony, 1968), which elevates its story of a gang succession struggle to the genre equivalent of Shakespearean tragedy, with career-peak performances given by Koji Tsuruta, Tomisaburo Wakayama, and Junko Fuji. It is as though Japanese were to revere the films Humphrey Bogart made with John Huston while ignoring the one called *Casablanca* he shot by that studio hack, Michael Curtiz.

By contrast, today's gang film directors face fewer barriers to international acceptance, using the genre to address, not the threat of Westernization to traditional values, but the globalization of Japanese society, particularly its criminal segment. Overseas attention, however, tends to focus on directors, such as Miike and Kitano, whose work is removed by both its excellence and eccentricity from the mainstream. Meanwhile Mochizuki, whose films are arguably more reflective of real gang life, has largely slipped through the cracks.

One film indicative of the new international approach is Takeshi Kitano's *Brother* (2002), in which the yakuza come to blows with the Mafia in Los Angeles's Little Tokyo. As his production company, Office Kitano, says on its web site: "[*Brother*] will challenge what has never been attempted in the Japanese cinema industry: to fuse the Hollywood film-making method . . . and Kitano's film-making as an auteur." In short, Kitano has made the first American mall-ready yakuza movie.

Brother presents the entire catalog of clichés characterizing Japan to the West since the heyday of "yellow peril" pulp: amputated pinkies, disemboweling, a severed head, suicide, and, in one memorable scene, broken chopsticks jammed up the nose of a rival hit man. Just about all that's missing is a *banzai* charge and *kamikaze* attack (though it considerately furnishes near-equivalents). *Brother* is also a typical Kitano film in its introverted compression—all chopped-up narrative and chopped-down performances. A plate of squid sushi in a soul food restaurant, it makes the Golden Age, by comparison, start to glow again.

DIRECTOR PROFILES & INTERVIEWS

Kinji Fukasaku (1930–2003)

Was Kinji Fukasaku a great director or merely a talented hack, who blew with the prevailing commercial winds while producing a genre gem or two amid the dross? For years the international critical jury didn't even sit on this question. Though Fukasaku turned out hit after hit over three decades, including the seminal Jingi Naki Tatakai (Battles without Honor and Humanity) series, he was all but ignored by foreign critics, who focused on his artier contemporaries, such as Nagisa Oshima, Shohei Imamura, and Masahiro Shinoda. (In Joan Mellen's 1976 book *The Waves at Genji's Door*, which contains a lengthy discussion of the postwar yakuza film, and the 1982 revised edition of Joseph Anderson and Donald Richie's history, *The Japanese Film: Art and Industry*, Fukasaku's name doesn't even appear.) Though his output was uneven—he churned out schlock to order rather than not work at all— Fukasaku revolutionized the yakuza movie genre with *Jingi Naki Tatakai* (1973). The film's grimly realistic portrayal of postwar hoods shook the genre out of its nostalgic longing for prewar verities and made it once again relevant to its materialistic, amoral times.

Rather than film the postwar chaos from the distancing viewpoint of the social anthropologist (Shohei Imamura), radical intellectual (Nagisa Oshima), or existential artist (Masahiro Shinoda), Fukasaku shot it like a cameraman on a reality show, getting down into the streets with his subjects and juicing his story with as much raw violence as he could get away with. Also, he rather liked his outlaws, though they might wear loud Hawaiian shirts, had bad table manners, and violated every commandment known to man. He didn't romanticize their code of honor—instead he exposed its fraudulence—but he admired their vitality and sheer cussedness. A bit of macho posturing was present in his just-one-of-the-bad-boys attitude, but there was also the pain and anger of the youth who had had his fill of official lies and adult hypocrisy, who realized that, in a world reduced to ruins and a society without values, the only law is survival. That youth was most alive—and defiant—in the five films of the Jingi Naki Tatakai series.

Now, three decades after the release of the series, critical winds have finally shifted, both in Japan and abroad. Fukasaku's work is now celebrated with retrospectives at major film festivals and cried up as the hot new thing on Internet message boards. Japanese critics proclaim Jingi Naki Tatakai as a classic of postwar Japanese cinema, right up there with the films of Kurosawa, Ozu, and Mizoguchi.

Fukasaku was born in Mito, the youngest of five children, in 1930. In 1945, with Allied warships bombing Mito and invasion seemingly near, the teenager slept at night with a sword near his pillow and in the daytime worked at a war plant. After the war, he began spending more time in movie theaters than school. His favorite films were French and the early work

© Mamiko Kawamoto

A master of gangster mayhem. Director Kinji Fukasaku transformed the yakuza genre with his Jingi Naki Tatakai (Battles without Honor and Humanity) series.

of Akira Kurosawa. In 1949 Fukasaku entered the first film department in Japan, at Nippon University. In his junior year, he transferred to the Literature Department, where he studied scriptwriting under Kogo Noda and Katsuhito Inomata.

Graduating in 1953, Fukasaku then joined Toei and, in June 1954, was assigned to the Toei Tokyo Studio as an Assistant Director (AD). He made forty films, working under such directors as Masahiro Makino, Yasushi Sasaki, Eiichi Koishi, Hideo Sekigawa, Shinji Murayama, and Tsuneo Kobayashi. In 1961 Fukasaku made his directorial debut with two featurettes, *Furaibo Tantei: Akai Tani no Sangeki* (The Drifting Detective) and *Furaibo Tantei: Misako o Wataru Kuroi Kaze* (The Drifting Detective 2), followed by his first full-length feature, *Hakuchu no Buraihan* (High Noon for Gangsters). All three films were released by Toei subsidiary New Toei. In 1962 Fukasaku directed his first film for Toei, *Hokori Takai Chosen* (The Proud Challenge), a suspense drama about a crusading reporter, played by Koji Tsu-

ruta, who unmasks dirty dealings between the Japanese arms industry and the American CIA.

In 1964 Fukasaku had a breakthrough hit with *Jakoman to Tetsu* (Jakoman and Tetsu), a drama set in a Hokkaido fishing village. Key to the film's success was Ken Takakura's energetic performance as the one-eyed outlaw Jakoman, battling against the frigid blasts of a Hokkaido winter. His follow-up film, *Okami to Buta to Ningen* (Wolves, Pigs, and Men, 1964), failed at the box office, however, and Fukasaku took a year-long hiatus, returning to the screen in 1966 with *Odoshi* (Threat), a kidnapping drama with an original script by Fukasaku and Ichiro Miyagawa. From that year until 1971, Fukasaku made a series of contemporary gang films for Toei, usually starring Koji Tsuruta, including *Kaisanshiki* (The Breakup, 1967); *Bakuto Kaisanshiki* (Gambler's Dispersion, 1968); and *Nihon Boryokudan: Kumicho* (Japan Organized Crime Boss, 1969).

In 1967, after signing a new nonexclusive contract with Toei, Fukasaku went to Shochiku to make the offbeat thrillers *Kuro Tokage* (Black

Lizard, 1968) and *Kurobara no Yakata* (Black Rose, 1969), starring transvestite talent Akihiro Maruyama (later Miwa). The former film was based on a stage play by Yukio Mishima and featured the writer in a cameo. In this same period, Fukasaku also directed the SF thriller *The Green Slime* (1968)—a U.S.-Japan co-production that later became a cult favorite abroad—and, together with Toshio Masuda, the Japanese scenes for the World War Two epic *Tora, Tora, Tora* (1970), after Akira Kurosawa made an acrimonious exit from the project.

Using the fee he received from Twentieth Century Fox for *Tora, Tora, Tora*, Fukasaku bought the rights to *Gunki Hatameku Motoni* (Under the Flag of the Rising Sun), Shoji Yuki's novel about a war widow's investigation into her late husband's service with the Imperial Army in New Guinea. The film of the same title as the book, with its *Rashomon*-like story line and brutal realism, earned Fukasaku critical praise and prizes both at home and abroad following its release in 1972.

That year Fukasaku returned to Toei to make two installments in the Hitokiri Yota (Street Mobster) series. Starring Bunta Sugawara as a rebellious gangster who violates gang code with a self-destructive impunity, the films marked a sharp break with the studio's *ninkyo eiga* conventions. They also brought Fukasaku to the attention of Toei producer Koji Shundo, who asked Fukasaku to direct a film based on the memoirs of a former gang boss about gang wars in postwar Hiroshima and nearby Kure. That film, *Jingi Naki Tatakai* resembles *The Godfather*—a huge hit in Japan—in ambition and scale but, shot in a semi-documentary style, is far more chaotic and headlong than Coppola's epic. Fukasaku's insistence on realism—in telling the truth about postwar gang violence and amorality—struck audiences as refreshing and new after a long season of *ninkyo eiga* romanticism—and *Jingi Naki Tatakai* became a big, influential hit.

Fukasaku made four sequels in quick succession, while other directors rushed out films in what came to be called the *jitsuroku rosen* (line of realism) style. After completing the first Jingi Naki Tatakai series in 1974, Fukasaku was persuaded to start a second, Shin Jingi Naki Tatakai (New Battles without Honor and Humanity), directing three of its four episodes. He also made *Jingi no Hakaba* (Graveyard of Honor, 1975); *Yakuza no Hakaba: Kuchinashi no Hana* (Yakuza Burial: Jasmine Flower, 1976); and *Hokuriku Dairi Senso* (Proxy War in Hokuriku, 1977) before the *jitsuroku rosen* boom ended.

Beginning in 1978, Fukasaku turned his attention from gangsters to SF dramas and historical epics, shooting *Yagyu Ichizoku no Inbo* (Shogun's Samurai, 1978); *Uchu Kara no Message* (The Message from Space, 1978); *Ako-jo no Danzetsu* (The Fall of Ako Castle, 1978); *Fukkatsu no Hi* (Virus, 1980); and *Makai Tensho* (Samurai Reincarnation, 1981), the latter two films for superproducer Haruki Kadokawa. Fukasaku's most critically acclaimed film of this period, however, was *Kamata Koshinkyoku* (Fall Guy, 1981), a black comedy set in the lower depths of the film world and starring Morio Kazama and Keiko Matsukata. The film swept domestic awards, as well as being named *Kinema Junpo* magazine's best film of the year—considered the highest honor in the Japanese film industry.

In 1992 Fukasaku returned to the action genre with *Itsuka Gira Gira Suruhi* (The Triple Cross), a frantically paced caper film that failed to impress at the box office, as did his next two films, the period dramas *Chushingura Gaiden Yotsuya Kaidan* (Crest of Betrayal, 1994) and *Omocha* (The Geisha House, 1998). In 2000 Fukasaku made a brilliant comeback with the dystopian action drama *Battle Royale*. Based on a best-selling novel about teenagers forced to play a murder game by a repressive government in a near-future Japan, the film attracted controversy even before its release. Diet members and even the Minister of Education

Kinji Fukasaku Interview (April 2002)

Q: You underwent some harsh experiences during and after the war. What effect did those experiences have on you as a person and a filmmaker?

A: You have to understand that war broke out the year after I was born [in 1930], when Japan invaded China. Japan was a small island country with no resources. It needed a resource-rich country like China to survive. England was doing the same thing, as were Germany and—the whole world was fighting these kinds of imperialist wars. These countries were struggling to survive. So, I was born in this storm of war and raised in the middle of it.

After the start of the war with China, Japan entered into the Tripartite Alliance with Germany and Italy to oppose the bloc led by America and England. The Allied powers were putting pressure on Japan to withdraw from China, so Japan joined that alliance as a means of resisting that pressure. It was doing what it needed to do to survive. Of course, Japan was completely defeated in the Pacific War. So, Japan was at war for fifteen years, from beginning to end. I was born and raised in the middle of that war—I got the whole nine yards. [laughs]

Q: Did you feel angry that Japan had lost the war?

A: I wasn't happy, but more than being angry I felt that there was no way Japan could have won. We had no weapons and the armaments factories were all destroyed. Also, there was nothing to eat, and the air raids had destroyed the cities. We had no planes to oppose the American air force that was bombing us. This was the exact opposite of what the army propaganda had been telling us. There was no way that we could have won.

Q: Did you feel that you had been deceived?

A: I wouldn't say "deceived"—I didn't know enough to be able to say I'd been deceived. I just thought it was strange. I realized that the military men and the politicians had all been liars. But the Japanese people, including the adults, couldn't say that while the war was going on.

Q: You were fifteen when the war ended.

A: Yes, I was a third-year student in junior high school.

Q: So, you had the experience of being educated under both the wartime and postwar system. One day you're saying *banzai* for the emperor, the next you're being taught about democracy.

A: During the war, we were taught to fight to the end and die. Not just the soldiers, but the children as well. We had no weapons, so we made spears out of bamboo. We had no thought of surrendering. We were going to fight to the death. We were taught that boys should die for the sake of the country, even if they were only fifteen years old. [laughs] That's the kind of education we had—and no one said anything against it. Our parents didn't tell us we had to die, but they didn't say anything against it either. If they had, they would have been taken away by the police. [laughs] They didn't say anything because they couldn't say anything. They had to be silent. Given that kind of education, we didn't think of death as something to be afraid of. We didn't know what it was. We did know that if things kept going the way they were, we wouldn't have anything to eat. We had no money to buy food. So, how were we going to get any? We were more worried about how we were going live than whether we were going to die.

Q: After the war, a lot of young men joined the gangs. I know that you never became a gangster [laughs], but were you tempted?

A: Before the war ended, adults started to lose control of their children—they could no longer tell their children what to do. There was nothing—no money, no food, no weapons to fight with. I think it was tough for the adults. [laughs] They had nothing and their children knew it.

I took the family sword and practiced with it until I thought I could cut someone with it. I really became serious about it. My friends were dying around me, some of them horribly—and a sword was completely useless. For my friends, it was a struggle just to fill their stomachs. Having those kinds of experiences, I suddenly felt that war was bad and that I'd had enough of the emperor. [laughs] So, what were we going to do? I felt that we had to rebuild Japan as a peaceful country, as hard as that might be, but the emperor and the politicians were just telling us to make war. Adults were teaching us how to die, but they didn't teach us how to live. When we asked them what we were going to do, they had no answer.

Living in the midst of those contradictions, being pulled one way and the other—that was my youth.

Q: Did movies help you to resolve those contradictions?
A: I wasn't allowed to watch movies. During the war, it was all right to watch Japanese films about how Japanese were going to win the war. They weren't very interesting, though. [laughs] But I never saw foreign films. Before the war, French, Austrian, and other foreign films were popular, as were American films. But I was forbidden to see them, even though I wanted to. I would pull my cap down low and try to sneak in the theater, but they would kick me out. [laughs]

Then, Japan lost the war and no one could stop you [from going in the theater]. People wanted to see films very badly—they had no other form of amusement. Not only adults but children saw films too, skipping school. Well, the schools had been burned down, so we had no choice. We snuck into the theaters—we didn't have any money of course. [laughs]

I was surprised when I saw my first foreign films. A lot of old French films were being released then, one after another. I thought, "So, this is what adults have been watching?" I was really moved. They were so interesting—any kind of film was interesting, really—the scenery, the history. With French films, there was also the cultural atmosphere. There were a lot of good films—Jaques Feyder's *La Kermesse Heroique* [Carnival in Flanders], Julien Duvivier's *Un Carnet du Bal* [Dance of Life] and *Pepe-Le-Moko*, Jean Renoir's *Les Bas-Fonds* [The Lower Depths], and *La Grande Illusion*. I was really surprised that people could think this way: They weren't telling lies—but the truth.

I also read a lot of old novels that I borrowed from my teachers. They would take down books from their shelves and say, "Read this, you'll learn something." That was the way a lot of teachers taught then, at least the ones who were serious. We would go to the teacher's house and borrow translations of famous literary works from around the world—Russian, French, English.

Q: I also heard that you liked the early films of Akira Kurosawa.
A: Yes, well, during the war he had to work within the military system—they would tell him what to make and cut his films. Then, the American Occupation came in and told him, "You can't make this or that"—especially period films. So, there's no way he was going to have friendly feelings toward the Occupation. American movies were a different story [laughs], but he didn't have much use for the American military.

Foreign films were so interesting back then—the way of thinking was so different. I thought it was no wonder that we lost. So, I became interested in films and didn't want to go to school. I didn't see any need for studying, as long as I had something like films to watch. I thought that if films were this interesting to watch, it would be even more interesting to make them. [laughs] I had no idea how, but I knew that there were people who made them.

Q: How did you happen to enter Toei?
A: To enter Toei, you had to have a college degree. So, I went to college and studied. My parents and siblings were all surprised when I told them I wanted to go into the movie business—they told me I had better give it up. [laughs] That's about what I expected—I'd been raised in a house where it was forbidden to see movies.

Q: That attitude wasn't limited to your family, was it?
A: No, that's the way it was all over, especially for junior high school students. If they were caught going to movies, they would get smacked on the face. Movies were shown in the dark where you had to be up to no good—smoking cigarettes and so on. So, kids who were caught at the movies were in for it. "No-goods make movies and no-goods watch them"—that was the adult attitude. "You'll never come to any good, watching movies"—that kind of thing. That's been the attitude for a long time.

Q: Did being from Mito have anything to do with it?
A: People in Mito are a bit *hesomagari* [cranky]. [laughs] In the Northern Kanto region when winter comes, the wind blows. There's not much snow, but a lot of dust. So, people from Mito, Gunma, and Tochigi tend to be like that winter wind, with stormy temperaments. A lot of yakuza come from there and people get into a lot of fights. Guys who can't fight aren't considered to be men. [laughs] That's the kind of place I was raised in, so I'm more the type who thinks with his body, not his head.

Q: That's the kind of experience that must have helped you when you started making films.
A: Violence is one basic element of films—it's

what you might call a pillar of filmmaking. Another is the "news" element—the social information that films convey. Still another is fashion. These are the three pillars of filmmaking, not just in Japan, but everywhere, with sex being a part of fashion. Of these three, the one that got across the quickest to the audience [when I started out] was violence. That was because Japan had lost the war.

Before and during the war, there were two big pillars. The first was violence, which was essential for period dramas, the biggest genre in the Japanese film industry. The second was romance, which was a big element in both period and contemporary films.

Q: Toei, though, made period dramas their specialty.
A: In the early days, though, the Occupation wouldn't let them make period dramas. During the war, there was a group of Japanese filmmakers working in Manchuria. After the war, they had to return to Japan. A lot of them got together and, because they had to eat, they decided to make something—and films were all they knew how to make. That's how Toei got started. After the war, there were three Japanese films companies: Toho, Nikkatsu and Shochiku. They were the mainstream of the industry at that time. Toei was a newcomer—a small, struggling company. The staff of Toei's Kyoto Studio were all veterans who had been making period dramas since before the war. When they started making them again, the audience welcomed them with enthusiasm. The Japanese audience had always liked period dramas. Toei wasn't the only one: Toho, Shochiku, and Daiei all started churning them out.

Q: You worked with a lot of directors when you were an assistant director with Toei, but I understand that the one you liked the best was Tsuneo Kobayashi. Why was that?
A: Kobayashi was a young director—only six or seven years older than me. He became a direc-

tor after the war. He had worked as a chief AD for [Akira] Kurosawa before he came to Toei. He had an interesting sensibility that appealed to me. When you're working as an assistant director on a boring film, you really feel like goofing off. But working with Kobayashi was interesting, so I didn't goof off as much. [laughs] I worked hard, and filmmaking became interesting for me.

Q: Because he listened to your opinions?
A: Yes, that's right. The older directors, the ones who had been directing since before the war, were harder to approach that way. The young ADs working for Kobayashi were full of enthusiasm, and he used a lot of their ideas. When a director uses your ideas, the job becomes more interesting.

Q: You made your debut as a director with a modern action film.
A: Toei made period films at its Kyoto Studio. But there was no period drama tradition at the Tokyo Studio, so there was a division of responsibility, with Kyoto getting all the period dramas. Tokyo got all the modern action films.

Q: Did you want to make period dramas?
A: Yes, I did, but Toei assigned people from the Kyoto area to the Kyoto Studio, people from the Tokyo area to the Tokyo Studio. That was the most logical way to do it. There were exceptions, though.

Q: About the time you started directing, Teruo Ishii came from Shin Toho with a more contemporary style of directing. Were you influenced by him at all?
A: Ishii came to Toei because Shin Toho went out of business. The directors for that studio went to various places—Toshio Matsuda went to Nikkatsu, while Teruo Ishii came to Toei. The studios hired them because they thought these directors could make interesting action films.

Toei was making more realistic films, mostly in the crime action genre. They were like French film noir. The basic style for such films is realism. Some directors developed their own style of realism, while others thought that realism was old fashioned and opted for dandyism instead. Ishii was one of the latter—his style was dandyism.

I was into something else—I'd been raised in Mito in a tough environment and happened to end up in a film studio, so my films tended to be rough around the edges. I was more along the lines of Godard or the director who made *Ashes and Diamonds* [Andrej Wajda]. They weren't into dandyism.

That's what was interesting about Toei at that time: Directors were trying various approaches. A lot of people, at Toei and elsewhere, were watching American films to learn how to make Hollywood-style entertainment, like the films of that ninety-five-year-old director who died recently—Billy Wilder.

Q: In the 1960s, Toei started making *ninkyo* films, which has a stronger element of fantasy.
A: That was because audiences were getting tired of period dramas. But the period dramas that were the easiest to understand were about yakuza. Westerns are the same way—a film like *Shane* is easy to understand.

Q: Most of them ended the same way—with the hero charging into the enemy gang's headquarters to kill the boss and anyone who got in his way.
A: Action movies—what you might call violent movies—always have to give the hero something to do, something to fight for. He has to kill the bad guys, there's no way around it. Good has to defeat evil. It's the same with French gang movies, with American gang movies. The pattern for all of them is the hero deciding how to fight and defeat his enemies, while trying to find a way of life—or death—that he can accept.

Q: True, that pattern is universal, but it can easily depart from reality.

A: That's often the case. Even American movies have that sort of unreality. The American style of heroism has its own approach to action: The hero saves the people he loves, while defeating the bad guys. In the traditional Japanese action films, the only choice of the hero is whether to die or go to prison. That leads to a very limited type of film, but everyone faces the same limitations when they make this type of film. Even American gang films are limited this way.

Q: What was the impact in Japan from the new type of violent films coming out of America in the late 1960s and 1970s—*Bonnie and Clyde* and *The Godfather*?

A: The same sort of thing was going on here. We thought that it was strange to have only noble heroes here, even though we were making films in Japan. We decided that it was all right to have heroes who weren't so noble. Those noble heroes were lies. Instead, we wanted the heroes to show us who they really were. Humphrey Bogart was popular in America about that time, though of course he had first appeared quite a bit earlier. So, we thought we'd try something similar in Japan. We made crime films that were like documentaries, Toei included.

Everywhere you looked then, film technique was making enormous strides, becoming more realistic. This happened from the late 1950s through the 1960s. In the 1950s, I was still an assistant director, but in the 1960s I became a director and consciously added these new techniques to my films. The American New Cinema movement arose because Hollywood films were no longer any good. You had films like *Bonnie and Clyde* and Arthur Penn's *Little Big Man*, starring Dustin Hoffman as the hero who was captured by an Indian tribe—that was a great film. It's interesting that American and Japanese filmmakers started making these kinds of films at about the same time. It was a strange period—we were in competition with each other, it seemed. We didn't want to lose to the Americans!

Q: The real breakthrough for you, and the *jitsuroku* genre in general, was *Gendai Yakuza: Hitokiri Yota*. It didn't do that well at the box office, but it had a big impact.

A: That was because of the hero. If he had been all good, the film wouldn't have been interesting. So, maybe it's all right if the hero does the worst thing in the film. The problem is, stars don't want a bad image, even Humphrey Bogart. By "bad" I mean an image that might say too much about their inner selves. Japanese stars were no exception—Koji Tsuruta didn't like that idea either. I had to find someone who wouldn't mind, and Bunta Sugawara was the one. He was in Shin Toho with Teruo Ishii; when that company went bankrupt he went to Shochiku and finally ended up at Toei but didn't do very well. I thought he might be the right one—he was slim and had those glittering eyes. He looked as though he could rape a woman. [laughs] Koji Tsuruta and Ken Takakura wouldn't do that sort of thing—but Bunta didn't mind.

Q: You two made a great combination, like Akira Kurosawa and Toshiro Mifune.

A: Kurosawa didn't like yakuza. Even though he had Mifune play violent roles, he would never have him rape someone in a film. He was from that kind of era. But people from my generation were raised in the black market, from the time we were kids. Rape was an everyday occurrence for us, so we didn't shy away from it on the screen. We wanted to do it. [laughs]

Q: The films you were making then seemed to reflect the reality of the yakuza world in a way that Koji Tsuruta couldn't portray.

A: They weren't yakuza so much as *gurentai* [delinquent gangs]. Yakuza need some kind of organization. If they don't have an organization behind them, they have no power, and with an organization, you have to have rules. If you have guys who violate the rules, you have to strangle them, kill them.

Q: It's a struggle for survival.
A: That's what makes it interesting.

Q: *Hitokiri Yota* also reflected the social background of its time. The Bunta Sugawara character was a rebel battling the police—the sort of thing that was making headlines then, with radical students doing the battling.
A: Yakuza are always thinking of ways of making their organizations bigger, so they can eat good food, sleep with beautiful women, and so on. Their way of life may look extremely anarchic, but it's also extremely easy to understand.

Q: It was easy to identify with the hero. Students at that time would go to the movie theaters and cheer for Ken Takakura. But what about *jitsuroku* films?
A: One film I made then, *Jingi Naki Tatakai*, reflects the reality of that time, the 1970s. When it came out, the student movement had already reached a dead end and the future looked unclear. There were [also] groups like the Japanese Red Army, attacking and killing each other. It all looked pretty hopeless. *Jingi Naki Tatakai*, which was pessimistic in a similar way, struck a chord—it came along at the right moment.

Q: I heard that [Toei producer] Koji Shundo wanted you for the film but was opposed by people at Toei's Kyoto Studio, where you were going to film it.
A: There were a lot of veterans on the Kyoto Studio staff—a lot of them had come up making period dramas. People like that didn't enjoy making a film about people who broke their promises and ran around being violent. They hadn't been trained to make movies that way.

They wanted something more aesthetic—so they looked for heroes [who could make their films look beautiful]. Koji Tsuruta fit the bill, as did Junko Fuji. Her sort of heroine was the Kyoto Studio's idea.

Q: Shundo was from the Kansai—did that make it easier for him to persuade them?
A: Shundo was basically their man. Even so, their films weren't working—audiences were tired of them. He thought that a Tokyo director could do a better job, so he asked me. A car needs two sets of wheels to get rolling. Two sets, not one—he was one set. I was the other.

Q: It must have been a big change for the Kyoto people. You were not only making a film on a new theme, but doing it a new way, using hand-held cameras and not worrying so much about the lighting.
A: That's true, I didn't worry so much about the lighting.

Q: I suppose the people there fought you about that.
A: Oh, they fought me, but you have to make something new. If you don't try a lot of new things, you can't make films that are truly new. For me, the interesting comes from the new. That goes for any art—you have to make it new. The old is boring because everyone already knows it.

Q: Kazuo Kasahara wrote the script for *Jingi Naki Tatakai*. Were his ideas in line with yours or did you have some differences?
A: We had our differences. Kasahara had been making *ninkyo* films straight along. Also, he was two years older than me—I was young enough to make the switch [to the new style] quickly; it took him longer. The people at Kyoto didn't like making films that way and at first Kasahara didn't rate my films very highly; but he realized that he had to do it my way if the studio was to have a future. So, we worked together, but the

jitsuroku boom didn't last very long, from 1972 until about 1975 or 1976, when the audience stopped coming.

Q: In casting *Jingi Naki Tatakai*, you used younger actors instead of Koji Tsuruta, Ken Takakura, and other veterans.
A: We cast younger people, such as Bunta Sugawara, who weren't well known—we got them from the *obeya* [the large common room where beginning actors slept]. We found some interesting characters that way. We worked pretty much by the seat of the pants. We kept going from the beginning of the 1970s until 1977 or 1978, when the boom died and we had to come up with something else.

Q: To make *jitsuroku* films, you had to find true stories. Was it difficult to find enough material?
A: Yes, the stories had to be realistic to a certain extent, but if audiences can see what's coming next they don't like it. Take fishermen for example—Japanese fishermen used to catch a lot of herring, but now because of global warming herring have stopped coming to Japanese waters and fishermen can't catch them. They've had to change their methods.

In the film industry, we used to cast this net called the period drama and draw up audiences. That's how the studios survived. When that no longer worked, they cast new nets called *ninkyo* films and got audiences the same way. Next came the net for *jitsuroku* films. Other companies had different nets—Shochiku had melodrama for example. Toho had a net called stylish cosmopolitan comedies, but all the nets started going bad in the late 1970s and 1980s.

Q: Yakuza movies especially—the studios stopped making them. One reason, I've heard, was that more women were coming to the theaters in the 1980s.
A: That's right. We had to make ourselves new nets and go out to the sea in a boat. It was the story of *The Old Man and the Sea*—we had to go where the fish were. We had to learn their habits—we had to study how to catch them. Movies are the same way. You can't catch women with yakuza. You have to find a net especially for women.

Q: In the 1990s, video films about the yakuza became popular, particularly with men. Show Aikawa and Riki Takeuchi became stars in those films, though Toei's were still the strongest. What do you think of these recent gang films?
A: I wish they paid more attention to the drama—if they did they would have better success. They're made with low budgets, on short schedules. Also they rework the few that are interesting to the point of exhaustion. That's no way to expand your audience or make interesting films, for that matter. But now there are guys like Beat Takeshi trying to come up with something different. That's what's interesting about films—there are always young people coming along with new ideas.

There are all sorts of ways to make films, so long as you bring out the potential of the material. There are always new films coming along and new talents making them. Kiyoshi Kurosawa is doing some interesting work. He's not just making violent action films but turning his attention to other genres and creating some interesting characters. He's experimenting—it's tough but he's keeping at it.

What is different about the younger directors is that they no longer submit projects to a studio. Instead, they're getting the money together themselves and making the kind of films they want. Japanese film companies don't have the energy they need to sell films, so these young directors are taking their films to foreign film festivals themselves. Then, if they get a prize, they bring it back to Japan and sell it.

Q: Takashi Miike is one example of that; he's getting more recognition abroad than he is in Japan.

A: He is popular abroad, isn't he? There's a fundamental difference between his approach and that of older directors. Young directors like him are making films that are first interesting to them. They're trying to make our line of work enjoyable. That's the way things are going now—in that sense young people have a lot of energy.

Q: But they have a hard time equaling the kind of energy you brought to your gang films in the 1970s.
A: Yes, it is tough. But [in 2000] the Rotterdam Film Festival screened fifteen of my films in a special section—the kind of thing foreign festivals used to do only for Ozu, Kurosawa, Mizoguchi, and people like that. Miike's films also got a good reception there.

A long time ago, I took *Jingi Naki Tatakai* to America for a screening. Five minutes after it started, a woman walked out of the theater and the man she came with ran after her. Pretty soon there was no one left in the theater. About five years ago, when the [L.A.] Cinematheque wanted to screen a special section of my films, I told them they'd better reconsider. [laughs] They told me that times had changed and they turned out to be right. When they screened my films, the audience gave me a standing ovation. I was astonished—I didn't think anyone would stand.

Q: Tastes have changed. *Battle Royale* stirred a lot of controversy in Japan, but abroad there was no problem.
A: The producers were afraid that they might get sued in America. They didn't want any trouble. I can understand their concern, given the situation of the schools over there.

Q: You still have the energy to make that kind of hit. Would you ever consider making another yakuza movie?
A: My yakuza movies come from my experiences when I was fifteen, in the burnt-out ruins

and the black market. I can't transfer that experience to the present. Dragging yakuza from that era of economic reconstruction into the present wouldn't work. There are no burnt-out ruins in Japan now. If I'm making fiction, I'd rather make a film like *Battle Royale*.

Q: That sort of story is more in tune with the times.
A: Today, it's a lot more interesting to make a film about young people. Adults are throwing up their hands at "young people today"—that's why.

Q: I see what you mean. If you had made *Battle Royale* with forty-two yakuza instead of teenagers, it would have been a totally different movie and not at all interesting.
A: Yakuza are already adults—they're using their heads, thinking about how to make money. Being a yakuza is a business. But if that's all it is—just a business—it's not going to make an interesting film.

Q: So, economics is a factor.
A: Definitely, definitely. A lot of yakuza today have gone to college—they've got brains.

Q: But leaving aside the yakuza, there are gangsters from China, Hong Kong, and elsewhere coming to Japan and working in places like Shinjuku.
A: That sort of thing is going on all over the world. Gangsters from America are going to Europe and encroaching on countries like Spain and France. Afghanistan is the same thing, though in a different sense. It's a vicious circle that ends in war. So, the Americans become the bad guys. [laughs]

Q: There's no sense of danger in Japan now.
A: Japanese are weak in that way—they think they're immune to that kind of danger. Anyway, those criminal organizations are invading Spain and France, slowly but surely. Now, the

Chinese, Korean, and Taiwanese Mafia are gradually encroaching on Tokyo. That kind of thing makes for a more interesting movie (than Japanese gangsters).

So, there are all kinds of possibilities, but the underworld is still central to film—that hasn't changed. The problem is how to fictionalize it.

Q: How do you appeal to modern audiences who have never known the reality of the gangs?
A: That has to come from your own consciousness, your own background. The gangsters in *The Godfather* were immigrants who had come to America from Italy. The same thing is happening in Europe now—people are coming from poor countries to rich countries. Crime is all they have, so they use it as a weapon. The Chinese and Korean Mafia are the same way. What makes them angry? Sad? How are their emotions rooted in their families?

Q: You could say the same sorts of things about both the Japanese and the immigrants coming to Japan.
A: Yes, they both have the same sorts of feelings—that's what make it interesting. The collision between the two sides is interesting.

Q: It's not just one-sided.
A: I did period dramas at one time, but big period dramas cost a tremendous amount of money. You have to use a lot of extras, and the characters have to wear armor—it's a lot of

trouble in various ways. With a yakuza movie all they have to do is walk. One guy walking alone is enough.

Q: But *ninkyo* films were period dramas of a sort. The setting was not the present day, but the Meiji, Taisho, and Showa Eras.
A: That's what linked them together, that period setting. That genre produced a lot of classics. They were made in a certain pattern, with an extremely limited story line. Yakuza were best suited for that sort of thing.

Q: From the beginning, you were trying to make something with a little more realism than the *ninkyo* films.
A: [Although] I didn't grow up with films, at some point I got interested in them and joined the film world. I never had any interest in *ninkyo* films, though—they were too old-fashioned.

I tried to find material that I thought would be interesting for an action movie. I found what I was looking for in the films of Kurosawa. He was the first one to go out into the burnt-out ruins with a camera. The money people at the studios thought that Japanese didn't want to see ruins, but that's all there was, that was all you could film. Kurosawa wanted to see what kind of interesting films he could shoot in the midst of those ruins, so that's what he did. That's our job—to record the reality around us.

publicly fretted about the effect its nonstop violence would have on its teenage target audience. That audience, however, lined up to see what all the shouting was about, despite the film's R-15 rating, while foreign film festivals competed to screen the most controversial Japanese film since Nagisa Oshima's *Ai no Corrida* (Empire of the Senses, 1976). In his eighth decade, Fukasaku had once again become the hot Japanese director of the moment. In Sep-

tember 2002, at a press conference announcing the production of *Battle Royale 2*, Fukasaku revealed that he was suffering from inoperable cancer and that the new film would be his last. He died on January 12, 2003, and his son Kenta took over as director.

FILMOGRAPHY

Battle Royale (2000); *Omocha* (The Geisha House, 1998); *Chushingura Gaiden Yotsuya*

Kaidan (Crest of Betrayal, 1994); *Itsuka Gira Gira Suruhi* (The Triple Cross, 1992); *Hana no Ran* (1988), *Shanghai Vance King* (1988); *Hissatsu 4: Urami Harashimasu* (Sure-Fire Death 4: We Will Avenge You, 1987); *Kataku no Hito* (1986); *Jinsei Gekijo* (Theater of Life, 1983), *Satomi Hakken-den* (Legend of the Eight Samurai, 1983); *Dotonborigawa* (1982), *Seishun no Mon* (The Gate of Youth, 1981); *Kamata Koshinkyoku* (Fall Guy, 1981), *Makai Tensho* (Samurai Reincarnation, 1981); *Fukkatsu no Hi* (Day of Resurrection, *The End, Virus,* 1980); *Ako-Jo Danzetsu* (The Fall of Ako Castle, 1978), *Uchu Kara no Message* (Message from Space: Galactic Wars, *Message from Space,* 1978), *Yagyu Ichizoku no Inbo* (Shogun's Samurai, *Yagyu Clan Conspiracy, The Yagyu Conspiracy,* 1978); *Doberman Deka* (Detective Doberman, *The Doberman Cop,* 1977), *Hokuriku Dairi Senso* (Proxy War in Hokuriku, 1977); *Shin Jingi Naki Tatakai: Kumicho Saigo no Hi* (1976), *Yakuza no Hakaba: Kuchinashi no Hana* (Yakuza Burial: Jasmine Flower, 1976); *Jingi no Hakaba* (Death of Honor, *Graveyard of Honor,* 1975), *Kenkei tai Soshiki Boryoku* (Cops versus Thugs, 1975), *Shin Jingi Naki Tatakai: Kumicho no Kubi* (1975); *Jingi Naki Tatakai: Chojo Sakusen* (1974), *Jingi Naki Tatakai: Kanketsuhen* (1974), *Shin Jingi Naki Tatakai* (1974); *Jingi Naki Tatakai* (Battles without Honor and Humanity, *Tarnished Code of Yakuza, War without a Code, The Yakuza Papers,* 1973), *Jingi Naki Tatakai: Dairi Senso* (1973), *Jingi Naki Tatakai: Hiroshima Shitohen* (1973); *Gendai Yakuza: Hitokiri Yota* (Street Mobster, *Modern Yakuza: Outlaw Killer, Bloodthirsty Man, The Code of the Killer,* 1972), *Gunki Hatameku Motoni* (Under the Flag of the Rising Sun, *Under the Fluttering Military Flag,* 1972), *Hitokiri Yota: Kyoken Sankyodai* (Yota the Killer: Three Wild Dog Brothers, 1972); *Bakuto Gaijin Butai* (Sympathy for the Underdog, 1971); *Chizome no Daimon* (1970), *Kimi ga Wakamono Nara* (If You Were Young: Rage, 1970), *Tora! Tora! Tora!* (1970); *Kurobara no Yakata* (Black Rose, *Mansion of the*

Black Rose, 1969), *Nihon Boryokudan: Kumicho* (Japan Organized Crime Boss, 1969); *Bakuto Kaisanshiki* (1968), *Gamma Sango Uchu Daisakusen* (The Green Slime, *After the Destruction of Space Station Gamma: Big Military Operation, Battle Beyond the Stars, The Battle of Space Station Gamma, Death and the Green Slime, Gamma #3 Big Military Space Operation,* 1968), *Kuro Tokage* (Black Lizard, 1968), *Kyokatsu Koso Waga Jinsei* (1968); *Kaisanshiki* (1967); *Hokkai no Abare-Ryu* (1966), *Kamikaze Yaro: Mahiru no Ketto* (Kamikaze Guy: Showdown at High Noon, 1966), *Odoshi* (1966); *Jakoman to Tetsu* (Jakoman and Tetsu, 1964), *Okami to Buta to Ningen* (Wolves, Pigs, and Men, 1964); *Gang Domei* (Gang 7, 1963); *Gang tai Gang* (Gang 3, 1962, *Gang tai G-men* (Gang versus G-Men, Gang 4, 1962); *Hokori Takaki Chosen* (The Proud Challenge, 1962); *Funky Hat no Kaidanji* (The Vigilante in the Funky Hat, 1961), *Funky Hat no Kaidanji: Nisenman-en no Ude* (Vigilante in the Funky Hat: 200,000 Yen Arm, 1961), *Furaibo Tantei: Akai Tani no Sangeki* (The Drifting Detective, 1961), *Furaibo Tantei: Misako o Wataru Kuroi Kaze* (The Drifting Detective 2, 1961), *Hakuchu no Buraikan* (High Noon for Gangsters, *Greed in Broad Daylight,* 1961).

Teruo Ishii (1924–)

One of Toei's more successful directors of the 1960s, whose stylish, fast-paced contemporary gang thrillers offered a sharp contrast to the studio's slower-footed, traditionally themed *ninkyo* films, Teruo Ishii has attracted relatively little critical attention either in Japan or abroad. Being neither an outrageous fantasist like Seijun Suzuki nor a gritty realist like Kinji Fukasaku, Ishii could be dismissed as a talented hack, making formula product to order while chasing Hollywood trends, but never quite catching up.

© Mark Schilling

The comeback kid. Teruo Ishii (left) and the author at the 2003 Udine Far East Film Festival, which screened six films from all periods of Ishii's career—the first-ever Ishii retrospective outside Japan.

True, Ishii did his share of hack work, turning out episodes of the popular Abashiri Bangaichi series with barely a pause: four alone in 1966, ten altogether between 1964 and 1967. But he was also a meticulous craftsman, master improviser, accomplished editor, and unregenerate dandy, whose films ranged from the witty and sophisticated to the outrageously strange, but were rarely boring.

Best known in the West for his *ero-guro* (erotic and grotesque) films of the 1960s and early 1970s, including one with the suggestive English title *The Joys of Torture* (*Tokugawa Onna Keibatsushi*, 1968), Ishii is in fact more various. Like the man he has called his directorial "brother," Jonathan Demme, Ishii has taken on a wide range of projects, from kiddy monster movies to sophisticated thrillers, while giving each one his personal stamp.

Born in Tokyo in 1920, Ishii was raised in the city's Asakusa District, where his father managed a cotton wholesaling business. In 1939 Ishii dropped out of Waseda Jitsugyo

High School and, three years later, entered the Toho Studio through a friend's introduction. He began as an assistant director but by the end of the war he was in Manchuria, taking aerial photographs for bombing runs. He joined the Shin Toho Studio on its founding in March 1947 and was once again assigned as an assistant director. Among his credits are Mikio Naruse's *Ishinaka Sensei no Gyojoki* (Conduct Report on Professor Ishinaka, 1950) and Hiroshi Shimizu's *Shiinomi Gakuen* (Shiinomi School, 1955). While working as a member of Shimizu's crew, Ishii studied script writing under Shin'ichi Sekizawa.

In 1957 Ishii made his directorial debut with *Ring no Oja: Eiko no Sekai* (King of the Ring: The World of Glory, 1957), a boxing film. He next turned his hand to the Super Giants SF fantasy series (1957–58), directing six of nine installments about supersized aliens come to earth to preserve world peace—the first of countless costumed Japanese superhero films and TV programs. His best-remembered films from his Shin Toho period, however, are the four entries in the Line series (1958–61)—thrillers that explored the contemporary Tokyo underworld in a semi-documentary style.

In 1961, with Shin Toho falling into bankruptcy, Ishii moved to New Toei, where he directed *Hana to Arashi to Gang* (Flower and Storm and Gang, 1961), a slyly comic heist movie whose box office success boosted Ken Takakura to stardom and spawned an eleven-part series. After this success, Ishii struck out into new territory, filming the Seicho Matsumoto mystery *Kiiroi Fudo* (The Yellow Land, 1961) and the William P. McGiven thriller *Rogue Cop*—called *Boss o Taose* (Kill the Boss, 1963) in Ishii's version. In 1963 he made his first period drama, *Showa Kyokakuden* (Tales of Chivalry in the Showa Era, 1963), a hit that helped fuel the *ninkyo* film boom.

In 1965 Ishii had his biggest smash of the decade with *Abashiri Bangaichi*, a prison-break movie based on Stanley Kramer's *The Defiant*

Q: You shot your first gang film in 1957, after moving from Toho to Shin Toho—the first film of the Line series.
A: That's right.

Q: The first postwar decade was the heyday of Hollywood noir. Did those films have an impact on you?
A: Not especially. When I was at Shin Toho, the president ran the studio as his personal fiefdom. He put his fingerprints all over the scripts, making a lot of comments. I hated that, so I wanted to write about a world he didn't understand, to shut him up. That's how the Line series came about—I wrote about something he didn't understand. The president was a big Kabuki person—he was a former *benshi* [silent film narrator] and so was very knowledgeable about Kabuki. He used to stick his nose into everything—I wondered what he needed a director for.

I didn't like being told what to do, so I looked for a world that the president wouldn't understand and happened to come up with the idea for the Line series. He had no idea what kind of world those films were taking place in, so he didn't say anything—and that's exactly what I wanted. [laughs]

Q: You explored the secret world of prostitution in *Sexy Line*. Did you have any trouble with Eirin [the industry censorship body]?
A: Not really, no. Eirin was willing to release [*Sexy Line*] just as it would any other film.

Q: Even so, there weren't many Japanese films at the time about the underworld.
A: Well, that's true. The subject matter may have been new.

Q: You left Shin Toho and went to Toei to make *Hana to Arashi to Gang* [Flower and Storm and Gang] in 1961. Was there a big difference between the two studios?
A: Yes, there was. I didn't really like Toei as a company, but my old studio went bankrupt, so I was in a jam. I thought, "Well why not?" The first film I did there was based on a work by Shinji Fujiwara—a gang film called *Hana to Arashi to Gang*. It wasn't exactly something new for me. I thought it would be an easy film to do, so I was rather casual about going to [Toei] to make it.

Q: The Line series was made with a documentary touch. *Hana to Arashi to Gang* had a bit of that as well, but I liked the way you combined comedy with the action. It struck me as something fresh for Japanese films at that time.
A: Is that so? Well, the Line series, especially the last one I did, *Sexy Line* [1961], had a comic touch as well. In *Hana to Arashi to Gang* as well, I wasn't saying, "This is the real underworld"—I was injecting a bit of humor into that situation. So, in a way it was an extension [of the *Line* films]. It wasn't a straight-ahead gang film but something more playful.

Q: You wanted to add entertainment value for the audience?
A: That was part of it. But I thought that if I enjoyed it, the audience would too—at least the people in the audience like me would enjoy it. That was my hope anyway. Most of the Toei action stuff I was asked to do was kind of crappy, so I hesitated at first. I thought, "I don't want to do this." Then, this material came along—it struck me as being somewhat different for Toei, so I took it on. I thought it was all right, that it was something I could do. The sort of stuff Toei was doing then was what kids today would call "uncool." [laughs]

Instead, I consciously tried to emulate what Nikkatsu was doing, especially the films they were making with Yujiro Ishihara. The costumes that Toei had in their costume department were no good, so I had them all remade. I borrowed a Nikkatsu poster of Yujiro and gave it to the costume people. I told them, "I don't want the pants to be any wider than these." I had them redo everything. Toei fought me, but their gang films were so different from Nikkatsu's—they were so uncool. [laughs] So, I had a problem with that. I wanted to make something that would blow their old stuff away.

Q: Did you film with Nikkatsu in mind as well?
A: What struck me about Nikkatsu's films were the costumes—the overall stylishness. The pants Toei was using were so wide and baggy. They were like knickers—the kind of things you wear with *tabi* [Japanese-style, split-toe socks, usually worn by workmen]. Or they would have characters pay a bill at a night club and say, "Keep the change." It was so stupid—as if none of the people making the films had ever been to a night club. So, I had a problem with that. The actors also had a problem with that. Some of them would say, "I can't say these lines." So, I cut all the problematic parts. [laughs] I wanted to make the dialogue a little more realistic, a little more stylish.

Q: That film was the first you did with Ken Takakura. At that time, he wasn't yet a star, though big things were expected of him.
A: Yes, that's true. Back then, most of Toei's production was at the Kyoto Studio. Toei was still making a lot of period dramas there, with people like Chiezo and Utaemon—big stars. The Tokyo Studio was lagging behind. That was only to be expected because period dramas were Toei's main thing. Then, gang films started to become more popular—and finally the positions of the two studios reversed. But until that happened, Tokyo was definitely number two and it was tough on Ken. When he joined the studio, they were making mainly period dramas, so he had a hard time.

Q: He did appear in various types of films, though, not just gang films.

A: But in the beginning he hardly ever appeared in Kyoto Studio films. Instead Ken was cast opposite Hibari Misora. He was rowing Hibari in a boat but not getting anywhere as an actor. So, when he had a chance to appear in a real leading role [in *Hana to Arashi to Gang*], he jumped at it. He did a great job in that film.

Q: He really seemed to grow as an actor in your films.
A: We got along pretty well—we were on similar wave lengths. We liked each other, so there was never any tension between us. We were like friends, which made it easy for him to work.

Q: I hear he was the type of actor who would try anything.
A: That's right—he would try anything. He wasn't the type to worry and fret. I would be frantically rewriting the script, just putting down whatever came to mind. He never knew what was going to happen next—and I didn't either. [laughs] We would just shoot anyway, but he put his trust in me. He would go along with me, no matter what.

Q: He still had something of a punk image at that time.
A: Yes, he was still young.

Q: Then, as he aged he acquired more dignity.
A: That's right. Sometimes, people will come to me and say they want to see one of his old videos. So, I'll watch it a bit with them and I'll realize how young he was then. He was a sort of punk at that age.

Q: Of course, there were Hollywood versions of the same thing—James Dean and Marlon Brando and so forth. Did they influence the way you shaped his image?
A: No, not all. I never thought of that sort of thing.

Q: I know that Takakura later developed this very Japanese macho image, but in your films he was something different.

A: I didn't deliberately try to do that—I just shot the way I wanted.

Q: Changing the subject a bit, you worked as an assistant director for Mikio Naruse and later said that he had been a big influence on you. How exactly did that influence appear in your films?

A: Well, when I was really in a jam and pressed for time, I would use what I had learned from him about technique. I would use a bit of the Naruse technique to slap together something in a hurry. No one noticed, but I had watched carefully Naruse at work and when I was in a bit of a spot, I knew how to get out of it. A lot of directors would worry about the next day's shoot if they didn't write out a storyboard the day before; but I would go to the set with nothing. [laughs] I always thought it was better to work with what I found on the set. Then, when I was really pressed for time, I would slide through with the techniques I had learned from Naruse. It was just something I did naturally—I had that technique in my bones, so to speak. I never worried about what to do next. So, in that way I had a kind of confidence.

Q: That's really an amazing ability.

A: Not really—it wasn't so hard. Storyboards create more problems than they solve. When you work according to storyboards, you're thinking you'll shoot a certain way. You've got something in your head. But with films, things don't always go the way you planned. When you try to film what you've got in your head you end up wasting a lot of time—and even then you don't get what you want. Instead, it's better to adjust to what you have to work with on the spot. If you go about it that way, just go with the flow, it's a lot easier. With storyboards, people often draw a window wherever they feel like—then they have to build a set and in-evitably someone says, "The window's not in the right place." It should be higher or lower or whatever. They end up wasting a lot of time with what I think is nonsense—and for very little result. That's why I'm not a big fan of storyboards. You think they're going to help things go more smoothly—but very often the reverse happens.

Q: Of course, finding the right location is more important than drawing the right storyboard.

A: That's right. It's very important. Naruse used to tell us that "it's all about finding the right location." You really have to find the right location. According to him, the location determines the stage setting or *mise en scène*. He often used to say that "no real director would leave the *mise en scène* to someone else." So, he would always decide it himself, not leaving it up to anyone else. He really believed the "*mise en scène* is the film." Once he made his decision, that would then determine where he would put his actors. He had all that in his head.

Q: It seems there are a lot more outdoor locations than studio sets in your films.

A: That's true. Besides Naruse, I worked as an assistant director for Hiroshi Shimizu. Shimizu also hated sets—he believed in shooting everything on location. Even for interior shots in a house—he would go to a real house. That may be pushing it too far, but. . . . He used to say that when you go on location you see sparrows fly under the eaves of the roof. When the wind blows, the trees sway and the leaves fly. That's nature—it's not something you can build on a set. He liked working in the midst of natural settings. He thought he could get better effects that way. I really came to like locations as well—so I've worked in that sort of setting more often than not, where I can incorporate more reality in the film.

Q: One example of that philosophy in action was *Tokyo Gang tai Hong Kong Gang*—you went abroad to shoot that one. I heard that you were in Hong Kong for about two weeks.

A: That's the longest period we were ever there. The first time was for only ten days. We did a bit of scouting for locations, but for the most part the first time we were there we just went out and shot. We had no budget for anything else. We didn't get permission to shoot—we just used a telephoto lens to steal the shots we needed. And back then, telephoto lenses were monsters—they weren't light the way they are now. Takakura carried that lens himself. Everyone had to work together because we were short on staff. We went with about ten people. Always on a shoot like that you have a script girl to keep records, but we couldn't take one. We just shot like crazy, but we had no records of what we had been doing. I was the only one who remembered what we had shot and in what order. [laughs]

Q: One thing that struck me about that film was how well you captured the atmosphere of Hong Kong—not just the tourist sights but the back streets where tourists never go.

A: That's true. We spent all of our time in the back streets. [laughs] I generally don't like the main streets. You just get the happy face of a city there, just the outward facade. But when you venture into the back streets, you get the real human flavor of a place—that's what attracts me to them.

Years after I filmed in Hong Kong with Toei, I went to Shochiku and again shot on location there. The Shochiku people were serious, straight-arrow types. When I said, "I want to shoot here," the cameraman would say, "If you shoot [these people] like this, I feel sorry for them." Or he would say something more intellectual, like, "This is a desecration of humanity." [laughs] I had to wonder what he was thinking. [laughs] I have a tough time getting along with serious people. [laughs] It's true that a lot of people in Hong Kong were living miserable lives back then. So, when I used them as

a backdrop, the cameraman thought it was a "desecration." He didn't want to shoot them. I thought he was a strange type of cameraman, but that's the kind of thing you run across in this business.

Q: Did you have any help from the Hong Kong film industry when you went?

A: No, none. We thought about asking for cooperation, but the companies there wanted a lot of money. Toei could never pay that much, so we had to do everything on our own. We ended up doing some strange things as a result. For example, they had these double-decker buses. We had a scene in which Takakura rides on one of them and various things happen. We went to the upper deck and just started shooting, like a news crew. When the conductor came to the upper deck, we had someone posted as a lookout who would give us a signal. We would turn off the electric power and try to look innocent. Then, when he left, we would start shooting again. [laughs] We did the same thing on the cable car they have there. We didn't pay one sen to anyone—we just shot on the sly, without permission from the police or anyone else. When a cop caught us, we would just pay him off. [laughs] It was a lot cheaper that way.

When we were in Hong Kong that time, a French movie crew came. They were really something, with a whole fleet of cars, contacting each other with walkie-talkies, pushing people out of the way. They were doing everything on a big scale. Of course, they were spending tons of money. We had all of ten people and were operating like a news crew, shooting everywhere without permission. [laughs]

Q: There is one scene where Takakura is shot and drops dead on the street, while the neighborhood kids gape at him. It's as though you shot that scene without rehearsal, with a hidden camera.

A: You're right—we shot it with a hidden camera. I thought that if someone dies on the street, a lot of people would gather around, but most of them looked totally indifferent. I wondered what would happen if someone really died. I thought, "This is a pretty cold place." [laughs]

When that scene was over, Ken said, "If you lost all your money in Hong Kong I wonder what would happen to you." I said, "Why don't we try it." He was wearing a very good watch—a Patek. We had him take it to Hong Kong pawn shops and ask how much he could get for it. He went to several shops, the idea being that a pickpocket had taken all his money and he had only the watch. He had to practically give the watch away. We came to the conclusion that if you were robbed there, it would be all over for you. Someone keels over, but no one comes over or asks what has happened. That's pretty scary. [laughs]

Q: After that, you returned to Hong Kong to shoot *Narazumono* [1964]. Was that also a short shoot?
A: That was the longest of any Hong Kong location shoot I did for Toei. We weren't so pressed for time and were able to bring enough people. The company was willing to spend more money, so it was a bit easier. But we arrived there on Chinese New Year, when the prices for hotels and everything else went up. Also, at the hotel about ten people came around for tips. [laughs] There was always a boy opening a door and holding his hand out. That bothered me a bit. We moved to Macao, but the hotels were also full. The production supervisor nearly had a fit. He ended up looking for what we call *minshuku* in Japan—cheap inns. He sent Ken Takakura to one, Tetsuro Tanba to another—we were scattered all over the place. The boats were the same way—some went on one, some on another. We couldn't get everyone together to shoot—it was a huge mess.

Q: You used Japanese actors for the Chinese roles. What was the reason for that?
A: It would have been a lot of trouble to use local actors. The company wouldn't pay for interpreters for one thing. Instead we had the [Japanese] actors learn Chinese and brought them over [to Hong Kong]. When Chinese people hear the dialogue, they'll probably find the pronunciation strange. But we thought, well, we're not going to release the film in China anyway, so we went ahead and did it that way.

Q: So, *Tokyo Gang tai Hong Kong Gang* and *Narazumono* were never released in Hong Kong?
A: I have no idea, but probably not—only in Japan. At that time, we weren't thinking about showing these films abroad.

Q: Now, of course, the Japanese film industry is thinking more about Asia.
A: Exactly. I was surprised recently to find out that one of my worst films has been shown abroad. I've had an article sent to me about it. I just wish now that I'd shot it more carefully. [laughs]

Q: You worked with Koji Tsuruta on the Gang series. He'd been a big star before he came to Toei. Was he harder to work with than Ken Takakura?
A: Yes, Tsuruta was. He was an argumentative type. He always wanted to hash things out. For me, it was a hassle. I laugh about it now, but he was into realism. Everything had to be real or he wouldn't go along. He would argue all the time, saying this or that was "strange," meaning not realistic. We would be frantically busy on the set when he would come to me with these objections. I would kind of laugh at him, but when he was working with [Tetsuro Tanba] and started complaining, Tanba would say, "All right, Tsuruta, enough is enough. Let's go, let's go—let's have a take!" That would shut him up

a bit. But he liked to argue—I really hate actors who do that.

Q: You ended up making a lot of films with him.
A: That's true, but I didn't really want to. The president of the studio liked to say, "When people who don't get along work together, they end up making a good movie." So, he'd force me to work with Tsuruta. [laughs]

Q: Tanba seems to be the opposite—an actor who could adapt himself to any situation. He's been in hundreds of films, but he shines in the ones he made with you.
A: He was a guy who would do anything. He was a complete contrast to Tsuruta. When Tanba came on the set, he'd say "I leave it all up to you" or "Use me any way you want." If I told him to face right, he'd face right—he would do anything I asked him.

Q: He was particularly interesting in *Juichinin no Gang* [1963], playing the young boyfriend of a powerful middle-aged women. Usually, that sort of character is weak and contemptible, but Tanba plays him as a strong-willed type, who speaks his own mind. Was that your idea?
A: I let him do pretty much as he pleased. [laughs] He was what the Chinese call a *taijin*—a kind of sage. He didn't let anything bother him. I told him to interpret the role any way he liked. I just let him run with it. So, I had no idea where he was going. [laughs] That made it more interesting. Instead of tying him down with detailed instructions, saying "do this or do that," I just gave him an outline of what I wanted-ed and let him take it from there. Within those limits, he was free. I got good results doing that.

Q: That film reminded me of *Ocean's Eleven*, the Frank Sinatra and Dean Martin film that was recently remade with George Clooney and Brad Pitt. Were you thinking of it at all when you made *Juichinin no Gang*?
A: No, not at all.

Q: The three female characters in that film are also interesting. In most gang movies, women play relatively subordinate roles, as girlfriends or bar madams or whatever. But in this film, the three women take part in the planning of the robbery and are equal to the men. Was that your intention, to beef up the women's roles?
A: Not really. The studio wanted an all-star cast—as many big names as possible. But with all those well-known actors in the cast, I had to give them something more than cameos. If you don't have a fairly meaty role for those types of actors, they won't appear in the film, no matter how much you negotiate. So, I shoehorned in big scenes for all the main actors—it was a huge hassle—and that's why the movie turned out the way it did.

Q: You also seemed to be trying something different in *Kaoyaku* [1965] in which Junko Fuji plays a club hostess who becomes the girlfriend of a deformed gangster, played by Kyosuke Machida. Fuji had a strong-willed, old-fashioned image in many of her films, but in this one she plays a softer, more modern type.
A: That film came out when Junko Fuji was still relatively unknown. She was the daughter of the producer, Koji Shundo—he asked me to give her a chance. I think that at the time she had hardly been in any films. Looking back at it now, I didn't use her very well—I feel sorry for her. I'm amazed that Shundo didn't get mad at me. [laughs] I really miscast her.

Q: Shundo was a big Toei producer who made a lot of *ninkyo* film, but you didn't work very much with him.
A: No, not very much. Shundo was usually at the Kyoto Studio—I was at the Tokyo Studio. When I went to Kyoto, he would often tell me to drop in at his place. He went out of his way to keep in touch—he really treated me well. Tokyo and Kyoto were different places, but he came [to the set] of several of my films. Kinji

Fukasaku was scheduled to direct *Kaoyaku*, but there was some disagreement between Fukasaku and the scriptwriter. Finally Shundo told me, "We're never going to get this settled, so I want you to take over." He brought the script to me and we talked it over. I told him I would do it, but I wanted to rewrite it a bit. So, I rewrote and shot it.

Later, he came to me with what at the time was an unthinkable request. Shintaro Katsu wanted to make a film called *Kaigun, Yokosuka Keimusho* [The Navy: Yokosuka Prison] at Toei. I was to write the scenario and Katsu was to star. Then, all of a sudden, Shundo came to me before we started shooting and said he wants me to quit that film and direct another one, starring Ken Takakura at the Kyoto Studio. "Why, what happened?" I asked. "I'm just about to start shooting with Shintaro Katsu." So, he switched directors and I went to shoot Ken in Kyoto. I asked him who he had hired to direct in my place. "Just leave that up to me," he said. "I'll get somebody." And that's what he did. Mr. Shundo would come at interesting times. [laughs]

Q: I heard that Shundo and Kinji Fukasaku didn't get along very well.
A: No, I never heard that. He generally got along well with everyone. He was a wonderful producer—I admired him. He was really precise—once he had made up his mind, that was it. That's why he was a great producer. He would call me in and I'd wonder, "What is it this time?" but when he started talking I'd suddenly be all ears. He had just the right tone, a very polite way of speaking—"Mr. Ishii we want to do so on and so forth for this picture, would you direct it for us?" I was surprised at how precise he was—he was one strong-minded individual. When we were filming on the set, he'd watch quietly, but I never saw him sit in a chair. He always stood, even if it was for one or two hours. Seeing that, I always felt that he was doing his best for the sake of the film.

I generally hate to fly, so I seldom get in an airplane or go abroad. Film festivals often send me invitations, but I never go. Once though, I had a location shoot in Hokkaido on a film for Mr. Shundo. Ken Takakura was starring in it. I had shot ten episodes of the Abashiri Bangaichi series in Hokkaido and had always gone there by train, while the staff flew. So, I had been on the train all by myself. This time as well I told Mr. Shundo that I wouldn't fly. Then, just before the train left the station, he said he would go with me, and so we rode together on the train. Mr. Shundo didn't want to take that train—he did it just to be with me. It was a long, tough trip—you had to take the night train and you'd arrive in Aomori in the morning. From there, you'd take the ferry to Hokkaido and then go from Sapporo to Abashiri. I was impressed that such an important producer would go with me all that way.

Someone came to interview me recently and when I told him that story, he said, "It wasn't because he wanted to be with you—he hated airplanes too." [laughs] "Oh really," I said. All that time, I'd felt he'd done me this great favor. I had to laugh. That was the first time I'd known about it.

Q: What about Kinji Fukasaku—he came to Toei a bit later than you did, but you were both directing modern gang films at the same time. In the interview book Shundo did with Sadao Yamane, Shundo said he was unhappy with Fukasaku at first because he was making films for himself, not the audience.
A: I'm a Fukasaku fan—I like him as a person. True, he was making films for himself, but I think that's wonderful. Some people can be successful doing that and some can't. He was one who could do it, who makes that approach work for him. I respect him for that—he's a wonderful person. I really love his films.

Q: He became famous abroad for his *Jingi Naki Tatakai* [Battles without Honor and Humanity] series, but you were making modern gang films with the same kind of documentary touch a decade earlier.

A: No, no, I've never thought about it that way. I'm a Fukasaku fan, but I don't care for the Battles without Honor and Humanity series. The first one or two are all right but after that they are hard to take. I prefer films like *Kamata Koshinkyoku* [Fall Guy, 1982]. I like his style of directing—it's just that I don't rate the Jingi Naki Tatakai films that highly. I admit that they're unique and stand out for their excellence, compared with other gang films, but I just find them hard to take.

Q: You worked with the same actors again and again, particularly Ken Takakura, Koji Tsuruta, and Kyosuke Machida. Was there any particular reason for that—or did it just make your job easier?

A: Well, some actors I just don't like. A lot of them I don't care if I never meet again. [laughs] I'm the type who doesn't like to suffer—I'd rather have it easy. So, if I like someone I want to work with him again and again. If I don't like someone, I don't want to work with him—it's that simple.

Q: But I suppose there were times when the studio decided the casting and you had to go along.

A: That's true, but I hated that. I would even quit a film rather than work with someone. For example, Koji Tsuruta—I never once asked to work with him, but we ended up making a lot of films together. I was forced to work with him, but even though I didn't like him I felt a bit sorry for him. I thought I should have done better by him.

Tsuruta starred in a film in the Gang series—*Hong Kong Gang tai Tokyo Gang*. In the original script, he was the focus of the story, but I rewrote the whole thing and gave half the story to Takakura. [laughs] I didn't even want to do half with [Tsuruta], but I thought I could

stick out that much with him and enjoy myself for the rest. That's how I persuaded myself to do it. Ordinarily, a star whose role I cut would make a big stink—go directly to the president of the company. "What do you think you're doing!"—that kind of thing. Tsuruta certainly had the power to do that, but he quietly went about his work. I felt bad about that—I thought I had gone a bit too far. "He has his good points too," I thought. Then, we worked together again, and I realized I couldn't stand him. [laughs]

Q: The way the film broke off in the middle reminded me of Stanley Kubrick's *Full Metal Jacket*. Perhaps he saw your film before he made his. [laughs]

A: I just wanted to get Takakura into it because I didn't like Tsuruta—that's all. Tsuruta starred in a yakuza film titled *Showa Kyokakuden* [Tales of Chivalry in the Showa Era, 1963]. When I heard the title I thought *kyokaku* sounded so uncool; so I said I didn't want to direct it, but the studio made me. I told the chairman [Shigeru] Okada, that I didn't care for Tsuruta, but Okada said "When people who don't get along work together, they make a good film." He talked me into it, against my will.

Just the thought of having to work with Tsuruta made me depressed, so I wrote in a role for Kanjuro Arashi. I thought that, with Arashi in the film, it would be easier to make.

Q: That was a *ninkyo* film—a genre that you usually had little to do with.

A: But the story itself was easy to do. I didn't feel any particular passion for it, but on the other hand it was about the demimonde in old Asakusa. I felt it was the kind of thing I could enjoy doing. Yasunari Kawabata had written some interesting things about Asakusa, such as *Asakusa Kurenaidan*. He described how the *chinpira* [apprentice gangsters] of that time looked, the kinds of clothes they wore. I found that old Asakusa demimonde fascinating.

Q: You had never done a period drama before, though—was that because you didn't want to?
A: Not really, but even when I was an assistant director I had never done a period drama, so I didn't have any experience.

Q: Changing the subject a bit, music played a big role in the gang films you made with Toei. The jazz scores gave them a very contemporary feeling. Masao Yagi was your main composer then—how did you get together with him?
A: I wasn't very knowledgeable about music. At that time, Toei had a person in charge of music who served as a kind of go-between, handling the musicians and deciding which composer would work best with which film. He would also negotiate with the musicians. Anyway, that person strongly recommended Masao Yagi to me. "Yagi is the only one for your films" and "You've got to meet him"—that kind of thing. He was extremely insistent, so I agreed to a meeting. Then, he told me that Yagi was in prison. When I asked why, he said, "He's in because of drugs." "What day does he get out?" I asked. Then, he said, "When he is using drugs, he's even better." "Well, all right," I said. [laughs]

So, anyway, that's how we got together. Even though I didn't know much about music, when I heard his stuff I knew that he really had it and that I wanted him to work for me. He was with me for a long time, all the way through the Abashiri Bangaichi series. He wrote the scores for all of them.

Q: The *Abashiri Bangaichi* theme song is famous, of course. It first appeared in *Kaoyaku*, where Ken Takakura sang it. Was it originally a folk song?
A: It was a song that prisoners sang. They would change the words, depending on who was singing it. Because it's a prison song, no one knows who the composer is. No one owns the rights to it.

Anyway, one day I was glancing at televi-sion, at some kind of documentary. There were two yakuza *chinpira* who had been in prison, but were now reformed. They were reminiscing and one of them said, "This is the song we used to sing." He played it on a guitar—not very well, I might add—and sang it. I listened to a bit of it and thought, "This is good." I quickly got my tape recorder and recorded it. Then, I had the TV station check out the song for me—it became the theme for *Abashiri Bangaichi*. I had Yagi listen to it and he said, "This is it." The theme song for *Abashiri Bangaichi* became a hit and several record companies, including Polydor, had famous singers record it.

Q: It's no secret that the basis for *Abashiri Bangaichi* is Stanley Kramer's *The Defiant Ones* [1958].
A: That's right, totally. When I saw *The Defiant Ones* I thought that I wanted to make a Japanese version. I was still with Shin Toho at the time. After that, I was hot to make that movie. I didn't have a script, but I wanted to make it. Then, the proposal for *Abashiri Bangaichi* came to me. When I first read it, I thought the story was too cheesy—it was just a melodrama. I told the studio I didn't want to make it, but I asked if it would be all right to change the story. They agreed, so I mentioned *The Defiant Ones* and asked if they would be interested in making a Japanese version. They gave their OK. After that, things went quickly. I didn't having anything down on paper but I had a good model to use for the story, so the script didn't take long to write.

Q: Was the Hokkaido setting your idea?
A: Hokkaido was our location from the beginning. I wrote the script without doing any location scouting. Then, when I went there, I knew I was in trouble. [laughs]

There's a scene in the film where the two convicts escape down a mountain on a railroad handcar. I thought that on a big island like Hokkaido, there was sure to be that kind of place, but when we went scouting for locations we couldn't find one. We made inquiries through the Toei chain in Hokkaido and checked out leads. We spent an entire month looking—the longest time ever for me. We finally ended up in Shintoku, a town with a famous horse market. It was a small town with a logging railroad that was just about to be torn up—the only one of its kind left.

I thought our problem was solved, so we went to Shintoku right away, but there were no inns in the entire town. The village association had built a kind of dormitory up in the mountains and we stayed there. People from the village office served as maids, making rice and laying out the bedding. The village people took good care of us, so we could shoot that scene.

Q: That chase scene was the most memorable part of the film. It must have been difficult to shoot.
A: It was a dangerous shoot for the actors, especially Tanba and Takakura. Neither of them complained—they stuck it out to the end. Tanba was staying at this dormitory up in the mountains. When he woke up early the first morning, he found that there was no heater in his room. He was an adult so he didn't get mad, but if it had been Tsuruta there would have been hell to pay. [laughs] He probably would have left. We were using every room in the place and some had no heaters—it was really tough. It was so cold that when you woke up early in the morning, you could see deer standing by the dorm, unable to move because of the snow. We brought cars up to the dorm and left them there overnight, but in the morning they wouldn't start—the engines were frozen. I thought, "I've come to some kind of ice box." [laughs]

Q: You shot ten installments of the Abashiri Bangaichi series. I thought it was interesting that you set the third, *Bokyohen*, in Kyushu. Was that to get away from the cold? [laughs]

A: No, not really. [laughs] The company told me they wanted me to make another installment right away. I told them I couldn't do it because it wasn't winter yet. They told me that as long as the theme song was on the soundtrack, it didn't matter—I could shoot anything. The business people were after me to do it and the studio people felt that if the business people were so insistent they didn't have much choice—they asked me to go along. That's why Abashiri Bangaichi moved to Kyushu. The wheels were already in motion, so I didn't have much choice. I didn't want to shoot it, but I was forced to by the higher ups.

Q: Which film in the series is you own favorite?
A: It's hard to say. Probably the first, because that's the one I worked hardest on, battling with the snow. After that, it became a routine—I just ground them out. Only on the first one was I serious for a change. [laughs] I had a hard time, though.

Q: You were making six or seven films a year then—that must have been a tough schedule.
A: I just went along with the flow. I had to do it that way, whether I wanted to or not. When I had a bit of free time, they would take me to an inn and shut the door. Then, I had to write a script. The head of the studio would come every day to see how I was doing, how many pages I had written. As I wrote each one, he would pick it up and read it. I thought "I've had it—I can't keep this up." But they wouldn't give me any rest.

Q: So, you felt like taking time off.
A: I didn't want to take time off so much as do a different kind of project—something other than the *Bangaichi* films. If I had been able to do other films together with the Bangaichi series. I wouldn't have minded so much. But all year long it was "*Bangaichi, Bangaichi*," until I was totally sick of it. I was so bored I was ready to do almost anything else. Another type of

film would have been a break, and I think I could have made twenty Bangaichi films and better ones too. Instead I got totally fed up—"*Bangaichi, Bangaichi, Bangaichi.*"

Q: Then, you went to Shochiku and made several films. Was that because you were fed up with Toei?
A: I needed a breather. I needed a different atmosphere.

Q: But for gang films, at least, Toei was number one.
A: That's true. I shot an action film at Shochiku but I realized that it wasn't working out. Pistols, for example. With Toei, you'd go to the set and there'd be a whole arsenal of pistols, loaded and ready to shoot. If you had a bad take, you'd just bring on more guns and go to it. Shochiku couldn't do that. If you had a bad take, getting ready for the next one would take an hour. It wasn't a company for making action movies.

Q: The Toei staff had plenty of experience in period dramas, so they were good at action choreography.
A: They were specialists. Shochiku on the other hand made home dramas. They shot one action picture a year. They weren't prepared for it, so it was impossible.

Q: You used the same actors again and again, but you changed cameramen frequently.
A: My cameramen all collapsed—they all got sick, so they couldn't work anymore. I didn't have any choice but to promote their chief assistant in their place.

Q: The pace was too hard for them?
A: That wasn't it. I didn't want to change, but they reached their limit. Now that I'm not working for Toei any more, I'll call up cameramen I used to work with at Shin Toho or who used to work for Nikkatsu and tell them I've

got a job for them. They'll say "I can't do it any more." "Why?" I'll ask. "I can't pick up the camera any more," they'll say. "I can't handle it." Then, I realize they're too old. I've got no sense of time, so I keep thinking that they can still do it but they get to the point where they can't. It's sad.

Q: You're also known for editing your films yourself.
A: Yes, I do just about all the editing myself. I get wrapped up in it.

Q: Is that the most important part of the filmmaking process for you?
A: Editing is the most fun—it's the part of the process I enjoy the most. When I'm on the set, I'm not so nervous. I just shoot away. Even when someone flubs up, I'll say "OK, OK." [laughs] I know I can fix it in the editing room. When I'm on the set, I always have editing in the back of my mind. People will say, "Is this all right?" and I'll say, "OK." They'll make a strange face, but I know I can cut the bad places, so I just keep shooting. [laughs]

Q: You have a style that carries over from film to film and your cameramen have to be aware of that, I suppose.
A: Sometimes I'll come across a cameraman who gives me trouble that way. Not that often, really, but if it happens I'll never work that guy again. Most of them understand what I'm trying to do, though.

Q: Also, some editors have a style that they want to impose on the film.
A: There are two types of editors. One type is a good cutter. If you say, "I want to cut it from here to here," he'll do it quickly and properly. Another type will try to cut it his own way—that I don't need. I'll say, "I don't need an editor, bring me a cutter." When an editor gets his hands on the film, chances are he'll cut out all the best parts. I just want him to cut to what I

consider the right places but if he does it differently, I'm sunk. I don't draw storyboards, so when shooting is done, all I have is the film.

Q: With the exception of the *jitsuroku* films by Kinji Fukasaku and others, the popularity of gang films began to decline in the 1970s. Did you regret that at all?
A: No, not all. It was fine with me. [The popularity] couldn't have continued forever—there had to be a change. When yakuza movies became hits, that's all they made, right? I found that strange—I thought the audience would have gotten tired of them sooner. They got tired too late, as far as I'm concerned.

Q: Directors like Kitano and Miike have become popular abroad for their gang films. Do you think they're bringing something new to the genre?
A: I haven't seen many of Kitano's films. I saw *Sonatine* [1993] but to be honest it bored me. I couldn't understand what everyone was making a fuss about—why they thought this film was so great. Jonathan Demme's films, on the other hand, are great—I can see why they win prizes. He gives me faith that some people are still making solid films out there. He's like a brother to me! When I see his early films, in particular, I get the feeling that we're brothers.
Kitano's films may be getting a lot attention now, but it's all a sham. They aren't going to last. Good films, like Demme's, will always be around. I really like Jonathan Demme's films.

Q: Did you have any close encounters with gangsters, especially when you were growing up? Were they familiar figures to you when you started making films about them?

A: I can't say that they were familiar figures. Back in the old days they had *kodan* and *naniwabushi* [traditional styles of storytelling]. They were like historical novels, telling stories about *giri-ninjo* and featuring characters like Kunisada Chuji and Shimizu no Jirocho. All of the so-called orthodox yakuza films come from those kinds of stories, the ones that say the yakuza don't involve the straight world in their quarrels—that paint a pretty picture of the gangs. Guys [of my generation] knew all that. There were also women who thought the yakuza were cool. Of course, none of that is true in reality. Kinji Fukasaku's *Jingi Naki Tatakai* brought that out in the open. That film smashed the image of the yakuza that had been presented in *kodan* and *naniwabushi*. That's why it was so fresh. Fukasaku's yakuza were the real thing. My yakuza were based on *kodan* and *naniwabushi*.

Q: What is your latest project?
A: I have five that I'm working on, but I haven't decided which one I'm going to make first. One of them is a gang film with Ken Takakura—a Japanese version of *Once Upon a Time in America*. It will cost a lot of money, but I am an easygoing type, so instead of raising it I'm just drifting along, thinking it will be good film to make if I get the chance. [laughs] Ken-san is still healthy and I'm still strong enough, so I'd like to make *Once Upon a Time in Japan*. The setting is the present, but the flashback scenes go way back. Once I shoot that film, I'll call it quits as a director. That will be my last. So, until I can shoot it, I have to keep going. [laughs]

Ones. Once again Ken Takakura starred, while his soulful rendition of the title song flew up the charts. Toei released a total of eighteen Abashiri Bangaichi films of which Ishii directed ten, before burning out in 1966. After directing one film for Shochiku, *Daiakuto Sakusen* (Big Villain Plan, 1966), he returned to the Toei fold, where he made a series of eight *ero-guro* films that instructed curious audiences on Japanese torture and sex practices through the ages. These included *Tokugawa Irezumishi Seme Jigoku* (Hell's Tattooers, 1969) and *Yakuza Keibatsushi: Lynch!* (A History of Yakuza Punishment: Lynch! 1969). In the mid-1970s, Ishii made martial arts movies with Shin'ichi "Sonny" Chiba—Toei's attempt to cash in on the popularity of Bruce Lee. The next hot trend was biker movies, which Ishii turned out until *Boryoku Senshi* (Violent Warriors, 1979), a film inspired by Walter Hill's *The Warriors*. Throughout the 1980s, he directed for television, not returning to films until 1991 with the Toei straight-to-video title *The Hitman: Chi wa Bara no Nioi* (The Hitman: Blood Smells Like Roses).

Ishii's feature comeback was *Tsuge Yoshiharu World: Gensenkan Shujin* (Gensenkan Inn, 1993), a four-part anthology film based on the work of underground comic icon Yoshiharu Tsuge. Ishii later helmed two more films based on Tsuge's *manga*, *Burai Heiya* (Vagabond Plain, 1995) and *Nejishiki* (Wind-Up Type, 1998). In 1999 Ishii released *Jigoku* (Hell), his vision of the netherworld, inspired by the hellish crimes of the Aum Shinrikyo sect, and in 2001 *Moju versus Issun Boshi* (Blind Beast versus Issun Boshi), another excursion into the strange, based on a story by Edogawa Rampo.

FILMOGRAPHY

Moju versus Isshun Boshi (Blind Beast versus Issun Boshi, 2001); *Jigoku* (Hell, 1999); *Nejishiki* (Wind-Up Type, 1998); *Burai Heiya* (Vagabond Plain, 1995); *Tsuge Yoshiharu World: Gensenkan Shujin* (Gensenkan Inn, 1993); *The Hitman: Chi wa Bara no Nioi* (The Hitman: Blood Smells Like Roses, 1991) (V); *Boryoku Senshi* (1979); *Wakusei Robot Dangard A tai Konchu Robot Gundan* (1977); *Bakuhatsu! Boso Yugi* (1976), *Boso no Kisetsu* (1976), *Kinkin no Lumpen Taisho* (1976); *Bakuhatsu! Bosozoku* (1975), *Daidatsugoku* (1975), *Jitsuroku 3 Okuen Jiken: Jiko Seiritsu* (1975); *Chokugeki! Jigokuhen* (Direct Hit! Hell Fist, *Executioner*, 1974),

Chokugeki! Jigokuhen: Dai Gyakuten (1974), *Gyakushu! Satsujin Ken* (Revenge! The Killing Fist, *Street Fighter Counterattacks!*, The Street Fighter's Last Revenge, 1974); *Gendai Ninkyo-shi* (1973), *Porno Jidaigeki: Bohachi Bushido* (1973), *Yasagure Anago Den: Sokatsu Lynch* (Female Yakuza Tale: Inquisition and Torture, 1973); *Hidirimen Bakuto* (1972), *Kyofu Kikei Ningen* (1972); *Genroku Onna Keizu* (1970), *Kaidan Nobori Ryu* (The Blind Woman's Curse, *The Haunted Life of a Dragon: Tattooed Lass*, Tattooed Swordswoman, 1970), *Kangoku ninbetsucho*, 1970, *Koroshiya ninbetsucho* (1970), *Noboriryu Tekkahada* (The Friendly Killer, 1970); *Edogawa Ranpo Taizen Kyofu Kikei Ningen* (1969), *Ijo Seai Kiroku Harenchi* (1969), *Menji Taisho Showa Ryoki Onna Hanzaishi* (1969), *Tokugawa Irezumishi Seme Jigoku* (Hell's Tattooers, 1969), *Yakuza Keibatsushi: Lynch!* (A History of Yakuza Punishment: Lynch! 1969), *Zankoku Ijo Gyakutai Monogatari Genroku Jokeizu*, 1969); *Onsen Anma Geisha* (1968), *Tokugawa Onna Keibatsushi* (The Joys of Torture, *Punishment of the Tokugawa Women*, 1968), *Tokugawa Onna Keizu* (1968), *Zoku Otoshimae* (1968); *Abashiri Bangaichi: Aku Eno Chosen* (1967), *Abashiri Bangaichi: Fubuki no Toso* (1967), *Abashiri Bangaichi: Ketto Reika 30-do* (1967), *Otoshimae* (1967); *Abashiri Bangaichi: Dai-setsugen no Taiketsu* (1966), *Abashiri Bangaichi: Hokkai-hen* (1966), *Abashiri Bangaichi: Koya no Taiketsu* (1966), *Abashiri Bangaichi: Nangoku no Taiketsu* (1966), *Daiakuto Sakusen* (Big Villain Plan, 1966), *Nippon Zero Chitai: Yoru wo Nerae* (1966), *Shinka 101: Koroshi no Yojimbo* (1966); *Abashiri Bangaichi* (A Man from Abashiri Prison, 1965), *Abashiri Bangaichi: Bokyohen* (1965), *Kaoyaku* (1965), *Zoku Abashiri Bangaichi* (1965); *Gokinzo yaburi* (1964), *Irezumi Totsugekitai* (1964), *Narazu-mono* (1964), *Tokyo Gang tai Hong Kong Gang* (Gang 9, *Tokyo Gang versus Hong Kong Gang*, 1964); *Ankokugai no Kaoyaku: Juichinin no Gang* (Boss of the Underworld: Gang of 11, Gang 5, 1963), *Boss o Taose* (Kill the Boss, 1963), *Gang tai G-men: Shudan Kinko Yaburi*

(Gang 6, 1963), *Showa Kyokakuden* (1963); *Gang tai Gang* (Gang 3, 1962), *Koi to Taiyo to Gang* (Gang 2, 1962), *Taiheiyo no G-men* (The G-men of the Pacific, 1962); *Hana to Arashi to Gang* (Flower and Storm and Gang, *Gang 1*, 1961), *Kiiroi Fudo* (1961), *Kiri to Kage* (1961), *Ren'ai Zubari Koza* (1961), *Sexy Chitai* (Sexy Line, 1961); *Jobachi to Daigaku no Ryu* (1960), *Kurosen Chitai* (Black Line, 1960), *Nyotai Uzumaki Jima* (Yellow Line, 1960); *Mofubuki no Shito* (1959), *Nippon Romance Ryoko: Sapporo Han* (1959), *Senjo no Nadeshiko* (1959); *Amagi Shinju Tengoku ni Musubu Koi* (1958), *Jobachi no Ikari* (1958), *Jotai Senbashi* (1958), *Shirosen Himitsu Chitai* (White Line, 1958), *Super Giants Jinko Eisen to Jinrui no Hametsu* (Spaceship of Human Destruction, *Super Giants 5*, 1958), *Super Giants Uchutei to Jinko Eisen no Kekitotsu* (Destruction of the Space Fleet, *Super Giants 6*, 1958); *Gonin no Hanzaisha* (1957), *Ring no Oja: Eiko no Sekai* (1957), *Super Giants Chikyu Metsubo Sunzen* (The Earth in Danger, *Super Giant 4*, 1957), *Super Giants Kaiseijin no Majo* (Invaders: From the Planets, *Super Giants 3*, 1957); *Super Giants* (The Steelman from Outer Space, *Super Giants 1*, 1956), *Zoku Super Giants* (Rescue from Outer Space, *Super Giants 2*, 1956).

Tai Kato (1916–85)

Tai Kato had his early defenders—Paul Schrader compared his *Jinsei Gekijo* (Theater of Life, 1972) to "the very best of Sergio Leone" (*Film Comment*, January 1974, p. 17)—but most critics, both in Japan and elsewhere, slotted him into the "genre director" category and passed him over for accolades and awards. At the peak of his career, in the 1960s and 1970s, Kato's period dramas and yakuza films were conspicuously absent from the Kinema Junpo Best Ten lists or the indexes of books by foreign film scholars.

If any of this bothered Kato, he never showed it, as he continued to make films that drew deeply from the traditions of Japanese popular cinema but differed markedly in style and quality from the usual run of studio product. Unlike directors who subverted genre conventions in the anarchic, antiheroic spirit of the times, Kato celebrated the *giri-ninjo* ethic and the gangsters who embodied it, in stories set in the comfortably distant prewar past. At the same time, he brought an emotional intensity and visual impact to these films that was uniquely his, with stylistic devices that bordered on the extreme.

An admirer of Yasujiro Ozu's low camera angles, Kato framed shot after shot from the point of view of a front-row, theater goer looking up at the stage—or a dug-in camera recording a cattle stampede—to both heighten tension and give his characters a presence larger than life. Where other directors might have fallen into excess or absurdity, Kato found a Kabukiesque grandeur.

Also, instead of filming his fight scenes with master shots to get everyone in the frame, while using long takes to avoid breaking up the action, as was then standard industry practice, Kato often went in the opposite direction, with tight shots and quick cuts. This approach may have reduced attackers to a swirling mass behind the foregrounded hero, but it brought the viewer into the heart of the action while highlighting key gestures and expressions—such as the implacable look on Junko Fuji's face when she plunges her short sword into yet another enemy hood.

Kato used his camera expressionistically to intensify the audience's encounter with the characters and their dilemmas—to make them directly experience the chaos of battle or the agony of parting. Rather than settle for the standard attitudes of genre melodrama, he created heightened moments that revealed the core of his characters' beings while placing them outside time, in monumental attitudes.

These stylistic elements, which he shared with the dramatists of Noh and Kabuki, gave his *ninkyo* films the feeling of belonging to another era. The same could also be said of Kato's fellow directors at Toei, such as Masahiro Makino and Kosaku Yamashita. Kato, however, differed from the rest in his treatment of women. Rather than one-sidedly exalt the hero as he manfully rejects the pleas of his wife or lover not to go to certain death or arrest, Kato acknowledges the woman's pain, while making clear that the hero is the cause of it. His heroines tend to be individuals, not collections of received attitudes, including clinging dependency. The men who destroy their happiness are shown as, not macho ideals, but lacking in crucial ways, though they may overcome a dozen enemies.

The relationships between the sexes in his films can hardly be called Westernized, but they are vital and balanced in ways not common in yakuza films, either then or now. No wonder Kato's best-remembered films are the three installments of the Hibotan Bakuto (Red Peony Gambler] series he made with Junko Fuji. Her Oryu is not only the most fully realized of yakuza movie heroines but the strongest in her relations with men, both friend and foe.

Kato was born on August 24, 1916, in Kobe, a port city in western Japan. His father was an importer, while his mother was the sister of film director Sadao Yamanaka. When his father's business went bankrupt, Kato was sent, at the age of five, to live with his grandparents in Nagoya. His parents tried to regain their financial feet by selling pottery in Tokyo; but following the Great Kanto Earthquake in 1923, they moved to Nagoya with Kato's younger brother and sister, and there his father resumed the import trade.

Kato entered the machinery course of a prefectural middle school but became interested in films, particularly the period dramas of Daisuke Ito. He dropped out in his second year and went to work for a trading house in Kyoto.

Tai Kato (1916-1985) at work, toward the end of his nearly five-decade film career. From the cover of *Kato Tai: Eiga o Kataru* (Tai Kato Talks about Films), a 1994 book of Kato's essays, speeches, and interviews.

Not long after, at the invitation of his uncle, Yamanaka, Kato went to Tokyo, where he became an assistant director at Toho. He was assigned to Mikio Naruse on *Hataraku Ikka* (The Whole Family Works, 1939) and other films. In 1941 he entered Kenkyu Kagaku Eiga (Science Research Films) and in 1944 Manei (Manchurian Film Cooperative), both documentary film companies. Drafted one week before the end of the war, he returned to Japan in 1946.

Not long after, Kato joined Daiei as an assistant director and was assigned to his idol Daisuke Ito on *Osho* (Chess Master, 1948) and Akira Kurosawa on *Rashomon* (1950). But as chief secretary of the company union, he acquired a "red" label and was fired from the studio. In 1951 Kato made his directorial debut with the swordfight drama *Kennan Jonan* (Troubles with Swords and Women), a co-production of Shin Toho and Takara Pro. In 1956 he joined Toei, where his first film was *Koizome Ronin* (Ronin in Love, 1957).

As a member of Toei's directorial rotation, Kato brought a new vitality and realism to the period drama genre, at times over the objections of studio traditionalists. For the 1958 *Kaze to Onna to Tabigarasu* (Wind, Women, and Hobo), Kato had his stars appear without makeup, employed live sound, and made abundant use of low angles and long cuts—all elements of his trademark style. He went on to direct some of Toei's most popular and acclaimed period dramas, working with studio stars Kinnosuke Nakamura and Hashizo Okawa. Among his better-remembered films from this period are *Honoo no Shiro* (Throne of Flame, 1960), a Japanized version of *Hamlet*; *Sanada Fu'unroku* (Brave Records of the Sanada Clan; *Sasuke and His Comedians*; *Tale of the Sanada Family*, 1963), a samurai musical whose failure at the box office nearly cost Kato his job; and *Kutsukake Tokijiro: Yukyo Ippiki* (One Man of the Gambler's Code; *Tokijiro of Kutsukake*; *Yukyo Ippiki*, 1966), one of many remakes of a 1929 *ninkyo* film classic by Kichiro Tsuji and accounted by critics as one of the best.

In 1965 Kato followed the studio shift to *ninkyo* films with *Meiji Kyokakuden: Sandai Shumei* (Blood of Revenge, 1965) whose story combined a passionate love affair between a gangster (Koji Tsuruta) and a prostitute (Junko Fuji) with the intrigues and battles of a bloody gang war. The result was high drama and a genre classic. In 1966 Kato made *Otoko no Kao wa Rirekisho* (History of a Man's Face; *A Man's Face Shows His Personal History*, 1966), the first of three films about the postwar gangs starring Noboru Ando, a real-life gang boss who had started his film career after a stretch in prison. Loosely based on Ando's experiences in the black market gang wars and their aftermath, the films had Kato's usual intensity, as well as a gritty realism, detailing the bloody struggles between Japanese and Asian gangsters scrambling for money and power among the postwar ruins. Ando later named the films he made with Kato as among his favorites—and the most truthful.

Starting in 1969 with *Hibotan Bakuto: Hanafuda Shobu* (Red Peony Gambler: Flower Cards Match; *Red Peony: The Hanafuda Game*, 1969), Kato directed three of the eight installments of the Hibotan Bakuto series starring Junko Fuji as the woman gambler Oryu, who goes about the country defending the weak and righting wrongs. Kato injected a distinctive lyricism into Fuji's encounters with her male love interests, played successively by Ken Takakura, Bunta Sugawara, and Koji Tsuruta, as well as staging her fight scenes with characteristic panache.

After Fuji's retirement in 1972, Kato made one more film for Toei, *Showa Onna Bakuto* (Woman Gambler of Showa, 1972), starring Kyoko Enami, before leaving the studio himself. He went to Shochiku, where he directed *Jinsei Gekijo* (Theater of Life, 1972); *Hana to Ryu: Sei'unhen Aizohen Dotohen* (The Blossom and the Sword, 1973); and *Miyamoto Musashi* (Sword of Fury, 1973)—all three the latest in a long series of remakes.

After the mid-1970s, Kato's output slowed as audience interest in gang films and period dramas waned. Among his late-career triumphs was *Hono-o no Gotoku* (Flames of Blood, 1981), a big-budget film set in the Bakumatsu Period. During this time, he was also shooting *Za Ondekoza* (Ondekoza, 1994), a documentary about the Ondekoza *taiko* (Japanese drum) troupe. The film was not released until 1994, however. Kato died on June 17, 1985, of liver failure, at the age of sixty-eight.

FILMOGRAPHY

Za Ondekoza (Ondekoza, 1994); *Hono-o no Gotoku* (Flames of Blood, 1981); *Edogawa Rampo no Inju* (Edogawa Rampo's Night Beast, 1977); *Miyamoto Musashi* (Sword of Fury, 1973), *Hana to Ryu: Sei'unhen Aizohen Dotohen* (The Blossom and the Sword, 1973); *Jinsei Gekijo* (Theater of Life, 1972), *Showa Onna Bakuto* (Woman Gambler of Showa, 1972); *Hibotan Bakuto: Oinochi Onegaishimasu* (Red Peony Gambler: Death to the Wicked, 1971); *Hibotan Bakuto: Oryu Sanjo* (Oryu's Visit, *Red Peony*

Gambles Her Life, 1970); *Hibotan Bakuto: Hanafuda Shobu* (Red Peony Gambler: Flower Cards Match, *Red Peony: The Hanafuda Game*, 1969); *Minagoroshi no Reika* (Gospel for Genocide, 1968); *Choeki Juhachi-nen* (Sentence: Eighteen Years, 1967); *Ahen Daichi Jigoku Butai Totsugeki Seyo* (Opium Heights: Hell Troop Attack! 1966), *Otoko no Kao wa Rirekisho* (History of a Man's Face, *A Man's Face Shows His Personal History*, 1966), *Hone Made Shaburu* (Suck to the Bones, 1966), *Kutsukake Tokijiro: Yukyo Ippiki* (One Man of the Gambler's Code, *Tokijiro of Kutsukake, Yukyo Ippiki*, 1966); *Meiji Kyokakuden: Sandaime: Shumei* (Blood of Revenge, 1965); *Bakumatsu Zankoku Monogatari* (Cruel Story of the Shogunate's Downfall, *Brutal Story at the End of the Tokugawa Shogunate*, 1964), *Shafu Yukyoden: Kenka Tatsu* (Fighting Tatsu: The Rickshaw Man, 1964), *Kaze no Bushi* (Samurai Vagabond, 1964); *Sanada Fu'unroku* (Brave Records of the Sanada Clan, *Sasuke and His Comedian, Tale of the Sanada Family*, 1963); *Tangesazen Ken'un Konryu no Maki* (Tangesazen: The Book of Ken'un and Konryu, 1962), *Mabuta no Haha* (Love for a Mother, 1962); *Kaidan Oiwa no Borei* (Ghost of Oiwa, *The Tale of Oiwa's Ghost, Oiwa no Burei*, 1961), *Asagiri Kaido* (Morning Fog Road, 1961); *Honoo no Shiro* (Throne of Flame, 1960), *Ayamegasa Kenka Kaido* (Ayamegasa: Fighting Road, 1960), *Oedo no Kyoji* (Gallant Youth of Edo, 1960); *Kogan no Misshi* (Mission to Hell, 1959); *Ronin Hakkei* (Ronin Eight Views, 1958), *Kaze to Onna to Tabigarasu* (Wind, Women and Hobo, 1958), *Genji Kuro Satsusoki: Byakko Nitoryo* (White Tiger Sword of Genji Kuro, 1958), *Hizakura Daimyo* (Tattooed Lord, 1958); *Koizome Ronin* (Ronin in Love, 1957); *Ninjutsu Jidenya* (Jindenya of the Ninja Arts, 1955), *Gyakushu Orochimaru* (The Counterattack of Orochimaru, 1955); *Hiyodori no Soshi* (Bulbul Storybook, 1952), *Shimizuko wa Oni Yori Kowai* (Shimizu Port Is More Frightening Than the Devil, 1952); *Kennan Jonan* (Troubles with Swords and Women, 1951).

Takeshi Kitano ("Beat" Takeshi) (1947–)

An actor, director, and television personality who redefined the yakuza film in the 1990s with a combination of black humor, minimalist stylistics, and extreme, at times eccentric, violence, Takeshi Kitano was born in 1947 in Tokyo and grew up with his two older brothers and older sister in Tokyo's Adachi Ward. His father, a house painter, was a violent drunk who left his family one step above destitution (though Kitano titled his eighth film *Kikujiro* in his honor). Kitano's main support in his childhood was his mother, a strict disciplinarian and fervent educator who had high ambitions for her sons. Though a bright boy, who managed to pass the entrance exam to prestigious Meiji University, Kitano was less interested in study than in sports, particularly baseball and boxing, and general hell-raising. (This phase of his youth was the background for his 1997 film *Kids Return*).

In college Kitano studied engineering but, influenced by the upheavals of the 1960s and following his own wayward impulses, was soon spending more time in Shinjuku coffee shops and bars than classrooms. Dropping out of college at the age of 19, he took a succession of odd jobs, finally drifting in 1972 to the Asakusa entertainment district with the intention of becoming a comedian. After getting a job as an elevator operator in the Asakusa France Theater, he apprenticed himself to one of the theater's leading comedians, Senzaburo Fukami, and became the theater's emcee. Progress up the entertainment world ladder was slow, however, until Kitano teamed with another young comedian to form the Two Beats comedy duo, with Kitano taking the stage name Beat Takeshi and his partner, Beat Kiyoshi. Using a unique brand of off-beat, off-color humor, the duo rose to nationwide popularity in the early 1980s, riding the crest of a stand-up boom.

© Office Kitano

Pearly gates or pearly whites? Takeshi Kitano (right) directing a scene from *Kids Return* (1996), his sixth film and the second in which he does not star.

The creative side of the duo, Beat Takeshi soon went his own way, both as a TV personality and actor, playing a sadistic camp guard in Nagisa Oshima's World War Two POW drama, *Senjo no Merry Christmas* (Merry Christmas, Mr. Lawrence, 1982)—and getting his first taste of international attention. In 1989 Kitano got his first chance to direct when a scheduling conflict forced Kinji Fukasaku to exit *Sono Otoko, Kyobo ni Tsuki* (Violent Cop, 1989). Kitano, who was to star as a rule-bending, violence-prone police detective, took over the reins and produced a dark, hyper-violent thriller, while administering most of the on-screen cuffs and blows.

Beginning with his second film, *3–4 X Jugatsu* (Boiling Point, 1990), Kitano amplified and refined what was to become his distinctive style, with its long takes, absence of camera movement, terse dialogue, pawky humor, and abrupt transitions to extreme, often deadly, violence. There is something ungainly, even amateurish, about this style (deliberately so— Kitano readily admits to bending and breaking film-making rules) but something compelling and revealing as well. Also, though Kitano is not always out to entertain, he does intend to surprise—and often catches his audience off guard, to amusing or shocking effect.

In *3–4 X Jugatsu*, he mixes wacky comedy and brutal violence in telling the story of two amateur baseball players who go to Okinawa to seek vengeance on a yakuza gang and find an unlikely ally in a psychotic gangster played by Kitano. The gangster, Uehara, is one of Kitano's scarier creations—a nearly mute stoic with a tight little smile, who suddenly erupts into frenzies of kinky sex or homicidal rage. He fits no mold and follows no model. Beside him even the suicidally out-of-control gangsters of Bunta Sugawara look almost boringly normal.

Kitano's break-out film, however, was *Sonatine* (1993), a gang film that begins conventionally enough, with Kitano as a tired-of-it-all capo sent to Okinawa to help an affiliate gang in a turf war. The capo, Murakawa, soon realizes that he is in over his head—and makes a quick exit to the countryside. Here, the film takes a turn to the absurd, as the gang's retreat begins to look like a segment from one of Kitano's variety shows, with Murakawa playing practical jokes of the crueler sort on his hapless underlings. These comic interludes alternate with violence, ranging from the sadistic to the surreal.

Though it failed to find an audience in Japan, *Sonatine* inspired raves in Europe—and Kitano was elevated to the front rank of the Japanese New Wave, with foreign critics evoking everyone from Ozu to Scorsese. Before he could properly enjoy his new-found fame, a motor scooter accident in August 1994 nearly killed him and left half of his face scarred and partly paralyzed. His disfigurement did not lessen his value as a movie tough guy, however—among his post-accident credits are Takashi Ishii's *Gonin* (1995); Ikuo Sekimoto's *Zankyo* (Remnants of Chivalry, 1999); and Nagisa Oshima's *Gohatto* (Taboo, 1999).

The accident also produced a change in his outlook, with Kitano reflecting publicly on his mortality and taking his film career with greater seriousness (even though his films were by no means always serious). From the Jim Carreyesque comedy of the pre-accident *Minna Yatteruka* (Getting Any? 1995) with its potty humor and pop culture in-jokes, Kitano shifted to the post-accident human drama of *Kids Return* (1996), with its unblinkered (if at times hilarious) reflections on the idiocy of contemporary youth, as well as the scarcity of second chances in gang life—and Japanese life in general. Also, in contrast to the stylistic mood swings and narrative ellipses of his earlier films, *Kids Return* is a highly integrated work. Its story of two teenage dropouts who are inseparable friends, until the boxing talent of one drives them apart, is so carefully structured and economically, if forcefully, told that the comparisons with Ozu are not totally absurd.

Kitano's masterpiece, however, is *Hana-Bi* (Fireworks, 1997), a film about a renegade cop out to salvage his conscience, even if he has to sacrifice his career—and life. With its stark, if

humanistic, worldview and spare but consistently gripping shotmaking, *Hana-Bi* represents a culmination of everything Kitano had learned as a director in his first six films. It was his biggest commercial and critical success, winning the Golden Lion at the 1997 Venice Film Festival—and cementing Kitano's reputation as the leading Japanese director of his generation. His followup, *Kikujiro no Natsu* (Kikujiro, 1999), was a semi-comic drama about a middle-aged man of uncertain occupation, played by Kitano himself, who takes a lonely little boy to find his long-lost mother. The parallels with Kitano's own life are obvious, as are many of the attempts at comedy and pathos.

Next came *Brother* (2000), a gang film intended as a frontal assault on the foreign market, with Kitano playing a fugitive gangster who flies to Los Angeles in search of his long-lost half-brother—and ends up bossing the brother's racially mixed gang. The violence comes thick and fast, as do images of sliced fingers, a severed head, a suicide by harakiri, and other Yellow Peril stereotypes. The film's key relationship, between the yakuza played by Kitano and the African-American gangsta played by Omar Epps, never quite clicks. The gangsta becomes fiercely loyal to the yakuza, though he is not much more than a comic-relief sidekick to his nearly mute boss. Not intended as a festival prize winner, *Brother* also did indifferent business at the domestic and foreign box office.

In 2002 Kitano took yet another radical turn with *Dolls*, a three-couple romantic drama, whose central story is loosely based on a famous Bunraku play. One of the side stories involves an elderly gang boss, who returns to a youthful love and finds her still faithfully making box lunches for him as she once did decades ago—before he callously abandoned her. The antique sentimentalism of this story extends to the rest of the film—and indicates that Kitano is now channeling, not Ozu, but D. W. Griffith.

Though at times highly stylized, the best of

his films point to closely observed realities, while serving as an emotional and moral autobiography for their director. They express both his nihilism—and inner child. (He often uses angels as a symbol, entirely without irony.)

While taking a romantic view of loner heroes that verges on self-regard of the bad-Hemingway sort, his films are refreshingly unbound by genre conventions. They are, in short, not mass-audience products but personal essays by a shy, brilliant man who happens to be an immensely popular celebrity—and thus possesses a power undreamed of by most of his directorial contemporaries. There is no one else quite like Kitano in the history of the yakuza movie genre—or for that matter, Japanese film.

FILMOGRAPHY AS DIRECTOR

Dolls (2002); *Brother* (2000); *Kikujiro no Natsu* (Kikujiro, 1999); *Hana-Bi* (Hana-Bi, *Fireworks*, 1997); *Kids Return* (1996); *Minna Yatteruka* (Getting Any?, 1994); *Sonatine* (1993); *Ano Natsu, Ichiban Shizukana Umi* (1992); *3–4 X Jugatsu* (Boiling Point, 1990); *Sono Otoko, Kyobo ni Tsuki* (Violent Cop, 1989).

FILMOGRAPHY AS AN ACTOR (FEATURE FILMS)

Zatoichi (2003), *Battle Royale II* (2003), *Battle Royale* (2000), *Brother* (2000); *Gohatto* (Taboo, 1999), *Kikujiro no Natsu* (Kikujiro, 1999), *Zankyo* (Remnants of Chivalry, 1999); *Tokyo Eyes* (1998); *Hana-Bi* (Hana-Bi, *Fireworks*, 1997); *Gonin* (The Five, 1995), *Johnny Mnemonic* (1995); *Minna Yatteruka* (Getting Any?, 1994); *Kyoso Tanjo* (Many Happy Returns, 1993), *Sonatine* (1993); *Erotique Kankei* (Erotic Liaisons, 1992), *Sakana Kara Dioxin!!* (Dioxin From Fish!!, 1992); *Hoshi o Tsugumono* (The Man Who Inherited a Star, 1990), *3–4 X Jugatsu* (Boiling Point, 1990); *Sono Otoko, Kyobo ni Tsuki* (Violent Cop, 1989); *Anego* (The Boss's Wife, 1988); *Comic Zasshi Nanka Iranai!* (Comic Magazine, 1986); *Yasha* (Demon,

1985); *Jukkai no Mosquito* (Mosquito on the 10th Floor, 1983), *Merry Christmas, Mr. Lawrence* (1983); *Danpu Wataridori* (Birds of Passage on the Truck, 1981), *Manon* (1981); *Makoto-chan* (Little Makoto, 1980).

Takashi Miike (1960–)

Most makers of straight-to-video movies—called V Cinema or OV in Japan—labor in obscurity, with only their industry peers and few devoted fans caring about the director's name on the box. For most, that obscurity is deserved; grinding out genre product on low budgets and impossibly tight schedules, they are little more than traffic managers, hired more for competence than creativity. Then, there is Takashi Miike, whose OV films may play in one Tokyo theater for all of two weeks but are screened and sold, despised and celebrated around the world.

Miike stands out from the herd, first and foremost, for his excess, which ranges from the laughably cartoony to the armrest-clutchingly horrific, and the retchingly gross. Yet, for all its indulgence in kinky sex, slaughterhouse gore, and action straight from the wilder *manga*, Miike's work has a propulsive energy, exuberant inventiveness, and unforced affection for even the dodgier of its characters that raises it above the level of traveling Geek Show. Does he harbor darker obsessions? Perhaps, but even in his more extreme moments, his fundamental attitude is often one of play, like a fourteen-year-old kid dreaming up exotic tortures with his buddies—that he would never dare try in real life. In Miike's world, the imagination, sick or otherwise, runs riot, while self-censorship is taboo.

Born in Osaka in 1960, Miike grew up in the working-class Kawachi District, where he was an indifferent student but an enthusiastic fan of pachinko, motorcycles, and rock music.

(His big ambition, he later confessed, was to become, not a director, but a rock singer.) After attending Shohei Imamura's film school in Yokohama (today called the Japan Academy of Moving Images), he worked as an assistant director for Imamura on *Zegen* (1987) and *Kuroi Ame* (Black Rain, 1989); for Kazuo Kuroki on *Tomorrow/Ashita* (1988); and for Hideo Onchi on *Shimantogawa* (1991).

In 1991 he made his directorial debut with the straight-to-video film *Topuu! Minipato Tai: Eye Catch Junction* (Squall! Miniskirt Patrol Force: Eye Catch Junction) and continued to turn out films for the video shelves. In 1993 he joined Excellent Films, a production company managed by producer and director Hidehiro Ito.

In 1995 Miike made his feature film debut with *Daisan no Gokudo* (The Third Gangster), starring Kiyoshi Nakajo. He upped the sex and violence ante in *Shinjuku Kuroshakai: China Mafia Senso* (Shinjuku Triad Society, 1995), the first of a trilogy about Japanese and Chinese gangs in today's urban Japan. His international breakthrough was *Gokudo Sengokushi: Fudo* (Fudoh: The New Generation, 1996), a gruesome, if blackly funny, revenge fantasy that was screened in the Toronto Film Festival's Midnight Madness section to acclaim and was later released on English-subtitled video.

He used overseas locations for the first time in *Gokudo Kuro Shakai Rainy Dog* (Rainy Dog, 1997), a hard-boiled essay on the life and death of an anti-social Japanese hitman in Taiwan. He returned to his native Osaka to film *Kishiwada Shonen Gurentai: Chikemuri Junjo-hen* (Boys, Be Ambitious: Blood Spray Pure Heart, 1997), the second in a comic series about delinquent teens in the city's working-class Kishiwada section. A video title he made that year, *Full Metal Gokudo* (Full Metal Yakuza, 1997), also had its comic moments, but its transposition of the RoboCop story to the yakuza world was drenched in blood as well—a by-now familiar Miike combination.

© Excellent Films

The shock jock of Japanese movies. Takashi Miike in a pensive pose.

His most ambitious film from this period was *Chugoku no Chojin* (The Bird People in China, 1998). Shot mostly on location in China's remote Yunnan Province, it was Miike's re-telling of the Shangri-La story, with a workaholic businessman and hot-tempered gangster finding an unlikely paradise in the mountains, where people as well as dreams can take wing. He even tried his hand at mainstream movie-making with *Andromedia* (1998), a pop idol movie featuring the girl group Speed.

In 1999, Miike accelerated his rise to international cult status with *Dead or Alive: Hanzaisha* (Dead or Alive), the first of a trilogy starring Show Aikawa and Riki Takeuchi. Though narratively connected only by their titles, the films displayed Miike's pop-culture sensibility and talent for outrageousness to the full, beginning with the opening sequence of the first film, a reeling, careening tour of the Tokyo underworld that featured murder, sodomy, and a gangster literally spilling his guts on a Chinese restaurant floor, all in a ten-minute span. But for all its absurdity, the series also examined Japanese and Asian cultures in collusion and—in the final film—in a full commingling, in a

Takashi Miike Interview (August 2000)

Q: You made four films last year [1999]. What drives you—other than the need to make a living?

A: I didn't become a director because there are things I want to express. Instead, I am looking for things to express. Even though I may be satisfied with my individual films, I always find something lacking in them—and that keeps me looking. One way, of course, is to look before shooting anything, but in my case I have to shoot first—I have to look while I'm shooting. That's why I have such a strong desire to make films. I'm always thinking while I'm in the process of shooting, working with the actors and so on. That's one way to learn how to make films.

Q: So, you're learning skills on the job?

A: I'm learning technique, but more importantly I'm meeting various types of people. I'm going to foreign film festivals where I can study foreign filmmaking methods and get ideas from the people I meet there. I also read novels, see other people's films, sample other arts, and absorb what I can from all of it. Mostly, though, I learn by being on the set and making films.

Q: What did you gain by attending Shohei Imamura's film school in Yokohama?

A: Now it's a vocational school with a strong curriculum, but when I was there it was a kind of *juku* [trade school]. We didn't study Imamura's filmmaking philosophy and methods directly. Instead, they taught us more generally about films. It was a school for training technical staff, not creative filmmakers. I made two films there, working as Imamura's assistant director. In the twenty years that school has been in existence, only three students have worked as Imamura's AD. My selection had nothing to do with my grades. I spent most of my time doing part-time jobs and playing—I hardly ever went to class. I wasn't a very serious student. [laughs]

Q: Imamura has said that he prefers the "bad students"—the ones who may look and act like street punks but have real creativity.

A: That may be something unique to Japan and not apply to other countries. Foreign filmmakers usually study hard and are well versed in cinematic modes of expression. They tend to be good at expressing themselves in other arts as well, be it writing novels or taking photographs. Japanese filmmakers, on the other hand, tend to be bad at expressing themselves. They have all these things they want to say locked up inside and when they make films, it all comes out. That's one big difference between Japanese and foreign directors. For foreign directors, filmmaking is often just one of several means of expression. They master cinematic techniques and use them rationally. Japanese directors tend to be a little more emotional and ambiguous, while relying less on knowledge and reason.

Q: The Japanese film industry has a rather dark image compared with television and advertising.

A: Film directors here are not particularly multitalented. Abroad, directors usually start as cameramen and work their way up. A lot of them can shoot and edit, score the music, and so on—they are multitalented. They're good at playing instruments, public speaking, writing novels, you name it.

I write scripts, but they're for my own use as a director—they're not as good as professionally written scripts. There are a lot of directors in Japan who couldn't make it abroad as creators.

Q: But your films have been well received abroad. Do you think foreign audiences really understand them?

A: Liking a film and understanding it are not necessarily one and the same. Just because people like my films doesn't mean I'm communicating what I want to say to them. I grew up watching Bruce Lee movies, but I didn't really understand the spirit behind Bruce Lee's fighting. I invented my own image of Bruce Lee. There is always a gap between a creator's intentions and an audience's feelings toward his creation. If you just want your film to be easy to understand, you can end up with something small minded and conventional. I prefer a bit of ambiguity, so that the audience can interpret the film in its own way.

A: I felt that, watching *Audition*. You can see it both as entertainment and as something more.

Q: The audience has the right to enjoy a film in its own way. I can't control their reaction—it's completely up to them. The moment you think you can get a certain reaction if you film a scene a certain way, your film is doomed. It may be important to have a clear-cut theme and be able to adequately express it in your film, but do you have to communicate your theme so that anyone can understand it? I have my doubts. You can see *Audition* in an up mood, in a down mood, with a lot of people, or alone at home. If a director says he wants people to see his film under certain conditions, he's kidding himself. I prefer films that I can see and enjoy in various ways. I don't enjoy films that telegraph their message so the audience will understand it in a certain way.

A: The ones that try to explain everything.

Q: That's right. I doubt whether the truth they're trying to push really exists. The director is trying to show a clear difference between good and evil, but because he wants to make his theme easy to understand he can't use a complex structure. Instead he has to use characters who are clearly good or clearly evil, who are courageous or cowardly. In trying to present a universal message, he ends up with something

more limited. You see the film once and you get everything out of it you're going to get.

Q: Japanese films are finding a wider audience abroad, yours included. Do you have any desire to go to Hollywood to further broaden that audience?

A: The environment for filmmaking is improving more rapidly abroad than in Japan, especially in terms of conditions and budgets. That said, I don't know whether I can make or even have to make a Hollywood film set in New York. I can make films my own way, but I don't know if that is what Hollywood wants. I have no real sense of what they would want me to make. I've had discussions with U.S. producers, but unless I have a clear idea of what they want, I can't work with them.

As you said, Japanese films are getting more attention and being released more often abroad. It's not because Japanese films are so wonderful, but because film festival directors and other people who are introducing Japanese films abroad think they are interesting. But they may tire of them. They may become interested in something else. A few people in foreign countries happen to be interested in our films now—so we have to make something for them now. We have to seize the moment.

Japanese producers and filmmakers don't understand that. They think Japanese films must be getting better because they are getter a better reception abroad, but that's not necessarily true. Japanese audiences are not giving Japanese films high marks—just certain people who introduce new films. They have been selecting Japanese films for several years now, but how long will that last? As long as Japanese film people don't understand that, this foreign interest in Japanese films will come to nothing. It won't continue this way forever, but they don't know it. They don't try to understand why this interest exists and develop a production strategy that will capitalize on it. That's a producer's job, but they aren't doing it.

In that sense, the Japanese industry is weak. It has no experience in translating the strengths of Japanese directors into foreign sales. Film industry people here just wait until they are invited somewhere and go there as visitors. There aren't many who go abroad in delegations, with business in mind.

Q: What are the main difficulties in working as a director in Japan? Raising money, of course, but what else?

A: Japanese directors are not only judged by how they direct. They have to live up to a certain image of what a director is and behave like "a Japanese director," whatever that means. I don't want these sorts of restraints on what I can and can't do.

The average budget for a mainstream Japanese film is about 200 or 300 million yen. If your budget is at that level, you're considered a first-class director. Once you reach that level and you're offered a film with a budget of 30 or 40 million yen, you're supposed to turn it down. Otherwise you're lowering yourself.

I don't feel that way. For me, a film that costs 400 million yen and one that costs 30 million yen can either be the same or totally different in terms of quality. It may be worth my while to make both. So, I do TV for Wowow [a satellite entertainment channel] or make a film backed by a local government with a zero budget. I don't believe that I shouldn't do certain types of films because I'm a big-deal director. So, I keep getting more work. [laughs]

I want to try different things in different genres. I keep getting offers from various places, so I can branch out in new directions. If you always stick to the same type of thing, you may work once a year or once every two years. But even a director who only works once a year can meet new people and get more job offers as a result. After sifting through offers, I make my choice and finally start shooting. Through these offers, I can also get an idea of what I want to do in the future. While developing these future projects, I'm making one film after another. It's an endless cycle.

Q: Compared with the number of Japanese young people who love pop music and attend concerts, the number who love Japanese films and see them in the theaters is quite small. The impact of films on the culture isn't what it used to be.

A: For Japanese today, Japanese films don't offer much stimulus. They find that stimulus in the new, but they don't see much that's new in Japanese films. In the average film here, the hero moves toward a climax that may be a bit out of the ordinary—that's it. There aren't any filmmakers or scripts that are making films new again, setting trends, showing people something that they haven't seen before. Japanese film people have this very conservative idea of what a film should be—and that's what they make again and again. Everyone is trying to make "film-like films"—they can't do anything else. There are enormously talented people outside the film industry who could challenge that way of thinking. Game designers, *manga* artists, musicians, designers, and even employees at ordinary companies, such as the car designers at Honda. They have a terrific sensibility, but the film industry doesn't appeal to them so they don't join it.

Q: Even so, there are Japanese directors, yourself included, who are having an impact. Takeshi Kitano, Rokuro Mochizuki, and Takashi Ishii are some of the names that come to mind.

A: But all of the directors you mentioned are not real film industry people. Kitano started as a comedian and still is one. He not making films as a professional but as an artist. Ishii, who was originally a *manga* artist, is the same way. Mochizuki's specialty was originally pink films. Kiyoshi Kurosawa is another outsider. These people do not belong to the group that considers itself film directors first and foremost, that only make feature films. They don't have that sort of pride. They're making the films they like, in the style they like, even if the budget is small.

There are still directors at Toho and other studios who are directors in the traditional sense, who would never make certain kinds of films, say V Cinema films. Their power is in decline, though. The directors who are being praised at foreign film festivals are from outside the film industry here. I'm the same way. I'm working in the video film industry—I'm not a film industry person. The people who are proud of having built the formerly first-rate Japanese film industry rarely leave Japan.

Q: The Japanese film industry can still make a film like *Popoya* [Railroad Man] a hit, but when I went to see it I was the youngest one in the theater—and I'm not exactly young.
A: That's one type of Japanese mass entertainment film. It's also part of the Japanese filmmaking tradition. Instead of art, you make something like *Tora-san* that will bring old people into the theater. That's one way to keep theaters filled and there's nothing wrong with it. But the film industry here is even losing the ability to make that type of film.

Anyway, there's a growing dissatisfaction, even among industry people, with the direction the industry is heading. That dissatisfaction is poured into low budget films that generate new types of explosions and eruptions. That energy is of a type you don't find in other countries.

Q: In your own films, such as *Audition* [1999] and *Gokudo Kuro Shakai Rainy Dog* [Rainy Dog, 1997], you present an image of Japan and the Japanese that is totally different from that in mainstream films, where the "gentle Japanese" stereotype prevails.
A: More than trying to say something about the Japanese in particular or humanity in general, I'm talking about one individual and those around him. In yakuza movies, I'm looking at

not just the hero, but the people who are cut down by the hero, who are not thought to have his appeal. For me, though, these guys have the same appeal as the hero. I like guys who can't become the hero. When I put the spotlight on them and really look at them closely, I find that they're expressing themselves differently from ordinary people, who just want to live normally and be happy. The bad guy is usually seen as sick and strange, but I think that's wrong. Everyone has that potential inside them.

For example, in Japan there's this phenomenon of kids who turn violent, who suddenly explode. People put the blame on violent films and video games like "Biohazard." That influence does exist, but for the mass media, games are bad, period. But people create games and people buy them. Something in human beings has taken the form of a particular game. It's not as though the game itself is bad. Children play games because there's something in them they want to see. The kids who play them are usually normal enough.

Why do they want to see that kind of violence? We have to answer that question. Otherwise, we end up simplistically saying that because kids are seeing that kind of thing, it's bad for them. Who is the bad influence? Not only the adults who created the games, but the kids themselves—everyone actually. All of us can see something of ourselves in those games. When we deny that, we end up denying the games and the media, as though we have no connection to either.

When I'm being written about in the mass media, I feel this tremendous sense of strangeness. Most media people don't see the stuff I make—that's what's fun about the indie world for me. Real adults don't see that sort of thing. And as long as they don't, they can't criticize me. I'm free. With only a few people watching [my films], I can do what I want. If my budgets become too big, I can't do that. If I had been in Hollywood doing what I like, I would be in big trouble by now. [laughs] In

Hollywood, you're asked to meet certain conditions, and you try your best to make a film in accordance with them, while expressing a bit of your individuality.

What I like, on the other hand, is not to be noticed too much—perhaps even to be ignored. I have a few fans who get what I am trying to do—that's enough. I thought I had found a way to express myself freely, by making the kinds of films I want to make on a low budget, but actually it's not that easy. Instead, I find that I'm getting more and more confused. [laughs] I sometimes think that I should stop for a while and think seriously about what I'm doing, but it probably wouldn't make any difference. As long as the jobs keep coming, I'll keep working. At any rate, given the conditions I'm working under now, no one's losing anything, even if no one knows what I'm doing. By that, I mean that my backers are recouping. As long as I can keep doing that, I'm basically free—and I'd like to become even freer.

If I can have my freedom, I don't mind working anywhere, even Hollywood. I've more or less had my own way so far, even when I'm asked to a job. In Hollywood, though, you have to make something Americans will understand. But if they just want me to do that, it's not going to work. It depends on the aim and theme of the project. When I finish the script it may be something only Asians will understand. I'll butt heads with the producers and that will be the end of the project.

Once I've made a big budget film, though, I think I'll be in a very different place from when I was making films for 40 or 50 million yen. I may be able to attract top-flight American staff to the world of V Cinema, where we make films for nothing and release them in one theater. I may be able to bring Hollywood explosion specialists and costume designers to Japan. I never studied when I was a kid and can't speak English at all, so I'm getting together with people who can handle English and understand films, and making various contacts.

Q: Hollywood doesn't try to keep anyone out because they can't speak English. It's a borderless world where only ability counts.
A: Even so, filmmakers in Hollywood can't do anything they want—there's too much money involved. For them, the Japanese way of making movies looks very practical. Here, you can make a film for 50 or 60 million yen. When they see that they say, well, maybe we can make our film for only 100 million yen. [laughs]

I'm still making V Cinema films, but now I have a chance to show them to people [in Hollywood]. I have a lot of fans there, some of whom are real *otaku* [fanatics]. I've met some of them, and we've talked about doing something together. My conditions for working with them are that I make something that interests me and that I have the freedom I need. I've made dozens of films and have worked as an assistant to a number of directors, so if someone asks me to make something, I can do it—technically I'm ready. But it's more fun for me to make a movie in Japan for 100 or 200 million yen than to make a film in Hollywood for 30 million dollars.

Producers of Japanese films have to hire members of our generation—but we don't have to make hits. Japanese movies rarely become box office hits anyway, so that makes it easier for us. We're freer. If fans are not going to come no matter what you make, you might as well make something interesting—but no one thinks that way. More directors should take advantage of the fact that their films are not going to be hits. Because they try anything to make a film a hit, they all end up making the same kinds of films. If a horror film becomes a hit, they all make horror films.

Q: After *Ring* [1998] became a hit, everyone started making something like it. But recent horror films have been pretty terrible.
A: That's because of the mentality of the investors. The investors are successful companies and individuals—they are your first audience, but the mental level of that audience is low.

They're investors, but they don't know what to put their money into. If *Ring*'s a hit, they'll make something like it—that's the level they're at.

Japanese movies are often called boring, but they're boring because the people who watch them are boring. The audience doesn't have any sense for what's good and what isn't. In the long run, that's reflected in the films.

The emergence of DVD may change that. It's definitely having an effect on films. If the younger generation starts watching a lot of DVDs, they'll get a good, strong grounding in films. With a DVD, you're getting an experience that's very close to the theater; you can see things that you can't see on video.

Also, once the new generation that has grown up playing video games comes into [the film industry] it will be interesting to see what kinds of films they make. Even if most people don't pay attention, the fans will enjoy themselves. Also, the investors won't lose anything. With indie movies, if you can make back your investment, you can have freedom. It not the same as trying to make a big hit, where you are under all kinds of pressures. You can't make progress without freedom. You can't perform miracles, you can't revive the business.

Q: All directors have their ups and downs; even the best don't always make masterpieces. How do you place yourself in that cycle—are you in the up phase now?

A: When a director surpasses the film that first attracted attention to his work, that's when he reaches the peak of his talent as a filmmaker. When you try to top what you've first been recognized for, using only the talent you have, you have to work like hell, while recruiting new brains and talents. That's how a Spielberg ends up with an *E.T.*, after films like *Duel* and *Jaws*. Once you've made a film like that, once you've won the acclaim of the world for it, it's sad, because it means you've passed your peak.

After that, everything is different, no matter what you try to do. You have to think about who you're going to work with, who your advisors are going to be. You have to find people who can serve as a tonic to your talent. You know that if you're left on your own, you're not going to top what you've done before. So, you work with a different producer, but the struggle you have surpassing your peak appears in your films. You may be enjoying yourself, but it's still tough. You lose the freedom that once made you excited in the real sense. So, you have to go beyond that, the way John Frankenheimer did, and do what you really want to do. But I don't know that success is really good for a director.

Q: In Japan, once a director has had a big success and rises in the industry, everyone starts calling him *sensei* (teacher). He starts to think that he's above the herd, that he's not an ordinary human being any more.

A: That's no good. You forget who you are, who's living in your skin. You end up just protecting the spot you're standing on. You want people to praise your work, not slam it. But your brain cells and muscles are linked. Your mental strength depends on your physical strength. Both come from the same cells. When you become short of breath climbing a flight of stairs that never gave you trouble before, your brain cells are also out of breath, though you may not realize it. A lot of the work involved in making films I can do naturally, like running up a flight of stairs. It's something I don't have to think about.

If you have young cells and a talent for making films, if you have a good script and good actors, then you have the right conditions for moving in a positive direction—but you have to create them yourself. Getting everything right is not just a matter of individual talent, though—luck is also involved. It's a kind of miracle when it happens. It's impossible to protect the position you gained from a miracle. It's as impossible as winning the lottery again and again.

Q: What has been your best experience as a director? That made you glad you're doing what you are doing?

A: When I finished my first original video, it was only supposed to be sold to video shops; there was no plan to turn it into a theatrical film. But when the video distributor saw it, he said he would put up the money to make a film version. So, it became a theatrical film and caught the eye of the directors of the Toronto Film Festival. It was shown there, where foreign audiences were able to see it for the first time.

This was my first foreign film festival—until then I had no interest in them. I had just been busy making films. In other words, I wasn't aware that I was climbing stairs—I was still young then. [laughs] When I saw that film in a theater with a foreign audience, I'd already seen it many times but I found it really interesting. Even though it was a film I knew backward and forward, I enjoyed it. When a film goes out into the world and starts to take on a life of its own, you get carried along with it.

You find something different every time you see it. Also, if I hadn't made that film I wouldn't have gone to Canada and met the people I did.

Q: That film was Gokudo Sengokushi Fudo [Fudoh: The New Generation, 1996]?

A: That's right, a yakuza movie. It was screened in the Toronto Midnight Madness section, for people who enjoy weird movies. [laughs] Anyway, the audience was there to enjoy themselves—and they enjoyed [my film], even though it was only a video. When I looked at the audience, I realized that the film was drawing a different sort of energy from them. I got a completely new take on it from their reaction. Films have no absolute limits—instead they have potentials and strengths the director never imagined.

Q: What has been your worst time as a director?

A: None. I'm just happy to be doing the job that I want to do. I've have some difficult moments, but I've never regretted anything.

future world where national borders have ceased to matter.

The film that made Miike truly notorious abroad, however, was *Audition* (1999), which began as a deliberately paced male fantasy about a middle-aged widower's search for a young, beautiful, traditionally minded bride—and ended as a horrific nightmare of sadistic depravity that sent the more delicate-minded scurrying from the theater. Miike's ultimate exercise in cinematic taboo shattering, however, was *Koroshiya Ichi* (Ichi the Killer, 2001), whose nerdish hitman hero sections his victims with a razor in his boot and climaxes as he kills. His nemesis, meanwhile, is a psychotic gangster who delights in torture and whose mouth, when the pins at its corners are removed, drops open in a huge, gaping rictus.

Miike also indulged his antic side with *Katakurike no Kofuku* (The Happiness of the

Katakuris, 2001), a musical comedy about a madcap family whose failing bed-and-breakfast keeps producing corpses, until they start digging graves at the arrival of each new guest. In 2002, perhaps to avoid typecasting as a directorial De Sade, Miike returned to the yakuza genre with *Shin Jingi no Hakaba* (Graveyard of Honor, 2002), a remake of the 1975 Kinji Fukasaku classic about a self-destructive gangster. He displayed his humanist side with *Kinyu Hametsu Nippon: Togenkyo no Hitobito* (Shangri-La, 2002), a comedy about the residents of a homeless camp who help a woebegone printer get back his business and life. Knowing Miike, however, more outrages are on the way—though the form they will take is anyone's guess.

FILMOGRAPHY

Gozu (2003), *Yurusarezaru Mono* (The Man in

White, 2003); *Sabu* (TV) (2002), *Part-Time Tantei* (TV) (2002), *Dead or Alive: Final* (2002), *Jitsuroku Ando Noboru Outlaw-den: Rekka* (Deadly Outlaw Rekka, 2002), *Kinyu Hametsu Nippon: Togenkyo no Hitobito* (Shangri-La, 2002), *Onna Kunishu Ikki* (2002), *Pandora* (2002), *Shin Jingi no Hakaba* (Graveyard of Honor, 2002); *Araburu Tamashii-tachi* (Agitator, 2001), *Family* (2001), *Katakurike no Kofuku* (The Happiness of the Katakuris, 2001), *Kikuchi-jo Monogatari: Sakimori-Tachi no Uta* (2001), *Koroshiya Ichi* (Ichi the Killer, 2001), *Visitor Q* (2001), *Zuiketsu Genso: Tonkararin Yume Densetsu* (2001); *Dead or Alive 2: Tobosha* (Dead or Alive 2: Birds, 2000), *Hyoryu-gai* (The City of Lost Souls, The City of Strangers, The Hazard City, 2000), *Tengoku kara Kita Otokotachi* (The Guys from Paradise, 2000), *Tsukamoto Shinya ga Ranpo Suru* (The Making of "Gemini," 2000) (V); *Audition* (1999), *Dead or Alive: Hanzaisha* (Dead or Alive, 1999), *Nihon Kuroshakai Ley Lines* (Ley Lines, 1999), *Salaryman Kintaro* (1999), *Silver* (1999) (V); *Andromedia* (1998), *Blues Harp* (1998), *Chugoku no Chojin* (The Bird People in China, 1998), *Kishiwada Shonen Gurentai: Bokyo* (1998); *Full Metal Gokudo* (Full Metal Yakuza, 1997) (V), *Gokudo Kuro Shakai Rainy Dog* (Rainy Dog, 1997), *Jingi Naki Yabo 2* (1997) (V), *Kishiwada Shonen Gurentai: Chikemuri Junjo-hen* (1997); *Gokudo Sengokushi: Fudo* (Fudoh: The New Generation (1996), *Jingi Naki Yabo* (1996) (V), *Kenka no Hanamichi: Osaka Saikyo Densetsu* (1996) (V), *Rakkasei: Peanuts* (1996) (V), *Shin Daisan no Gokudo II* (1996) (V), *Shin Daisan no Gokudo: Boppatsu Kansai Gokudo Wars* (1996) (V); *Bodyguard Kiba: Shura no Mokushiroku 2* (1995) (V), *Daisan no Gokudo* (1995) (V), *Naniwa Yukyoden* (1995) (V), *Shinjuku Kuroshakai: China Mafia Senso* (Shinjuku Triad Society, 1995); *Bodyguard Kiba: Shura no Mokushiroku* (1994) (V), *Shinjuku Outlaw* (1994) (V); *Bodyguard Kiba* (1993) (V), *Oretachi wa Tenshi Ja Nai* (1993) (V), *Oretachi wa Tenshi Ja Nai 2* (1993) (V); *Ningen Kyoki* (A Human Murder Weapon, 1992) (V), *Last Run* (TV) (1992); *Lady Hunter: Koroshi no Prelude* (1991) (V), *Topuu! Minipato Tai: Eye Catch Junction* (1991) (V).

Rokuro Mochizuki (1957–)

Many yakuza movie heroes have love lives of one sort or another; few have passionate affairs. The focus of the action is on the streets, not the bedroom. *Tateyaku* (traditional macho) types, such as the ones Ken Takakura portrayed in 1960s *ninkyo* films, have little to do with women as a matter of principle. Inheritors of the samurai code, the *tateyaku* regards romance as a weakness, something to be avoided by manly men. The heroes of Rokuro Mochizuki may be able to kick gangster ass with the best of them, but they are also capable of romantic passion in ways that set them apart from the yakuza crowd. Some, in fact, are not yakuza at all but on the fringes of the underworld, much like the heroes of Elmore Leonard.

Mochizuki, a veteran of Japan's huge porn industry, sees sex and all the accompanying emotions as simply human—and thus an inescapable part of his heroes' lives. His films may depict love at its extremes—with lovers wounded and even degraded to the core of their beings—but rarely as a mere sideshow. This approach may flout genre rules, but it sets his films apart. They are adult in ways that the films of many of his agemates, busy making violent fantasies for grown-up boys, are not. This does not mean that Mochizuki ranks feelings over fight scenes—he films action with a gut-clenching impact—but he rejects both the old *tateyaku* idealism and the newer *manga*esque sensibility of his contemporaries, whose heroes are cool cartoons.

Born in 1957 in Tokyo's Shinjuku Ward, Mochizuki entered the prestigious Literature Department of Keio University but dropped out in 1977 and spent several years scuffling

© Miura Photo

Director Rokuro Mochizuki is the creator of a new, grittier image of the yakuza loner.

Lewd Private Life, 1985) and *Aido Ningyo Ikasete* (Sex Slave Doll: Make Me Come, 1986).

In 1987 Mochizuki started his own production company, E Staff Union, and proceeded to churn out more than 120 adult videos. In 1991 he made *Skinless Night*, a poignant semi-autobiographical film about a veteran porn director who recalls the dreams of his youth—and longs to escape from the life. Screened both in Japan and at the Berlin, Vancouver, and Chicago Film Festivals, *Skinless Night* proved to be Mochizuki's stepping-stone to feature filmmaking. In 1992 he made the video film *Kahanshin Boso Senshi Gokuraku Hunter* (The Wild Warrior of the Lower Body: Pleasure Hunter) and in 1993 *Gokudo Kisha* (The Wicked Reporter, 1993), with Eiji Okuda playing a gambling-addicted, horse-racing reporter. Though given only a token theatrical release, *Gokudo Kisha* won popularity and critical accolades for its gritty portrayal of contemporary lowlife and generated a three-part series.

Mochizuki continued to work primarily for the straight-to-video market, making films in the yakuza and erotic genres. His 1995 *Shin Kanashiki Hitman* (Another Lonely Hitman, 1995), starring Ryo Ishibashi as a hitman who falls in love with a drug-addicted whore, was selected as Best Film at the Japan Film Professional Awards. Mochizuki also won the Best Directors prize that same year for *Kitanai Yatsu* (Dirty Guy, 1995), a film about an ex-yakuza extortionist whose daughter is kidnapped by a gang boss—and extortion target.

In 1997 Mochizuki released *Onibi* (The Fire Within) a film about a middle-aged hitman who falls in love with a younger woman and tries to go straight but takes on one last job for his new lover. Screened at many festivals abroad, the film further heightened Mochizuki's international profile. That same year, he made *Mukokuseki no Otoko: Chi no Shukaku* (Pinocchio: A Man without Nationality), whose salaryman-turned-Mafioso hero tries to make a killing with stolen fashion designs. Though

through a series of low-paying jobs. At the age of twenty-four, he began attending the Image Forum film school in Tokyo. One of his teachers, Katsu Kanai, invited him to assist with a film he was making, but production was canceled and Mochizuki once again found himself adrift. A script he wrote under Kanai caught the eye of director Genji Nakamura, who made it as *Shojo Nawa Ningyo* (Girl Rope Doll) in 1983. Mochizuki began working for Nakamura's Kenji Pro production company as an assistant director, while continuing to write scripts for pink and *roman poruno* (soft porno) films. In 1985 he made his directorial debut with *Honban Video Hagu* (Fuck Video: Strip), an adult film produced by the Million company. He also directed the adult films *Onanie Musume: Midarana Shiseikatsu* (Masturbation Girl: My

Rokuro Mochizuki Interview (September 2002)

Q: After having made so many films about the yakuza, are you fed up with them?
A: Not fed up. Yakuza are also human beings. I haven't made many films that make gangsters look cooler than the ordinary run of humanity. I've made a few, as jobs I took on, but not anymore. When you see yakuza up close, you realize there aren't any good ones. [laughs] The worst ones move up in the ranks. The yakuza I make films about aren't the ones who are advancing and becoming powerful—instead they're the dropouts. I don't want to make films about the yakuza elite.

Q: A lot of directors do present the yakuza as cooler than everyone else, don't they?
A: Yes, there are films—and not only Japanese films, that make gangsters look cool, even though they're bad people. It's as though the films are saying "bad is cool." I don't agree with that—bad is bad.

Q: You've been in the movie business for nearly twenty years now, ever since you left college.
A: I never graduated—I dropped out of Keio University.

Q: In the beginning, you made a lot of pink and adult films. Was that your only way into the industry?
A: At the time they were making both pink films and Nikkatsu *roman poruno*. When I was young, Nikkatsu *roman poruno* was thought to be the easiest way to get a start as a director. I had absolutely no problem with that, but adult videos were something else again—I wondered whether I was making the right choice. I thought I might never make a straight movie. But I liked movies, and I knew that if I wanted to keep making them, it was either the sexy stuff or nothing. To be honest, I wouldn't have kept doing it for nearly twenty years if I didn't like the sex and the women. [laughs] You've got to like that sort of thing to keep at it so long. When I was young, I rationalized that I had to make porno if I wanted to make movies. But now I really like it. [laughs]

I made adult videos for about five years. I shot one in about two days—I just churned them out. I learned how people in that business think—not just the women, but the men too. How they get jealous of each other—all that sort of thing. Also, because it's a business, I learned how ugly money is, how many hassles it causes. With adult videos, I didn't just get a taste—I did it for five years and by the end I knew just about all there was to know. That was a plus for me. After that, when I made straight movies, I was wise to a lot of things. How money can corrupt. How rotten people can be. How bad things can get.

The bubble economy burst around that time. The adult video business was made up of small production companies and when the recession hit I had a rough time, economically and in other ways. By economically, I mean people ripping me off. When things were going well for me, it made certain people jealous and when things were not going well . . . Well, people I thought were my best friends became my worst enemies. Seeing all that was an education for me, you might say. It influenced me.

Q: When I saw your first straight film, *Skinless Night*, I thought that this was one film you had to make for yourself. I heard that when you were writing it, you wondered whether you could ever put it on the screen.
A: Yes, that's the way I felt about it. When I first started making adult videos, I told myself that I would direct a film like [*Skinless Night*] someday. I thought I even might make some money from it. It wasn't easy, but I was able to shoot it because it was still the bubble economy era and I could raise the money. I guess you could say I was lucky. After that I had a lot of money problems, so I was lucky to make that film when I did.

Q: After that, you started making straight films.
A: My next one was *Gokudo Kisha* [The Wicked Reporter, 1993].

Q: It wasn't the usual film about the underworld—the hero wasn't a yakuza, for one thing. It reminded me of the American author Elmore Leonard, who often writes about characters on the fringes of the underworld, in a realistic style.
A: I tried to make it as stylish as possible, because it was that type of story. I could have made it just as a gambling movie, but I wanted to film people in the *shitamachi* [the old Tokyo downtown] who are barely scraping by. I want to film people who have no way out.

Q: The hero becomes addicted to gambling and ruins his life as a result. Was there anything autobiographical about that character?
A: I'm not a gambler, but when I made that film I gambled quite a bit, for research purposes. I wanted to find out what it was like and why people found it interesting. I never really liked it, though. I'll play cards or mah-jongg with friends, but that's about it. This was just when the bubble burst or maybe just before.

Q: The film came out in 1993.
A: That was when the phrases "new rich" and "new poor" entered the language. I thought the only thing you could put money into and expect to get a good return on was gambling. It's hard to imagine today, but people suddenly found themselves divided into financial winners and losers. The only way for the losers to get back into the game was through gambling. I thought that would make an interesting theme for a movie.

Q: That was your first film with Eiji Okuda, who later appeared in other films for you. He struck me as rather depressed in that movie. [laughs]
A: He's a cosmopolitan guy—not very macho. That's my impression of him as an actor. In person, he's not depressed at all. But he has this sophisticated air about him.

Q: That was my first impression, anyway. Then, when I saw him in Tatsumi Kumashiro's *Bo no Kanashimi* [Hard-Head Fool, 1994], I realized he had this stubborn quality as well.
A: That's true. He's very particular about his likes and dislikes—that's part of his appeal. He's the kind of actor who can play any role.

Q: You've been making films with him for some time now. What keeps drawing you back to him—does his image fit the kinds of films you're trying to make? Or is there a more personal chemistry at work?
A: We get along well in our personal lives. I've been influenced by him. When I made *Minazuki* [1999], I was thinking of a different actor, but he had a scheduling conflict and couldn't do it so I went with Okuda instead. He's a wonderful actor and I want to keep working with him.

Q: He's also quite good in love stories, *Minazuki* being a good example.
A: That he is. I understand why women don't want to get nude for love scenes, but men are the same way. Love scenes are really raw, right? There are a lot of people who don't want to expose themselves that way. Once men reach a certain age and level of fame, they won't take off their briefs. [laughs] They just won't do it. [Okuda] doesn't have that kind of macho pride. He's got a talent for bed scenes. When he's with a woman, he's not trying to be macho. Also, he's got a slim body that matches whatever age he happens to be in the film. Even though he's in his forties, he can play an average guy in his thirties or twenties. If he looked as though he were working out every day, he couldn't do that, though. [laughs]

Q: The audience can identify with him, in other words.
A: Yes, that's what I like about him.

Q: On the other hand, Yoshio Harada often played cool characters when he was younger. He had the right face for it.
A: And a good body as well.

Q: But in *Onibi* [The Fire Within, 1997], he shaved his head almost bald and looked like an average, middle-aged man. Was there a reason for that?
A: I started writing that film the year Aum Shinrikyo [members released poison gas on the subway trains]. I wondered why people kill each other. Especially members of Aum, who were about my own age. They didn't look like bad people. Why would apparently ordinary people do that kind of thing? As I said, I was really wondering why people kill. I had a model in mind for Harada's role—a guy named [Noriyasu] Kunihiro. When I met him, I thought, "This is a killer."

Q: He was a hitman?
A: Yes, a hitman. I really couldn't understand why he killed people—and that's what motivated me to make the film. He didn't have any good reason that I could see. He didn't do it for pride or country—he did it for nothing. Some people have to kill when they reach a certain boiling point—and that's how I presented him in the film. What made it a kind of fable was Kunihiro's nickname—Hi no Tama, which means fireball. That's what Kunihiro had inside him and what Show Aikawa and Eiji Okuda had in that film. If you have that fire, you either die or get stronger. There aren't many people like that now. *Onibi* is not exactly action packed, but in the climax Aikawa and Okuda face off against each other with pistols. The story is about men who are out to destroy themselves, men with a fire inside that consumes them.

I also like love stories. There was a movie several years back called *The Piano*, about a classical pianist. It was called *The Piano Lesson* in Japan. One thing I often wondered, even before I saw that film, was why classical musicians have this look of ecstasy on their faces. Pianists, violinists—they all have this look of ecstasy. I wanted to put that look on the screen, at least once.

Q: The hero of *Onibi* is not an ordinary yakuza—he's got a spiritual quality to him.
A: Kunihiro in the film is not supposed to be the real man—he's just modeled on him. The real man has been in prison for about twenty-five years altogether, starting when he was in reform school. He got out, killed someone, and went back in again. Then, he got out, killed someone, and went back in again. In Japan the law may have changed recently, but yakuza used to get the death sentence when they had killed three people. It's different for ordinary citizens. In the yakuza world, you can kill up to three other gangsters in gang wars and so on. After the third one, though, you die.

Before I met the man who was the model for Kunihiro, I wondered how scary he would look, but he was like a middle-aged guy who runs a used book store. He was like a librarian. He had been in prison for about twenty-five years and had come to like classical music and books. His penmanship was superb. But there was something a bit strange about him. He wasn't crazy, but there was something missing. He didn't have whatever people have that makes them hurt each other.

Q: I wanted to ask you about the role of music in your films—it seems to be very important to you.
A: Well, film itself strongly resembles music. For me, the structure of a film is like a musical score.

Q: The music in your films is often quiet. You don't pound away at the audience like Shinya Tsukamoto and a lot of other younger directors.
A: We used only classical music for the score of *Onibi*—a lot of Mendelssohn. We got some complaints about that—a yakuza movie with

classical music. [laughs] Well that's what I wanted to use.

Q: In *Shin Kanashiki Hitman* [Another Lonely Hitman, 1995] Ryo Ishibashi played a different kind of lonely guy.
A: In the yakuza world, they make the new members undergo a kind of training period. They live together and the older guys teach them. But while they're teaching them, they're also observing, to see if the new guys are suited to the life. For example, if they see that a guy is good at making money, they'll keep him on that career path because it's profitable for the gang. The guys who become hitmen are all only good at whacking people. Otherwise, their productivity is zero—they're taken care of, so they'll be there when they're needed. But yakuza are essentially terrorists—that's why everyone listens to them. So, the hitmen are well taken care of—it's just that they don't have any other talent. It's hard for them to move up into the yakuza elite—they just don't have a lot of interest in that.

Q: Ishibashi's character is like that as well, but he's loyal more to his own version of the gangster code than to the gang. He not killing for the *oyabun*, but for his own reasons.
A: That's true. Ishibashi says good-bye to the *oyabun* in that film—he goes his own way.

Q: It's a modern take on the *giri-ninjo* ethic, not like that of the old yakuza films.
A: I suppose so. The hero doesn't have a lot of interest in living in the yakuza world. He's a sad, tragic character. He thinks he can escape and find something better.

Q: In the third act, Ishibashi goes into the gang office and takes money from his boss, but he's holding a video camera, instead of a gun. That must be a first for a yakuza movie. [laughs] Was that your idea?
A: That's right. I put that [scene] into a script

for a yakuza comedy I was writing and [the producer got mad at me]. [laughs] I was thinking of the film as a comedy, but he wanted something more serious. He told me not to make fun of yakuza in the script. But I thought it would be more interesting if [Ishibashi] carried a camera.

When I first told Ishibashi about the camera, he was a little surprised. But when I explained why I wanted him to do it, he thought it was an interesting idea. When we started shooting the scene, there was a lot of tension [on the set]. Ishibashi was worried that he couldn't do the scene properly if he didn't have a pistol. To walk into a gang office with only a video camera, you have to be pretty pumped. You have to have a high level of adrenaline or you can't do it.

Q: You brought that tension across well, I thought. You take a similar approach in another of your yakuza films. One is *Gedo* [The Outer Way, 1998], which strictly speaking is not a yakuza film, but it does have a lot to say about the way the gangs operate.
A: That was a video film. Another was *Koi Gokudo* [A Yakuza in Love, 1997], which I made with Okuda. I wanted to film a kind of yakuza *Les Amants du Pont Neuf* [The Lovers on the Bridge]. [laughs]

Q: Did you have any trouble getting it made?
A: Have you seen it? In the middle of it, Okuda becomes his mother. In other words, he becomes possessed and enters into this trance state. His mother appears and her words come out of his mouth. When I wrote that scene, the producer begged me to cut it. I asked him to let me shoot it and then, if it wasn't any good, I said I would cut it. But when we edited the film, he let me keep it.

Q: Are you relatively free to shoot what you want?
A: Being hired to shoot a yakuza film itself

means that you're not free. I don't make films with my own money so I have to listen to other people. That's the way the movies have always been—you're not totally free to do what you want. I know what I want and don't want to do with a given project, but I'm not so talented that I can do everything. I have to work within certain limits. It's not as though I like yakuza so much. Do you know the word *gokudo*? It basically means to follow a given path to the end— to master a certain art. I don't necessarily believe yakuza are doing that, but I like making films about people who are outside mainstream society, following their own path.

I have two films I want to shoot but haven't yet—they were canceled because of various problems. One is about an erotic artist who was painting these extreme pictures in the Taisho Era [1912–26]. Another is about a *rakugo* [comic monologue] performer, an eccentric guy who wears contemporary clothes but speaks old-fashioned Japanese—"*yo gozansu*." [laughs] I'm interested in that kind of person. It's not that I have no interest in ordinary people, but I'm not interested in ordinary people who take up dancing, for example. If I make a dance movie, I want to make it about dancers. But in general I'm interested in outsiders and outlaws—people who are doing whatever it takes to survive.

Q: You create characters who are totally different from those in ordinary yakuza movies. I'm thinking of the yakuza played by Kazuki Kitamura in *Minazuki*. That guy is almost psychotically violent, but he has an ability to love as well. As a character, he's about as extreme as you can get.
A: When I took that film to foreign film festivals, I was asked about the violence. Japan is a peaceful country without a lot of violence. Instead of street fights, you have people who lose it—who go on rampages. There's even a word for it—*kireru*. It's a sickness. In that film, I wasn't depicting violence as such but that kind

of sickness. There are even children who are afflicted with it. They aren't usually delinquents, but gentle-spirited types who like flowers and music. When Kitamura is feeling mellow he cooks for people—he's not hopelessly insane.

Q: Kitamura has babe-magnet looks, but he also has a certain ambiguity—you can't be sure what he's thinking. He can be the soul of sensitivity one moment, explode with rage the next.
A: He is extremely serious. I don't know about his relationships with women, but when it comes to work he is extremely serious. He'll ask me to do one more take and, when the take is over, ask me how he did, with this serious expression on his face. He's not fishing for compliments—if he can't solve whatever problem he has [with his performance], the next day is not going to go well for him. He's totally dedicated to acting.

Q: In *Chinpira* he's not the usual *chinpira* type but more like a kid doing a part-time job.
A: That movie was based on a *manga* with a strong sexual theme. The way I explained it to Kitamura, his character is a sexual angel. I told him his penis was like a syringe. He goes around injecting all the women he can find. When he sees a woman who is in pain, he gives her an injection. [laughs] Women in their teens, twenties, thirties, and forties appear in the film. He doesn't have sex with the teenager, but when he sees a woman in trouble he tries to help her.

Kitamura asked me if the film was just about sex. [laughs] It's about sex in certain scenes—and for those scenes I needed an actor who had the right sort of sexual power. An actor who can do a good sex scene is an actor who can do a good love story, I think. In other films, Kitamura only does action roles—he's studied karate, so he's good at that. I see a lot of action scenes and most of them aren't that scary, but he really nails them—he's so fast. Action scenes are important, so you need an actor who can do them well and he's definitely one who can.

Q: Takashi Miike has been getting a lot of attention abroad, but not for his talent with love scenes. He usually turns them into S&M sessions. [laughs]
A: [Miike] and I get along well, but he does go over the top sometimes. I think he knows that himself—he's stopped using that particular pattern.

Q: He's been making more conventional films recently—*Shin Jingi no Hakaba* [Graveyard of Honor, 2002] and *Togenkyo no Hitobito* [Shangri-La, 2002]—the film about the homeless camp.
A: He's become a bit more serious. He knows that the crazy Miike World he created is getting old.

Q: I don't know whether he planned it or not, but his crazier films got him noticed abroad. Do you have any ambitions in that direction yourself? Also to make films abroad the way he has?
A: I haven't had the chance yet. For the past two years, I've had a string of bad luck. My company went under and the top person had to be replaced. Several movies I was just on the verge of making got canceled. The movie about the erotic artist was one. I still want to make it—the theme hasn't become stale for me yet.

If I keep at it a bit longer, I'll be back on track. Next year [2003] I plan to make a film based on the life of a science-fiction novelist. Having three film projects wash out has been a shock, but I can still make them by the time I'm fifty.

Usually you don't get that many second chances with films, do you? Kon Ichikawa remade his *Burma no Tategoto* [Harp of Burma, 1956], but that's a rare case. I wasn't able to make some films I wanted to make, but the rea-

son, I think, is that I was trying to do too much too soon. If I take my time and try to do them right, maybe I can still get them made.

Q: Did you like yakuza films when you were growing up?
A: I loved Kinji Fukasaku's stuff. When I was in junior and senior high school, I started to become interested in films, both foreign and Japanese. I liked ATG [Art Theater Guild] films, but I also loved Toei [yakuza films] and *roman porno*.

Q: Fukasaku was one of your favorites?
A: I liked his films about yakuza antiheroes. The films that came before, by Ken Takakura and other people, fell into a certain pattern. But when I look at some of those films today—the ones by [Masahiro] Makino are really incredible. Also, Junko [Fuji] is beautiful and a wonderful actress.

Q: The films Fukasaku was making in the early 1970s seemed like the real thing—he even had real gangsters coming to his sets and appearing before the cameras.
A: One film I remember from that time—it came along after Fukasaku's gang films—was *Nihon no Don: Yakuza Senso* [The Don of Japan: Yakuza War, Sadao Nakajima, 1977]. Someone asks the don, "What's going to happen to Japan?" I didn't want to hear that kind of question from a yakuza. [laughs] Fukasaku was really great in that way—he wasn't pretentious.

Q: Fukasaku used yakuza movies to present an underground history of postwar Japan. He wanted to broaden his scope—to examine society as a whole, not just the yakuza. You seem to have a similar ambition—to depict post-bubble Japan in your films.
A: That may be true, but Fukasaku is a director I greatly respect—I don't put myself on his level at all. He's like a god to me—a truly great director.

Q: You mentioned liking foreign films. Were you influenced by *The Godfather* and other Hollywood gang films?

A: *The Godfather* is a truly interesting film. It's about the gang world elite and their encounters with fate. When the characters meet their moment of fate, they're totally alone. I love that film—it's one of the ten best ever made.

Q: A lot of people feel that way. By comparison, Toei's yakuza films from that period didn't get much recognition in Japan or anywhere else. They were considered strictly commercial pictures and never won prizes.

A: Some of my yakuza films got made because they weren't Toei films. [laughs] A producer at Gaga wanted me to make the type of yakuza film that Toei would never make. I have worked with Toei, though. The guy who asked me to cut the scene of Eiji Okuda becoming his mother was a Toei producer. He also told me not to have Ishibashi bring the video camera into the gang office in *Shin Kanashiki Hitman*. But when Ishibashi said he would do it, the producer laughed and said OK, so he wasn't all bad. [laughs]

Q: A lot of young Japanese directors are taking their work abroad now and more of them are working abroad. Do you have any plans to do that?

A: No, I don't have any plans to work abroad at the moment. Films are a universal medium though. I don't know how many more years I can keep making films, but I'd like to try making one with foreign partners. I have an idea for such a film—it's about a sushi chef. There are a lot of Japanese working as sushi chefs in America now, aren't there?

Q: Yes, there are.

A: Ichiro and Nomo aren't the only ones trying hard to make it over there—sushi chefs are too and I'd like to make a film about them. The title is *Sushiman*. In recent decades, the image

of Japan abroad has changed from geisha and Fujiyama to sushi. Americans have even started to say that they're tired of Japanese-style sushi. They've started American-style sushi schools—they're trying to take the Japanese out of sushi. That would make an interesting story I think.

Q: Sushi doesn't only belong to the Japanese anymore, that's true.

A: There's something strange about the sushi business in general. In Japan, sushi costs as much as 3,000 or 5,000 yen a piece. That's insane. Sushi was originally a fast food, so a lot of Japanese have their doubts about the sushi mystique. Tuna sushi is really delicious, but one tuna can sell for as much as 5 million yen. What is that about? I'm not criticizing the guys who sell it, but it's still strange.

The guys who are really supporting the underworld are the ones who take women to eat expensive sushi. [laughs] They're the ones who keep the gangs going. I first realized that when I was doing a job in Aomori Prefecture—it sort of hit me. Remember Muneo Suzuki, the Diet member who was caught smuggling tuna from Russia? I wonder if it's all right to say this? He had a close relationship with the yakuza. Usually one tuna goes for 5 million yen in the Tokyo fish market. You can buy the same tuna in Russia for 1 million yen, bring it to Tokyo, and sell it for 3.5 million yen.

Q: That's quite a profit.

A: For a 1 million yen investment you get 3.5 million yen back. Can you think of another business like that?—I don't think so. After they arrested Suzuki, the price of tuna soared in the Tokyo fish market. He was smuggling it in like crazy with his yakuza partners, though the whole truth hasn't come out yet. Sushi shop owners and gourmets can't survive without that kind of guy. I like to eat good food too, but I think it's stupid to pay an absurd price for it. For one thing, I don't have that kind of money. For another, I think it's insane to be spending tens of thousands of yen on fish. Compared with Japan, American sushi shops are reasonable.

Q: What are you making now?
A: A film about Kamachi Yamada, a boy who died when he was seventeen. He died twenty years ago, leaving behind poems and paintings.

Q: In the form of a journal?
A: Not a journal—he left behind a huge amount of work. He wrote about taking entrance exams at the age of seventeen, problems with the opposite sex, that sort of thing.

Q: It seems to be quite different from your other films.
A: That's right, there's no sex or violence. Instead, it's about this boy who spent a year after junior high studying for his high school entrance exam because he failed to get into the best high school in the prefecture—his first choice. He was a bright boy but for some reason couldn't pass the exam and had to spend a year studying as a result. This was about twenty years ago, when Japan's system of *hensachi kyoiku* [evaluating students only by their place on the testing curve] was getting underway. He was among the first generation of kids to lock themselves up in their rooms [in response to this system]—the so-called *hikikomori*. Another was the notorious serial killer, Miyazaki, though he was living in Niigata when he committed his crimes. I'm setting my story in the present day, though.

Half the film comes from [Kamachi's] life and half comes from stories of kids today who are causing various problems. I feel that kids who stab people with knives and otherwise make trouble have something in common with kids who lock themselves in their rooms. There are already a lot of films about delinquents. There are also a lot of films about the problems of dumb kids who can't study. This is a film about a kid who can study but has problems anyway.

Q: He was of your generation.
A: I'm about four or five years younger—he would be about forty now if he had lived.

Q: So, in a way it's the story of your generation.
A: In a way it is, I suppose. Another reason I'm making it is that I don't especially like yakuza—I want a change of pace. Until now I've just been looking up at people who are older than me. I was interested in what I might be like in the future, when I was their age. I'm not particularly old now [laughs], but I want to look at kids who are younger than me.

Q: You want to look back at your own past?
A: Yes, look back. Also, I'm concerned about the situation of kids today. People my age already have fifteen- and sixteen-year-old children. By depicting children of that age, I'm also depicting their parents. That's my generation, so I have a natural interest in the subject.

admirably ambitious in its attempt to internationalize the yakuza genre, the film was one of Mochizuki's few failures, filled with amateurish acting and cross-cultural miscues.

His more successful followup was *Koi Gokudo* (A Yakuza in Love, 1997), a comedy about a yakuza who is more devoted to chasing women than whacking rivals. It was the first Mochizuki film to be distributed by a major company, Toei. Based on books by Yukio

Yamanouchi, a former lawyer for the Yamaguchi-gumi, *Shin Kanashiki Hitman*, *Onibi*, and *Koi Gokudo* have been called, perhaps ironically, Mochizuki's "no-good, middle-aged yakuza" trilogy.

Mochizuki further pursued the theme of middle-aged loners searching for new lives in *Gedo* (The Outer Way, 1998) and *Minazuki* (Everyone's a Moon,1999). The latter, starring Eiji Okuda as a sad-sack restructured salaryman and Takami Yoshimoto as the sex worker he falls in love with after his wife abandons him, was Mochizuki's most harrowing depiction of sex and violence at the edge. In 2000, he took a new turn with *Chinpira* (Chinpira/Two Punks), which featured Kazuki Kitamura as a *chinpira* who regards his gang duties as a part-time job, while administering sexual healing to the women who come his way—except for a self-destructive runaway he decides to save.

Struggling with professional troubles in the new millennium, including the bankruptcy of his production company and cancellation of two film projects, Mochizuki has slowed from his one-time pace of two feature releases a year. In 2002 he filmed *Kamachi*, a biography of a poet and painter who became a generational legend following his death at seventeen.

FILMOGRAPHY

Jam Films (segment *Pandora: Hong Kong Leg*, 2003), *Zankyo Densetsu: Haodo* (2002), *Konjaku-denki-ka* (2002), *Jitsuroku-Aomori Koso* (2002), *Kamachi* (2002); *Shishi no Ketsumyaku* (2001), *Giso Satsujin* (2001), *Chinpira* (Chinpira/Two Punks, 2000), *Kishiwada Shohen Gurentai Toku-betsu Hen: I Had a Dream* (2000); *Minazuki* (Everyone's a Moon, 1999), *Tsuka to Kinpatsu* (Money and Blondes, 1999); *Gedo* (The Outer Way, 1998), *Gokudo Zangeroku* (Mobster's Confession, 1998); *Koi Gokudo* (A Yakuza in Love, 1997), *Mukokuseki no Otoko: Chi no Shukaku* (Pinocchio: A Man without Nationality, 1997), *Onibi* (The Fire Within, 1997); *Shin Gokudo Kisha: Niguema Densetsu* (New Wicked Reporter: The Story of Niguema, 1996); *Debeso* (Apron Stage, 1995), *Kitanai Yatsu* (Dirty Guy, 1995), *Shin Kanashiki Hitman* (Another Lonely Hitman, 1995); *Gokudo Kisha* (The Wicked Reporter, 1993); *Skinless Night* (1991); *Aido Ningyo Ikasete* (Sex Slave Doll: Make Me Come, 1986); *Honban Video Hagu* (Fuck Video: Strip, 1985), *Onanie Musume: Midarana Shi-seikatsu* (Masturbation Girl: My Lewd Private Life, 1985).

Seijun Suzuki (1923–)

A director once dismissed as a light-minded studio hack with visual flair, Seijun Suzuki now looks like an avatar whose influence crosses borders and genres. His aestheticized, absurdist worldview, depicting the boundaries between reality and dream that constantly shift as the code of the tough guy devolves into choreographed grotesquerie, not only brilliantly reflected the Sixties' go-go excess, but foretold the course of much of popular culture over the next three decades, both in Japan and the West. While the films of many of his more engaged contemporaries, with their ripped-from-the-headline narratives and leftist social advocacy, now look dated, the best of Suzuki's work still has the power to amuse and amaze.

His one unarguable masterpiece from that period, *Koroshi no Rakuin* (Branded to Kill, 1967) is not a gang film, strictly speaking. Its hitmen are not gangsters but freelance operators ranked in a strictly graded hierarchy, with the hero beginning the film as Number Three. Nonetheless, *Koroshi no Rakuin* is a parody of the gang film's eat-or-be-eaten ethic, as well as the macho will-to-power of its characters. This attitude is also apparent in *Tokyo Nagaremono* (Tokyo Drifter, 1966); its story of a gangster coming selflessly to the aid of an aged (and unreliable) former boss may be a genre standard but, in Suzuki's hands, becomes a wild ride that segues into fantasy or, depending on the viewer's mood, hallucination.

Perhaps, as certain detractors have argued, Suzuki was simply having a bit of fun at the expense of his studio, with no deeper purpose than to amuse himself and his coterie of fans. But his reinventions (or trashings, if you will) of genre conventions, as well as his surreal, anarchic vision, have since inspired directors as different as John Woo and Jim Jarmusch (who dedicated *Ghost Dog* to him, while paying homage to several of his more famous shots). In their borrowings from pop culture and their

© Ogura Jimusho

The sage of Japanese movies. Grinding out action films for Nikkatsu in the 1960s, Seijun Suzuki created Kabukiesque climaxes and Dadaesque excursions into the absurd, all on the studio dime.

rearrangements of reality, many young Japanese directors are also far more Suzukiesque than they are Ozuesque or Oshimaesque, even if they have seen none of Suzuki's films. He doesn't tower as a sui generis genius so much as he infiltrates and insinuates.

Born in Tokyo's Sumida Ward on May 24, 1923, Suzuki was given the first name Seitaro. His father was a manufacturer of bicycle bells, a family business that Suzuki was groomed to inherit. In 1941 he graduated from a Tokyo middle school and took the entrance examination for Koa Gakuin (Asian Development Institute), with the aim of going to Indochina. He failed and studied independently for a year. During this period, he saw several films that made a strong impression on him, including Erik Charell's *Congress Dances* (Der Kongress Tanzt, 1931) and Hiroshi Inagaki's *Edojo Saigo no Hi* (The Last Day of Edo Castle, 1941). He finally entered Hirosaki High School in Aomori Prefecture but was drafted in December 1943 and started naval officer training. As a member of a weather observation unit, he was sent to the Philippines and Taiwan. A transport

ship on which he was serving was sunk by an Allied warplane, and he drifted for several days in Philippine waters before being rescued. By the end of the war, he had advanced to the rank of Acting Sub-Lieutenant but had developed a deep distrust of authority—as well as an acute sense of life's randomness.

Returning to Japan in 1946, Suzuki entered Hirosaki High School and graduated in 1948. He took the entrance exam for the University of Tokyo but failed and, at the urging of a friend, entered the film course of the newly founded Kamakura Academy. In September that year, he passed an assistant director's test at the Shochiku Ofuna Studio. Suzuki began work in October, with his first assignment being Minoru Shibuya's *Shushin Imada Kiezu* (Red Lips Not Yet Faded). He later worked for other directors but in 1951 was assigned exclusively to Tsuruo Iwama, a melodrama specialist.

In 1954, Suzuki transferred to Nikkatsu Studio, which had recently restarted film production after a long hiatus. He worked with several directors but primarily with Hiroshi Noguchi, a maker of program pictures, including *Ore no Kenju wa Hayai* (My Gun Is Quick, 1954). In 1956 Suzuki directed his first film, the musical melodrama *Minato no Kanpai: Shori O Wagate Ni* (Harbor Toast: Victory Is in Our Grasp, 1956). With *Ankokugai no Bijo* (Beauty of the Underworld, 1958) he began using the professional name Seijun.

In 1959 he directed *Suppadaka no Nenrei* (Age of Nudity), the debut of Kei'ichiro Akagi, an up-and-coming Nikkatsu star who was to die two years later in a go-cart crash. Ironically, Akagi's character, a young rebel without a cause, is killed in a motorcycle accident. Suzuki later praised the film as "relatively real." He also made several action films with Koji Wada, another Nikkatsu star with a large fan base among the young.

Suzuki's breakthrough, however, was 1963's *Yaju no Seishun* (Youth of the Beast), starring Jo Shishido as a disgraced former police detective who poses as a hitman to infiltrate two yakuza gangs and learn the truth about a senior detective's death. Though the story was typical cop-on-a-mission stuff, the film looked unlike anything then coming off the Nikkatsu lot, with flamboyant visuals (including a one-way mirror in a gang-run club that covers the better part of a wall) and action at once comic and cool (typified by the memorable scene of the hero fighting off baddies while hanging upside down from a chandelier).

With his next film, *Akutaro* (The Bastard, 1963), Suzuki began an association with art director Takeo Kimura that would help him further refine his distinctive style. That year, Suzuki also shot his first *ninkyo* film, *Kanto Mushuku* (Kanto Wanderer, 1963). Akira Kobayashi stars as a gambler who becomes involved in the tangled lives of an impulsive *chinpira* and his older sister—a professional card cheat who scams suckers together with her lantern-jawed husband. Working with Kimura and cameraman Shigeyoshi Mine, Suzuki incorporated Kabukiesque touches throughout the film. His stylistics reached a height of audacious beauty

in the climactic showdown, as primary colors flooded across the screen to express the hero's turbulent emotions.

He incorporated similar elements in the gang films *Hana to Doto* (The Flower and the Angry Waves, 1964) and *Irezumi Ichidai* (Life of a Tattooed Man; *One Generation of Tattoos*; *White Tiger Tattoo*, 1965). Both told conventional tales of gangster outrage and vengeance, while saving the visual pyrotechnics for last. In *Tokyo Nagaremono* (Tokyo Drifter, 1966), Suzuki became more audacious, using splashy primary colors and other Pop Art touches throughout the film, while revving up the story to a mind-spinning speed and even throwing in a comic barroom brawl straight out of a John Ford Western.

During this, his most fertile period, Suzuki made *Kenka Elegy* (The Born Fighter; *Elegy to Violence*; *Fighting Elegy*, 1966), a film about a pure-hearted youth, played by Hideki Takahashi, who sublimates his hyperactive sex drive by brawling and, in one scene, pounding the piano of his inamorata with his erection. The film burst with comic energy, while delving into the psychology of its high-spirited hero. In the end, the character joins an uprising of rightist army officers that, in February 1936, attempts to topple the government and install a military dictatorship. The boy who loves fighting finally has a real fight on his hands.

In his next film, *Koroshi no Rakuin* (Branded to Kill, 1967), Suzuki took his stylistic experiments to brilliant new extremes. The hero, Goro Hanada (Jo Shishido) is violently ascending the hitman hierarchy when a half-Japanese, half-Indian woman with a death wish (signaled by the dead bird hanging from the rearview mirror of her sports car) hires him for a job. When he botches it—a butterfly lands in front of his rifle scope at the crucial moment, he begins a Kafkaesque descent into terror and death, while falling hopelessly in love with his mysterious employer. The film, which begins as another wacky parody of hard-boiled

Seijun Suzuki Interview (March 2003)

Q: I see you got the question list.
A: These are difficult questions. You're trying to give me a hard time. [laughs]

Q: I'm sorry. [laughs] First, I'd like to ask something easy—are you working on a new film now?
A: Well, I've got plans, but I can't get anyone to make them. The film industry is in a difficult situation now. What's this book going to be about, by the way?

Q: It's on yakuza movies, from the silent days to the present, including yours of course.
A: Why are you interested in yakuza movies?

Q: I wonder why? [laughs] I've seen hundreds and I'm getting tired of them. [laughs] Well, it's an important genre of Japanese films, one that no one has ever written about at book length in English. Many books have been written in English about Hollywood gangster films and the people who make them, but not yakuza films.
A: Are yakuza films so different?

Q: I think they are, especially in the way they treat the theme of *giri-ninjo*. In movies about the Mafia, it's usually a *jingi naki tatakai* [merciless struggle for survival], not much *giri-ninjo*. [laughs] When you made your first yakuza movie, *Kanto Mushuku* [Kanto Wanderer, 1963], the genre was already quite popular, especially the *ninkyo* films in which the *giri-ninjo* theme was central. Did you have any problem with that theme?
A: Yes, I did, but I was working for Nikkatsu. When a director got a film from that studio he couldn't very well turn it down. Ninety percent of the time he couldn't say "no." If he really hated it, he could refuse to direct it, though.

Q: So you didn't want to put up a fight.
A: That was the studio policy. It wasn't just me—other directors had to make [yakuza films] as well.

Q: Did you have any particular interest in making them? Or did you feel that if you had to make them, you wanted to make them differently?
A: My first one [*Kanto Mushuku* (Kanto Wanderer, 1963)] was a remake of a film *Chitei no Uta* [Song of the Underground] by my teacher, Hiroshi Noguchi. Noguchi's film was really good, so I didn't want to compete with it directly. Since my film was a remake, I tried to make it different.

Q: It was different, particularly in the *nagurikomi* [climactic fight] scene, where you used a Kabukiesque style that was unlike Toei's or anyone else's.
A: Yes, it was different, but it reflected the studio style. Toei films at that time usually contained some element of social criticism. Even though they were yakuza films, they commented on social problems. But there was none of that in Nikkatsu films. They were *mukokuseki* ["borderless"]—the period or the place didn't matter. Nikkatsu films were interesting that way.

Q: *Mukokuseki* also meant that they had a certain foreign flavor.
A: Yes, there was that as well.

Q: But your films had a "Kabuki flavor."
A: [Laughs] That's true. I couldn't very well turn them into Shakespeare. [laughs] They were Japanese films after all, so I ended up using Kabuki.

Q: It been said that *ninkyo* films all derive from the *Chushingura* story, which was a favorite of the Bunraku and Kabuki stage. So you have that connection.

A: That's right. It's all Japanese culture, that goes without saying. The Japanese spirit and various other things are all found [in yakuza films]. They're a sort of rag-and-bone shop of Japanese culture.

Q: *Kanto Mushuku* was set in the Meiji period wasn't it?
A: But as I said, the period didn't matter. It could have been the Taisho or Showa period. [Yakuza films] were fundamentally entertainment. The audience could imagine any period it wanted, as long as it wasn't the present. [The films] were supposed to be entertainment—there was nothing realistic about them. Kabuki is the same way—both [Kabuki and yakuza films] are surrealistic.

Q: With Kabuki plays at least the style is consistent, but in your yakuza films there are stylistic breaks. Suddenly the audience is plunged into what seems to be a dream. Did the studio have any idea you were going to do that?
A: No, not all. The studio came to me with a script and asked me to make it. But whatever I cooked up after that was up to me—the studio had no idea what I was doing until I was finished. The producers let the director do his job and didn't interfere. The set was the director's territory.

Q: I've heard that once you started shooting a film, you didn't go home, you didn't change your clothes—for you it was the film and nothing else.
A: From the time I got the script until I began shooting I had about one or two weeks. If I had had three months to prepare I could have given it plenty of thought, but when I was making these films for Nikkatsu I had to decide the [set-ups] for next day's shooting the day before. It would have been better if I had a long preparation time like Kurosawa, but at least I could draw the storyboards. No-name directors like me had zero time, so I had no choice but to stay

up all night and never go home. We wouldn't start shooting a film on the set—instead we would begin with the locations, while the production designer and his people were preparing the set.

Q: I suppose you had to work closely together as a team to keep all the gears turning.
A: I wouldn't call it "teamwork." I let everyone think on their own, without worrying about anyone else. I wanted them to come to me with their ideas. The director should be the one who coordinates, not dictates. For example, if the production designer had an idea that I felt wasn't any good, I didn't have to use it. I think it's better for everyone to have different ideas.

Q: Your production designer, Takeo Kimura, had a reputation as an idea man. It's hard to imagine some of your films without him.
A: Well, I wouldn't go as far as that, but it was convenient to have people like him around, because they came up with ideas. He was always hitting me with one idea or another. A lot of production designers are silent types, but Kimura liked to gossip. He wouldn't talk about films—just trivia. [laughs]

Q: Would you consult with your cameraman?
A: Not really—I just talked to myself. [laughs] When we were filming I would tell [the cameraman] what he needed to know, but otherwise I just joked around. [laughs]. I wanted to lighten the overall mood. The director's job is to create an atmosphere that makes it easy for everyone to work.

Q: Did you have any say-so in the casting?
A: Not really—I had to use Nikkatsu's contract actors. I had no choice as to who I could cast.

Q: Akira Kobayashi was perfect for *Kanto Mushuku*, though. There was a certain purity about him that seemed to fit the material—and he looked the part as well.

A: Well, I had to think about which costume would be right for each actor. Because I was making a yakuza movie I had to come up with a costume that would fit that type of character. There's no book that can tell a director how to do that. Also, actors have to become whatever role they are asked to play, be it a yakuza or whatever, based on the script. But actors like Akira Kobayashi, Jo Shishido, and Hideki Takahashi had their images to consider as well—after all, we were making program pictures.

Q: They had to live up to audience expectations I suppose. The audience was coming to see Akira Kobayashi, not the character he was playing, but after a while they also started coming because they wanted to see a Seijun Suzuki picture.
A: No, not at all. That never happened.

Q: But you had your fans didn't you?
A: A few, but nearly everyone came for the actors. If more had come [for me] I would have become a major director. I could have shot whatever I wanted.

Q: But even though you were making program pictures, you were doing things that made you stand out. One example is *Nikutai no Mon* [Gate of the Flesh, 1964], which is set in the postwar underworld. I was struck by not only the style but the sensuality of that film. It was quite different from the usual take then on the postwar period.
A: The studio wanted to a make a skin flick, that's all. [laughs] We couldn't make real porno back then, though.

Q: A similar film from that period was *Kawachi Carmen* [Carmen from Kawachi, 1966], another film about women in the flesh trade, though done in a style that reminded a lot of people of the French New Wave.
A: You're talking about the guy who made *Breathless* aren't you? I'm often compared to Godard. I did see *Breathless*—it was an interesting film—but nothing else by him.

Q: There is definitely a connection between that film and *Koroshi no Rakuin* [Branded to Kill, 1967], which is your most famous film abroad. Not just the New Wave–style editing, but the sets, costumes, and casting. Was there any particular reason for that?
A: Well, they were both made by the same director. I had my own way of shooting that carried over from film to film.

Q: Was your individuality something that you tried to stress? In other words, did you want to make not just Nikkatsu films, but Seijun Suzuki films?
A: Not really. I was just trying to grind out program pictures. I wasn't trying to stand out from anyone else.

Q: You didn't have the leeway?
A: More than not having the leeway, I just didn't think about it. Nikkatsu had a double-bill system, so I did worry about what sort of film I would be paired with and what sort of actors would appear in it, but I didn't feel like rebelling against the system.

Q: You were more concerned with making your own films interesting.
A: That's right.

Q: More interesting for the audience than for yourself?
A: That's right, for the audience. They were the ones paying my salary. When I thought about making the film more interesting and suspenseful, it was all for the audience. I was there to serve them.

Q: Did that extend to your yakuza films? Did you get to point where you became sick of making them?
A: I had to follow studio policy. Otherwise I

would have had to quit. When Nikkatsu started to make youth films with actors like Sayuri Yoshinaga, I had to go along. Everything depended on studio policy.

Q: Even so, you went above and beyond the call of duty. When I watched the climactic fight scene in *Irezumi no Ichidai* [One Generation of Tattoos, 1965], with the complex choreography, the coordination of the colors, and the use of unusual angles, I was impressed by the thought and planning that must have gone into it. You weren't just grinding that one out.

A: I couldn't make a new film interesting or suspenseful if I just copied the previous one. I had to make a yakuza film that was different from *Kanto Mushuku*. Even so they ended up resembling each other, but I tried to make them different. I didn't want people to say that I was making the same old thing.

Q: That difference is especially noticeable in the last ten minutes or so, when Hideki Takahashi seems to enter a dream world.

A: That's right—at the end it gets into a Kabuki groove.

Q: Did you have to do a lot of rehearsing to get the timing right? Every movement seemed to be tightly choreographed.

A: Well, it was an action film—the actors had to get everything right the first time. I couldn't do retakes. The actors' concentration was really important.

As for why I used a Kabuki style, in foreign films the camera stays on the principal character. When he stands up and goes somewhere the camera follows him. Wherever he goes, the camera is waiting. But we do it differently here [in Japan]. In Kabuki they show everything at once. The interest is in seeing where and how the actors enter and exit. They appear right in front of you and go off somewhere in the distance. The continuity comes from the unity of atmosphere. On the other hand, in American films the continuity comes from the movements of the individual characters. That's the big difference. What we make here is a series of pictures, so the movement of any one character is secondary. It's hard to explain—I can't really put it into words.

Q: Was the theater more influential for you than films?

A: Not at all. Of course you can't shoot a scene like [the one in *Irezumi Ichidai*] without being aware of Kabuki, but it wasn't an influence exactly. I also didn't see a lot of films. If you're going to make them you shouldn't become addicted to them. Kabuki is the same way. You shouldn't become so addicted to something that you lose sight of everything else. That goes for you too, Mark—you shouldn't become addicted to yakuza movies. [laughs]

Q: I understand that better than anyone. I've seen enough of them. [laughs]

A: That's good—you'd better give them up. [laughs]

Q: But now that I've started writing a book about them, I have to finish it.

A: I feel sorry for you. [laughs]

Q: When you made *Irezumi no Ichidai* the fight scenes were serious business, but in *Tokyo Nagaremono* [Tokyo Drifter, 1966], the mood became lighter. You seemed to be parodying the genre, with the story taking second place. How did you come to make it that way?

A: When I made that film, I had to work the theme song, "Tokyo Nagaremono," into the story a certain number of times. Everything started with that song—I was told to put it in as much as possible. When you have to use a song like that, the story ceases to matter. The main thing is to get the audience to remember the song.

Q: Besides the song, what people remember

about that film is the style. Tetsuya Watari wearing a powder blue suit—it was a strange get-up for a yakuza. [laughs]

A: A hero has to look stylish. If he dresses like a bum he's not a hero anymore. That went for the hero in *Tokyo Nagaremono* as well.

Q: Also memorable was the night club set, with the huge hanging mobile that looks like a donut and changes colors. Was it there just for design purposes or for another reason?

A: The production design people came up with that. The space needed filling, so I asked [Takeo] Kimura to do something. He hung that thing there—that's all there was to it.

Q: Again, surrealism.

A: That's right.

Q: And the big fight scene in the bar—it seemed to come straight from a Hollywood Western.

A: That's right—it was supposed to be like a saloon [brawl] in a Western.

Q: How did the audience react? Did they understand the humor?

A: I have no idea. I never go to the theater. The studio knew, though.

Q: What was the studio's reaction? When the studio executives screened the film, did they say they couldn't release it?

A: That's right, but they had to release it. They had nothing else to replace it with.

Q: Then came *Koroshi no Rakuin*, which wasn't really a yakuza movie.

A: It was a Mafia movie. The hero was on the run alone. It was the story of a man who had escaped from America.

Q: In the beginning he is quite cool, but gradually you start to feel sorry for him.

A: That's no good—you shouldn't feel sorry for

a movie hero. [laughs] I agonized over that one too much, I should have filmed it with a lighter touch.

Q: The hero's wife livened things up quite a bit though. How did you get her?

A: Nikkatsu actresses wouldn't take off their clothes back then, so I had no choice but to go outside the studio and cast Mariko Ogawa. I ended up using her again after that film.

Q: Did you have any trouble getting her to do what you wanted?

A: I usually don't tell actors to do this or that. I let them do what they want. I only say something when they go off track. But in general I leave them alone—that's better for the film, I think. A movie ends up a certain way because of fate. You never thought you would find a certain type of actress but there she is. It's like a chance encounter. Along comes a girl you had never imagined.

The other girl in that film [Annu Mari] was also not from Nikkatsu. I didn't want a Nikkatsu actress [for her role], so I had to go outside the studio. I wish she had been more voluptuous, though—she was a little underdeveloped. [laughs]

Q: That film seemed to reflect the social background of the time, including the Vietnam War and all the questioning of values that accompanied it. It didn't even seem to be set in Japan—it had an "international" feeling to it.

A: It was made when student protests were at their height. "Don't cry for me, Mother" was a popular catch phrase. The kids involved in the student movement liked that kind of film. Yakuza films were popular then, in the midst of university riots. It was that kind of time.

Q: New types of antiheroes were also becoming popular, such as Clint Eastwood's Man With No Name in the spaghetti Westerns. In Japan the traditional heroes played by Ken Takakura

were still popular, but by 1967 the time was ripe for the hero Jo Shishido played in *Koroshi no Rakuin*, who become more and more un-heroic as the film progressed.
A: I wonder about that, though it's true I did want to make a new type of Nikkatsu film. To be brief, I wanted to kill off the hero. I finally shot it so you couldn't tell whether he was alive or dead at the end. In Japanese films then you couldn't kill off the hero, but I tried to come as close as I could.

Q: But the studio honchos found the movie incomprehensible.
A: They couldn't make heads or tails of it.

Q: It ended up being your last film with Nikkatsu, though now it's your most popular one abroad.
A: The story is easy to follow.

Q: Looking back on your Nikkatsu career, are there any films you are particularly fond of?
A: I made them in various genres—yakuza, *ninkyo*, and erotic. I can't say which ones I like. I like all of them in some ways and I dislike all of them in others. Also, some of the actors in those films are still alive. If I say I like one film, then the actors in the others will get mad at me, so I can't say anything. [laughs]

Q: The Nikkatsu films shown abroad are all from the latter part of your career with the studio. Are there any of the earlier ones that you would like to see revived?
A: No, not really.

Q: After you left Nikkatsu, a new, more realistic type of yakuza film became popular, led by Kinji Fukasaku's Jingi Naki Tatakai series. Of course, you didn't like realism in your own work, but what did you think of those films?
A: I didn't like them. Why do you have to make a film a record of real life? It's all right if you can make it entertaining, the way Fukasaku did,

but Nikkatsu's yakuza movies, including the ones I shot, were entertainment films.

Why can't they still make ones like them today? There are no actors now who can play the lead in yakuza movies. I don't see any actors in Japan who equal Ken Takakura or Bunta Sugawara in terms of charisma and style. Without the right actors, you can't make yakuza movies. Also, the stories may still revolve around *giri-ninjo*, but you have to find new ways to shoot them or what's the point?

Q: They're still turning them out, though. Takashi Miike recently filmed a remake of *Jingi no Hakaba* [Graveyard of Honor]. He's often compared to you, in the way he suddenly switches from a realistic narrative to surrealism.
A: I've haven't seen any of his films. I have to learn more. [laughs]

Q: When you left Nikkatsu, you had had your fill of yakuza movies. The films you made after that, such as *Zigeunerweisen* [1980], *Kageroza* [Heat Shimmer Theater, 1981] and *Yumeji* [1991] seemed to unfold in a dream world.
A: That's right, a dream world.

Q: Were these the kind of films you wanted to make at Nikkatsu, but couldn't?
A: That's right. Toward the end [of my time there] I wanted to make the kind of films that couldn't be made at Nikkatsu. That includes films about ghosts and other types of strangeness.

Q: The setting of those films was the Taisho era [1912–26]. You also used that period for some of your Nikkatsu films.
A: That I did. It was Japan's Belle Epoch, different from both the Meiji [1868–1912] and Showa [1926–89] eras. The Taisho was a period that glorified freedom. Of course, there was control from above, but within certain bounds the common people were free. There were anarchists, Bolshevists, and terrorists. It was an

age of ideology. On stage there was opera and new types of theater.

Q: You took a break from directing in the 1990s, though you appeared as an actor in other people's films. Then you made *Pistol Opera* [2001], which was advertised as a remake of *Koroshi no Rakuin*, but really wasn't.
A: It's totally different. At first I thought I would shoot a remake of *Koroshi no Rakuin* with a male actor in the lead, but when I started working on it, I gradually turned it into something quite different. The lead became a woman.

Q: Makiko Esumi—she's an unusual actress, quite stylish but not the most feminine type.
A: I had a problem with that—she wasn't sexy. [laughs] I wish she had a bit more sex appeal. Well, she had what she had—there's wasn't much I do about it.

Q: Also, *Pistol Opera* was shot more in the style of your 1980s films than your Nikkatsu films.
A: That's true. The Nikkatsu films were shot in the studio. The ones I made later were not. That makes a big difference.

Q: With the later ones you had more freedom.
A: But I was cut off from the skills that the studio had developed over a period of many years.

Q: So you think the era of yakuza films is really finished?

A: As long as they don't have the right stories and the actors. If you have the right story you can make something interesting, but both Nikkatsu and Toei's yakuza movies are pretty much finished. What they're making now are modern yakuza films, not ones set in the Taisho period. I don't have any interest in modern yakuza.

Q: I'd like to see an old-fashioned *nagurikomi* [one-against-all fight] scene again.
A: When [yakuza] go up on the space shuttle, they won't have any room for *nagurikomi*. [laughs]

Q: Do you still want to make films?
A: Not really—you need to be physically strong. I get tired too easily. [laughs]

Q: Of course there are directors like Fukasaku who keep going until the end.
A: He had no choice—he had already started shooting [*Battle Royale 2*]. If he hadn't started shooting, he would have been sick in bed. My teacher, Noguchi, also died during a shoot. He was fifty-seven.

Q: Directors all want to work until the end. Kurosawa was that way as well.
A: I think it's better to die like an ordinary person. It's often said that actors should die on the stage, but if you look at it objectively, dying on the job just causes problems for those around you. I don't need that.

---

conventions (the hero gobbles cooked rice instead of downing booze), finally sails into a bizarre realm in which dream (or nightmare) merges with reality—i.e., the hero's ambition to become Hitman Number One metamorphoses into a monstrous, deadly joke with his life as the punch line.

Koroshi no Rakuin, however, did not endear Suzuki to Nikkatsu president Kyusaku Hori, who found the film "incomprehensible." He gave Suzuki his walking papers and denied supporter Kazuko Kawakita permission to screen thirty-seven of his films in a retrospective. This later decision resulted in a court case, but though Suzuki had the sympathy of many colleagues and fans he found film work hard to come by. After a decade-long gap, he returned to the screen with *Hishu Monogatari*

(A Tale of Sorrow and Sadness, 1977) for Shochiku. By this time, he was sporting the white goatee that was to become his trademark. (He had also shed some of the eccentric personal habits that he was known for in his early years as a director, such as never bathing, brushing his teeth or changing his clothes during a shoot.)

Suzuki's comeback culminated with *Zigeunerweisen* (1980), a ghost story set in the early years of the twentieth century in which the barriers between the dead and living dissolve. The film won numerous awards, including the jury prize at the Berlin Film Festival. Suzuki made more films in widening intervals over the next two decades, but none in the gang genre. In 2001 he released *Pistol Opera*, a remake of *Koroshi no Rakuin* that starred Makiko Esumi as a hitwoman and Mikijiro Hira playing an older version of the Goro Hamada character. Static, mannered, and self-indulgent, the film was nonetheless made with Suzuki's uniquely stylish panache. Suzuki has also appeared in other director's films in recent decades, usually playing a version of his puckish, sage-like public personality.

FILMOGRAPHY

Pistol Opera (2001); *Kekkon* (1993); *Yumeji* (1991); *Capone Oi ni Naku* (Capone Cries a Lot, 1985); *Lupin Sansei: Part III* (TV series) (Lupin III: Part III, *Lupin III: The Gold of Babylon*, 1984); *Kageroza Heat Shimmer Theater* (Heat-Haze Theater, 1981); *Zigeunerweisen* (1980); *Ana no Kiba* (The Fang in the Hole, 1979); *Hishu Monogatari* (A Tale of Sorrow and Sadness, 1977); *Mira no Koi* (TV) (A Mummy's Love, 1970); *Otoko no Naka ni wa Tori Ga Iru* (TV) (There's a Bird Inside a Man, 1969); *Koroshi no Rakuin* (Branded to Kill, 1967); *Kawachi Carmen* (Carmen from Kawachi, 1966), *Kenka Elegy* (The Born Fighter, *Elegy to Violence, Fighting Elegy*, 1966), *Tokyo Nagaremono* (Tokyo Drifter, *The Man from Tokyo*, 1966); *Akutaroden: Waruihoshi no Shita Demo* (Stories of Bastards: Born Under a Bad Star, 1965), *Irezumi Ichidai* (Life of a Tattooed Man, *One Generation of Tattoos, The White Tiger Tattoo*, 1965), *Shunpu-den* (Story of a Prostitute, 1965); *Hana to Doto* (The Flower and the Angry Waves, 1964), *Nikutai no Mon* (Gate of Flesh, 1964), *Oretachi no Chi ga Yurusanai* (Our Blood Will Not Forgive, *Our Blood Won't Allow It*, 1964); *Akutaro* (The Bastard, 1963), *Kanto Mushuku* (Kanto Wanderer, *The Woman Sharper*, 1963), *Tantei Jimusho 23: Kutabare Akutodomo* (Detective Bureau 2–3: Go to Hell, Bastards, 1963), *Yaju no Seishun* (The Brute, *Wild Youth, The Young Rebel, Youth of the Beast*, 1963); *Ore ni Kaketa Yatsura* (The Guys Who Put Money on Me), *High-Teen Yakuza* (1962); *Hyakuman Dollar O Tatakidase* (Million Dollar Smash-and-Grab, 1961), *Kaikyo, Chi Ni Somete* (Blood-Red Water in the Channel, 1961), *Muteppo-daisho* (A Hell of a Guy, 1961), *Sandanju no Otoko* (The Man with a Shotgun, 1961), *Toge O Wataru Wakai Kaze* (The Wind-of-Youth Crosses the Mountain Pass, 1961), *Tokyo Kishitai* (Tokyo Knights, 1961); *Kemono no Nemuri* (Sleep of the Beast, 1960), *Kutabare Gurentai* (Fighting Delinquents, 1960), *Mikko Zero Line* (Clandestine Zero Line, 1960), *Sono Gososha O Nerae* (Aim at the Police Van, 1960), *Subete Ga Kurutteru* (Everything Goes Wrong, 1960); *Ankoku no Ryoken* (Passport to Darkness, 1959), *Love Letter* (1959), *Suppadaka no Nenrei* (Age of Nudity, 1959); *Ankokugai no Bijo* (Beauty of the Underworld, 1958), *Aoi Chibusa* (Young Breasts, 1958), *Fumihazushita Haru* (The Boy Who Came Back, *The Spring That Didn't Come*, 1958), *Kagenaki Koe* (Voice without a Shadow, 1958); *Hachijikan no Kyofu* (Eight Hours of Terror, 1957), *Rajo to Kenju* (The Naked Woman and the Gun, 1957), *Ukigusa no Yado* (Inn of the Floating Weeds, 1957); *Akuma no machi* (Satan's Town, 1956), *Hozuna wa Utau: Umi no Junjo* (Pure Emotions of the Sea, 1956), *Minato no Kanpai: Shori O Wagate Ni* (Harbor Toast: Victory Is in Our Grasp, 1956).

ACTOR PROFILES & INTERVIEWS

Show Aikawa (1961–)

The biggest star of the 1990s New Yakuza boom, with a cooler, drier presence than an older generation of yakuza heroes, Show Aikawa was born in 1961 in Tokushima Prefecture, the son of a Self-Defense Force pilot. In 1967, when Aikawa was five years old, his father died in a mid-air collision. He and his younger brother and sister were raised by their mother in her native Kagoshima Prefecture. Left largely to his own devices while his mother ran a coffee shop near a Self-Defense Force base, Aikawa became something of a neighborhood terror. But in junior and senior high school, he channeled his considerable energy into athletics, particularly judo and gymnastics.

Rejecting the call of a local yakuza to join a gang, Aikawa left Kagoshima in 1980 for Tokyo to attend a trade school. Soon after arriving, he got a job as a part-time reporter for *Pop Teen* magazine, covering the Tokyo youth scene. With his carefully sculpted "regent" hairdo and trademark leather jacket and pants, Aikawa may have been a throwback but was hardly alone: "rollers"—kids who adopted the look and attitude of 1950s rebels—were a small but growing presence on the Tokyo street and club scene. Joining a group of zoot-suited street performers who did everything from push-ups in unison to sophisticated dance moves, Aikawa soon became an underground sensation. An offshoot of the group, Issei Fubi

Sepia, debuted in 1984 with Aikawa taking a prominent role. A singing and dancing ensemble with a harder edge than the typical J-Pop boy band, Issei Fubi Sepia toured, released CDs, and appeared on television, but it never crossed over to mainstream success.

Though a star of the group with a budding solo career, Aikawa was tiring of the grind when he was invited to appear in a TV drama, "Tonbo," starring pop singer Tsuyoshi Nagabuse. His performance as Nagabuse's gang underling led to other offers and, following the breakup of Issei Fubi Sepia in 1988, Aikawa concentrated on his acting career. His breakthrough was a starring role in Banmei Takahashi's *Neo Chinpira Teppodama Byu* (Neo Chinpira: Zoom Goes the Bullet, 1990), the first entry in Toei's V Cinema straight-to-video series. The film became a hit with video store customers, and Aikawa became a rising star in the burgeoning video movie industry.

He solidified his acting reputation—and shed his pop-star-turned-actor image—with his performance in Tatsumi Kumashiro's *Bo no Kanashimi* (Hard-Head Fool, 1994) as the ice-cool gang associate of the mad-dog ex-con played by Eiji Okuda. After winning the Mainichi Blue Ribbon's Best Supporting Actor award for his work in this film, Aikawa continued to churn out gang action films for the video shelves, notably the hit Shuraba ga Yuku (The Carnage Comes, 1995–present) series, while occasionally venturing into theatrical

Show Aikawa Interview (August 2002)

Show Aikawa is one of the hardest-working men in Japanese movies but one that most Japanese moviegoers have rarely seen unless they are fans of OVs. They would know Aikawa as the gangster glaring down from the boxes of dozens of yakuza films, including the *Shuraba ga Yuku*, *Shakingu* (Loan King), and Katte ni Shiyagare!! series. Meanwhile, young foreign fans know Aikawa as the coolest of the new generation of Japanese movie tough guys, who works with the coolest of the Japanese New Wave directors, such as Takashi Miike (*Gokudo Kuro Shakai Rainy Dog, Dead or Alive*) and Kiyoshi Kurosawa (*Kumo no Hitomi, Hebi no Michi*).

In the meantime, he keeps churning out films at a mad rate—more than 140 since his first, Seiji Izumi's *Kono Mune no Tokimeki o* (The Throbbing of this Breast) in 1988, and mostly in starring roles. On August 8, 2002, following the release of his latest film, *Kinyu Hametsu Nippon: Togenkyo no Hitobito*, Aikawa was taking a brief break, which meant talking to the media in the morning at the Daiei headquarters and filming a TV drama later in the day.

In person, he looked fit, rested, alert, vibrant—a walking advertisement for workaholism. His clothes were fashionably casual, his manner open and friendly, but Aikawa was also radiating something more than warmth. Call it an avidness not just to experience but to engulf the world. A man in a hurry, in other words—and still only forty-one.

Q: In your autobiography *Ore, Furyohin* [Me, the Reject], you say that you can't speak Kansai dialect in a film, but in your latest, *Togenkyo no Hitobito*, you were speaking it.
A: I was speaking it, but not very well. [laughs] There are a lot of types of Kansai dialect. The type I was speaking may exist, but it's going to give real Kansai people the creeps. [laughs] I'm from Kagoshima and I get the creeps when people who aren't from Kyushu try to speak the Kyushu dialect. More than what they are saying, the intonation is hard on the ears. The same is true when I speak Kansai dialect.

Q: The character is from the Kansai, so I guess you had no choice.
A: I feel that the film is a kind of new development for me. It's different from the films of Kiyoshi Kurosawa and some of the other directors I've worked with—it's a human drama, but at the same time it's got laughs. That's what people like in terms of content—they all love human drama.

Q: It's good to take a break from violence once in a while, isn't it? [laughs] The first film of yours I saw was probably *Rainy Dog*—and that had a human drama element as well.
A: That was a good film.

Q: You liked it too?
A: Yeah, I liked it, I also like *Dead or Alive*. That was another human drama.

Q: Each film in the series was quite different. In the first film, you played a detective who was also a devoted family man. That was one of your more memorable roles.
A: Yeah, that detective was a real homebody.

Q: Was it an easy film for you to do?
A: Even though the detective had a family, there was a loneliness about their dinner table. There were a lot of meal scenes in that film and there was a certain realism to them. You could really understand what was going on—you could see the atmosphere of that family. You could see how lonely they were. That loneliness underscores the detective's violence.

Q: In the third film, you were not playing a human being but a robot. Did you enjoy that?

A: I loved it! It was completely unreal. I could shout about all these taboos that you're not allowed to talk about in daily life. And there are so many of them. Taboo things aren't necessarily bad. Things you really ought to make a noise about are often suppressed by Japanese tradition, Japanese society. The ones who can make that noise in Japan are the yakuza. The whole Dead or Alive series is all about getting things out in the open. With that kind of outlaw character, you can make that kind of noise.

Q: Miike's film may have their outlandish elements, but there's also an honesty—they're saying what people really feel.
A: There's a human quality to them. That kind of thing strikes a strong chord with me.

Q: On the other hand, with Kiyoshi Kurosawa's films, you're in this strange nonhuman world. [laughs]
A: He uses that style to put across his message—but with a soft voice, not a loud one. But they both surprise you, even though one is soft and one is loud.

Q: The first Kurosawa film you appeared in was the first episode of the Katte ni Shiyagare series—a comedy. It's the kind of film you would not expect now from Kurosawa, but I thought it was interesting the way he did it.
A: Yeah, it was an interesting film! But whatever Kurosawa makes is interesting. I hadn't done much of that kind of thing before, but the script grabbed me. I knew it would work as a movie—it got me really excited. There were a total of six films in the series and they were all interesting.

Q: You are becoming better known abroad. Are you thinking of selling yourself more aggressively abroad? Of appearing in foreign films?
A: I'm not really that eager to work abroad, but I'm really happy that more films made in Japan are being sent overseas. If I'm asked to work abroad, I might do it. If I don't have to worry about the language problem and can speak Japanese, I would definitely be interested.

Q: You tried directing a few years ago with *Bad Guy Beach*. Then, recently, you produced *Rush!*, though Takehisa Zeze directed. Are you interested in doing more directing?
A: Maybe once every five years. It takes an incredible amount of energy, so I have to recharge my batteries before I can do it again. If you haven't made a number of films already, you get crushed by all the demands made on the set. The job is completely different from acting—you have to tell people what to do; you have to be in control. With acting you just have to be there and play your role—you just have to do what the director tells you. As a director, you have to take charge—you're a kind of manager. When I directed, I not only had to do my own role but blend it together with the performances of everyone else. That takes a lot of energy.

Q: But Woody Allen has somehow managed to do it for years. Tell me about *Rush!* What was the experience of making that one like?
A: I was involved in the production of *Rush!* from the planning stage. I even wrote a treatment and spent about five months working on it before I handed the piece to the scriptwriter.

Q: *Rush!* was released as a theatrical film, so I can understand why you spent more time on it. But with V Cinema it seems that you're doing one after another.
A: I'm getting projects from all over. I generally know what my schedule is going to be for about half a year ahead. So, if I get an offer, I have about half a year to prepare.

Q: The shooting schedules for OV movies are usually pretty short, aren't they—about three weeks? The preparation period must be important.

A: It's the most important part of the process. During preparation, I talk to the director and we decide what kind of movie we are going to make. Once shooting starts, I'm just on the run. So, what happens before that is very important. If I stop to think on the set I'm finished. So I do my thinking in the month before.

Q: When you prepare for a role, do you have to imagine everything about the character—his background and so on? Do you have it all figured out before shooting?

A: That's right, before shooting. I have to figure out three or four things about the character or I can't prepare for the role. For example, I have to know his blood type; the month, day, and year he was born; how many brothers and sisters he has; what his home life was like growing up. Once I know those kinds of things, I can understand what kind of human being he is. If his blood type is O, he'll smoke this kind of cigarette—I'll figure it all out.

Q: The character you play in *Shangri-La*—the "mayor"—is rather mysterious. How did you get a grip on him?

A: Yes, he's mysterious. I didn't try so hard to pin him down. I thought I would make him a little vague, a little mysterious. He had cigarettes, but he didn't take them out of his case. Even so, I put different kinds of cigarettes in the case. [laughs]

Q: That devotion to detail wasn't limited to your character in the film. Even the homeless village looked as though people were really living there.

A: Crew members were staying there. We were worried about bikers coming and wrecking everything, so they had to stay there a week to protect it.

Q: Even the printing shop looks as though its been used for years.

A: Well, the printing shop was supposed to make phony checks for use in the scam. The kind of place we found that could do that was old. There were these huge bugs running around the place—it must have been dozens of years old.

Q: It reminded me of the printing shop in the Tora-san series—it looked as though it hadn't changed in years. Also, the film describes the whole process of making those checks very carefully.

A: That's important.

Q: Does that sort of realism matter a lot to you?

A: Of course, it's better to have it—it really helps to have a sort of precision. If I don't have it, then my performance suffers. It makes it easier for me [to get into a role]. For example, the barrel that we used for a bathtub in the film. It made a big difference having that barrel. When I washed my face in it, my skin became all white and thin—it was really strange. I was homeless, but my face was white and thin—that looked so real. What looked strange then was to have a black, dirty, sunburned face.

Q: So, you looked like the real thing.

A: No one could tell the difference.

Q: I heard that when Kinji Fukasaku was making *Jingi Naki Tatakai* the local yakuza came to the set to give him and the others advice—so he was able to get that sense of realism into the film.

A: They used to do that, didn't they, with the gambling scenes and so on. When they filmed the ceremony for the changeover to a new boss, everyone was wearing the correct period clothes. They were still doing that kind of thing in the 1960s and 1970s—having everyone wear period clothes. They would also film those formal introductions [when new people came to the gang headquarters].

Q: They had a certain way of holding out their hands, a certain speech they had to deliver.

A: They didn't have business cards, which didn't really start becoming popular in Japan until the 1960s. Then, they were suddenly everywhere and [yakuza] stopped doing that kind of formal introduction.

Q: You had to say not only your name but where you were from, what kind of job you had, and so on.
A: They didn't have business cards to give to people then. When the cards came in, the introductions went out. A yakuza told me that. When I asked him why they didn't do the introductions anymore, he said it was the business cards—when people got them, they thought they had everything they needed. But yakuza with business cards just don't look cool.

Q: When I interviewed a boss with the Sumiyoshi-kai several years back, he gave me his business card, with all the details. I don't think the American Mafia would be so upfront.
A: No, they probably wouldn't. Japan is smaller so you know who someone is and where they are from right away. In America you don't, because it's so big. Even in Chicago, you wouldn't know.

Q: You grew up in Kyushu—I heard that you had some contact with the yakuza there.
A: Well, I was in a small town. The yakuza there would recruit the more alert guys like me and use us as gofers. When I was about to graduate from high school, I was invited to join a gang—but I got scared and ran. [laughs]

Q: Did you ever wonder what would have happened if you had accepted?
A: If I had accepted, I would probably be a yakuza now. The yakuza in Kyushu don't get into people's faces as much as they do elsewhere. They're in the entertainment business, putting on sumo tournaments, pop concerts, and that kind of thing. They do a lot of jobs to promote the community—they're not like the yakuza on TV.

Q: Were you attracted to yakuza movies?
A: I loved yakuza movies! I wouldn't become a gangster myself, but I thought they were so cool. Men seem to get excited by that kind of thing: cut or be cut, kill or be killed. It's like little kids with a superhero—I had this "wow" reaction. Of course, [the yakuza] were anti-heroes, but it felt good [to see them in action]. They lived by the *giri-ninjo* code.

Q: Yes, back in the old days, but now it's a bit different, isn't it?
A: The environment around the yakuza has more or less changed, but the sort of yakuza I play are mostly ones who still abide by the old *giri-ninjo* code.

Q: When you were coming up, you starred together with a lot of older actors. Were there any that you wanted to model yourself on?
A: Not really, there was no one person that I wanted to be like. From the viewpoint of the older actors, I may have been something strange. The reaction was like "Aikawa what are you doing here?" [laughs] In other words, I hadn't done any acting, but suddenly, bang!, there I was. I was a singer—I didn't have much interest in acting, but when I was asked to try I thought it might be interesting so I thought I would give it a shot. And then all of a sudden there I was.

That's how I got started, so from the viewpoint of the other [actors], it may have seemed strange. As for acting, I felt that I shouldn't think so deeply about it, but just do it. But when I started doing it, I realized that I had to think more deeply about it. It was so tough that I thought it would take me ten years to get anywhere. I hit a wall and wondered how I would ever get over it.

Now, almost ten years have passed. I feel that I should rethink what I'm doing. With age, you somehow achieve a better balance—you start to figure out your priorities. But as for acting, I've recently started to feel that, number one, I ought to go back to the starting line.

More than theorize about acting, I'm looking to find something about a character that interests me, that I can identify with. For example, say you have a killer. I want to know why he killed people. If I feel that I might do the same thing he did, that's great. If I can't identify that way, well . . .

Q: In your autobiography, you said that you couldn't play a homosexual—is that still true?
A: I wonder. Why do they become that way? I don't mind talking about it, but if someone came here and said "play [a homosexual]," I don't think I could do it. [laughs]

Q: Right, but when you played a Korean in Junji Sakamoto's *Shin Jingi Naki Tatakai*, you were getting outside yourself and into the role of a foreigner.
A: That's true—I had no idea of what it was like over there. I talked about it with [Tomoyasu] Hotei [who played one of the leads], and we came up with a back story—that I had only been in Japan four years, but from the moment I arrived, [Hotei] had been a big help to me. At a time when I knew from nothing about Japan, he took me under his wing. I felt that I owed him something for that. There was a limit, though—if he were no good, that would change things. That [back story] didn't appear on camera, but it was my starting point. That's how I was able to get a handle on the role. I had a conversation with the director as well, and he agreed with my back story. Once I had a clear idea of how [the character's] human relationships would be affected by the fact he was a foreigner, I was in the world of *giri-ninjo*. I had my character.

Q: Did you go to Korea, get to know some Koreans and do other research of that kind?
A: I have some Koreans among my acquaintances. I'm from Kagoshima in Kyushu where there aren't a lot of Koreans, but the temperament of people [from Kyushu and Korea] is

similar. For example, if [Koreans] don't like something they don't like it—and they'll tell you so loud and clear. They're more straightforward than the Japanese, but people in Kyushu are that way, too. Adults will tell kids to stop—and mean it. Adults are not under the thumbs of their kids. You don't see kids treating adults like fools or physically attacking older men, the way you do elsewhere in Japan. In Kyushu adults are respected for being adults and that's the way it is in Korea as well. Over there, juniors defer to their seniors—they're very strict about that. So, Kyushu and Korea have that in common.

Q: When I went to Korea for the first time, several years ago, I was struck by some of the cultural differences with Japan. For example, juniors are not supposed to smoke in front of their seniors.
A: That's also true in Kyushu—you have to ask your senior before you smoke. [Gestures with imaginary cigarette], "Please, may I?" [laughs]

Q: In the third episode of the Dead or Alive series, you played a robot—so you had even a larger jump to make. Not just a different culture, but a different world. [laughs]
A: It was tough. I was supposed be a military robot passing himself off as a human being, and I had to make it look convincing somehow. I had a lot of trouble dealing with the character's emotional tug-of-war—the conflicted feelings he had because he was a robot who was halfway to being human. At the same time, I was having a bit of fun with it, because the character was a robot. But in general, it was really a painful process.

Q: I'd like to ask you about your family background a bit. Your father died when you were young, and you were raised by your mother. I understand she had a big impact on you.
A: Yes, it was probably big. I was never scolded by a man, but until I was in high school my

mother used to pound me. [laughs] I wonder what would have happened if a man had done the same thing? If it had been a man, I probably would have resisted more. When a woman hits you, it's kind of a joke. But by the time I was in high school, she was too scared to hit me. She was worried that I'd hit her back. [laughs] When I was in high school, I thought I was stronger and could handle myself—so the balance of power shifted.

But at the same time, I remember feeling sorry for her because I had been so bad in elementary school. I had finally arrived at an age when I could understand how bad I had been, after all. When she got mad at me, it was because I was in the wrong—she had nothing to feel sorry for. I'm really thankful for that. I didn't understand then, but when I became an adult I realized that adults have to tell children no, for the good of both of them.

Q: You have five children. With that big a family, you probably feel that you can't fall down on the job.
A: Yes, that's a big factor. I worked when I was single and the pace hasn't really picked up since I was twenty-four. But as you get older, your reaction to exhaustion and tiredness changes—there's a difference between your mid-twenties and your forties.

So, the amount of work hasn't changed so much. But, though I haven't declined physically or spiritually, when I come back home, it's nice to know that someone is there. If I came back exhausted and hungry to an empty house, it would be tough to get ready for the next day.

Also, having a family means I can't give up. It's as though the kids are pushing me, telling me to keep trying, but not in so many words.

Q: Acting is usually an unstable profession, but you churn out films like a conveyor belt. [laughs]
A: But it's definitely a job with its ups and downs. So, it's good that I have someone at home telling me to go out and do it. That helps me buckle down. There is a limit, though, and I don't want to exceed it. When people come to me with an offer while I'm doing a film, I'll tell them to come back later. Otherwise the new job will affect the job I'm doing now. I have to know my limits and do one job at a time.

Q: Do you feel you've reached a point in your career that, instead of waiting for offers to come to you, you have to seek out the sort of films you really want to make?
A: It gets boring just doing what people ask you to do—that goes for both acting and singing. So, even though I'm doing a job that someone has brought me, I try to bring my own ideas to it. I have to do that or I can't do that job. If I were to just do what I'm told, I'd be gone in a year or two. What do I do? If I see something that looks interesting, I'll do it, whether it's a starring role or not. Kurosawa or some other director will sometimes ask me to try something—maybe just a small role. If it looks interesting and worthwhile from the script, I'll do it. We may fight quite a bit over how I'm going to do it, though.

Q: Still, it's amazing that you never seem to tire of it. [laughs]
A: [laughs] I guess not. But really, I never get the same role twice. I've done about 145 films, but no role has been the same as the other. That's strange, isn't it? Even if the scripts are similar, the age of the characters and the settings are different, so the way I approach each role varies. It's like eating spaghetti every day, but each day the taste is different. I eat rice and miso soup every day, but somehow it's not the same as the day before. It's like that with acting.

Q: When you started, you were playing *chinpira*, but now you're playing *oyabun*—or a mayor, like the character in *Togenkyo no Hitobito*.
A: I'm not quite an *oyabun* type yet. [laughs] Take a character like Honjo [in the Shuraba ga

Yuku series]. He's a mixture of *oyabun* and *chinpira*. He seems to have a sense of responsibility, but he really doesn't. Instead, he is under pressure from everyone, so he feels he has no choice. I find that kind of thing interesting. He's actually quite lazy, but people are telling him to do this and that, so he feels compelled to go along. "Well, if you say so"—that kind of thing. Everyone is waiting for him to make a move.

Q: Even so, he takes good care of people.
A: That's right—he takes good care of people. That's why he can attract a woman who has the same quality. She tells him that that's his good point. So, they have that in common. [laughs]

Q: In Hollywood, veteran actors start their own companies and develop their own roles.
A: They do that, don't they—but it would be impossible in Japan.

Q: Impossible?
A: Almost. There used to be a few companies like that in Japan, but they all went bust. That's true not only in Japan but in America as well, isn't it?

Q: But America is a bigger market—it makes it easier to do that sort of thing.
A: The Japanese film industry has only Japan, when you come down to it. If you were to spend a year making a film here, you might end up with a hit but it's impossible to get that much time. As long as people in the studios don't want to make that kind of film—it's impossible for one individual to do it.

Q: In your autobiography you say that, even given how bad conditions are here, you don't want to lose to Tom Cruise. In other words, that cut for cut, scene for scene, you can make films that will give audiences the same value as the ones Tom Cruise makes in Hollywood.
A: That's right. I may lose to Travolta, though.

He's too strong for me. [laughs] The conditions here are tough, but it doesn't mean we can't beat [Hollywood]. If we keep trying, we can achieve good results. So, all we can do is keep trying. Now that I'm past forty, it's time for me to buckle down and stayed focused.

Q: After Ken Takakura turned forty, he stopped making yakuza films and went in another direction, appearing in only one film a year, if that. He became a sort of icon.
A: He did, didn't he? Ken-san being Ken-san, he could do that. That's all right, if you're over sixty, but I'm not there yet. I like making films. Getting into a rhythm and making as many films as I do is tough, but the moment one is finished I feel so happy. I get a real feeling of satisfaction. Or a feeling of relief—"It's finally over!" [laughs] I just keep going, from one to another. Why not? Being in your forties now isn't like being in your forties, thirty years ago. Forties is still young.

Q: When Koji Tsuruta was in his forties, he was already playing *oyabun*—he really aged quickly.
A: That's right. But I'm still young looking— and as long as I keep looking this way, there's no problem. In this business, it's not how old you are, it's how old you look. So, I'll just keep on going the way I've been going. It's still not physically too much for me.

Q: You've said that when you're performing together with other actors, you don't want to beat them—a tie is good enough.
A: That's right—a tie is good enough.

Q: Have you ever felt that you've lost?
A: Yes, sometimes. When someone's really great, I feel so pissed off! But that's OK— there's still tomorrow. There are still a lot of actors who can make me feel that way. Sometimes the director notices it. Or I get home and realize I got my ass kicked by Shohei Nomura. [laughs]

Q: Who's been the easiest director to work with?

A: The easiest? I've never fought with any of my directors—I'm too scared. [laughs] I thought that Tatsumi Kumashiro was really great.

Q: You worked with him on *Bo no Kanashimi*. It was his last film—he was in bad shape from emphysema when he made it.

A: He was on the verge of death. I asked him to eat honey, so he wouldn't die. He said, "Why do you want me to eat this stuff and get healthy?" He was incredible—even though he was dying, his eyes were still shining.

Q: Which director had you do the most takes?

A: That would have been [Kiyoshi] Kurosawa—he had me do thirty-seven takes once. Before that [Seiji] Izumi had me do twenty-four. That was my first film—*Kono Mune no Tokimeki* [The Beat of My Heart, 1988]. It took me from morning 'til noon. I thought, "Movies aren't any fun." [laughs] I also worked with him on the first three films of the Shuraba ga Yuku series and on the Shakkin series. He's a genius at getting a movie underway. He's a director's director. There aren't that many like him left. He's very careful about getting it right. We would go to the top of the mountain in Kyoto to shoot! I felt that with him I was in good hands. I like that type of director.

Q: Better than the ones who just want to get it done, no matter how?

A: He's very serious. Usually, though, he shoots very quickly, any old way. Then, suddenly something comes over him. "Do you think we can film here?"—sort of thing. Before that, he's just shooting away like the wind. [laughs] He runs a tight set, but the shooting goes quickly, like whoosh!

Q: What's Miike like to work with? I've heard he likes to improvise on the set.

A: Miike has the entire film in his head. He's so quick! He doesn't give you time to think. For an actor, though, he's easy to work with. Kurosawa also has the movie in his head before he begins. He makes continuity drawings of all the scenes. You have to do it exactly the way he says. He works amazingly fast. Those two stand out from the rest.

Q: In *Hebi no Michi* and *Kumo no Hitomi*, Kurosawa adds an element of horror you don't find in most yakuza movies. There's something creepy about them.

A: Creepy is right. They aren't really like yakuza movies. The pace is slower, for one thing. They're amazing films. Miike is easier to understand. He gives it to you straight.

Q: His last film before *Togenkyo no Hitobito* was *Shin Jingi Naki no Hakaba* [Graveyard of Honor, 2002], starring Goro Kishitani as Rikio Ishikawa. I wanted to see you in that role, though.

A: Really? Well, I'm kind of sorry I didn't get that one. [laughs] But that's all right.

Q: Are there any roles that you really wanted to play but couldn't because of scheduling or other problems?

A: Yes, there have been a few. The timing wasn't right or the director didn't want me. For example [Miike] probably used Kishitani because [Miike] thought [Kishitani] would be interesting in that role. That's fine with me—[Miike] had a responsibility to the project. I'll do something else with him. I don't like the "it's gotta be me" attitude. If something comes along, fine. When you do it that way, you can give a stronger performance, I think.

When I saw *Jingi Naki Tatakai* [Battles without Honor and Humanity, 1973], I got mad. It was so good! Why can't I do something like that! You need that kind of competitive feeling, I think. Even now, I want to do something that great, with that kind of speed and human drama.

Q: You said the actor from that period you most resemble is Shin'ichi "Sonny" Chiba. When [Atsushi] Murota asked you to play a role the way Chow Yun-Fat would, you said it was easier to imagine yourself as Sonny Chiba. [laughs] He's really popular abroad, as you may know. He's appearing in the new Quentin Tarantino film, *Kill Bill*.
A: He's a great actor. We recently appeared together on a TV variety show and he was so funny. He said we ought to work together. Me with Sonny Chiba! [laughs]

Q: He was known for his martial arts skills. That's the kind of thing foreign producers expect of Asian action stars, even now.
A: I've been asked that myself. One Hollywood producer asked me if I could jump from a 40-meter mast. I told him no. [laughs]

Q: Maybe Jackie Chan could do it. Anyway, thank you very much for your time.
A: Thank you.

films, including Shohei Imamura's *Unagi* (The Eel, 1997), the winner of the Palme d'Or at the 1997 Cannes Film Festival.

In 1995 Aikawa made his first film as a director, replacing Banmei Takahashi in *Bad Guy Beach*. Also about this time, he began a long

Show Aikawa—The definition of yakuza cool in the nineties.

and fruitful association with Kiyoshi Kurosawa and Takashi Miike, two leaders of the Japanese New Wave. His films with Miike include *Gokudo Kuro Shakai Rainy Dog* (Rainy Dog, 1997) and the *Dead or Alive* trilogy (1999–2001). With Kurosawa he made the six films of the Katte ni Shiyagare!! (Suit Yourself or Shoot Yourself, 1995–96) gang comedy series and *Kumo no Hitomi* (Eye of the Spider, 1997) and *Hebi no Michi* (Serpent's Path, 1997)—a pair of thrillers whose chilling atmospherics and off-beat stories of revenge are echoed in Kurosawa's international hit *Cure* (1997).

Since the start of the new millennium, Aikawa has expanded his professional activities, playing a Korean gangster in Junji Sakamoto's *Shin Jingi Naki Tatakai* (Another Battle, 2000) and producing and starring in Takehisa Zeze's *Rush!* (2001), a wacky caper film whose scrambled-chronology story line was developed from Aikawa's treatment. He also played the mysterious "mayor" of a homeless community in Takashi Miike's drama *Kinyu Hametsu Nippon: Togenkyo no Hitobito* (Shangri-La, 2002). But though he no longer portrays a gangster—or even a human being—in every outing (see *Dead or Alive Final*), Aikawa is indelibly identified with the OV gang film, which accounts for most of his lengthy (145 titles by last count) filmography.

More of a star than an actor, Aikawa may

still swagger and glare like the black-leathered punk he once was but does so with an intensity and dynamism that compels respect on the screen—and attention in front of it. Also, though they are still macho men of the old school in their dealings with fellow gangsters, Aikawa's heroes are capable of wry humor and even family feeling, to an extent rare among the stone-faced gangsters of a previous generation. The break dance moves, however, have gone into permanent storage.

Noboru Ando (1926–)

One of the few gang movie stars, in Japan or elsewhere, who was a gangster in real life, Noboru Ando was born in 1926 in Higashi Okubo, Tokyo, the oldest of four children. His father was of samurai descent, a circumstance Ando describes in detail in his autobiography *Jiden Ando Noboru* (2001). He attended primary school in Yokohama and, in 1941, entered an elite junior high school in Manchuria, where his father was working. But Ando was expelled after seven months and returned to Tokyo, to live with relatives. He enrolled in another junior high school but was expelled again after three months. During this period, he was running with other delinquents in Tokyo, fighting and thieving—the latter activity earned him a stretch in Tama Reformatory. In December 1943, Ando joined the military as a pilot trainee and in June 1945, after completing training, volunteered for a unit in Kurihama that trained frogmen for suicide missions. But the war ended before he could be sent into action.

Returning to Tokyo, Ando resumed his old outlaw ways amid the ruins and the black markets. Somehow, he found time to pass the entrance exam to Hosei University, but Ando preferred the streets to the classroom and finally dropped out in May 1948. Known for his talents

as a brawler, with a straight razor his weapon of choice, Ando got a taste of his own medicine later that year when a Korean gangster slashed his left cheek, leaving a long scar that would later become his on-screen trademark.

In 1952, Ando formed his own gang, the Ando-gumi, whose core members were mostly college-boys-gone-bad like Ando himself. Formally called Azuma Kogyo, the gang had more than three hundred members at its peak and ruled in the Shibuya District of Tokyo. Ando's top lieutenants, distinguished by the gray suits they wore as a badge of membership, were not adverse to using violence when necessary. But Azuma Kogyo itself operated as a legitimate company, with its main business being real estate and entertainment, including the management of cabarets and night clubs. Ando and his crew were thus forerunners of the "economic yakuza" (*keizai yakuza*) who would later serve as the villains in countless gang movies.

Ando's biggest moment of notoriety came in June 1958, when a hitman sent by Ando himself shot Hideki Yokoi, a prominent, if shady, businessman. Yokoi had neglected to pay back 20 million yen of a 30 million yen loan—and Ando and his gang had been hired to collect. When Yokoi refused to come across, and insulted Ando in the bargain, Ando decided that more forceful persuasion was necessary. The hitman's bullet, which was intended as a warning, nearly killed its victim—and Ando went on the lam, with the police in hot pursuit. The media detailed every move of the ensuing nationwide manhunt, as well as the arrests of dozens of Ando-gumi members. On his thirty-fifth day as a fugitive, Ando was arrested in Hayama. He ended up serving a six-year sentence. Shortly after his release, in December 1964, he formally dissolved his gang, citing feelings of responsibility toward a dead gang member.

In 1965 Ando found a new career as an actor, appearing in Yoshio Yuasa's *Chi to Okite* (Blood and Rules), a Shochiku film that told

Noboru Ando was a gang boss who became a star for Toei in the 1960s, reprising his real-life adventures on the big screen.

the story of Ando's gang, with Ando playing himself. The film was a big hit, and Ando starred in four more films in the Okite series over the next two years, none reaching the box office heights of the first. In 1966 Ando made *Otoko no Kao wa Rirekisho* (History of a Man's Face, *A Man's Face Shows His Personal History*) with director Tai Kato, a film about two wartime comrades, a Korean and Japanese, who end up on opposite sides in the postwar gangs. The film was a success, and Ando appeared in two more by Kato in quick succession: *Ahendaichi Jigoku Butai Totsugekiseyo* (Opium Heights: Hell Squad Attack, 1966), which described army corruption in wartime

China, and *Choeki Juhachinen* (Sentence: Eighteen Years, 1967), which exposed the inner workings of the gangs in the postwar black market. In these three films, Ando expressed the loneliness, desperation, and feral toughness of many men of his generation against a social backdrop of general lawlessness. They were to be career highlights.

In 1967 Ando signed with Toei and, starting with *Choeki Juhachinen*, appeared in contemporary gang films helmed by the studio's leading studio directors, including Teruo Ishii (*Abashiri Bangaichi: Fubuki no Toso*, 1967; *Gendai Ninkyoshi*, 1973) and Kinji Fukasaku (*Nihon Boryokudan Kumicho*, 1969; *Bakuto Gaijin Butai*, 1971; *Gendai Yakuza: Hitokiri Yota*, 1972; *Shin Jingi Naki Tatakai*, 1974; *Jingi no Hakaba*, 1975). In 1971 Ando starred in Toho's first yakuza film, Hideo Gosha's *Shussho Oiwai* (Prison Release Celebration). In 1973 Ando reprised his gangster past in Junya Sato's *Jitsuroku Andogumi Shugekihen* (The True Story of the Ando Gang: Attack) and in 1976 retold the story of his fugitive days in Noboru Tanaka's *Ando Noboru no Waga Tobo to Sex no Kiroku* (Noboru Ando's Record of Flight and Sex). In the latter film, he acted out his sexual adventures while on the run.

After appearing in Sadao Nakajima's 1979 *Socho no Kubi* (The Big Boss's Head, 1979), Ando largely retired from acting. While working occasionally as a producer on Shun'ichi Kajima's *Kizu* (Bruise, 1988) and Seiji Izumi's *Koiko no Mainichi* (Koiko's Days, 1988), Ando also devoted himself to writing, churning out novels about the gangs as well as how-to books on fashion and sex. During his acting heyday in the 1960s and 1970s, Ando pursued a second career as a singer but stopped making records when he left the screen.

In 1997, with Seiji Izumi's *Jitsuroku Shinjuku no Kao: Shinjuku Gurentai Monogatari* (The True Face of Shinjuku: The Story of the Shinjuku Delinquent Gangs), Ando resumed his acting career, this time for the straight-to-

Noboru Ando Interview (March 2002)

Q: How did you get into acting, in 1965, with Shochiku?
A: To be brief about it, I was broke.

Q: A producer from Shochiku approached you, quite soon after you'd dissolved your gang?
A: Yes, that's right.

Q: I suppose there was a big difference between what you'd experienced as a gangster and what you were asked to do in front of a camera.
A: Yes, but it couldn't be helped. I just did what the director asked me.

Q: After making eleven films with Shochiku, you moved to Toei.
A: Yes, it was a Toei producer who persuaded me to switch—Koji Shundo. He made interesting films and I was fortunate enough to be in many of them.

Q: I heard that he hung around a lot with yakuza and it was even said he'd been a yakuza himself.
A: He *was* a yakuza. [laughs] They were all yakuza at that company. [laughs]

Q: What was the main difference between the two studios for you?
A: Toei really understood the type of movies they were trying to make. They had good directors working for them. I just listened to what the directors wanted me to do. That's how I learned my job as an actor.

Q: Did you feel their films were more realistic?
A: I don't know about that. Toei's yakuza films were like period dramas—the samurai swordplay films. They were about *giri-ninjo*, the conflict between duty and feelings. That same theme, again and again.

Q: Which director did you more enjoy working with?
A: Tai Kato was something special. He was always watching us closely, through the camera. He liked to shoot from low angles. He also paid a lot of attention to the background details. The films I made with him were some of my best.

Q: Did you find it hard to make the transition between being a gangster and being an actor?
A: Not really. In Japanese, the only difference between "yakuza" and "*yakusha*" (actor) is one hiragana character. All yakuza have to be actors to survive.

Q: How did you get involved with the gangs to begin with?
A: I was in the Japanese navy—one of the suicide squadrons, but then the war ended and I was on the street, with no job, nothing. I had no idea what was going to happen to me—it was that kind of time. So, I joined the gangs to survive. I knew I was doing something wrong, but I was young and wild, so I didn't care—and I went bad as a result. The other gangsters were the same way—they could see no future for themselves. They had nothing to lose. For me it was a 180-degree turn from the suicide squadron. Suddenly, I had absolutely nothing. So, I did what I had to do to live.

Q: When you were arrested by the police after being on the run because of the Yokoi shooting, did you think you'd had it as a yakuza, that you couldn't live that way any longer?
A: Not really—living as a yakuza was easy for me.

Q: Did you decide to break up your gang because you felt you couldn't fight the current of the time?
A: Partly that. Also, one of my people had been killed, and I felt sorry for his mother. She told me that if I had been there for him, he wouldn't

have died. Listening to her, I really felt as though I had done wrong by him. It's easy to keep doing what you've always done. Living as a gangster had been easy for me. But now I was seeing the reality of what I had done—that a mother had lost her only child, a child she had raised on her own. That's what made me decide to quit, more than anything.

Q: In the movies, gangsters who try to quit the life find it difficult.

A: They always say that, don't they?—that no one can quit entirely. When I announced the breakup of my gang, the police didn't believe me—they told me it was a coverup.

Q: But having left the life, you had to work.

A: I didn't know what would happen after I made the decision to quit. Like someone once said, once you let go of the cliff, all you can do is wait for things to take their course. By that I mean, you're holding on to the cliff like this [demonstrates] but once you let go and start falling, you have no idea what's going to happen next. When I quit, I didn't have anything lined up. I wasn't thinking, "Well I can become a bureaucrat or something." [laughs]

Q: But you ended up making fifty-some films for Toei.

A: Fifty-one—and now I'm making video movies. I even sell them myself.

Q: The video movies came in about ten years ago. They make them the way Toei used to make its gang program pictures, using young actors and directors.

A: With videos, they shoot everything in one week. When I was [working at Toei], they would take forty-five days or at least a month. The films had more depth back then. They told a different kind of story. Now, they just knock them off. With video, they're all just knockoffs. Pink videos are the same way—it's getting to the point where no one is buying them.

Q: But some of the directors of gang films—feature films, as well as videos—are becoming better known abroad, such as Kitano and Miike.

A: Oh, really?

Q: You haven't seen their films?

A: I have—no comment.

Q: What about the younger actors? Anyone you particularly like?

A: Koichi Iwaki is one. I've worked with him on several films. He's one of the best [of the younger ones].

Q: You've said that the most important element in a film is the script.

A: If it's a good script, yes. A script for a film is like a design for a house. If you have a bad design, you end up with a bad house. The same is true of films; if you have a bad script, there's no way you can make a good film. With a bad script, the film is going to be bad, no matter who appears in it. Now, they'll make anything if they can shoot it in a week and make money on it. But just making any kind of crap is no good. People get tired of watching it and then where are you?

Q: Did you ever think of writing scripts yourself?

A: I've read a lot of scripts and tried writing them, but for some reason I just can't do it. I've written a lot of manuscripts [for books], though. I've written books that have been the basis of scripts.

Q: Which do you enjoy more now, writing or making films?

A: I like taking it easy. [laughs] But making movies is easier for me.

Q: Are there any stories you'd particularly like to make now, based on your own youth, for example?

A: There's a film I like called *Once upon a Time*

in America. I've told Toei that I'd like to make something like that, but it would cost a lot of money.

Q: Also, it would be hard now to find directors and actors who understand the yakuza world as it was then.
A: It would be tough. There's nothing like that now. Tokyo after the war was like a burnt field. You can't find that kind of scenery now.

Q: Speaking of money, how much do those video films cost to make?
A: Not much really—about 50 million yen. You can't show that kind of film in a theater, so they don't spend any money on them.

Q: But the one you're thinking of making would cost many times that, I'm sure. Who would you like to play you?
A: That, I don't know. Someone who is an artist, not just a name.

video market. Once again the films were mainly high fictionalized retellings of his gangster glory days. In 2002 he appeared in Shun'ichi Kajima's *Jitsuroku Ando Gumi Gaiden Garo no Okite* (The True History of the Ando Gang: Rules of the Starving Wolf) and served as a "supervisor" on Takashi Miike's *Jitsuroku Ando Noboru Outlaw-den: Rekka* (Deadly Outlaw: Rekka).

Junko Fuji (1945–)

The biggest female star of the yakuza movie genre, who dominated men on the screen and in the audience with her cool sensuality and forceful presence, Junko Fuji was born in 1945 in Wakayama as the third child and younger daughter of Koji Shundo, later a Toei producer. After spending her early childhood in Wakayama, she and her family moved to Osaka, where Fuji attended local schools with her older brother and sister. As a teenager, Fuji was a fervent fan of the all-female Takarazuka Theater Troupe and dreamed of entering its training school. Beginning in junior high school, she studied dancing, singing, and acting at an Osaka school for child actors and models, as well as the Yamamura style of *buyo* (Japanese dance).

When Fuji was seventeen her family moved to nearby Kyoto. Soon after, she and older sis-

ter, Nobuko, began appearing on a local TV show, *Hai Hai Mahine*, as regular "cover girls" (i.e., eye candy). Fuji also visited the Toei Kyoto Studio, where she attracted the attention of Masahiro Makino, a veteran Toei director and long-time associate of her father. When Makino invited her to appear in one of his films, Shundo was at first reluctant to give his approval—he wanted his daughter to have a "normal" life as a wife and mother. But Shundo acquiesced when he realized she intended to have a show business career, with or without Toei.

Fuji made her screen debut in Makino's *Hashu Yukyoden: Otoko no Sakazuki* (Tales of Hashu Chivalry: A Man's Sake Cup, 1963). In her first year with Toei, she appeared in ten films, including Sadaji Matsuda's *Shingo Bangai Shobu* (Shingo's Unexpected Battle, 1964) and Makino's *Nihon Kyokakuden* (An Account of the Chivalrous Commoners of Japan, 1964), while making regular appearances in dramas seen on public broadcaster NHK and the TV Asahi network.

By the middle of the decade, Fuji was the leading actress on the Toei lot, playing the love interest of Koji Tsuruta and Ken Takakura in a long string of *ninkyo eiga*. Her male costars usually portrayed stoic loners, who placed their gang obligations over their romantic inclinations—and the films ended without a clinch, let alone a bed scene. Unlike the many yakuza movie actresses of the time, whose range

© 1969 Toei Company, Ltd.

While remaining impeccable in her kimono, Junko Fuji (right) handily disposes of any number of male attackers in *Hibotan Bakuto: Tekka Baretsuden* (Red Peony Gambler: Biography of a Gambling Hall, 1969).

extended from faux naiveté to hysteria, Fuji projected a natural dignity and authority—one could imagine her on the Takarakuza stage as a prince or warrior—but without sacrificing her femininity. This combination thrilled her male fans, who elevated her to the top rank of Toei stars. "[My fans] are seeing an ideal woman, the personification of *yamato nadeshiko* [pure and virtuous Japanese womanhood]," Fuji told an interviewer. "The audience feels a kind of security in that, which I think is fine. . . . But still it's strange seeing that woman on the screen and realizing that it's me." (Inomata and Tayama, *Nihon Eiga Haiyu Zenshi: Joyo-hen*, p. 207.)

From 1968 to 1972, Fuji reached the height of her popularity as the star of the eight-part Hibotan Bakuto (Red Peony Gambler) series. She played Oryu, a woman gambler who, beginning with Kosaku Yamashita's *Hibotan Bakuto* (Red Peony Gambler, 1968), travels the country seeking revenge for the murder of her *oyabun* father. Though having a soft spot for the lone yakuza, played by Ken Takakura or Koji Tsuruta, who comes to her aid at critical moments, she is implacable in her determina-

tion, as well as deadly with a sword when faced with a small army of enemy gangsters. The three series entries directed by Tai Kato are standouts, highlighting both the power and sensuality of the Oryu character.

Her own favorite among her films with Kato, however, was *Meiji Kyokakuden Sandai Shumei* (Blood of Revenge, 1965) in which she played a prostitute who falls in love with Koji Tsuruta but becomes a pawn in a gang power struggle. "I personally like the type of woman that I played in the film better than the strong women [I usually play]," said Fuji. Her moment at the summit was not long, however. In 1972 she married Kikunosuke Onoe, a Kabuki actor she met while appearing in the hit NHK drama *Minamoto no Yoshitsune* and, after making Masahiro Makino's *Kanto Hizakura Ikka* (The Hizakura Family of Kanto, 1972), she retired from the screen. With her departure, the popularity of Toei's *ninkyo eiga* went into decline and a search to find a successor proved fruitless.

Fuji, who has since changed her professional first name from Junko to Sumiko, did not quit show business entirely. She later hosted a daytime talk show and returned to films in 1989, playing opposite her old Toei co-star Ken Takakura in Yasuo Furuhata's melodrama *A Un* (Buddies). She also starred as a geisha house proprietor in Kinji Fukasaku's *Omocha* (The Geisha House, 1998).

Shintaro Katsu (1931–97)

An actor whose off-screen exploits were as colorful as his starring roles, Shintaro Katsu was born in 1931 in Fukagawa, Tokyo, into a theatrical family. His father, Katsutoji Kineya, was a popular performer of *nagauta*, a traditional epic song form, while his older brother became film star Tomisaburo Wakayama. Katsu began practicing *nagauta* and *shamisen* (a traditional string instrument) at an early age and, at the age of 17, launched a career as a professional *nagauta* singer under the name Katsumaru Kineya.

After touring the United States for six months, Katsu joined the Daiei Studio and made his screen debut in Katsuhiko Tasaka's *Hana no Byakkotai* (Byakkotai) in 1954. Another newcomer at Daiei, Raizo Ichikawa, raced up the ladder faster, however. In 1955 Ichikawa's performance as Kiyomori no Taira in Kenji Mizoguchi's *Shin Heike Monogatari* (New Tales of the Taira Clan) made him a star, while Katsu was still scraping along in minor roles. After standing in Ichikawa's shadow for years, Katsu began to emerge in 1960 when he landed the part of the blind villain in Kazuo Mori's period drama hit *Shiranui Kengyo* (Shiranui the Masseur), a precursor to his most famous role as the blind swordsman Zatoichi.

Katsu's true breakthrough, however, was Tokuzo Tanaka's 1961 *Akumyo* (Tough Guy) in which he played a lone wolf gangster with a short temper but a good heart. Despite his rotund physique, Katsu was an explosive presence on the screen, battling crowds of opponents with his bare fists, knocking them over like ten pins. The film was a hit, generating a total of fourteen episodes. Soon after, Katsu married Tamayo Nakamura, his *Akumyo* co-star. In 1962 he starred in Kenji Misumi's *Zatoichi Monogatari* (The Tale of Zatoichi), launching a signature series that ran for twenty-six episodes, until 1989. Katsu played the title character, a blind masseur who likes gambling, women, and money but has an uncanny skill with a sword—in short, a fictional extension of Katsu's own earthy, hedonistic personality. The high point of the films was Zatoichi's climactic sword battles with sighted opponents, who underestimated their blind foe until they tasted his steel.

In 1965, Katsu started a third series with Yasuzo Masumura's *Heitai Yakuza* (The Hoodlum Soldier). Portraying a gangster sent to a regiment near the Soviet frontier in 1943, Katsu once again broke heads with abandon, but the film's dramatic mainspring was his relationship with an intellectual corporal, played by Takehiro Tamura. Initially occupied with keeping his obstreperous subordinate out of trouble, the corporal comes to appreciate his courage and strong sense of justice. The series ran for eight installments, until 1968.

In 1967, with Daiei sliding toward bankruptcy, Katsu set up his own production company, Katsu Production. In 1971 he produced, directed, and starred in *Kaoyaku* (The Big Boss), a rogue-cop-on-a-mission movie that critics savaged and audiences ignored but was later praised as a bold departure from genre conventions. He also produced several TV series, including one based on his *Zatoichi* films.

Beginning in the mid-1970s, Katsu took longer and longer breaks from the screen. He was offered a lead role in *Kagemusha*, Akira Kurosawa's 1980 comeback film, that might have relaunched him on the international stage. But Katsu quarreled with the director on the first day of shooting and left the set, never to return. After making his last film in Japan,

Kazuo Kuroki's 1990 *Roningai*, Katsu became a tabloid regular, getting himself arrested for marijuana possession in Hawaii and struggling with mountainous debts. He died on June 21, 1997, of cancer.

Though hardly a leading-man type, Katsu enjoyed tremendous popularity with male fans, portraying larger-than-life outsiders who may break every rule but usually prevail through sheer force of personality, as well as their talent for meting out mayhem. He provided an appealing fantasy figure for salarymen slaving to create the Japanese economic miracle.

Katsu's long, hard apprenticeship—in his early days at Daiei he was forced to ride in the bus with the crew while contemporary Raizo Ichikawa was chauffeured about in a limousine—gave him a certain hunger that came across on the screen and added to his common man appeal. Also, his "king of the night" antics, which generated countless tabloid stories about his drinking, womanizing, and law breaking, cemented his reputation as a figure out of his own movies. In Katsu's case, art and life were truly one. By the end, he was no longer making films—or even seeming to care. Who needed fiction when life supplied all the drama his outsized ego demanded?

Akira Kobayashi (1937–)

Endowed with brooding good looks reminiscent of the young Elvis, but a cooler, drier presence on the screen, Akira Kobayashi was born in 1937 in Setagaya Ward, Tokyo, the son of a lighting director. A star judoist at Mejiro High School in Tokyo, he followed in his father's footsteps and joined Nikkatsu in 1956. After making his screen debut in Yuzo Kobayashi's *Ueru Tamashi* (Hungry Spirit, 1956), Kobayashi appeared in a succession of minor roles. He first attracted attention for his performance as punkish young bartender to Yujiro Ishihara's

bar manager in Buichi Saito's *Sabita Knife* (Rusty Knife, 1958). About that time Nikkatsu publicists began calling him "Mr. Dynamite," with the tagline on one poster proclaiming "You never know when he's going to explode!" In Japanese, this nickname became "'Mite Guy" (Maito Guy).

Though regarded as a younger version of Yutaro Ishihara, a major Nikkatsu star, Kobayashi had a working-class, up-from-the-streets appeal that contrasted sharply with Ishihara's well-born, college-educated, Golden Boy sheen. Kobayashi began to get larger roles, as a troubled youth in Seijun Suzuki's *Funihazushita Haru* (False Step Spring, 1958) and a boxer in Toshio Masuda's *Onna o Wasurero* (Forget about Women, 1959), while making an impression with his performance of the latter film's theme song. His big break came in Buichi Saito's *Nangoku Tosa o Atonishite* (Leaving behind Tosa of the South, 1959) in which he portrayed a yakuza who tries to go straight but returns to his old life to revenge insults to his lover. Boosted by Peggy Hayama's hit recording of the title song, the movie became a box office success,

Now a hot talent, Kobayashi appeared in the nine-part Wataridori (Bird of Passage, 1959–62) series, playing a wanderer wearing a fringed jacket and playing a guitar who moseys into a country town, sides with the good townsfolk against bad gangsters and other evildoers, and wins the affection of a local maiden (played in all but one installment by Ruriko Asaoka). His singing in this series made him a pop sensation, while his romance with co-star Asaoka made him a tabloid weekly by-word. When he married pop diva Hibari Misora in 1961, upsetting all expectations, the weeklies had another field day. (Asaoka exited the Wataridori series soon after.)

After marrying the biggest name in Japanese show business, who sold records and movie tickets at a furious pace, Kobayashi found himself battling a massive inferiority complex. He even publicly denounced acting as "unmanly" and set himself up as president of a production company. The marriage failed, however, and in 1965 Hibari announced their divorce (though it was later revealed that the couple had never bothered to legalize their living arrangements).

Despite his personal troubles, Kobayashi continued working steadily for Nikkatsu, starring in the five-installment *Nagaremono* (Wanderer, 1960–61) series, which had the same basic stranger-in-town premise as the Wataridori films, and the six-installment *Ginza Maitogai* (Ginza Might Guy, 1959–63) series in which he played a Ginza tough guy who rights wrongs. He also portrayed traditional yakuza types in *Kanto Yukyoden* (Legend of Kanto Chivalry, 1963); *Kanto Mushuku* (Kanto Wanderer, 1963); *Hana to Doto* (Flower and the Angry Waves, 1964); *Shima Wa Moratta* (Retaliation, 1968); *Kenka Bakuto: Jigoku no Hanamichi* (Conflict, 1969); *Bakuto Hyakunin* (One Hundred Gamblers, 1969); *Arakure* (Tough, 1969); and *Koiki Boryoku: Ryuketsu no Shima* (Widespread Violence: Bloody Territory, 1969).

Kobayashi remained loyal to Nikkatsu, even as the studio's fortunes declined; but after it stopped production, he joined Toei in 1972. In a departure from his old dashing image, the actor played a calculating, cold-blooded yakuza boss in Kinji Fukasaku's *Jingi Naki Tatakai: Dairi Senso* (Battles without Honor and Humanity 3: Proxy War, 1973) and *Jingi Naki Tatakai: Chojo Sakusen* (Battles without Honor and Humanity 4: High Tactics, 1974). In the late 1970s Kobayashi left film to concentrate on television work and business interests, including a golf venture that later went belly up. In the 1990s, he resumed his film career, appearing in Seiji Izumi's *Shuraba no Densetsu* (Legend of Carnage, 1992) and *Minbo no Teio* (Emperor of Violence, 1993). Abroad he is best known for his Seijun Suzuki and Kinji Fukasaku films. Chow Yun-Fat has claimed

Cover my back. Akira Kobayashi (left) and Hideki Takahashi in a poster for *Ketto* (Bloodbath, 1967).

him as an influence, particularly in Chow's portrayal of a cool killer in John Woo's *A Better Tomorrow*.

Hiroki Matsukata (1942–)

A versatile, powerful performer in his early career—the personification of bearish macho in his middle years—Hiroki Matsukata was born in 1942 in Oji, Tokyo, the son of popular period drama star Jushiro Konoe (1916–77) and the older brother of actor Yuki Meguro. In 1960, while still in high school, Matsukata joined Toei, his father's studio, and made his screen debut in Shigeaki Hidaka's *Jyunanasai no*

仁義が生きて帰ってきた。

ド首領を殺った男

松方弘樹
田村英里子
山口達也
多岐川裕美
池上季実子
川谷拓三

久桂 陽 子
大 龍
史 孝
白野真正史
成田口モヒロー
志賀 勝

綿引勝彦
中尾 彬
山城新伍
梅宮辰夫
菅原文太
夏八木 勲

ヤクザ30年、男の決算。

監督/中島貞夫

© 1994 Toei Company, Ltd.

Hiroki Matsukata stars in Toei's "last yakuza movie,"
Don o Totta Otoko (The Man Who Shot the Don, 1994).

Gyakushu: Boryoku o Buttsubuse (Counterattack at Seventeen: Crush the Violence, 1960). In 1961, Matsukata was sent to Toei's Kyoto Studio to play *nimaime* (romantic leading man) roles in period dramas, including the first two episodes of Masahiro Makino's Jirocho Sangokushi (Jirocho's "Three Countries at War," 1963) series. He was often cast together with Kinya Kitaoji, another son of a popular actor who would also later make a mark in gang films.

With the start of the yakuza *eiga* boom, Matsukata began to exchange his *chonmage* (topknot) for a gangster's *haramaki* (belly band), appearing in *Bakuto* (Gambler, 1964) and *Showa Zankyoden* (Remnants of Chivalry in the Showa Era, 1965). In 1966, he starred as a young gangster in Sadao Nakajima's *893*

Gurentai (Yakuza Hooligans)—a film inspired by Jean Luc Godard's *Breathless*, down to its Belmondo-like hats and shades. In 1968 he made an impression as an extortionist punk in Kinji Fukasaku's *Kyokatsu Koso Waga Jinsei* (Extortion Is Our Life).

Matsukata also appeared in two episodes of Fukasaku's five-part Jingi Naki Tatakai (Battles without Honor and Humanity, 1973–74) series. Before the first film was greenlighted, Matsukata was cast in the lead role of Hirono but was later replaced by Bunta Sugawara. Playing Itai, a *wakagashira* (sub-boss) of the Yamamori-gumi, Matsukata had a memorable death scene: shot by hitmen while buying a gift for his child, he expired on the floor of a toy shop. In *Jingi Naki Tatakai: Kanketsuhen* (Battles without Honor and Humanity 5: The Final Episode, 1974), he rose from the dead to play the gang boss Ichioka, a power-hungry schemer with the look of a sly wolf.

Matsukata continued to star in gang films over the next two decades, including Fukasaku's *Kenkei tai Soshiki Boryoku* (Cops versus Thugs, 1975); *Hokuriku Dairi Senso* (Hokuriku Proxy War, 1977); and Toei's "last" yakuza *eiga*, *Don o Totta Otoko* (The Man Who Shot the Don). As a regular on Takeshi Kitano's popular 1990s variety show, *Genki Ga Deru TV*, Matsukata charmed a new generation of fans as a good-natured, if comically clueless, middle-aged man. This was a far cry from his youthful peak, when he played greedy, violent, and crude antiheroes with unmatched brio and force.

Jo Shishido (1933–)

Best known in the West for his work as the rice-gobbling hitman in Seijun Suzuki's *Koroshi no Rakuin* (Branded to Kill, 1967), Jo Shishido was born in 1933 in Osaka's Kita Ward, the third of four sons and one daughter. His younger brother later became the actor Eiji

Go. Shishido attended schools in Tokyo and Miyagi Prefecture and, after high school graduation, entered the theater course of Nihon University's Arts Department in 1952. In March 1954, he successively auditioned for Nikkatsu's New Face contest—one of twenty-one who passed, out of eight-thousand applicants. Dropping out of college, he entered Nikkatsu and began appearing in bit roles.

He made his true debut, under his own name, in Seiji Hisamatsu's *Keisatsu Nikki* (Policeman's Diary, 1955), as a young patrolman who takes on a police chief, played by Masao Mishima, in a *kendo* (Japanese fencing) bout. Noting that a Shishido was a villain in the popular novel *Miyamoto Musashi*, his studio bosses wanted him to change his name to something more suitable for a rising young actor they envisioned as a romantic lead, but he refused.

In 1957, unhappy with his blandly handsome features, Shishido underwent plastic surgery to flesh out his cheeks, giving him a more ruggedly masculine look. Soon after, he started getting larger parts, mainly as bad guys in action films. Appearing opposite Akira Kobayashi in the Wataridori (Bird of Passage) series and Kei'ichiro Akagi in the Kenju Buraicho (Record of Pistol Criminality) series, both money earners for Nikkatsu in the early 1960s, Shishido rose to national popularity, with the nickname "Ace no Jo."

Following Akagi's death in a go-cart accident in 1961, Shishido found himself thrust into the Nikkatsu action star rotation. His first starring role was in Buichi Saito's *Rokudenashi Kagyo* (Dirty Work, 1961), a comic buddy film co-starring Hideaki Nitani. The film was a success and Shishido quickly made two more Kagyo films: *Yojimbo Kagyo* (Bodyguard Work, 1961) and *Suketto Kagyo* (Helper Work, 1961). He also starred in *Hayauchi Yaro* (Fast-Draw Guy, 1961) as "the third-fastest draw in the world—0.65 seconds."

But while cavorting in these and other comic action roles, Shishido also honed his

© 1969 Nikkatsu Corporation

All-Star line-up. The versatile Jo Shishido (top, third from left) stars with Hideki Takahashi (bottom center) in *Ninkyodo: Bakuto Hyakunin* (The Way of Chivalry: One Hundred Gamblers, 1969).

tough-guy loner image in Seijun Suzuki's *Yaju no Seishun* (Youth of the Beast, 1963). Shishido played an ex-cop who infiltrates two yakuza gangs in an attempt to clear both his name and that of a superior who was found dead in a double suicide with a call girl. Shishido carried the film with an appealing mix of impudence and intensity, while remaining blithely oblivious of Suzuki's parodic shenanigans.

Shishido worked with Suzuki on several other films in the 1960s, including *Tantei Jimusho 23: Kutabare Akutodomo* (Detective Bureau 2–3: Go to Hell, Bastards, 1963) and *Nikutai no Mon* (Gate of Flesh, 1964). But internationally his most famous role was that of "Hitman Number Three" Goro Hamada in

Suzuki's *Koroshi no Rakuin* (Branded to Kill, 1967). Famous as the film that got Suzuki fired from Nikkatsu, *Koroshi no Rakuin* also did little for Shishido's career at the time. His character's life-or-death struggle to rise in the hitman hierarchy, while pursuing a half-Japanese, half-Indian femme fatale, did not impress at the box office. Shishido later reminisced about going to see the film with friends—and finding almost no one else in the theater.

In the late 1960s, Nikkatsu's entire action lineup began to fall from favor and Shishido found roles harder to come by. He appeared in the films of other studios, while shifting the focus of his activities to television, where he could give his comic talents full play. During this period, he also starred in Nikkatsu's "new action" films, including *Yakuza Wataridori: Akuto Kagyo* (Yakuza Bird of Passage: Bad Guys' Work, 1969), an all-star vehicle for Shishido, Akira Kobayashi, and Tetsuya Watari, and *Ryuketsu no Koso* (Bloody Battle, 1971), playing an ex-con who takes revenge after his gang is crushed by a larger rival.

In 1971, for the first time in eighteen years, Shishido found himself without a studio contract. He appeared in Toei's *jitsuroku* gang films, including Kinji Fukasaku's *Jingi Naki Tatakai: Kanketsuhen* (Battles without Honor and Humanity 5: The Final Episode, 1974), as an out-of-control gang boss. After yakuza movies began to decline at the box office in the mid-1970s, Shishido put his hard-boiled screen persona into storage. Over the next two decades, he worked primarily as a TV personality, while making occasional forays into films, including Nobuhiko Obayashi's *Tenkosei* (Transfer Students, 1982); *Noyuki Yamayuki Umibeyuki* (Bound for the Fields, the Mountains, and the Seacoast, 1986); and *Onna Zakari* (A Mature Woman, 1994).

In the 1990s, Shishido returned to his tough-guy past, playing a gruffly avuncular detective *sensei* to Masatoshi Nagase's scruffy P.I. in Kaizo Hayashi's *Waga Jinsei Saiaku no Toki*

(The Most Terrible Time in My Life, 1994); *Haruka Jidai no Kaidan o* (The Stairway to the Distant Past, 1994); and *Wana* (The Trap, 1996).

Shishido had the requisite swagger and insolence for his roles as hitman, gangster, or rogue cop, but his easy grin, quick wit, and puffy-cheeked charm also made him a natural for comedy. He was the perfect choice for Suzuki's assaults on genre convention, which reached their outrageous height in *Koroshi no Rakuin*. Instead of winking his way through the material, he threw himself into his role with a glittery-eyed fervor that underscored the absurdity of his situation and surroundings. At the same time, he revealed the sweaty, desperate human being behind the tough-guy mask. Three decades later, in Kaizo Hayashi's Mike Hama series, the urgency of his earlier performances had given way to hammy self-parody. He was a living legend—and knew it all too well.

Bunta Sugawara (1933–)

A riveting presence as a rogue gangster in the *jitsuroku rosen* films of the early 1970s, who later mellowed into a comic trucker and underworld elder statesman, Bunta Sugawara was born in 1933 in Sendai, a city in northern Japan. His artist father divorced his mother when Sugawara was four and moved to Tokyo. Sugawara was raised by his stepmother, whom he had regarded as his birth mother. His discovery of the truth, on the brink of adolescence, was a shock he preferred not to discuss in later years.

When Sugawara was in the fourth grade, he was sent to Sendai, as part of a wartime government policy to evacuate children from major urban areas. He studied at a Sendai elementary school until he was in the sixth grade, when the war ended. He later attended local junior and senior high schools, where he was considered

© 1973 Toei Company, Ltd.

Bunta Sugawara boils out of the sea in a publicity still for the Jingi Naki Tatakai (Battles without Honor and Humanity) series.

an elite student, despite doing little studying. Reunited with his stepmother after years of wartime separation, he clashed with her frequently but couldn't take his rebellion too far, as he later reminisced "because she was feeding me." (Inomata and Tayama, *Nihon Eiga Haiyu Zenshi*, p. 292).

After a year of study to prepare for his college entrance exams, Sugawara entered Waseda University's evening law school prep course, leaving him free to work during the day. With no financial support coming from home, he took manual labor jobs to scrape by. In his second year, Sugawara was dropped from the rolls for failing to pay his school fees. After a period of heavy drinking and frequent job changes, he began to work as a model in 1956—his first steady employment. He continued to make the rounds of the Ginza bars, however, and according to later rumors supplemented his income by pimping.

In 1958, at the age of twenty-five, he was scouted by the Shin Toho Studio and made his screen debut in Teruo Ishii's *Hakusen Himitsu Chitai* (White Line, 1958). Though Shin Toho promoted him and fellow hunks Tatsuo Terashima and Teruo Yoshida as "the handsome towers," the studio went bankrupt in 1961, and the three "towers" joined Shochiku. Sugawara was cast in Masahiro Shinoda's *Shamisen to Otobai* (Shamisen and Motorcycle, 1961), but when the actor stayed out drinking with a female acquaintance and came late to the first day of shooting, Shinoda fired him. Sugawara got other roles but didn't make an impression until his performance in Keisuke Kinoshita's *Shito no Densetsu* (The Legend of a Desperate Struggle, 1963). His strangely glittering eyes—the result of a hangover—caught the director's attention, but the film failed at the box office.

With the backing of former gang boss and Toei star Noboru Ando, Sugawara joined the Toei Studio in 1967. His first role was in Teruo

Bunta Sugawara Interview (December 2002)

Q: I'd like to go back to the beginning, if you don't mind. When I interviewed Kinji Fukasaku, he told me how much his war experiences had affected him. He was in Mito at the end of the war, when it was being bombed by the Americans—he saw the destruction of war first hand. Did you have similar experiences?
A: Fukasaku-san and I are about the same age—he's three years older. We had the same types of experiences. The difference is that he was in the third year of junior high when the war ended, while I was only in the sixth grade. After Japan's defeat in the war, everything fell apart. I was only a child then, so I only had a child's understanding of what was going on, but I know what Fukasaku went through.

Q: He said that he became very familiar with violence. He also remembers being angry at the adults who had taken Japan into the war. The angry feelings he had then later exploded in his films. You're from Sendai—how was it growing up there? Did you have similar feelings?
A: Fukasaku-san would stress that, wouldn't he? The violence he experienced back then made an extremely strong impression on him—you could say that it traumatized him. Well, in discussing his own films, he would logically talk about that sort of thing. Mito is a place that encourages *bu*—the martial spirit—which is about not just violence but also strength of character. Fukasaku-san may have felt the influence of this spirit strongly when he was a child.

Q: Do you mean that he liked to fight?
A: I don't think so—not him.

Q: What about you?
A: My part of the country, Tohoku, isn't like that all. When Japan was at war, *shobu* [the martial spirit] was encouraged throughout the country. It was quite different from now. I was strongly influenced by that spirit, but I didn't necessarily express it in yakuza movies.

Q: Were you a movie fan when you were young?
A: There were movies theaters during the war, but they weren't places for children.

Q: Fukasaku said something similar—that adults smacked kids for going to the movies.
A: My parents wouldn't let me go to movie theaters or coffee shops. I started going to movies after the war—there wasn't any other kind of entertainment. From about a decade after, the war movies were it.

Q: What did you watch mainly—American films or Japanese films?
A: They started making Japanese movies right after the war. It was a bit strange because everyone was so poor. I still don't understand how they were able to start making [movies] so quickly. What about America? I suppose they were able to get up to speed quickly because they won the war.

Q: That's right, Hollywood was flourishing then.
A: There weren't any yakuza movies, though now that I think of it there was Kurosawa's *Yoidore Tenshi* [Drunken Angel, 1948], with Toshiro Mifune. I suppose you could call that a yakuza movie.

Q: Were there any that you particularly liked?
A: They showed a lot of old foreign movies from before the war. They were cheap—you could see them for 20 or 30 yen. That would be about 200 or 300 yen in today's money. You would go down into the basement to some dirty theater like the Meigaza and watch double or triple bills. There were also big, nice theaters, but no one had the money to go to them.

Q: Are there any titles you particularly remember?

A: I remember nearly all of them. I saw *The Grand Illusion* and nearly everything by Duvivier. Everything by Rene Clair. I also watched American Westerns—prewar movies by John Ford. Films starring Ronald Reagan. I saw everything and anything. Movies were more popular than they are now—there was no other form of entertainment. The cities were starting to revive and they were building a lot of theaters, but even so they were always full.

Q: Did you think of becoming an actor back then?

A: No, not at all.

Q: You became an actor at the age of twenty-five, after dropping out of Waseda University and working as a model.

A: It was by chance. I was working at various jobs when I was asked to appear in a film. I thought of it as another kind of part-time job. I tried it and kept doing it. I still think that I might have been better off if I had gotten out while I still had the chance. [laughs]

Q: When you joined Shin Toho you were able to playing leading roles fairly quickly.

A: I was cast in leading roles right from the beginning. I was able to become a star while I was at Shin Toho—I got lucky. I appeared in films that no one remembers today, though. The studio folded after two years. After that, I went to Shochiku and wasn't so lucky.

Q: In 1967 you went to Toei. How did you feel about joining that studio? Did you feel that you had to start again from square one?

A: Shin Toho went under and I didn't see any future at Shochiku, though I was never fired. They would have let me hang around if I wanted, but at low pay. I didn't get any good parts. I saw that it wasn't any use continuing, then I got a break.

Q: From Noboru Ando.

A: From Ando-san.

Q: How did you happen to meet him?

A: Ando-san made a movie about his life—Yoshio Yuasa's *Chi to Okite* [Blood and Rules, 1965]—in which he played himself. I played the role of Kei Hanagata—a leader in Ando's gang who ends up getting killed. That's how I met Ando-san. That film turned out to be his big break—he made one film after another after that, while I fell behind. I got a few of his leftovers. Maybe "leftovers" isn't the right word—I appeared with him in several pictures, particularly for Shochiku. Then, Ando-san got an offer from [Koji] Shundo, a Toei producer, to come to Toei and he accepted it. This would have been in 1967. After going to Toei, he starred in Tai Kato's *Choeki Juhachinen* [Sentence: Eighteen Years]. He could do that because he didn't have an exclusive contract with Shochiku. Anyway, when he went to Toei he took me with him.

Q: Ando had been a real yakuza, though by the time he started acting he had quit the gangster life. When you started playing yakuza you had not only Ando but others around you from that world—role models, you might say. Were you close friends with them?

A: I had yakuza friends. Not just Ando, but guys who were still gangsters. We used to go drinking together. It was the same in America, wasn't it—actors [who played gangsters] had real gangsters as friends? I would meet them at bars—at places where I was a regular. Several of them were regulars at well—we'd say hello to each other.

Q: Did you ever find them scary?

A: Not really—they'd come in alone, as customers. I was a customer as well. It wasn't as though they would put a knife on the counter and start drinking. [laughs] They would drink the same as anyone else. Nobody would know who they were.

Q: Where did you go?

A: Shinjuku, Shibuya—any of the entertainment districts. I didn't have any money then, but I used to go a lot anyway. I would get friendly with them and we'd go drinking at another bar. We'd walk around and drink together. The way they carried themselves really impressed me. They were different from other people, from the people who came from acting schools. I wasn't consciously aware [of the impact they were making on me], but it may have naturally appeared in my acting.

Q: Especially in the Hitokiri Yota series—you played a violent character who seemed to be right off the streets.

A: I made a lot of suggestions to Fukasaku [who directed the two films in that series]. I told him how a yakuza would act in a certain situation. It wasn't something I made up. It wasn't something I got from a book. I made a lot of suggestions and he was interested in what I had to say. "Oh really, I didn't know that"—that kind of thing. I would say, "You don't shoot a gun looking cool like that." I didn't want to do it the way Ken-san did, which was something like Kabuki. Guys who had never [held a gun] would do it like that, but I didn't want it to look pretty—I wanted it to look real. I've never been in a street fight myself, but I'd seen them. I'd go out drinking late at night and see guys fighting with each other. So, I knew what it was like.

Q: Even so, you had a different look in your eyes from the other people around you, as though you had done things that they hadn't.

A: That's because I was a slow learner. [laughs]

Q: What do you mean by "slow learner"?

A: I stopped going to classes and had no way to eat—not even a part-time job. Maybe you don't understand what I mean—but there was nothing. Even a job as a bartender in a dive would have been OK. Instead, I ended up working as a kind of errand boy. I hated that, so I tried something else and, when I'd scratched up

some money, I'd go drinking. I was living on ramen and stuff like that. If I woke up the next day without any money, I'd go out and look for a job. That's the kind of life I was living.

Q: It wasn't exactly good for your health, was it?

A: I wasn't doing it because I liked it.

Q: You had a long period of scuffling, even after you became an actor. Did you ever think of quitting?

A: When Shin Toho folded, I thought that was it for me. There was no one asking me to join [their studio]—I wasn't that popular. There are still a lot of actors like that running around.

Q: You were a later bloomer. By the time you really became big, you were getting up there in age. Did you feel any sense of desperation—that you had to make up for lost time?

A: Not really. I wasn't the type to brood over things like that. I'm still not.

Q: You didn't think you had to sell yourself.

A: No, not at all. I'm not the type who's always thinking of what to do next—maybe that's why I've lasted so long. When Shin Toho folded, a lot of guys were afraid that they could never make a living acting, so they ended up doing something else—and succeeded at it.

One was Honda of the Honda Theater in Shimokitazawa. We were both actors together at Shin Toho. He saw that it wasn't working out and started a bar. He expanded to several locations, made a lot of money, and built the theater. He became a success by actively clearing a path for himself. Me, I was at a loss. Even so, I never became negative—I thought something would turn up eventually—and that's what happened. I was picked up by Shochiku, and when that didn't work out, I met Ando-san. There were a lot of struggling actors like me around Ando at the time but for some reason he favored me. He would ask me if I was free and when I said I was—that I didn't have a job, he'd ask me to come with him. I'd go with him to his apartment and we'd eat together.

Q: You got your break with the Hitokiri Yota series by playing a character who didn't follow the *ninkyo* code and didn't fit into any organization. In other words, a new type of yakuza dirty hero.

A: Yakuza aren't as cool [as their image in the movies]. The character was a *chinpira*—a punk. I was really just a punk with a good body. I could put a better complexion on it, but that's what I was—I was playing at being a tough guy. I called myself a struggling student, who was paying my own way through college, but if I'd really been one, I would have studied harder, gotten a scholarship and wouldn't have had to quit school.

Q: What did you study in school?

A: I entered the Law Department—I just ended up there, because that's the way the college entrance system worked then. When you applied to Waseda University, you had to write your first- and second-choice departments. My first choice was the Literature Department, my second was the Business Department, but I ended up with my third or fourth choice. I didn't have any excuse.

Q: When you got your break with the Hitokiri Yota series, *ninkyo* films were starting to fade. Films that tried to portray the yakuza more realistically were becoming popular, even though they weren't quite what were later called *jitsuroku* films. Did you feel that you happened to come along at the right time, when your type was in demand?

A: I guess you could say that. Fukasaku was not having a lot of success at Toei then—there were a lot of directors above him, who were making *ninkyo* films and doing well with them at the box office. I was getting starring roles at Toei, but there were a lot of people above me—big stars like Ken-san and Koji Tsuruta and Tomisaburo Wakayama. There was no way I could compete with them. I talked with Fukasaku and other people who were his age and on the same career track, such as Sadao Nakajima and [Norifumi] Suzuki. I told them that I would never get anywhere if I did the same thing as [the studio's established stars]. I'd never be number one—I'd always be number two or three. I had to do something they couldn't—and that was to play a *chinpira*.

Q: As you said, Fukasaku was relatively young then, as were the actors he worked with. They weren't big stars yet, like Takakura and Tsuruta. *Jingi Naki Tatakai* itself was a sort of gamble.

A: The guys who were older than me, like Ken-san and Tsuruta-san, had made their names with *ninkyo* films. Those films weren't as stylized as Kabuki, but they followed a certain formula. The hero wore Japanese clothes and carried a sword; there was a clear difference between right and wrong, with right always winning in the end. Before I joined Toei, I saw those films in the theater and thought they were great. They had a certain visual beauty— they were wonderful in a lot of ways. But if I were to make films like that, with all the competition I had, I could never measure up. The same was true of Fukasaku—no matter how hard he tried, he couldn't surpass the directors who came before him. So, we had to do something different—and we came up with *Jingi*.

Q: Did you think it was going to be such a hit? Fukasaku ended up making a total of five films in the series. You played the most important character, Shozo Hirono. Did you feel that there was something special about the films when you were making them?

A: When I made the first film of that series, I had already starred in a number of films and was getting some attention. If you look at the back issues of *Shukan Sankei* (Weekly Sankei), you'll see that the Jingi Naki Tatakai series ran in 1972 or 1973. About six months before the movie came out, I was on the cover of the magazine together with Tatsuo Umemiya. I was happy because it was my first cover photo, so I bought the magazine when I rode the Shinkansen. I was gazing at it with satisfaction when I saw the first installment of the Jingi Naki Tatakai series advertised on the cover. It was also listed in big characters in the table of contents, so it caught my eye. I don't know why, but I liked the title—it made an impression on me. The article was a true story, written in the style of a journal. It was announced as the first of a series, again in big characters. I thought it was really interesting. When I arrived in Kyoto, I gave the magazine to [Koji] Shundo [a Toei producer] and told him to read it. He was playing mah-jongg at the time, so I left the magazine with him and told him the article would make a good movie.

Q: So, you were the one who gave him the idea.
A: Two or three days later, I asked Shundo if he had read the article and he said no. So, I bought another copy of the magazine and asked him to read it. He reluctantly agreed, but after reading the article Shundo said it was really interesting. I asked him to let me appear [in a film based on it]. I also asked him to use Goro Kusakabe as a producer and Fukasaku as a director. "I can't use Fukasaku," he said. When I asked why, he said that Fukasaku didn't make hits. Instead, he was making films like *Gunki Hatameku Motoni* [Under the Flag of the Rising Sun, 1972]—difficult films about social issues that didn't make any money, so Fukasaku got a bad reputation as a director.

Before that he had made a film called *Hitokiri Yota: Kyoken San-kyodai* [Yota the Killer: Three Wild Dog Brothers, 1972] that got some attention, but he was still just another young director. Shundo said that any number of others, like Yamashita and Ozawa, would be better but I said, "No, no, it's got to be Fukasaku." When I asked him if he'd seen *Hitokiri Yota*, he said he hadn't. After Shundo saw it, he said that the film was interesting and that he would take my advice and go with [Fukasaku]. Then, he asked Kasahara-san to

write the script. It wasn't a jigsaw puzzle exactly but somehow the pieces fit together. The script was good, the director was good, and the actors were good.

Q: I heard that they were initially thinking of another actor for the role of Hirono—Hiroki Matsukata. This is the first time I've heard that you were cast from the start.
A: Not just *Jingi Naki Tatakai* but a lot of movies have various stories told about them. America has the same sort of story, such as the one about Coppola butting heads with his producer when he made *The Godfather*. Some strange and interesting legends get born that way. Coppola and the producer may have collided, but Coppola never said yes to him.

Q: When you were reading the article on the Shinkansen, did you see yourself in the role of Hirono [the fictional name of Mino, the gang boss who wrote the journal on which the article was based]?
A: No, I wasn't thinking that far ahead. I just knew that the story was interesting.

Q: When I see the Jingi films, I get the feeling that I'm seeing behind the curtain of the yakuza world.
A: Until then, yakuza movies, especially the *ninkyo* films, were highly idealized. The Hollywood Westerns also idealized the cowboy. John Wayne and James Stewart played heroes who were glorified versions of the real thing. But not everyone was playing that sort of hero. There were also the bad guys.

Q: Then, you had the dirty heroes, like the ones played by Clint Eastwood.
A: There was something fresh about what he was doing.

Q: The Jingi films seemed to suit the mood of the times. *The Godfather* had become a big success, as had Clint Eastwood movies—in Japan as well as America. Did you feel that you were playing a Japanese version of Clint Eastwood? Did you think that you were competing with what was coming out of Hollywood?

A: There was no way that we could touch *The Godfather*. That film had a certain history behind it, as well as so many wonderful things going for it, including its visual beauty, editing, script—I could only be envious. Japanese filmmakers are still far behind in that way.

Q: Do you mean they haven't been trained properly?

A: It's become worse now. Asian filmmakers, like the ones in Taiwan, are trying a lot harder.

Q: You made the Jingi films at a rapid pace—three in 1973 alone. You finished all five in two years.

A: Not only me but everyone around me was working like crazy. I was making ten films a year.

Q: All yakuza films.

A: That's right, nearly all yakuza films. A few were erotic. The fans gradually got tired of them—there were just too many. They did well until about 1975, but after that they went downhill. By 1980 the genre was dead.

Hollywood did a good job of changing the way it made films. With Spielberg and Coppola taking the lead, a number of directors said good-bye to the old Hollywood ways. It wasn't something that one person could do, but together they were able to pull it off. They were making road movies, The Godfather films, SF movies, and doing well at the box office with them. They created a new wave. Or you might say, the river started flowing in a different direction—it became a new river.

In Japan as well, the audience was changing, but nobody was doing anything about it. By the time they realized what was going on, the river had dried up and the flow had stopped. There was no one like Coppola to start a new wave, to make reforms.

Q: At least Fukasaku was trying.

A: He made a little wave. It wasn't big enough to bring about major changes.

Q: Even so, the Jingi films have since been widely shown abroad. Do you consider them to be representative—the films you want to be remembered by?

A: I've never made anything that deserves being called "representative." Everyone makes a big deal about the Jingi films, but the whole thing started with me happening to buy a *Shukan Sankei*.

Q: If you hadn't bought that magazine, someone else might have made the film. Or it might have never been made at all. So, in a way it was a stroke of luck. You mentioned the cover with you and Tatsuo Umemiya—that of course was for a completely different film.

A: Yes, completely different. Umemiya had become famous for his Furyo Bancho [Wolves of the City] series, while I had made several *Hitokiri Yota* movies. We were both in the news at the time, so they asked us to appear on the cover. They had Makoto Wada draw caricatures of us.

Q: Hirono, the character you play in the Jingi films, goes through a lot of changes. Also, a lot of time passes—more than two decades in the course of the series. Was it hard for you to express those changes?

A: I wasn't really thinking of that while I was working. Our society changed any number of times after the war and it's still changing. In the midst of all these changes, the characters are mixing it up with each other—it's more interesting than just seeing a bunch of gangsters without the context. There's a connection between them and the ordinary society in which they live. It's like printing a photo on photographic paper—without the paper you're not going to get a good photo. But no one was thinking in those terms back then. We were all young.

Q: Even so, your character did change from the first film, when he was a wild street punk, to the later ones, when he was a gang boss.

A: That's true. [The *Jingi* films] were on a smaller scale and don't measure up as works of art, but they resemble what was great about the *Godfather* films in that way. The first *Godfather* film centers on Marlon Brando as the Godfather. In the second and third, the focus shifts to Al Pacino. The period changes as well, with the story about a young gangster coming from Italy to America with nothing and then, by hook or crook, building a big crime family. It's film as a recorder of history.

The *Jingi* films also show how the characters follow a certain path. Japan has lost the war, the society has fallen into chaos, and in the midst of all this are these young guys who have become gangsters. The films present a picture of Japan as it was at that time—though they deal with the yakuza, they're not only about them. Even in straight society, people were cheating one another. People would go off with a rucksack to buy rice and potatoes, but bad sorts would cheat them and steal what they had. Some would even kill to get what they wanted. Because the films included that kind of thing, they were something more than the ordinary yakuza movie. It was fun to be part of that.

Q: I got that impression watching the third installment of the series—*Dairi Senso* [Proxy War, 1973]. It was like a Shakespearean history play, with all the betrayals and wars. It goes not only behind the curtain, but the curtain behind the curtain. Today's friend is tomorrow's enemy, while today's enemy is tomorrow's friend.

A: That's why the series title, Jingi Naki Tatakai, is so important. Unfortunately, it wasn't someone at Toei who thought of it, but someone at the weekly magazine. I was trying to come up with a title, but I didn't. Instead, it was this reporter. Well, they were probably all sitting around and someone blurted it out. That's how it started—it's a famous title.

Q: The two big bosses in the series—Yamamori and Uchimoto—are comically weak types. I had to wonder why anyone would give up their lives for those two. On the other hand, your character, Hirono, was stronger.

A: Maybe too much so—he was too good to be true.

Q: He put more emphasis on the gang code.

A: He had to because he was the hero. I wonder how he would have acted in real life. I never asked Mino [the real-life boss on whom Hirono is based] how he felt about it. If I met him now—we're both getting on—I'd like to ask him for the true story.

Q: Hirono is just trying to protect what he has—his territory in Kure—not move up in the ranks.

A: If you want to move up, as either a businessman or a politician, you can't always play by the rules. You have to push people aside or sacrifice them. Even if you're not conscious of it, you end up doing that kind of thing. The films are symbolically expressing a fundamental law of human life.

Q: Eat or be eaten.

A: That's human history. They're still fighting wars, aren't they? Politicians are still cheating and betraying each other. They betray the betrayers—it happens all the time. There's nothing unusual about it.

Q: The *Jingi* films are not just yakuza movies—they say something about the society as a whole.

A: There are a surprisingly small number of films that really tell the truth, including the truth about the dark side of humanity. Instead, they make films that prettify reality. Politicians also do the same thing, but the reality behind the curtain is something else—a dirty battle for power.

Q: Wasn't the same thing true of the studio system back then, with both directors and actors struggling for position? The hierarchy was rather strict. Didn't they have to fight dirty to get ahead?

A: I suppose so. Some people were quite frank about it. Some people were more clever. Some people stood aloof. There were some actors and directors I liked. There were others I kept my distance from. I won't name names, but I also don't want to gloss over what went on.

Q: When you made the *Jingi* films, you were working with actors, like Akira Kobayashi and Jo Shishido, who had come from Nikkatsu. How was it working with them?

A: They provided a kind of stimulus. They brought a different flavor, you might say. Also, Mikio Narita was trained in *daiei* [the composition of poems on a set theme], Asao Koike in *shingeki* [so-called "new drama" that originated in the early decades of the twentieth century], while Takeshi Kato was from the Bungakuza Troupe. Then, there was the crowd from Nikkatsu, as well as guys like me who belonged to no one school or group. That mixture is what made it interesting.

Q: Everyone was allowed to shine—there was no one star who dominated.

A: That was something new at Toei. Until then there was one star who was on stage from beginning to end. Hollywood was the same way. Now, though, you don't always have one star on the screen. American films were the first to change—now it's not strange for the star to be absent for scenes at a time. In Japan, though [*Jingi*] was the first film to change to that style. That gave a fresh stimulus to society.

Q: Unfortunately, your films weren't widely shown abroad back then. One Kosaku Yamashita film [*Yamaguchi Gaiden Kyushu Shinko Sakusen* (The Untold Story of the Yamaguchi Gang: Strategy for the Advance into Kyushu, 1974)] was released in the States as *The Tattooed Hitman*, but it was cut to pieces and didn't find an audience. Did that bother you? Were you sorry that the film didn't do better?

A: No, not at all. That was the times. It was like baseball—[Japanese players] didn't have a big desire to play in the Majors and [Japanese actors] didn't have a big desire to act in foreign movies. I didn't have it myself. Now, though, I'd love to try it. [laughs]

Q: After that, you appeared in the Truck Yaro [Fireball on the Highway, 1975–79] series, which were comedies. Were you getting tired of yakuza movies and eager to try something different?

A: No, I didn't think of it that way. Kinya Aikawa happened to bring me a weekly magazine and told me, "You've got to do this." It was a photo spread of all these trucks, decorated with bright lights and flashy designs—the boom for this sort of thing had just started. I told him, "If you bring me [a movie], I'll do it." So, he showed the magazine to a Toei producer, who said he wanted to make a movie—and it became a hit.

Q: Well, you do have a talent for comedy.

A: No, not at all. [laughs] The other guy [Aikawa] was the funny one.

Q: A lot of the characters you played were men of few words—they express themselves with their eyes instead. Was that hard for you—to have to get by without words?

A: Not really—I enjoyed it. I didn't intend it that way—but I was always being asked to keep it short. Basically, the proper way to make films is without a lot of words—to tell the story with images. A play can only communicate to the audience with words. Movies, on the other hand, can express what you want to say with an image, say of a dog or flower. Given film's visual power, actors shouldn't have to say too much. If you're filming a lot of talk, you might as well freeze the picture and use narration. With Shakespeare, you have to communicate everything with words, from beginning to end—and that's wonderful in its own way. But movies are different.

Q: When I interviewed Show Aikawa, he told me that in preparing for a role he didn't rely only on the script but tried to imagine how many brothers and sisters his character had, what sort of cigarettes he smoked—all these details. Of course, that sort of backstory doesn't appear in the script. Did you try to think of what sort of childhood Hirono had?

A: I really can't remember. I suppose I gave it some thought, but not a lot. There are various types of actors. Some study a role very seriously. Some even have all their teeth pulled, so they'll look older.

Q: Or get fatter and then thinner, like De Niro.

A: That's right—that's one type. Then there's another type who goes with what they happen to be feeling at the moment. If somebody asked me to pull my teeth out, I would quit. [laughs] An actor is essentially a kind of con artist. Even though he knows nothing about a certain line of work, he pretends that he does. It a pretty childish business actually. A lot of fishermen and various other people are risking their lives, devoting themselves to their jobs. Guys like me have never been a yakuza and never killed anyone, but we play killers. Even though we've never been on a boat, we play fishermen. No matter how good an actor is or how much he prepares, he's never going to beat a real fisherman—for the fisherman it's a way of life. So, I don't like to brag about what I do or think about it too much—what's the point? If I can get people to fall for a bit of trickery on the screen, that's enough.

But saying that, I have to admit that there are a lot of great Japanese and foreign films that have stood the test of time, that I can see over and over. In the end, though, it's all made up—it's not reality.

Q: Marlon Brando is famous for hating acting—for saying it's not a man's line of work.

A: There are actors like that in Japan, too, but it leaves a bad taste in my mouth when I hear them say that. If you feel that way, you ought to quit. On the other hand, actors like De Niro, who starve themselves for a role, are great.

Q: Have you given up on yakuza movies entirely? Do you think the genre is finished?

A: It's finished. If you don't have the right framework, you can't make new yakuza movies.

Q: By framework, do you mean having a studio behind you?

A: No, that's not what I mean. I'm talking more about having a certain sensibility—that's more important. Now, they're just making these films to score at the box office. They're making them so that they can ride a trend. Young actors and directors are forced to work within that framework, so I feel sorry for them. In my time, we didn't have such a solid framework, but we did have drive and desire and were allowed a certain amount of freedom. Of course, some had the attitude that anything went, as long as it made money.

Even before the war, people like [Tsumasaburo] Bando and Kanjuro Arashi were making leftist films, experimental films, something different from the commercial films of the time. They were somewhat restricted in what they could do. They had to make entertainment, but as long as they did well at the box office they could try something a little different. That was true in my time as well, but basically we were working in a capitalist system, so there was always pressure to make money. But they would also allow us space to do something personal, something artistic. So, once in a while, something interesting would suddenly appear, like a flash in the dark.

Kurosawa-san's films were like that. He came up in the capitalist system but was allowed to make the kinds of films he wanted, such as *Yojimbo* [1961] and *Yoidore Tenshi*

[Drunken Angel, 1948]. He would make about one film a year. That wouldn't be allowed now—no one has the money. They would worry about taking a loss. But it was all right back then. Maybe somewhere someone will start making films like that again, including new yakuza films, but now wherever I look there's no money.

Q: Are you looking to make that kind of film yourself?
A: Well, as I told you before, if you only have one rocket going up and bursting, it's boring. A fireworks display means one explosion after another. That's what makes people happy—a fireworks display. I don't mean a series necessarily.

You've got to have a foundation to work from—but unfortunately that sort of foundation no longer exists at Toho, Toei, or Shochiku. They've become exhibitors—that's it.

Q: I recently interviewed an old colleague of yours, Teruo Ishii, who told me that he'd like to make a Japanese version of Sergio Leone's *Once upon a Time in America*.
A: That was a good movie.

Q: He's getting on in age but is still full of energy. You worked with him on a number of films, didn't you?
A: That's right.

Q: How was he to work with, compared with Fukasaku?
A: Well, we were in the same company [Shin Toho] when it went bankrupt and we both ended up on the streets. I worked with him on Toei's *Abashiri Bangaichi* series, so we have that in common. Ishii worked as a director but never rose to the top [the way Fukasaku did]. I wonder why. Ishii had the same sort of power—but he had a different touch. He was somewhat of a fish out of water at Toei.

Q: Ishii made a lot of films with Takakura, but he added a comic touch to them. His films were a bit out of the ordinary compared with the usual Toei product.
A: He never really got along with the top people at Toei. Ishii was one of those people who don't quite fit into the *donburi* [rice bowl], if you see what I mean. He didn't quite belong in the organization.

Q: How about you? Were you inside or outside the rice bowl?
A: I was inside. [laughs] I could have gone either way. I was flexible—or half-assed. [laughs]

Q: You're best known for the *Jingi* films, but are there any others that you wish were better known?
A: I liked *Kenkai tai Soshiki Boryoku* [Cops versus Thugs, 1975], another film I made with Fukasaku. Kazuhiko Hasegawa's *Taiyo o Nusunda Otoko* [The Man Who Stole the Sun, 1979] was also interesting. I played a detective in both—the complete opposite of what I usually did. I think an actor has to always be ready to reverse direction. When people have typed you as a yakuza, play a detective or school teacher.

Q: Have you ever thought of working with a young director and actors? I'm thinking of the way Jo Shishido played a *senpai* [senior] to Masatoshi Nagase's detective in Kaizo Hayashi's Mike Hama films. That role revived his career and introduced him to a new generation of fans.
A: I hadn't thought about it, but if someone were to come to me with an interesting idea, I would do it. If it's boring, though, I won't. That's the stance I'm taking now—I turn down more offers than I accept. I've become lazy. [laughs] I see acting as a kind of mimicry, but it doesn't mean I'll do anything. It's got to be interesting.

Q: How about getting together again with Fukasaku or Ishii or one of the other old-timers from Toei?

A: I could see doing that. But if it's just *senko hanabi* [toy fireworks] that fizzles and sparks and is over in a minute, then I wouldn't be interested. The Japanese film industry is like a dry river bed. A river is only a river when it flows. Films are the same way. When you have a steady flow [of films], something interesting may pass by. In the river it could be a fish, in the movie business, an idea. When the river dries up, there's nothing—all you can see is rocks. Those are the kind of conditions young directors are working in now. They have to patiently strike out on their own, pile up rocks on the bank of the dry river bed, send up a rocket, and clap their hands—alone. I feel sorry for them—it's a sad sight.

How is it in America? They have a flowing river, with various people by the banks. There are a lot of worthless American movies, but there are some good ones, too. And they're not just sending up one rocket. They have a solid foundation and organization. The American movie river will never dry up, just as the Mississippi River will never dry up. The Japanese movie river has dried up, I'm sorry to say. It will be hard to get it flowing again.

Q: Have you seen many Japanese movies recently?

A: No, though there are some that I'd like to see. There's one called *Kao* [Face, 2000] that I wanted to see but missed. I'd like to find things by good, young directors. But I don't like movies that feel artificial or overly intellectual. I don't like the types of films that get sent to film festivals. I'm extremely orthodox in my tastes. I like *The Godfather* or *Once upon a Time in America* or, among Japanese movies, *Yoidore Tenshi*. Films that are the best of the mainstream.

Q: What do you think of the newer yakuza movies, such as the one starring Show Aikawa?

A: You can't call them yakuza movies. Yakuza movies ended with me. The ones that came after are something else. They're either remakes or V Cinema.

Q: What about Junji Sakamoto's *Shin Jingi Naki Tatakai* [Another Battle, 2000]?

A: I had nothing to do with that one. It left a bad taste in my mouth. I wouldn't have minded if they had made a proper movie, but there already was a *Jingi*. They were just going after an easy score—that shows a lack of guts and ambition. Young actors and directors may be making various types of action movies, but they can't make a yakuza movie now. It would be all right if they were to use what was good about the old movies, but no matter what Toei and the other companies do, they can't get it right—the films don't do well at the box office. Just remaking old movies with young actors and directors doesn't work—that whole mentality is wrong.

Q: There's even been a remake of *Jingi no Hakaba* [Graveyard of Honor, 1975].

A: That was Tetsuya Watari's film—it was somewhat different from the usual Toei film.

Q: Takashi Miike is the director of the new one.

A: I understand what Miike is trying to do, but I feel sorry for him. He wants to make a real movie, but he can't. All he can make is V Cinema—that's the state the Japanese film industry is in now, as you know. In America, they've changed from the old Hollywood style to a new way of making films. As a result, American films are making progress in terms of both quantity and quality, but not Japanese films. It's not *jingi no hakaba* [the graveyard of honor]; it's *eiga no hakaba* [graveyard of the movies].

Ishii's *Abashiri Bangaichi: Fubuki no Toso* (A Man from Abashiri Prison: Battle in the Blizzard, 1967). His performance in Kosaku Yamashita's *Gokudo* (Gangster, 1968) in which he played the underling of a gruff *oyabun* (Tomisaburo Wakayama), impressed studio bosses and Sugawara began to get larger parts. His first starring role was in Yasuo Furuhata's *Gendai Yakuza: Yotamono no Okite* (The Code of an Outlaw, 1969), as an ex-con who ends up battling his own gang. Sugawara starred in all five subsequent series installments, portraying wild-dog gangsters who are put down in the last reel. The last, Kinji Fukasaku's *Gendai Yakuza: Hitokiri Yota* (1972), made the biggest splash; Sugawara's brand of on-screen wildness set a standard that no other actor of his era could match.

His image as a bull-headed flouter of *ninkyo* rules made Sugawara a logical choice for the lead in Kinji Fukasaku's seminal hit *Jingi Naki Tatakai* (Battles without Honor and Humanity, 1973). As the ex-soldier-turned-gangster Shozo Hirono, Sugawara completely inhabited the role. His nearly two decades of scuffling had prepared him to portray a man who has lost everything but is determined to struggle on, whatever the odds—or the body count.

Though the leading exemplar of the new antihero that *Jingi Naki Tatakai* and other *jitsu-roku rosen* films spawned, Sugawara's reign at the yakuza movie summit was short. As gang films began to fade at the box office in the mid-1970s, he shifted career gears, playing the lead in the ten-installment Truck Yaro (Fireball on the Highway, 1975–79) comedy series, as a trucker who falls in love anew in every episode but never gets the girl. He also appeared in gang films throughout the next two decades, including Toei's "last" yakuza film, *Don o Totta Otoko* (The Man Who Shot the Don, 1994) and the first entry of the popular video series *Shuraba ga Yuku* (The Carnage Comes, 1995).

Ken Takakura (1931–)

Born in 1931 in Fukuoka, Ken Takakura grew up in the shadow of war and was still only in junior high school when Japan surrendered. He graduated from Meiji University with a degree in commerce and entered Toei after passing the studio's second New Face audition. He made his screen debut in Fujio Tsuda's *Denko Karate Uchi* (Lightning Karate Strike) in 1956, but audiences were slow to warm to the comic salarymen he portrayed on the screen. Takakura himself felt miscast in such roles, as he later confessed to an interviewer: "They didn't really ly suit me," he explained. "More than safe and secure salarymen, characters who had been cast out of society and were on the run were more my style" (Inomata and Tayama, *Nihon Eiga Haiyu Zenshi: Danyu-hen*, p. 183).

The director who finally made Takakura a true superstar was Teruo Ishii. Playing an escaped convict in Ishii's 1965 hit *Abashiri Bangaichi* (A Man from Abashiri Prison), Takakura found both his groove and audience. "Teruo Ishii is probably the man who made me what I am today," said Takakura. (ibid., p. 183.) Toei ended up releasing eighteen installments of the Abashiri Bangaichi series over the next eight years, of which Ishii directed eleven.

Another signature series for Takakura was Nihon Kyokakuden (An Account of the Chivalrous Commoners of Japan), which ran for eleven episodes from 1964 to 1971. The first nine were directed by Masahiro Makino and, together with the Bakuto (Gambler) and Hishakaku series, were instrumental in launching the *ninkyo* film boom. Takakura usually played a pure-hearted gambler or workman who finds himself battling greedy, unscrupulous yakuza or businessmen. Even though his character lives an outlaw life, he upholds justice, as defined by the *ninkyo* code.

Yet another popular Takakura series was *Showa Zankyoden* (Remnants of Chivalry in the

© 1969 Toei Company, Ltd.

Classic gangster chic. Ken Takakura plays a wandering yakuza who finds himself on the wrong side in *Hibotan Bakuto: Hanafuda Shobu* (Red Peony Gambler: Flower Cards Match, 1969).

Showa Era), which ran for nine installments from 1965 to 1972. The directors were Toei stalwarts Kiyoshi Saeki (five episodes), Masahiro Makino (three), and Kosaku Yamashita (one).

In most episodes, Takakura played a gangster named Hidejiro Hanada who allies himself with a gang that upholds the good old *ninkyo* ways but is fighting for its existence against a money- and power-hungry rival. Hanada usually begins each film as the putative foe of a gangster named Jukichi Kazama (Ryo Ikebe), but by the end they are firm friends, going off to fight the rival gang together. Hanada also usually wins the affection of a beautiful-but-long-suffering woman, played in several episodes by Junko Fuji.

These three series sustained Takakura's superstardom throughout the 1960s yakuza movie boom, while making large contributions to Toei's bottom line. After more realistic gang films became popular late in the decade, however, Takakura found box office success increasingly elusive and Bunta Sugawara took his place as the studio's top male star. In the first half of the 1970s, Takakura tried to broaden his range, even playing a criminal in Junya Sato's thriller *Shinkansen Daibakuha* (The Bullet Train, 1975). Although a hit in France, the film flopped in Japan.

After leaving Toei and going freelance in 1976, Takakura portrayed a disgraced detective out for revenge in Junya Sato's mystery thriller *Kimi yo Funmu no Kawa o Watare* (Cross the River of Indignation, 1976); an ex-con in search of an old love in Yoji Yamada's *Shiawase no Kiroi Handkerchief* (The Yellow Handkerchief of Happiness, 1977); and a detective who loves and leaves three woman in Yasuo Furuhata's *Eki* (Station, 1981). But though these and other post-Toei films were box office successes, he never quite regained his earlier career momentum.

Hollywood filmmakers found in Takakura a bankable (in Japan) star, who could give characters comic shadings without compromising their essential dignity. His reasonable facsimile of fluent English was another plus. Credits include Robert Aldrich's *Too Late the Hero* (1970); Sydney Pollack's *The Yakuza* (1975); Ridley Scott's *Black Rain* (1989); and Fred Schepisi's *Mr. Baseball* (1992). Still active in his seventh decade, Takakura appeared in the hit Toei melodramas *Poppoya* (Railroad Man, 1999) and *Hotaru* (2001), playing elderly role models whose words may be few, but whose hearts beat warm and true.

Despite his image as the Japanese John Wayne—a rock-jawed embodiment of core values and an unabashed traditionalist—Takakura has been more various in his long career. In the beginning, he impersonated everything from charming scapegraces, such as the scandal sheet reporter in the Hibari Misora vehicle *Kashi no Onna Ishimatsu* (The Female Ishimatsu of the Fishing Harbor, 1961), to comic schleps, such as the gap-toothed trucker in Teruo Ishii's *Juichinin no Gang* (Eleven Gangsters, 1963). Playing *chinpira*, he exuded a punkish arrogance and nonchalance that stood in sharp contrast to the more sober-sided types around him. But he could explode into action with power and grace, while looking privately amused by the bodies falling around him.

Takakura reached the heights of his popularity, however, portraying wanderers or fugitives who adhere quietly but fearlessly to the *ninkyo* way. Also, in contrast to Koji Tsuruta's *nimaime* types, who could give themselves heart and soul to a woman, Takakura's yakuza heroes were inevitably *tateyaku* (heroic leading man) characters, who stoutly resisted romantic passion and usually bade farewell to their love interest in the last reel.

But as merciless as he could be toward his on-screen enemies—famously asking them to "please die" (*shinde moraimasu*) before slicing them to ribbons—Takakura never quite lost his boyish sincerity; it was a quality that humanized even his toughest characters. He was also a straight shooter in real life, freely admitting to interviewers that, as a nongambler and nondrinker, he was nothing like his characters. "I could never become a yakuza," he told one interviewer, "I just played them to make my fans happ." (ibid., p. 182).

Riki Takeuchi (1964–)

Owner of the best sneer in the Japanese movie business and among its hardest-working actors, with more than 170 screen credits, Riki Takeuchi was born in Oita Prefecture in 1964.

After graduating from high school, he worked in an Osaka bank for two-and-a-half years. He then left for Tokyo and tried his luck in show business. In 1986 he made his first screen appearance in Nobuhiko Obayashi's *Kare no Otobai, Kanojo no Shima* (His Motorbike, Her Island), starring as a biker who finds romance on the road. That same year, he appeared in two more Obayashi films: *Noyuki Yamayuki Umibeyuki* (Bound for the Fields, the Mountains, and the Seacoast) and *Nihon Junjoden Okashina Futari* (The Strange Couple, The Strange Pair), as well as Hideo Gosha's *Gokudo no Onnatachi* (Gang Wives)—his first gangster role. Takeuchi appeared frequently in TV dramas in the late 1980s and early 1990s, including the Fuji TV megahit *101 kaime no Propose* (The 101st Proposal), playing a variety of roles but often serving as a male love interest.

In films, his big break came in 1992 with *Nanba Kin'yuden Minami no Teio* (Tales of Nanba Finance: Emperor of the South), a straight-to-video film based on a popular comic. Takeuchi played Kinjiro Manda, an Osaka loan shark who lends money to the type of people who can't go to banks, including gangsters and other underworld types. Though willing to squeeze debtors—and welshers—with the best of them, Manda is a soft touch for those genuinely in need. Takeuchi's first film set in his native Kansai, *Nanba Kin'yuden Minami no Teio*, spawned a long-running series while launching Takeuchi on his career as the "King of Video" (a title hotly disputed by the equally hard-working Show Aikawa). By fall 2002, the series had passed the forty-episode mark and was still going strong.

In 1991 Takeuchi co-starred with Tsuyoshi Ihara in *Jingi* (Chivalry), a yakuza buddy movie directed by Keiji Hasegawa, with Takeuchi playing a *chinpira* with an eye for the ladies, and Ihara, a University of Tokyo graduate down on his luck. The resulting series had reached thirty-one episodes by fall 2002. Takeuchi also starred in *Nobody* (1994), OV veteran Tochi-

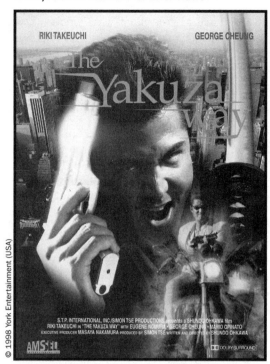

Coming to America. Riki Takeuchi (center) as a gangster on a mission of revenge in Los Angeles in *The Yakuza Way* (1998).

the Dead or Alive series (1999–2001). Though still a snarler on screen, Takeuchi fits right into Miike's wacko worldview, with his gravity-defying quiff adding the right surreal touch. Takeuchi was also impressive, but in a different way, in Miike's *Jitsuroku Ando Noboru Outlaw-den: Rekka* (Deadly Outlaw: Rekka, 2002), playing a gangster out to avenge the death of his long-haired, sage-like boss. He displays a wider range than the usual gang film antihero—after a homicidal rampage he looks shattered and apologetic in a most un-yakuza way. Heavier and puffier than when he started his film career a decade-and-a-half ago, Takeuchi also bore a striking resemblance to Bill Clinton in this film—not to mention late-period Elvis. The "King of Video," however, still has a long way to go before he can fit into the jumpsuit of the "King of Rock 'n' Roll." Not that he needs to—Takeuchi is marketing his own line of clothing and accessories, all taken from his films, in stores across the country as well as on his web site at http://www.rikitakeuchi.com/new/news.html.

Koji Tsuruta (1924–87)

A king of the Toei lot for more than a decade and the ultimate on-screen exemplar of the *ninkyo* film's *gaman* (tough-it-out) creed, Koji Tsuruta was born in Hamamatsu, Aichi Prefecture, in 1924. He was raised in Osaka by his grandmother following his parents' divorce and his mother's remarriage. Attending a commercial high school, he ran with a delinquent gang and neglected his studies, finishing second from the bottom of his class. Once in a movie theater, he got into a quarrel with students from another school and ended up fighting them all, though they were a dozen to his one.

Despite his mediocre grades, Tsuruta managed to enter Kansai University and, in May

michi Okawa's feature debut, as a former-*chinpira*-turned-salaryman who, with two of his colleagues, starts a war with a yakuza gang. The film later screened abroad and was released on a subtitled DVD by Vanguard International Cinema. Among other Takeuchi films released in English-subbed DVDs are the four films in the Tokyo Mafia series, Kosuke Suzuki's *Blood* (1998), and Shundo Okawa's *The Yakuza Way* (1999), a U.S./Hong Kong/Japan co-production featuring Takeuchi as a yakuza in L.A. getting revenge after a drug deal goes wrong.

His best-known films abroad, however—and certainly among his best work—are the ones he made with Takashi Miike, including *Gokudo Sengokushi Fudo* (Fudoh: The New Generation, 1996) and the three installments of

1944, joined the naval air corps. After passing a test for pilot trainees, he accumulated sixty-eight hours of flying time and rose through the ranks to lieutenant. He volunteered for a suicide squadron that operated out of the Yokosuka air base but was never called to fly. When the war ended, nearly one-third of his squadron mates had died—and Tsuruta suffered ever after from survivor's guilt. "I survived but my comrades were at the bottom of the ocean," he later said. "I have never been able to forget that" (Inomata and Tayama, *Nihon Eiga Haiyu Zenshi*, p. 100).

After the war, Tsuruta entered Hirokichi Takada's Theater Troupe and toured the provinces as an actor. At Takada's recommendation, he joined Shochiku and in 1948 made his screen debut in Tatsuo Osone's *Yukyo no Mure* (The Herd of Gamblers). He won a large following among female fans as a *nimaime* for his handsome face and moody presence. A role in Yasujiro Ozu's *Ochazuke no Agi* (Flavor of Green Tea over Rice, 1952) exposed him to the work of a cinematic master and made him impatient with the trash he had been appearing in. "I realized how worthless it was," he later said (ibid., p. 101).

In 1952 Tsuruta left Shochiku to set up his own production company, but found success elusive. Also, a highly publicized romance with a rising young actress, Keiko Kishi, ended badly when Shochiku forced the couple to break up—a blow so devastating that Tsuruta temporarily went into hiding. He enjoyed considerable success as an independent, however, working for every studio but Nikkatsu in a variety of roles, including student soldiers who sacrificed their all for their country.

In 1960 he joined Toei and starred in Kiyoshi Saeki's *Sabaku o Wataru Taiyo* (The Sun that Crosses the Desert). His breakthrough role, however, was as a fugitive gangster in Tadashi Sawajima's *Jinsei Gekijo: Hishakaku*, a 1963 hit that launched the *ninkyo* film boom. Tsuruta became the pillar of the Toei yakuza

© 1971 Toei Company, Ltd.

The heart of the Toei *ninkyo eiga* lineup. Ken Takakura (left) and Koji Tsuruta are ready for battle in *Ninkyo Retsuden: Otoko* (Ninkyo Biography: A Man, 1971).

lineup for the next decade, starring or guest starring in nearly a film a month at his peak. Tsuruta also enjoyed remarkable success as a singer, releasing a string of hit records. Among the biggest was Masato Fujita's and Tadashi Yoshida's *Kizudarake no Jinsei* (A Life of Pain) in 1966. Fujita's lyric, "You may think I'm an old-fashioned guy," became a popular catchphrase and further boosted Tsuruta's already enormous popularity.

Among his best-remembered films during this decade were *Hokori Takaki Chosen* (The Proud Challenge, 1962); *Bakuto* (The Gambler, 1964); *Nihon Kyokaku Den Ketto Kanda Matsuri* (Bloody Festival at Kanda, 1966); *Meiji*

Kyokakuden: Sandaime Shumei (Blood of Revenge, 1968); and *Hibotan Bakuto: Isshuku Ippan* (Red Peony Gambler: A Bowl of Rice and a Place to Sleep, 1968).

Despite being the hardest worker in the Toei lot, who rarely turned down a project, Tsuruta had his preferences. Though he dutifully played variations of the noble stoic in film after film, he did not easily make the transition to the more realistic depictions of gangsters that became popular in the late 1960s. Thus came the charge by his critics that Tsuruta was an actor of limited range. Within that range, however, he was unsurpassed, creating an image of ideal Japanese manhood as compelling as John Wayne's American version. His air of loneliness and melancholy, of being set apart from the ordinary run of mankind by his suffering and sacrifices, appealed both to women, who longed to share his pain, and men, who admired the way he endured it.

Tsuruta brought more to his roles than an attitude; he embodied core values with sincerity and conviction. When he strode off to meet near-certain death at the hands of his enemies in the service of a higher ideal, he was living out the central drama of his youth—and indirectly his entire generation. "Ninkyodo is a moral philosophy that every human being should follow," he said in a March 1971 interview with *Kinema Jumpo* magazine. "Be considerate, do your duty, keep your promises and respect your seniors. Know right from wrong and never cheat anyone."

Tsuruta was no Boy Scout, however. He could wield a sword with deadly authority, make the sparks fly in a love scene, and shed tears of hot grief at the death of a lover. This combination of stylish macho toughness and sensitive male sex appeal served him well for decades. But even after his star started to fade in the 1970s, he refused to admit defeat, doggedly playing gang bosses and other authority figures, albeit with dwindling frequency. He made his last film for Toei, *Saigo no Bakuto* (The Last Gambler) in 1985. On June 16, 1987, Tsuruta died of lung cancer, at the age of sixty-two.

Tatsuo Umemiya (1938–)

Able to play anything from comical schemers to cold-blooded killers, usually with a dash of wit and roguish charm, Tatsuo Umemiya was born in 1938 in Manchuria, then a Japanese colony. While still a university student, Umemiya won Toei's fifth New Face contest in 1958 and made his screen debut in 1959 in Tsuneo Kobayashi's *Haha to Musume no Hitomi* (The Eyes of Mother and Daughter). After starring as the title character in Hideo Sekikawa's two-part SF epic *Yusei Oji* (Prince of Space, 1959) and appearing in the Tsuneo Kobayashi thriller *Kodo 7000 Meter Kyofu no 4 Jikan* (Altitude 7000 Meters, Four Hours of Terror, 1959), Umemiya became a regular in Toei's contemporary and period gang films, usually in supporting roles.

Umemiya rose to stardom in Yukio Noda's *Furyo Bancho* (Wolves of the City, 1968), playing the leader of a Hells Angel-like motorcycle gang, the Capones. The film was a hit and spawned a sixteen-part series. Starting with the fourth episode, Makoto Naito's *Furyo Bancho Okuri Okami* (Wolves of the City: Wolves Following Women, 1969), the series acquired a distinctly comic flavor. Umemiya also played a memorable supporting role in Kinji Fukasaku's *Jingi Naki Tatakai* (Battles without Honor and Humanity, 1973) as Wakasugi, a Doi-gumi *wakagashira* who befriends the hero, Hirono (Bunta Sugawara) in prison—but later changes his allegiance. He also appeared in several other Fukasaku films, including *Chizome no Daimon* (Bloody Coat of Arms, 1970); *Jingi no Hakaba* (Graveyard of Honor, 1975); and *Yakuza no Hakaba: Kuchinashi no Hana* (Yakuza Burial: Jasmine Flower, 1976).

In 1975 Umemiya launched his TV career with the drama *Zenryaku Ofukurosama* (To Get to the Point, Dear Mother) and worked in other popular TV drama series. Meanwhile, his film career continued to flourish, even after the end of the yakuza *eiga* boom. In the 1990s, Umemiya returned to the yakuza movie genre, with roles in *Don o Totta Otoko* (The Man Who Shot the Don, 1994); *Yakuzado Nyumon* (A Yakuza Primer, 1994); and *Shuraba ga Yuku 4: Tokyo Daisenso* (The Carnage Comes 4: The Big Tokyo War, 1997).

Although Umemiya was a Grade-B star, as a supporting actor he was a valuable presence, particularly in Toei's contemporary gang films, adding his unique blend of hustler smarts and slickness to the at-times crude macho proceedings. He could also chill, however, with flashes of soulless amorality or deadly cruelty. The very image, in other words, of the modern gangster, for whom the *jingi* code is little more than a flag of convenience.

Tomisaburo Wakayama (1929–92)

The older brother of Shintaro Katsu and a star in his own right for his portrayals of fearless, out-of-control gangsters, Tomisaburo Wakayama was born in 1929 in Fukagawa, Tokyo. After finishing high school, he began practicing *nagauta* and, at the age of twenty, became a professional *nagauta* performer under the name Tomisaburo Wakayama. Joining the Shin Toho Studio in 1954, Wakayama made his acting debut in Tai Kato's *Ninjutsu Jiraiya* (Ninja Master Jiraiya, 1955). Though he soon advanced to larger roles, Wakayama found true stardom elusive (brother Shintaro Katsu was then waging a similar struggle at Daiei).

Discouraged with his progress at Toho, Wakayama left for Toei in 1959 and Daiei in 1962. By this time, Katsu had become a star, playing the blind swordsman Zatoichi, and

Fire and fury. Tomisaburo Wakayama as a fighting priest in *Gakuakubozu: Nenbutsu Sandangiri* (The Wicked Priest: The Triple Cut of the Nenbutsu Prayer, 1970).

Wakayama was hoping to duplicate his success. At the urging of Daiei president Masaichi Nagata, Wakayama changed his professional name to Kenzaburo Jo and played a variety of roles, from buffoons to villains. He even starred with Katsu in *Zoku Zatoichi Monogatari* (The Return of Masseur Ichi, 1962), a billing that made a media splash. In 1966 he returned to Toei, resumed the name Tomisaburo Wakayama and appeared in Shigehiro Ozawa's *Bakuchiuchi* (Gambler, 1967), the first film in a ten-part series starring Koji Tsuruta. Wakayama's real breakthrough came in the fourth installment, Kosaku Yamashita's *Bakuchiuchi Socho Tobaku* (Big Gambling Ceremony, 1968), in which he

カラー作品

昭和やくざ系図 長崎の顔

血で血を洗う宗家三代目襲名！

激怒と悲嘆が

の任侠

Ready when you are. Tetsuya Watari (front) and Noboru Ando prepare to cross swords in a poster for *Showa Yakuza Keizu: Nagasaki no Kao* (Lineage of Yakuza in the Showa Era: The Face of Nagasaki, 1969).

played an ex-con denied his rightful promotion to *oyabun* of his old gang. His all-stops-out performance electrified audiences and helped make the film a well-remembered classic.

Now a full-fledged Toei star, Wakayama appeared in several hit series including Gokudo (Gangster, 1968–74, eleven episodes); Goku-aku Bozu (The Priest Killer, 1968–71, five episodes); Hibotan Bakuto (Red Peony Gambler, 1968–72, eight episodes); Silk Hat no Oyabun (Silk Hat Boss, 1970, two episodes); and his most famous abroad, Kozure Okami (Baby Cart, six episodes, 1972). Produced by brother Katsu's Katsu Production, this blood-drenched action series featured Wakayama as a lone-wolf warrior who trundles his young son

about the country in a cart seeking vengeance against the evil clan that murdered his wife and destroyed his livelihood.

Unlike other Toei stars who quickly faded out when the yakuza movie boom ended, Wakayama kept busy with films, TV dramas, musicals, and even two Hollywood films: John Berry's *Bad News Bears Go to Japan* (1978) and Ridley Scott's *Black Rain* (1989). His last role was as a boxing coach in Junji Sakamoto's *Ote* (Checkmate, 1991). Wakayama died of a heart attack on October 1, 1992.

At his worst a shameless ham, at his best Wakayama was an actor of passion and vitality, who inhabited his roles totally and brought conviction to even hackneyed material. His forceful presence gave Toei's yakuza films a fresh charge at a time when they were falling into stale mannerism. Today, there is no one in Japanese films remotely like him and it is hard to imagine a successor.

Tetsuya Watari (1941–)

Handicapped by illness and unfortunate timing, but a magnetic presence on the screen and an actor of unusual skills, Tetsuya Watari was born in 1941 in Awaji Island, Hyogo Prefecture. His younger brother was actor Tsunehiko Watase. After completing his secondary education at a boarding school, Watari entered the elite Aoyama University in Tokyo. On graduating, he took a test to be a Japan Airlines pilot but failed. In 1964 he was scouted by a publicist for Nikkatsu and joined the studio.

Watari made his screen debut in Isao Kosugi's *Abare Kishido* (Wild Kishido, 1965). With his boyish good looks, long legs, and brooding intensity, he was tagged from the start as the second coming of the 1950s idol and studio savior Yujiro Ishihara. Watari appeared in several remakes of Ishihara hits, including *Arashi o Yobu Otoko* (The Man Who Called the Storm,

1966); *Hoshi Yo Nagekuna: Shori no Otoko* (Stars Don't Cry: The Champion, 1967); *Hino Ataru Sakamichi* (The Sunlit Slope, 1967); and *Kurenai no Nagareboshi* (The Velvet Hustler, 1967). In the last film, he played a boozing, womanizing gangster, modeled on Jean Paul Belmondo, who falls for the lovely fiancée of a missing businessman. The film was Watari's personal favorite. The 1960s, however, were a different, darker era than Ishihara's 1950s, and the remakes did not reach the box office heights of their models.

Watari's breakthrough role was in the Burai (Hoodlum, 1968–69) series as Goro Fujita, a lone-wolf gangster based on a real-life model of the same name, whose memoirs became a best seller. The six-part Burai series was a hit with audiences and made Watari one of Nikkatsu's last action stars. His best-known Nikkatsu film abroad, however, was *Tokyo Nagaremono* (Tokyo Drifter, 1966), Seijun Suzuki's Dadaesque genre send-up. Watari plays a gangster who defends his gone-straight former boss against the machinations of murderous rivals. Forced to live on the run, he becomes involved in increasingly bizarre situations, including a barroom brawl straight out of a Hollywood Western. To his credit, Watari handles the film's absurdities with the merest hint of a wink, playing the powder-blue-suited hero with his trademark intensity.

In 1971 Watari left Nikkatsu and joined Ishihara Pro—Yujiro Ishihara's production company. While continuing his film career, he played the title role in the NHK TV series *Katsu Kaishu* but fell seriously ill and left the show in the middle of the season. After a year of recuperation, Watari made his screen comeback as an out-of-control yakuza in Kinji Fukasaku's *Jingi no Hakaba* (Graveyard of Honor, 1975). His sensational performance, highlighted by a scene in which he chews his dead lover's bones in front of his startled *oyabun*, earned him a secure place in the genre pantheon.

After appearing in Fukasaku's *Yakuza no Hakaba: Kuchinashi no Hana* (Yakuza Burial: Jasmine Flower, 1976), Watase left the films for television, appearing in the long-running cop shows *Daitokai* (Big City) and *Seibu Keisatsu* (Seibu Police). In the 1990s, Watari made a comeback to the big screen, with starring roles in Takao Okawara's *Yukai* (Abduction, 1997) and Yukio Fukamachi's *Nagasaki Bura Bura Bushi* (Nagasaki Strolling Song, 2000).

A Homansu (1986)

Scr.: Shoichi Maruyama, Yusaku Matsuda. *Dir.:* Yusaku Matsuda. *Prod.:* Toei, Kitty Film. *Main cast:* Yusaku Matsuda, Ryo Ishibashi, Chieko Hirasawa, Satomi Tezuka, Paul Maki, Yoko Agi, Renji Ishibashi, Eichi Kudo, Nobuya Hayama. 99 mins.

STORY

Tall, silent drifter (Yusaku Matsuda) rolls into Shinjuku with no money and no memory—only a big, bad motorbike, a sleeping bag, and an enormous pair of shades. (In the film's poster, Matsuda looks like a Japanese Ray Charles in leather.) His air of impenetrability and invulnerability verges on the catatonic, but it attracts the attention of Yamazaki (Ryo Ishibashi), a tough-but-understanding gang boss who is caught in the middle of a gang power struggle and looking for an out.

The drifter, Fu, may seem beyond it all—sleeping rough with the homeless and brushing off punches from Yamazaki's puny henchmen as though they were buzzing flies—but he takes a liking to Yamazaki. He enters his new friend's world—and reveals himself as an inhumanly efficient fighting machine. He also happens to be catnip to women, bedding a chatty club hostess with hardly a word—just his macho charisma. But even with this superman at his side, Yamazaki cannot change the iron law of gang life: eat or be eaten.

CRITIQUE

Based on a comic by Marei Karibu and Akio Tanaka, *A Homansu* was Yusaku Matsuda's only film as director. The strangeness of the title—a combination of "aho" (a Kansai dialect word for "fool") and "performance"—is reflected in the oddness of the film, a hybrid of yakuza programer and dystopian SF, reflecting the then-fashionable musings on the humanity of artificial entities, be they *RoboCop*, *Terminator*, or Ridley Scott's replicants. The film was also a showcase for its star, who underscored the ultra coolness of his character at every opportunity (Fu even slept with his shades on), while laying on steamy underworld atmospherics with a trowel.

This approach—maximalist in its macho romanticism, minimalist in its dialogue, and over the top in its violence—resembles that of Takeshi Kitano, though Matsuda's camera acrobatics and cartoony excesses are quite un-Kitano-like. Viewed today, *A Homansu* verges on camp, though Matsuda brings an intensity to his mechanical mute act that partly compensates for his self-indulgences. Playing Yamazaki, a young Ryo Ishibashi displays the same coiled power and stoic intelligence that would inform his later gang films, including Kitano's *Kids Return*. He also happened to be one of the few actors who could hold his own with Matsuda. For one thing, he looked almost as cool in shades.

Abashiri Bangaichi (1965)

A MAN FROM ABASHIRI PRISON

Scr./Dir.: Teruo Ishii. *Prod.:* Toei. *Main cast:* Ken Takakura, Hiroshi Nanbara, Tetsuro Tanba, Toru Abe, Kunio Tanaka. 92 mins.

STORY

Shin'ichi Tachibana (Ken Takakura) is serving a three-year stretch in Abashiri Prison in Hokkaido—the Siberia of Japan. On work details, he is cuffed to Gonda (Hiroshi Nanbara), a five-time loser and all-round bad character. Tachibana gets into beefs with Gonda and a yard boss, Yoda (Toru Abe), but generally keeps his nose clean. A lawyer (Tetsuro Tanba) takes a liking to him and puts in a request for Tachibana to see his sick mother.

Then, when he has only six months to serve on his sentence, Yoda, Gonda, and other cons make an escape attempt, jumping off a prison truck and running into the woods. Still chained to Gonda, Tachibana is forced to go along. When the lawyer hears that his model prisoner has gone missing, he feels betrayed—and when he learns that Gonda has attacked his wife, he goes berserk—and vows to hunt the pair until he captures them, dead or alive.

CRITIQUE

Abashiri Bangaichi was modeled on *The Defiant Ones*—the 1958 Stanley Kramer prison-break movie, starring Tony Curtis and Sidney Poitier—but set, not in the sunny South, but in Hokkaido in the dead of winter. The action scenes also differ distinctly from their Hollywood models. In one, Tachibana and Gonda pump for their lives on a railroad handcar, flying down a snow-covered Hokkaido mountain, with the lawyer on another handcar in hot pursuit, potting away at them with a shotgun. In another, Gonda and Tachibana have the desperate idea of cutting the chain that binds them by lying next to a rail as a train passes over, with Tachibana on the track, Gonda on the shoulder.

In addition to the action, a big draw for contemporary audiences was the theme song "Abashiri Bangaichi" (Abashiri Prison), sung by the husky-voiced Takakura—a Japanese companion piece to Johnny Cash's "Folsom Prison Blues" that became a well-remembered hit and featured in all ten of the series episodes helmed by Ishii. Another draw was Kanjuro Arashi playing an elderly con who reveals himself as the legendary *oyabun* Onitora—and proves that he still deserves his fearsome reputation as a fighter. Active in films since 1927 and a period drama star for decades, Arashi became a fixture in the Abashiri Bangaichi series.

A smash hit, the film propelled Takakura to superstardom, while Ishii went on to make ten Abashiri installments. After the tenth, *Abashiri Bangaichi: Fubuki no Toso* (A Man from Abashiri Prison: Battle in the Blizzard), he turned over the reins to other Toei directors, who filmed another eight entries, ending in 1972.

Abashiri Bangaichi: Bokyohen (1965)

A MAN FROM ABASHIRI PRISON: GOING HOME

Scr./Dir.: Teruo Ishii. *Prod.:* Toei. *Main cast:* Ken Takakura, Noaki Sugiura, Kanjuro Arashi, Kunie Tanaka. 88 mins.

STORY

Freed from Abashiri Prison, Shin'ichi Tachibana (Ken Takakura) returns home to Nagasaki to pay his respects at his mother's grave. There, he becomes friendly with Emi, a half-Japanese, half-African-American girl, and decides to go straight for good. Soon after, he learns that the boss of the Asahi-gumi (Kanjuro Arashi), to whom he owes an obligation, is fighting a waterfront turf war with the Yasui-gumi, whose boss (Toru Abe) had cut him a new navel in the previous film. Tachibana decides to throw his lot in with the Asahi-gumi, even if he has to go back to prison for it. After several confrontations with Yasui-gumi thugs—and the murder of the Asahi *oyabun*—Tachibana strides off to fight the entire gang himself and take the life of that human snake, Yasui. First, though, he has to get by Joe (Naoki Sugiura), a tubercular hitman who is Tachibana's equal as a sword fighter.

CRITIQUE

The third *Abashiri Bangaichi* film and widely considered by Japanese critics and fans to be the best, *Bokyohen* made such a hit at the box office that the producers decided to spin out the Abashiri films into a series, one that ran for eighteen installments.

A highlight is the matchup between Ken Takakura and Naoki Sugiura as Joe. In their first encounter Sugiura, dressed in white and coughing into a handkerchief, challenges Takakura on the docks, calling him a yakuza. When Takakura denies it, Sugiura points to a tattoo on his arm and says, "If you're not a yakuza, what is that?" Takakura replies by taking out a lighter and burning off the tattoo while humming a tune. Sugiura blanches—and beats a hasty retreat. The climactic fight scene between this pair is modeled on a similar showdown between Burt Lancaster and Gary Cooper in the 1954 Robert Aldrich Western *Vera Cruz* in which the seeming winner is standing with a grin on his face—and suddenly collapses.

Ishii made a specialty of mixing East and West in his films but seldom to cooler—if occasionally ludicrous—effect as in *Bokyohen*. Someone, for example, should have suggested that he cast a real African-American as Emi, instead of hiring a Japanese kid and blacking her up. The ghost of Al Jolson shouldn't haunt a yakuza movie.

Adrenaline Drive (1999)

Scr./Dir.: Shinobu Yaguchi. *Prod.:* Kindai Eiga Kyokai, Gaga Communications, Nihon Shuppan Hanbai, There's Enterprise. *Main cast:* Masanobu Ando, Yutaka Matsushige, Hikari Ishida. 112 mins.

Shinobu Yaguchi's *Adrenaline Drive* will look familiar to those who have seen the director's two previous features, *Hadashi no Picnic* (Down the Drain, 1993) and *Himitsu no Hanazono* (My Secret Cache, 1997). All are picaresque in form with heroes who are lovable goofs, but *Adrenaline Drive* represents an advance.

Yaguchi has always been a crowd-pleasing idea man, whose high-concept plots could fly at a Hollywood pitch meeting, but in earlier films his storytelling reach often exceeded his technical grasp. In *Adrenaline Drive*, he has finally mastered the art of making every yen count on the screen. If not quite Hollywood-slick, the film is a more accomplished entertainment than anything he has attempted so far.

Even so, *Adrenaline Drive* has story problems that in Hollywood would probably not have survived the second rewrite. Yaguchi gives his narrative game away too easily and occasionally sacrifices logic altogether. I am usually not interested in picking holes in plots: I go to movies to be seduced, not convinced—but in *Adrenaline Drive* the holes are too big to ignore. In the end, though, the ride is worth it. Yaguchi fuels his film with sharp, sympathetic observations about his characters and the madly acquisitive society in which they live.

His hero is Satoru Suzuki (Masanobu Ando), an employee at a rent-a-car company who, distracted by the teasing of a sadistic superior, smacks a company car into the rear of a Jaguar. The driver, a menacing gangster named Kuroiwa (Yutaka Matsushige), drags poor Satoru to the gang office to extract an extortionate payment for damages. A gas explosion at the office, however, leaves Satoru as the only ambulatory survivor. He is rescued by Shizuka Sato (Hikari Ishida), a nurse who has rushed to the scene from a nearby convenience store. A mousy type in a semi-permanent daze, Shizuka is shocked by the carnage but manages to help Satoru out of the ruined building. He, however, is thinking less about saving his hide than swiping a box filled with 200 million yen in yakuza loot. When the ambulance carrying Satoru, Shizuka, and Kuroiwa crashes, Satoru scoops up the spilled money, with Shizuka's reluctant assistance. Before they can make a clean getaway, they are spotted by a semi-conscious Kuroiwa.

Satoru and Shizuka soon find themselves being pursued by the gang's surviving *chinpira* (played by the Jovi Jova Comedy Troupe), who have no intention of turning over the loot to Kuroiwa, their erstwhile boss. They are also goofballs who let Satoru and Shizuka escape and flee to the countryside. Realizing that if he wants the job done right he has to do it himself, Kuroiwa hobbles out of the intensive care unit in search of the fleeing couple, who by this time are enjoying their windfall at a resort hotel and falling in love.

Satoru and Shizuka are predictably careless with the loot (Shizuka hauls her share around in a knapsack) and predictably smitten with each other. They also spend their small fortune in the usual ways: fancy designer clothes, expensive jewelry, and a room with a view, while Shizuka undergoes the usual transformation from bespectacled nerd to babe in a red mini-dress.

Several of the plot twists are head scratchers. Why, for example, does a friendly sommelier that Shizuka encounters suddenly make off with her knapsack, without knowing what is in it? His grab exists solely to start another idiotic chase.

Matsushige Yutaka looks the part of Kuroiwa, with the skull-face, slicked-back hair, and doom-laden voice of a Japanese Christopher Walken. But Yutaka can also get laughs by arching his eyebrows in exasperation while trapped in a neck brace that resembles a fiendish Lego construction.

If Yaguchi wants to be the next Masayuki Suo, i.e., a maker of intelligently crafted, entertaining mainstream films, he should hire a producer with a Suo-like, steel-trap mind. He is too much like his hero, who may win Shizuka but can't quite keep both feet anchored to planet Earth.

Akumyo (1961)

TOUGH GUY

Scr.: Yoshikata Yoda. *Dir.:* Tokuzo Tanaka. *Prod.:* Daiei. *Main cast:* Shintaro Katsu, Jiro Tamiya, Tamao Nakamura, Yoshie Mizutani. 93 mins.

STORY

Tough guy Asakichi (Shintaro Katsu) falls for Kotoji, a prostitute at a brothel on Matsushima Island, near Osaka. He also gets into a fight with a fast-talking local gangster named Motoru no Sada ("Motor Sada," played by Jiro Tamiya) and beats him to a pulp. This feat wins Asakichi the favor of Motor's boss—as well as Motor himself, who becomes Asakichi's sidekick.

Kotoji escapes from Matsushima but is captured and sold to a brothel on Innoshima, in Japan's Inland Sea. Asakichi and Sada ride off to her rescue. But when they spirit her away in a boat, they are swept back by the tide and forced to take refuge at an island inn. A dandyish local gang boss, King Silk Hat, and his minions are on their trail, but the mistress of the inn—a gang boss in her own right—takes their side.

CRITIQUE

Based on a popular serial novel, *Akumyo* spawned a sixteen-part series and launched the rough-hewn Katsu to stardom, after years of indifferent success in period dramas for Daiei. Though not a leading-man type—even at this early stage of his career Katsu looked as though he had spent too much time at the bottom of the rugby scrum—he had a vitality that boiled off the screen. In *Akumyo*, Katsu plays a brawler who obliterates opponents with thudding fists, not martial arts finesse. His Asakichi is an oak-hearted (if oafish) type, who exudes a roguish sexual charm. As Motoru no Sada, Jiro Tamiya provides the good looks that Katsu lacks, as well as an easy-going appeal that balances (offers relief from?) Katsu's full-bore personality.

Not intending to make a continuing series, the producers killed off Tamiya's character in the followup *Zoku Akumyo* (Tough Guy II, 1961) but had to resurrect him for the third film, *Shin Akumyo* (The Unknown, 1962), as Sada no Motoru's younger brother.

American Yakuza (1994)

Scr.: Max Strom, John Allen Nelson. *Dir.:* Frank Cappello. *Prod.:* First Look Films. *Main cast:* Viggo Mortensen, Ryo Ishibashi, Michael Nouri, Franklyn Ajaye, Yuji Okumoto, Christina Lawson, Robert Forster, Nicky Katt, John Fujioka. 96 mins.

STORY

Ex-con Nick Davis (Viggo Mortensen) gets a job driving a forklift in a warehouse. Soon after he starts, he witnesses a shoot-out between Japanese gangsters and American hoods. Nick saves the life of one of the Japanese and takes him to his fleabag of a hotel to recover from his wound. The Japanese, Shuji Sawamoto (Ryo Ishibashi), is grateful for Nick's help, but Sawamoto's men take him away before he can properly thank him.

Nick is fired from the warehouse when his prison record is discovered. He runs into Sawamoto, who offers him a job with his "import company." Nick learns that Sawamoto and his crew are engaged in a turf battle with the local mafia, lead by one Dino Campanela (Michael Nouri). After a tense meeting with Campanela to discuss a recent hit on one of Sawamoto's crew, Nick decides that Campanela ordered it—and prepares for war.

Sawamoto takes a liking to Nick, though his underlings make no attempt to hide their distrust. But when the gang war begins, Nick stays loyally by his new employer. Nick goes to a fish market where he meets Sam (Franklin Ajaye)—an FBI agent. Nick, it turns out, is an agent himself, working undercover. "You do whatever it takes to stay deep," Sam tells him—whatever "whatever" means.

Tendo (John Fujioka), the boss of Sawamoto's gang, arrives in town—and Nick finds himself being watched. The Japanese still don't trust him completely, it seems. Then, when the FBI breaks up a gun deal in which Sawamoto's gang is involved, Nick gets caught in the crossfire between the yakuza and FBI agents. He wounds several of the latter and escorts his biggest doubter in the gang, the perpetually sneering Kazuo (Yuji Okumoto), to safety. Nick also makes off with a bag of money—an even more important achievement in his bosses' eyes. Sawamoto gives Nick a spacious apartment, with a promise of more to come.

Nick becomes better acquainted with Yuko (Christina Lawson), the gorgeous interior decorator Sawamoto has hired for him. Meanwhile, Campanela orders one of his underlings, Vic (Nicky Katt), to take out Tendo—and promises to buy him a house in return. Nick uses his influence with a border guard to make Sawamoto's smuggling business safer. The "guard," however, is Sam. Sawamoto now trusts Nick so much that he makes him a full-fledged yakuza—a first for a non-Japanese. After the induction ceremony, Nick spends a glorious night with Yuko.

Nick's FBI superior, Littman (Robert Forster), tells him that he is off the case. The Campanela gang is about to launch a full-scale war on the yakuza—and Littman doesn't want Nick caught in the middle. Where, Nick wonders, do his loyalties lie? With Sawamoto, who has supported him every step of the way—or with the FBI, who could care less if Sawamoto lives or dies?

CRITIQUE

Though a straight-to-video programer, *American Yakuza* strives for the look of a studio film, with tight action choreography, slick MTV-style editing, and a thrumming score by David C. Williams that shouts "epic." Also, the film takes its theme of East-West friendship seriously, a welcome development in 1994 when the long season of "Japan bashing" in the U.S. was still a recent memory.

That said, star Viggo Mortensen is a nullity with a chiseled jaw, who acts with all the energy of a bored teenager hanging out in the mall. When he answers "yeah" to Ryo Ishibashi's offer to join the gang, it's as though he's been asked if he wants fries with his burger.

As the gangster Sawamoto, Ishibashi hits the right emotional notes, even though he delivers most of them in a foreign language. He cannot, however, make up for his co-star's lack of affect and the pedestrian storyline, which is lifted more from John Woo and male-bonding movies than from anything in Japanese gang films. In fact, the entire premise—that a white-bread American can become a full-fledged yakuza, complete with *sakazuki* (literally, wine cup) initiation ceremony, is absurd.

In yakuza movies, *gaijin* (foreigners) may have their uses but usually take a bullet by the second reel. Real-life yakuza are little different; like their Sicilian counterparts, they only admit those with the right blood to the inner sanctum. Blue-eyed blondes, even ones with male model looks, need not apply.

Ankokugai no Kaoyaku (1959)

THE BIG BOSS

Scr.: Motosada Nishikame. *Dir.:* Kihachi Okamoto. *Prod.:* Toho. *Main cast:* Koji Tsuruta, Akira Takarada, Toshiro Mifune, Mitsuko Kusabue, Yumi Shirakawa, Keiko Yanagawa, Seizaburo Kawazu, Akihiko Hirata, Makoto Sato, Hideyo Amamoto. 102 mins.

STORY

A finance company president is shot in his office and a waitress sees the face of the hitman's driver as he pulls away from the scene. The driver, as it turns out, is Mineo Komatsu (Akira Takarada), who sings jazzy pop numbers at a club full of screaming young women. He and his older brother Ryuta are members of Yokomitsu-gumi, whose boss (Seizaburo Kawazu) ordered the hit. When the boss finds out that the police are trying to ID the driver, he tells Ryuta to make his brother stop singing— or else. But Mineo refuses to listen to his brother's warnings and entreaties; his singing career is just taking off and he wants to go straight. "You want to go straight, too," he tells Ryuta. "You just won't admit it."

Kurosaki, the boss's top lieutenant, orders a garage man, Kashimura (Toshiro Mifune), to fix the get-away car to avoid police detection. Kashimura is reluctant to do the gang's dirty work, but Kurosaki puts the arm on him. Ryuta again urges Mineo to follow gang orders, but the stubborn singer says that, if push comes to shove, he will go to the police.

Meanwhile, Ryuta must take care of gang business. He and another Yokomitsu gangster, Tsudo (Akihiko Hirata), pay a visit to a foreigner whose gambling club is encroaching on their territory. When the foreigner pulls a pistol on them, they beat him up and trash his club. Soon after, Ryuta visits the home of a loyal gang member who has just been released from prison—and learns that he has been killed. The grieving father blames Ryuta, but who is really responsible?

Kurosaki goes to Kashimura with another job; the gang is going to whack the waitress, who is close to ID'ing Mineo—and a car will be the weapon of choice. Later, a hitman runs her over after she leaves the restaurant. Knowing that the gang regards him as a traitor and potential snitch, Mineo toys with giving himself up but listens to the urgings of his pregnant wife and Ryuta to go into hiding. When the boss and Kurosaki ask Ryuta to tell them

Mineo's whereabouts, he says he doesn't know, but they don't believe him. To put pressure on Ryuta, the gang kidnaps Ryuta's disabled son and assigns a gimlet-eyed enforcer, Goro, to deliver the news and make sure Ryuta doesn't try anything funny. But Ryuta finds allies in unexpected places—and moves toward a decisive showdown with the boss, Kurosaki, and his minions.

CRITIQUE

The second film in the eight-part Ankokugai (Underworld) series and the first of three installments directed by Kihachi Okamoto, *Ankokugai no Kaoyaku* solidified Okamoto's reputation as an action director in the Hollywood mode. Set in a postwar Japan of fancy foreign cars, glitzy night clubs, big houses, and Westernized pop music, the film is less about the struggle between *giri* and *ninjo* that would occupy so many later yakuza films and more about fast-paced suspense, building to an explosive climax. Okamoto makes liberal use of off-kilter camera angles and extreme close-ups, while creating underworld characters that range from the smoothly sophisticated to the dangerously eccentric but rarely conform to traditional yakuza type. Instead, they are "international" in a way reminiscent of the heroes of Nikkatsu's *mukokuseki* action films of the 1960s.

The exception, as might be expected, is Koji Tsuruta's Ryuta, who is sincere and upright in the standard heroic manner, though his loyalty to his Machiavellian boss is far from absolute. Also, his agonizing over his gang's dirty deeds, including a drunken debauch that ends with his collapse into the sympathetic arms of a club mama-san, is a departure from the stern face Tsuruta's characters usually presented to the world.

Toshiro Mifune's much-put-upon garage owner is likewise a change from the wild and wily samurai Mifune portrayed for Akira Kurosawa. A common-man type who may cringe before bullying gangsters, but quietly seethes at their methods, he is, given Mifune's star billing, a surprisingly minor character. In portraying this worm that finally turns, Mifune displays a range not always apparent in his stoic samurai roles. The film itself, however, is little more than a fast paced, slickly constructed entertainment that often devolves into weepy melodrama, while offering a fascinating glimpse at the evolution of Japanese pop music in the swingin' 1950s.

Asu Naki Machikado (1997)

END OF OUR OWN REAL

Scr.: Toshiharu Maru'uchi, Akimasa Niima, Hidehiro Ito. *Dir.:* Koji Wakamatsu. *Prod.:* KSS. *Main cast:* Ken Kaneko, Koji Matoba. 95 mins.

Koji Wakamatsu was once known as the "King of the Pinks" for grinding out dozens of porno pics in the "Flower Power" era and after. He was also the quintessential 1960s rebel, whose *Kabe no Naka no Himegoto* (Skeleton in the Closet), a 1965 film about a voyeuristic high school boy who rapes and kills a housewife, got a seal of disapproval from the Eirin censorship board, but created a success de scandal at the Berlin Film Festival—that forced Eirin to relent. Now three decades later, in *Asu Naki Machikado*, Wakamatsu is not blazing new territory but reverting to genre form, though in this case the genre is noir thriller, not *pinku eiga*.

As usual with Wakamatsu, sex and violence are much in evidence, as is a rough affection and sure feel for the byways of Tokyo's meaner streets. Missing, however, is a fresh take on his much-filmed theme of underworld betrayal and revenge. Ever the pro, Wakamatsu produces an entertainment that should please its target audience—salarymen looking to chill out with 95 minutes of boom-boom and bang-bang, but his approach is more reminiscent of 1977 than 1997.

Tetsuji (Ken Kaneko) operates a screw machine in a small machine shop by day and works as a drug runner for a gangster named Sasaki by night. This routine is interrupted, however, when a deal goes wrong: Tetsuji is ripped off and Sasaki ends up dead. Realizing that he is an amateur in over his head, Tetsuji does not try to search for the killers. Nonetheless, the bag man for the buyers, a cold-eyed, hot-tempered *chinpira* named Koga (Koji Matoba), suspects Tetsuji was in on the job. When Koga finds him, he nearly fillets him with a knife. Tetsuji, however, persuades Koga that he too was a victim and together they try to find the gangsters who made off with their drugs and money.

They learn that the thieves were taking orders from Koga's boss, a squat, bulldog-faced *sokaiya* (corporate extortionist) named Murakawa. Enraged, Koga and Tetsuji vow to get Murakawa and, after bulling their way into his office, Tetsuji beats him with a tire chain. Murakawa survives and declares war on Koga and Tetsuji. With the heat on, the women in their lives, including Koga's lover, who happens to be Murakawa's secretary, begin to melt away. This unlikely pair learns that they can only depend on one another.

As Koga, Koji Matoba has a way of glaring up through his eyelids that is pure essence of *chinpira*. Playing Tetsuji, newcomer Ken Kaneko is still the spoiled slacker of Takeshi Kitano's *Kids Return*—and is not yet ready to carry a film on his own. Compared with Matoba's raging punk, he is little more than a pretty-boy nullity.

Wakamatsu does not try anything new with his tried-and-true, male-bonding material. The point-of-view shots with a handheld camera are reminiscent of vintage Godard, while the quick-draw contests in drug hand-over scenes are recycled from countless TV cop shows. Also indicative of Wakamatsu's reluctance to move with the times is his treatment of the film's women, who serve mainly as objects for displaying the heroes' prowess in bed. Not surprisingly, the one with the strongest charac-

ter, Koga's world-wise lover, ends up selling him out. A sweet trap in an unapologetically retro movie.

Bakuchiuchi Socho Tobaku (1968)

BIG GAMBLING CEREMONY

Scr.: Kazuo Kasahara. *Dir.:* Kosaku Yamashita. *Prod.:* Toei. *Main cast:* Koji Tsuruta. Tomisaburo Wakayama, Junko Fuji, Nobuo Kaneko. 95 mins.

STORY

The year: 1934. The *oyabun* of the Tenryu-gumi, who controls gambling in Tokyo's Koto Ward, suddenly dies and the issue of succession must be settled. A leadership conclave picks the upright, ever loyal Nakai (Koji Tsuruta) as the next boss of bosses, but he declines, saying he is not a direct disciple of the fallen *oyabun*. Instead, Nakai nominates Matsuda (Tomisaburo Wakayama), the next in line, who is serving a stretch in prison. The crafty Senba (Nobuo Kaneko), Nakai's senior, puts forward the lower-ranking, but smooth-talking Ishido (Hiroshi Nawa)—and carries the day.

When the burly, hot-tempered Matsuda is released from the slammer, he is enraged to hear that he has been denied his rightful place at the top. Nakai, ever the peacemaker, tries to persuade him that what is done is done and succeeds—for the moment. Then, a Matsuda underling (Shin'ichiro Mikami) attacks Ishido—and the uneasy truce begins to fall apart. When Nakai's wife (Mitsuko Sakuramachi) tries to patch things up, she gets herself killed. Nakai still urges caution, but Matsuda, by now in no mood to listen, bursts into a gang succession ceremony and demands justice. Instead, Senba punishes him with expulsion from the gang and orders him to whack Nakai. Though Nakai has been a selfless ally, Matsuda feels obliged to obey Senba, who has been like an uncle to him. But Senba feels no obligation to anything but his own ambition.

The lion made him do it. Koji Tsuruta is ready to burst into action in a poster for *Bakuchiuchi Socho Tobaku* (Big Gambling Ceremony, 1968).

CRITIQUE

The fourth installment in the ten-part Baku-chiuchi series, *Bakuchiuchi Socho Tobaku* is considered the crowning glory of Toei's *ninkyo* films. In the March, 1969 issue of *Eiga Geijutsu* magazine, Yukio Mishima described it as a drama that "resembles the ancient tragedies—it breathes with a human reality." But though the film may not approach Sophocles, it exudes the essence of the stoic, self-sacrificing *ninkyo* ethic, rising above standard genre tropes to true pathos, as when Nakai, in obedience to gang code, slips a knife into Matsuda, a man he feels a genuine affection for—and Matsuda, having salvaged his pride, accepts his foreordained death with a smile.

Nakai, in a spectacular display of forbearance, kills four people he had no intention of harming, out of obligation, before he finally explodes and goes after the one who really deserves death: the human slime Sendo. "Would you murder your own uncle? Have you forgotten the way of *ninkyo*?" a cowering Sendo demands. "I don't know anything about the way of *ninkyo*," Nakai replies before he plunges in the blade, "I'm just a low-down killer." A classic line by the best in the business at the gangster game: Koji Tsuruta.

Bakuto Gaijin Butai (1971)

SYMPATHY FOR THE UNDERDOG

Scr.: Fumio Konami, Hiroo Matsuda, Kinji Fukasaku. *Dir.:* Kinji Fukasaku. *Prod.:* Toei. *Main cast:* Koji Tsuruta, Noboru Ando, Tomisaburo Wakayama, Kenji Imai, Rin'ichi Yamamoto, Akiko Kudo. 93 mins.

STORY

Part One: *Oretachi no Rirekisho* (Our History). Gunji (Koji Tsuruta), the former top lieutenant of the Yokohama-based Hamamura-gumi, gets out of prison after a ten-year stretch to find the gang dissolved and its members scratching out precarious livings on the fringes of straight society. The cause of their woes is the Daito-kai, a gang of "economic yakuza" led by the diminutive, imperious Oba and his slick right-hand man, Kaizu. The Hamamura *oyabun* formed an alliance with the Daito-kai, but when the Hamamura gang fought a turf war with the rival Kohokukai, Oba and his gang cynically played one side off against the other, with the aim of becoming the supreme powers on the Yokohama docks. Gunji finally attacked the Kohokukai headquarters alone—and ended up in prison for his trouble.

Gunji rounds up four members of his old gang and goes to Oba to demand 500 million yen for the Hamamura-gumi's contribution to the Daito-kai's current prosperity. Oba, over Kaizu's objections, agrees to Gunji's demand. Ever the politician, Oba would rather neutralize Gunji than fight him. Instead of using the money to reestablish the gang in Yokohama, Gunji proposes to go to Okinawa, where there is still gang territory open for the taking.

Oba faces a threat from another source, however, when Kudo (Noboru Ando), a Kohokukai stalwart, tries to assassinate him. The Daito-kai boss narrowly escapes, while Kudo, though wounded by Oba's men, manages to get away—and ends up at the old Hamamura-gumi headquarters, where Gunji and his crew protect him from the rage of Daito-kai avengers.

Part Two: *Oretachi no Nawabari* (Our Turf). Gunji and the gang arrive in Naha, Okinawa, and scout the local competition. The one-hundred-man Hamateru-gumi runs the docks, while the sixty-man Gushiken-gumi controls the nightlife district. A weasely broker sources U.S. military liquor from a foreign supplier and sells it to the clubs. Meanwhile, the bearish gang boss Yonabaru (Tomisaburo Wakayama) and his thuggish associate Jiru (also known as "Wild Dog") range over the island with their gang of Okinawans and dream of taking over Naha for themselves.

Gunji decides that the broker and his *gaijin*

Life and death in Okinawa. A poster from *Bakuto Gaijin Butai* (Sympathy for the Underdog, 1971), featuring (from left) Tomisaburo Wakayama, Tsunehiko Watase, Koji Tsuruta, and Noboru Ando.

pals are the easiest prey. A barroom shoot-out results in several dead *gaijin* gangsters and the agreement of the terrified *gaijin* boss to let Gunji and his pals run the bar. Gunji and Kudo then go to a sit-down with Hamateru and Gushiken but get into a beef with the latter, and Gushiken ends up with a knife in his belly. A shaken Hamateru agrees to give Gunji Gushiken's territory.

A triumphant Gunji encounters an Okinawan hooker (Akiko Kudo) who reminds him of his old girlfriend—the one who abandoned him after he went to prison. The attraction is mutual. Love does not bloom undisturbed, however; bent on ousting Gunji from Gushiken's turf, Hamateru enlists the support of Jiru and Yonabaru. Yonabaru, who hates Japanese mainlanders, bursts in on Gunji and his crew but is stopped by Kudo's pistol He leaves with a new appreciation for the newcomer's guts.

Jiru is still determined to whack them, however—and leads a night attack on their hotel that Gunji's gang repels with the loss of two members. Gunji manages to capture Jiru, however, and, after a dramatic standoff with Yonabaru's gang in the Okinawan countryside, releases him in exchange for Yonabaru's promise to let them live in (relative) peace.

Part Three: *Oretachi no Kyuteki* (Our Enemies). Kaizu arrives in Naha with a phalanx of Daito-kai gangsters to meet Hamateru. He proposes that the two gangs unite to take over Okinawa, with Hamateru standing to double his current profits. Hamateru agrees, but Yonabaru sees Kaizu and his crew as more foreign invaders. Yonabaru goes to Gunji and asks him whose side he will take in the coming war: that of the Okinawans or the mainlanders? Gunji decides to stand with the Okinawans—while plotting his revenge on his Daito-kai enemies.

CRITIQUE

The ninth of ten installments in the Bakuto (Gambler) series (1964–71) and one of two directed by Kinji Fukasaku, *Bakuto Gaijin Butai* is a transitional film, with a classic theme of righteous revenge but filmed in a contemporary setting in the realistic style that Fukasaku was to later perfect in the Jingi Naki Tatakai (Battles without Honor and Humanity) series.

The film has an incongruous feel, as though John Ford were to plunk John Wayne in the middle of 1960s Manhattan, wearing Raybans but thinking like a nineteenth-century cowboy. Though their greatest triumphs are only recently behind them, stars Koji Tsuruta and Tomisaburo Wakayama both look superannuated. Tsuruta is a waxworks figure in a pair of shades (which he even wears in bed), while Wakayama is a dissolute bear who gets by on his growls. In contrast to his co-stars' tired posturing, former real-life gangster Noboru Ando exudes an ethereal cool that hardly qualifies as acting at all but feels earned—and at least belongs to the decade in which the film is taking place.

The lackluster performances of the two leads may have been due to the absurdity of the material, which mixes classic genre conventions—such as the good gangsters taking on overwhelming odds—and modern weaponry. Jiru and his minions fire off hundreds of semi-automatic rounds at Gunji and his crew, at near point-blank range, miss with nearly everyone—and are finally overcome by one determined gangster with a knife.

Meanwhile the foreigners serve the same function as Asians in old Hollywood movies about the Mysterious East, i.e., as convenient foils for proving the heroes' moral and racial superiority. Nonetheless, the film has Fukasaku's characteristic energy, as well as a firm grasp of the central reality of underworld life: eat or be eaten. But how did Gunji and his quixotic band of losers end up lounging by the poolside at that luxury hotel? This is one of the several mysteries that *Bakuto Gaijin Butai* never satisfactorily explains.

Bakuto Kaisanshiki (1968)

GAMBLER'S DISPERSION

Scr.: Fumio Konami, Norio Nagata. *Dir.:* Kinji Fukasaku. *Prod.:* Toei. *Main cast:* Koji Tsuruta, Fumio Watanabe, Tetsuro Tanba, Seizaburo Kawazu, Harumi Sone. 90 mins.

STORY

In October 1964, a law is passed eliminating the gangs and, soon after, the police swing into action, arresting key members of the Iwasaki-gumi, a waterfront gang in Kamihama (actually Yokohama). The Iwasaki *kumicho* (boss) and his *kigyo kanbu* (manager of corporate affairs) call a press conference to announce that the latter, Karasawa (Fumio Watanabe), is leaving the Iwasaki-gumi to start a legitimate shipping business.

Kuroki (Koji Tsuruta), the Iwasaki *wakaishu gashira* (second-in-command), gets out of prison after an eight-year stretch and meets the Iwasaki *kumicho* (Seizaburo Kawazu), who tells him that the gang has become a legitimate company as well, with the members working as stevedores. Confessing that his health is fragile, Iwasaki asks Kuroki to take over if anything should happen to him. "I know you want to go straight," Iwasaki tells him, "but please consider my offer."

Kuroki meets his old *kobun* (underling), who greet him with open arms (save one youngster, Isao, who does not recognize him) and renews an acquaintance with Sachiko (Masayo Mari), who is now running a successful *gaijin* bar. Kuroki recalls rescuing her from a gang of GI attackers many years ago. "Times have changed," she tells him. He also visits Karasawa, who claims that he has gone straight—but doubts whether his former Iwasaki comrades can do the same. "Once a yakuza, always a yakuza," he says scornfully.

Karasawa, however, is determined not only to leave the Iwasaki-gumi behind but eliminate it as a rival. Knowing that his former *kobun* wants to crush him, Iwasaki rages at Karasawa

when he meets him at a party—and collapses with a heart attack. Kuroki takes over the gang. With dock jobs drying up—the result of Karasawa's machinations—the Iwasaki-gumi is forced to go to Karasawa for work. He gives them an impossible deadline for unloading a ship in the expectation that they will fail and ruin what remains of their reputation.

Kuroki is determined to beat the deadline, but one of his foremen quarrels with a stevedore. When the stevedore retaliates by swinging a load of cargo at his head, the foreman falls from the ship to his death on the dock below. Seeing his body, the Iwasaki men start to thrash the culprit, but the other stevedores come to his rescue, and Kuroki nearly has a riot on his hands. He defuses the situation, but the next morning the stevedores find the corpse of their comrade in the water, beaten to death by Iwasaki thugs. When they attack the Iwasaki headquarters, the police intervene, but not before the mob reduces the building to rubble—and effectively destroys the gang's hope of revival.

Learning that Karasawa is behind their recent troubles, Kuroki decides to restore the fortunes of the gang by challenging Karasawa to a gambling duel. Karasawa refuses the invitation and instead calls the cops down on Kuroki. To eliminate his rival for good, he hires a degenerate addict (Tetsuro Tanba) to pop him. But Kuroki proves hard to discourage or kill. Instead, he becomes more determined than ever to have it out with Karasawa, gangster to gangster.

CRITIQUE

The sixth of ten entries in the Bakuto series (1964–71), *Bakuto Kaisanshiki* updates the conventions of the *ninkyo eiga* to the present day. Once again, Koji Tsuruta plays the virtuous gangster returned to a Westernized, modernized world in which only money and power matter. But in the setting of mid-1960s Yokohama—with the Iwasaki gangsters wearing construction helmets and relaxing at rock bars, and the "economic yakuza" Karasawa wearing tailored suits and spouting modern management clichés—he is less the returning hero than the ghost at the banquet. All he knows are the old ways and all he can do is cling to them as his world crumbles around him. Instead of the usual chivalric fantasy, *Bakuto Kaisanshiki* is an elegy for a dying breed.

The film has more moral shades than the typical *ninkyo eiga*, with members of the good gang going wrong, while the leader of the bad gang is portrayed as an intelligent realist (though he eventually exposes himself as a cowardly weasel). Also, while celebrating the nobility of Kuroki's *ninkyo* code, the film offers little hope that it can survive in postwar society. It is a foretaste of Fukasaku's films of the 1970s, which reveal that code as a sham—and have no place for a Tsuruta, who already looks weary of it all though he is only in his mid-forties.

As Karasawa, Fumio Watanabe does not slither like the usual *ninkyo eiga* villain but instead seethes at the stupidity of his rivals, who refuse to understand that the world has passed them by. While tough enough to be a credible gangster, he is sleekly arrogant as the modern entrepreneur, who knows that to be a success one has to look it—and feel entitled to it. He is an avatar of the coming bubble era.

Blood (1998)

Scr.: Daisuke Tengan. *Dir.:* Kosuke Suzuki. *Prod.:* Nikkatsu. *Main cast:* Riki Takeuchi, Noboru Takachi, Mai Oikawa, Hakuryu, Sei Hiraizumi. 90 mins.

STORY

A hitman, Kizaki (Riki Takeuchi), is about to clip a gang boss, the saturnine Ri (Hakuryu), when the boss's men get the drop on him. While subjecting Kizaki to various tortures, Ri accuses the hitman of selling him out. Dangling from the ceiling like a side of (about-to-be-slaughtered) beef, Kizaki begs for a bullet. Ri, however, has other plans for him—which Kizaki thwarts by making a miraculous escape.

Ri visits Dr. Kamiyama (Noboru Takachi), who has diagnosed him with terminal bone cancer—but has yet to inform him. After being discovered on a riverbank, more dead than alive, Kizaki is brought into Kamiyama's emergency room. The doctor saves his life but tells him he will probably never use his right hand again. The police, led by the determined detective Yoshihara (Sei Hiraizumi), are after both Ri, a kingpin in the Chinese Mafia, and Kizaki, who has been working for Ri under an exclusive contract.

Then Kamiyama's wife Yuki (Mai Oikawa) tells her husband she is three-months pregnant. He is less than overjoyed by the news. He knows that Kizaki is really Takuya Nakajo, a close friend of his youth and Yuki's former boyfriend. He is also aware that Takuya took the rap for a murder the doctor committed in saving Yuki from a rapist and that he owes him for his subsequent career and marriage. Now, Takuya has returned to haunt him.

After Kamiyama tells Ri that he has six months to live—news Ri accepts with a chilling equanimity—a cop questions him about his relationship with his gangster patient. Kizaki fends off a Ri-dispatched killer and escapes from the hospital. Kamiyama offers to hide him—and informs Kizaki that he has married Yuki. Then, Yuki discovers that Kizaki is really Takuya—and tells her husband that she wants to meet him. Kamiyama, tortured with conflicted feelings about his wife and friend, fearful of heat from the police and Ri, starts to melt down.

Then, Yuki is kidnapped by Ri, who has learned about Kamiyama's and Kizaki's pasts. Ri orders Kamiyama to kill his old friend or he will never see his wife again. The doctor reluctantly agrees but can't bring himself to pull the trigger. Hitmen sent from Ri try to finish the job—and one of them ends up killing

Kamiyama. Kizaki survives—and vows to terminate his former employer.

CRITIQUE

A straight-to-video action title starring the indefatigable Riki Takeuchi, *Blood* wants very much to be a John Woo movie, from its friends-who-become-enemies story line to Riki's two-gunned heroics and the shower of bird feathers as his bullets hit their marks. Woo, however, had not only done this sort of thing to death by the time *Blood* hit the video racks, in 1998, but with more energy and imagination.

Even so, scriptwriter Daisuke Tengan and director Kosuke Suzuki manage to raise *Blood* a cut above the usual V Cinema product, though Tengan overly relies on the convenient coincidence and Suzuki, on vertigo-inducing camera moves. In most gangster revenge flicks, good and evil appear in the gaudiest of primary colors. Tengan, however, presents them in subtler shades, while providing his principals with credible motivations for their various eruptions and breakdowns. Also, Suzuki gives the film the polished look of a more generously budgeted feature, while injecting an arty touch or two, such as filming Kizaki's escape from Ri's executioners entirely in a frontal long shot, in semi-darkness, somewhat like a Balinese shadow play.

Meanwhile, Riki Takeuchi glowers and growls as he does in dozens of other V Cinema cheapies, though he provides a few surprises, as when he buys guns from a foreign dealer in accented but natural-sounding English. The best performance, however, is that of Sei Hiraizumi as Yoshihara, who brings a bedrock integrity and weary dignity to what could have been a standard, dogged-detective turn.

The film's worst mistake is using young actors for the flashbacks who look nothing like Takeuchi and Noboru Takachi. Who, especially, could replace Takeuchi—and his utterly distinctive quiff?

Bo no Kanashimi (1994)

HARD-HEAD FOOL

Scr.: Tatsumi Kumashiro, Hidehiro Ito. *Dir.:* Tatsumi Kumashiro. *Prod.:* Excellent Film, Unitary Kikaku, Hero, TMC. *Main cast:* Eiji Okuda, Hakuryu. 120 mins.

In *Bo no Kanashimi*, Tatsumi Kumashiro shows one way to revive the flagging yakuza genre: fine-edged character portrayal, dirty realism, and irony-laced nihilism that plunges us into the heart of yakuza darkness.

Bo delivers rude shocks with calculated effectiveness. "You want blood and sleaze?" it seems to say. "We'll show you blood and sleaze you'll never forget." And it does. At the film's premiere at the 1994 Kyoto International Film Festival, members of the audience reacted to certain scenes by covering their eyes or emitting audible groans of dismay (I was one of them). The film's focus, however, is less on extreme sex and violence per se than the dilemma of a yakuza facing a mid-life crisis. After taking fall after fall for his gang and spending eight years in the slammer, Tanaka (Eiji Okuda) feels that it's payback time. Instead, the boss gives him the back of his hand. The old boy's favorite is Kurauchi (Hakuryu), a smooth-talking, fashionably dressed "economic yakuza" who believes in making yen, not war.

Tanaka, however, is a warrior of the old school. He may look like a rumpled middle-aged salaryman (a young woman he wants to turn out as a hooker tells him he looks like a "department manager at an electronics company"), but Tanaka still breaks heads with the best of them. Jumped by two *chinpira* from a rival gang, he reduces his attackers to heaps of whimpering flesh, while barely breaking a sweat.

The boss appreciates Tanaka's talent for violence but also fears him. After treating him to dinner at a fancy restaurant, the boss suggests that Tanaka set up his own subgang under the umbrella of the *honke* (main gang). Tanaka, rightly, sees this as a ploy to ease him aside and give Kurauchi a clear path to the gang succession. He decides to fight back.

A film that turned out to be Kumashiro's last—he died soon after its 1994 release—*Bo* is too episodic in structure, too distracted by its various subplots to be a well-made gang movie; but it gives us, in Tanaka, an antihero who is as fascinating in his human complexity as he is strange in his habits and repulsive in his actions. Somewhat stir-crazy after all the years in prison, Tanaka talks to himself constantly, giving us a running monologue on his plans, suspicions, and fears. He coolly orders the murder of a skin-headed spy for a rival gang and, together with his housewife mistress, plots to corrupt a beautiful young woman with amphetamines and sex. In his struggle against Kurauchi, he is even capable of planning his own knifing and, after the deed is done, sewing up the gaping wound.

But though scary and brutal, Tanaka is without pretensions, has no use for authority or conventions, and adheres strictly to his own yakuza code. He is the antihero's antihero, down to his close-cropped (and very hard) head—and his skill at tying off a suture. Eiji Okuda can be the glummest of actors—one feels like handing him a prescription for Prozac—but in Tanaka he has found a role suited to his talent for understatement and emotional honesty.

But though *Bo no Kanashimi* may offer a vivid portrayal of a gangster's inner life, it is not always a pleasant film to watch, unless your idea of erotic fun is a woman exciting herself to orgasm while her lover describes a stabbing in gory detail. But whether you giggle, slaver, or walk out in disgust, *Bo no Kanashimi* will leave an impression. After seeing this movie, I have a new appreciation for the infinite variety of human sexuality—and the possible uses of a needle and thread.

Brother (2000)

Scr./Dir.: Takeshi Kitano. *Prod.:* Office Kitano. *Main cast:* Takeshi Kitano, Omar Epps, Claude Maki, Masaya Kato. 114 mins.

Despite its Los Angeles setting and the presence of American actor Omar Epps in a starring role, *Brother* is all Takeshi Kitano in nearly every frame, meaning about as non-Hollywood as you can get. Instead of Hollywood hyperkineticism, Kitano opts for the same quirky mix of frontal compositions and elliptic editing, minimalist dialogue and uninflected acting, brutal violence, and pawky comedy that have characterized his style for more than a decade. The typical Hollywood action film is all extroverted expression, the typical Kitano film, all introverted compression—and never the twain shall meet.

At the same time, he has included nearly the entire catalog of clichés that have characterized Japan to the West since the heyday of "yellow peril" pulp, including amputated pinkies, a disemboweling, a severed head, a suicide, and, in one memorable scene, broken chopsticks jammed up the nose of a rival hit man. Just about all that's missing is a *banzai* charge and *kamikaze* attack (though the film, considerately, furnishes near-equivalents). It's hard, however, to imagine American mall rats tuning in to Kitano's brand of bleak macho romanticism. They may buy the severed digits but not the chopped-up narrative or chopped-down performances. Culturally, this film is a plate of squid sushi in a soul food restaurant.

The hero is Yamamoto (Kitano), a yakuza subboss who is left with two choices after a defeat in a gang war: get whacked or get lost. He decides, wisely, to fly to Los Angeles to find his long-lost, half-brother Ken (Claude Maki). On his first day in L.A., however, he gets involved in a street beef with an African-American man nearly twice his size, who tries to shake him down for $200. Grabbing a broken bottle, Yamamoto cuts his opponent a new eye socket

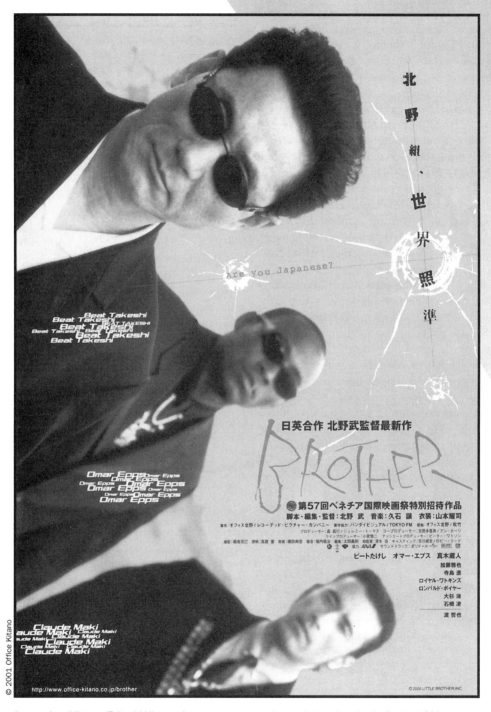

International lineup. Takeshi Kitano plays a gangster on the run in Los Angeles in *Brother* (2001). Omar Epps (center) and Claude Maki co-star.

and goes on his way, without having changed his expression or mussed his black designer suit (courtesy of Yohji Yamamoto).

Speaking not a word of English—or hardly a word, period—Yamamoto quickly tracks down Ken, who is dealing drugs with a black gang. One gangster, Denny (Omar Epps), is wearing an eyepatch and greets Yamamoto with a suspicious stare. This bad moment passes, however, when Ken assures Denny that his big brother didn't do the deed. "All Japanese look alike," he jokes. This, as it turns out, is the beginning of a beautiful friendship. Yamamoto, whom everyone is soon calling "Aniki" (older brother) in imitation of Ken, establishes his tough-guy credentials by clipping members of a rival gang.

With Aniki as the muscle and brains, Ken and his homies become powers in the drug trade, as well as allies with the handsome, ruthless Shirase (Masaya Kato), the gang lord of Little Tokyo. Instead of battling roaches in a crummy apartment, they are living large, cruising the streets in a stretch limo and shooting hoops in a spacious penthouse office. Aniki, however, wants to take on the Italians, who still hold the keys to the drug kingdom. He wants, in short, to live his version of the American dream. Once war is declared, it's hell in the Pacific all over again.

Brother has its moments of lyricism and pathos, as well as a few laughs and chills, but it never develops momentum either as a thriller or an essay on East-West friendship. Aniki rarely ventures from his shell (save to explode), while Denny never becomes more than a trash-talking sidekick. The ending, which aspires to soul-wrenching catharsis, is simply an embarrassment. Kitano may have gone to America, but he clearly needed to get out more.

Burai Yori Daikanbu (1968)

GANGSTER VIP

Scr.: Kaneo Ikegami, Keiji Kubota. *Dir.:* Toshio Masuda. *Prod.:* Nikkatsu. *Main cast:* Tetsuya Watari, Chieko Matsubara, Mitsuo Hamada, Tamio Kawachi, Kyosuke Machida, Kayo Matsuo. 93 mins.

STORY

Goro Fujikawa (Tetsuya Watari) goes to prison after stabbing Sugiyama (Kyosuke Machida), a hitman for the Ueno-gumi—thus repaying an obligation to the rival Mizuhara-gumi. Sugiyama, however, was Goro's senior and friend at the reform school where they both spent much of their boyhoods.

When Goro gets out after three years, the gang boss, Mizuhara (Michitaro Mizushima) and one of his lieutenants (Mitsuo Hamada) welcome him warmly, but the gang itself is in sad shape. Then, after a miraculous recovery, Sugiyama gets a cool reception from the Ueno gang and learns that his lover (Kayo Matsuo) has been forced to sell herself into prostitution. Angered at what he considers ingratitude, Sugiyama leaves the gang.

Meanwhile, Mizuhara and Ueno (Yoshio Aoki) call a truce to their war, but as a peace condition, Ueno demands that Mizuhara cut Goro loose—and Mizuhara agrees, for the survival of the gang. Now that they are both free agents, Goro and Sugiyama renew their friendship.

Yukiko (Chieko Matsubara), a runaway girl, attracts a gang of Ueno *chimpira* with impure intentions, but she is rescued by Goro—and starts to pursue him. Goro rejects her as unsuited for the yakuza life, but she remains determined. Finally, he decides to go straight and live with her. They are about to leave Tokyo together with Sugiyama and his lover, but at the station they are attacked by Ueno gangsters and Sugiyama dies protecting Goro. Then, another Mizuhara gangster who wants to follow in Goro's footsteps and leave the gang is killed.

Goro flees with the two women, but Ueno gangsters are in hot pursuit.

CRITIQUE

The Burai series, of which *Burai Yori Daikanbu* is the first installment, was based on the memoir of Goro Fujita, a real-life gang boss, with Tetsuya Watari playing Goro. Unlike the gangsters of Toei's *ninkyo eiga*, who lived and died by the *giri-ninjo* code, Goro is a lone wolf, who makes up the rules as he goes along. Although *Burai Yori Daikanbu* follows the general genre pattern, the big fight scene at the end is not the usual cathartic, precisely choreographed ballet (featuring Ken Takakura as the prima), but a free-for-all brawl, with Tetsuya Watari fighting in a downpour with the desperation of a cornered cat. By the end, he is muddied and bloodied but still standing, if barely, a cat who has clawed his way to an uncertain victory.

This feral quality, combined with youthful looks, set Watari apart from Toei's top yakuza stars, who were older and belonged to a different era. Chieko Matsubara, a refugee from Nikkatsu's *seishun eiga* (youth movies) who plays Watari's love interest in the film, underscores this difference with her air of unsullied purity and innocence. Watari, however, plays Goro in a dark, fatalistic funk, perhaps the result of battling serious illness at what should have been the height of his career. Call it Nikkatsu noir.

Chinpira (1996)

Scr.: Shoji Kaneko, Toshiyuki Morioka. *Dir.:* Shinji Aoyama. *Prod.:* Taki Corporation, Tsuburaya Eizo. *Main cast:* Takao Osawa, Dankan, Reiko Kataoka, Chikako Aoyama, Ryo Ishibashi, Susumu Terajima. 100 mins.

STORY

Yoichi (Takao Osawa), a tall, rangy *chinpira* from Shikoku who looks like a college boy gone bad, gets into a fight with a flame-haired junkie in a club toilet. When Yoichi's boss, Otani (Ryo Ishibashi), hears that the junkie has left his set of works in a stall, he drives a chopstick into his ear—and draws it out bloody. The club manager, Michio (Dankan), takes a liking to the gutsy Yoichi, while Yoichi is attracted to Yuko (Reiko Kataoka), the girlfriend of Masao (Susumu Terajima), a gang *aniki* (senior).

Yoichi gets into trouble for not properly greeting Masao on the street. Later, at the gang office, Masao tries to punish Yoichi for his presumption, but his victim-elect resists the attempt—a violation of the gang code that rouses Masao to fury. After this bruising encounter, Yoichi tells Michio he is ready to quit, but Michio, while admitting he could never become a gangster himself, urges Yoichi to wait.

One evening Yoichi encounters Masao and Yuko in a parking lot in the midst of a lover's quarrel. He beats up Masao and, after the chastened gangster speeds away in his car, confesses his feelings to Yuko—and she reciprocates. Then, Yoichi and Michio go into business as bookies with Otani's backing. Michio develops a crush on Otani's slinky wife, Miya (Chikako Aoyama), but does nothing about it, while Yoichi gets into a bar fight with Masao that Yuko breaks up by pouring water on the combatants. Despite the gap in their ages—Michio is thirty-five to Yoichi's early-twenties—they work well together, after a rough start, and are soon shaking down a welshing customer with practiced ease.

Michio finally finds himself alone with Miya, who loses no time in seducing him. She asks him why he never became a yakuza. "I'm too scared," is his answer. Soon after, Yoichi and Yuko talk about starting a new life together. Yuko wants him to leave the gang and the city, but Yoichi resists.

Masao becomes a made man and a subboss in Otani's gang. Not long after, when Yoichi goes to Otani's apartment on business, Otani stabs him with a sword. This arrogant kid needs to be taught a lesson, Otani has decided. Tending to his wound, Yuko again begs him to go straight, but Yoichi refuses.

Otani rages at Miya for her suspected infidelity, but before he can learn the truth, he ends up dead—and Yoichi and Michio realize that they have to make their respective moves—or lose the chance forever. Michio steals the gang's money, perhaps to keep Miya in the manner to which she is accustomed— and Masao and his crew are soon on his trail.

CRITIQUE

A remake of a 1984 Toru Kawashima film of the same title and based on a script by movie Dead Legend actor Shoji Kaneko, Shinji Aoyama's *Chinpira* resembles Kaneko's 1983 gang drama *Ryuji* in its plotless structure and its outlaw hero Yoichi, a *chinpira* from Shikoku who casually but stubbornly defies gang rules and dares anyone, senior or no, to stop him.

Aoyama's take on the story of Yoichi and his friend Michio—a middle-aged punk too timid to make the leap to full-fledged yakuza—is coolly minimalist, but not in the style of Takeshi Kitano, with his peculiar mix of black humor and shock violence. Instead, Aoyama presents moments of emotional transformation amid the pettiness and grimness of gang life in an understated manner reminiscent of directorial idol Robert Bresson. Aoyama's lead, Takao Osawa, is in the Bresson mold: male-model handsome but somehow hollow and bland, even in his rages. As Yoichi, he projects an arrogance that comes from not only being the biggest babe magnet in the room but being able to thrash the tough guys who mistake his prettiness for weakness.

In the hands of most directors, a character like Dankan's Michio would be comic relief: the gang wannabe who becomes absurdly attracted to the boss's woman. Aoyama, however, takes him seriously—and his quirky brand of courage (or foolhardiness) compliments Yoichi's and gives *Chinpira* another narrative arc

—the turning of this worm propels the film to its climax.

Kaneko's portrait of a doomed gangster in *Ryuji* may have a documentary-like power, but Aoyama's odd couple have a poignancy of their own. Misfits in the gang world, they try to build one of their own, without quite realizing that the walls are closing in.

Chinpira (2000)

CHINPIRA/TWO PUNKS
Scr.: Masaya Ishikawa, Koki Hirayama. *Dir.:* Rokuro Mochizuki. *Prod.:* Groove Corporation. *Main cast:* Kazuki Kitamura, Tomoro Taguchi, Yoko Hoshi, Naoto Takenaka, Akaji Maro, Kiyori Miyamae, Hiroyuki Nagano. 109 mins.

STORY
Osamu (Kazuki Kitamura) is putting up stickers for a call girl service, when he sees punks chasing a girl, Keiko (Yoko Hoshi). He rescues and takes her to his girlfriend Yumi's apartment. When Yumi (Kiyori Miyamae) returns from her job as a club hostess, she is not pleased to find the newcomer—and that night makes noisy love to Osamu as a way of asserting her claim, while the girl listens silently on the couch.

The punks find Keiko and Osamu, but he saves her from their clutches again. When one, who claims to be her boyfriend, says he has lost face, Keiko bites off part of her little finger to compensate.

Keiko soon leaves the apartment but is caught and returned to the boss (Hiroyuki Nagano) of the Tsukishima gang. Funami (Tomoro Taguchi), Osamu's boss, whose gang belongs to the boss's organization, tries to extort money from an executive (Ren Osugi) that Funami accuses of insider trading. Meanwhile, Osamu discovers a young girl at the beach trying to kill her cat. He finishes the job for her— and she tells him she wants to sell her virginity to the highest bidder. Osamu agrees to help her.

A hitman tries to whack the boss as he comes out of a club with Keiko. A rival gang is apparently making its move, with support from a Kansai mob. Funami plans strategy with an elderly gang advisor (Akaji Maro) and later consults with a powerful boss (Naoto Takenaka), who is taking a neutral position. "Gangsters," he says, "will be gangsters." Funami, a rational type, is getting tired of the crazy yakuza life and tells Osamu he is not cut out for it. Osamu agrees.

Osamu tells the young girl, Yayoi, that he will pay her 300,000 yen to have sex with him. She rejects him—exactly the reaction Osamu was hoping for. Not long after, a client at a club where Yumi works as a hostess asks her to become his mistress for 300,000 yen a month. She says she will consider it. Keiko is infatuated with Osamu, while the boss is infatuated with her. When Funami learns that she has been calling Osamu on her mobile phone, he tells Osamu to get another one. He also warns him not to work behind his back.

The boss, who remains in the dark about Keiko's feeling for Osamu, calls him into his room and orders Osamu to make love to Keiko who, he says, "wants a real man." Reluctantly, Osamu complies as Keiko goes into ecstasies and the boss looks glumly on. Osamu meets the young girl Yayoi again, and she asks him what he sees in sex. He tells her that when she becomes an adult she'll understand—but there's no hurry.

A war threatens to break out when a hood from a rival gang is hit. Funami tries to keep the peace with a payment to the wounded man. But he can't keep the lid on indefinitely; another hitman makes an attempt on the boss's life—but Osamu stops the bullet. Funami suspects a rat, a lieutenant in the Tsukishima gang who has been talking to the enemy.

Keiko comes to visit Osamu at Yumi's apartment—and gets a cold reception from Yumi. Soon after, Keiko escapes from the boss's clutches; taking out a gun, she orders the boss's driver to take her to the station. The boss blows up at Funami and Osamu and threatens them with expulsion from the gang. Osamu, however, only wants to follow after Keiko.

CRITIQUE

Based on a *manga* by Ayumi Tachihara, *Chinpira* is yet another of Rokuro Mochizuki's meditations on a loser who would finally rather be a lover than a gangster. But unlike his previous films on this theme, such as *Shin Kanashiki Hitman* and *Onibi*, his hero is not a battle-weary veteran of the gang wars but a *chinpira*—an apprentice gangster. Whereas Mochizuki's middle-aged heroes knew the gangs' *jingi* code, even though they were less than strict in honoring it, Osamu is loyal to the Tsukishimagumi boss the way he would be loyal to a manager at McDonald's if he were a burger flipper. He has a stronger relationship with Funami, his immediate boss, but acts less like a *kobun* than Funami's cheeky younger brother—to Funami's displeasure.

As played by Kazuki Kitamura, the nearest the Japanese gang film has come to Brando, Osamu glides through the gang world with an insolence that is at once knowing and boyish—a combination women find irresistible. Though forever either in trouble or on the verge of it, he has just enough wit to avoid serious—or fatal—consequences.

Unlike Tomoro Taguchi's Funami, a normal type who tiptoes uneasily around the childishly impulsive boss in the interests of his career, Osamu is essentially a drifter who knows he can get by on his looks—and lets the rest take care of itself. There is no tragedy in his dilemma, but there is a certain justice in his fate that makes the ending of *Chinpira* satisfying, if somewhat enigmatic. It is not clear that the damaged Keiko is the love of his life—he may well glide away from her as well—but at least he likes her enough to deserve her. In a world divided between the users and the used, the betrayers and the betrayed, that spark of humanity is worthy of a modicum of happiness.

Choeki Juhachinen (1967)

SENTENCE: EIGHTEEN YEARS

Scr.: Kazuo Kasahara, Shin Morita. *Dir.:* Tai Kato.
Prod.: Toei. *Main cast:* Noboru Ando, Asao Koike,
Hiroko Sakuramachi, Tomisaburo Wakayama,
Shinobu Chihara, Masaomi Kondo. 92 mins.

STORY

The year: 1945. The place: Tokyo. Kawada (Noboru Ando) and Tsukada (Asao Koike) are demobilized soldiers trying to scratch out a living in the rubble, while helping the families of their dead comrades. Naturally, they turn to the black market, selling rice and other stolen goods, with the U.S. military a prime target. Then, they are caught red-handed at a heist and, with the cops closing in, Kawada selflessly helps Tsukada make a getaway. He ends up in prison, while Tsukada launches a company with himself as president. His aim—to build a cooperative market for the members of his army unit's Survivors' Association.

While in prison, Kawada carries a torch for Hisako (Hiroko Sakuramachi), the pure-in-heart younger sister of one of his dead comrades. He also gets on the wrong side of Funawaka (Tomisaburo Wakayama), a brutal, corrupt guard, and Funawaka's prisoner cronies. Kawada ends up in solitary, while Tsukada, now more of a gangster than a businessman, rakes in the yen and starts to take more than a friendly interest in Hisako.

The widows and mothers of the Survivors' Association? Tsukada sells them out with nary a second thought, until one elderly woman commits suicide out of despair. When Kawada hears about Tsukada's double dealing, he calls him on it. Kawada coolly replies the world has changed while Kawada has been in prison— and business is business. Kawada flies into a

rage and his one-time friend becomes an enemy.

Ken'ichi (Masaomi Kondo), Hisako's wild younger brother, is thrown into the same prison as Kawada. The kid quickly gets himself into trouble with both the guards and inmates for his unruly ways and, though Kawada tries to protect him, he is nearly beaten to death. Ken'ichi's savior is an idealistic young prison official determined to fight the corruption and cruelty of Funawaka and his kind (including the prison warden).

When Tsukada fails to seduce Hisako—she is waiting faithfully for Kawada's release—he resorts to skullduggery, telling Ken'ichi that Kawada had his lustful way with his sister. Ken'ichi goes on the attack, but Kawada keeps his cool—and brings the youngster over to his side. Tsukada, however, is determined to have Hisako, even if it means whacking Kawada.

CRITIQUE

The third film Tai Kato directed starring former gang boss Noboru Ando, *Choeki Juhachinen* is loosely based on Ando's own postwar experiences in Tokyo's underworld, with a heavy overlay of violence.

Though Ando is not one of Kato's most charismatic leads—he is a convincing gangster but a wooden actor—Kato brings out his stoic endurance, feral power, and capacity for rage. The strongest performance in the film, however, is that of Masaomi Kondo as the suicidally defiant Ken'ichi. Think Paul Newman in *Cool Hand Luke*, but without the "cool."

Asao Koike is reliably villainous as Tsukada, though his underhanded attempts to steal Hisako and kill Kawada are pure melodrama— all he needs is a mustache to twirl. Even so, *Choeki Juhachinen* is the prison movie at its rawest, with Kato's cons and screws more than holding their own against classic Hollywood's. George Raft may flip a better coin than Noboru Ando, but Ando has the cooler scar— and the deadlier stare.

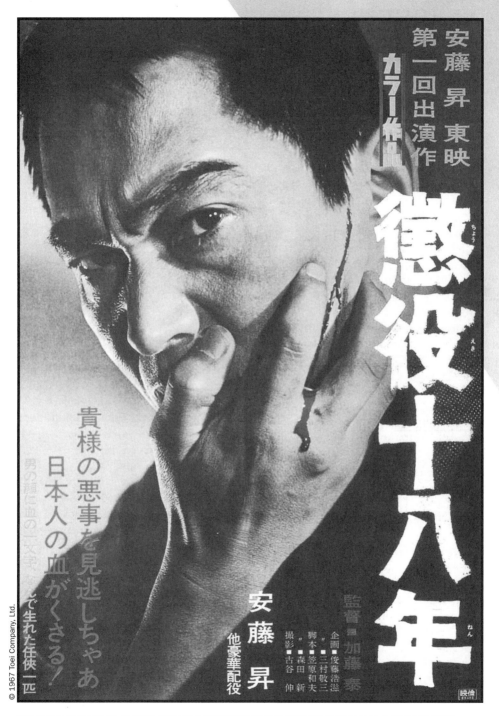

The cruelest cut of all. Noboru Ando in a poster for *Choeki Juhachinen* (Sentence: Eighteen Years, 1967).

Chuji Tabi Nikki (1927)

DIARY OF CHUJI'S TRAVELS

Scr./Dir.: Daisuke Ito. *Prod.:* Nikkatsu. *Main cast:*
Denjiro Okochi, Eiji Murakawa, Hideo Nakamura,
Motoharu Isogawa, Kichiji Nakamura, Seinosuke
Sakamoto, Naoe Fushimi, Ranko Sawa, Asako Mi-
tsuyama. 94 mins.

The only existing version of the long-lost trilogy by Daisuke Ito, *Chuji Tabi Nikki* (Diary of
Chuji's Travels) contains an episode from Part
Two and half of Part Three. The hero, Kunisada Chuji, was based on a real-life Edo era
gambler whose exploits made him the subject
of story and song—a latter-day Robin Hood,
albeit one who came to a more tragic end.
Chuji was born in 1810, the second son of a
farmer in Kunisada Village, in today's Gunma
Prefecture. At the age of seventeen, he killed a
man in a quarrel and, fearing that his family
would also be punished for his crime, ran away.
Drifting to Kawagoe, in today's Saitama Prefecture, he apprenticed himself to a powerful
gambler named Omaeda. Using his wit, charisma, and formidable fighting skills, Chuji became a boss gambler himself.

In 1836, when Chuji and twenty of his men
were traveling to Shinano, a province in today's
Nagano Prefecture, they got in a fight with
guards at a barrier checkpoint. Though surviving this altercation, Chuji became a fugitive—
and lived on the run for nearly thirteen years.
In 1849, tiring of his long travels, he returned
to his home province, where he suffered a
stroke. When the authorities got wind of his
whereabouts, they arrested him in the summer
of 1850 and took him to Edo. There, he was
tried, convicted, and sentenced to death. Early
in 1851, he was crucified at the same barrier
checkpoint he and his men had attacked so
many years ago.

Chuji Tabi Nikki is based on a *kodan* center-
ing on Chuji's final fugitive days and conclud-
ing with his arrest. Considered the finest
period drama of the silent era, it was lost for
many years, until eight of twenty-six reels were
discovered in 1991 and restored by the Japan
Film Center. As the first of the surviving reels
begins, Chuji (Denjiro Okochi) is working as a
head clerk (*banto*) for a rich sake merchant,
Kihei (Motoharu Isogawa). Ginjiro (Eiji Murakawa), the merchant's son and heir, is a wastrel
and constant worry. Meanwhile, the merchant's
beautiful daughter Okume (Ranko Sawa) is en-
amored of Chuji, who is tempted to return her
affections. He would never think, however, of
betraying his master's trust. Instead, Chuji loyally serves his interests, including bailing the
son out of trouble at a gambling den run by an
evil yakuza.

When Chuji's true identity is revealed,
Kihei apologizes for treating such a famed outlaw as a mere clerk. Chuji, on the other hand,
expresses his wish to grow old and die in his
master's service. It is not to be—he must flee
before the authorities come to arrest him.
Chuji, however, is in poor health. Though he
manages to cut his way out of town, he suffers
from attacks of palsy and is forced to stop in
Akagi, in today's Gunma Prefecture. When
Chuji's men hear the news about his flight, they
rally around him, as does his long-suffering
lover, Oshina (Naoe Fushimi).

Laying the invalid Chuji on a pallet, his
men carry him from a temple where he has
been staying to Kunisada Village—his birth-
place. Worried that a traitor among them may
give away Chuji's hiding place, his men move
him to a storehouse at Jokoin Temple. The police are alerted, however, and surround the
storehouse. Chuji's men battle valiantly—but it
is no use: they are too few and the police are
too many. Determined to fight it out to the
end, they gird for the enemy's final charge.

As played by Denjiro Okochi, among the
most popular of the early *jidai geki* (period
drama) stars, Chuji is a figure of great natural
dignity and authority—but one far removed
from the wooden samurai stereotype. Though
capable of piercing intensity—his large, staring

eyes communicate volumes while his slab of a face moves not a muscle—he could unwind for a clownish romp with children or a tender, if awkward, pas de deux with the sake merchant's daughter.

But though the pathos of Chuji's end—and Okochi's skill in portraying the dying outlaw at bay—was key to the film's success with its contemporary audience, among the most impressive scenes for the modern viewers are those displaying cinematographer Hiromitsu Karasawa's bravura camera work. In action scenes, Karasawa races along with the contestants, breathlessly capturing the rush and clash of battle.

There is much formal beauty of a quieter sort as well in the movie, including an extended sequence among rows of huge empty sake barrels that seems to unfold in a strange dream. Dwarfed by their gargantuan set, the actors begin to describe circles themselves—children even play a game of ring-around-the-rosie. Simply to advance his plot, Ito could have chosen a more generic setting, but the barrels give the scene's main players—Chuji and Okume—a grander, if more desolate, stage for their fumblings at passion.

Intended as popular entertainment, *Chuji Tabi Nikki* is also an eloquent expression of an aesthetic that was to vanish with the coming of sound, though both Ito and Okochi were to survive the transition to the new medium. The story of Chuji did as well, including the 1960 Senkichi Taniguchi film *Kunisada Chuji* (The Gambling Samurai) starring Toshiro Mifune. Still, Ito's version, with Chuji resisting arrest to his last chilled breath, remains the benchmark—and makes it easier to understand why authorities of a later decade decided that Chuji and similar romantic outlaws were not fit heroes for a nation about to march obediently—and disastrously—to war.

Dead or Alive: Hanzaisha (1999)

DEAD OR ALIVE

Scr.: Ichiro Ryu. *Dir.:* Takashi Miike. *Prod.:* Daiei. *Main cast:* Show Aikawa, Riki Takeuchi. 105 mins.

Is Takashi Miike a hard-pressed hack, a hard-driven genius, or something in-between? Miike may not be quite the Balzac of Japanese cinema, but is an ambitious, uninhibitedly experimental type who loves his work—and usually succeeds in making it interesting. In *Dead or Alive: Hanzaisha* (Dead or Alive), Miike starts with a fast, funny romp of a montage that presents the Kabukicho of his imagination in all its hyper-sexual and hyper-violent glory, while jump-starting the story with minimum wasted motion and maximum cool.

If only the rest of the film were this good—but it isn't. Instead, Miike eases back into standard genre melodrama, interspersed with inspired moments, then speeds up to a sensational if absurd finish. What, I wonder, could he have done if he'd spent the last year making 105 brilliant minutes (*Dead or Alive's* running time), instead of grinding out four—count 'em—four feature films. What if . . . ?

His leads are Show Aikawa and Riki Takeuchi, who have defined gangster style for the 1990s the way Ken Takakura and Bunta Sugawara did for the 1960s and 1970s. In *Dead or Alive*, Aikawa plays a detective whose beat is Kabukicho, Japan's biggest, baddest nighttime playland. As the film begins, he is investigating the spectacularly gross murder of a gangster in a Chinese restaurant, the latest victim of a turf war between two powerful gangs, one Japanese and one Chinese.

With his spiky hair, his shades, and his attitude, Tajima could pass for the bad guys he is chasing. But he is, as we soon see, a dedicated cop and family man, who is scuffling to raise 20 million yen for his teenage daughter's heart transplant operation in the United States. (He is also a traditional Japanese male, who rejects out of hand his wife's offer to work.)

Shades of difference. Riki Takeuchi (left) and Show Aikawa square off in *Dead or Alive: Hanzaisha* (Dead or Alive, 1999).

cop and one gangster can stop them, both for reasons that go beyond professional ambition and pride. Unwitting allies at first, they become the bitterest of enemies—and finally collide in a showdown to end all showdowns.

Aikawa and Takeuchi play their accustomed tough guy roles with their usual flair. Both have the faces, in repose, of dissipated choirboys, but Takeuchi has the best punk glare in Japanese movies, while Aikawa has a coiled power beneath his bland, weary mask. In *Dead or Alive*, Aikawa stretches beyond the standard parameters of the tough-guy hero to something approaching normal humanity. True, his cop doesn't spend much time with his worried wife and chronically ill daughter, but he at least acknowledges their existence and tries to include himself in it.

The heart of the movie, however, is the gathering clash between Takeuchi and Aikawa, one that Miike builds to *manga*esque proportions and beyond. Either he didn't know he was undercutting the tension he had been building for the last hundred minutes with goofiness straight out of a Dragonball Z cartoon, or he didn't care. A hoot? Perhaps, but Miike is capable of more.

Don e no Michi (2003)

THE ROAD TO BOSSDOM

Scr: Ichiro Otsu, Tsuchihiko Takadataku. *Dir:* Shigeru Ishihara. *Prod:* Sugar Enterprise. *Main cast:* Kentaro Shimizu, Hideo Nakano, Shinya Hashimoto, Kojiro Honjo, Rikiya, Hakuryu, Akira Kobayashi. 125 mins.

Shigeru Ishihara's *Don e no Michi* (The Road to Bossdom) is a throwback to the glory days of the *jitsuroku* (realistic) gang film, in more ways than one. First, several of its veteran actors were active during the subgenre's 1970s heyday. Akira Kobayashi, in particular, was a major star during this period, first for Nikkatsu and

Meanwhile, another drama is unfolding as Ryu'ichi (Takeuchi), the gangster grandson of a Chinese "war orphan," meets his straight-arrow younger brother (Michisuke Kashiwaya) at the airport on his return from the States. The next day, following a wild welcoming party on a rain-soaked beach, Ryu'ichi takes his brother along as an unwitting accomplice to an armored car heist that results in the death of one zealous cop and the theft of several heavy cases of cash. The brother is appalled, but Ryu'ichi is pleased; he now has the money he needs to grab a big share of the drug market and challenge the established gangs for supremacy in Kabukicho.

Two of these gangs, however, are about to end their war and form an alliance. Only one then for Toei. Though he had the looks of a Japanese Elvis, right down to the bedroom eyes and crooked smile, he was a cooler, drier presence than the King in the Jingi Naki Tatakai (Battles without Honor and Humanity) films he made for Kinji Fukasaku.

Second, its story of a gang succession struggle comes from a manga that ran in *Tokushu Manga Topics* from 1978 to 1980. Its creator was Kazuhiko Murakami, a Kansai-based writer whose work, especially his long-running *Showa Gokudoshi* (History of the Showa Gangs), reflected the knotty, violent realities of ongoing local gang wars.

The film, however, unfolds in the present, beginning with a police raid on a gambling game run by the Shimada-gumi. Suspecting a rat, two hoods from the Shimada gang, Sakurai (Kentaro Shimizu) and Kanazawa (Hideo Nakano), grab two suspects—businessmen who were at the game that fatal night. They extract the information that the rival Byakko-kai (White Dragon) gang was behind the snitch. Sakurai and Kanazawa whack Otsu (Shinya Hashimoto), a high-ranking Byakko-kai gangster, in reprisal, but in the ensuing gunplay Kanazawa is wounded—and volunteers to take the rap for both of them.

Naturally, the Byakko-kai is outraged by this turn of events, but their boss, Shirosaki (Kojiro Honjo), decides that the beef is not worth a war. Instead, to calm troubled waters, he calls on Mitamura, the boss of the Mitamura-gumi and a gang world elder.

But just when the two gangs are about to formalize a truce, shocking news arrives: Narita (Rikiya), the bearish, husky-voiced second-in-command of the Shimada-gumi, has been clipped in the elevator of his apartment building by hitmen from the Otsu-gumi, a Byakko-kai subgang. The truce forgotten, the two sides square off for battle.

Wanting to head off a bloodbath that is sure to attract the attention of the police, Sakurai goes to Shirosaki's house alone and asks him to take responsibility for Narita's death by resigning. Impressed by Sakurai's resolve, as well as by the dynamite he has strapped to his body, Shirosaki agrees, on condition that Sakurai join with Shirosaki's successor, the saturnine Ochi (Hakuryu), in gang brotherhood. Shirosaki sees Sakurai as a comer—and wants the Byakko-kai to be on his good side. Sakurai agrees.

Ochi proves to be powerful ally, bent on whacking anyone who threatens Sakurai and his rise to power. His exertions on behalf of Sakurai, however, causes resentment among members of the Shimada-gumi, who decide to mount a coup d'état. The road to the top, he discovers, is rockier than he had thought.

Where Fukasaku's Jingi films were bursting with a wild, chaotic energy that seemed to well up from the tough postwar streets, *Don e no Michi* plays slowly and sedately, with its mostly over-forty cast engaged in more sitdowns than shoot-outs. This may reflect reality—the gangs are graying together with the rest of the population—but gives the film a middle-aged feel.

As Sakurai, singer-turned-actor Kentaro Shimizu tries to make with the macho fireworks, but being a beefy, if deeply tanned, fifty, he lacks a certain spring in his step. He compensates by overacting, but bulging eyes and a clenched jaw do not a yakuza movie hero make. Meanwhile, Shigeru Ishikawa, who was born in 1940 but made his directorial debut only in 1998, with an entry in the Hissatsu samurai action series, adds little in the way of visual pizzazz, though his orthodox, spell-it-out approach makes it easier to tell his large cast apart without a scorecard.

The best thing in the film is Kobayashi, who exudes the sort of relaxed charisma that the camera—and audience—loves. Why have the years been so good to him—and so bad to the *jitsuroku* films that once seemed the genre's last, best hope?

Don o Totta Otoko (1994)

THE MAN WHO SHOT THE DON

Scr.: Hiroji Takada. *Dir.*: Sadao Nakashima. *Prod.*: Toei, Toei Video. *Main cast*: Hiroki Matsukata, Eriko Tamura, Tatsuya Yamaguchi, Isao Natsuyaki, Yumi Takigawa. 116 mins.

Horai (Hiroki Matsukata) has spent the last eighteen years in prison for killing a rival gang's boss. Just before his release, however, a fellow inmate attacks him with a knife. With the timely help of a young con named Kazu (Tatsuya Yamaguchi), Horai survives but knows that someone out there doesn't like him. Who could it be? When he finally gets out, though, he wants, not revenge, but a new life. It will not be easy. The gangster who went with him on the hit, Okido (Isao Natsuyaki), is now the powerful boss of a nationwide syndicate; he wants to do right by Horai, who did time for them both. Through his subordinates, Okido offers him the position of senior advisor, along with the perks of women and foreign travel. Who could resist?

Horai, that's who. He tells Okido's boys that they can keep their meaningless title; he still wants out. Through Kazu, he has found a job as a cook in a night club and, through a chance meeting, a young admirer, a jazz singer named Jane (Eriko Tamura). Happiness beckons.

If this were the true story of an ordinary hood, it might end here. But Horai is not ordinary; he is a throwback to the days when yakuza were still romantic outlaws with a code of honor. When he gets out of prison, his first act is to visit his old *oyabun*'s grave. When he realizes that the pretty woman in kimono offering incense at a nearby tombstone is the daughter of the boss he killed (he is mistaken, but no matter), he bows his head and says that a lifetime will not be enough to work off his *on* (obligation). When he meets the woman later at a club—she is the above-mentioned Jane—he takes the mike and wows the young crowd with an emotion-drenched *enka* (Japanese ballad) number dedicated to his dead wife. This old dude has soul!

He really does. Matsukata swaggers and growls the way John Wayne used to amble and drawl, with a born authority and style. He can also play with his macho dinosaur image, taking a pratfall or two; but when the occasion calls for it, he becomes a demon god in a baggy suit. But even Matsukata's star presence can't overcome the film's idiot plot, juvenile action sequences, and retrograde stereotyping of its female characters. Why, for example, didn't Horai have better information about Okido's acts and intentions while he was in the slammer? The movie paints him as a latter-day Urashimataro (Japan's Rip Van Winkle), but even a slow-learning yakuza would eventually find out that the country's biggest boss had a daughter with said yakuza's supposedly devoted wife.

Why does Jane, the film's representative of modern womanhood, spend so much of the movie in the weepy-clingy mode, mooning after Horai? She seems to exist solely as a wish fulfillment for middle-aged men. Even Kazu's mother (Yumi Takigawa), who runs a high-class *ryokan* (Japanese-style inn) at Kyushu's Unzen hot springs without mussing a strand of her perfectly coifed hair, plaintively tells Horai that *yappari* (as one might expect), the place is too much for a mere woman to manage on her own.

Don o Totta Otoko is meant to be not a realistic portrayal of the gangs or the society on which they prey, but a fairy tale for adults—or rather men who long for a simpler world in which good triumphs over evil (and women know their place). Unfortunately, the film's brand of simplicity has come to look simplistic—and dated. Matsukata deserves better: a growl like his is a terrible thing to waste.

Freeze Me (2000)

Scr./Dir.: Takashi Ishii. *Prods.:* KSS, Nikkatsu.
Main cast: Harumi Inoue, Kazuki Kitamura, Naoto Takenaka, Shunsuke Matsuoka, Shingo Tsurumi.
101 mins.

Chihiro may have made the worst possible choices in men at one point in her life, but this OL ("office lady") with the boyishly cut, copper-colored hair, and cute, punkish-looking face is not about to let her past mistakes ruin her present, which is happier than she once dared hope. Chihiro has a job she likes and a man she wants to marry—a goateed colleague who is good-looking and nice, if a bit slow.

Then, it all falls apart. A gangster named Hirokawa (Kazuki Kitamura) comes calling and forces his way into her apartment. She recognizes him, with horror, as a participant in a gang rape that still haunts her nightmares. With a terrifying insouciance, he tells her that her other two rapists are on their way for a reunion. Their leader, Baba (Naoto Takenaka), has just been released from prison and is eager to take up where he left off.

When her boyfriend (Shunsuke Matsuoka) pays an unexpected visit and hears Hirokawa's version of the rape, he leaves in anger and confusion. Not content to destroy her personal life, Hirokawa then creates a scene at her office designed to get her fired. By this time, the audience is aching for the catharsis of Hirokawa's violent end and director Takashi Ishii delivers. Chihiro now has a body to dispose of and time is pressing—the other rapists might arrive any moment. Then, she notices the big empty space inside her fridge. . . .

Despite the grotesquery of Chihiro's unusual choice of hiding places, Ishii's primary aim is not laughs. Still and silent, Hirokawa has become, as Chihiro notes with delight and awe, ethereally beautiful. In life a monster, in death he has become a frozen specimen of ideal manhood—as well as a perfect listener. Now that her life has been returned to zero, she decides

to keep him. Every girl needs someone she can talk to, at least until the next visitor comes calling.

Kazuki Kitamura plays Hirokawa to chill perfection, with a feral energy and charisma. Shingo Tsurumi and Naoto Takenaka are creep-inducing as the other two rapists, but their moral monsters have a familiarity (Takenaka has been playing variations of his for years) that lessens their impact. It doesn't help that Chihiro uses the same basic murder method for all three. Boiled down, *Freeze Me* is the "Three Pigs" story with the numbers reversed. There is, however, nothing childish about Ishii's vision of evil, which is at once universal and specific. His demons would be familiar to Thomas Aquinas, but their attitudes and actions reflect the reality of today's Japan, where stalkers too often prey unhindered and unmentioned.

Fukushu: Kienai Kizu Ato (1997)

THE REVENGE: THE SCAR THAT NEVER FADES

Scr/Dir.: Kiyoshi Kurosawa. *Prod.:* KSS. *Main cast:* Show Aikawa, Shun Sugata, Chikako Kobayashi, Kazuyuki Senba, Kunihiko Ida, Kiriko Shimizu, Tonbo Zushi. 80 mins.

STORY

A former detective, Anjo (Show Aikawa), works with a team of hitmen. A job goes wrong, with several of the hitmen being hit themselves. Anjo and an excitable colleague, who says he shot a traitor in their midst, deliver the goods—a white box full of drugs—to a yakuza boss, Yamanobe (Kazuyuki Senba). The delivery goes wrong as well, with the colleague and boss ending up dead and Anjo, the survivor, wondering what is going on.

Anjo is pursued by a young detective, Nishi (Kunihiko Ida), who suspects that Anjo was involved in the Yamanobe hit. From his chief

(Ren Osugi), Nishi learns that Anjo's wife was killed five years ago by loan sharks—and Anjo has been taking revenge on them ever since, with Yamanobe being victim number four. Nishi confronts Anjo with his suspicions, but Anjo defies him. "Officially, I no longer exist," he says. "You can't arrest someone who doesn't exist."

Anjo's day job is working at a recycling center. Living alone in a run-down apartment, he makes the acquaintance of an attractive upstairs neighbor, Mitsuko (Chieko Kobayashi), who attends design school. When he asks her for a school catalog from five years before, she refuses him—at first.

Nishi meets Anjo again and asks for his help on a case. "We're on your side," he says, but Anjo is not yet sure he can trust him. Anjo hangs out with Yoshioka (Shun Sugata), a loudmouthed scam artist and the boss of a small gang. But though he plays *shogi* (Japanese chess) with Yoshioka, Anjo is less eager to play along with his schemes.

Mitsuko asks Anjo to be her model for a design she is making. Anjo, though embarrassed, agrees—and their relationship deepens. Soon after, Anjo gets the catalog he has been asking for, and comparing it with a list of names he received from Nishi, finds one he wants: a powerful businessman named Ogasawara (Tonbo Zushi). Anjo, however, becomes nervous when he finds Mitsuko poking around his apartment—the relationship is deepening too far.

Anjo breaks into Ogasawara's house, where he is living with his daughter, Fumie (Kiriko Shimizu). The old man is bedridden and on the point of death, but Anjo mercilessly interrogates him about his wife's murder and decides to spare him—for the time being. When Yoshioka's latest scheme falls through, he rages at his *kobun*—and drives off with Anjo into the countryside. Yoshioka nearly falls asleep at the wheel, but they survive their adventure—and part to meet their respective destinies: Anjo to kill and Yoshioka to . . .

CRITIQUE

The second of the two-part Fukushu video film series, *Fukushu: Kienai Kizu Ato* (The Revenge: The Scar that Never Fades) is hard-boiled action in Kiyoshi Kurosawa's usual manner, with a subdued but edgy mood of menace and controlled but strong performances by the principals, particularly the reliable Show Aikawa. The scattershot plot distracts from the main story thread—Aikawa's relentless search for revenge—but Kurosawa keeps the tension level high. He uses Aikawa's cool ex-detective and Shun Sugata's hot-tempered gang boss as human time bombs, ticking away throughout the film. Sugata's explodes with a bigger noise, but Aikawa's blasts pack a greater chill.

The minimalist stylistics, including the static camera placements, many middle-distance shots, and small number of cuts, as well as the injections of pawky humor, seem inspired by Takeshi Kitano. But the most memorable scenes, including the untimely end of the bedridden businessman, verge on horror—and are pure Kurosawa.

Full Metal Gokudo (1997)

FULL METAL YAKUZA

Scr.: Itaru Era. *Dir.:* Takashi Miike. *Prod.:* Excellent Films. *Main cast:* Takeshi Caesar, Yasushi Kitamura, Yuichi Minato, Shoko Nakahara, Ren Osugi, Tomoro Taguchi, Koji Tsukamoto, Tsuyoshi Ujiki. 102 mins.

STORY

Keisuke (Tsuyoshi Ujiki) is not the bravest or smartest *chinpira* in the gang but is fiercely loyal to his boss, Tosa. One day the boss leaves on unexplained business and gives his wallet to Keisuke—a gesture that touches the young *chinpira*'s heart. Tosa attacks and kills the boss of a rival gang with a sword—and is sentenced to seven years in prison.

While his boss is serving his time Keisuke

proves an inept gangster. When he visits a deadbeat to collect on a loan, the deadbeat's wife chases him away with a knife. When he tries to make it with his hostess girlfriend, he comes up limp. When he is assigned to whack a rival, he clings to his fellow hitman in fear. When he tries to overawe a gang of punks with his yakuza status, they beat him to a pulp. He refuses to quit, however, because he feels obliged to Tosa. When Tosa is finally released from prison, Keisuke is waiting. But when they drive to a reunion with the old gang, hitmen are waiting for them. They whack both Keisuke and Tosa—and everything goes black.

When Keisuke wakes up, he finds himself in a laboratory and, spotting a bathtub full of body parts, decides to make his escape on a bicycle. He is hit by a car and lands in a park—with the same punks who had creamed him before. This time, however, he creams them, with an ease that surprises and delights him. He has somehow become a mean fighting machine! Then, it starts to rain and Keisuke starts to smoke like an overheated engine. He collapses—and wakes up back in the lab.

This time a mad scientist (Tomoro Taguchi) is there, dressed in a yellow trenchcoat and wearing a knowing smile. The scientist tells Keisuke that he is now a cyborg, made from the remains of two bodies (his brain and Tosa's heart) and various metal parts. "I want to make you a full metal human," says the scientist. "I would rather die," Keisuke replies. He changes his mind, however, when he realizes that, with his new superpowered body, he can get revenge on the traitors who killed him and Tosa. The scientist gives him metal to eat, carves a tattoo on the metal patches on his back (to match the one on his skin), and shows him how to survive in his new body. As soon as the tattoo is completed, Keisuke embarks on his mission—which he has to complete before he turns into a robot completely and loses all human feelings—including rage.

He learns, though, that revenge is not as sweet—or as easy—as he had hoped. When a rival gang boss (Ren Osugi) tells him that his own gang was responsible for Tosa's death, he doesn't know who to believe. How could the boss of bosses betray Tosa, one of the best men in the organization? Failing to find answers, he goes to the beach to sort out his thoughts—and his life. There, he encounters Tosa's former lover (Shoko Nakahara), praying by his grave. She says she wants to forget the past and needs Keisuke's help to do so. He wants to respond, physically and every other way, but how can a man/metal monster find human happiness?

CRITIQUE

A straight-to-video parody of *RoboCop*, *Full Metal Gokudo* ranks among Miike's most fully realized comic creations, as well as a film that anticipates much of his later work. Compared with such cinematic outings (and offenses) as *Koroshiya Ichi* (Ichi the Killer) and *Audition*, *Full Metal* is mild; its gore effects are relatively few and laughably primitive (perhaps deliberately so), while the action scenes, though clever (if occasionally clunky), do not reach the *manga*-esque heights of later Miike.

Not that it matters—the film may use the 1987 Paul Verhoeven SF thriller as a template, but it is Miike in every frame. Its story comes less from a dark vision of a crime-ridden near future than Japanese comics and TV shows with a schlump-turned-superhero theme. (Keisuke's new metal body, with its rippling muscles, looks like a steal from *Masked Rider*). Another obvious inspiration is Shinya Tsukamoto's *Tetsuo* films with their visions, set to the pounding beat of industrial noise, of humans morphing into avenging metallic monsters.

Unlike many of his models, the transformed Keisuke remains Keisuke—still a schlump despite his new ability to drop kick opponents into the next decade. Reading "Pinocchio" at the seaside, he longs to become "real," which means being able to feel. But to survive in the Darwinian yakuza world, he

© 1998 Film Partners

Love on the run. Mirai Yamamoto and Takeshi Kaneshiro in *Fuyajo* (Sleepless Town, 1998).

must also grow up—and get smart. *Full Metal Gokudo*, however, is less a deep-think essay on what it is to be human than a zany marriage of genres, by a director with an original comic mind, who is still more interested in entertaining than outraging his audience. In short, a good Miike to begin with.

Fuyajo (1998)

SLEEPLESS TOWN

Scr./Dir.: Lee Chi Ngai. *Prod.:* Kadokawa Shoten/ Ace Pictures. *Main cast:* Takeshi Kaneshiro, Mirai Yamamoto, Sihung Lung, Kippei Shiina, Eric Tsang, Shu Ken. 122 mins.

Fuyajo is a vehicle for Takeshi Kaneshiro, the half-Japanese, half-Taiwanese actor who first came to attention in the films of Wong Kar-Wai and has since become a hot action star. In *Fuyajo* he plays a hustler of his own ethnic background, who becomes mixed up in a Chinese gang war in the Kabukicho entertainment district of Tokyo, while pursuing a passionate, volatile affair with the former lover of the man he is trying to kill.

Based on a best-selling novel by Seishu Hase, who worked as a bartender in Golden Gai, the seedy heart of Kabukicho and met many of the underworld types he later wrote about, *Fuyajo* accurately depicts the ethnic stew that Kabukicho has become, as well as the growing influence there of Chinese gangs. Filming on an open set that recreates Kabukicho down to the barfing salarymen, director Lee Chi Ngai has created a vision of Japan's most notorious playspot at once familiar and strange. This disjunction is not so much from atmospherics—though Lee sees Kabukicho through a filter of gaudy exoticism absent in local films about the place—as approach. His film is a glimpse of a new borderless world in which Japan is merely a backdrop to the war of its Chinese gangsters.

That war, however, has little in common with the usual ultraviolent dustups in Hong Kong films. Instead, *Fuyajo* focuses on the labyrinthine intrigues of its three contending gangs and the love affair of its two principals, saving most of its gunplay for the last fifteen minutes. It is finally more of a romance than a thriller, though its two narrative strands tend to cancel each other out, leaving a not-so-romantic romance and a not-so-thrilling thriller.

The main problem is the lack of chemistry between the two leads. Kaneshiro gets it on with co-star Mirai Yamamoto in scenes of frenetic love-making but doesn't connect with her. For most of the film, he regards her more as an annoyance or a threat than a lover.

As the film begins, Liu Chien-yi (Kaneshiro) is scraping out a living by fencing stolen goods in Kabukicho. A former protégé of Yang Wei-min (Sihung Lung), the don of the local Taiwanese Mafia, Liu went independent when he realized that his mixed blood barred him from full acceptance by clannish gang society. He becomes embroiled in its quarrels, however, when Wu Feng-ch'un (Kippei Shiina), a former fellow gangster, returns to Tokyo after killing the top lieutenant of Yuan Ch'eng-kuei (Eric Tsang), the dome-pated boss of the Shanghai Mafia. Yuan orders Liu to pop Wu in return, with the proviso that if he can't complete the job in three days Yuan will have him popped instead. When Liu goes to his godfather for help, Yang refers him to Tsui Hu (Shu Ken), the hot-headed boss of the Beijing Mafia. Liu quickly realizes, however, that only his survival skills, including his talent for deceit, can save him in the three-way battle for supremacy.

At this worst possible moment, Wu's Nagoya girlfriend, Natsumi (Yamamoto) slinks into his life. Claiming that Wu abused her, she tells Liu that she has come to sell out her old boyfriend—and Feng-ch'un has followed her to Tokyo to stop her. It soon becomes apparent, though, that Natsumi sees Liu as not only an instrument of revenge but a replacement lover. Liu, in turn, wonders if she is playing the same head games with him that she plays with everyone else.

As a mid-shoot replacement for Riona Hazuki, who left the set citing artistic differences with Lee, Yamamoto is so flirty and clingy that she impresses more as a Kaneshiro groupie than a woman of the world plotting seduction. Also, she lacks the aura of danger that made Hazuki ideal for this femme fatale role. Kaneshiro gives no indication that Yamamoto's lack of star wattage bothers him; instead, he ends up supplying enough for both. What should have been a poignant story of love and betrayal becomes a slickly produced, oddly bloodless one-man show.

Gang tai G-men (1962)

GANG VERSUS G-MEN
Scr.: Shigeru Tajima. *Dir.:* Kinji Fukasaku. *Prod.:* Toei. *Main cast:* Koji Tsuruta, Yoshiko Sakuma, Tetsuro Tanba, Shin'ichi "Sonny" Chiba, Tatsuo Umemiya. 83 mins.

STORY
The Tokyo cops are battling a murderous, predatory gang but conventional tactics are getting them nowhere. Then, a veteran detective has the idea of fighting fire with fire by asking a former yakuza of his acquaintance to head up an elite squad of undercover agents. Their aim: penetrate the innocently named Sanritsu Kogyo (Sanritsu Entertainment) and soften it up for the kill. But his man, Tojima (Koji Tsuruta), is running a small trucking company with his wife (Yoshiko Sakuma) and has no desire to return to his old life, even temporarily. Then, the gang wrecks one of Tojima's trucks and roughs up his employees, including his wife's impulsive younger brother, Osamu (Shin'ichi "Sonny" Chiba). Tojima decides the best way to battle his new enemy is to join his old one—the cops.

He recruits a motley crew that includes a former pro boxer, an expert car thief, a veteran safecracker, and a straight-arrow detective with

188 / FILM REVIEWS

a fast draw, while rejecting Osamu, despite his earnest pleas to join. Tojima thinks the kid lacks the cool head needed for dangerous work. He is right about the risks—when Tojima and his crew, posing as the revived Tojima-gumi, start to stake out a territory, Tatsumura (Tetsuro Tanba), the Sanritsu boss, launches a counterattack that nearly takes Tojima out—until Tojima is unexpectedly rescued by a young gangster (Tatsuo Umemiya) intent on whacking him for an ancient grudge. Then, Tojima saves his life and the hood agrees to become his bodyguard.

Tatsumura consolidates his hold on power by clipping the old Sanritsu chairman, who had agreed to become Tojima's ally. Then, Osamu goes undercover by joining the Sanritsu gang. Tojima reluctantly agrees to let him become the G-men's "seventh samurai" but learns that Sanritsu is raking off huge profits by selling bootleg liquor to the clubs and cabarets in its territory. Sanritsu gangsters pursue their Tojima tail in a wild car chase. They shoot the driver, but he survives after Tojima's bodyguard removes the bullet. Deciding to crack down, Tatsumura kidnaps Tojima's wife and demands that his rival get out of the gangster business. Osamu tries to rescue her but is caught. Tojima goes to the Sanritsu headquarters to demand his wife's release but is forced to witness the torture and murder of Osamu.

Tojima then announces that he is breaking up the gang, but his driver steals a car and follows a Sanritsu delivery truck to the factory where they are producing liquor. When Tojima and his gang try to sneak into the building, they are caught by Tatsumura, who has been alerted by a traitor in their ranks. Tied and locked in a boiler room, they can only await their fate. The traitor, however, has a change of heart—and sacrifices himself to save them.

CRITIQUE

The second film in Toei's Gang series and the seventh in director Kinji Fukasaku's career,

Gang tai G-men (Gang versus G-Men) is, with its brisk pace, crisp editing, and vivid performances, reminiscent of the work of Fukasaku's Toei *senpai* Teruo Ishii, who helmed the first series installment and was to become the studio's main director of modern gang films over the next decade. The story may be a pulpy farrago of old Warner crime thrillers and Akira Kurosawa's *The Seven Samurai*, but Fukasaku films it with a youthful energy and verve, together with hints of the realism characterizing his work in later years. The scene of Osamu's death at the hands of Tatsumura and his crew is a brutally effective example of Fukasaku's talent for ripping away the mask, though he does not stint on the macho melodrama.

Koji Tsuruta does his standard turn as the good man driven to desperate deeds, while Tetsuro Tanba is characteristically saturnine as the evil gang boss. One standout is Shin'ichi "Sonny" Chiba as the never-say-die Osamu, licking his lips with boyish impudence even as he is being battered by Sanritsu thugs. Though intended as a reprise of Toshiro Mifune's peasant samurai in Kurosawa's classic, Chiba's performance has an anarchic charge all its own. Think a youthful Jerry Lewis as an action star instead of a comedian.

Also notable is a young Tatsuo Umemiya as the hitman-turned-bodyguard; his carefully sculpted quiff goes well with his pretty-boy face, cool presence, and slick moves. Not yet the pudgy, smart-mouthed smoothy of his later Toei gang films, he is nonetheless a star, even as he tries to play the loyal subordinate to Tsuruta's beleaguered gang boss.

Gedo (1998)

THE OUTER WAY

Scr.: Kazuhiko Kobe, Jun Takada. *Dir.:* Rokuro Mochizuki. *Prod.:* Image Factory IM. *Main cast:* Hakuryu, Amiko Kanaya, Akaji Maro. 99 mins.

STORY

Koichi Himuro (Hakuryu), a veteran police detective, is cashiered from the force as a scapegoat in a *sokaiya* (corporate extortion) bribery scandal, taking the rap for his corrupt superior. Riding a train into the countryside, he encounters a garrulous old man who is collecting trash—Kuwata (Akaji Maro). Getting off, Koichi walks down an empty white road through a field of ripening plants—a symbol of his new beginning.

Satoru Kojima, a young city hall bureaucrat dispatched from Tokyo, is running for office. After Sunday services at a local temple, he makes a speech full of boyish sincerity, and his supporters pass out *omiyage* (presents) to worshippers. Passing by, Himuro watches as they pay off the temple priest in the parking lot. Later, Kojima, a voluptuous young woman, and one of his female campaign workers, Mika Kuwana (Amiko Kanaya), hike to a lonely hilltop, where Kojima photographs the two women in the nude, including poses with dildos and S&M gear.

Back home, Mika is using Kojima's photographs to construct a porno web site—and crying at her own humiliation, when Himuro bursts into her room—and offers her 3 million yen to aid what has become his one-man investigation into Kojima's dirty dealings. Mika, misjudging his offer as a payment for her body as well as her cooperation, disrobes.

Soon after, Himuro happens upon two *chinpira* who have been driven from an old woman's property after unsuccessfully trying to persuade her to sell it. He ends up playing mahjongg with them—and tells them that he will do anything for money. Later, he has a meeting with their boss at the gang office—and encounters the old "cleaning man" Kuwata, who turns out to be a semi-retired gangster. Together, they return to the old woman's house, where Himuro pretends to rout one of the *chinpira* with a pistol. Impressed, the old woman agrees to sell—and Himuro receives a handsome payment for his services (and extracts a similar one for Kuwata).

Himuro becomes a regular visitor at Mika's. She resists the intrusion at first but begins to confide in him, telling him that she is through with Kojima and too far gone into corruption to be saved. Himuro tells her that, as long as she's still worried about it being too late—it's not too late. Himuro continues his campaign against Kojima, even invading his house, tying him up and threatening to rape his wife. When Himuro proves to the wife that her husband is sexually aroused by the rape scenario, she decides to leave him.

The local TV station runs a report on hazardous waste dumping—one of the gang's businesses. The bosses suspect that Kuwata's "clean up" campaign is going to get them into more trouble. Soon after, Himuro tells Kuwata that they ought to leave town. Kuwata refuses; he loves it too much—and wants to "get rid of all the trash here."

Unknown to Himuro or anyone else, Kuwata decides to extend his campaign to Kojima, mailing him a threatening letter—and saying he will expose him to the media unless he comes up with 100 million yen. The gang gets wind of Kuwata's extortion scheme—and asks Himuro to kill him. "You said you would do anything for money didn't you?" asks one boss. "The old man is going to die soon anyway—you might as well be the one to benefit." Himuro is sorely tempted.

CRITIQUE

Though not strictly a gang movie, Rokuro Mochizuki's *Gedo* (The Outer Way) is one of the most incisive and unsparing studies ever made of how the gangs draw the unsuspecting (or all-too-willing) into their orbit—and how closely they have woven themselves into the fabric of Japanese politics, business, and even religion. In most gang movies, the outsider hero operates in a parallel world that has only a tenuous relationship with the audience's own.

Despite its satiric and even farcical elements, *Gedo* offers no such "it's only a movie" assurance. Even Akaji Maro's eccentric "clean-up man" ends up trying to seize the main chance.

Everyone has dirty hands in this film, though Mochizuki provides a ray of hope in Mika, who climbs from the depths of self-abasement by trusting and finally loving the disgraced detective Himuro. Her savior remains an enigma, however. Seemingly disdainful of money and all the corruption it spawns, he is nonetheless irresistibly drawn to the flame of self-annihilation. Playing this all-but-lost soul Hakuryu gives little away behind his bland expression and hooded eyes, while creating sympathy for Himuro's tough, resourceful, and deeply lonely character.

When his final test arrives, in the form of a hit on Kuwata, his decision is not obvious. If Himuro accepts, he will be one with the corrupt forces he has spent the entire film battling against. If he refuses, he is dooming himself to eternal marginality, as the entire community is either tacitly on the side or in the grip of the corrupters. "People like you perform a useful social function," says the gangster ordering the hit. Knowing the society—and himself—as he does, how can Himuro say no?

Gendai Yakuza: Hitokiri Yota (1972)

STREET MOBSTER

Scr.: Yoshihiro Ishimatsu, Kinji Fukasaku. *Dir.:* Kinji Fukasaku. *Prod.:* Toei. *Main cast:* Bunta Sugawara, Mayumi Nagisa, Noboru Ando, Asao Koike, Noboru Mitani, Keijiro Morokado. 92 mins.

STORY

Isamu Okita (Bunta Sugawara) is released from prison after serving a long stretch for violent crimes, including the slashing of a prison yard boss. A fellow prisoner and ally, Taniguchi (Noboru Mitani), gets out the same day and is greeted by his wife, whose face is horribly scarred. Spooked, Okita takes leave of his friend, who has apparently opted for the straight life.

Okita is enjoying a wild session with a massage parlor prostitute when he is rudely interrupted by another client—a *chinpira*. A fight ensues that soon moves outside and involves the *chinpira*'s entire gang. Okita beats them to a standstill—and they all end up drinking together at a pub. As a gesture of friendship, his new friends hire another girl for him—the fiery Kinuyo (Mayumi Nagisa), who recognizes Okita as a participant in a gang rape that traumatized her many years ago. She moves to stab him with a knife, but he wrenches it away and Kinuyo runs out of the club to an abandoned building nearby, with Okita following behind. Here, she reminds him, is where he raped her. His look of contrition softens her—and they end up having sex.

Kizaki (Asao Koike), a veteran gangster, has watched Okita in action and likes what he sees. He approaches Okita with a proposal: they start their own gang, using the local *chinpira* as shock troops to carve out territory. Their two rivals in the town—the dominant Takigawa gang and the insurgent Yato gang, once a Yokohama-based *gurentai*—have reached a modus vivendi, with the former running gambling games and massage parlors and the latter managing a "leisure building." "They've become too peaceful," says Kizaki. "It's time to shake things up."

Okita reluctantly agrees to go along and soon he and his band of *chinpira* are wreaking havoc on the town's coffee shops and bars and beating up any Takigawa gangsters they encounter. The Takigawa *oyabun* (Keijiro Morokado) rages at his men for losing to a mere bunch of punks, but they can't stop Okita's depredations. Finally, Takigawa's hoods corner Okita and his gang, but the boys are saved by the Yato *oyabun* (Noboru Ando)—who steps out of his building with his crew and tells the

Takigawa *daigashi* (gambling house manager), Karasawa (Nobuo Yana) that he is invading Yato territory. Okita is anything but grateful—he doesn't want to be obligated to anyone, let alone a rival like Yato.

Escaping from another inter-gang dustup, Okita encounters Taniguchi, who hides him in his ramshackle house. Soon after, Okita is shot by one of Takigawa's men and carried by his gang into Kinuyo's bar. Takigawa gangsters surround the place, but once again Yato rides to the rescue—and proposes a merger. Kizaki is willing to accept, but Okita, even on the brink of death, resists. Yato nods in understanding: "He's the way I used to be," he says.

At Kizaki's urging, Okita gives in and the two gangs unite, with the newly merged gang, the Sakura-kai, getting their long-desired slice of turf. With peace restored, Okita becomes restless and takes up with a pretty hostess. When Kinuyo finds out, she goes wild, assaulting the other woman and being assaulted by Okita in turn. After a ferocious quarrel, they make up—and enjoy a brief idyll in Kinuyo's wreck of a room.

Then, a Kansai gang, the Saiei-kai, moves into town, with the assistance of the Takigawa gang. Driving through a gathering of these rivals, Okita and his *chinpira* plow into them and Okita insults the Owada *oyabun* (Asao Uchida), the Saiei-kai leader, to his face. Okita refuses to apologize, even after his protector, Yato, presents a cut finger to Owada in contrition. When Yato threatens to expel him if he doesn't bend a knee, Okita says he never wanted to join with Yato in the first place. Soon after, Saiei-kai gangsters begin arriving by plane and train, with the aim of wiping the Sakura-kai out of existence.

CRITIQUE

The sixth and final installment in the Gendai Yakuza series, *Gendai Yakuza: Hitokiri Yota* brought director Kinji Fukasaku to the attention of producer Koji Shundo, who was im-pressed by the film's nonstop action and gritty realism and decided to hire Fukasaku to direct *Jingi Naki Tatakai*, the seminal film that launched the *jitsuroku rosen* boom.

The film also proved a star-making vehicle for Bunta Sugawara, whose performance as Isamu Okita was not only physically explosive but revealed the soul of a gangster who, raised on the streets, could only express himself with violence. As the prostitute he rapes—and falls in love with—Mayumi Nagisa equals him in wildness, though hers is more tinged with desperation. In most on-screen yakuza romances, the power balance tilts toward the male, not so in *Hitokiri Yota*. Nagisa's Kinuyo is more than a match for Sugawara's Okita—the gangster who has never known love or limits. Though often described as a warm-up for Fukasaku's later work, especially the 1975 *Jingi no Hakaba* (Graveyard of Honor), *Hitokiri Yota* is among his strongest statements about the lawlessness of the postwar period—and the children of despair it produced.

Gokudo Kuro Shakai Rainy Dog (1997)

RAINY DOG

Scr.: Seigo Inoue. *Dir.:* Takashi Miike. *Prod.:* Daiei. *Main cast:* Show Aikawa, He Jianxian, Chen Xianmei. 94 mins.

In the 1990s, more Japanese films took on an Asian complexion, as Japanese contacts within the region grew and Asians flooded into Japan in increasing numbers. Takashi Miike's *Gokudo Kuro Shakai Rainy Dog* follows this trend in its Taipei setting and contingent of Taiwanese actors. But instead of simply adding Asian spice to his product, Miike explores Taiwan's underworld from the viewpoint of an insider, albeit one alienated from the human race. He makes no attempt to exoticize or caricaturize his Taiwanese for Japanese consumption. Instead, he

Show Aikawa finds love and death awaiting him in Taiwan in *Gokudo Kuro Shakai Rainy Dog* (Rainy Dog, 1997).

allows them to be themselves, assuming rightly that his gangsters and whores need no cross-cultural filters to be understood. He tells a noirish tale of a Japanese hitman's life that exudes attitude, with spare, stylish atmospherics. Like its hitman hero, *Rainy Dog* makes no excuses and takes no prisoners. Though suffused with macho romanticism, it goes easy on the macho self-regard and self-pity. The ending hits the right note: stark, downbeat, zero cool.

Yuji (Show Aikawa) scrapes out a living as a hitman for a Taipei gang. Living in a shabby apartment and surfing the Internet on his computer, he is a loner who seems to have little need of or use for human contact. When his boss—a crude, dangerous man—calls him his son, his face remains an unreadable mask; all Yuji cares about is the cash. One day a former girlfriend appears at his door and, with a desperate abruptness, leaves him with a boy (He Jianxian) that she claims is his son.

While the boy tags after him, Yuji goes calmly about his business: blowing away a rival gangster who is eating lunch with his family and after collecting his payment, taking home a pretty young hooker named Lily (Chen Xianmei). Meanwhile, the boy is sleeping on flattened cardboard in the rain, snuggling a puppy he found in the street.

Child abuse? Certainly, but Yuji smiles with amusement at the boy's persistence and throws him a towel for his drenched body. When Yuji finds a briefcase full of cash after whacking a rival boss, he even becomes generous, offering to fulfill Lily's dream of escaping to a place drier than her monsoon-soaked homeland. Together with the boy, they go to a lonely beach, with the gang's remaining members in hot pursuit. Taking shelter in a wartime pill-box, they wait for the never-ending rain to stop. During this period of enforced intimacy, they begin to show traces, however faint, of family feeling. Then, the skies clear and the deadly chase resumes.

Rain is a constant presence in the film, both circumscribing Yuji's life and symbolizing his dilemma. Continuing for days and weeks, the wetness seeps, inexorably, into everything. In Taiwan's climate and underworld society, the stranger can never quite come out of the rain. It finds him, and if he is in the wrong place at the wrong time, can kill him. As Yuji, Show Aikawa combines mute stoicism with minimalist charm and cool-dude theatrics, such as the neat way he whips his gun out from behind his white trenchcoat. His best prop, however is his shades. With them, he looks debonairly menacing; without them, he has the face of a dissipated choirboy. Anybody know where I can get a pair?

Gokudo no Ane: Reiko (1994)

GANG LADY: REIKO
Scr./Dir.: Kazuo Komizu. *Prod.:* KSS. *Main cast:* Naomi Kawashima, Katsuya Kobayashi. 90 mins.

Gokudo no Ane: Reiko (Gang Lady: Reiko) would seem to have a progressive story line for a yakuza flick: after a yakuza boss is shot by rival hoods, his young wife takes over the gang and gets revenge. But the movie, we soon see, is utterly traditional in its attitude toward its heroine and her situation. As played by Naomi Kawashima, Reiko is devoted to and dominated by her husband. After he becomes a wheelchair-bound vegetable, she not only ministers to his needs lovingly, massaging his withered muscles and washing his rigid face, but submits her will to his unspoken thoughts. She's like a political wife who, after her husband's death in office, takes over his job, while pledging to continue his policies. (She is, however, occasionally tempted to put him out of his misery.)

As director and scriptwriter Kazuo Komizu makes clear in scene after scene, Reiko is a hot number; we get our first glimpse of her—covered by a muscular tattooed back—in the throes of erotic ecstasy. She later reprises the heaves and moans when she gets a tattoo of her own, out of loyalty to her man; the blend of exquisite pain and passion in this scene will delight S&M aficionados.

Reiko's gang of young, pure-hearted yaku-za, the Tomioka-gumi, battle a gang of bad yakuza, the Kitano-gumi, who shot the Tomioka boss. The baddies' leader (rock DJ Katsuya Kobayashi) is a blustering slimeball who wants to build a resort complex with his ill-gotten gains. Standing in his way is an old peasant woman, Reiko's friend, who owns a strategic parcel of land. When Reiko refuses to use her influence to help the slimeball buy it, he bulldozes the site anyway. Despondent, the old woman leaps off a cliff.

The next outrage is not long in coming. A Kitano-gumi *chinpira* rapes the foreign girlfriend of Kenzo, a hot-blooded Tomioka-gumi stalwart. When Kenzo sees the *chinpira* forcing her into a car after the rape (he wants a second go), he mistakenly assumes that she is cheating on him. Discovering the pair in a restaurant, together with the slimeball and his boys, he blows them away with a homemade gun. But when he pulls the trigger on the slimeball, the gun explodes in his face, killing him. This means war!

Despite the obviousness of the story and awfulness of some of the acting (Kobayashi is the worst offender), the film has its entertainingly bizarre moments. The most bizarre is the final showdown in which the good guys, armed to the teeth, charge the bad guys across an open field, while a bulldozer rumbles behind them (perhaps to clear away the human debris), and Reiko leads a *taiko* ensemble in some rousing martial drumming. Midway through the performance, the drummers don what appear to be white goalie masks, perhaps to deflect flying bullets. Here, I thought, is one Japanese movie not likely to find a foreign audience—unless Woody Allen writes the subtitles.

Gokudo no Onnatachi (1986)

GANG WIVES
Scr.: Hiroshi Takada. *Dir.:* Hideo Gosha. *Prod.:* Toei. *Main cast:* Shima Iwashita, Rina Katase,

Naomi Kawashima stands by her yakuza man in *Gokudo no Ane: Reiko* (Gang Lady: Reiko, 1994).

Akiko Kana, Riki Takeuchi, Kei Sato, Masanori Sera, Masataka Iwao, Mikio Narita, Masao Komatsu. 120 mins.

STORY

Wives and girlfriends of Domoto-gumi gangsters gather at a club to party. Presiding over the festivities is Tama (Shima Iwashita), the wife of Awazu (Kei Sato), a jailed gang subboss. Mako (Rina Katase), her younger sister, is working at another club, where she attracts the attention of a talent agency president, Sugita (Masanori Sera). When he suddenly proposes marriage, the club mama-san warns her that he may not be what he seems. Mako returns home, where she lives with her father, the gruff, chain-smoking owner of a small machine tool shop. A handsome *chinpira* who hangs around the shop is infatuated with Mako, but she will have nothing to do with him.

Tama tries to set up an *omiai* (meeting for the purpose of marriage) between Mako and the son of a rich real-estate company president. Mako resists, but Tama wants her out of the *mizu shobai* ("water trade") world. She also wants her father to give up his business, which is only piling up debts, and retire.

The boss of the Domoto-gumi, the biggest gang in Japan, dies, and a power struggle ensues. The winner is Kakinuma (Masataka Iwao), the gang *wakagashira*. The losing faction forms the Koryu-kai, a new gang, to continue the struggle under the leadership of the wily Koiso (Mikio Narita). Awazu is about to be released from prison. Once considered a candidate for gang boss, he has the potential to change the power equation. Koiso comes to Tama to ask her help in recruiting her husband as an ally, with the promise of making him Koryu-kai chairman. Tama accepts his offer—and becomes a power in her own right.

Mako becomes engaged to the real-estate heir—but is not sure she is doing the right thing. Meanwhile, Koiso is plotting to whack Kakinuma, using an outsider, Sugita, to make the hit. He has the right combination of guts and anonymity. Sugita begins training his men for the job.

On holiday in Hawaii, Mako meets Sugita and goes with him to his hotel room. There, he reveals his gang tattoo—and makes violent love to her. When Mako returns to Japan, she learns that her father's shop had been robbed and the *chinpira* had caught the thief. Mako tells her sister that she can't marry the real-estate heir and confesses that she has found a new man. Tama quickly susses the fact that he is a gangster. Kakinuma is shot by Sugita's crew and taken to the hospital. One of the crew members, Kawase (Masao Komatsu), is arrested at the scene. Mako, who met Kawase in Hawaii, realizes that Sugita was involved in the hit. When she confronts him, he asks her to marry him—and threatens to kill her if she refuses. He finally confesses to the hit—and tells Mako that he wants to be the Japanese Capone.

Sugita and Mako are celebrating their impending wedding with members of the Sugita-gumi when the police arrive to question him about his connection to Kawase. Soon after, Tama visits Domoto's widow—the gang matriarch. She tells Tama that there have been too many victims in the gang war—and that Tama might be the next one. Tama is relaxing in a club with other gang wives and girlfriends when two hitmen come in. Tama shoots at them and they escape.

As the war intensifies, Sugita decides to go to Osaka and lay low. He doesn't want Mako to go with him—it's too dangerous. Koiso's wife (Akiko Kana) pays a call on Tama; she's worried that Awazu is after her husband and asks Tama to intervene. She promises to consider it. Hitmen attack the Sugita-gumi. Mako makes a narrow escape, but several gang members are not so lucky. Sugita confronts Koiso on the latter's yacht, wanting to know who whacked his crew. Koiso insists that he doesn't know—but promises to investigate. Sugita threatens to return if anything else happens.

Authoritative style. Shima Iwashita looks stunning in a red kimono in a publicity still for *Gokudo no Onnatachi: Akai Kizuza* (Gang Wives: Blood Ties, 1996).

Mako goes to Tama to talk about Sugita. Tama tells her he deserves to die—and urges her to find someone else. Mako says she will never give him up—and draws a gun on Tama. Now enraged, Tama dares her sister to shoot and when she can't, they start to fight, punching and tearing at each other in Tama's elegant apartment. Meanwhile, another sort of fight—for the leadership of the gang—is moving toward its climax.

CRITIQUE

Based on a best-selling book by investigative journalist Shoko Ieda, *Gokudo no Onnatachi* may not have been the first yakuza movie to feature women as its main characters, but its combination of sex, action, intrigue, and a rare behind-the-scenes look at women in the gangs made it a box office hit—and spawned the most successful gang film series of the 1980s. Ieda, who had a bit role in the film, proclaimed herself pleased with the result, though the film's treatment of the Osaka gang war, which Ieda herself witnessed as part of her research, was highly fictionalized.

Hideo Gosha, a specialist in costume dramas that celebrate female sexuality, charges the film with more eroticism than the typical yakuza *eiga*, contrasting the earthy, curvaceous sensuality of Rina Katase's Mako with the sophisticated, delicate beauty of Shima Iwashita's Tama, a vision in kimono—but hell to cross. He has less success resolving the glaring gap between these two radically different types, who seem to have come from not only different eggs but different universes.

Iwashita dominates the film, sweeping confidently through a male-dominated world, while refusing to hide her femininity. The obvious parallel is with Junko Fuji's wandering gambler in the Hibotan Bakuto series. Despite her shoot-out with two hitmen and epic brawl with Katase, Iwashita's Tama is less a Fuji-like fighter than a commanding presence, who may use her husband's position in the gang as a stepping-stone to power but is a true leader, not a mere placeholder. One could as easily imagine her managing a corporation as bossing a gang; she has the right combination of intelligence, charisma, and force of personality—an older sister/wife/boss who not only knows best—but how best to get her way. Millions of yakuza movie fans became her willing acolytes.

Gokudo no Onnatachi: Kejime (1998)

GANG WIVES: DECISION

Scr.: Hiroji Takada. *Dir.:* Sadao Nakajima. *Prod.:* Toei. *Main cast:* Shima Iwashita, Rina Katase, Riki Takeuchi, Fumie Hosokawa. 116 mins.

One day in 1986, Toei producer Goro Kusakabe was on the train thumbing through weekly magazines when he came across an article by journalist Shoko Ieda about the lives of gangster girlfriends and wives. Ieda had spent a year living among her subjects, becoming their friend and confidante and having several close encounters with an ongoing gang war. Kusakabe saw that many of the women in Ieda's stories were neither exploited products of the sex industry nor squelched victims of feudalistic relationships but strong personalities who had learned to assert themselves in a macho world. Here, he decided, was a movie.

That movie, *Gokudo no Onnatachi* (Gang Wives), became a hit following its release that November. One reason for its success was its unusual subject matter; another was its realism: *Gokudo* followed the outlines of Ieda's reportage fairly closely. Still another explanation was star Shima Iwashita. Elegant and stately, possessed of a steely will and cool intelligence, Iwashita's gang-boss wife was a match for any yakuza tough guy. After starring in seven of nine series installments and thoroughly implanting her gang-wife image in the public mind, Iwashita decided that the tenth *Gokudo* film, subtitled *Kejime* (Decision), would be her last.

Directed by Toei veteran Sadao Nakajima, Iwashita's farewell performance is of a piece with her others, though she is not playing a continuing character (given the high mortality rate of the male characters in the series, this is understandable). Once again, she impersonates the wife of an Osaka *oyabun* with a swagger and haughtiness that defines the essence of camp. Picture Bette Davis in a kimono. But unlike Davis, who often swept everything before her like a force of nature, Iwashita is an ensemble player who shares the spotlight with several other actresses, notably the voluptuous and equally formidable Rina Katase.

In the latest installment, Iwashita's husband heads the Idei-gumi, a large gang based in south Osaka and three subgangs that have formed a close alliance. One day a premed stud named Ginji (Riki Takeuchi), the boss of a sub-gang, is murdered while working out in a gym. Following this hit, the gang's cohesion begins to erode. Ginji, it turns out, borrowed money from a local trust bank for a resort hotel he was building. Then, the economy turned sour. Drowning in bad debt, the bank went belly up and stopped payment on his loan. Desperate for funds, Ginji used his last trump card: information he had secretly obtained about a 5-billion-yen stash that a gang director had accumulated on the sly.

The question is, who ordered the hit? The cops arrest the hitman, a "guest" member of the Idei-gumi, who promptly snitches on Idei for putting out the contract. Idei's wife (Shima Iwashita) believes that her husband has been set up: Ginji had been like a son to him. But if he didn't order the hit, who did? She decides to find the real culprit and prove her husband's innocence. Naturally, she enlists the support of the other gang wives.

The story serves as yet another star vehicle for Iwashita, while supplying enough action thrills and sexual oomph for the genre's core fans. The film's women are thus a varied lot: the wives played by Iwashita and Katase project an admirable firmness, while a *zaftig* bank teller (Fumie Hosokawa) who becomes the plotter's accomplice is made of baser, more pliable, clay. Those hoping to see their first feminist yakuza film will have to wait. Also, those hoping to revel in ultraviolence will be disappointed. Nakajima may film the bang-bang scenes in operatic slo-mo, but a John Woo he is not.

Nonetheless, the film has Iwashita. Watching her calmly squeeze off a round at an assault weapon-wielding gangster, without mussing a hair of her impeccable coiffure or crinkling a line on her still exquisite face, one has to admire a presence that goes beyond mere acting. Now in the fourth decade of her career, Iwashita is still the reigning diva of Japanese film.

Gokudo Sengokushi Fudo (1996)

FUDOH: THE NEW GENERATION

Scr.: Toshiyuki Morioka. *Dir.:* Takashi Miike. *Prod.:* Gaga Communications. *Main Cast:* Shosuke Tanihara, Kenji Takano, Riki Takeuchi, Marie Jinno, Tamaki Kenmochi, Toru Minegishi, Miho Nomoto, Takeshi Caesar, Mickey Curtis. 99 mins.

STORY

The Yasha and Fudo gangs face off when a Fudo drug runner is clipped by Yasha hitmen. The son of the Fudo boss (Toru Minegishi) gets his own back—and gets his father in trouble with the Nio-kai, the gang that controls all of Kyushu. The Nio-kai overlords tell the Fudo boss he is responsible for bringing the two gangs to the brink of war and demand an act of contrition. Fudo responds by whacking off the head of his son and presenting it to the Nio-kai bosses. Unfortunately, his younger son Riki, still an impressionable boy, is watching in silent horror as Fudo commits this most heinous of crimes.

Time flies and Riki (Shosuke Tanihara) is now a teenager with revenge on his mind. He plans to assassinate the men who ordered his brother's murder to commemorate the tenth anniversary of his death. The means he chooses, however, are most unorthodox, including the use of grade school boys as hitmen, poisoned coffee served by a pretty gas station attendant, and a poison dart that wings its way to its target from the vagina of a schoolgirl stripper.

While all this mayhem is unfolding, Riki is posing as a good student in a rough high school. (His thug of an English teacher, on finding a kid with a racing form, bangs the boy's head against the desk until his face is covered in blood.) At night, however, Riki is the swaggering *wakagashira* of the Fudo-gumi.

The plan works to perfection. Riki even makes the English teacher cower, while recruiting a new ally: a Polynesian man-mountain with the improbable name of Akira Aizome (Kenji Takano). Finally, on the tenth anniversary of his brother's death, Riki and Aizome visit the temple where the twin patriarchs of the Nio-kai hold forth—and Riki reduces them to puree. Now all that is left is to kill his father—but the elder Fudo has plans of his own, namely to hire a pickle-eating hitman named Gondo (Takeshi Caesar) to take out his son. Gondo does his work with a relish—and soon Riki's people are being blown up, blasted through windows, and otherwise dispatched.

Meanwhile, lurking in the shadows, is Noma (Riki Takeuchi), a slick, super-bright Kobe gang boss who plans to take over not only all of Kyushu—but the world.

CRITIQUE

The first in a trilogy, *Gokudo Sengokushi Fudo* was also the first of Miike's films to come to international attention. In a way that is by now familiar, but in 1996 startlingly new to foreign audiences who thought Takeshi Kitano the last word in edgy gangster movies, Miike trashed every conceivable genre convention and social taboo. In place of the old gangster (and indeed Japanese) ideal of family loyalty, he portrays a father who murders his older son for power, after which his younger son lusts to repay him in kind. Instead of staying grounded in classic one-against-all fight scenes, with macho bravado on full display, the film takes flight to a bizarre fantasy land where kids kick around a severed head for fun and the neck of a poisoned gang boss explodes in a Vesuvian blood spray.

It's the blackest of black humor, taken to extremes that invite either fan worship or disgust. Though Miike was inspired by the comic on which the film was based, as well as by other pop culture phenomena, the excess is all his own. There is a cartoony dimension to the film, as when Riki recovers from a multistory fall into Tokyo Bay as quickly as Wile E. Coyote does from his encounters with the Road Runner. But it never descends to camp; Miike takes his revenge story seriously, even when subverting it with gruesome gags.

He is, however, no Kitano-like romanticist, glorying in his hero's lonely, if manly, end. Instead Miike is closer in sensibility to Seijun Suzuki and Teruo Ishii, who made the best of the bad job of grinding out yakuza programers by indulging their taste for the outrageous. In *Fudo*, however, Miike is still groping for the style that he would later bring to such films as *Dead or Alive: Final* and *Koroshiya Ichi*. His violent pyrotechnics often have a cheesy, shot-on-the-cheap look, as though he couldn't be bothered to make the tubes squirting blood from the gang boss's neck look less like tubes. Nonetheless, there is propulsion to *Fudo* that carries it over its technical rough spots, as well as a frisson of unhealthy—and unholy—fascination with the dark side. How many other directors could make patricide look cool—or would even want to try?

© 1995 Bunkasha. Image Factory IM

From darkness into the light. Five desperate men take on the mob in Takashi Ishii's *Gonin* (1995).

Gonin (1995)

Scr./Dir.: Takashi Ishii. *Prod.:* Bunkasha, Image Factory IM. *Main cast:* Koichi Sato, Naoto Takenaka, Jinpachi Nezu, Kippei Shiina, Masahiro Motoki, Beat Takeshi. 109 mins.

Takashi Ishii's *Gonin* tries to shock the unshockable much the way *Pulp Fiction* did, with violence that is not merely in your face but at your throat. He differs from Tarantino, however, in the approach to his material and attitude toward his audience. Whereas Tarantino is the hip trickster, subverting genre conventions and playing with his audience's head, Ishii is the *otaku* of sex and violence, who puts his obsessions on screen and takes his audience to the end of the night. To put this difference in another way, Tarantino directs from the neck up, Ishii from the neck down, with a particular emphasis on the region of the solar plexus.

In making a film about a gang of losers and outcasts who take on the yakuza, Ishii rode on the wave of "New Yakuza" films that flooded the video shops in the mid-1990s. But *Gonin* is also an Ishii film. While assaulting the senses with violent, erotic, and hallucinatory imagery, it explores the borderlands of revenge, lust, and sanity. Few directors venture so far, or know the terrain so well. Those expecting to unwind with two hours of mindless bang-bang are in for some rude jolts.

A disco owner named Bandai (Koichi Sato), who was once a bubble-era comer, is now a loser, up to his handsome jowls in debt to the yakuza. They harass him, humiliate him, and threaten his life. Desperate for a way out, Bandai encounters others also at the ends of their individual ropes: a strung-out salaryman (Naoto Takenaka), who has been restructured out of a job; a former police detective (Jinpachi Nezu), who has just been released from prison; a hot-headed boxer-turned-pimp (Kippei Shiina), who is on the outs with the mob; and a gay blackmailer (Masahiro Motoki), who is still in love with Bandai, though he suspects that the disco manager sold him out to the cops.

Bandai recruits this motley crew to rob the yakuza office at gun point. Amazingly, they make off with nearly 1 million yen. The enraged yakuza hire a hitman (Beat Takeshi) to hunt down the robbers, one by one. The standard recipe for movies of this kind calls for a large dollop of macho humor, a pinch of redeeming qualities for the good guys, and a fiery climax in which the star and a buddy or two emerge victorious. In making *Gonin*, however, Ishii threw the recipe away. The good guys are not charming scapegraces (though Saito, Nezu, and Motoki are convincing hard guys) and the big confrontation degenerates into a bloody mess. The ending? Don't ask, but I doubt that Hollywood will buy the remake rights.

What this film lacks in genre clichés, it more than makes up for in high-charged drama. Ishii's directorial trademark has always been intensity and, in *Gonin*, he pushes his actors to their emotional and physical limits, until they reek of sweaty fear and vibrate with hot rage. He edits for speed, tension, and immediacy, until we feel that we are running across the table top, heart in mouth and gun in hand, toward a nonplussed gang boss.

In probing his characters' psyches, however, Ishii abandons realism for flights of sophisticated dream (or nightmare) imagery, using cuts that approach the subliminal in their brevity. Does he go over the top with ultraviolence? Does he indulge in displays of macho melodrama? Does he oversell his movie's dark, bleak, nihilistic message? Yes, yes, and yes. But, to paraphrase Blake, the road of excess leads to an extraordinary film.

Gorotsuki (1992)

TOUGH GUYS

Scr.: Yasuhiro Horiuchi. *Dir.:* Yasuhiro Horiuchi. *Prod.:* Hero Communications. *Main cast:* Masanori Ikeda, Yoshiyuki Omori, Naoko Amihama, Aiko Asano. 97 mins.

Akira (Masanori Ikeda), a smart-mouthed college student, and Ryo (Yoshiyuki Omori), a lunk-headed reform school graduate, meet cute in a Roppongi disco. Just released from juvenile detention, Ryo bulls his way in and begins dancing wildly to celebrate his new-found freedom. Akira scolds him for breaking the house rules. Soon, they are outside, trading insults and punches. As they are tumbling about, a rolled-up magazine makes contact with Akira's skull. The two boys look up into the angry face of a fat, long-haired yakuza. From this beginning, we expect a tongue-in-cheek look at the underside of Japanese life. But not quite: *Gorotsuki* has too many rough edges and too much gritty honesty to be just another funny gangster movie. Its yakuza are neither scar-faced clowns nor noble outlaws, but the real thing. Director Yasuhiro Horiuchi may have shot *Gorotsuki* on the cheap, but its technical flaws, if anything, enhance its semi-documentary feel.

The boys end up in the same gang—Akira because he wants money and women, Ryo because his father forces him to join, in the hope that gang discipline will straighten him out. They are set to answering the phones, cleaning the office, and performing other chores. Inevitably, they screw up and incur the wrath of their seniors. With slaps upside the head and *manga* throws across the room, these scenes are funny in a Three Stooges way.

But while getting laughs at the boys' expense, the film shows how they make choices that change their lives. In most films about bad boys, their criminality is a given; they start bad and become worse. In *Gorotsuki*, however, the bad boys are not sure that they want to become bad men. The rewards, including overseas trips and yakuza groupies, are often outweighed by the unpleasantness. Confessing their doubts to each other, Akira and Ryo become friends.

As they graduate from gofers to apprentice gangsters, they are introduced into the gang's real dirty work. Akira is sent to collect money from an old woman living alone in a ramshackle house; Ryo is told to rape a young girl for the filming of a porno video. Horiuchi presents these scenes matter-of-factly, minus moralizing. This, he says, is what the yakuza do; this is the kind of men they are. Instead of angels with dirty faces, he gives us thugs with dirty souls.

As Akira, Masanori Ikeda projects not only a pretty-boy charm but the toughness required of a yakuza recruit. Yoshiyuki Omori plays Ryo as a bull-headed wild man. This, we think, is the type who becomes a real yakuza. But Ryo also wants to live. Is being a gangster, he asks, worth getting killed for? From such basic questions and unvarnished answers is *Gorotsuki* made. This shouldn't come as a surprise considering its creator, Shoko Ieda, who wrote the book of reportage on which it is based, spent two years living the yakuza life. Yasuhiro Horiuchi got his start as a porno director, a profession not free of underworld connections. His first straight feature may disappoint fans who prefer the genre's romantic conventions. For the rest of us, though, *Gorotsuki* is a sobering initiation into the mean reality of the gangsters' world.

Hana to Arashi to Gang (1961)

FLOWER AND STORM AND GANG

Scr.: Kan Saji. Dir.: Teruo Ishii. Prod.: New Toei.
Main cast: Ken Takakura, Koji Tsuruta, Mitsue Komiya, Mamoru Ogawa, Shigeko Arai, Nijiko Kiyokawa, Shinjiro Ebara, Harumi Sone, Ryuji Oki, Takamaru Sasaki. 84 mins.

STORY

Smiley Ken (Ken Takakura), a member of the Kawakita-gumi, finishes a three-year stretch in prison and reunites with his wife Sawa (Mitsue Komiya), who runs a bar for foreigners and has a police record as well. In fact, her older brother Hong Kong Joe (Koji Tsuruta), her mother Masa (Nijiko Kiyokawa), and her younger brother Masao (Mamoru Ogawa), all live on the wrong side of the law. Yamafuji (Ryuji Oki), a boss who came into the gang world about the

same time as Smiley but has since risen higher, recruits Smiley for a bank robbery and asks him to assemble a crew to pull it off. With the money for this job, Sawa says, Smiley can go straight. Meanwhile, the gang's big boss, Kawakita (Takamaru Sasaki) asks Joe to have Masao whack someone for him. Masao, a punk kid, proves unequal to the task and Joe has to come to his aid. Even so, Masao boasts of his exploit to his girlfriend, Keiko (Shigeko Arai), who is proud of him for killing his first man.

Sawa enlists Masao for the bank heist, together with Gakutai (Shinjiro Ebara) and Whisper (Harumi Sone), two punks who loathe each other. It doesn't matter to her if one kills the other after the job—it will leave more loot for the rest.

Yamafuji, Smiley, and the rest of the crew plan and execute the robbery. Everything goes smoothly, until Whisper "accidentally" shoots Gakutai inside the bank. Then, while they are making their getaway, Masao runs off with the money. Whisper suspects a family scheme to cut out him and the others. Yamafuji tells Smiley to retrieve their ill-gotten gains—or else.

Masa asks Kawakita not to pop her son or she will spill his secrets to the police. She then returns to her home in Osaka, where Masao and Keiko are hiding—and tells him he'll be killed unless he gives back the money. Sawa asks Smiley if he really intends to whack her brother. He feels caught between a rock and a hard place. Gakutai escapes from the hospital, just before Whisper arrives to give him the coup de grâce. He calls Yamafuji, saying he'll go to the cops unless he gets his share right away. Smiley offers to pony up—and pleads with Yamafuji to spare Masao. Gakutai sends a boy to collect the money and, though Kawakita hoods follow him, makes a getaway.

Smiley asks Kawakita to let Masao live if he returns the loot. Kawakita agrees on one condition: that Sawa stay with him. She, however, is visiting her mother in Osaka. Smiley goes to get her—and together they search for the money bag. Masa, however, is too clever for them. Joe is relaxing on a yacht with his blonde girlfriend, Masao, and Keiko, when Yamafuji and Kawakita hoods arrive in a speedboat. While they are searching the yacht, Masao and Keiko make their escape. Soon after, Whisper visits Smiley at the club and tells him the boss wants Masao dead—or Smiley will die in his place.

CRITIQUE

The first film Teruo Ishii made after coming to Toei in 1961, *Hana to Arashi to Gang* launched an eleven-part series that ran until 1967, while propelling Ken Takakura, whose career had been faltering, on the road to stardom. This comic caper film has no heroes—only scoundrels of varying degrees, deceiving and double crossing each other until the final reel. Its moral: A family that steals together, stays together. Also, the real brains in the film belong to Mitsue Komiya's Sawa and Nijiko Kiyokawa's Masa—women who are two iron-willed peas from the same wayward pod.

None of these elements were common in Toei's films at the time: the studio was still known mainly for its samurai period dramas. But with *Hana to Arashi to Gang*'s success behind him, Ishii moved to the front rank of Toei directors, a position he held for more than a decade. Seen today, the film still amuses with its clever twists, brisk pace, and colorful characters, whose mugging is more reminiscent of *Guys and Dolls* than the usual Japanese gang film. This is not Ishii trying and failing to ape Hollywood conventions but a smart, stylized Japanese adaptation of them.

The film occasionally floats up into the silly-sphere; but no-nonsense performances by Komiya and Kiyokawa anchor it to earth, while Ken Takakura's turn as the stuttering, spineless, but good-hearted Smiley gives it vitality and charm. Not a great whacked-out genre parody like Seijun Suzuki's *Tokyo Nagaremono* (Tokyo Drifter), *Hana to Arashi to Gang* is nonetheless an entertaining precursor.

Hana to Doto (1964)

FLOWER AND THE ANGRY WAVES

Scr.: Kazuo Funabashi, Kei'ichi Abe, Takeo Kimura. *Dir.*: Seijun Suzuki. *Prod.*: Nikkatsu. *Main cast*: Akira Kobayashi, Tamio Kawachi, Chieko Matsubara, Hiroyuki Nagato, Naeko Kubo, Osamu Takizawa. 92 mins.

STORY

The time: the Taisho Period (1912–26). The place: Asakusa, a popular Tokyo entertainment district. Ogata (Akira Kobayashi), a former yakuza, is working as a common laborer. Then, his past arrives in the form of a mysterious man in a cape (Tamio Kawachi)—a hitman for a rival gang. Meanwhile, Manryu (Naeko Kubo), a popular geisha who has her pick of clients, becomes sweet on Ogata, even bankrolling a successful gambling spree. This favoritism stirs the wrath of Izawa (Teruo Miyabe), a yakuza who wants Manryu for himself.

Ogata is working for the Murata-gumi, which has won a big construction job from Daito Denryoku, an electric power company. The Tamai-gumi, with which Izawa is allied, is angling to steal the job away, however. Ogata is inadvertently drawn into this struggle when he knocks down an old man who seems to be trespassing on the work site—and learns that he is Mr. Shigeyama (Osamu Takizawa), an industry fixer and Murata ally. Shigeyama takes a liking to Ogata, whom he sees as a man of spirit—a rare being in the corrupt modern world.

Ogata reunites with Oshige (Chieko Matsubara), a waitress in a small restaurant and, unknown to everyone around her, his wife. Manryu takes an instant dislike to Oshige, whom she senses is a rival for Ogata's affections. The struggle between the Murata-gumi and its yakuza rivals heats up when gangsters invade the work site and wreak havoc. The mysterious man in a cape makes an appearance and Ogata gives chase, but the stranger escapes. Izawa tries to buy Manryu's affections, but she rejects his pile of cash. He also quarrels with Ogata

The moment of truth. Akira Kobayashi unsheathes his knife as Chieko Matsubara looks on in a poster for *Hana to Doto* (Flower and the Angry Waves, 1964).

and accuses him of being a yakuza. Ogata uncovers his tattooed back, proving Izawa right.

Ogata urges the Murata *oyabun* to seek a peaceful resolution to the dispute with the Tamai-gumi. "We are construction workers, not yakuza like them," says Ogata. "They don't care who they kill." Murata replies that they must fight or lose the construction job to their rivals. In the ensuing battle, Ogata at first stays behind but later joins the fray, proving his ability with the sword as he cuts down gangster riflemen who are plunking Murata laborers.

To avoid more bloodshed, the two rivals agree to split the work and hold a ceremony to cement their new relationship. They celebrate with a dice game, but the dealer—the mysterious caped man, but without the cape—is a cheater; Ogata catches him trying to substitute loaded dice for the legit ones. But the dealer quickly palms the loaded dice and Ogata is accused of trying to sabotage the peace agreement. The Murata *oyabun* later beats him to a pulp, while demanding to know if he really is, as a gangster at the dice game charged, a yakuza.

Ogata, his face now horribly disfigured from the beating, finds out that Murata, for whom he was willing to sacrifice his life, is plotting to have him killed. At the urging of his mentor, Shigeyama, Ogata decides to make his escape with his wife, Oshige. By this time, however, not only the caped man but the police are on his trail. Oshige urges Ogata to save himself, but he is determined to live with her as husband and wife. First, he has to get both of them out of town alive.

CRITIQUE

The second pairing of Seijun Suzuki and Akira Kobayashi, following the 1963 *Kanto Mushuku* (Kanto Wanderer), *Hana to Doto* (Flower and the Angry Waves) unfolds in Suzuki's beloved Taisho Era Asakusa, whose colorful demimonde echoed both old Japan and the new cultural influences from the West.

Though the story, with its conflict between the salt-of-the-earth construction workers and grasping gangsters, is standard genre material, Suzuki films it with characteristic theatrical flair. The hitman played by Tamio Kawachi, with his cape, bolero hat, and Man of Mystery air, is the most obvious example, although Suzuki admits that the costume was the idea of Takeo Kimura, the production designer who also co-wrote the script.

Similar scenes include the escape of Oshige and Ogata from Asakusa and the final confrontation in Niigata. The former is accomplished in the midst of masked revelers, who add a fantastic note of unreality to the proceedings. The latter unfolds amid sculpted mounds of snow that, together with the Kabukiesque action choreography, lift the story into another, heightened, dimension. Characters struggle for their lives within a setting of stark, bizarre beauty, kill and die with a stylized grace. Suzuki films all this without an obvious wink, but the very abruptness of the shifts from the straightforward to the surreal indicates an antic, subversive spirit at work.

But compared with Suzuki's later outrages, *Hana to Doto* is still well within the bounds of film industry and social conventions, from its story of true love thwarted by fate to Ogata's spurning of the feisty, rule-defying geisha Manryu for the weepy, pure-hearted serving girl Oshige (though given that Ogata happens to be married to the latter, his choice is undoubtedly honorable). Even so, certain story choices betoken a more unconventional, if not outwardly rebellious, attitude. One is the vicious beating by the supposedly "good" *oyabun* that leaves half of Ogata's face a grotesque mess. Was Suzuki having a joke at the expense of his handsome star—or simply trying to give the audience a jolt?

Harukana Jidai no Kaidan o (1994)

THE STAIRWAY TO THE DISTANT PAST

Scr.: Daisuke Tengan, Kaizo Hayashi. *Dir.:* Kaizo Hayashi. *Prod.:* For Life, Film Detective Office. *Main cast:* Masatoshi Nagase, Haruko Wanabuchi, Francoise Morechand, Tetta Sugimoto. 101 mins.

Second in a series about a street-wise P.I. (Masatoshi Nagase) in Yokohama, Kaizo Hayashi's *Harukana Jidai no Kaidan o* (The Stairway to the Distant Past) has the look of a retro chic fashion spread for *Cut* magazine. It is photographed with a touch of calculated daring, a dash of piss elegance, and a large dollop of post-modernist attitude. The world of old yakuza flicks and noir thrillers is knowingly restored as a design motif.

Image for image, Hayashi is the most visually gifted, unmistakably individual younger director working in Japan today. Three minutes into a Hayashi film and you know who made it; his directorial signature is as unmistakable as Spielberg's. But what, exactly, are you watching? As a cinematic storyteller, Hayashi is a terrific fashion photographer. The images come first, the content, second. His films tend to dress in tired gags, stock sentiments, and creaky plot devices in the garb of arch whimsy and coy romanticism. Hayashi thinks he's covering his bets by not taking his genre parodies too seriously. But his winks at the audience can't hide the insubstantiality of the proceedings.

Mike Hama is a scapegrace P.I. who drives a Nash Metropolitan and works out of an office in the Nichigeki Theater, a Yokohama landmark since 1952. As the film starts, he is scraping bottom; his only client is a foreign matron (Francoise Morechand) who wants him to find her itsy-bitsy dog. While he is on the prowl for the pooch, loan sharks repossess his Nash. Then, Mike's long-lost mother (Haruko Wanabuchi) returns to work at a Yokohama strip joint and the Black Dog Society, a gang of naturalized Asians, starts a turf war with the "White Man," a boss-of-bosses who always dresses in white and has run the riverfront rackets since the Occupation days. When Mike's friends walk in on Mom's show and cops discover dead gangsters by the river—losers in a quarrel with the White Man's minions—Mike finds himself drawn into a past he would rather forget, a tangled web of crime and passion he would rather avoid.

As Mike, Nagase spends much of the movie shouting at the top of his voice and sounding like a teenager in the throes of a snit fit. His tough-guy posturing as he tangles with the cops, who want to use him as a snoop, and the White Man's wise guys, who want him dead, is mildly comic but unpersuasive. When Mike is about to invade the White Man's riverside lair and his cab driver buddy gives him a derringer that looks like a host club cigarette lighter, the movie plunges to a nadir from which it never quite recovers. Before Hayashi films another gangland shoot-out, he would be advised to rent a few *Dirty Harry* tapes for pointers on tough guy weaponry. Somehow, though, I don't think Nagase will ever master an Eastwoodian sneer.

Be that as it may, *Harukana* has its pleasures, including Yuichi Nagata's gorgeous photography (nighttime Yokohama has never looked so pulp-thriller mysterious), a razor-sharp comic turn by Shiro Sano as a gang-boss-turned-politician, and a chilling performance by Tetta Sugimoto as the "Red Man," the White Man's merciless red-clad enforcer. Also, Hayashi seems to have had a ball filming Mike's cinematic adventures in his Yokohama wonderland. If he can translate that enthusiasm into on-screen excitement instead of attitude aimed at Parco charge card holders, we may have reason to look forward to Part Three.

Shades, leather, and a Nash Metropolitan. Masatoshi Nagase as a down-at-the-heels, but stylishly turned-out, private investigator in *Harukana Jidai no Kaidan o* (The Stairway to the Distant Past, 1994).

Heitai Yakuza (1965)

HOODLUM SOLDIER

Scr.: Ryuzo Kikushima. *Dir.:* Yasuzo Masumura. *Prod.:* Daiei. *Main cast:* Shintaro Katsu, Takahiro Tamura, Keiko Awaji, Eiko Taki, Mikio Narita, Yutaka Nakamura, Kyu Sazanka, Toshitaro Kitajiro, Asao Uchida. 103 mins.

STORY

The time: 1943. The place: Manchuria, near the Russian front. The film opens with a shot of a skeleton—a Japanese soldier. The scene shifts to the barracks of the Kanto Army. A new recruit arrives—a burly former yakuza named Kisaburo Omiya (Shintaro Katsu). Knowing that he is likely to be trouble, his superiors put him under the care of Private First Class Arita (Takahiro Tamura), an intellectual who hates the army but has learned how to cope with the system.

Omiya quickly gets into trouble for insolence but takes the resulting insults and slaps calmly—he has seen far worse in the gangs. Arita, on the other hand, admires his new charge's honest and fearless nature and becomes determined to protect him. Omiya quarrels with a squad of artillerymen in the bath and punches out the entire lot. Corporal Kurogane (Toshitaro Kitajiro), a college man like Arita, punishes Omiya with a brutal beating. When Arita finds out, he reminds Kurogane how he has been in the army longer—Arita has four years of service to Kurogane's two—and is thus his superior, even though he is of lower rank. Taking this as his cue, Omiya stomps Kurogane, earning his undying enmity.

Their three months of training over, Omiya and the other new recruits are marched 300 kilometers to a new post. Omiya proves to be as poor a marcher as he is a good fighter. Arita helps him survive this ordeal, however—and the two men become friends. At the new post, Kurogane catches Arita alone, tells him his claim to being an Army *senpai* is a lie—and beats him to a pulp. When Omiya hears, he and Arita go to find Kurogane—and Omiya ends up fighting a dozen or so artillerymen at once. His superiors get wind of this brawl—and Omiya is confined to camp.

Arita hears that Omiya has gone AWOL, but soon tracks him to an officer's brothel, where he is enjoying the favors of Otomaru (Keiko Awaji). Chief Warrant Officer Nakazawa (Asao Uchida) orders Arita to punish Omiya. Arita makes a half-hearted attempt to beat Omiya—then Omiya pounds himself with a brick so Arita won't lose face. Soon after, Private Nogi (Yuji Moriya) deserts; a sensitive type, he has had his fill of the beating and bullying. Omiya, Arita, and the others find him—shot by his own hand. His comrades hide this fact from their superior and Nogi gets a soldier's funeral. When Omiya learns that a squad of cooks beat Nogi just before he deserted, he goes after them alone. A worried Arita finds him drinking with his erstwhile enemies; after a titanic brawl, they have decided to call a truce.

Midori (Eiko Taki), another prostitute at Otomaru's brothel, tells Arita that the cooks have been selling sugar and other scarce supplies. Soon after, he discovers Omiya in yet another one-against-all rumble with the cooks, who are armed with shovels and other weapons. Omiya and Arita survive this and other narrow scrapes, but the war situation deteriorates and they and their comrades are shipped off to certain death. Then, Omiya comes up with a plan for getting them through the rest of the war alive.

CRITIQUE

Based on a novel by Yorichika Arima and the first in a nine-part series (eight from 1965 to 1968 and a final film released in 1972), *Heitai Yakuza* has elements of a typical service comedy, Japan division, including all-in brawls featuring star Shintaro Katsu, that made the film a crowd-pleasing hit. But scriptwriter Ryuzo Kikushima and director Yasuzo Masumura also incorporated a penetrating critique of the Imperial Army in wartime, especially the tyranny of the stronger over the weaker—and the brutal punishments meted out to those who deviated from the norm (or even those who didn't).

Arita, the intellectual who is the conscience of the film, proclaims his hatred of the army and all of its works, but he and the other characters do not question what they are doing in Manchuria in the first place. Their existence centers entirely on their own small, harshly Darwinian society: the world outside the camp, including the war they are ostensibly fighting, hardly exists. This narrowing of focus, as well as many of the incidents in the film's picaresque story line, have the ring of reality. It's an exaggerated reality, with Katsu lumbering through the film like a giant in a folk tale, but reality for all that.

The yakuza has often been called one of the last institutions in Japan that preserves the "true Japanese spirit" (*yamato damashi*), but Katsu's Omiya is, despite the army's glorification of that spirit, a misfit, a loose cannon. Though a hardened fighter, used to the harsh code of gang life, he is supremely unimpressed by the army's hierarchies and rules. He respects only those who deserve respect, risks his life only for fights he can understand. In short, he could give two farts about the emperor's war. This makes him highly dangerous to an organization that is built on unquestioning obedience—and enforces that obedience with fear. Katsu's performance—earthy, but never merely buffoonish—is among his best, while co-star Takahiro Tamura shines as his elite, if rebellious, protector—who is occasionally in need of protection himself.

Hibotan Bakuto: Hanafuda Shobu (1969)

RED PEONY GAMBLER: FLOWER CARDS MATCH

Scr.: Motohiro Torii. *Dir.:* Tai Kato. *Prod.:* Toei. *Main cast:* Junko Fuji, Ken Takakura, Tomisaburo Wakayama, Kanjuro Arashi, Kyosuke Machida, Kanbi Fujiyama, Asao Koike. 98 mins.

STORY

The setting: Nagoya in the middle of the Meiji Period (1868–1912). A wandering woman gambler, Oryu (Junko Fuji), arrives at the headquarters of the Nishinomaru gang and, in an elaborate greeting in formal Japanese, asks for their hospitality. The elderly *oyabun*, Sugiyama (Kanjuro Arashi), welcomes her, but his gang is in trouble—the rival Kanahara-gumi is vying with them for the lucrative gambling concession that raises money for the Atsuta Shrine. A calculating type, Kanahara has even enlisted the support of a powerful Diet member, with the intention of taking over in Nagoya.

A complication arises when Sugiyama's son Jiro, a pure-hearted, unworldly college student, proclaims his love for Yaeko, Kanahara's daughter. Seeing an opening in his power struggle with the Nishinomaru gang, Kanahara takes Jiro hostage. Meanwhile, Otoki (Yoshiko Sawa), a female gambler who had earlier cheated Oryu in a card game to raise money for her blind daughter's eye operation, feels remorse when Oryu forgives her—and tries to return the favor by helping Jiro escape. Kanahara's gangsters kill her in their frantic pursuit of the hostage, but with Oryu's aid, Jiro and Yaeko flee to Osaka.

Hanaoka (Ken Takakura), a wandering gangster staying with the Kanaharas, chases them on horseback, but when he stops their carriage Oryu comes to their defense, short sword at ready. Hanaoka, sensing that he is on the wrong side of the quarrel and feeling something more than gangsterly affection for Oryu, backs down, and the young couple complete their journey in safety.

He still feels an obligation to his hosts, however, and when Kanahara orders him to kill Sujiyama he has no choice but to comply. Then, a top Nishinomaru lieutenant is killed and Oryu, having reached the limit of her patience with these nefarious goings-on, decides to take on the entire Kanaharu gang. On the way to the showdown, however, she gains two unexpected allies.

CRITIQUE

Hibotan Bakuto: Hanafuda Shobu (Red Peony Gambler) is the third installment in the eight-part Hibotan Bakuto series and one of the three directed by Tai Kato. Its story of star-crossed lovers may be familiar—a gangland "Romeo and Juliet"—but Kato's style, with its rapid cross-cuts, low angles, and extreme close-ups, is utterly distinctive.

In the first scene, in which Oryu rescues a blind girl from an on-rushing train, the cutting and composition are reminiscent of the Odessa Steps sequence in Eisenstein's *Battleship Potemkin*: bursting with drama and intensity, with one iconic image following another in blinding succession. His trademark low-angle shots are in abundant evidence throughout the film. For one, of a Nagoya bathhouse, he ordered his crew to dig a hole for the camera, which meant drilling through asphalt. Also, notable is Kato's use of visual markers to create atmosphere and comment on the action. One memorable example is the locomotive steam that, blowing down from a railroad bridge, marks major transitions in the lives of the characters, while suggesting life's transience.

Kato's style well conveys the chaos of battle, while imparting a certain grandeur to the heroes, but he also uses it to good effect in his tenderer scenes, notably the first meeting of Oryu and Hanaoka in the rain. She offers him an umbrella, he reluctantly accepts, and, as he takes it their fingers touch. Kato moves in for a close-up that underscores the significance of this encounter for the stoic Hanaoka. (His idea of a pick-up line is, "When I touched your fingers, I was reminded of my dead mother.") What might have been a corny overstatement in the hands of another director becomes, in Kato's, a charged, poignant moment.

Hibotan Bakuto: Oinochi Itadakimasu (1971)

RED PEONY GAMBLER: DEATH TO THE WICKED

Scr.: Norifumi Suzuki, Tai Kato, Morimasa Owaku. *Dir.:* Tai Kato. *Prod.:* Toei. *Main cast:* Junko Fuji, Koji Tsuruta, Tomisaburo Wakayama, Kyosuke Machida, Kanjuro Arashi, Hiroshi Nawa, Akira Shioji, Seizaburo Kawazu, Kimiko Kamioka, Hosei Komatsu, Ken'ichi Okubo. 93 mins.

STORY

Wandering gambler Oryu (Junko Fuji) saves an elderly hunchbacked man, Yasujiro (Akira Shioji), from a band of men intent on murdering him. He says he is innocent of their accusations of thievery—and Oryu chooses to believe him. When Oryu wins big in a gambling game, the dealer accuses her of cheating. She denies it—and proves that the dealer is the cheater instead. In the midst of the ensuing uproar, the gambling den master, the Omaeda *oyabun* (Kanjuro Arashi), arrives to calm the troubled waters—and warmly greets Oryu, an old friend.

The Tomioka *oyabun* (Seizaburo Kawazu) is profiting from the presence of an armaments factory in his village, even though the smoke and waste water are ruining the farmers' fields. The village, Daigo, is also home to Yuki Kikujiro (Koji Tsuruta), a gangster who was once a farmer himself. He and Oryu become acquainted after she sees him praying at the grave of his wife. Oryu takes a liking to him and, when he invites her to visit his village, she accepts.

Four months later: their demands rejected, the farmers are battling the police when Oryu arrives in Daigo. Despite the turmoil, she gets a warm greeting from Yuki's sister Ofumi (Kimiko Kamioka). Meanwhile, Yuki is earnestly negotiating with the factory owner (Ken'ichi Okubo) and the military representative, Captain Hatanaka (Hosei Komatsu). When he says that the farmers have reached the limit of their patience and may become violent, Hatanaka accuses him of traitorous talk—and beats him nearly senseless.

A nearly comatose Yuki is brought home by his *kobun* but still has the presence of mind to greet Oryu—and urge forbearance to his men. One, Goro (Kyosuke Machida), refuses to listen and attacks the carriage in which the factory owner and captain are riding. He is captured but rescued by Oryu, and together they make a narrow escape. The factory owner and Tomioka *oyabun* visit Yuki and offer the farmers compensation if they end their protest. Yuki insists that money will do nothing to end the pollution, but the farmers' representative decides that the offer is better than nothing—and decides to accept it.

The offer of compensation, Tomioka later tells Yuki, was just a ploy. When Yuki says they can't do business if that is the case, Tomioka tells him to face reality—the factory will stay whether he wants it or not. Later, the captain, factory owner, and Tomioka plot to get rid of Yuki, using one of Yuki's trusted men, Oyama (Hiroshi Nawa) to set the trap. In return, they will make Oyama boss of Yuki's gang and marry him to Ofumi—a long-cherished dream.

Yuki goes to rescue Goro's niece, who has been sold into prostitution by her desperate mother. On his return, he is attacked by hired assassins, though the one who plunges in the fatal sword is Tomioka himself. Oryu has been working as a dealer at a gambling game in nearby Takasaki, oblivious to events in Daigo. When she hears the news, Oryu rushes back—but before she can get revenge for Yuki's death, Oryu has to learn the identity of the killers and untangle the web of conspiracy woven by the plotters.

CRITIQUE

The seventh installment in the Hibotan Bakuto (Red Peony Gambler) series and one of three directed by Tai Kato, *Hibotan Bakuto: Oinochi Itadakimasu* (Red Peony Gambler:

Death to the Wicked) takes a burning topical issue—the environmental devastation wrought by rapid industrialization—as the mainspring of its plot. Kato's approach is less didactic than humanistic, however. Close-ups of smoke belching from a factory chimney and dirty water pouring into a farmer's field are suggestive, but his true focus is on the human cost of the pollution—and the human vipers who perpetuate it.

As such, the film would seem to be a typical *ninkyo* genre morality play, with self-sacrificing good battling money-grubbing evil. In most *ninkyo* films, however, the heroes know who the villains are from the first act. In *Oinochi Itadakimasu*, the heroine, Oryu, and her allies must first unravel the mystery of Yuki's death before they can righteously descend on the perpetrators. Also, the ways the perpetrators use and turn on each other add another layer of complexity—and made the final comeuppance even more richly deserved.

More than its plotting, however, the film is notable for its pathos, as when Ofumi (Kimiko Kamioka), just saved from sexual slavery, tells her rescuer, Yuki, that she feels unfairly blessed—all of her friends have already been sold. That comment, more than the film's dirty streams and belching smoke, brings home the destruction of individual lives in the name of national strength and prosperity.

Irezumi Ichidai (1965)

ONE GENERATION OF TATTOOS
Scr.: Kinya Naoi. *Dir.:* Seijun Suzuki. *Prod.:* Nikkatsu. *Main cast:* Hideki Takahashi, Kotobuki Hananomoto, Akira Yamanouchi, Hiroko Ito, Masako Izumi, Kayo Matsuo, Yuji Odaka, Hosei Komatsu. 87 mins.

STORY
Tetsu (Hideki Takahashi) of the Owada-gumi kills the boss of a rival gang. Before Tetsu goes

into hiding he leaves money for his younger brother Kenji (Kotobuki Hananomoto), an aspiring artist. Kenji, however, decides to follow—luckily so, because the Owada *oyabun* ordered a hit on Tetsu to silence him—and comes along just in time to shoot the hitman. Kenji offers to give himself up, but Tetsu has a better idea—escape to Manchuria.

When they reach a port, they are cheated out of their traveling money by a fast-talking broker, Yamano (Hosei Komatsu). They also encounter a detective who is on the look-out for criminals trying to cross the Japan Sea to Manchuria. They may forget his face—but not his distinctive red shoes. Near the port, Tetsu asks a construction foreman for a job—and ends up fighting him over an insult. After a bruising battle under a water wheel, the foreman decides that Tetsu is all right after all—and hires both him and Kenji as members of the Kinoshita-gumi.

Soon after, Kenji becomes infatuated with the wife (Hiroko Ito) of the Kinoshita boss—and asks to draw her nude. She tells him coyly that she only undresses for the bath—which he takes, correctly, as an invitation. He is fascinated with her, he later tells his brother, because she reminds him of their dead mother. When Kenji's drawings are discovered by his fellow workers, they create an uproar. Meanwhile, Tetsu is becoming better acquainted with the boss's daughter, the saucy Midori (Masako Izumi). When she asks him to strip for her—she wants to see his manly back—he refuses.

Yamano plots to bring in a yakuza gang, the Akamatsu-gumi, to steal the Kinoshita-gumi's plum job—a tunnel construction project. When the Akamatsu thugs arrive, they pick a fight with the Kinoshita-gumi laborers, but the battle ends inconclusively. Meanwhile, the police, including the red-shoed detective, are busy tracking down Tetsu and Kenji. The foreman refuses to give them up, but Ezaki (Yuji Kodaka), a Kinoshita manager who is in love with Midori and jealous of Tetsu, tries to undermine the brothers with his boss by exposing Tetsu as a gangster and fugitive from justice.

Kinoshita, however, takes their side, even after discovering that Kenji has made a nude statue of his wife and Tetsu has been seeing his daughter. When Owada gangsters arrive to whack the brothers, Kinoshita helps them escape to the docks, where they successfully elude their Owada pursuers. Kenji, however, decides to return for one last rendezvous with the boss's wife. On the way, he is spotted, pursued, and killed by Akamatsu gangsters. Tetsu arrives in time to give a sip of sake to his dying brother. Receiving a sword from an old yakuza, he strides alone to the Akamatsu headquarters to take his just revenge.

CRITIQUE

A conventional yakuza programer through much of its eighty-seven-minute running time, *Irezumi Ichidai* (One Generation of Tattoos) makes an astonishing transition to the surreal in its climactic showdown sequence, among the most famous in Seijun Suzuki's oeuvre. When Kenji is cut down, red light floods across the room. After he dies, Tetsu, wearing a black-and-white *happi* coat, pops open a Japanese-style umbrella with a flourish and rushs out into the rain.

Soon after, he encounters and battles a mysterious opponent in a straw cape. The stylization of the swordplay is pure Kabuki, with beauty all, realism nothing. The opponent turns out to be an elderly yakuza that Tetsu had earlier befriended. His gift of his sword to Tetsu is a passing of the *jingi* spirit in the form of a beloved weapon, across generations.

Invading the Akamatsu headquarters, Tetsu throws open a series of first blue and then yellow *fusuma* (paper doors) and rushes through, past sword cuts and pistol shots, until he reaches the inner sanctum. The sequence is a tour de force of breathtaking speed and flawless timing, drenched in primary colors. His fight to the death with the Akamatsu boss, shot from

below through a sheet of glass, is another bravura bit that ends spectacularly when Tetsu, avoiding a spear thrust, falls backward out of the house into the garden in the midst of a downpour.

After killing his man, Tetsu's torn garment parts to reveal his tattoo in all of its glory. Then, he slowly pries his fingers from the sword—proof of his superhuman effort. In this moment, Suzuki the cult legend was born. No one then working rivaled his audacity—or could imagine trying. By making gorgeous Japanesque spectacle out of genre clichés, Suzuki was not only issuing a frontal challenge to studio convention but bringing Japanese cinema into the international avant garde.

Jingi Naki Tatakai (1973)

BATTLES WITHOUT HONOR AND HUMANITY
Scr.: Kazuo Kasahara. *Dir.:* Kinji Fukasaku. *Prod.:* Toei. *Main cast:* Bunta Sugawara, Hiroki Matsukata, Tatsuo Umemiya, Nobuo Kaneko, Kunie Tanaka, Tamio Kawachi, Eiko Nakamura, Hiroshi Nawa, Masataka Iwao. 99 mins.

STORY

The year: 1947. The place: Hiroshima and nearby Kure, which have been reduced to rubble by American bombings, including the atomic blast that ended the war. Shozo Hirono (Bunta Sugawara) is a demobilized soldier wandering through the black market, when he encounters American soldiers raping a Japanese woman. In the ensuing struggle to save her, he bonds briefly with Wakasugi (Tatsuo Umemiya), a member of the Doi-gumi.

Soon after, Hirono becomes involved in a beef between several of his old Kure friends and local gangsters, who have been lording it over the black market. He shoots a crazed gangster (Masataka Iwao) who comes at him with a sword—and ends up in prison. There, Hirono reunites with Wakasugi and becomes

Bunta Sugawara glares from behind a long knife in a publicity still for *Jingi Naki Tatakai* (Battles without Honor and Humanity, 1973).

his blood brother in a ceremony that is his effective initiation into the gang.

Released, he is greeted by his old crew, now members of the Yamamori-gumi, and even by Yamamori (Nobuo Kaneko) himself, who praises Hirono for his stand-up behavior. Hirono joins the gang, with a bright future ahead of him as one of Yamamori's most trusted men. The Yamamori-gumi and its main Kure rival, the Doi-gumi, have been living in uneasy co-existence but split over a tight city council race. The Yamamori gang enjoys a big pay day sabotaging the election of a candidate supported by the Doi gang—but earns their enmity when word gets out. Thus begins a gang war that is to last twenty years.

In the ensuing jockeying for advantage, Wakasugi leaves the Doi-gumi and joins the Yamamori-gumi, while Kanbara (Tamio Kawachi) of the Yamamori-gumi becomes a spy for the Doi-gumi. When the conflict escalates, Yamamori decides to whack Doi (Hiroshi Nawa), but the only one brave (and foolish) enough to take the contract is Hirono. After pulling the trigger and running off, Hirono holes up alone until Kanbara comes to take him to a new hideout—and nearly gets him killed by Doi gangsters.

Hirono makes his escape but is later nabbed by the police and sent to the slammer again. While behind bars, he is visited by Wakasugi, who says he is fed up with Yamamori's weasely ways. Not long after, Wakasugi, on the run himself after clipping the traitor Kanbara, is killed when police invade his hideout. But who gave him up?

When Hirono gets out, he finds himself in the middle of a feud between Yamamori and his *wakamono gashira* (second-in-command), Sakai (Hiroki Matsukata), over the stimulant drug trade, caused when Sakai discovered Yamamori duplicitously dealing drugs after forbidding his underlings from doing the same. Yamamori wants Hirono, but he has just started to breathe free air and refuses. "Sakai is wrong, but you're wrong too," Hirono says on his way out the door; but he can't stay neutral in the dispute—and the body count continues to escalate.

CRITIQUE

Based on Ko'ichi Iiboshi's *Shukan Sunday* magazine series on the life and times of Kozo Mino, a Kure gang boss, *Jingi Naki Tatakai* (Battles without Honor and Humanity) became a studio-saving hit for Toei and a career milestone for director Kinji Fukasaku. The film had a difficult birth, however. When producer Goro Kusakabe and scriptwriter Kazuo Kasahara approached Mino about making a movie—his writings about the Hiroshima gang war had been the basis for the *Shukan Sunday* articles—he flatly refused permission. Criticized by his fellow gangsters for his revelations about the gangs' inner workings, Mino didn't want any more trouble. Using patient persuasion, Kusakabe and Kasahara were able to change his mind—the fact that Mino and Kasahara had been in the same navy unit as Mino helped, as did a declaration by a powerful Hiroshima gangster that anyone who touched Mino would have to answer to him.

Koji Shundo, the Toei producer who supervised the studio's gang film output, encountered another hurdle when he proposed Kinji Fukasaku as the director. His Toei colleagues opposed the choice, saying that Fukasaku could not make the material "interesting," i.e., commercial enough. Shundo overrode their objections and was proven right when the film

became a hit. With *Jingi Naki Tatakai*, Fukasaku was not just shooting a script but telling the story of his generation, who as teenagers had experienced Japan's defeat in war and scrambled to survive in the aftermath, with no values but those of the street. Clear-cut heroes and villains did not exist in such a world, a truth that Fukasaku had been forced to suppress in his early gang films for the studio.

In *Jingi Naki Tatakai*, however, he filmed the realities of the postwar period as he saw them, using handheld cameras, zoom lens, natural lighting, and various types of film stock to create the gritty, chaotic look of period news footage. Fukasaku had tried similar techniques in the 1972 *Gendai Yakuza: Hitokiri Yota* (Street Mobster), the film that made Shundo hire him, but in *Jingi Naki Tatakai* Fukasaku was working on a larger scale with a more complex narrative—and the impact was correspondingly greater.

While supplying the violence Toei fans had come to expect—two arms are lopped off in the opening scene, with accompanying gushers of blood—Fukasaku underlined the absurdity of the Hiroshima gang war with the craven Yamamori more interested in saving his own hide than upholding *giri-ninjo* ideals. The comedy doesn't undercut the drama; if anything it underlines the film's central message that, in understanding the modern gangs in particular and the modern world in general, Machiavelli, not the *jingi* code, is the more reliable guide.

Jingi Naki Tatakai: Hiroshima Shitohen (1973)

BATTLES WITHOUT HONOR AND HUMANITY 2: FIGHT TO THE DEATH AT HIROSHIMA

Scr.: Kazuo Kasahara. *Dir.:* Kinji Fukasaku. *Prod.:* Toei. *Main cast:* Bunta Sugawara, Kin'ya Kitaoji, Meiko Kaji, Shin'ichi "Sonny" Chiba, Asao Koike, Hiroshi Nawa, Mikio Narita, Tatsuo Endo. 100 mins.

STORY

The year: 1952. The place: Hiroshima. After the postwar years of desperate poverty, the Korean War brought prosperity to both Japanese society and Japanese gangsters. One young outlaw, Shoji Yamanaka (Kin'ya Kitaoji), has yet to benefit from the boom, however; back on the streets after a stretch in prison, he is hungry and broke. But when the young man tries to get a job at a restaurant, he instead gets into a beef with one of the patrons—Otomo (Shin'ichi "Sonny" Chiba), the mad-dog son of the Otomo Rengo-kai boss. A wild brawl ensues, with Yamanaka getting the worst of it at the hands of Otomo and his crew. He is rescued by Yasuko (Meiko Kaji), a waitress he hit on, who happens to be the niece of the Muraoka-gumi boss. Muraoka takes a liking to Yamanaka—the kid has spirit, if not sense—and makes him a member of his gang.

The junior Otomo, an ambitious, if reckless, type, plans to wipe out the rival Muraoka gang and take over the Hiroshima rackets. His father, however, is an old-fashioned type who wants to follow the gang's original trade, gambling, and keep the peace with the Muraoka-gumi. Unable to take no for an answer, the son quarrels with the father—and is expelled from the gang. Undeterred, Otomo starts his own gang, the Otomo-gumi, and sets up his own gambling operation. Seeing this as a violation of his turf, Muraoka tells Otomo either to fold his tent or face the consequences. But Otomo finds a protector in Tokimori (Tatsuo Endo), a *shatei* (lieutenant) of the Muraoka-gumi.

Meanwhile, romance has bloomed between Yamanaka and Yasuko, who is the widow of a suicide pilot—and is thus considered unmarriageable by gang traditionalists, including her gang boss uncle. Undeterred, Yamanaka makes his mark as a gang hitman—an occupation he finds congenial. Then, he takes a contract on the traitor, Tokimori, who, hearing of his death sentence, goes to a Kure gang boss, Yamamori (Nobuo Kaneko), for protection. Yamamori in turn asks a former *kobun*, Hirono (Bunta Sugawara), to hide the fleeing gangster. Hirono, who is running a struggling scrap business, is at first reluctant but Yamamori's money persuades him.

The power struggle between the Otomo and Muraoka gangs degenerates into all-out war and the body count rises. Yamanaka tries to whack Otomo but fails—and is cornered by the cops. Though sentenced to a ten-year stretch, he refuses to give up Yasuko, while her uncle is violently opposed to their union. Then, Yamanaka escapes but finds a cold reception from his old gang. He's forced back on the streets, where a police manhunt awaits him.

CRITIQUE

The second installment in Kinji Fukasaku's *Jingi Naki Tatakai* series has only a tenuous connection to the first, with the scene of the action shifting from Kure to Hiroshima. Bunta Sugawara makes a brief appearance as Hirono—the focus of the previous film—but the hero is Kin'ya Kitaoji's Yamanaka, a romantic loner and loser in the classical mold. Following an iron rule of the series—and Japanese popular culture in general—Yamanaka is doomed from the moment he falls in love.

Kitaoji plays Yamanaka with a raw, wide-eyed intensity but is no match for Shin'ichi "Sonny" Chiba as mad-dog Otomo. Sporting a wide-brimmed hat, sunglasses, and a loud aloha shirt, Otomo is the ultimate gangster dandy, a strutting assault on good taste. Grinning maniacally, acting erratically, and swinging a wooden sword with lethal intent, he is also the ultimate gangster bad ass, who would eat Mike Tyson's children for breakfast and ask for seconds.

In a just world, he would die a slow, excruciating death. In Fukasaku's film, with its stern Darwinian realism, he not only lives but flourishes. Meanwhile, the pure-spirited, love-struck Yamanaka is repeatedly betrayed by his gang superiors, who use him when it is convenient, discard him when it is not. Though not as strong as the first film in the series, the second has its highlights, including a scene in which the stone-broke Hirono is unwittingly treated to fried dog meat by his hungry *kobun*—and is surprised when a starving pooch refuses a piece. In *Jingi Naki Tatakai: Hiroshima Shitohen* only the human world is truly dog-eat-dog.

Jingi Naki Tatakai: Dairi Senso (1973)

BATTLES WITHOUT HONOR AND HUMANITY 3: PROXY WAR

Scr.: Koichi Iiboshi, Kazuo Kasahara. *Dir.:* Kinji Fukasaku. *Prod.:* Toei. *Main cast:* Nobuo Kaneko, Akira Kobayshi, Mikio Narita, Bunta Sugawara, Tsunehiko Watase, Yasuhiro Suzuki, Takeshi Kato, Shingo Yamashiro, Tatsuo Umemiya, Tetsuro Tanba. 119 mins.

STORY

The year: 1960. Sugihara (Yasuhiro Suzuki), second-in-command in the Muraoka-gumi, the biggest gang in Hiroshima, is popped by a hitman over a gambling dispute. Sugihara was regarded as a likely successor to the Muraoka-gumi boss Tokio Muraoka (Hiroshi Nawa), who is recovering from illness. Sugihara's sudden death thus leaves a power vacuum. Among those in a position to fill it are Muraoka-gumi *wakagashira* Matsunaga (Mikio Narita) and *kanbu* Takeda (Akira Kobayashi). Also in the running is Uchimoto (Takeshi Kato), Sugihara's *shatei* (lieutenant) and the boss of the Uchimoto-gumi. But fearing that he might share Sugihara's fate, Uchimoto rejects Takeda's offer of support for a revenge strike, opening the way for a power struggle.

Meanwhile, Hirono (Bunta Sugawara) is running his scrap business in the port of Kure. After he punishes an underling, Saijo (Takuzo Kawatani), for stealing scrap (he wanted to buy

his woman a TV set), Saijo cuts off his left hand in remorse. Then, a gang elder, Okubo (Asao Uchida), approaches Hirono about affiliating with Yamamori (Nobuo Kaneko), the boss of the Yamamori-gumi. Hirono decides to accept the offer.

Not long after, Uchimoto asks Hirono's help in forming an alliance with the Akeishi-gumi, a powerful Kobe gang. Uchimoto also reveals his ambition to take over the Muraoka gang. Kuramoto (Tsunehiko Watase), a young laborer, slices off the ear of a professional wrestler in a street brawl. Later, Kuramoto's former teacher approaches Hirono about taking the youth into the gang. "He might have a future as a gangster," the teacher says. Hirono agrees to give him a try. Hirono learns that Yamamori has been selling his scrap without his approval. When Hirono complains, the boss is dismissive: "If you don't like it, you can leave the gang."

In June 1961, Uchimoto visits Kobe and enlists the Akeishi-gumi as an ally. He now owes allegiance to two masters: Akeishi (Tetsuro Tanba) and Muraoka—a no-no in the yakuza world, but as Hirono explains, "Uchimoto is a businessman." When Muraoka discovers Uchimoto's treachery, he is enraged. Meanwhile, Uchimoto is angry at Hirono for revealing his alliance with Akeishi. Soon after, the Muraoka-gumi and Yamamoro-gumi unite. Later, celebrating the alliance at a cabaret, Yamamori scolds Uchimoto in front of everyone for his disloyalty—until Uchimoto starts sobbing in humiliation. He later lashes out at Hirono. "If you want to get me," says Hirono, "I'm waiting."

Two gangs in Iwakuni, the Hamazaki-gumi and Komori-gumi, start a war. Led by Yamamori, Hiroshima gangsters ride to the aid of the Hamazaki gang but Hirono changes his mind, and Yamamori's plan comes to nothing. Muraoka, Takeda, and other gangsters dodge a firecracker tossed into the gang office, thinking it is a bomb. They blame Uchimoto for the stunt and soon after Muraoka announces that he is returning Uchimoto's *sakazuki* cup, thus cutting their gang ties. Soon after, Hayakawa, an Uchimoto *kanbu* disgusted by his boss's weakness, receives an invitation to join the Yamamori gang—and is sorely tempted to take it.

The Hamazaki and Komori gangs reconcile, while Uchimoto becomes a *shatei* of the Akeishi-gumi. Yamamori, who had planned to ally with the Akeishi gang himself, is angry at Hirono for what he perceives as the latter's interference. To redress the power imbalance, he makes Takeda his *wakagashira*, while allowing him to negotiate an alliance with the Shinwa-kai—the Akeishi gang's Kobe rivals. As the battle lines between the Uchimoto and Muraoka forces and their allies solidify, an all-out war seems all but inevitable.

CRITIQUE

The third installment in the Jingi Naki Tatakai series, *Dairi Senso* (Proxy War) is as labyrinthine in its plottings and counter-plottings, alliances and betrayals, as anything in Shakespeare's history plays, though the deals go down in earthy Hiroshima dialect, not Elizabethan English. This is not to say that the film is all dark mutterings in smoke-filled rooms: plenty of action of the rougher sort exists, including a particularly ferocious thrashing that Hirono, the series' dirty hero, delivers to a larcenous underling.

Even so, the film's in-depth investigation of an inter-gang power struggle (and by extension, similar power struggles in Japanese business, government, and academia) is its raison d'être. This investigation is highly instructive, especially for anyone with an interest in strategic games. We see the gangster executive class as, not noble warriors or brutal thugs, but wily survivalists, whose first law is "eat or be eaten."

The leaders of this struggle—Takeshi Kato's Uchimoto and Nobuo Kaneko's Yamamori—are comically weak, with Uchimoto regularly dissolving into tears and Yamamori cravenly quivering at the first threat of physical harm. That they can command the loyalty of the more macho types around them is one of the film's richer ironies. Its center, however, is Bunta Sugawara's Hirono, who skillfully maneuvers to his own advantage against more powerful adversaries (including his putative allies). He has come a long way from being the hot-blooded hood of the first film, who acted first and regretted later. As he has learned so painfully, brains—and a keen nose for the prevailing winds—trumps brawn every time.

Jingi Naki Tatakai: Chojo Sakusen (1974)

BATTLES WITHOUT HONOR AND HUMANITY 4: HIGH TACTICS

Scr.: Kazuo Kasahara. *Dir.:* Kinji Fukasaku. *Prod.:* Toei. *Main cast:* Bunta Sugawara, Nobuo Yana, Toshio Kurosawa, Takashi Noguchi, Takeshi Kato, Renji Ishibashi, Nobuo Kaneko, Masataka Naruse, Katsu Shiga, Kunie Tanaka, Akira Kobayashi, Tatsuo Umemiya, Asao Koike, Hiroki Matsukata, Shin'ichi "Sonny" Chiba. 101 mins.

STORY

The year: 1963. The place: Hiroshima and nearby Kure. The Uchimoto-kai and Hirono-gumi, both affiliated with the larger Akashi-gumi, are engaged in a ferocious turf war with the Yamamori-gumi and Hayakawa-gumi, which are allied with the Shinwa-kai. Meanwhile, straight society is getting ready for the 1964 Olympics and busily building the Japanese economy, with Prime Minister Ikeda's plan for doubling incomes within the decade serving as a blueprint. Longing for peace and prosperity after the years of postwar chaos and poverty, straight citizens no longer regard the yakuza with their old tolerance. They want a crackdown and the police give it to them, with the ambitious aim of driving the gangs out of business.

The gang war heats up, however, with both sides recruiting allies for the big showdown. Hirono (Bunta Sugawara), the boss of the Hirono-gumi, and Uchimoto (Takeshi Kato), the boss of the Uchimoto-kai, approach Okajima (Asao Koike), the *oyabun* of the Hiroshima-based Yoshinishi-kai, for help. Okajima at first intends to stay neutral, but Iwai (Tatsuo Umemiya), a lieutenant of the Akashi-gumi, wins his reluctant support.

Meanwhile, in nearby Kure, the Hirono-gumi and Makihara-gumi, whose boss, Makihara (Kunie Tanaka), is an ally of Yamamori (Nobuo Kaneko), are engaged in almost daily tit-for-tat. Then, a Hirono soldier, Kawanishi (Nobuo Yana), is whacked by Matoba (Masataka Naruse), a soldier of the Makihara gang. Hirono wants to attack Yamamori, whom he suspects is behind the hit but the police arrest him at his headquarters before Hirono can carry out his plan.

Then, Okajima is clipped while at a hot spring for a class reunion. The shooter is Yoshii (Katsu Shiga), a soldier for the Yamamori-gumi. Reeling from this double blow, the Hirono and Uchimoto alliance is forced on the defensive. The young bloods of the Uchimoto gang, incensed by their boss's cowardly caution, join with Fujita (Hiroki Matsukata), a tubercular but still fiery soldier of the Okajima gang, to unleash a secret counterattack. The streets of Hiroshima become a gang battlefield until the police start to round up of the leaders. Has all the bloodshed been in vain or will the gangs live to fight another day?

CRITIQUE

This fourth installment of the Jingi Naki Tatakai (Battle without Honor and Humanity) series is a swan song for the postwar gangs, forced on the defensive by a prosperous middle-class that is no longer as accepting of their old violent ways. The American analogy would be the Hollywood elegies for the end of the Old West, with the schoolmarms setting the tone and the cowboys roped into respectability (or carried off to Boot Hill).

Bunta Sugawara's Hirono is the film's central symbol of this change. Cornered by dozens of cops in his headquarters, he gives himself up for a parole violation—and spends another seven years in Abashiri Prison in Hokkaido. The feral hood of the first film has become, in the fourth, the wised-up con who knows that, whatever course his future criminal career may take, his days of roaming wild are over. But though Hirono may be (at least partly) tamed, there are still crazies on the loose, such as Hiroki Matsukata's Fujita, who may be coughing his lungs out but is still ready to go to war for, not only face, but the evil joy of it. Even in a society in which a washing machine, a refrigerator, and a TV—the Three Sacred Treasures of postwar consumerism—have become everyone's birthright, the gangster spirit lives on.

Jingi Naki Tatakai: Kanketsuhen (1974)

BATTLES WITHOUT HONOR AND HUMANITY 5: THE FINAL EPISODE

Scr.: Kazuo Kasahara. *Dir.:* Kinji Fukasaku. *Prod.:* Toei. *Main cast:* Bunta Sugawara, Kinya Kitaoji, Hiroki Matsukata, Ken'ichi Sakuragi, Kunie Tanaka, Goro Ibuki, Shingo Yamashiro, Nobuo Kaneko, Jo Shishido. 99 mins.

STORY

To survive a police sweep that has put many of its leaders in jail, the Hiroshima gangs reorganize themselves as a political organization called the Tensei-kai, appointing the Yamamori-gumi boss (Nobuo Kaneko) as the first chairman. The gangs thus assume a new, peaceful face, but this is only a mask to fool the police and straight society. Behind the guise, the old struggle for power continues.

The mask begins to drop with the ascension of the Tensei-kai's second chairman, Takeda

(Akira Kobayashi), the boss of the Takeda-gumi. His appointment of the young Matsumura (Kinya Kitaoji) as acting chairman (*kaicho dairi*), over several senior candidates, is opposed by some of the bosses; they fear that Takeda is plotting to take control of the Tensei-kai, with Matsumura serving as his second-in-command. The leaders of the opposition are the sly, scheming Hayakawa (Junkichi Orimoto) and the impulsive-but-dangerous Otomo (Jo Shishido), who once fought an all-out war with the Muraoka gang.

Meanwhile, Ichioka (Hiroki Matsukata), the boss of the Kure-based Ichioka-gumi and a *kyodaibun* (gang brother) to Hirono (Bunta Sugawara), who is serving time in Abashiri Prison, plans to widen this crack in Tensei-kai solidarity and break the gangs' back. Ichioka begins by ordering a hit on Sugita (Yasuhiro Suzuki), a Teisei-kai lieutenant. With Hayakawa as his ally and go-between, Ichioka then exchanges vows of gang brotherhood with the tempestuous Otomo, bringing into existence a three-gang faction large enough to challenge the Tensei-kai. Soon, Hiroshima is once again embroiled in gang war.

Even the young bloods of the Hirono gang join the fray, though their boss is in prison. One of their first tasks is to kill Makihara (Kunie Tanaka), the boss of a rival Kure gang, who has recently been released from jail. Hirono is finally freed, but before he can retake command of his gang, he is approached by Takeda, who urges Hirono to retire—with the aim of peacefully removing a possible threat. Hirono, however, distrusts Takeda's protestations of sincerity and rejoins his old gang. Soon after, hitmen from the Hayakawa-gumi spray bullets into a car in which Matsumura and his lieutenant Eda (Shingo Yamashiro) are riding. Eda is killed, but Matsumura survives—and becomes determined to take revenge on his foes. The twenty-year Hiroshima gang war is about to reach its bloody climax.

CRITIQUE

In bringing the *Jingi Naki Tatakai* (Battles without Honor and Humanity) epic to a conclusion, director Kinji Fukasaku and scriptwriter Kazuo Kasahara weave a tale of intrigue, treachery, and murder worthy of sixteenth-century Florence. Akira Kobayashi is particularly noteworthy as Takeda, the Tensei-kai chairman whose sangfroid is only matched by his inscrutability and duplicity. In sharp contrast to his phlegmatic boss, Kinya Kitaoji's Matsumura impresses one as intelligent but self-destructively volatile. His outbursts express a dangerous sincerity—and inject a welcome vitality into proceedings that might otherwise have been too middle-aged. (Imagine Al Pacino's Michael Corleone crossed with James Caan's Sonny.)

Playing Otomo, Matsumura's blustering mortal enemy, Jo Shishido provides an instructive example of the dangers of hubris. The sort of outrageous behavior that might have been tolerated in the traditional world of the *ninkyo eiga*—think Wakayama Tomisaburo—is fatal in the new world of the corporate gang, where cooler and smarter heads prevail. In the end, the gangs survive, but the old free ways of the early postwar years die away. Though not a nostalgist in the Coppola mold, Fukasaku depicts the passing of an era with starkness and force.

Jingi no Hakaba (1975)

GRAVEYARD OF HONOR

Scr.: Tatsuhiro Kamoi. *Dir.:* Kinji Fukasaku. *Prod.:* Toei. *Main cast:* Tetsuya Watari, Tatsuo Umemiya, Hajime Hana, Yumi Takigawa, Noboru Ando, Meika Seri, Eiji Go, Kenji Imai. 94 mins.

STORY

The year: 1941. A young gangster, Rikio Ishikawa (Tetsuya Watari), joins the Ikebukuro-based Kawada-gumi. Two years later, he is arrested and sent to a reformatory in Hakodate—his first, but not last, stretch in jail. Back on the streets of Shinjuku, Ishikawa steals the takings of rival yakuza from a shoe repair scam. Caught, he is forced to apologize to their *oyabun*.

He then meets Imai (Tatsuo Umemiya), a fellow gangster who complains that *sangoku-jin*—Koreans, Chinese, and other Asian nationals freed from second-class citizenship by the Occupation—are lording it over the Japanese. Soon after, Imai's gang gets into a quarrel with Korean gangsters over money stolen from a gambling den. In the subsequent street battle, Ishikawa ducks into the room of Chieko (Yumi Takigawa), an apprentice geisha, to avoid the fighting, but leaves in time to be arrested with Imai and the other brawlers. Thrown into the same cell, the Japanese and Korean gangsters resume their fight, but Ichikawa, Imai, and the other Japanese are soon put back on the street by the cops, who need their help in controlling the uppity *sangokujin* hoods.

Imai, Ishikawa, and the gang celebrate their freedom with a wild party after which a drunken Ishikawa breaks into Chieko's room again and rapes her—a prelude to love. The scene shifts to a political rally in Shinjuku, where a prominent *tekiya* leader, Nozu (Noboru Ando), is running for city council—another indication of the growing power of the gangs.

In a cabaret, Ishikawa picks a fight with and knifes the Shinwa-kai *oyabun*. He escapes but is scolded by his own *oyabun*, Kawada, for causing unnecessary trouble. With the Kawada-gumi and Shinwa-kai now at loggerheads, Kawada asks Nozu for advice. Nozu tells him to use the Americans, who control the flow of goods to the black market, to get the edge on the Shinwa-kai. A month later, however, Nozu loses the election by 5,000 votes, a bitter defeat.

At a gambling den, Ishikawa sees a prominent politician receive a loan from the gangsters in charge. When Ishikawa asks for a loan, however, they toss him out—and he torches

their boss's car in revenge. Ishikawa is beaten severely by Kawada for causing yet more trouble and goes to Iwai's place to recover. He comes back later—and stabs Kawada. Ishikawa is sent into prison and expelled from the yakuza world for ten years.

Two years later, in October 1948, Ichikawa is released. He is greeted by Imai, who gets into trouble with the other gangs for sheltering him before his term of expulsion ends. With all avenues closed to him in Tokyo, Ishikawa goes to Osaka, where he contracts tuberculosis and becomes a drug addict. He befriends a drifter named Kosaki (Kunie Tanaka), who becomes his partner in petty crime.

Ishikawa, however, can't stay away from Tokyo or stop committing new outrages. He ends up killing Imai—and is arrested by the police (with the assistance of the yakuza, who toss rocks at Ishikawa and Kosaki in their hideout). He is sentenced to ten years in prison, and soon after Chieko commits suicide. Ten days before, she had been legally registered as Ishikawa's wife. Ishikawa feels twinges of guilt—and an even stronger longing for oblivion.

CRITIQUE

Released in 1975, *Jingi no Hakaba* (Graveyard of Honor) is similar in theme to Kinji Fukasaku's 1972 *Gendai Yakuza: Hitokiri Yota* (Street Mobster). Both films feature mad-dog heroes, who violate the rules of yakuza society and pay the inevitable price. The two films also serve as bookends to the peak of Fukasaku's career. But while *Hitokiri Yota* was an installment in a six-part series that launched Bunta Sugawara to stardom, *Jingi no Hakaba* was a standalone film, based on a true story and featuring an already established star, Tetsuya Watari.

Both films take the outlaw-against-the-establishment theme to new limits, with their heroes battling not only the usual underworld enemies, but the entire world; *Jingi no Hakaba* plunges to darker depths, however. While Sugawara's Yota goes out in a blaze of crazy glory, Watari's Ishikawa ends as a lost soul, whose epitaph, carved on the wall of his cell, is *"Owarai—sanjunen baka sawagi owatta"* (What a laugh—the thirty-year party is over.) He is not only wild at heart but possessed of a death wish, not just untamable but unmoored from human society—and taking down any who cling to him.

Ishikawa begins the film as a boy who has seen too much, been loved too little. Offered love by Chieko, he can feel but not respond until she herself is past saving. In the film's most memorable scene, he eats her bones as a gesture of, if not quite remorse, a hunger that can now never be satisfied. It is appalling, this hunger, which is that of a man who fears nothing because he has lost everything. Most gang films romanticize the gangster's courtship of death. *Jingi no Hakaba* rejects the illusion of an honorable end (or a cool one); Ishikawa dies with, not a grand gesture, but a plunge into stark oblivion.

Jinsei Gekijo: Hishakaku (1963)

THEATER OF LIFE: HISHAKAKU

Scr.: Kinya Naoi. *Dir.:* Tadashi Sawashima. *Prod.:* Toei. *Main cast:* Koji Tsuruta, Yoshiko Sakuma, Ryunosuke Tsukigata, Ken Takakura, Tatsuo Umemiya, Hideo Murata, Ryuji Oki, Yoshi Kato. 95 mins.

STORY

The time: The mid-Taisho Period (1912–26). The place: A prison cell where Kakutaro Koyama, nicknamed Hishakaku (Koji Tsuruta), listens to a new prisoner in the next cell, protesting his innocence. Meanwhile, he remembers another time, another place. The scene shifts to a brothel in Yokohama, where Hishakaku persuades his lover, the courtesan Otoyo (Yoshiko Sakuma), to escape. They make their way through the snow to a hideaway in Fukagawa, a Tokyo pleasure quarter,

but Hishakaku is called away to help his benefactor, the Kokin *oyabun* (Yoshi Kato), in a struggle with a rival gang, the Oyokodas—whose members include Hishakaku's former comrades.

Even though he is only a "guest" of the gang, Hishakaku goes with two Kokin men, one of whom is the master swordsman Miyagawa (Ken Takakura), to the Oyokoda headquarters. In the ensuing melee, Hishakaku stabs the rival *oyabun* and makes his escape alone. He is taken in by Kiratsune (Ryunosuke Tsukigata), an old yakuza who is living with the son (Tatsuo Umemiya) of his late boss. The son is attending Waseda University and intends to become a novelist. When the police come calling, Kiratsune covers for Hishakaku—and earns his undying gratitude.

Leaving Otoyo in the care of another ally, Narahei *oyabun* (Michitaro Mizushima), Hishakaku gives himself up to the authorities. Otoyo, who believed Hishakaku's promise to go straight, is distraught. Later at a summer festival, Narahei and Otoyo encounter Kokin *oyabun*. Soon after, the old *oyabun* is shot—and Otoyo realizes to her horror that Narahei is responsible.

Otoyo runs away and becomes a maid in a teahouse. Narahei and his men find and try to silence her, but she is rescued by Miyagawa, now working as a rickshaw man following the breakup of the Kokin gang. When she collapses with a fever, Miyagawa nurses her back to health, and they become lovers. Then, Otoyo learns that he was a yakuza—and discovers that she was Hishakaku's woman. Overcome with shame, Otoyo runs away and enters a brothel. After a long search, Miyagawa finds and asks her to escape with him, but she can't forget Hishakaku.

Then, Kiratsune comes with money to pay off her debt to the brothel—and learns about her relationship with Miyagawa. He tells Hishakaku this when he gets out of prison, after a three-year stretch. Together, they go to the fishing village that is Kiratsune's old home, where Hishakaku intends to make a new start. There, he confronts the contrite Miyagawa and Otoyo. When Miyagawa offers to cut off a finger in apology, Hishakaku tells him, "Even if you cut them all off, it wouldn't satisfy me," but ends up forgiving him and Otoyo.

Miyagawa then single-handedly takes on the Narahei gang in revenge for the murder of his old *oyabun* but is killed. When Hishakaku hears of his death, he first takes on the local gangsters who have insulted him and Kiratsune, then returns to the city to settle accounts with Narahei.

CRITIQUE

Tadashi Sawashima's *Jinsei Gekijo: Hishakaku* (Theater of Life) became one of the big hits of 1963—and launched the 1960s ninkyo *eiga* boom. Two sequels followed in quick succession, completing a three-part series, all based on a novel of the same title by Shiro Ozaki. Among other directors who mined the novel for film material were Tomu Uchida (*Jinsei Gekijo: Seishunhe* for Nikkatsu, 1936, and *Jinsei Gekijo: Hishakaku to Kiratsune* for Toei, 1968); Tai Kato (*Jinsei Gekijo* for Shochiku, 1972); and Kinji Fukasaku (*Jinsei Gekijo* for Toei, 1983).

But though Sawashima's film set the *ninkyo eiga* pattern, its focus is less on the tug-of-war between *giri* and *ninjo* than on its triangular love story. Yoshiko Sakuma, who was having an affair with co-star Koji Tsuruta at the time of filming, pulls out all stops as Otoyo, the prostitute who loses two lovers to the *ninkyo* code. Unlike most actresses in similar roles, who choke back tears over their men's self-destructive actions, Sakuma howls with despair and refuses to be consoled.

By comparison, co-stars Tsuruta and Ken Takakura go through what will become familiar stoic motions in the coming years, though these two future icons inject the film with sensual passion (Tsuruta) and brash energy (Takakura). Meanwhile, silent period drama

star Ryunosuke Tsukigata is superb as the wise old yakuza who embodies the traditional values that the modern world is fast forgetting. The ending, which comes midway through Tsuruta's climactic one-against-all fight with the bad *oyabun*'s gang, is cinematic coitus interruptus—and an obvious ploy for a sequel.

Jinsei Gekijo: Hishakaku to Kiratsune (1968)

THEATER OF LIFE: HISHAKAKU AND KIRATSUNE

Scr.: Goro Tanada. *Dir.:* Tomu Uchida. *Prod.:* Toei. *Main cast:* Koji Tsuruta, Ryutaro Tatsumi. Ken Takakura, Junko Fuji, Sachiko Hidari. Hiroki Matsukata, Shogo Shimada, Rin'ichi Yamamoto. 109 mins.

STORY

Hishakaku (Koji Tsuruta), a *kyakubun* (visitor) with the Kokin gang, frees his lover Otoyo (Junko Fuji) from a brothel run by boss Oyokota (Tatsuo Endo)—and consequently brawls with Oyokota's gang, accompanied by Miyagawa (Ken Takakura) and other Kokin gangsters. After killing several of Oyokota's men, including a former *anikibun* (elder brother) who has betrayed him, Hishakaku flees, with the police in close pursuit, and takes refuge in a strange house. There, he encounters Kiratsune (Ryutaro Tatsumi), an old man who calmly invites him in, gives him sake, and advises him to give himself up. Struck by the nobility of the old man's character and the sageness of his advice, Hishakaku does as he says.

Four years pass and Miyagawa is in love with Otoyo, who went into hiding after Hishakaku's arrest. When he finds that she is Hishakaku's woman, he wants to run away with her but Otoyo hesitates—and disappears again. Then, Hishakaku gets out of prison and, with Kiratsune's support, reunites with Otoyo and Miyagawa. When an Oyokota hitman (Rin'ichi

The big five of the Kokin Clan. Ken Takakura (left) and Koji Tsuruta (right) flank a gang lantern in this poster for *Jinsei Gekijo: Hishakaku to Kiratsune* (Theater of Life: Hishakaku and Kiratsune, 1968).

Yamamoto) gets wind of Hishakaku's whereabouts, he comes to whack him—but Miyagawa stands in his way. When the hitman takes refuge with a local gang, Miyagawa pursues him—and is cut down in turn. Now, it is Hishakaku's turn to take revenge against the killers of his friend.

CRITIQUE

Based on a novel by Shiro Ozaki, Tadashi Sawashima's 1963 *Jinsei Gekijo: Hishakaku* launched the 1960s *ninkyo eiga* boom. Two more films followed in quick succession, completing a three-part series. Tomu Uchida's 1968 *Jinsei Gekijo: Hishakaku to Kiratsune* is based on the same novel as the previous films but not a continuation. Interestingly, Uchida also made *Jinsei Gekijo: Seishunhen* (Theater of Life) in 1936 for Nikkatsu, again using the Ozaki novel as material. His Toei film, however, is taken from the last third of the book.

Though a typical Toei product in its casting and story line, *Jinsei Gekijo: Hishakaku to Kiratsune* is a cut above for its restrained, complex interplay of friendship and love, self-interest and self-sacrifice, as well as for its layered, resonant performances, particularly by Tsuruta as Hishakaku. Though often playing a stoic who endures much for the sake of the *ninkyo* code—which those around him usually honor more in the breach than the observance—Tsuruta was also one of the great screen lovers of the postwar period. And his performance in *Jinsei Gekijo* brings out both sides of his screen persona to powerful effect. In one early scene, he even sings a wistful children's song to Junko Fuji's Otoyo that expresses both the depth of his passion and his despair with life on the run.

A veteran star of the Shingeki stage, Ryutaro Tatsumi impresses as the sagely servant Kiratsune, who takes the gangster Hishakaku under his wing while nurturing the scholarly ambitions of his dead master's son, played by Hiroki Matsukata. He also utters one of the film's more memorable lines: "The only thing a yakuza has to look forward to is a red kimono [of the condemned prisoner] or a white kimono [of the corpse]" *(Yakuza no ikusaki wa akai kimono ka shiroi kimono ka sore igai ni ne yo).*

Jitsuroku Ando Gumi Gaiden: Garo no Okite (2002)

THE TRUE HISTORY OF THE ANDO GANG: RULES OF THE STARVING WOLF

Scr.: Toshiyuki Tabe. *Dir.:* Shun'ichi Kajima. *Prod.:* Toei Video. *Main cast:* Noboru Ando, Show Aikawa, Masayuki Imai, Hiroyuki Watanabe, Nanako Okochi, Noriko Aota. 90 mins.

Most Hollywood movie gangsters have had little or nothing to do with the gangs in real life. Even George Raft, notorious in 1930s Hollywood for his underworld connections, got his break as a Charleston dancer, not a hood. Then, there is Noboru Ando, who was not only a real gangster but had a real gang movie career, appearing in fifty-one films for major studios in the 1960s and 1970s, while acting out versions of his own story in such films as *Jitsuroku Ando-gumi: Shugekihen* (The True Story of the Ando Gang: Attack, 1973) and *Ando-gumi Gaiden: Hitokiri Shatei* (The Untold Story of the Ando Gang: The Killer Brother, 1974). His first film, the 1965 *Chi to Okite* (Blood and Rules) recounted the rise and fall of his gang, the Ando-gumi, with Ando starring as himself—and became a big hit for the Shochiku Studio.

As an actor, Ando may have had the deadest of dead pans, but his quiet air of menace made the more extroverted types around him look like poseurs. It helped that he had a scar running from the corner of his mouth to his left ear, acquired in a youthful brawl with a Korean gangster. Ando knew he was the real deal and saw no need to out-Method Al Pacino to prove it. Instead, he just did what came naturally—and the fans kept coming back for more. "In

Japanese, the only difference between 'yakuza' and '*yakusha*' [actor] is one hiragana character," Ando once told me. "All yakuza have to be actors to survive."

Ando, who was born in 1925, is still making yakuza movies, but for the video shelves, not the theater screens. Also, he is now playing, not the tough guy hero, but the gangland elder. His latest film, *Jitsuroku Ando Gumi Gaiden: Garo no Okite* (The True History of the Ando Gang: Rules of the Starving Wolf), is yet another recounting of his underworld adventures, with Ando doing the narrating. Dressed in an elegant gray kimono, surrounding by attentive listeners in a beautiful Japanese-style house, he looks less like a former wise guy, more like a retired statesman revisiting the scenes of his youth.

The main subject of his reminiscences, however, is Kei Hanagata, a top lieutenant of the Ando-gumi who lived fast, died young, and left a beautiful corpse. With his trademark dark shades and white clothes (including a snazzy white felt hat), and his legendary refusal to fight with anything more than his fists of steel, Hanagata was yakuza cool personified. Following his death at the age of thirty-two in 1963, he became the subject of several films. The director of the latest, Shun'ichi Kajima, also featured Hanagata in his 1993 gang comedy *Shuraba no Ningengaku* (The Anthropology of a Fight Scene). Played with swaggering panache by Shinji Yamashita, this Hanagata, Ando later claimed, was the closest of all the movie versions to the real thing. *Garo no Okite*'s Hanagata is Show Aikawa, the biggest star in the OV industry, who can walk his character's strutting walk with the right presence and authority. When he strides to another showdown, coattails billowing behind, he's so flagrantly *kakko ii* (cool) that even fashion-phobes in the audience will mutter an involuntary "wow."

The story starts in 1945, with Japan in ruins and the survivors scrambling to making a living by any means necessary, legal or no. Among

© 2002 Toei Video

Former gang boss Noboru Ando (left) reminisces about old partner in crime Kei Hanagata (Show Aikawa), in *Jitsuroku Ando Gumi Gaiden: Garo no Okite* (The True History of the Ando Gang: Rules of the Starving Wolf, 2002).

them are students who may have entered elite universities but prefer busting heads to cracking books. One is Hanagata (Aikawa), a boxer and rugby player; another is Izawa (Masayuki Imai), who runs with the Ando-gumi, a *gurentai* that rules Shibuya. After an all-out brawl in which they end up battling the police instead of each other, Hanagata and Izawa become fast friends. Ando (Hiroyuki Watanabe) also takes a liking to Hanagata despite his loose-cannon rep, and asks him to join the gang.

Though Hanagata rises quickly in the gang hierarchy and even acquires a wife (Nanako Okochi) and a baby son, he remains the romantic who loves a good rumble and refuses to set up a legitimate front, despite the advice of the more level-headed Izawa. After killing a fat *chinpira* in a street fight, Hanagata is sentenced to three years in prison. When he gets out, his wife is gone, but his gang welcomes him back—and he soon picks up where he violently left off, with his motto being "do unto others before others do unto you" (*yararetara yarikaesu*). His wild ways, however, incur the displeasure of Izawa's shrewish wife (Noriko Aota), who wants him not only out of her life but out of the world. He doesn't know it, but she is his most dangerous opponent.

Hanagata finally goes over the line when, in a drunken rage, he breaks up a cabaret run by a colleague from the Ando-gumi and adds insult to injury by slapping the staff around. When Izawa wife's hears, she gives one of the slapped a gun and dares him to do his worst. Pissing his pants with fear, the *chinpira* shoots Hanagata outside of a club and runs for his life. *Yararetara yarikaesu*. But the Hanagata saga does not end here—rising like a phoenix in soiled whites, he transforms from man into legend.

This is sure-fire stuff, but it is also an often-told story and Kajima does nothing particularly new with it. One problem is the film's bare-bones budget, which necessitated the use of present-day cars and backdrops for their period equivalents, undercutting authenticity. (There is something distracting about 1950s gangsters piling into a Benz that looks as though it had just rolled off the Yanase lot.) Another is a script that does little more than string together incidents, like an Ando-gumi Greatest Hits CD. Among the saving graces is Aikawa, who may be too puffy for a young man's role but still gives good action, including one memorable scene in which he defiantly guzzles sake at a *yatai* (outdoor stall) while blood pours out of his punctured stomach. Hanagata, wherever he is, would probably be proud.

Jitsuroku Ando Noboru Outlaw-den: Rekka (2002)

DEADLY OUTLAW: REKKA

Scr.: Shigenori Takechi. *Dir.:* Takashi Miike. *Prod.:* Toei Video. *Main cast:* Riki Takeuchi, Yuya Uchida, Ken'ichi Endo, Renji Ishibashi, Rikiya, Kazuya Nakayama, Daijiro Harada, Shin'ichi "Sonny" Chiba, Tetsuro Tanba. 96 mins.

This month's film by the insanely prolific Takashi Miike, *Jitsuroku Ando Noboru Outlaw-den: Rekka* (Deadly Outlaws: Rekka) is a yakuza thriller with the by-now-standard supercharged beginning and ending. The story in-between, about a gang power struggle, "supervised" by former gang boss and legendary Toei star Noboru Ando, is uncharacteristically twisty, however. It's as though after *Koroshiya Ichi* (Ichi the Killer)—that feature-length wallow in madness, deviance, and gore—that Miike realized he was in danger of being typed as Mr. Geek Show and drew back into, if not normality, a semblance of conventionality.

The opening is that gang genre standby: the assassination of an *oyabun* by an anonymous hitman. Because this is a Miike film, the hitman is shot running at a breakneck pace through the streets, as Joe Yamanaka's rock score pounds, then leaping into space. As the hitman comes flying over a roof in slo-mo, both guns out, he blasts the *oyabun*'s bodyguards and finally the long-haired *oyabun* (Yuya Uchida) himself. The old boy is hard to put down, however, throttling the hitman with both hands even as round after round slams into his body. Then . . . but why spoil one of Miike's cooler effects? It's enough to say that the boss ends up dead, while the hitman ends up with a most unusual necklace.

Naturally, this hit enrages the surviving Sanada-gumi members, particularly Kunisada (Riki Takeuchi), a fire-eating gang lieutenant who regarded the *oyabun* as a surrogate father. Back on the streets after a stretch in prison, Kunisada goes on the hunt for the killers together with his doggedly faithful, second-in-command Shimatani (Ken'ichi Endo) and the rest of his crew. The contractor of the hit, Kunisada learns, is Otaki (Renji Ishibashi), the boss of the rival Otaki-kai and a degenerate swine. Whacking Otaki will start a war—not that Kunisada cares. He and Shimatani move on the attack, while finding time to bed two Korean girls drifting about the big city.

Meanwhile, Kunisada's Sanada-gumi colleagues, including the gravel-voiced Kugihara (Rikiya) and smooth-talking Iguchi (Kazuya Nakayama), are maneuvering for the top spot behind his back—and intend to use him as cannon fodder. Scheming on the other side is Nakajo (Daijiro Harada), an Otaki-kai capo whose loyalty to his slithery boss is less than absolute. Serving as mediator is Hijikata (Shin'ichi "Sonny" Chiba), a Bando Rengo boss who seems to be the soul of neutrality, while playing both sides against each other for his own ends. Observing these plottings and counterplottings is a gang elder known only as Gozen (Tetsuro Tanba), who may be cloistered in his mountain retreat but sees and knows all.

Needless to say, Kunisada gets his man, with a grimly clever ruse that belies his out-of-control image, and becomes the target of the same Otaki hitmen who whacked Sanada. These two, however, are not the only ones who want him and those around him dead. As outrage follows outrage, Kunisada's anger grows until he is ready to annihilate his enemies with a display of firepower that would do the U.S. military proud.

After appearing in more than 170 films, usually as a yakuza, Riki Takeuchi is a practiced hand at the sort of scowls and explosions the part of Kunisada requires. Miike, however, pushes Takeuchi beyond his usual mannerisms, as when, armed with a crowbar, he lays waste to a gang of mocking hoods and finishes the slaughter with a manic, woebegone glance at his stunned girlfriend, exposing the needy little boy behind the tough-guy mask. This sort of I-couldn't-help-it-please-forgive-me look is utterly un-yakuza, though as he grows older and pudgier, Takeuchi is taking on an uncanny resemblance to Bill Clinton.

Also, while supplying the sort of over-the-top action his fans have come to expect, such as firestorms that consume entire buildings, Miike is more interested in the film's complex intrigues than its slam-bang effects. Is this just another phase—Miike taking a breather before plunging again into the pop-culture cesspool—or is he finally growing up?

Juichinin no Gang (1963)

ELEVEN GANGSTERS

Scr./Dir.: Teruo Ishii. *Prod.:* Toei. *Main cast:* Koji Tsuruta, Naoki Sugiura, Ken Takakura, Shinjiro Ehara, Kyosuke Machida, Hideo Taka, I George, Toru Abe, Tatsumi Umemiya, Yoko Mihara, Reiko Hitomi. 91 mins.

STORY

Gondo (Koji Tsuruta) and Betto (Naoki Sugiura) have the brilliant idea of robbing a steel tubing plant in Hamamatsu—much easier, they think, than knocking over yet another bank. The target: the 500 million yen payroll for the plant's eighteen thousand employees. The date: the twenty-fourth, just before pay day. First though, they have to recruit a crew for the job—two alone won't do. Betto, a smooth operator in a white trench coat and shades, hires Sawakami, a rough-hewn trucker, to drive the get-away truck for the equivalent of three year's salary. Meanwhile, Gondo recruits Ebina (Shinjiro Ehara), an old pal who runs a bar and asks him to bring two more robbers on board, for 4 million yen each. He also borrows some needed cash from Miwa (Michiyo Kogure), a wealthy woman living in baronial splendor with her younger lover (Tetsuro Tanba).

Then, Mayumi (Yoko Mihara), a cabaret hostess, hears enough about the job from the suddenly flush Sawakami to become curious. At the behest of her boss (Toru Abe), who is also wondering how a drunken slob like Sawakami happens to be walking around with 10,000-yen notes, she follows his benefactor, Betto, all the way to Tokyo. No fool, Betto catches her, makes her confess—and takes her to bed. Meanwhile, Gondo buys weaponry from a low-life dealer (I George) and visits his hard-working mother and fresh-faced sister.

The gang gets together for a final strategy session at Miwa's mansion. A tolerant sort, especially where her own money is concerned, Miwa pitches in with advice. Meanwhile, Yuki (Reiko Hitomi), a cabaret singer who is Gondo's girlfriend, volunteers to drive. The day of the heist all goes well: Gondo, Betto, and the rest of the crew pay a surprise visit to the plant office and make off with the cash. But then the getaway starts to go wrong.

CRITIQUE

Released in January 1963, *Juichinin no Gang* (Eleven Gangsters) was intended as a crowd-pleasing caper flick with an all-star cast, headlined by Koji Tsuruta and Naoki Sugiura. Tsuruta, better known for his stoic hero roles, is convincingly ruthless as the gang leader, while adding his characteristic gravitas to the proceedings. Sugiura, with his slick look and cool exterior, embodies the film's swinging 1960s mood, while Ken Takakura, who has yet to enter his screen icon phase, plays amusingly against type as the slack-jawed truck driver with the silver front tooth.

The three female leads also impress. Wives and girlfriends in yakuza films are usually clingy types, with little or no existence independent of their gangster significant others. This trio, however, takes an active role in the heist, while more than holding their own with the men around them. Eiren, the industry censorship board, fretted that the film might "mislead youth" because its crooks were too attractively clever and brought their heist off too

easily. Also, critics of the time pointed out the film's close resemblance to the Rat Pack vehicle *Ocean's Eleven*, although Frank, Dean, and the gang would have never deigned to rob a steel mill. In 1963, however, Las Vegas casinos were beyond the dreams of even the best and brightest Japanese thieves.

Kamikaze Taxi (1995)

Scr./Dir.: Masato Harada. *Prod.*: Pony Canyon. *Main cast*: Kazuya Takahashi, Mickey Curtis, Koji Yakusho, Reiko Takahashi. 150 mins.

Masato Harada's *Kamikaze Taxi* depicts the plight of ethnic Japanese from South America who have come to Japan to find a prosperity denied to them in the land of their birth. As we learn from the interviews with returnees that open the film, they often encounter prejudice in finding housing and work, even though they are Japanese by blood and statute. The reason? They talk and act differently, listen to different music, and eat different food. They aren't "real" Japanese.

Kamikaze Taxi touches other thematic bases as well, including the meltdown of Japanese politics, the Neanderthalism of certain Japanese politicians, the spread of drugs in Japanese society, and the rise of self-help movements, including the inevitable spiritual snake-oil peddlers. But though Harada may probe at contemporary society's ills, his central concerns are the universal ones of friendship and loss, love, and revenge. His characters are searching for meaning and connection on society's fringes but finding both in short supply. The price of the search, they discover, can be isolation and even death.

Tatsuo (Kazuya Takahashi) is a cocky *chinpira* whom his yakuza bosses are grooming as a pimp. But the first hooker he supplies to an elderly conservative politician returns from her date beaten half to death. When Tatsuo's girl-

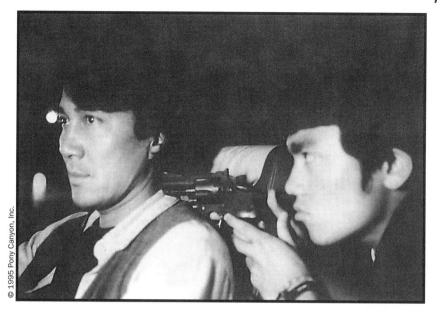

© 1995 Pony Canyon, Inc.

Taking the cab driver for a ride. Koji Yakusho (left) as a cabby and Kazuya Takahashi as a *chinpira* in *Kamikaze Taxi* (1995).

friend protests, a pony-tailed boss named Animal (Mickey Curtis) kills her as Tatsuo looks on. Enraged, Tatsuo seeks revenge by breaking into the politician's house with his *chinpira* pals and stealing a large pot full of money.

The gang *anikibun* soon trace them to the countryside villa where they are hiding out and begin executing them one by one. Firing at his pursuers, Tatsuo makes his escape, together with several of his crew. He is the only one to emerge from the woods alive, however. Vowing to stage a kamikaze raid on the gang headquarters, he finds a taxi and orders the driver to take him to a town on the Izu Peninsula. But the Japanese-Peruvian driver (Koji Yakusho) can't read the map. "A foreigner!" Tatsuo groans.

Calm where Tatsuo is excitable, quiet where Tatsuo is loud, the driver seems at first a Third World innocent, lost and out of place in the midst of First World sophistication and corruption. But as they travel through the countryside, stopping for occasional gun battles, the driver emerges as a tower of inner strength. Tatsuo and the hooker (Reiko Takahashi), who later joins this odyssey, come to respect that strength. The driver, in turn, takes

Tatsuo's side. By the time Tatsuo makes his raid, they are no longer passenger and driver, but allies.

The driver is a familiar type in Hollywood films, the minority father or older brother figure (African-American, Native American, you name it) who sets the young majority hero straight. But *Kamikaze Taxi* takes us beyond surface ethnicisms to the heart of contemporary Japan. The ride is long, winding, and occasionally bumpy, but the sights along the way are extraordinary.

Kanto Mushuku (1963)

KANTO WANDERER

Scr.: Yasujiro Yagi. *Dir.:* Seijun Suzuki. *Prod.:* Nikkatsu. Main *cast:* Akira Kobayashi, Hiroko Ito, Daizaburo Hirata, Chieko Matsubara, Sanae Nakahara, Taiji Tonoyama, Toru Abe, Keisuke Noro, Yunosuke Ito. 93 mins.

STORY

A trio of schoolgirls is attracted to a handsome yakuza, Katsuta (Akira Kobayashi), of the

Ito-gumi. They also make the acquaintance of Diamond no Fuyu (Daizaburo Hirata), a young *chinpira* with the gang. But only one of the three, Hanako (Sanae Nakahara), can stand to watch Diamond get tattooed—a painful procedure that sends the other girls fleeing. Eager to learn more about the yakuza world, Hanako goes with him to a gang-run gambling game. The comically clumsy dealer, Tetsu (Keisuke Noro), takes a liking to her—and Diamond has a rival. The police raid the game and arrest Hanako but let her off with a warning. Tetsu later runs into Hanako on the street—and persuades her to help him work a variant of the badger game. Picking up a strange man at the train station, Hanako lures him to a room, but Tetsu makes a botch of it and Hanako finds herself in more trouble than she can handle. Katsuta chances to meet Tatsuko (Hiroko Ito), a professional scam artist he first encountered four years ago at a *ryokan*. There, he exposed her and her male partner—and was slashed on the cheek by the latter for his trouble. He still wears the scar—and cherishes the memory of their brief affair.

Katsuta asks Tetsu about Hanako, who has dropped out of sight. Tetsu says he doesn't know where she is. They go looking but fail to find her. They end up staying at a hotel, where a gambling game is underway. Tetsu wants to play, but Katsuta suspects the game is fixed. Tetsu goes anyway—and Katsuta eventually follows. He finds Tatsuko together with her husband—the lantern-jawed Okaru Hachi (Yunosuke Ito), who is winning with an ingenious scam that involves a cigarette case with a mirror surface. After the others have left, Katsuta challenges him to a gambling duel. Okaru Hachi accepts—and uses yet another scam to win.

Tatsuko is hiding Diamond, her younger brother. He is still obsessed with Hanako—and when he finally meets Katsuta, demands to know what has happened to her. Katsuta doesn't know, however. Meanwhile, Katsuta is still wrestling with his own feelings for Tatsuko (just as she is wrestling with her feelings for him).

A power struggle is brewing between the Ito-gumi and the rival Yoshida-gumi, which has been muscling in on the former's gambling business. The short-tempered, short-sighted Ito boss (Taiji Tonoyama) suspects Katsuta of disloyalty. Though sorely tempted to quit the whole yakuza business, Katsuta feels a sense of obligation to the gang—and is willing to face Yoshida and his entire crew alone to prove it. Finally, the Ito boss is whacked by a hitman— and Katsuta swings into action.

CRITIQUE

Directed by Seijun Suzuki, *Kanto Mushuku* (Kanto Wanderer) was the second film to use Taiko Hirabayashi's novel as inspiration, after Hiroshi Noguchi's 1956 *Chitei no Uta* (Songs from the Underground). In making his first *ninkyo eiga*, however, Seijun Suzuki created a look that owed little to previous gangster films, much to Suzuki's beloved Kabuki. Working with art director Takeo Kimura and cameraman Shigeyoshi Mine, Suzuki incorporated Kabukiesque touches throughout the film, beginning with Akira Kobayashi's theatrically painted eyebrows and knife scar. It is in the third act, however, as Kobayashi strides to his long-destined confrontation with the rival gang—that Suzuki's stylistics reach their height of audaciousness, with primary colors splashing boldly across the screen to express the characters' turbulent emotions.

Red, for example, signals Kobayashi's determination to stake all for the *ninkyo* code. When he invades a rival gang's gambling den and slices two enemy gangsters with his sword, one falls back against the *fusuma* (sliding doors) in the background. As it collapses, a solid band of red light floods in, framing Kobayashi in a white loincloth.

Whether this bold use of color deepens the film is questionable; the emotions remain conventional, the plot, with its clash of duty and inclination, all-too familiar. Nonetheless, Suzuki's departures from genre norms were more than attention-getting stunts, bringing as they did a new beauty and vivacity to the screen, as well as mythological dimension of a type often hinted at in earlier films but rarely presented with such confidence and craft. There was also a pranksterish element to Suzuki's work, however, that became more evident with each passing film, reaching its climax in the 1967 *Koroshi no Rakuin* (Branded to Kill)—a mad adventure in genre-bending that effectively ended his studio career.

Kaoyaku (1965)

BOSS

Scr.: Kazuo Kasahara, Kinji Fukasaku, Teruo Ishii. *Dir.:* Teruo Ishii. *Prod.:* Toei. *Main cast:* Koji Tsuruta, Ken Takakura, Kyosuke Machida, Shinjiro Ebara, I. George, Yoshiko Sakuma, Yoshiko Mita, Junko Fuji, Toru Abe, Minoru Oki, Meicho Soganoya. 91 mins.

STORY

A contract to prepare reclaimed land for a major development project is up for grabs and the Kanto Josei-kai aims to snag it, as does the Kansai Doshi-kai, a gang trying to establish itself on Kanto turf. The boss of the Kanto Josei-kai, Hiyama (Toru Abe), assigns Nakagami (Koji Tsuruta) and Hayami (Ken Takakura) to the task of winning the contract and thwarting the Kansai gang. The Koda-gumi, a subgang of the Kansai Doshi-kai, stands in their way.

With the help of Kashiwada (Minoru Oki), a gangster-turned-bar-owner pal, Nakagami meets Kosugi (Meicho Soganoya), the local boss, who has the power to fix the contact but tells Nakagami that he hates yakuza and wants nothing to do with his or any other gang. Soon after, Hayami goes to meet the town mayor, with the intention of bullying him into submission, but runs into Mayumi (Yoshiko Mita), an old flame who is Kashiwada's younger sister. He pursues Mayumi, but she says she wants nothing more to do with him—though her look of longing as he saunters away sends a different message.

The mayor is intimidated into awarding the contract to Nakagami and work gets underway. Then, Nakagami hears, from a nosy reporter who is hot for Mayumi, that the officials are preparing the site, not for dairy farming as he had been led to believe, but a housing development. Nakagami goes to Tokyo, with Hayami following close behind, to persuade Hiyama to do the job properly—otherwise the development will be built on unstable land.

Meanwhile, Koda gangsters attack the construction site, setting a truckload of fuel barrels on fire and otherwise raising havoc. When Nakagami makes his plea, Hiyama laughs in his face—he has already made a deal with an unscrupulous developer. Gangsters dispatched by Hanaoka (Shigeru Amachi), Hiyama's second-in-command with designs on the top, wipe out Nakagami and Hiyama's crew, and Hiyama himself is killed by a Kansai Doshi-kai hitman.

The Kanto bosses hold a meeting to choose a successor and, over Hanaoka's objections, settle on Nakagami. They hear that the impulsive Hayami had threatened the developer and stolen documents—news that might scuttle the entire construction project. As the new boss, Nakagami has to confront Hayami but instead of whacking him, proposes making an unusual offering to the Kansai gang. Hayami resists at first, but decides to go along with Nakagami's plan, as the two gangs prepare for a final showdown.

CRITIQUE

Kaoyaku was originally a project of Toei uber-producer Koji Shundo, with Kazuo Kasahara assigned to script and Kinji Fukasaku to direct, but Kasahara and Fukasaku had a falling out, Fukasaku left the picture, and Teruo Ishii was brought in as a replacement. Scheduled as Toei's New Year's film for 1965 and featuring the studio's two biggest stars, Koji Tsuruta and Ken Takakura, *Kaoyaku* was conceived from the start as a major film—one too big to kill. Ishii shot it with his usual panache, though he could do little with the hackneyed love story, with Yoshiko Mita as the virginal school teacher attracted to Takakura's crude-but-charismatic gangster. Even so, Ishii's staging of the climactic scene, with the two long lines of gangsters confronting each other on reclaimed land by Tokyo Bay, is strikingly bold, with a helicopter shot pulling back from the battling hoods to reveal the rising sun at daybreak. Plenty of symbolism there.

Also noteworthy is Junko Fuji as the perky club hostess who takes a liking to a fiery gangster with a disfiguring facial scar, played by Kyosuke Machida. Fuji would soon emerge as a major star, playing strong women with tender hearts, but here she is uncharacteristically malleable—and kittenishly sexy.

Ishii used the tune that Takakura hums in the film (and that Mita later plucks out on the piano as he listens outside her window) as the theme song for his next film, *Abashiri Bangaichi*. Once again Takakura sang—and made both the song and the film smash hits.

Karakkaza Yaro (1960)

AFRAID TO DIE

Scr.: Ryuzo Kikushima. *Dir.*: Yasuzo Masumura. *Prod.*: Daiei. *Main cast*: Yukio Mishima, Ayako Wakao, Keizo Kawasaki, Eiji Funakoshi, Takashi Shimura, Yoshie Mizutani. 96 mins.

STORY

A convict, Takeo Asahina (Yukio Mishima), narrowly escapes a hitman posing as a visitor. The contractors of the hit are the Sagara-gumi, whose current boss Takeo nearly killed three years ago. When his release date approaches,

he begs prison officials to extend his sentence: Takeo knows the Sagara gang is still gunning for him. Prison rules are prison rules, however, and he has to leave at the appointed time.

Takeo escapes his waiting killers by a ruse and slips into town. Holing up at a movie theater run by his gang, he reunites with his lover Masako (Yoshie Mizutani), a nightclub singer. The reunion, however, does not go smoothly; Takeo has sussed the fact that Masako has another man. Nonetheless, he takes her pearls, which he can pawn for much-needed cash.

Yoshie (Ayako Wakao), the theater cashier, brings lunch to her union activist brother—just as yakuza thugs arrive to break up the strike he is leading. In the ensuing battle, both Yoshie and her brother are taken into custody by the police. The Sagara-gumi boss (Jun Negami)—Takeo's intended victim—hires a hitman from Hokkaido to dispose of Takeo. His name: Masa the Asthmatic (Shigeru Kamiyama).

Takeo meets with his *oyabun*, Hirayama (Takashi Shimura), and Aikawa (Eiji Funakoshi), a law school grad, who is his gang brother. The *oyabun* tells Takeo he must kill Sagara before Sagara kills him—and gives him a gun. When Takeo protests that he has just been released from prison, Aikawa agrees to do the job.

Aikawa sees his girlfriend, who works at a drug store. She tells him about a new cancer drug that has been pulled off the market after several patients died. A shipment of the drug has been lost, however, and the company, she says, would pay a lot to get it back. Worried about Aikawa's gang troubles, she urges him to give up the yakuza life and go with her to Osaka, where they can marry and start over.

Masa trails Takeo and tries to shoot him, but Takeo escapes with a nonfatal wound. He is treated by a doctor—a former gangster. Soon after, Sagara hoods torture the doctor, who tells them that a gangster named Nozawa stole the shipment. All they have to do now is relieve Nozawa of his prize—and start negotiating with the drug company.

Takeo and Yoshie become lovers, even though Takeo once fired her and, when she demanded her job back, beat her. She thinks she can reform him and tells her brother, now in jail, that she wants to spend the rest of her life with Takeo. He, however, is in no hurry to get married. When Takeo discovers Sagara's daughter alone in a park, he kidnaps her and tells her father that he will exchange the child in return for the cancer drug. They make the swap in Tokyo Station and, with a gang godfather serving as peacemaker, agree to cease hostilities and split the take from the drug company extortion scheme.

Hirayama dies and Yoshie announces that she is pregnant. Takeo tells her to get an abortion and she reluctantly agrees but has second thoughts at the abortionist's. They leave, but not before Takeo is spotted by Masako—who is now working for Sagara. Takeo tries to slip Yoshie a German abortion drug, but she suspects a trick and spits it out. When Takeo confesses, she tells him she will have the baby no matter what. Then, he hears that Sagara has kidnapped Yoshie's brother. "He means nothing to me," he tells Sagara—but in fact he does. Takeo is in too deep; he has even started to want the normal life that is Yoshie's dream.

CRITIQUE

A film that could have been a little more than a gimmick—writer Yukio Mishima gets his wish to play a yakuza on the screen—*Karakkaza Yaro* (Afraid to Die) is a surprisingly effective thriller that rewrites genre rules. Instead of coddling Mishima, then a national celebrity, director Yasuzo Masumura ran him through long rehearsals and numerous takes until he nailed each scene to Masumura's satisfaction. A spartan type, Mishima heartily approved of this nonstar treatment.

Also, instead of a stereotypical noble gangster, Mishima's Takeo is a misfit and cad. Though he struts around in a black leather jacket and greets trouble with a lopsided grin,

he is less macho than he pretends. Instead of killing the rival gang boss who is so obviously out to kill him—the course of action his *oyabun* recommends as befitting the gangster code—he uses various ruses and stratagems to survive. Meanwhile, Takeo treats his girlfriend Yoshie abominably, even trying to trick her into an abortion.

Playing this un-hero, Mishima gives a performance that, for all its stiffness and outright strangeness, is nonetheless committed: he never tries to coast or wink at the material. As Yoshie, Ayako Wakao brings a commendable professionalism to what must have been a difficult assignment (Mishima reportedly got carried away in their on-camera quarrels—and she had bruises to prove it.). Masumura filmed *Karakkaza Yaro* with his usual panache, bringing it to a memorable (if decidedly off-beat) conclusion on a moving escalator—a chilling evocation of a fantasy that Mishima had long held dear and was to fulfill a decade later, in far more grisly form.

Katte ni Shiyagare!! Godatsu Keikaku (1995)

SUIT YOURSELF OR SHOOT YOURSELF: EXTORTION PLOT 1

Scr.: Kiyoshi Kurosawa, Kuniho Yasui. *Dir.*: Kiyoshi Kurosawa. *Prod.*: KSS. *Main cast*: Show Aikawa, Koyo Maeda, Natsumi Nanase, Shun Kanda, Ren Osugi, Kinuko Horaguchi. 80 mins.

STORY

Yuji (Show Aikawa) and Kosaku (Koyo Maeda) are *chinpira* who do the gang's dirty work, such as putting the squeeze on an indebted garage owner. Punks from another gang accuse the boys of trying to steal their business—and give chase. Yuji is caught, beaten—and finds himself on a bed in a nursery school, getting treatment from an angelic teacher (Natsumi Nanase). Yuji is smitten—and barely listens when

Kosaku tells him that he wants to marry "Candy"—a hostess at a local club. The next day, Yuji goes back to the nursery school to give flowers and candy to the teacher. "I was just doing my job," she says. But Yuji insists. "This is the first time I've felt this way," he tells her—and she accept the gifts.

Yuji turns over a new leaf, getting rid of his girlie magazines and liquor. But when Kosaku shows up that night with "Candy"—she turns out to be the nursery school teacher, moonlighting at the club. Her real name, she tells the befuddled Kosaku is Ryoko. She is working a second shift, it turns out, to make 30 million yen for her father's kidney transplant operation. She breaks up with the boyish Kosaku, but Yuji is still definitely interested—and offers to help Ryoko raise the cash.

The lanky bespectacled Matsuura (Shun Kanda) appears on the scene: A former doctor who botched an operation on Ryoko's father, he happens to be desperately in love with Ryoko. She, however, calls him a *binbogami* (god of poverty) who has never brought her anything but bad luck. While acknowledging the label, he tags after Ryoko and her newfound friends.

A slinky female fixer named Yuko (Kinuko Horaguchi) encounters Yuji and Kosaku at their favorite hangout and, hearing Matsuura's sad story, offers him 30,000 yen to pose as a yakuza and extort money from a middle-aged man engaged in hanky-panky with a hostess. Yuji and Kosaku go along for moral support, which Matsuura needs because, as a yakuza, he is a total flop. Trouble comes calling in the form of a crew of real yakuza, who demand that Ryoko pay 2 million yen on her gambling debt. She had been indulging in some off-track betting and lost big. Yuji offers to slice off his little finger in recompense—but the yakuza want the money instead.

Yuko comes up with another job: a drug delivery. Yuji, Kosaku, and Ryoko pick up the white powder from a drug runner and take it to a women's only club, where a nervous Ryoko makes the handover. Mission accomplished? Not quite—Ryoko substituted camembert cheese for 50 million yen in dope. A lantern-jawed gangster working for the drug buyers kidnaps Matsuura and, when Ryoko comes to rescue him, nabs her too. Now, it's up to Yuji and Kosaku to save the day.

CRITIQUE

The first entry in the six-part Katte ni Shiya-gare!! series, *Godatsu Keikaku* (Extortion Plot) is, given director Kiyoshi Kurosawa's subsequent reputation as a horrormeister, a surprisingly light-footed comedy, with an ingeniously twisty story line. Playing a straight man to Koyo Maeda's scatterbrained *chinpira*, Show Aikawa deftly moves between his comic scenes, including his love-at-first-compress encounter with Natsumi Nanase's nursery school teacher, and the sort of action heroics for which he is better known.

Most yakuza comedies turn their funny gangsters into clowns, blowing their credibility as tough guys. Aikawa's dry, sly presence, with the hint of toughness in his sandpapery voice and crooked grin, gives the film the ballast it needs to keep from floating off into the ether. Kurosawa also draws a performance from Natsumi Nanase that, with its combination of spaciness and spunk, provides the right balance to Aikawa—and makes their romance work at least as a plot device, if not as a passionate reality.

Also, Kurosawa films the more serious scenes, particularly Ryoko's drug delivery, with the sort of chilling tension that later became his trademark. Few directors could make a back look so menacing or a tossed can of dope take on, in mid-air, such life-or-death significance. The throw ends in farce, but Kurosawa never drops the ball—*Godatsu Keikaku* remains a pleasure from beginning to end.

Kawaita Hana (1964)

PALE FLOWER

Scr.: Ataru Baba. *Dir.:* Masahiro Shinoda. *Prod.:* Shochiku. *Main cast:* Ryo Ikebe, Mariko Kaga, Takashi Fujiki, Shin'ichiro Mikami, Eijiro Tono, Seiji Miyaguchi, Kyu Sazanka, Naoki Sugiura, Muga Takewaki. 96 mins.

STORY

Muraki (Ryo Ikebe) is released from prison after serving a three-year term for murder. He is unrepentant, however. Human beings impress him as little more than beasts, with no reason for living beyond mere survival. Why, he muses, is it so bad to kill them?

At a gambling den, he encounters a smartly dressed young woman who bets aggressively, while studiously ignoring the men around her. Muraki is intrigued, though his next stop is the house of his long-suffering lover, Shinko (Chisako Hara), where he has a passionate, if troubled, reunion. The old spark is gone, replaced by Shinko's doubts about her path in life. Muraki sees the mysterious woman gambling again and later, at an outdoor stall, makes her acquaintance. Her name is Saeko (Mariko Kaga) and she wants bigger action. Muraki asks a friendly gang brother, Chiba (Naoki Sugiura), if there are any games in town that can give it to her. Soon after, however, he is nearly killed by a punk with a knife. Who put the punk up to it and why?

The would-be hitman is Jiro of the Yasuoka-gumi, whose boss, Yasuoka (Eijiro Tono), is tight with Muraki's own *oyabun* (Seiji Miyaguchi). Yasuoka comes to apologize, but Muraki remains suspicious. Shinko tells Muraki that a straight-arrow salaryman wants to marry her. "That's good," is his laconic reply. Now that Saeko has come into the picture, he is ready to let Shinko fade out of his life. Jiro comes to apologize to Muraki—"I was only trying to make a name for myself," he says. Muraki calls him a fool but forgives him.

When Muraki meets Saeko again, she questions him about his past. Why did he kill? "That wasn't a crime," he tells her. "Just survival. It's kill or be killed." People, he adds, are crap—and he is too. Soon after, they go to a high-stakes game, where Muraki locks eyes with a hollow-cheeked gangster whose cool, appraising gaze spells trouble.

Yasuoka complains to Muraki's *oyabun* that a new organization, Funaba Kogyo, is muscling in on his territory. The *oyabun* offers Muraki as a third-party negotiator and Yasuoka agrees. Approached about the negotiating job, Muraki is reluctant but finally agrees. He meets the Funaba Kogyo rep, a weasely hotel manager who gives him nothing but excuses. After the meeting he spies Saeko with an obviously well-heeled group—and susses that she is a rich girl looking for kicks. Saeko and Muraki go for a ride in her sports car—and she asks him if he uses drugs. She wants to try them. He calls her an idiot—and gets out of the car.

Muraki stays away from Saeko, hanging out instead with a half-Japanese *kobun*, Ryo, but the mutual obsession with gambling draws them back together. A police raid at an inn sends Muraki and Saeko flying under the covers of a futon, but Muraki refuses to take advantage, to Saeko's disappointment.

A hitman darts knives at Muraki in a dark alley and he narrowly escape with his life. Soon after, Chiba tells him that Saeko and Ryo have been spotted together. Muraki has a disturbing dream about being chased—and finding Saeko and Ryo, masked, in bed, enjoying a revel of sex and drugs. Soon after, a member of his gang is whacked—and Muraki volunteers to whack the killer. This, he tells Saeko, is better than drugs. Does she want to come along?

CRITIQUE

Based on a novel by Shintaro Ishihara, Masahiro Shinoda's *Kawaita Hana* (Pale Flower) had a difficult birth. Its downbeat, nihilistic tone displeased not only Shinoda's Shochiku bosses, who shelved the film for eight months before releasing it in March 1964, but also the industry censorship board, Eirin, which tagged it with an adults-only rating. The resulting controversy drew crowds and made *Kawaita Hana* an unlikely hit.

Filmed in stygian black-and-white, with Toru Takemitsu's atonal score jaggedly underscoring the on-screen alienation, *Kawaita Hana* was not intended as a crowd-pleaser, however. Viewed today, its vision of underworld life in postwar Tokyo does not look like the stuff to inspire moral crusades. Its one scene of wild dissipation is a dream sequence that is more suggestive than exploitative.

Nonetheless, the noir atmospherics, with their skewed angles and looming shadows, create an ever-hovering cloud of menace, while Ryo Ikebe's strong, low-key, performance as the gangster Muraki provides an emotional anchor to the at-times over-wrought proceedings. Mariko Kaga's spoiled rich girl on a spree, buzzing about in her sporty convertible and laughing gaily at the absurdity of it all, is something of a crock, but her big, liquid eyes light up the screen with defiance and arrogance, while evoking the postwar Nietzschian mood, with its long, deep stare into the void.

Keisho Sakazuki (1992)

SUCCESSION CEREMONY

Scr.: Hiro Matsuda. *Dir.:* Kazuki Omori. *Prod.:* Toei. *Main cast:* Hiroyuki Sanada, Ken Ogata, Yuko Kotegawa. 119 mins.

STORY

When an elderly boss of bosses decides to step aside in favor of a middle-aged underling, a young gangster named Yoshinari (Hiroyuki Sanada) is given the tough job of persuading the *oyabun* (Ken Ogata) of an affiliate gang to serve as the *baishakunin*—a kind of emcee—at the succession ceremony. This *oyabun* is the second choice after the first one fell ill. Being

considered second best is, we are given to understand, an unbearable blow to yakuza pride.

When Yoshinari arrives at the *oyabun*'s country home, he finds him to be a pleasant, amiable fellow. He also discovers that the stunner he tried to pick up on the way is the *oyabun*'s wife (Yuko Kotegawa). Yoshinari's troubles, however, don't begin until this pair arrives in Tokyo. The first choice makes a miraculous recovery and Yoshinari has to tell the second *oyabun* that his services are no longer required. Now Number Two *oyabun* is really insulted. He gets roaring drunk, crashes a funeral, and starts a one-man riot. Soon after, the first choice collapses again and the second *oyabun* gets another chance. By now, Yoshinari knows that he will need a miracle of his own if he is to shepherd his sake-loving charge successfully through the ceremony.

CRITIQUE

The script by veteran Hiroo Matsuda has promise, but *Keisho Sakazuki* (Succession Ceremony) doesn't realize it. The beginning, with its wild race through the countryside—Yoshinari and his frantic superior are late for an appointment with the *oyabun*—points the film in the direction of farce. But director Kazuki Omori, whose credits include two Godzilla films, turns the movie in the direction of soap opera.

The second *oyabun*, it so happens, is not a W. C. Fields comic drunk but a Ray Milland (*Lost Weekend*) tragic drunk who becomes painful to watch. His wife, however, is fed up. A former OL (office lady or female assistant), she once embezzled 70 million yen for him and spent three years in prison as a result. Look, she complains, how he is paying her back! This veering between the silly and the serious keeps *Keisho Sakazuki* from taking off. We cringe at the confessions and keep waiting for laughs that never quite arrive.

The key scene, however, is the ceremony itself and Ken Ogata, as the drunk *oyabun*, brings

---

it off splendidly, illuminating the spirit behind the mummery. Though his hands may tremble with the DTs, he manages to gut through, calling on his reserves of yakuza pride. Throughout the film, we have seen the gangsters' buffoonish side. Now, we get a different, more intimate view of their world.

I was reminded of sportswriter Bill Murray's observation about a Hell's Angel: "Planted on the back of his hog, this oaf acquired instant grace." Ogata's *oyabun* undergoes a similar transformation, but one that expresses not only an individual will but group continuity and solidarity. For one moment in a patchwork of a movie, we see the glue that holds the gangs together.

Kids Return (1996)

Scr./Dir.: Takeshi Kitano. *Prod.:* Office Kitano, Bandai Visual. *Main cast:* Ken Kaneko, Masanobu Ando. 108 mins.

Takeshi Kitano's *Kids Return* is ostensibly about the attempts of two present-day high school dropouts to make their fortunes on society's fringes. Its point of view, however, is that of a middle-aged man looking back at his own younger days and telling the kids in the audience that life is tough and unforgiving. The film's mood, however, is anything but harsh. Though Kitano is famously fed up with the younger generation, he has an evident affection for his two no-account heroes. They are, as he mentions in the program notes, modeled on boys he grew up with—1960s throwbacks in 1990s dress.

Despite its air of being suspended between eras, *Kids Return* is the most observant, poignant, and nuanced of Kitano's six films, though it shares their wry understatement and quirky, pranksterish inventiveness. Like most of us, his heroes find it easier to change their circumstances than their characters. Whether wearing a boxer's trunks or yakuza's luminescent silk shirt, they are forever the teenage punks whose idea of a good time is to defiantly weave around the schoolyard on a bike while their classmates endure a trigonometry lesson.

Though Kitano has been guilty of gratuitous violence (*Sono Otoko Kyobo ni Tsuki* [Violent Cop]), patronizing sentimentalism (*Ano Natsu, Ichiban Shiziikana Umi* [A Scene at the Sea]), and auteurist self-indulgence (*Sonatine*), there has always been a welcome strain of emotional and intellectual honesty in his work. Unlike directors whose only aim is to make us feel good, Kitano tells us how he thinks and feels, without worrying whether the mass audience will accept his often nihilistic messages.

In *Kids Return*, however, he tries harder to meet mainstream expectations halfway, without softening his downbeat story line. The two heroes—the loudmouth Masaru (Ken Kaneko) and his quiet follower Shinji (Masanobu Ando)—exhibit the same raunchy, cruel sense of humor familiar to viewers of Kitano's innumerable TV comedy shows. They dangle a handmade doll, complete with bobbing penis, from the school roof to their classroom window or shake down classmates for spare change by making them jump up and down like so many jammed piggy banks. Their aim is to spend as little time as possible in class and as much time as possible eating noodles, drinking beer, and sneaking into dirty movies.

One day, a favorite victim brings a protector—a professional boxer—who promptly wipes the sneer off Masaru's face and dumps him on his arrogant rear. Soon after, Masaru drops out of school to train at a local boxing gym. Shinji tags along and discovers, to his surprise, not to mention Masaru's, that he is a natural boxer. After Shinji cleans his clock in a sparring bout, Masaru quits the gym in disgust and becomes an apprentice yakuza.

The two friends drift apart. Shinji continues to move up the boxing ranks, while Masaru learns the gangster's violent trade. The film also follows the post-high-school careers of the boys' "victim" classmates, including a meek loner who longs futilely for a pretty coffee shop waitress and ends up driving a cab and two fledgling *manzai* comedians who crack lame jokes about their high school teachers to audiences of uncomprehending pensioners.

It's not hard to guess Shinji's and Masaru's respective fates: the movie is framed as flashback from their unpromising present. Ironically, the only ones who succeed are the *manzai* duo—Masaru and Shinji's former marks. As a full house roars at their jokes, we can see Kitano looking back at his own past as a *manzai* comedian—and hear him having the film's last laugh.

Kishiwada Shonen Gurentai (1996)

BOYS, BE AMBITIOUS

Scr.: Chong Ui Shin, Masayuki Azuma. *Dir.:* Kazuyuki Izutsu. *Prod.:* Shochiku, Yoshimoto Kogyo. *Main cast:* Takashi Okamura, Hiroyuki Yabe, Nanako Okochi, Nenji Kobayashi, Hakuryu. 106 mins.

Aren't Japanese kids basically docile, nonviolent types, whose rebellious poses are little more than fashion statements? Perhaps not, if Kazuyuki Izutsu's *Kishiwada Shonen Gurentai* (Boys, Be Ambitious) is any indication. Based on an autobiographical novel by Riichi Nakaba, a long-distance-trucker-turned-author, the movie is a nearly plotless account of youths growing up in Kishiwada, a tough working-class district of Osaka. The time is the mid-1970s, the violence, nearly nonstop. The two boys at the center of the film—Kotetsu (Takeshi Okamura) and Chunba (Hiroyuki Yabe)—are forever either beating the bejesus out of some hapless punk or getting the bejesus beaten out of them. There is no rhyme or reason to this tit for tat, other than the age-old

commandant of gang warfare: "do unto to others before others do unto you."

Usually in this sort of film, the heroes either go down in a blaze of antisocial glory or arrive at the edge of the abyss and decide to pull back. *Kishiwada*, however, has almost no arc at all; Kotetsu and Chunba like fighting the way Ichiro likes swinging a bat and Nomo likes throwing a ball. It's their release, their form of self-expression, their raison d'être, even when a gang of punks is using their skull for soccer practice.

At the same time, they follow certain rules in their war games: Kotetsu may smash a brick into a gang boss's face and Chunba may gong a punk with a steel plate, cleverly concealed in his school bag, but neither would do anything truly nasty, such as bully a wimp or whack a rival. They are restrained less by moral strictures than the gut feeling that going over the line would spoil their fun.

This utter lack of melodrama or moralizing, combined with naturalistic dialogue, delivered in a thick Kishiwada dialect, gives the film an air of authenticity. When a rival gang ties the boys to a fence and pelts them with stones, Chunba, Kotetsu, and their buddies wisecrack and hurl insults at their tormentors. This is no TV comedy routine, however; the anger and defiance are real. Our heroes are not only funny guys but tough, independent types, who live by their own don't-care code.

More than straight reminiscence, the film is a cry of defiance against the middle-class ethic of work hard, get ahead, follow the rules (note that its ironic English subtitle is *Boys, Be Ambitious*). The heroes are layabouts who ride the academic escalator from public junior high school to bottom-of-the-barrel commercial high school. From there, they drift into the fringes of the yakuza underworld and through a series of menial jobs. Chunba conducts a desultory relationship with Ryoko (Nanako Okochi), a sultry transfer student, but his real interests lie elsewhere, in head-banging and daydreaming about exotic, far-away places, like Kurobe Dam.

Chunba is, however, going exactly nowhere —and director Izutsu clearly approves. The film, in fact, overglamorizes the heroes' feckless life-styles, making the beatings with various blunt objects look about as dangerous as a Three Stooges routine. *Kishiwada* also shows us the origin of the rough-and-tumble Kansai style of comedy that dominates the TV airwaves. The next time I see one TV comedian slap the other upside the head and let fly with insults in the Kansai dialect, I'll reflect that, although they may not have passed the exams to the right schools, they are now making more than ten of their Tokyo University-graduated contemporaries combined. There is a kind of justice in this world.

Kizuna (1998)

TIES

Scr.: Teruhiko Arai. *Dir.:* Kichitaro Negishi. *Prod.:* Toho. *Main cast:* Koji Yakusho, Yosuke Saito, Yoshiro Kato, Ken Watanabe, Yumi Aso, Katsuo Nakamura, Hoka Kinoshita, Mansaku Ikeuchi, Kimiko Tsuchiya, Ikuko Kawai. 123 mins.

Though advertised as a yakuza thriller, Kichitaro Negishi's *Kizuna* is really more a melodrama in which gunplay is less important than the tangle of relationships that bind the hero, a former yakuza turned businessman, to his old life in ways not easily escaped. The Japanese audience loves a puzzle plot, the more convoluted the better, and *Kizuna* gives it to them. Meanwhile, the ex-gangster moves inexorably toward his destiny, driven by love, friendship, and a sense of duty. Like so many Japanese heroes, he is ultimately alone, ultimately doomed.

The ex-gangster is Takaaki Ise (Yakusho), now the president of a company that manages clubs and restaurants. He still has close ties, though, to his old gang, the Sasaki-gumi.

When a long-time Sasaki confederate, Fuda (Yosuke Saito) shows up, stabbed in a gang dustup, Ise helps him. The gang is fighting a turf war with the rival Kuhara-gumi and Fuda is one of the casualties. Ise also meets Fuda's wife, Kyoko (Yumi Aso), an old flame whom he has been trying, without much success, to forget. With her marriage unraveling, she is eager to renew her acquaintance with Ise.

A few days later, Ise sees a newspaper article about the murder of a scandal-sheet writer (Yoshihiro Kato). The gun used in the slaying, the article says, was also used to murder a loan company president ten years earlier. The gun had been Ise's. He had given it to a friend (Hoka Kinoshita) with orders to throw it into the ocean. Why is it turning up now? He goes to the friend, now a restaurant manager, to find out.

Meanwhile, the cops, led by the glinty-eyed Detective Sako (Ken Watanabe), are hot on the trail of the killer. They discover that the victim had 13 million yen in the bank and question his club hostess girlfriend (Kumiko Tsuchiya), who tells them he suddenly came into money. They suspect he was killed because he had put the arm on the wrong person. It doesn't take Sako long to dig up a suspect—Ise. But the detective also discovers that there seem to be two Ises, one of whom may be dead, the other a fake.

Why did the writer end up with a bullet in his heart? Why does Ise want to return to the gang life? The answers lie deep in the past, in a house on the Inland Sea, where Ise lived with a seaman stepfather and a younger half-sister, who later became a famous violist. This half-sister (Ikuko Kawai) has no idea Ise is alive— and is willing to sacrifice everything to save her reputation.

Negishi does a workman-like job of transferring Toru Shirakawa's best-selling novel, *Umi wa Kawaiteita* (The Sea Dried Up), to the screen. Given all the twists and turns of the plot, it's not surprising the film plays slower than the typical Hollywood thriller, though

Negishi keeps the focus squarely on the film's central relationships. In one key scene, he stops the action entirely as Koji Yakusho's Ise watches his sister perform on stage. In its mixture of loving pride and aching regret, remembrance and determination, his face tells us all we need to know about his motivation—and ultimate fate.

Koroshiya Ichi (2001)

ICHI THE KILLER

Scr.: Sakichi Sato. *Dir.:* Takashi Miike. *Prod.:* Omega Project, Omega Micott. *Main cast:* Tadanobu Asano, Nao Omori, Shinya Tsukamoto, Sabu, Mai Goto, Hoka Kinoshita. 128 mins.

Violence has replaced sex as the last frontier, edgewise—and Takashi Miike knows it. This directorial outlaw has rapidly pushed the violence ante to heights that look, depending on one's point of view, sickening, awe-inspiring, or absurd. Despite the hints of fetishism in his work—he has the same kind of thing for body piercing that Hitchcock had for icy blondes—Miike has an antic and even humanistic side. He's like the naughty kid whose idea of fun is dreaming up neat tortures but would never think of wielding the pliers and meat skewers himself.

His latest claim to the world edginess title is *Koroshiya Ichi* (Ichi the Killer), a gang thriller based on a cult comic by Hideo Yamamoto. The hero is a wimp who has transformed himself into a deadly fighting machine—and stokes the fires of rage with tears of remembrance for boyhood humiliations. Though reminiscent of *Crying Freeman*, a popular *manga* and *anime* about a crying hitman, *Koroshiya Ichi* adds a new, perverted twist: the hero climaxes every time he kills.

The serious strangeness of Ichi is only the beginning; it's as though Miike and his staff sat up nights trying to top each other with fresh outrages. The splatter is so over the top—certain shots are a broom's-eye view of the slaughterhouse floor—that the movie becomes a grotesque *gaman taikai* (endurance contest). That said, if you happen to share Miike's warped sense of humor (and to some extent, I am ashamed to say, I do), you will enjoy the way he propels the violence far, far beyond anything a Hollywood director would dare. Or the film will leave you staring at the screen in stony-eyed disgust. There's not much middle ground.

The boss of the Anjo-gumi and his young lover are murdered, and the survivors, led by Anjo's hot-blooded top lieutenant, Kakihara (Tadanobu Asano), boil through Shinjuku in search of revenge. Because this is a Miike film, the vics are not only slaughtered but sliced, diced, and spattered from floor to ceiling. Included in the gang's three-man clean-up crew is Jijii (Shinya Tsukamoto), a shifty-eyed man of indeterminate age who takes a grim pleasure in his work.

The hitman, it turns out, is Jijii's protégé—the aforementioned Ichi (Nao Omori), a doe-eyed shlump who works as a waiter in a coffee shop. Though Jijii's willing tool, Ichi is a delicate type who was traumatized by bullies when he was a lad (or at least thinks he was). He also happens to be in love with Sarah (Mai Goto), a pink salon hostess who is routinely brutalized by her pimp (Hoka Kinoshita). But while the pimp is beating Sarah to a monstrous pulp in their apartment, Ichi is standing outside, writhing in agony—and ecstasy. The boy clearly has problems.

So, does Kakihara, whose face is crisscrossed with scars and mouth splits into a horrible rictus when he loosens the pins that hold the corners, like a demon from an old folk tale. He pursues his boss's killer with an eerie calm, punctuated by eruptions of fiendishly inventive cruelty. When Jijii fingers a hood from an affiliate gang (Susumu Terajima) as the probable perp—the Anjo gang stole his profitable porno video business—Kakihara has him strung up with meat hooks, like a flying bat, and douses him with boiling oil. At Jijii's urging, Ichi goes on more rampages, cutting his victims to shreds with a blade concealed in his boot. Meanwhile, Kakihara conducts his own investigation, using the services of a straight-arrow former cop (Sabu) who is prone to homicidal rage. As the body count mounts, we see a showdown coming: Ichi versus Kakihara.

Tadanobu Asano, as Kakihara, is this extreme movie's grinning malevolent center. Usually cast as a quiet type who seethes with inner fire, Asano plays the flame-haired gang boss with a chilly psychopathic glee. If Miike had used him to better purpose, instead of playing gruesome games with prop innards, *Koroshiya Ichi* might have been more than the latest exhibit in his Traveling Geek Show.

Kunisada Chuji (1958)

Scr.: Shinji Yuki, Hajime Takaiwa. *Dir.:* Shigehiro Ozawa. *Prod.:* Toei. *Main cast:* Chiezo Kataoka, Kotaro Satomi, Ryunosuke Tsukigata, Yumiko Hasegawa, Eitaro Shindo, Kensaku Hara. 95 mins.

STORY

The time: The Tempo Era (1830–40). The place: Joshu or present-day Gunma Prefecture. Poverty stalks the land, while tax collectors carry out merciless exactions. Men are driven to sell their wives and daughters into prostitution and families to commit group suicide. The local magistrate, Takegaki (Kyushuo Abe), is a vain, corrupt man, who drives starving farmers from his gates.

One night, preparing for bed, he has an unexpected visitor: Kunisada Chuji (Chiezo Kataoka), a local gambling boss. When Chuji humbly asks Takegaki to give the people tax relief, the flustered magistrate tries to drive him away, first with words and then a sword. In-

stead, Chuji cuts down Takegaki and makes his escape to nearby Mount Akagi, where he hides with his followers.

Guards catch an old man, Kiemon (Kenji Usuda), trying to bring supplies to Chuji. His daughter pleads for his release, to no avail. When Chuji hears this, he decides to rescue Kiemon. In the attempt, one of his followers, Asataro (Kotaro Satomi), inadvertently attracts the attention of the enemy and a fight ensues, with Chuji making a narrow escape. Asataro's comrades accuse him and his uncle of treachery and the young man leaves the camp in disgrace. Chuji, however, expresses his trust.

Asataro comes to his uncle (Ryunosuke Tsukigata) with the intention of taking the older man's life, but hesitates at the critical moment. The uncle, a gambler, tells Asataro that he has long expected to die this way—and drives in the sword himself, even though he is innocent of wrongdoing. Asataro returns to camp with his young nephew Kantaro and his uncle's head—and the ones who had doubted him now express their contrition. Soon after, the camp is attacked—and Chuji and his men are forced to fight for their lives. They prevail, but Asataro is killed.

The mountain has become too dangerous, Chuji decides—he must escape on his own. Taking Kantaro, he goes down into town. There, he finds Osen (Yumiko Hasegawa), an old acquaintance who is now running an inn. After thwarting thieves claiming to be his men, Chuji asks Osen to take care of Kantaro. Chuji is afraid that, if he raises the boy, Kantaro will end up a yakuza like him. She agrees and Chuji departs.

On the Shinshu Road, Chuji comes across Kiemon trying to hang himself. The old man has been swindled by a powerful *oyabun*, Yamagata (Eitaro Shindo), to whom he has sold his daughter. Chuji goes to Yamagata's in the guise of Kiemon's humble friend and begs the *oyabun* to lend the old man 100 ryo. When Yamagata arrogantly refuses, Chuji accuses him of chicanery and reveals his true identity. Yamagata's attitude abruptly changes; he not only agrees to lend the money but releases the old man's daughter from her contract, simply on Chuji's word to "pay later." After Chuji departs, however, Yamagata's harridan of a wife accuses him of cowardice. Angry and humiliated, Yamagata vows to get revenge.

CRITIQUE

One of the many films based on the life of a famous Edo Era outlaw, Shigehiro Ozawa's *Kunisada Chuji* features Chiezo Kataoka in the title role. A prewar samurai action star who became a pillar of Toei's *jidai geki* (period drama) lineup in the 1950s, Kataoka was already in his midfifties when he played Chuji. In the early scenes, he leaves much of the swashbuckling to others, particularly Kotaro Satomi as the young gangster who must prove his loyalty. Instead, Kataoka is the *oyabun* father figure, ruling over his underlings with a firm but benevolent hand.

His principal adversaries in the film, the corrupt magistrate Takegaki (Kyushuo Abe) and the avaricious *oyabun* Yamagata (Eitaro Shindo), are also middle-aged men, but buffoonish types who have a taste for the soft life and are no match for Chuji either physically or spiritually. Though Kataoka's performance is overripe—he doesn't speak so much as nosily suck air and emote—he also embodies the Japanese masculine ideal, over-fifty division. Also, in his scene with Yamagata, Kataoka shows why Kunisada Chuji deserves his Robin Hood reputation, in a bravado turn that more than makes up for his ponderous theatrics earlier in the film.

Kurenai no Nagareboshi (1967)

THE VELVET HUSTLER

Scr.: Toshio Masuda, Kaneo Ikegami. *Dir.:* Toshio Masuda. *Prod.:* Nikkatsu. *Main cast:* Tetsuya Watari, Ruriko Asaoka, Jo Shishido, Ryotaro Sugi, Kayo Matsuo, Chiyo Okumura, Tatsuya Fuji, Masahiko Tanimura. 97 mins.

STORY

Goro (Tetsuya Watari) shoots at Kajima, a Tokyo gang boss, from his red convertible—and the boss's car plunges through a concrete railing to oblivion. Goro goes into hiding and one year later is working for a Kobe gang, the Seki-gumi. Among his rackets is steering American military men, straight from Vietnam, to a gang-run bar. Meanwhile, Goro fends off a local cop, Usu, who knows his game and is determined to put him behind bars. Kojima, a jewel dealer newly arrived from Tokyo, scorns Goro's guidance—a mistake, as it turns out. Meanwhile, Goro's bar hostess girlfriend, Yukari (Kayo Matsuo), throws herself at him, but he could care less. "I'm tired of women," Goro says. ". . . I want to go back to Tokyo." Soon after, Kojima turns up dead—and his suitcases full of money have gone missing.

Keiko Shirakawa (Ruriko Asaoka), the daughter of the jewel company president, arrives in Kobe to investigate Kojima's death. She tells Usu that she was engaged to Kojima—but only at her father's insistence. Later, Keiko visits Seki Industries, the gang's front company, where she meets Goro, taking his ease alone. At first he denies knowing Kojima, but her haughty beauty attracts him—and he ends up helping with her search. His real aim, however, is to bed her, but Keiko soon figures out his game. She finds him fascinating, however—especially after she learns that he is a yakuza. A hitman (Jo Shishido) who has been stalking Goro ends up shooting Goro's comic sidekick Keebo, while Koko, a friendly local prostitute, looks on in horror.

Goro and Usu take Keiko to the morgue to ID Kojima. After viewing the remains of her fiancé, Keiko asks Goro to show her the town. When Usu informs Goro of Keebo's death, Goro keeps the news from Keiko but after she confesses her love to him, runs out on her. He can understand Kajima sending a hitman after him—but why kill Keebo, who has no connection to Kajima? He is determined to find the hitman—and learn the truth.

CRITIQUE

In its chilled-out take on genre conventions, verging on flippant self-parody, Toshio Masuda's *Kurenai no Nagareboshi* (The Velvet Hustler) is reminiscent of Seijun Suzuki's *Koroshi no Rakuin* (Branded to Kill) and *Tokyo Nagaremono* (Tokyo Drifter), though it lacks their stylistic flair. Instead of Suzuki's predilection for mixing genres (the brawl in a Western saloon in *Tokyo Nagaremono*) or plunging headlong into the collective unconscious (the death imagery in *Koroshi no Rakuin*), Masuda is content to wink at the clichés of 1960s action movies, without trying hard to improve on them.

That said, Tetsuya Watari plays the gangster Goro with an engaging mixture of brashness and nonchalance, motor-mouthed cool and hot-headed passion. He has able foils in Jo Shishido's hitman, with his dark suit, shades, and comically unflappable air, and Ruriko Asaoka's rich girl, with her impeccably stylish wardrobe, frankly appraising glance, and deadpan wit. A refreshing change from the female stereotypes who populate so many yakuza films, she is more than a match for Goro—and, by being the only one to call his bluff, wins his respect. But though Watari and Asaoka's sexual sparring may lift the film above the genre average, its story of a hitman-on-the-run remains little more than an excuse for Watari's antics. Realism, emotional or otherwise, is not an issue. How many hitmen, of whatever era or nationality, sail off to work in a spiffy red convertible and hum as they take aim?

Kuro no Tenshi, Vol. 1 (1998)

BLACK ANGEL, VOL. 1

Scr./Dir.: Takashi Ishii. *Prod.:* Shochiku. *Main cast:* Riona Hazuki, Reiko Takashima, Jinpachi Nezu, Yoshiyuki Yamaguchi. 106 mins.

In *Kuro no Tenshi, Vol. 1* (Black Angel, Vol. 1), Takashi Ishii takes his lead from *La Femme Nikita*, *Natural Born Killers*, and other films whose deadly protagonists are female. The "black angel" of the title is a woman who witnessed her father's murder as a child—and has become a relentless killing machine bent on revenge. Ishii puts his visually extravagant, emotionally overcharged stamp on every scene. He also has cast Riona Hazuki, the bad girl of the Japanese film business, as his Dark Angel—a wise choice. She projects the right combination of steamy sexuality and cold menace—not an easy assignment for a young actress who, only four years earlier, was playing a kitten-fondling child concubine in Masahiro Shinoda's *Sharaku*. *Kuro no Tenshi* is trash with panache that thankfully aspires to be nothing more. Slap it into the machine, pour a finger of Jack Daniels, and turn the critical facilities to low.

The story begins with the assassination of the heroine's father, a gruff, gray-haired *oyabun*, in his own home by a pair of hit women. Six-year-old Ikko is asleep when the shooting starts but witnesses enough of the bloodshed, including the horrifying killing of her mother, to be permanently traumatized. Saved by Mayo (Reiko Takashima), a sultry hitwoman belonging to her father's gang, the girl Ikko is spirited to the United States, where she spends the next fourteen years.

Switch to the present. The gang boss is now Nogi (Jinpachi Nezu), a former lieutenant of Ikko's father. Smart, dapper, and ruthless, Nogi ordered the hit that brought him to power and Ikko knows it. Getting off the plane at Narita with a gay *sansei* (third-generation Japanese) companion named Zill (Yoshiyuki Yamaguchi), Ikko has only one thought: Kill

Smoke gets in your eyes. Riona Hazuki takes on the mob in Takashi Ishii's *Kuro no Tenshi, Vol. 1* (Black Angel, Vol. 1, 1998).

Nogi and anyone who gets in her way. Nogi, however, is a hard target. In addition to the phalanx of underlings who shadow his every move, he has an ally in Ikko's sister-in-law (Miyuki Ono), who has, to Ikko's disgust, become his lover. Ikko soon discovers another disturbing change: Mayo, the woman she once so fervently admired, has become Nogi's drug-addled sex slave.

Enraged, Ikko blasts her way into Nogi's headquarters, a spacious, sparely decorated warren that looks like a modern art museum with most of the exhibits removed. She fails in her mission and is captured but rather than do the intelligent thing—kill her as he would a rabid beast—Nogi decides to toy with her. Bad mistake, of course: Ikko is soon on the loose and plotting her next move. Meanwhile, Mayo, her nearly moribund will stirred by Ikko's return, begins to free herself from her addiction and realize where her true loyalty lies. When these two women warriors finally join forces, even a yakuza army could not stop them. Nogi is a few divisions short.

Though the ending is never in doubt, Ishii provides plenty of flagrant sex and flamboyant violence to distract us on the way to the predictable conclusion. In his equal-opportunity world, big strapping yakuza are easy marks not only for the bullets but the flying kicks and slamming punches of Ikko and Zill. Lithesome rather than fearsome, Hazuki plays her fight scenes with Chinese operatic energy and flair. As the gay street kid Zill, Yoshiyuki Yamaguchi displays a fighting style more inspired by break-dance moves than karate *kata*, but equally devastating.

Meanwhile, Ishii pumps up the noirish atmospherics for the film's action scenes, most of which takes place at night in smoky dives or driving rain. He is also adept at using an off-kilter camera angle or traveling crane shot to heighten tension and deepen suspense, though he cannot disguise the familiarity of the proceedings. Given his affinity with the material, Ishii will no doubt make other volumes in the Kuro no Tenshi series. I hope, though, that next time he sends his Black Angel on a less clichéd assignment.

Kutsukake Tokijiro (1929)

Scr.: Satoshi Kisaragi. *Dir.:* Kichiro Tsuji. *Prod.:* Nikkatsu. *Main cast:* Denjiro Okochi, Koichi Kuzuki, Yoneko Sakai, Sukesaburo Onoe, Motoharu Isogawa. 63 mins.

STORY

An *oyabun* asks his loyal *kobun* Mutsuda no Sanjo (Koichi Kuzuki) to take over the gang while he's away in prison. Sanjo vows to protect the gang with his life but as the days lengthen, more and more *kobun* drift away. Finally, the remaining three, claiming they can't make it as gangsters anymore, quit, leaving only Sanjo. Somehow, he must feed his wife Okinu (Yoneko Sakai) and his young son Tarokichi (Sukesaburo Onoe), while worrying about a rival gang determined to wipe him off the face of the earth. Then, comes the crowning blow—Okinu announces that she is pregnant. Sanjo decides to get away while the getting is good—and return later to reclaim his territory.

Meanwhile, three gangsters are on their way to kill Sanjo. They are joined by Tokijiro (Denjiro Okochi), a wandering gambler whom they intend to use as a lookout. Tokijiro wants in on the action, but reluctantly agrees to wait. Arriving at Sanjo's house, the three gangsters announce themselves and try to break in, but Sanjo drives them away. Fleeing to Tokijiro, they beg him to help. Though having nothing against Sanjo, Tokijiro has an obligation to the *oyabun* who gave him food and shelter—which he considerately explains to Sanjo before drawing his sword.

In the ensuing fight, Sanjo is mortally wounded. The gangsters want to kill his wife and child as well, but Tokijiro stops them. Enraged, they flee. Knowing that Tokijiro was only acting according to the *ninkyo* code, Sanjo asks him to care for his family and, when Tokijiro agrees, dies. Tokijiro, Okinu, and Tarokichi wander about the country, falling farther and farther in penury. Tokijiro has vowed to give up the yakuza life—and no other doors are open

to him. He finds a *shamisen* on a dead traveler and, arriving in a town, plays for passersby. He gets into a quarrel with local gangsters but escapes with the aid of Hatcho no Kashimoto (Motoharu Isogawa), a boss gambler.

The gangsters Tokijiro quarreled with track him to the inn where he is staying with Okinu and Tarokichi, but the innkeeper's wife ejects them. The innkeeper then makes Tokijiro a proposal: hire out as a fighter in an inter-gang battle. The fee is one ryo—a huge sum—and Tokijiro readily agrees. The innkeeper has second thoughts when he hears that Tokijiro has quit the gang life, but Tokijiro insists. He needs the money to feed his new family. When he goes off to fight, however, Okinu goes into labor—and realizes that she is dying. The old innkeeper finds Tokijiro in the midst of a heated battle and gives him Okinu's message: return at once—or never see her again in this life.

CRITIQUE

As an early example of the *matatabimono* genre of films about wandering gamblers, as well as the original model for the *ninkyo eiga* of the 1960s, *Kutsukake Tokijiro* has inspired a total of seven remakes, the latest by Tai Kato in 1966. The original features *jidai geki* star Denjiro Okochi as Tokijiro in a performance that may have been more stylized than those of a later generation of *ninkyo eiga* heroes but was nonetheless physically dynamic and emotionally expressive. A *tateyaku* (traditional macho) star, with a large frame and ruggedly masculine bearing, Okochi was also able to express Tokijiro's growing affection for Okinu and Tarokichi without resorting to the hackneyed tricks of silent screen melodrama.

Tokijiro's story set the pattern for many later *ninkyo eiga*, from his initial dilemma—he must fight and possibly kill a stranger to repay an obligation to an *oyabun* he barely knows—to his willingness to sacrifice himself for two "obligations" he has come to love. The story of Sanjo is also typical: he readily takes over the gang in his *oyabun*'s absence but is helpless in the face of his *kobun*'s desertion. Many later "good" *oyabun* share his weakness in the face of adversity (or treachery), making necessary the intervention of the "outsider hero."

Only sixty-three minutes long, *Kutsukake Tokijiro* moves along briskly under Kichiro Tsuji's unobtrusive direction, though the narrative structure is unusual: the hero, Tokijiro, does not make his first appearance until well into the first act. Also, by later standards, the action scenes are almost comically hurried—a flurry of swords, scurrying figures, then over. Even so, Okochi is the real thing—he gives us a clear look into the old soul of a Japanese warrior.

Kyohansha (1999)

PARTNERS IN CRIME

Scr./Dir.: Kazuhiro Kiuchi. *Prod.:* Toei, Toei Video, Tohoku Shinsha. *Main cast:* Naoto Takenaka, Yuya Uchida, Kyoko Koizumi, Mikio Osawa. 102 mins.

Kazuhiro Kiuchi's *Kyohansha* (Partners in Crime) has "international" written all over it. The look and mood are reminiscent of Hollywood thrillers at their most baroque, as though Kiuchi has been channeling everyone from David Fincher to John Woo. The hero is a Japanese-Brazilian gangster named Carlos (Naoto Takenaka) who sprinkles his perfectly fluent, if hardly polite, Japanese with Portuguese. The villain is Elder Gilyak (Yuya Uchida), a blonde-haired hitman of indefinite origin who prefaces his usually flawless Japanese with phrases in tough-guy English. Even the weaponry is pure Hollywood; instead of the usual generic shooters, the characters sport customized hardware that could have been lifted from Arnold Schwarzenegger's personal prop collection.

I rather doubt, though, that *Kyohansha*'s producers have international ambitions. The film is pitched squarely at a domestic audience, who will presumably not care that its foreign characters are about as authentic as beef curry. The story from director and scriptwriter Kiuchi—the creator of the popular *Be Bop High School* comic—is pure *manga* in which the realities of international crime in Japan count for less than macho romanticism, cool stylistics, and violent action. That said, the film has some striking images, including shots of Kyoko Koizumi's bare feet as she silently stalks the hitman that carry a surprising erotic charge. (Are Kiuchi and cameraman Seizo Sengen foot fetishists—or is it just me?)

Kiuchi's 1991 *Carlos* described the title character's one-man battle with a yakuza gang in which he wreaked bloody havoc and wound up with an eight-year prison term. As *Kyohansha* begins, Carlos is back on the streets. Rather than accept him for deportation, the Brazilian cops substitute a look-alike at the airport and tell him never to darken their country's door again. Carlos decides to pick up where he left off eight years earlier and finish his quarrel with the Yamashiro-kai, which has become obscenely wealthy and powerful in the interim. First though, he stops at a noodle restaurant for a meal. Just as he is about to dip his chopsticks into the bowl, however, a wooden sandal plops into it. Its wearer—a waitress named Satomi (Kyoko Koizumi)—is being beaten by her brute of a husband. Carlos calmly takes the sandal, slams it down on the husband's forearm, and makes his exit. Satomi, determined to escape the hell of her marriage, is close behind and ends up joining Carlos on his quest.

Driving to a Yamashiro-kai office, they encounter a gang subboss whom Carlos once shot—and is now dying from the bullets of his former comrades. The gangster offers Carlos a suitcase full of cash and asks him to take care of his two *kobun*. He agrees. After a gun battle, Yamashiro-kai thugs retrieve the money, but Carlos isn't going to surrender his inheritance so easily. He declares war, again, on the entire gang. Rather than risk another fight, the Yamashiro-kai boss decides to hire the hitmen brothers Elder (Uchida) and Younger Gilyak (Mikio Osawa) to whack Carlos. It will be a war to end all gang wars.

Naoto Takenaka is best known for his comic roles, including the goofy Latin dancer of *Shall We Dance?* but he often plays darker characters as well, and Carlos is among the darkest. Takenaka is an acquired taste—his self-regard can grate—but he is also a gifted chameleon who brings an explosive force to his portrayal of Carlos. I would have liked him more, though, if he had dropped the bad Portuguese and called himself Suzuki.

Level (1994)

Scr.: Tetsuya Matsushima and Takuro Fukuda. *Dir.:* Tetsuya Matsushima. *Prod.:* Image Factory IM. *Main cast:* Toru Nakamura, Bengal, Shiori Sakura, Ryo Ishibashi. 84 mins.

Made as a vehicle for action star Toru Nakamura, Tetsuya Matsushima's *Level* explores the world of Tokyo *pachisuro* shops with a knowingness and spare romanticism reminiscent of the novels of Elmore Leonard. The story is classic Leonard—a man on the fringes of the underworld becomes caught in its grip and must find his own way out. Tomita (Nakamura) is a salaried drone working for a company that designs computer games. When his estranged father dies, he inherits his *pachisuro* parlor and the problem of what to do with it. Though Tomita has never tried the game—a made-in-Japan marriage of pachinko ("*pachi*") and slot machine ("*suro*")—he finds that he enjoys the business (especially when the store manager [Bengal] shows him how to rig a machine so the tokens pour out). Also, Tomita cannot leave the parlor's loyal employees in the lurch. He decides to change careers.

It doesn't take Tomita long to realize that customers will come more often if he gives them slightly better odds and his employees will work harder if he treats them as partners, not wage slaves. Soon, the money is rolling in and everyone is happy. That is, except for Tomita's sloe-eyed girlfriend (Shiori Sakura), who doesn't like his transformation into a profit-obsessed businessman; the local *pachisuro* parlor owners, who see Tomita's success as a threat; and the local yakuza, who want their share of the take. Tomita, however, insists on going his own way. One day he finds himself with a garbage bag over his head and feet thudding into his kidneys. Where does he go from here?

Matsushima knows how to plot, pace, and ratchet up the tension, but his real interest is character and its complications. *Level* is not only a macho fantasy about a lone hero taking on yakuza bad guys but the story of a man wrestling with his dark side and not always winning. "Desire is a dangerous thing," Tomita says at one point. By the end, we know what he means.

Nakamura is the latest pretender to the crown of the late Yujiro Ishihara—the legendary film and TV action star whose nickname was "Tough Guy." He has Ishihara's long legs, good looks, and air of danger simmering beneath the boyish surface. But whereas Ishihara embraced traditional values, Nakamura is a chilled-out product of contemporary Japan. A tough guy, yes; a warm, sentimental guy, no. He charges up the film with his scorn and rage.

In the hard-boiled genre, the female roles are usually formulaic filler—and *Level* is no exception. As the girlfriend, Shiori Sakuri is given little to do but pull long faces and fret. The best of several strong supporting performances is that of Ryo Ishibashi, who in a cameo as a scary yakuza boss turns a cane into a weapon of terrifying power. In many Japanese gangster movies, the mob is little more than a pose or a joke. In *Level* it is a malevolent reality.

In gang films of the 1990s aloha shirts were out and Armani was in. Toru Nakamura (left) and Ryo Ishibashi square off in *Level* (1994).

Matatabi (1973)

THE WANDERERS

Scr.: Kon Ichikawa, Shuntaro Tanigawa. *Dir.:* Kon Ichikawa. *Prod.:* Ichikawa Productions, ATG. *Main cast:* Isao Bito, Ken'ichi Hagiwara, Ichiro Ogura, Reiko Inoue, Akiko Nomura, Tadao Futami. 96 mins.

STORY

The period: The teens of the Tempo Era (1830–44). Three apprentice gangsters—Genta (Ichiro Ogura), Shinta (Isao Bitoh), and Mokutaro (Ken'ichi Hagiwara)—wander across the countryside in search of employment—or simply something to fill their stomachs. They make comically elaborate self-introductions to the steward of an *oyabun* but are really only peasant boys with pretensions, who have no standing in the yakuza world.

But, as the narration explains, in exchange for a rice bowl and place to sleep, they must put their lives at the service of their *oyabun* host, according to the *jingi* code. This is no hollow gesture, as a night attack on the *oyabun*'s house makes clear. The trio survives this fight without serious mishap, driving off the attackers, though they hardly distinguish themselves. Instead of slicing their opponents with grace and ease, they hack at them in blind terror. Back on the road, they encounter an open-air gambling game in progress. Sensing easy prey, they drive off the gamblers and snatch their money—or rather grub in the dirt for coins.

They lodge at the home of another *oyabun*, the oily Bangame (Tadao Futami). There, Genta encounters his father, Yasukichi (Toshimitsu Omiya), who scrapes out a mean living squeezing debtors—but the father scolds his son for becoming a *toseinin* (wandering gambler).

Genta also meets—and later rapes—Okumi (Reiko Inoue), the young wife of a nasty older man who is in debt to Bangame. Soon after, he visits his father, who is now living with a new mistress, the pudgy Oharu (Akiko Nomura).

Genta resists her blandishments and rejects her offer to live with them.

Genta visits Okumi again—and this time she makes love with him willingly. Complications arise when Bangame discovers that Yasukichi has been plotting against him—and orders Genta to kill him. With Shinta's urging ("It's your duty!"), Genta complies, cutting the old man's neck in a frenzy. But instead of praising him on a successful job, Bangame throws him and the others out—he cannot, he says, abide a parricide.

Accompanied by Okumi, the trio hits the road again, traveling to Genta's village. There, Genta finds his old home in ruins and everyone gone, save his younger brother, a boy who does not recognize him. Soon after, Okumi is approached by a man sent by her father, who urges her to return home and marry the suitor —but she kills him instead. Suffering from an infected foot, Shinta cannot walk any farther. Desperate for money, Genta takes Okume to an inn, where he sells her into prostitution— but promises to return for her. Meanwhile, Shinta dies of the infection. Genta and Mokutaro take to the road again and go off to meet their destinies—or dooms.

CRITIQUE

Based on a television drama that Kon Ichikawa directed in 1962, *Matatabi* (The Wanderers) may, from its plot summary, sound like the gloomiest of yakuza melodramas. Its trio of young gangsters are pathetic losers all, whose only reward for adhering to the *jingi* code is poverty, humiliation, and death. Its central figure, Genta, kills his father at the command of a boss who views him as little more than a convenient tool. Though Genta's lover sacrifices everything to be with him, he does not hesitate to prostitute her to feed his stomach. Even his end is pathetic and absurd.

The film, however, plays like a black comedy, with the trio being less tragic heroes than three slacker stooges, Isao Bito's Genta being the most clueless of all. Unlike the period gangster films of Toei and other studios that unfold in stately rhythms derived from traditional theater, *Matatabi* clips along, spurred by the soundtrack's pounding *taiko* drums. The intent is to expose the idiocies of the gangster code, within the framework of a straight-faced narration that purports to educate the audiences on the now-exotic customs of the nineteenth-century yakuza. The contrast between this narration and the reality of what we see on the screen—the formal self-introductions that devolve into farce, the life-or-death battles that are little more than frantic brawls—is amusingly sharp, if at times overly obvious.

As *Matatabi* progresses, however, the situation of the wanderers becomes too desperate to admit easy laughs. Even so, the film never loses its vigor or mordancy. Its critique of the old yakuza way also echoes the larger struggle then being waged in Japan and elsewhere against the American adventure in Southeast Asia—yet another example of an inflexible mind-set (peace with honor!) leading to disaster and death.

Meiji Kyokakuden: Sandai Shumei (1965)

BLOOD OF REVENGE

Scr.: Akira Murao, Norifumi Suzuki. *Dir.:* Tai Kato. *Prod.:* Toei. *Main cast:* Koji Tsuruta. Junko Fuji, Minoru Oki, Masahiko Tsugawa, Toru Abe, Shingo Yamashiro, Yoshiko Nakamura, Kanjuro Arashi. 90 mins.

STORY

The year: 1878. The place: The Osaka Kenka Matsuri (Fighting Festival). Emoto (Kanjuro Arashi), the boss of the Kiyatatsu-gumi is stabbed by an unknown assailant while watching the procession. Suspicion falls on the boss of the Hoshino-gumi (Minoru Oki) and his slithery lieutenant Karasawa (Toru Abe), who are trying to move in on Kiyatatsu's construc-

tion business, but proof is lacking. Even so, Emoto's hot-tempered son Haruo (Masahiko Tsugawa) is ready to start a war.

Meanwhile, Emoto's top lieutenant, Asajiro Kikuchi (Koji Tsuruta), is falling in love with the beautiful Hatsue (Junko Fuji), a prostitute in the pleasure quarters. But Hatsue, deep in debt to Karasawa, is not free to start a new life. Then, after a night of passion with Hatsue, Asajiro returns to gang headquarters to find his boss on the verge of death. When he dies, Asajiro is in line to become the new boss, the third since the gang's founding. He tries to make peace with the disgruntled Haruo for the good of the gang, but on the day of his succession ceremony Asajiro suffers a personal blow when Hatsue is forced to go off with Karasawa. Not stopping at this insult, the Hoshino-gumi escalates its war against its Kiyatatsu rivals, even trying to kill Haruo. Finally able to stand the humiliation no longer, Asajiro goes off alone to settle his score with Hoshino, Karasawa, and the entire gang.

CRITIQUE

Regarded by Japanese critics as a genre masterpiece, Tai Kato's *Meiji Kyokakuden: Sandai Shumei* combines high romantic drama and all-out action, filmed with Kato's trademark low angles and long cuts to extract every last ounce of emotion. The film was scripted and shot in only eighteen days, after Kato was brought in at the last minute to replace the original director, Shigehiro Ozawa.

Though released as just another program picture, *Sandai Shumei* is filled with scenes that have been treasured for decades by yakuza movie fans. In one, Harue gives Asajiro two peaches from her parents' garden, after returning from her father's funeral. This is a gesture filled with pathos, given that she must return to the brothel—and Karasawa's attentions. In another scene, set in Osaka's Nakanoshima Park, she urges Asajiro to run away with her, but he refuses. He feels guilty for not arriving in time for his *oyabun*'s death because of the night he spent with her. "I'm a stupid guy, but this is the only life I know," he says. Duty once again triumphs over personal feeling, as it must in the world of the *ninkyo eiga*.

Minazuki (1999)

EVERYONE'S A MOON

Scr.: Yasuhiko Arai. *Dir.:* Rokuro Mochizuki. *Prod.:* Nikkatsu. *Main cast:* Eiji Okuda, Kazuki Kitamura, Takami Yoshimoto. 114 mins.

Rokuro Mochizuki is a maker of films about middle-aged men on the fringes of society, at the ends of their respective ropes. Their stubborn integrity, however, has a certain appeal, especially to the younger women who enter their lives. The hero of Mochizuki's *Minazuki* (literally, *Everyone's a Moon*) would seem to be a departure from his usual pattern. A slump-shouldered salaryman named Suwa (Eiji Okuda) comes home one night to find that his wife Sayoko has fled, taking his life savings and leaving only a cryptic note: "Everyone was a moon. I've reached my limit. Good-bye." Suwa contacts Sayoko's younger brother Akira (Kazuki Kitamura), a gangster who is surprisingly sympathetic to his plight. What, we wonder, does this stud with the spiky hair and flower-print shirts see in this nerd, who lives for his computer and walks as though he has just stepped off a lunar lander?

Akira tries to console his disconsolate brother-in-law by taking him to a pricey hostess club and, when that doesn't do the trick, to a soapland (massage parlor). Suwa's *sopujo* (soap girl, or masseur) is Rinko (Takami Yoshimoto), a foxy little toughie who has seen and done it all. She takes a liking to this over-age innocent, who is pining for his runaway wife and is amusingly awkward in his first attempt at cheating. But she also senses a tremendous hunger—for what she can't say. She discovers, though, that

appearances to the contrary, this middle-aged guy is a terrific lover.

Far from being ordinary, Suwa turns out to be the most out-there Mochizuki hero of all. When Suwa's company goes bankrupt, leaving him without a job or yen to his name, he moves in with Akira and gets an accounting job with a gang bossed by Akira's old school friend. A suave type with a reptilian smile, the boss tells Suwa that the job is strictly a favor—and that Akira is too wild to be a member of the gang. Then, after a turbulent bout of lovemaking that begins with kicks and jabs and ends in frantic transports, Rinko asks Suwa to move in with her—and he accepts.

Their love nest soon becomes a hell, however, when Akira calls Rinko (whose real name is Yumi) a mercenary slut who is only after Suwa's nonexistent retirement allowance. As Suwa looks on, Akira forces her to engage in humiliating sex. Despite the disillusions and humiliations, this odd trio stays together. One reason is a shocking act of expiation by Akira that may turn a few stomachs. Another is a shocking murder, again committed by Akira, that may turn a few more.

On a tip from one of Akira's loan-shark acquaintances, they begin to search for Suwa's wife, who ran away with her young gangster lover, to a town near the Japan Sea. She's finally tracked down to an inn called Minazuki, run by the gangster's mother, and they start a stakeout. Camping near the sea, the three form stronger bonds, come to new understandings. Suwa takes long solitary walks along the coast to toughen up his scrawny body. He even romps with Yumi in the surf and plays new sexual games with her. But though he no longer desires revenge against his wife, he wants to ask her one question: What did she mean by "moon"?

Working from a tightly constructed script by Yasuhiko Arai, Mochizuki uses the standard yakuza genre elements of sex and violence as tools to strip his characters to their essential

selves. Minus his socially defined roles as duti-
ful husband and loyal employee, Suwa is at first
as helpless as a pet rabbit ejected from its cage
(a comparison Yumi quickly notices). Instead of
trying to crawl back inside, however, he hops
off clumsily into the unknown. From pathetic
zero he becomes, if not a typical hero, a man in
his own peculiar right.

Akira and Yumi undergo the same process
of deepening and change. Mochizuki may show
them at their worst—Akira as a stone-cold
killer, Yumi as a degraded whore—but never
simply as monster and victim. While not trying
to excuse their actions, he illuminates them in a
stark, sympathetic light. Neither an exploiter
nor an ideologue, Mochizuki is interested in
the truths that human beings reveal in the extremes of lust and rage, need, and despair.

There is nothing extreme about his methods, however: he rejects both Kitanoesque
minimalism and Miike-esque maximalism in
favor of a documentary-like clarity and immediacy. If any of his shots unsettle, it is not because he is jamming them into our optic nerves
but because he has captured his characters'
most emotionally naked moments. As Suwa,
Eiji Okuda provides most of those moments.
Though he has played similar roles before,
Okuda brings a new level of mastery and conviction to his end-of-the-tether portrayal. He
builds his characterization from the inside out
with inspired touches, from Suwa's goofy, lop-
ing walk to the hunch of his narrow shoulders,
as though he were an old man walking into a
cold wind. This "moon" makes *Minazuki* a
work of brilliance.

Minbo no Onna (1992)

THE GENTLE ART OF JAPANESE EXTORTION
Scr./Dir.: Juzo Itami. *Prod.:* Toho, Itami Film. *Main
cast:* Nobuko Miyamoto, Akira Takarada, Yasuo
Daichi, Masahiro Murata. 123 mins.

The title of Juzo Itami's *Minbo no Onna* (The
Gentle Art of Japanese Extortion) is a classic
teaser. Before the film's release, the average
Japanese probably could not have told you the
meaning of *minbo*. A contraction of *minji
kainyu boryoku*, *minbo* is cop talk for gangsters
ripping off nongangsters through various
scams. Punchy and racy, it sticks in the mind,
while evoking the movie's world. But what
about *Minbo no Onna* the movie, as opposed to
Minbo no Onna, the cleverly branded product?
As do all Itami's films, it stars his wife, Nobuko
Miyamoto. She is the *minbo no onna*: a lawyer
who specializes in helping businesses deal with
the yakuza.

Minbo begins as a smart, fast-paced, nimbly
acted comedy. A high-class Tokyo hotel loses a
bid to a rival to host a summit meeting. The
reason? The yakuza are conducting their business—including shakedowns of clients who
have fallen behind in their loan-shark pay-
ments—in the lobby. The hotel manager (Akira
Takarada) assigns two employees—an athletic
bellboy named Wakasugi (Masahiro Murata)
and a wiseacre pencil pusher named Suzuki
(Yasuo Daichi)—to a yakuza task force. Wakasugi and Suzuki have no idea how to handle the
boys in the razzle-dazzle suits, however. The
yakuza, who sense weakness the way sharks
scent blood, soon realize the hotel is easy meat.

Minbo no Onna is a manual of a movie; the
first part, with its funny confrontations between the bumbling good guys and sneering
bad guys, is the "how not to" chapter. The second, when the lawyer finally appears on the
scene, is the "how to" chapter. Dressed impeccably in Armani, the lawyer tells the two-man
task force that their attempts to pay off the
yakuza are as futile as throwing bits of meat to
a hungry man-eating shark. Firmness—and
electronic gear for catching the gangsters in
the act—are essential.

But won't the yakuza feed them to the fish-
es, they ask? She laughs in their faces. Gangsters almost never use violence against

nongangsters, she explains. Roughing up civilians is not only against the gangster code but bad for business. For all their bluff and bluster, gangsters are businessmen first, who have no desire to spend unnecessary time in the slammer. This is good to know, but Itami's didactic impulses overwhelm his movie-making instincts. We get the point long before his film winds its way to its foregone conclusion.

Like all self-help books, *Minbo no Onna* wants to give us confidence that we can solve a problem we consider overwhelming, but, like so many of those books, it makes the solution seem unrealistically easy. (As Itami's own experience proved—his "disrespect" for gangsters in the film inspired several hoods to knife him outside his Tokyo home, nearly killing him.) His wise guys are posturing caricatures. They are clever enough, in a low sort of way, but not very bright. They make indictable threats for the hotel's video camera, even though they know it is recording their every snarl. The movie's plunge into deep dramatic waters also fails to convince. We can laugh at Itami's cartoony characters, but when he asks us to shed a tear for them we balk. We see the manipulative hand of the cartoonist too clearly.

Itami did his homework for *Minbo no Onna*; he interviewed dozens of yakuza-afflicted businessmen and *minbo* experts. He also made the film a hit. But he couldn't surpass *Ososhiki* (The Funeral) or *Tampopo*. Those early films were fresh, funny, delightfully skewed. *Minbo no Onna* seems to come from the tape recorder—and an exhausted imagination.

Mukokuseki no Otoko: Chi no Shukaku (1997)

PINOCCHIO: A MAN WITHOUT NATIONALITY

Scr.: Shoichi Maruyama. *Dir.:* Rokuro Mochizuki. *Prod.:* Toei Video. *Main cast:* Ryo Ishibashi, Ai Oyokawa, Sansei Shiomi, Dan Li, Kazuki Kitamura, Koh Takasugi. 94 mins.

STORY

Shinya Kuroki (Ryo Ishibashi) arrives at Narita Airport from New York. A former elite salaryman working for a big trading company, he comes out of the terminal dressed as a Buddhist monk, complete with a wide straw hat covering his face. Soon after, two foreigners also come out the doors—hitmen for the Gepetto Family, one of the three biggest Mafia clans in New York. They are met by Kenta, a yakuza who will help them find their prey: Kuroki, or as he is better known in New York mob circles, Pinocchio. Kuroki is also wanted by the FBI, which regards him as a witness who can break the power of the Gepettos and associates. With the help of the Japanese police, they intend to find him.

Aoi (Sansei Shimi), the Japanese detective acting as a liaison with the FBI, visits Kuroki's father and asks him to notify the police if Kuroki comes to call. Aoi, it turns out, was on the basketball team with Kuroki in high school and also his friend in college but has since lost track of him. Six years ago, Kuroki went to work in his firm's New York office and, in rescuing a colleague's botched business deal, became enmeshed in the mob.

Meanwhile, the Japanese police try to bust a Taiwanese drug ring, but their opponents destroy all their computer files—and finally each other—before the cops can close in. This big loss of face does not please Aoi—or the FBI man who is impatient for results on the Kuroki case. Kuroki has greater success in breaking into the office of a clothing company run by Taiwanese mobsters—and offering them stolen designs from a famous New York maker for 50 million yen. Miss Lee (Dan Li), the slinky Taiwanese woman who is in charge, agrees to the deal.

Kuroki turns up at a riverside restaurant now run by the son (Kazuki Kitamura) of an old friend. The place is empty when a beautiful woman, Ritsu Omori (Ai Oyokawa), saunters in. Kuroki makes her acquaintance and takes her out for an evening of dining and dancing.

Later, at a hotel, he learns that she is Japanese-American, with nonstandard sexual tastes. On their next night out, Kuroki and his new girlfriend encounter the two hitmen in a restaurant. Kuroki greets them like old friends—but with the unexpected aid of Ritsu, makes his escape.

The Taiwanese mobsters try to cheat Kuroki on the payoff and, when he calls them on it, pursue him through the back streets of the Ginza. Aoi, who has been on stakeout, is close behind. Kuroki loses the Taiwanese but later encounters Aoi. After a bit of cat-and-mouse, Kuroki and Aoi finally have a conversation and Aoi asks his old friend to turn himself in to the FBI. Kuroki says he will consider it—but has some business he wants to take care of first. That, as it turns out, includes another meeting with his dodgy and dangerous Taiwanese business partners—and a showdown with his two would-be assassins.

CRITIQUE

A followup to his well-received *Shin Kanashiki Hitman* (Another Lonely Hitman), Rokuro Mochizuki's *Mukokuseki no Otoko: Chi no Shukaku* (Pinocchio: A Man without Nationality) is an ambitious attempt to internationalize the yakuza movie. How many Japanese directors, including the adventurous Miike, would have made their hero a salaryman-turned-Mafioso? Or use stolen fashion designs as a plot MacGuffin?

That said, *Mukokuseki no Otoko* is one of Mochizuki's few failures, with a parade of cultural stereotypes and missteps that range from the laughably lame to the offensive. Leaving aside the question of whether a Japanese Mafioso is even a possibility, the film's view of the mob—with its don named Gepetto and its "Mutt and Jeff" hitman blustering through Tokyo—more properly belongs in a comedy. The two FBI agents pursuing the hero are little better; the man is a cartoon racist and the woman, though supposedly a Japanese-American, speaks heavily accented English and suspiciously fluent Japanese, while having no identifiable American characteristics, save for shouting "yes" in bed. The foreign actors, who seem to be local hires, are uniformly atrocious. Meanwhile, the Taiwanese characters are slithery, murderous types from Central Casting, though Chinese actress Dan Li, a familiar face in Japanese video movies, works up an amusingly campy air of menace as the mysterious Miss Lee.

Ryo Ishibashi, a rock vocalist when he is not playing gangster, does not overly embarrass himself as the wise guy on the run, delivering his English lines with something resembling understanding and assurance—but does he really have to sing "O Sole Mio" while one of his would-be hitmen dances with his girlfriend? Something from the oeuvre of Tony Bennett would have been more Mafioso-ish—but then, anything close to cultural accuracy and sensitivity would have meant making another movie.

Narazumono (1964)

THE UNTAMED

Scr./Dir.: Teruo Ishii. *Prod.:* Toei. *Main cast:* Ken Takakura, Tetsuro Tanba, Naoki Sugiura, Shinjiro Ebara, Toru Abe, Takashi Shikanai, Kenji Imai, Yoko Mihara, Risa Takami, Yoko Minamida, Mariko Kaga. 98 mins.

STORY

Nanjo (Ken Takakura) comes to Hong Kong to whack a local gangster and, after accomplishing his task, goes to a pre-arranged hotel room to collect his payment. Instead, he discovers the corpse of a woman on the bed. He goes to question Mao (Toru Abe), the Chinese gang boss who contracted the hit, but on the way tries his luck at an arcade coin-toss game and wins the grand prize: two bags of trinkets, including a mysterious can. A beauty in a clingy

Chinese dress, Ming-lan (Yoko Mihara) offers to buy the can from him in flawless Japanese, but Nanjo refuses her offer—and later finds a small fortune of opium in it.

The next day, he entrusts a young maid at his hotel with the can and goes to meet Ming-lan. In exchange for the can, he wants her boss, Chiang (Tetsuro Tanba), to divulge Mao's whereabouts. Ming-lan, however, wants the can for herself—and is willing to betray her boss to get it. She and her boyfriend, Zhou (Takashi Shikanai), go to Nanjo's hotel to find the can—and Zhou kills the maid in the course of a brutal interrogation. The old woman who runs the hotel walks in at the wrong moment, and they buy her silence.

Hearing that Mao is in Yokohama, Nanjo boards a plane for Japan, but his quarry eludes him and slips back into Hong Kong (not before an interlude in a love hotel with a saucy young Japanese hooker (Mariko Kaga). Hot on Mao's trail, Nanjo returns to Hong Kong—and learns about the maid's murder. He extracts the truth from the old woman, but his anger at her duplicity gets the better of him and he has another corpse on his hands. Nanjo then meets Chiang in Macao and fights him in an epic brawl, but when Nanjo learns that Ming-lan has been playing a double game, he and Chiang make up and become allies.

The Hong Kong police, however, are after Nanjo for the two murders. He escapes to a slum where he encounters a Japanese undercover detective (Naoki Sugiura) who is trying to break up Mao's drug ring and a tubercular Japanese hooker, Akiko (Yoko Minamida), whom he saves, temporarily, from death. With information from Chiang, Nanjo finally runs Mao to earth—but gets less than a welcome reception.

CRITIQUE

Soon after, making *Tokyo Gang tai Hong Kong Gang*, Ishii returned to Hong Kong for *Narazumono* (The Untamed), which in development was an ambitious project with location shoots planned for Indonesia, Seoul, and Las Vegas. Much of the action, however, occurs in Macao, including Nanjo and Chiang's fight at the ruins of Saint Paul's Cathedral—a major tourist site then off limits to film crews. The two male leads, Ken Takakura and Tetsuro Tanba, display none of the martial arts moves that were to characterize Hong Kong films in later years; instead, they have a slugfest in the then-approved Hollywood style.

Ishii cast his Japanese "repertory company," including Naoki Sugiura, Yoko Mihara, Shinjiro Ebara, and Toru Abe, in nearly all the Chinese roles, much the way Hollywood of the time presented Yul Brenner and Anthony Quinn in a wide range of "exotic" guises. Ishii's actors, however, spoke more dialogue in Cantonese than Hollywood would have then considered necessary.

Ken Takakura does his standard turn as the punkish gangster who can't be tempted or fooled but is a dirtier hero than Hollywood would have permitted in the early 1960s. Even Marlon Brando, Paul Newman, Steven McQueen, and other screen rebels of the era weren't into battering old ladies to death. Takakura, however, compensated by sucking tubercular blood from the throat of the choking Yoko Minamida—a good deed that turned the stomachs of the film's contemporary critics but helped make *Narazumono* a standout among Ishii's Toei gang films. It justifiably remains one of his favorites to this day.

Nihon Kuroshakai Ley Lines (1999)

LEY LINES

Scr.: Ichiro Ryu. *Dir.:* Takashi Miike. *Prod.:* Daiei. *Main cast:* Show Aikawa, Samuel Pop Aning, Michisuke Kashiwaya, Kazuki Kitamura, Dan Li, Ren Osugi, Tomoro Taguchi, Naoto Takenaka, Koji Tsukamoto, Hua Rong Wong. 105 mins.

STORY

Two brothers, half-Japanese and half-Chinese, are living on the edges of the law in the Japanese countryside. The violent-tempered older brother, Ryu (Kazuki Kitamura), suddenly decides to leave for Tokyo, together with his stuttering, eccentric friend Chan (Tomoro Taguchi). Younger brother Shunri (Michisuke Kashiwaya), a quiet, studious type, stays behind but then changes his mind and tags along. In the big city, this trio meets a Chinese hooker, Anita (Dan Li), in a red dress, who entices them into a room, locks them in, and makes off with their money. She is beaten by her pimp for the trouble—he suspects she is earning behind his back.

Back on the street again, the boys meet Bobby (Samuel Pop Aning), a black speed dealer. He introduces them to his boss (Show Aikawa), who hires them as dealers. Roaming Shinjuku, they earn their first yen. Meanwhile, Anita services a salaryman with unusual sexual tastes—and gets more than she bargains for. Ryu wants to go to Brazil, but black-market passports are expensive. How to raise the money? Not long after, Shunri spots Anita, staggering down the street after another beating from her pimp. She proposes paying him back with sex and he accepts. Meanwhile, Ryu and Chan are getting thrashed by gangsters, whose boss, Wong (Naoto Takenaka), rules this corner of Shinjuku and takes exception to their presence. Shunri finds them and takes them to Anita's apartment. She has sex with both and, afterward, all four sleep together, reconciled at last.

Ryu finds a man who says he can smuggle them out of the country for 2 million yen. A boat is leaving from Kawasaki on Friday and they plan to be on it. Assisted by Bobby, Ryu buys guns with the intention of ripping off Wong. Not long after, Ryu and his crew burst into the restaurant where Wong's gangsters are counting their loot and make off with most of it. Escaping on scooters, they are ambushed by

Bobby and his boss but manage to shoot their way out. However, Chan is fatally wounded. Driving a stolen car, they take him to a temple in the countryside, where he dies. Shunri takes Chan's share of the loot to his mother—but is discovered by Wong's men and brutally murdered. Ryu is also chased but manages to escape. Together, he and Anita head for Kawasaki—and a new future.

CRITIQUE

The third in Takashi Miike's trilogy of films about Japanese and Chinese gangsters—*Shinjuku Kuro Shakai China Mafia Senso* (Shinjuku Triad Society) and *Gokudo Kuro Shakai Rainy Dog* (Rainy Dog)—*Ley Lines* is half the way in Miike's transition from the sort of macho minimalism made popular by Takeshi Kitano in the 1990s to the extravagances and outrages of his early millennial work. The elegiac long shots of vicious beatings, the deadpan reaction shots, and the ironically punchy accordion music are of the Kitano style—and make us believe, in the opening scenes at least, that we are going to see another blackly humorous, mercilessly violent essay on outlaw life, in a minor key and with a downbeat ending.

Miike soon betrays these expectations with a whirlwind tour of the Shinjuku night streets that is as jittery and jumpy as a bad speed trip, a horrific S&M sex session that features an enormous syringe, a glimpse through a speculum, and bloodcurdling screams. The finale includes a lingering closeup of pooling blood and a leap into what may or may not be a dying vision of bliss. These are not images usually found in the Kitano canon—but are immediately identifiable as Miike.

Matching the visuals are the film's out-there characters. Naoto Takenaka, as the gang boss, relaxes by listening to Chinese fairy tales in a candlelit room—but goes berserk at the least provocation. Tomoro Taguchi, as a Harpo Marxist sidekick, is tongue-tied, childish, and irrepressibly lecherous. In combining these disparate elements, Miike may trash credibility—his Shinjuku exists nowhere outside his film, but his vision is also entertainingly inventive, blackly funny, and touched with an unexpected spirituality.

Nihon Kyokakuden: Naniwahen (1965)

Scr.: Tatsuo Nogami. *Dir.:* Masahiro Makino. *Prod.:* Toei. *Main cast:* Ken Takakura, Koji Tsuruta, Kotami Satomi, Hiroyuki Nagato, Ryutaro Otomo, Yoko Minamida, Kaoru Yachigusa. 98 mins.

STORY

The year: 1921. Shuji Fujikawa (Ken Takakura), a *daigashi* (gambling house manager) with the Nitto gang of Yokohama, comes to Osaka to retrieve the ashes of his younger brother, who died in an accident working on the docks. One of his brother's co-workers, Tora (Hiroyuki Nagato), takes him to the gravesite on a lonely patch of land. There, Fujikawa reminisces, saying that his brother was an independent type who, three years earlier, left Yokohama to seek his fortune.

Fujikawa thanks Tora and the other stevedores for the kindness they showed his brother—and asks if he can work with them for a while, loading coal. They are happy to oblige (partly because he gave them a much-appreciated bottle of sake) and help him get a job with their foreman, Wadajima (Hideo Murata), whose boss (Asao Uchida) leads the Handagumi. The Handa-gumi, however, has competition—Naniwa Unso, whose *oyabun*, Niizawa (Ryutaro Otomo), and top lieutenant (Bin Amatsu), are unscrupulous gangsters. Fujikawa soon butts heads with this rival gang by forcing their cheating paymaster to give the stevedores what he owes them. Fujikawa is pursued by Naniwa thugs but is rescued by Wadajima, who takes a liking to Fujikawa and asks him to join his gang.

Tora is in love with a young teahouse prostitute, Oshin (Yoko Minamida), who is in turn coveted by Niizawa. Enraged by the thought of Oshin being stolen away from him, Tora vows to pay off her debt and free her. No longer capable of leading the gang, the elderly Handa *oyabun* wants to turn it over to Wadajima. Handa's estranged son, Terukoma, wants no part of the business, despite Wadajima's entreaties. In trouble with the law, Terukoma is arrested by the police and taken away. (He is later freed and repents.)

Niizawa bribes the stevedores to come to work for him. Many accept, but Tora and other Handa loyalists resist. Needing to complete a big job for the navy, Wadajima finds himself shorthanded—the object of Niizawa's recruiting drive. As if that weren't bad enough, Wadajima is ambushed and shot by unknown assailants. Was Niizawa responsible?

Then, Fujimura (Koji Tsuruta) returns to the Naniwa Unso headquarters after an absence of five years—and renews his acquaintance with Chiyo (Kaoru Yachigusa), a senior to Oshin at the teahouse. He is, however, given a cold reception by Niizawa, who sees him as competition for the gang leadership. Wadajima dies of his wounds and the old *oyabun* asks Fujikawa to take his place. Fujikawa agrees, to everyone's jubilation. Tora and Oshin decide to escape but are pursued by Niizawa's men. They kill Tora and, soon after, Fujimura hears that Niizawa has raped Oshin. Fujimura goes to the gang headquarters to investigate—and finds her dead. He also learns that Niizawa is responsible for the death of Wadajima—an old friend. Fujikawa and Fujimura, though barely acquainted, join forces to attack Niizawa and his minions for their many outrages.

CRITIQUE

The second installment in the eleven-part Nihon Kyokakuden series and one of nine directed by Masahiro Makino, *Nihon Kyokakuden Naniwahen* follows the standard pattern of honest workers being threatened by slimeball gangsters, with Ken Takakura playing a yakuza exemplifying the *ninkyo* code—and selflessly siding with the workers. The narrative focus of the film, however, is less on its feuding gangs than its loving couples, beginning with Hiroyuki Nagato's stevedore and Yoko Minamida's prostitute, whose doomed romance has antecedents in Kabuki.

Also paired are Koji Tsuruta and a flirtatious young Kaoru Yachigusa (who is now playing grandmothers) and Ken Takakura and Wakaba Irie as the giggly proprietor of an outdoor stall, their relationship providing little more than comic relief. As usual in a Makino film, several big action scenes explode on the screen before the final showdown, all staged with characteristic dynamism and precision. The dramatic highpoint, however, is Nagato's self-sacrificing death, milked for maximum pathos.

Nihon Kyokakuden: Shiraha no Sakazuki (1967)

Scr.: Sadao Nakajima. *Dir.:* Masahiro Makino. *Prod.:* Toei. *Main cast:* Ken Takakura, Junko Fuji, Kenji Sugawara, Hiroyuki Nagato, Minoru Oki, Kayo Matsuo, Yuriko Mishima, Gen Shimizu, Junko Miyazono, Bin Amatsu. 95 mins.

STORY

The time: the beginning of the Showa Era (1926–89). Shuji Okita (Ken Takakura), a wandering yakuza, is traveling with his sick wife (Junko Fuji). He stops a truck, whose rough-but-kindhearted driver, Ishikawa (Hiroyuki Nagato), agrees to take the wife to the nearest hospital, where she is diagnosed with pneumonia. The company Ishikawa works for, Togawa Unso, operates in the port city of Choshi, in Chiba Prefecture. The owner, Togawa (Kenji Sugawara), is a former yakuza who is being challenged by a former lieutenant, Nejime (Bin

Amatsu), now the boss of a rival trucking company. Nejime offers to buy out Togawa—and decides to crush him if he refuses. Togawa, however, says he can't do business with a man who is still a gangster.

Both are engaged in a battle to control the lucrative fish shipping business from the port. Hand carts are giving way to trucks, throwing the carters out of work. Nejime predicts that Togawa will join them in six months or less. His plan is to bribe the fish dealers who hire the trucks and, to seal the deal, marry the daughter of the Dealers' Association chairman (Gen Shimizu). (She objects but no matter—to her father she is only a bargaining chip.)

Meanwhile, Nejime has eyes for Fumie (Kayo Matsuo), the luscious wife of Enatsu (Minoru Oki), a Togawa-gumi lieutenant now in prison. She is raising her young son alone—and is in need of the financial helping hand Nejime is so willing to provide. He also tries to undermine Togawa by hiring away his drivers, beginning with Ishikawa, whose girlfriend Yumeko (Junko Miyazono) is in debt to Nejime. Ishikawa agrees, though it breaks his loyal heart to abandon the kindly Togawa. Then, the driver of one of Togawa's trucks is involved in a fatal accident—another of Nejime's schemes. When Ishikawa finds out about the accident, he goes to Togawa's office and tells his old boss that Nejime is to blame. He is ready to kill Nejime in revenge, but Okita, who feels indebted to Ishikawa for saving his wife's life, restrains him. No matter, soon after, Togawa is stabbed and killed by Nejime's men. Okita takes the body to Nejime's office—and offers to pay the debt owed by Yumeko.

Enatsu, released from prison, returns together with a Togawa-gumi brother, Daigoro (Junzaburo Ban). Soon after, however, his wife commits suicide out of shame because she has succumbed to Nejime's advances. Putting two and two together, Enatsu and Daigoro invade Nejime's office with the aim of taking revenge, but both are shot and killed by a Nejime underling. When Okita hears this news, he decides to finish what they have started.

CRITIQUE

The sixth installment in the Nihon Kyokakuden series, *Nihon Kyokakuden: Shiraha no Sakazuki* may star Ken Takakura, but the supporting cast makes a stronger impression, starting with Bin Amatsu, as Nejime. With his over-ripe good looks and air of slithery arrogance, Amatsu is persuasive as both the seducer of Kayo Matsuo and the corporate shark who destroys those he does not first devour. Though his character is typical of the series' rogue gallery—an "economic yakuza" who has abandoned the gangster code (as if he ever adhered to it in the first place)—Amatsu gives him a sensual dimension that most *ninkyo eiga* villains lack.

Also outstanding is Junzaburo Ban as Minori Oki's companion on both his return from prison and fatal attack on the Nejime headquarters. A period drama veteran, Ban makes his salty character more than the standard comic sidekick. Facing off against dozens of enemy gangsters, he wields his sword to deadly effect. When one hood tries to ambush him, Ban pats him on the head as he might a naughty boy—while ramming a blade into his side.

In the climactic *nagurikomi* (showdown) scene, Ken Takakura slashes through the rival gang with more than usual fierceness and dash. Perhaps after hanging in the background for much of the film, he decided to show the audience who was the real star of the show. As usual, Masahiro Makino choreographs the action less for realism than high drama.

Nihon Boryokudan: Kumicho (1969)

JAPAN ORGANIZED CRIME BOSS

Scr.: Fumio Konami, Norio Osada, Kinji Fukasaku. *Dir.:* Kinji Fukasaku. *Prod.:* Toei. *Main cast:* Koji Tsuruta, Bunta Sugawara, Noboru Ando, Ryohei Uchida, Tomisaburo Wakayama. 97 mins.

STORY

The Tanno-gumi, a powerful Kansai gang, is expanding from its Osaka base into the Kanto region. As part of this plan, it forms an alliance with the Yokohama-based Hamanaka-gumi. Meanwhile, local bosses unite in a new organization—the Kanto Rengo—to resist the Tanno invasion. One member is another Yokohama gang, the Sakurada-gumi, which goes on the attack against their Hamanaka rivals. Tsukamoto (Koji Tsuruta), the Hamanaka second-in-command, is released from prison after an eight-year stretch and, on his way to the gang's waterfront headquarters, breaks up a scuffle between Hamanaka and Sakurada gangsters—and breaks a few Sakurada heads in the process.

Soon after, however, the Hamanaka *oyabun* is mortally wounded in a car explosion. Before he dies, he asks Tsukamoto to take over the gang—and tells him that the alliance with the Tanno gang was a big mistake. Tsukamoto is about to settle matters with the Sakurada assassins—when Kazama (Bunta Sugawara) returns to the gang headquarters, having already accomplished the necessary mission of revenge—and received a fatal cut. Tsubaki (Ryohei Uchida), a top Tanno lieutenant and one of Tsukamoto's friends from his old *gurentai* days, urges Tsukamoto to continue the alliance. But Tsukamoto tells both him and his boss that he intends to go it alone. He's had enough bloodshed and knows that further involvement in the turf war will only result in more.

The power-hungry Tsubaki decides to form a new coalition with another local gang, the Hokuryu-kai, whose amphetamine-addicted boss Miyahara (Tomisaburo Wakayama) is only too happy to move on the Sakurada gang's Yokohama territory. Meanwhile, the Tanno *oyabun* is enlisting the support of a powerful political fixer to pave the way for the Hokuryu-kai's Yokohama invasion. Soon Miyahara and his gang are battling their Sakurada rivals on the streets and eyeing their next target: the Hamanaka-gumi.

After a brawl in a bar on Hamanaka turf, Miyahara's crew snags a hostage—a young Hamanaka gangster. Tsukamoto goes alone to the Hokuryu-kai headquarters to free him—and wins the reluctant respect of Miyahara for his boldness. Surviving a cut to the forehead from Miyahara's sword, Tsukamoto is nursed back to health by Kazama's widow—and comes to share her futon.

The Hokuryu-kai breaks their Sakurada rivals with a successful, if bloody, attack on their headquarters. Now desperate, the Kanto Rengo decides to take out Tanno. Their hit-man (Noboru Ando) wounds Tanno while he is strolling in a park, but in the ensuing shoot-out a foreign woman is killed. The hitman ends up at the Hamanaka headquarters—and Tsukamo-to agrees to take him in, while the boss of the Kanto Rengo casually abandons the man to his fate. Reluctant to put his rescuers in danger, the hitman leaves the Hamanaka headquarters with his wife, but both are gunned down by Tanno pursuers. Tanno discovers that the Hamanaka gang hid the hitman—and decides that the gloves will have to come off.

CRITIQUE

Kinji Fukasaku's first film after returning to Toei in 1969, *Nihon Boryokudan: Kumicho* (Japan Organized Crime Boss) features a line-up of top Toei stars. Unlike the *ninkyo eiga* that Toei had churned out so successfully throughout much of the decade, the film was set in present-day Japan and told a ripped-from-the-headlines story about modern gang warfare. Also, though Koji Tsuruta plays an upright, old-fashioned gangster—a suit-and-tie version of the countless *ninkyo eiga* heroes who had lived and often died by the *jingi* code—the film clipped along more briskly than the typical stately *ninkyo eiga*. As an explanatory device,

Fukasaku used the sort of TV news clips, with a Walter Winchell-like announcer providing narration, that later became his trademark in the Jingi Naki Tatakai (Battles without Honor and Humanity) series of the 1970s.

To many yakuza film fans, Tsuruta represents the old guard, Fukasaku the new, but Tsuruta is well cast in the role of a gangster Rip Van Winkle returning to a changed world. He provides several of the film's more memorable lines and scenes, including his stoic running of the gauntlet in the Hokuryu-kai headquarters and his reply to his lover, who has been begging him to go straight: "A yakuza is always a yakuza," he says. No argument there.

No Way Back: Toso Yugi (1995)

NO WAY BACK
Scr./Dir.: Frank Cappello. *Prod.:* Toei Video, Tohoku Shinsha, First Look Films. *Main cast:* Etsushi Toyokawa, Russell Crowe, Michael Lerner. 92 mins.

A co-production between Toei Video, Tohoku Shinsha, and First Look Films, Frank Cappello's *No Way Back* may race over the same treacherous ground covered by other Japan-U.S. culture gap thrillers, including *Rising Sun* and *Black Rain*, but it avoids most of the usual jingoistic potholes, while offering smartly paced, tightly constructed genre entertainment. The film, Cappello's second for Toei Video's V America video series, has a familiar thriller arc. When the son of a Mafia boss is murdered, an FBI agent (Russell Crowe) arrests a New York-based yakuza (Etsushi Toyokawa) that he suspects of ordering the hit. But the revenge-bent boss (Michael Lerner) kidnaps the agent's seven-year-old son and demands the yakuza in exchange for the boy's life. Deciding that his son is more important than his career, the agent flies off to a rendezvous in Los Angeles, with his captive in tow. But on the way, the yakuza hijacks the plane and, protesting his innocence, escapes across the desert. The agent gives chase but begins to wonder who is right: the Mafia boss and the whole FBI? Or a Japanese gangster trying to save his own neck?

Cappello, who also wrote the script, may have hit a few wrong cross-cultural notes, including a yakuza lair that looks like a dark, metallic knockoff from the *Blade Runner* set, but tells his story with a blend of taut action and dry humor. Also, unlike Hollywood filmmakers who see the conflict between their Japanese and American characters in terms straight from a "Japan-bashing" book (if not directly based on one), Cappello personalizes the agent's pursuit of his yakuza suspect. Though they may begin the movie viewing each other as stereotypes—the yakuza, of course, is sneaky, duplicitous, and cold—by the end they know each other intimately and have disposed of the usual East-West cant. Billed as a chase film, *No Way Back* is really a buddy movie with an East-meets-West twist.

Etsushi Toyokawa plays his yakuza with post-modern cool while rejecting genre clichés. Crowe underplays the tough-guy heroics, while bringing a coiled power and quotidian credibility to his role. The only distraction is Helen Slater as a stewardess whose mind is a stew of New Age mumbo-jumbo, girl scout platitudes, and corny old songs. She clowns valiantly but is more embarrassing than amusing. Perhaps her character is a Japanese producer's idea of real air-headed Americana.

Nobody (1994)

Scr./Dir.: Tochimichi Okawa. *Prod.:* New Wave. *Main cast:* Riki Takeuchi, Hideo Nakano, Masaya Kato, Hiromi Nakajima, Jinpachi Nezu. 100 mins.

The straight-to-video market has generated an interesting class of hybrids: gang films that are targeted primarily at video fans but have the stars and production values of theatrical movies. Screenwriter and director Toshimichi Okawa indicates he is fully aware of this fact by shooting much of his first feature, *Nobody*, in TV-friendly close-up. But he has also made a stylish thriller that gets beneath its characters' skins and in its audience's faces in some original ways. As the movie approaches its violent climax, the film becomes manipulative and slightly absurd, but *Nobody* never loses its grip.

Three friends are having a drink in a trendy-looking bar. Former *chinpira*, they are now junior execs in a big advertising company, designing ad campaigns for a home security company. Reminiscing about the bad old days, Nambu (Riki Takeuchi) makes a snide remark about the three yakuza sitting at the next table. The yakuza, however, have rabbit ears. The ensuing confrontation ends peacefully enough, and the three men leave the bar unscathed; but when Onishi (Hideo Nakano) returns to retrieve his umbrella, he gets stomped by the wise guys. Their gangster instincts aroused, the ad execs vow revenge.

Okawa peels this scene to its emotional core, showing the fear, anger, and male pride flickering over his heroes' faces. The pacing is deliberate, the air of danger, palpable. His heroes, we see, are fully aware of the risks and not altogether sure that they want to run them. Though the theme—little actions have big consequences—may be common enough, the film charges it to a high pitch. Revenge, however, does not come easy. Onishi and Taki (Masaya Kato) feel that chasing around after gangsters is not something adults do. But when they encounter one of the yakuza in a dark underground passageway, they beat him, Nambu kills him, and the victim's pals find out. The hunters become the hunted.

The pace picks up, the plot twists multiply, and tension escalates. Finally, Taki has to confront his barroom acquaintances alone. Along the way to this showdown, he meets a sultry

NOBODY

MASAYA KATOH/JIMPACHI NEZU/RIKI TAKEUCHI
HIDEO NAKANO/HIROMI NAKAJIMA/YUMI NISHIYAMA

誰もいない―。
乾ききったこの街で男たちは出会ってしまった。
そしてルールのない死のゲームが始まる―。

© 1994 New Wave

Entering a tunnel of no return. Three *chinpira*-turned-ad-execs battle gangsters in Tochimichi Okawa's *Nobody* (1994).

model (Hiromi Nakajima) who won't take no for an answer and a cop (Jinpachi Nezu) who seems to know more than he is telling. Okawa may lean heavily on thriller clichés, including the tiresome one of the never-say-die villain, but creates an atmosphere of omnipresent fear. I've seldom seen a Mercedes Benz as scary as the one in *Nobody*, like a low-slung, wide-jawed, gray-metal beast, quite naturally the yakuza car of choice.

Oedo Gonin Otoko (1951)

FIVE MEN FROM EDO

Scr.: Fuji Yahiro, Shinichi Yanagisawa, Yoshikata Yoda. *Dir.:* Daisuke Ito. *Prod.:* Shochiku. *Main cast:* Tsumasaburo Bando, Utaemon Ichikawa, Isuzu Yamada, Mieko Takamine, Ryunosuke Tsukigata, Teiji Takahashi, Kokichi Takada, Masao Mishima, Reizaburo Yamamoto. 133 mins.

STORY

Under Tokugawa Iemitsu (1604–51), the third shogun, peace has spread across the land. This is bad news for the *hatamoto* class—warriors who are now finding their services unneeded. One clan of the Edo *hatamoto*, the Shiratsuka-gumi, takes out their frustration with their lot by invading a theater in Yoshiwara and disrupting the play. They are confronted by Chobei Banzuin (Tsumasaburo Bando), the leader of the Edo *machi-yakko* (townsmen who have banded together to resist the depredations of the *hatamoto* and are forerunners to the yakuza). The chief of the *hatamoto* is Jurozaemon Mizuno (Utaemon Ichikawa), a haughty man who nonetheless backs down under Chobei's withering gaze. As the disgruntled *hatamoto* leave the theater, they have a new enemy: Chobei and his men.

Mizuno is scheming to make a match with a princess—and to sweeten the deal, offers her precious plates that are an ancestral treasure. The princess, however, is less than impressed

with the plates, as well as with Mizuno's proposal. One of Chobei's men, the impetuous young Gonpachi (Teiji Takahashi) takes a liking to the lovely Oiran—a courtesan whose price is far beyond what he can afford. But Gonpachi manages to insinuate his way into her presence—and heart. She chooses him to "initiate" her into her profession, in the presence of *hatamoto* who are vying for this honor. Soon after, Gonpachi gets into a street fight with several samurai—and barely escapes with his life. Chobei reproaches him for stirring up violence, though Gonpachi protests he was not to blame.

An old *hatamoto* visits the local daimyo (feudal lord), Okubo (Reizaburo Yamamoto), to complain about the threat to their livelihood. Okubo assures him that he is thinking of the *hatamoto*'s welfare but the old man refuses to be pacified. If the Shiratsuka-gumi falls apart, chaos will result, he warns. He also visits Chobei, who has little sympathy with his proposal to use the *hatamoto* as peacekeepers. He and his men are already protecting the townspeople—they do not need to ally with the *hatamoto*, especially if the latter are to be senior partners.

Mizuno's plan to sell the plates is opposed by Okinu (Mieko Takamine), who manages his household. Seeing that she has aroused his fury, she retreats—and stumbles over the box containing the plates. When the agent for the sale, Kondo (Masao Mishima), demands to see the plates, Okinu counts them—and discovers one broken. Incensed, Mizuno comes at her with his sword. Wounded, she falls to her death in a well.

When Gonpachi hears this story, he tells it to the managers of the Kabuki theater. If they stage the story as a play, he reasons, the humiliation will enrage Mizuno and his *hatamoto*. This will in turn bring on the decisive clash Gonpachi desires—and is sure the Banzuin-gumi will win. The theater presents the play based on Okinu's story, and it creates a tremendous sensation. In retaliation, Mizuno and his men kidnap the female-role actor, or *onnagata* (Gonjuro Kawarasaki), who played Okinu. Chobei goes alone to rescue him, knowing full well he will probably never return.

CRITIQUE

Released in 1951 to celebrate Shochiku's thirtieth anniversary as a studio (and Daisuke Ito's thirtieth year as director), *Oedo Gonin Otoko* (Five Men from Edo) combines two famous *kodan* that have been told and retold over the centuries in various forms. One is best known as *Bancho Sarayashiki*, a Kabuki play by Kido Okamoto about the housemaid Okinu, who breaks a precious plate belonging to her master, Harima Aoyama. He drowns her in a well in retribution and her ghost returns to haunt him, counting the plates until she comes to the one with the fatal crack.

Another of the narratives concerns Chobei Banzuin, a seventeenth-century *ronin* (masterless samurai) who rose to power in Tokyo as a labor broker and gambling boss. A leader of the *machi-yakko*, he has long been celebrated as a Robin Hood figure. As played by silent-era star Tsumasaburo Bando, Chobei is a charismatic figure, deferring to the higher status of Mizuno and his *hatamoto* cronies but fearless in their presence. Though Bando is hardly a dashing swashbuckler—that role is filled by Teiji Takahashi as the young bravo Gonpachi—Bando dominates the screen, particularly in his final showdown with Utaemon Ichikawa's Mizuno. Confronting Mizuno at his mansion, with dozens of *hatamoto* waiting in the wings to run him through, Bando defeats his man with the sheer force of his personality in contrast to later generations of *ninkyo eiga* stars, who would wade into similar situations with swords flashing.

Daisuke Ito, who began directing in 1924 and completed his last film in 1970, made *Oedo Gonin Otoko* into a crackling entertainment, with strong performances from a veteran cast. The ending is somewhat anticlimactic though, with its limp make-peace-not-war message. This is understandable, given that, at the time of the movie's release, Japan was under Occupation rule and the film industry was required to celebrate democratic values and pacifist politics, even in a film about the grandfather of all yakuza dons.

Onibi (1997)

THE FIRE WITHIN

Scr.: Toshiyuki Morioka. *Dir.:* Rokuro Mochizuki. *Prod.:* Gaga Productions. *Main cast:* Yoshio Harada, Show Aikawa, Eiji Okuda, Reiko Kataoka. 101 mins.

Rokuro Mochizuki's *Onibi* (literally, will-o'-the-wisp) is a character study of a man on the cusp of a new beginning—and the edge of an abyss. Yoshio Harada's performance as the hero—an aging hitman who wants to go straight—is his best in years. Harada has long played macho-life-force types, at times with a swagger verging on self-parody. In *Onibi*, however, his hitman is weary, weathered, and at the end of his tether, but competent at the grisly trade. He sincerely wants to start a new life but clings to old gangster virtues. Though a sad figure, the underworld equivalent of the restructured salaryman, he is at the same time a noble figure, who goes to his self-appointed doom with his eyes open, defiant to the end.

Onibi begins with Noriyasu Kunihiro (Harada), fresh out of prison, offering incense at the grave of his old boss. He wants no part of the old gang or his old profession, however. Having served two stretches for murder, he knows that three-time losers in his line of work get the noose. He needs a job though and, when a junior member of his old gang (Show Aikawa) offers him one as a gang chauffeur, he takes it. The boss (Eiji Okuda), a stylishly

A song in the key of a hitman's life. Yoshio Harada as the hitman and Reiko Kataoka as his pianist lover in *Onibi* (The Fire Within, 1997).

dressed, coolly urbane type, apologizes to Kunihiro for this demotion in status. "It's only until you get your touch back," he says.

Kunihiro shows that he never lost it when, at the boss's request, he walks into the office of a rival gang that has welshed on a loan. Grabbing a gun jammed against his forehead, he turns it on the welshers and forces them to pay. This display of bravado wins him the gratitude of the boss and the reward of a night with the pretty young pianist at a hostess club. Unexpectedly, he and the pianist, Asako (Reiko Kataoka), hit it off. Also unexpectedly, the gang cuts him loose; the boss wants to avoid a war with the customers Kunihiro so rudely interrupted—bad for business, don't you know. So, Kunihiro has to go. This termination is, at first, a blessing in disguise. Together with Ayako, Kunihiro moves into a new apartment and finds a new job as a journeyman printer. But his old calling still has a hold on him he can't resist. And his first client is his new girlfriend.

Onibi has a narrative arc of a hundred other yakuza flicks (as well as such Hollywood movies as Dustin Hoffman's *Straight Time*), but

it is less a throwback to genre conventions than a quietly brilliant reworking of them. Director Rokuro Mochizuki provides the required tension and thrills—the staging of the gunplay scenes is as joltingly realistic as any in recent Japanese films—but the amount of bloodshed is surprisingly small.

Instead of racheting up the body count, Mochizuki concentrates on the way circumstance shapes character and relationships. By the end of the film, we feel a kinship with this middle-aged man who does not want to give up hope but cannot shake off his past. Though his line of work may be unusual, his dilemma is familiar, his end, tragic. His will-o'-the-wisp is one we are also chasing.

Otoko no Monsho (1963)

SYMBOL OF A MAN
Scr.: Hisataka Kai. *Dir.:* Akinori Matsuo. *Prod.:* Nikkatsu. *Main cast:* Hideki Takahashi, Masako Izumi, Yukiko Todoroki, Kenjiro Ishiyama, Asao Koike. 96 mins.

STORY

Ryuji Oshima, the young son of a gang boss, witnesses an attempt on his father's life that ends in the bloody death of the would-be assassin. The year: 1931. Ryuji has become a doctor and is firmly determined never to follow in his father's footsteps, though he loves and respects him. Meanwhile, his father (Kenjiro Ishiyama) still has dreams of Ryuji succeeding him and marrying the pretty, vivacious Hanako (Masako Izumi), a servant girl who has become like a daughter to him.

Saiga, the boss of a rival gang, enviously eyes the festival run by the Oshima-gumi. One day, he tells his *kobun*, it will be theirs. Soon after, a wild-eyed gangster from Kobe stabs one of Saiga's men. The bleeding gangster is rushed to a clinic, where Ryuji successfully treats his wound, while his attacker, Kono, throws himself on the mercy of the Oshima *oyabun*, an old acquaintance—and tearfully explains why his attack was an act of righteous revenge. Saiga's men spy Oshima guiding Kono to safety and an enraged Saiga goes with the police to Oshima's headquarters, determined to get answers. Oshima's second-in-command, Kanzo, tells the police that there's been a mistake—and knowing him to be a man of integrity, they take him at his word. Saiga, however, is not so easily convinced.

Kanzo escorts the grateful Kono to the station, while Ryuji decides to go to the mountains to work as a mining camp doctor. Haruko strenuously opposes this decision, saying that his father needs him; but Ryuji refuses to listen. Soon after, the local power balance changes when Kiyo (Yukiko Todoroki), the formidable female boss of the Murata-gang, allies herself with Saiga, on the condition that they do nothing to harm Ryuji.

At the mining camp, Ryuji finds a local gang, the Izawa-gumi, working hand-in-hand with the mine owner to exploit the miners. Serving as foremen, the gangsters ruthlessly suppress complaints about low wages and harsh conditions. Ryuji sides with the miners—and finds himself on the wrong side of the gang; a dangerous place to be. He is saved by the timely intervention of an elderly emissary from the Oshima gang, who reveals Ryuji's true identity to the Izawa hoods—and urges him to come back home. Ryuji refuses.

Soon after, Ryuji hears that his father has been stabbed. He rushes to his side—too late to save his life. He confronts Saiga, the main suspect, who challenges him to a roll of dice for the honor of conducting next year's festival. Kanzo, suspecting a scam, intervenes—and finds unexpected backing from Kiyo. At the funeral, Kanzo tells Ryuji the shocking news that Kiyo is his birth mother.

Soon after Ryuji takes over the gang, the army offers him a lucrative job on a war plant construction project. Ryuji even reunites with an old friend from the mine, the irrepressible Tatsu (Asao Koike). But he must still deal with the envious Saiga, who considers the construction site his territory—and will kill to prove his point.

Kiyo tells Ryuji that he is not up to the task of defending his turf—and offers to do it for him. She confesses that she always regretted leaving him and was overjoyed at his decision to become a doctor. Ryuji however, tells her he can never go back to his old life and shows her his new tattoo—blue waves roiling over his back. "This is a symbol of manhood [*otoko no monsho*]," he says. First, though, he must prove he has the right to wear it.

CRITIQUE

The first in a ten-part series that ran from 1963 to 1966, *Otoko no Monsho* (Symbol of a Man) was also Nikkatsu's first *ninkyo* film—an attempt to play catchup with genre leader, Toei. Fortunately, the film was a hit, giving the career of star Hideki Takahashi a new trajectory, away from his earlier roles as a *seishun eiga* (youth movie) hero.

In *Otoko no Monsho*, he is still playing a

The doctor is in. Hideki Takahashi plays a doctor who takes over his father's gang in *Otoko no Monsho* (Symbol of a Man, 1963).

pure-hearted youth of a type familiar from his *seishun eiga*. His Ryuji may flash a gangster's tattoo but remains stubbornly idealistic and pacifistic, even in the face of repeated outrages from the rival gang boss, who always dresses in Western-style clothes and dispatches foes with a pistol—both symbols of his moral turpitude. It's as if Al Pacino's Michael Corleone were never to go over to the dark side.

The simplistic good-versus-evil story line is complicated by Ryuji's relationship with Kiyo—the matronly gang boss who turns out to be his birth mother. Struggling against her attempts to reclaim and dominate him, Ryuji plays out a psychodrama that had its echoes in the postwar, middle-class family, where workaholic Dad seldom showed his face and overprotective Mom pushed her sons to greater educational and professional heights.

Ryuji's childhood trauma—as a boy he watched his father kill an attacker who had broken into their home—is used to explain his later reluctance to use violence, even when he is justified in doing so by the gang code. He seems to be acting out the national trauma following the wartime bombings, which gave the Japanese a permanent war allergy. Being a *ninkyo* movie hero, he finally overcomes his pacifism—but just barely and only under extreme provocation. His hands remain clean to the end.

Otokotachi no Kaita E (1996)

THE MAN WITH TWO HEARTS

Scr.: Tatsumi Kumashiro, Hidehiro Ito. *Dir.:* Hidehiro Ito. *Prod.:* Excellent Film. *Main cast:* Etsushi Toyokawa, Yuna Natsuo, Keiko Takahashi. 120 mins.

In 1996 Etsushi Toyokawa was Japan's hottest male movie star. One indication was that his fans called him simply "Toyoetsu," thereby elevating him to the ranks of the superstars who,

like royalty, need only a single name (Elvis, Marilyn, Madonna). Given his following, it was inevitable that someone would produce a Toyokawa vehicle. That someone was Hidehiro Ito, a former director of soft porn for Nikkatsu and a long-time associate of Tatsumi Kumashiro, a Nikkatsu colleague. Kumashiro was going to film his script for *Otokotachi no Kaita E*—a study of a yakuza with a split personality—but died of pneumonia in February 1995, before he could begin shooting and Ito took over the project. *Otokotachi* is thus a Kumashiro film in absentia.

Toyokawa plays a "Dr. Jekyll and Mr. Hyde" in modern yakuza dress. In his primary incarnation, he is Sugio, a wimpish former piano tuner who has somehow become an underling in a yakuza gang. With his conservative suits, boyishly tousled hair, and meek demeanor, Sugio is as out of place in a gang as a nun in a Las Vegas casino.

We know, however, that the film is not going to be a yakuza version of *Sister Act* when Sugio's cheek starts twitching in a coffee shop and he transforms into a sneering tough guy, who abuses the waitress for bringing him the wrong (i.e., Sugio's) order. This is Matsuo, Sugio's other half, who is a subboss in the same gang and who, with his flashy clothes and take-charge attitude, does belong in the yakuza milieu.

Toyokawa manages his Jekyll-Hyde metamorphosis well and inhabits both characters thoroughly. He is equally convincing as Sugio, who mildly accepts a contemptuous brushoff from his girlfriend (Yuna Natso) and as Matsuo, who later brutally beats and rapes her, while converting her to the delights of sado-masochistic sex. (The conversion, a loathsome convention in movies of this type, does not convince.)

But instead of examining the real difficulties of living with what has come to be called Multiple Personality Disorder, *Otokotachi* plunges us into the melodramatics of a gang war and Sugio/Matsuo's tangled romance with a vampish nightclub singer (Keiko Takahashi). Working with cinematographer Noboru Shinoda, Ito uses muzzy color tones and floating tracking shots that underline Sugio/Matsuo's confusion and anxiety. He also enlivens the film with tightly choreographed fight scenes (though Sugio/Matsuo gets jumped in dark alleyways too often) and steamily photographed bed scenes.

Otokotachi, however, cannot overcome the strangeness of its premise: two gangsters in one body and, incredibly, one gang. Ito tries to get around this absurdity by making the other characters, including Sugio/Matsuo's confederates, regard his transformations with barely a blink of the eye, as though the poor fellow were suffering from an annoying tick. It's as though Clark Kent were to change into his Superman outfit at a *Daily Planet* editorial meeting while Perry White cracks wise about Kent not needing carfare. Ito may have filmed his former mentor's script as a tribute but should have first thought seriously about a rewrite, beginning from page one.

PornoStar (1999)

Scr./Dir.: Toshiaki Toyoda. *Prod.:* Little More, Tokyo Theater, Filmmakers. *Main cast:* Koji Chihara, Onimaru, Akaji Maro, Rin Ozawa, Tetta Sugimoto. 98 mins.

The title of *PornoStar* is misleading. Instead of a made-in-Japan *Boogie Nights*, Toshiaki Toyoda's debut feature is a violent fantasy about life and death in the lower depths of Shibuya. Also, while populated by recognizable Shibuya types, from tanned hustlers to teenage skateboarders, the film is an essay on the gang rites of blood and brotherhood that has as little to do with the realities of the Shibuya scene circa 1999 as *The Good, the Bad, and the Ugly* did with realities of life in the Old West.

PornoStar's hero is Arano (Koji Chihara), whom we first meet striding through the Shibuya streets carrying a mysterious gym bag and knocking aside passersby with brute indifference. A tall, rangy kid in a hooded khaki jacket, with a hawk-like face and impassive gaze, Arano looks so out of it as to be scary, if darkly funny. A Clint Eastwood–like stone killer, he knifes a bad-mouthing yakuza and after his victim stumbles into the office of a gang boss (Akaji Maro) and collapses, he casually steps over his writhing body, while the boss and his underlings look on with wide eyes and gaping mouths.

Arano, however, meets his match not only in the boss, a bald growler who runs a discount ticket shop as a front, but in Kamijo (Onimaru), a long-haired *chinpira* who operates a date club with his crew of Shibuya bad boys. Business has been falling off, however, and the boss has been turning up the heat; Kamijo is open to anything that brings in the yen. Though better-socialized and better-focused than Arano, he is equally cold-blooded. Kamijo knows Arano is a nutcase but feels that he has his uses. Soon, Arano is running with the gang while continuing to seethe with blank, dangerous rage.

There is a story of sorts, revolving around a stash of LSD, that Kamijo and his boys snatch from a pair of foreigners, and a rivalry with a gang of grown-up yakuza in colorful suits headed by a lantern-jawed boss (Tetta Sugimoto). The real focus, however, is on the uneasy relationship between Arano and Kamijo and Arano's quixotic pursuit of his own justice, whose code is "if it bothers me, kill it." He is searching for a kind of purity—his battle cry is *"Yakuza wa iranai"* (I don't need yakuza)—but finds his sword of righteousness turned against him.

First-time director Toyoda tries to inject pathos into this story, but he also wants to maintain its black comic tone while piling up the bodies. His execution is uneven, with more

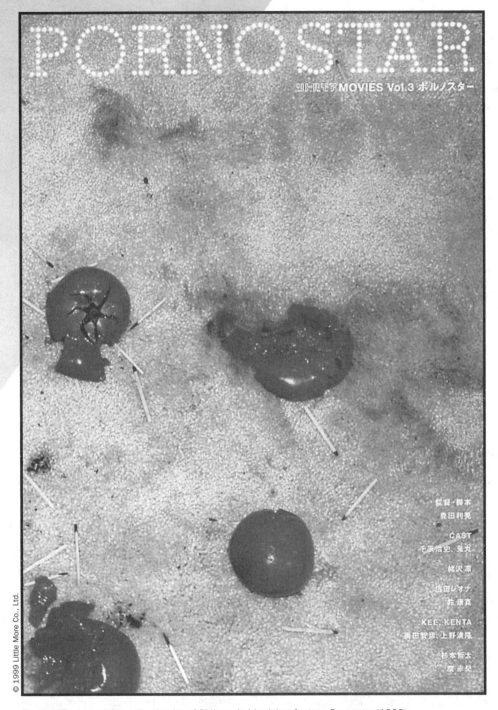

Toshiaki Toyoda explores the depths of Shibuya in his debut feature *Pornostar* (1999).

crude shocks than clever jolts. The film, however, contains moments of beauty and revelation. One is when the gang is celebrating its snatch of the stash with an orgy that includes a dip in a hot tub with a floating hookah. More striking than the writhing bodies are the hundreds of tomatoes floating in the tub and scattered about the floor, like so many symbolic victims waiting to be squashed.

Another begins after Arano and a date club employee named Alice (Rin Ozawa) make off with the stash, and she leaves him alone in an alley while she goes to sell it. Hours pass but Alice does not return. Arano looks up at the night sky and a shower of knives rains down on him. The knives turn into raindrops and Arano gets thoroughly drenched and feels spiritually cleansed.

There are other such moments, but do they add up to a movie? Not quite, but both Koji Chihara, a member of a popular *manzai* comedy act, and Onimaru, a former gangbanger who made his acting debut in Masashi Yamamoto's *Junk Food*, are strong, distinctive presences. Also, Toyoda, despite his self-indulgences, knows how to connect with an audience. I only wish that he would put away the *manga* and the Tarantino tapes for a while and get better acquainted with his true cinematic soul brother: Jean Cocteau.

Ryuji (1983)

Scr.: Akio Suzuki. *Dir.:* Hide Kawashima. *Prod.:* Production Ryuji. *Main cast:* Masaji Kaneko, Koji Kita, Kinzo Sato, Eiko Nagashima. 92 mins.

Though not a James Dean-like icon, Masaji Kaneko had a Dean-like career: short, intense, and fruitful, though in his case the fruit was only one film, the 1983 *Ryuji*. Kaneko was a struggling stage actor when he wrote the script for a film about a yakuza who tries to go straight. Together with director Hide Kawa-

shima, Kaneko assembled the staff and cast, all unknowns, and began filming on a shoestring budget. *Ryuji* cinematographer Michihiko Kawagoe reminisces how an assistant director came up to Kawashima and told him that, having used up their loan-shark credit, they couldn't borrow money to buy film stock. "All right," said Kawashima. "We'll use one take per scene."

Somehow Kaneko and Kawashima managed to finish *Ryuji* and, after major distributors turned it down, found a few small theaters to screen it. A week after it opened, Kaneko died of cancer at the age of 33. *Ryuji* failed at the box office but won a slew of awards, including best actor prizes for Kaneko, and became a cult classic. Few actors ever walked the gangster walk with Kaneko's combination of credibility and pathos. This performance came not only from research—Kaneko temporarily joined a gang as a *chinpira*—but from his rightness for the part.

Kaneko's Ryuji lives on intimate terms with violence and death—an acquaintance that gives him power over the straight world, which deeply fears both. A losing battle with cancer may not have been the same as a life in the gangs, but it made Kaneko understand Ryuji's mentality, including his large capacity for rage and tenderness. Despite his rail-thin body and hollow-eyed face, his Ryuji dominates any room he walks into. At the same time, he also knows he has hit bottom, with the grime of the streets in his soul. He is the ultimate end-of-the-tether man.

Ryuji is a feared subboss in a Shinjuku gang, who trims high rollers at private roulette sessions. His two *kobun*, Hiroshi (Koji Kita) and Nao (Kinzo Sato [now Sakura]), are fiercely loyal if not exactly suited for the gang life. Hiroshi has an un-gangster-like weakness for bargain sale clothing, while Nao beats up the wrong hood and, when he tries to slice off his little finger in atonement, fluffs the job, and ends up with a bleeding mess.

© 1983 Production Ryuji

Yakuza family values. Masaji Kaneko plays a gangster trying—and failing—to go straight in *Ryuji* (1983).

Three years earlier, Ryuji's liking for the rough stuff landed him in the slammer. When his wife Mariko (Eiko Nagashima) begged her parents for bail money, they gave it to her on the condition that she leave her no-good husband. Back on the outside, Ryuji learned the truth and raged at Mariko for selling him out. Now, he is living alone and tiring of the hustle. The money is rolling in, but what's the point?

With the help of a former yakuza who runs a bar, he goes straight and reconciles with his wife. Instead of shaking down quaking debtors, he drives a truck for a liquor dealer and in the evenings teaches his toddler daughter the ABCs. Life is wonderful—but of course it can't last. True to the film's indie roots, the color is grainy; the editing, patchy; the soundtrack, out of sync. Also, several of the actors, particularly Kinzo Sakura as Nao, ham it up shamelessly.

Even so, something sets *Ryuji* apart from hundreds of other yakuza flicks. The hero is not just another tough guy, but a man who has a real inner life and an actual home. We see Ryuji laughing at TV comedians, heaving beer crates, and making passionate love to his wife.

We see him in all his moods, from dark anger to beaming bliss. We come to like him. Thus, the ache we feel when he succumbs to the pull of the old life again. We want him to resist it, even as we understand why he can't. The scene in which he makes his decision and wordlessly communicates it to his wife pierces to the heart. It is one of several reasons why this film has lived long after its creator's death. As the film's poster says, "Ryuji Forever"—indeed.

Shiawase ni Naro ne (1998)

LET'S GET HAPPY

Scr./Dir.: Akio Murahashi. *Prod.:* KSS, Cinema Haut. *Main cast:* Show Aikawa, Masumi Sanada, Tsunehiko Watase, Morio Kazama, Seijun Suzuki, Naomasa Musaka, Narimi Arimori, Ryo Amamiya. 115 mins.

In art, limitations have their uses. What one loses in sweep and scale, one can gain in compression and expression. Thus, Picasso's Blue Period. Thus, the less-is-more aesthetic of much of Japanese art, including the cinematic art of Yasujiro Ozu. Akio Murahashi's *Shiawase ni Naro ne* (Let's Get Happy) is a cleverly conceived, if overlong, attempt at genre stretching within a similarly self-locked cage. A veteran TV scriptwriter, Murahashi has made a yakuza movie that plays like Sidney Lumet's *Twelve Angry Men*; i.e., a drama unfolding in a limited time and space, with the pressure building as minutes tick by.

One difference between Murahashi's film and Lumet's is its tone: light, comic, even farcical. But while his yakuza gang may find itself in a ridiculous situation—dragged into a war the day before it is to dissolve—his gangsters are not merely comic grotesques. Posing nobly one moment, calculating cravenly the next, they reveal much about the contradictory impulses of real human beings in extreme situations.

The story begins with Kyohei (Show Aikawa) videotaping the congratulations of his colleagues in the Yamamuro-gumi on his upcoming wedding. He is quitting the gang to marry the sweet, innocent (of gang connections) Chikako (Masumi Sanada) and become a sushi chef. Most of the other gang members, including boss Yamamuro (Tsunehiko Watase) and subboss Kiuchi (Morio Kazama), are following him into the straight life. Under pressure from the law and a bad economy, the Yamamuro-gumi plans to disband the next day.

Then comes a TV news flash: the boss of the rival Sasajima-gumi has been knifed to death. They realize with a sickening certainty that one of their number, the absent Hiroshi, made the hit. Soon after, an elderly fixer (Seijun Suzuki) comes calling with an ultimatum from the Sasajima-gumi: either deliver up the head of boss Yamamuro or 100 million yen in cash by tomorrow morning. What a choice—but what else can they do? Then, they hear, from Hiroshi himself, that the Sasajima-gumi is preparing for war. Instead of going gently into the good night, they might be hurried into an early grave.

The hot-headed Otaki (Naomasa Musaka), a subboss who opposed disbanding, wants to fight. Kiuchi, however, insists that it's better to pay the 100 million yen than commit group suicide. Yamamuro has the money, locked up in a safe in his office, but his leggy, luscious wife Rie (Narimi Arimori) has the key—and no intention of giving up a long-promised life of leisure. She urges Yamamuro to run off to Europe. What if they gave a gang war and nobody came? But Yamamuro knows that the reach of his enemies is long. Also, he has his honor to consider. Somehow, he can't take the fatal step out the door.

No one can, in fact: the entire story unfolds inside the Yamamuro-gumi headquarters. This goes against the genre grain: a yakuza movie without the atmospherics of gambling dens, hostess clubs, stretch limos, and other gangster-friendly environments is like a Western without wide-open spaces. Murahashi, however, moves deftly from one pilot complication to the next, including the unexpected arrival of a gang member (Ryo Amamiya) just released from prison and the sudden appearance of a citizen's group who correctly suspects that the gangsters are up to no good.

Murahashi throws too many narrative balls up in the air and juggles them too long. But compared with all the yakuza movies that haven't changed their three-ball acts in decades, *Shiawase* is a welcome change. The cast revels in what is essentially an actor's showcase. Morio Kazama is particularly good as Kiuchi, who reveals a strength of character not immediately apparent from his wishy-washy exterior. He gives weight to what is an otherwise lighter-than-air entertainment.

The funniest character is Narimi Arimori as Yamamuro's wife. Her hot little vamp with a heart of ice may be a cliché, but she charges the film with a sexy verve and fine, dry comic talent. Her constant and unexplained changes of costume, from resplendent kimono to slinky designer gown, are a touch worthy of Monty

Python—yet another indication of a movie made by a creative mind, not a formula.

Shin Jingi Naki Tatakai (2000)

ANOTHER BATTLE

Scr.: Hiroshi Takada. *Dir.:* Junji Sakamoto. *Prod.:* Toei. *Main cast:* Etsushi Toyokawa, Tomoyasu Hotei, Ittoku Kishibe, Koichi Sato, Tai'ichiro Toyama. 109 mins.

Of all the yakuza movie series Toei produced in its heyday, few had the impact of the Jingi Naki Tatakai (Battles without Honor and Humanity) series. Based on true accounts of gang wars in early postwar Hiroshima, the first film of the series, directed by Kinji Fukasaku and released in 1973, realistically depicted the Darwinian power struggles of the era. Instead of a noble hero adhering to the *jingi* code, the series lead, Bunta Sugawara, played a hood whose only law was survival. Instead of the deliberate pace of earlier yakuza movies, *Jingi* unspooled in a style reminiscent of TV news, with a handheld camera breathlessly recording the chases and punchups.

Now, after a gap of twenty-one years, Toei has revived this venerable franchise with *Shin Jingi Naki Tatakai* (Another Battle). Realizing that turning the clock back to 1973 was not an option (Fukasaku, though still active, had long since said good-bye to the series), the studio hired Osaka-born Junji Sakamoto to direct the new installment. Best known for his boxing films (*Dotsuitarunen* [Knockout], *Tekken*, *Ote* [Checkmate], *Boxer Joe*), Sakamoto has an indie sensibility quite different from that of Toei's older generation of directors. Whether quirkily brilliant (*Dotsuitarunen*) or ham-handedly eccentric (*Tekken*), his films rarely follow genre rules. An Osaka native who has shot film after film in that region, Sakamoto is intimately acquainted with his characters and their Kansai milieu.

That understanding is much in evidence in the new film, which is set in present-day Osaka. It is also, however, a sprawling, ambitious epic: *The Godfather* with a Kansai accent. While faithfully reflecting the labyrinthine power politics of the gangs, it recaptures some of the dynamism of Fukasaku's classic series. Kadoya Kaneo (Etsushi Toyokawa) and Tochino Masatatsu (Tomoyasu Hotei) are childhood friends who have grown up and gone their separate ways. Kadoya is a subboss in a powerful Osaka gang; Tochino is a club owner who hates the gangs and all their works. When he was a boy, Tochino watched as two loan collectors from a local gang dunked his father, a poor Korean worker, in a filthy ditch. Tochino plunged a knife into the back of one of the hoods, but his rage still burns.

The paths of these old friends intersect in the midst of a gang succession struggle. When the big boss dies, his right-hand man and anointed heir is too old and ill to take over, leaving the job open to the gang's Number Three, the saturnine Awano (Ittoku Kishibe). First, though, Awano has to win over his colleagues, which means lining their pockets. He also has to contend with Nakahira (Koichi Sato), a younger rival who ranks below him in the gang hierarchy but matches him in ruthlessness. When Nakahira's henchmen put the squeeze on Tochino, he refuses to be cowed. Meanwhile, Kadoya is monitoring Nakahira's moves for his *oyabun* (boss), Awano. Then, Kadoya's own crew is attacked by a Kyoto gang connected to Nakahira's. The gloves come off and the bodies start to fall. Despite his yakuza allergy, Tochino is forced to take sides.

Rock musician Hotei may have the requisite permanently pissed-off air, but his Tochino is an outsider whose connection with the main events of the film remains mostly peripheral. Also, the fierce devotion of Toyokawa's Kadoya to his Oscar Wildeish boss lacks motivation—a Michael Corleone he isn't.

That said, Sakamoto keeps the energy level

新・仁義なき戦い。

ヘイコラ生きて、なんぼのもんじゃ。

A study in contrasts. Etsushi Toyokawa (left) and Tomoyasu Hotei play childhood friends who end up on different sides of the law in *Shin Jingi Naki Tatakai* (Another Battle, 2000).

high, while allowing his talented cast to stretch beyond usual genre limits. I particularly liked Tai'ichiro Toyama as the languid, druggy Nakahira henchman who makes the memorable comment, "For 100 million yen, I'd kill Nakahira myself, even if I had to use a rusty sword." Such honesty is refreshing and an indication that, nearly three decades after *Jingi Naki Tatakai* first exploded on the screen, Fukasaku has found a worthy successor.

Shin Jingi Naki Tatakai: Bosatsu (2003)

ANOTHER BATTLE: CONSPIRACY

Scr.: Izuru Narashima. *Dir.:* Hajime Hashimoto. *Prod.:* Toei. *Main cast:* Nenji Kobayshi, Katsunori Takahashi, Ken Watanabe, Daisuke Ryu, Higashinari Kochi, Katsu Shiga, Renji Ishibashi, Mari Natsuki. 110 mins.

In 2000 Junji Sakamoto revived the venerable Jingi Naki Tatakai series with *Shin Jingi Naki Tatakai* (Another Battle). Set in the Japan of the new millennium, the film is a sprawling, ambitious epic that has its moments but lacks the urgency of its predecessors. Toei, which produced both Fukasaku's film and Sakamoto's followup, has now continued the new series with *Shin Jingi Naki Tatakai: Bosatsu* (Another Battle: Conspiracy). Directed by newcomer Hajime Hashimoto, the new film has little in common with the previous one other than its title, Kansai setting, and convoluted story line.

Working from a script by Izuru Narashima, Hashimoto updates the series for a new era in which the gangs have adopted the trappings of modern business, right down to laptops and spreadsheets. The fuel propelling the narrative, however, is the standard genre blend of obligation and ambition, alliances and betrayals, fear and violence. Unfortunately, the welter of plot complications, with fixers fixing the fixers, as briefcases of cash fly back and forth, obscures the story's core relationships. By the end, when all is revealed, we have become too confused to care. Also, though the payoff for all the machinations is clever enough, the bitter laughter as the curtain comes down rings hollow—and the audience files out feeling had.

The story begins with the New Year's celebration of the Oda-gumi, a gang under the umbrella of the Sahashi-gumi, the largest underworld organization in western Japan. The boss, Oda (Nenji Kobayshi), may look the picture of vigorous middle-aged manhood but, for reasons of his own, plays the part of the garrulous codger. At a cabaret, he regales his underlings with tales of his war exploits, though at the time, as one of them informs us, he had barely graduated from nappies. Whatever the reason for the old-man act, pressure is building on Oda to anoint his successor. The two leading candidates are, ironically, the best of friends. One is Yahagi (Katsunori Takahashi), who not only looks the part of the rising young gang executive, with his smooth manner and immaculately tailored suits, but has a sterling track record running the gang's semi-legitimate business activities. His mentor is Sugimori (Daisuke Ryu), the cold-blooded second-in-command of the Sahara-gumi, whose weapons of choice are yen notes.

The other is Fujimaki (Ken Watanabe), a gangster in the old, violent mold, with a short fuse and no fear of anyone alive, including Oda, though he regards Yahagi more as a younger gang brother than a rival. Meanwhile, Yahagi supports Fujimaki, not only out of deference to his seniority but also because he believes the older man is the better for the job. The gangs are really all about violence, he explains to Sugimori, and Fujimaki uses it more effectively (if indiscriminately) than anyone else in the Oda-gumi. Oda, however, is reluctant to cede power to Fujimaki, whom he regards as a loose cannon. In fact, knowing the usual fate of discarded gang bosses, he is far from ready to retire—though he slyly hides his intentions. Instead, he names his Number Three, the easily manipulated Sanada (Higashinari Kochi), as his successor, baffling Yahagi and outraging Fujimaki. Seeing his ambitions in Osaka thwarted, Fujimaki shifts the base of his operations to Nagoya, invading the territory of the local Ryumon-kai.

The weak-willed, Ryumon-kai boss, Maeda (Katsu Shiga), seems to be easy prey for Fujimaki—but he has the backing of the Domyo-kai, a Kanto-based gang whose leader, Watarai (Renji Ishibashi), has no love for either Fujimaki or the Oda-gumi. Working with Sugiura, he devises a plot to destroy both the Ryumon and Oda gangs. The two gangs, it turns out, are feuding over not only territory or pride but a big deal involving a failing construction company. The spoils are rich and both Sugiura and Watarai are determined to get their share. Meanwhile, Oda is biding his time and playing both sides against the middle, as the chaos builds and violence rages. These machinations and counter-machinations put a strain on Yahagi and Fujimaki's friendship. By this time, the power game now has more than two players—and the two men become unwitting pawns.

Playing Yahagi and Fujimaki, Katsunori Takahashi and Ken Watanabe, respectively, are a well-matched set, though they are hardly equals. Whereas Takahashi has the look of a pop star manqué, Watanabe's Fujimaki is the real deal—a scowling Nio statue brought to life, with the physical presence to intimidate anything that crosses his path (or simply blast it aside with those football lineman's shoulders). Fujimaki shows his human side, however, with his wife, a whiskey-voiced, sweets-gobbling toughie played by Mari Natsuki. This odd coupling—Natsuki as the profane, wise-up older sister to Fujimaki's impulsive younger brother—is one sign that the film is not on autopilot.

Yet another is Nenji Kobayashi's performance as the foxy Oda, who seems to be a few cards short of a full deck but is really the dealer in a game of three-card monte. Though too young by at least a decade for the role, Kobayashi plays it with great comic brio, though he nearly gets lost in the film's wheels within wheels. Oda may have the last laugh—but by then we have almost forgotten the joke.

Shin Jingi no Hakaba (2002)

GRAVEYARD OF HONOR

Scr.: Shigenori Takechi. *Dir.:* Takashi Miike. *Prod.:* Daiei, Toei Video. *Main cast:* Goro Kishitani, Narimi Arimori, Ryosuke Miki, Shingo Yamashiro, Tetsuro Tanba. 131 mins.

Takashi Miike's *Shin Jingi no Hakaba* (Graveyard of Honor) was inspired by Kinji Fukasaku's 1975 film about a gangster who violates the gang code with an impetuosity that ends in his downfall and death. Based on reportage by Goro Fujita, Fukasaku's film was relentlessly dark, in a way seldom seen before or since. Rising from a sick bed that had kept him away from the screen for a year, Tetsuya Watari played the hero, Rikio Ishikawa, as a hollow-eyed man plunging through life like a wounded beast. His last words, scrawled on the wall of his cell: *"Owarai, sanjunen no baka sawag owattai"* (What a laugh—the thirty-year party is over).

While Fukasaku's film was set in the war and early postwar years, Miike's begins in the bubble era and unfolds in the post-bubble recession. The shadow of poverty and social chaos so present in the earlier film is thus absent in the new one. The first close encounter of Rikuo Ishimatsu (Goro Kishitani) with the gangs is a shootout in a fancy Chinese restaurant where he works—a shootout he ends with contemptuous ease, saving Sawada (Shingo Yamashiro), the boss of the Sawada-gumi. He is rewarded with admission to the gang as an underboss, thus skipping the bother of an apprenticeship. A very bubble-era beginning in other words. Unfortunately, Ishimatsu has zero impulse control. Other gangsters get steamed when things go wrong: Ishimatsu explodes.

His first encounter with Chieko (Narimi Arimori), the woman who becomes his long-suffering lover and common-law wife, is typical. Meeting her at the hostess club where she works, he invites her to a karaoke session. Once inside the booth, he brutally rapes her, wiping her blood on the club's posted rules as he walks out. This is a man who does not know the meaning of "no." Naturally, this being a yakuza movie, she falls in love with him.

Sent to prison for whacking a gangster who welshed on a gambling debt, Ishimatsu becomes pals with Imamura (Ryosuke Miki), an underboss with the rival Giyu gang. When he gets out, after five years, not only his old crew but Imamura and Chieko are waiting. Life, for the next eight years, is good. Ishimatsu rises in the gang hierarchy, while the economy falls into recession. Then, one day, when he comes to Sawada for a 10-million-yen loan (Chieko wants to open a club of her own), he is given what he considers a runaround by his gang seniors and sends several of them to the hospital in a fit of rage. This is a whackable offense—and one that turns out to have been totally unnecessary. (Sawada was willing to give him the money but had to go to the dentist for a toothache.)

Ishimatsu goes to Imamura for help and his friend agrees to hide him, but Sawada-gumi gangsters soon track him down. He escapes their wrath and later sneaks into Sawada's house to confront him about the loan—and ends up killing him. "The game is over," says one gangster on hearing the news. Ishimatsu, however, refuses to be taken off the board; instead, he wants to eliminate as many other pieces as possible.

The director, Takashi Miike, is mainly known abroad for films like *Audition*, *Koroshiya Ichi* (Ichi the Killer) and *Visitor Q* that frontally assault the audience with sadistic violence and sex, bodily fluids, and gore. But as Miike has proven several times in his career, most notably in the 1997 *Gokudo Kuro Shakai Rainy Dog* (Rainy Dog) and now with *Shin Jingi no Hakaba*, he can present emotions as well as effects, with something resembling empathy and insight, even if his subject is closer to a clinical case than a romantic loner. Yes, the film is twenty minutes too long and violent in ways not mass-audience friendly, but it is also among Miike's strongest.

Working from a script by Shigenori Takechi, Miike may not explain Ishimatsu's background—he is mad and bad from his first scene—but goes deeper than Fukasaku into his hero's tortured affair with Chieko. What seems at first a crude S&M fantasy—a weak reed of a woman submitting to the strong will of her macho master—evolves into something stranger and more complex. These two, we come to see, need each other to live out their scenarios of self-destruction to the limit. As you degrade me, you complete me. The film is really a love story.

As Ishimatsu, Goro Kishitani (*Returner*, *All under the Moon*) is every inch the modern Japanese gangster, right down to his sculpted eyebrows and tightly wound punch perm curls. He is a viper of a man, who strikes mercilessly and senselessly but is also capable of courage. Having started the game, he plays it to the hilt, one piece against a dozen. What finally breaks him is not fear of his enemies but loss of the only thing he loved. Watari's character ended as a lost soul, gnawing on his lover's bones in front of his horrified former comrades. Kishitani is equally lost but smiling beatifically as he leaps into the void. Free at last.

Shin Kanashiki Hitman (1995)

ANOTHER LONELY HITMAN

Scr.: Toshiyuki Morioka. *Dir.*: Rokuro Mochizuki. *Prod.*: Gaga Communications/Excellent Film. *Main* cast: Ryo Ishibashi, Kazuhiko Kanayama, Asami Sawaki, Tatsuo Yamada, Tetsuya Yuki. 105 mins.

STORY

Takashi Tachibana (Ryo Ishibashi) pops the boss (*kaicho*) of a rival gang in a Chinese restaurant, and in the process accidentally kills a woman. After ten years in prison, he is released and greeted by members of his old gang. They assign a young *chinpira*, Ryuji (Kazuhiko Kanayama), to him, install Tachibana in a hotel, and send a hooker to his room. When the hooker, Yuki (Asami Sawaki), fails to arouse him, she apologizes, but Tachibana blames himself; he isn't used to the outside world yet. The next day, they go to an amusement park and Tachibana begins to unwind. On their return that evening, however, Yuki's jealous boyfriend, a yakuza, beats her in the street. Tachibana comes to her rescue and pounds the boyfriend to a bloody pulp.

Tachibana visits the office of his old gang, the Hirayama-gumi, where he is told that they have made peace with their old rivals and gone legit. Afterward, Ryuji tells Tachibana that he is skeptical about the supposed truce, saying that it's only a matter of time until the gang is swallowed up by its ostensible partners. While the Hirayama-gumi is still involved in traditional gangster activities, such as loan sharking (one client is threatened with the extraction of his internal organs for transplants if he doesn't pay up), its hopes for big money rest on a golf course construction project.

Yuki's boyfriend, his broken nose bandaged, drives up to Tachibana on the street and taunts him. What, he asks, did Tachibana get out of killing the rival gang's boss and taking a ten-year rap? Tachibana dumps a garbage can on him—but can't answer his question. Later, cleaning his pistol, Tachibana happens on a recruiting ad for fishermen in the newspaper. He tears it out and saves it. Tachibana begins working for the gang as an enforcer, while unbeknown to him, the gang begins a new business: selling cigarettes soaked in stimulants to night club patrons. When he finds that Yuki has been doing drugs, he decides to make her go cold turkey. He ties her to the bed, buys water for her to drink and a puzzle to play with, and hires a woman to babysit her while he is away. Yuki rages against him and even asks him to kill her, but he persists.

He and Ryuji get into trouble with the higher ups by dealing too harshly with hoods from Dekata Kogyo—a business ally the Hirayama-gumi is anxious not to go to war with. Tachibana cuts off his little finger and presents it to the Dekata boss, who beats him with a wooden sword. Soon after, the golf course deal falls through. Ryuji and Tachibana quit the gang and raid the gang office to extract a "retirement allowance" from the bosses. Tachibana and Yuki make their escape by car, while Ryuji decides to stay behind. Tachibana stops to see his young daughter, who gives him her muffler—and leaves him in tears. He also visits his mother and sister. His mother, calling him a killer, rejects his offer of money, but his sister, more sympathetic, takes it. On the road, Tachibana reads a newspaper article saying that Ryuji has been arrested for killing a Hirayama-gumi boss. He and Yuki press on to the dock where they plan to board a boat—and embark on a new life. But fate intervenes.

CRITIQUE

Based on a novel by Yukio Yamanouchi, a former lawyer for the Yamaguchi-gumi, Rokuro Mochizuki's *Shin Kanashiki Hitman* has no narrative relationship with the 1989 Haruo Ichikura film *Kanashiki Hitman* (Lonely Hitman). The story—about a hitman who cannot fit back into his old gang after a stretch in prison—resembles that of *Onibi* (The Fire Within), the 1997 film that is Mochizuki's masterpiece. It also has counterparts in dozens of other gang films, but Mochizuki takes it in a more realistic direction than usual.

Despite being a hero in the standard

romantic loner mold, Tachibana is less self-sacrificing martyr than a man who lives by his own version of the gang code, while seeing all too clearly the venality of his Hirayama-gumi superiors. He severs a finger not out of fear or loyalty, but because, according to that code, it is a necessary act. He is also willing to discard the gang life for love—a choice seldom made by an older generation of gangster heroes.

Tachibana's love for a drug-addicted whore redeems him. In saving her from herself, he is in fact saving himself—or at least expiating the guilt he feels for shooting an innocent victim. His *shatei*, Ryuji, regards him as a kind of role model—a throwback to the days when gangsters were really gangsters, not just crooked businessmen. But Tachibana has no illusions about the worth of his work for the gang; his only desire is to get out. Though he very much wants to live (as indicated by his videotaping of his "retirement announcement" to fend off retribution), he cannot escape an organization that only wants to use—and discard—him. His end, more than those of most yakuza heroes, approaches pathos.

Shinjuku Kuro Shakai China Mafia Senso (1995)

SHINJUKU TRIAD SOCIETY

Scr.: Ichiro Fujita. *Dir.*: Takashi Miike. *Prod.*: Daiei. *Main cast*: Kippei Shiina, Tomoro Taguchi, Takeshi Caesar, Eri Yu. 101 mins.

STORY

Cops investigate a murder scene in Shinjuku—the vic has been beheaded by a sword. The MO (modus operandi) is that of a Chinese gang—the Dragon's Claw. The scene shifts to disco where, in a back room, a bearded man is getting a blow job from a pretty-faced boy. The cops break in and the boy flees through the disco. A pursuing cop is tripped by a girl and, the boy, running down an alley, slashes the neck of a cop who tries to stop him. At police headquarters the cops interrogate the bearded man, who seems to speak only a Taiwanese dialect. A policewoman conducts a body cavity search of the girl, Ritsuko Katsura (Eri Yu)—and draws a blank. When Ritsuko threatens the cops, one slams a folding chair down on her face.

The madball cop is Tatsuhito Kiritani (Kippei Shiina), the son of a Chinese woman and Japanese "war orphan" who, as a child, had been left behind by his parents in Japan's chaotic retreat from China at the end of World War Two. Concerned about his father's failing health, Tatsuhito offers him money—won on a kick-boxing bet—to underwrite a move to Shizuoka. Tatsuhito's younger brother, Yoshihito, is working as a lawyer for Ritsuko, who wants revenge for her broken nose and disfigured face. She has sex with a giant of a Chinese gangster—and urges him to kill Tatsuhito.

The big man's boss, however, is the diminutive but fearless Wang (Tomoro Taguchi), who walks into a meeting with a rival gang alone, threatens war, and on his way out, flashes the boss (thus revealing that he has been wearing nothing but a trenchcoat). Tatsuhito interrogates the bearded man again and finds out he can speak Mandarin but still refuses to talk. Tatsuhito drags him to a room, where a diminutive cop proceeds to bugger him. The man spills when Tatsuhito threatens to stop the sex.

Wang makes a payoff to an elderly Japanese mama-san, who complains about the amount—so Wang plucks out her eye. Soon after, Wang is ambushed by yakuza from the Yamane-gumi but makes his escape in a car driven by Yoshihito. Tatsuhito, who has been on stakeout watching all this, runs after the car. He catches up at a light, but Yoshihito pulls away, nearly running him over. Wang's gang decides to cooperate with the Yamane-gumi in a kidney smuggling operation, with a going price of 30 million yen per operation. Meanwhile, Tatsuhito goes to Taiwan to learn more about Wang. A Taiwanese cop tells him that Wang killed his father when he was fourteen and was sent to a notorious mental hospital. Tatsuhito also learns that Wang gets his kidneys from healthy children—the parents consent to the operation for the money.

The scene switches to Wang's Shinjuku flat, where he sleeps with the pretty-faced boy. Wang washes his bloody hands but can't get them clean. Back in Japan, Tatsuhito frets about Yoshihito, who has disappeared. He goes to the kick boxing gym to investigate but is nearly beaten to death by yakuza, who turn him over to Wang.

The second-in-command of the Yamane-gumi (Masahiro Sudo) asks the pretty-faced boy about Wang—then pays for a blow job with a knife. Wang learns that the Yamane-gumi has been cheating him on the kidney business and his boyfriend has been talking to Ishizaka. Soon after, Wang's gang invades the kick boxing gym and blows away their yakuza partners. Ritsuko takes pity on Tatsuhito; he is the first man, she says, to ever make her climax. She nurses him until he is ready to continue his search for his brother—and take revenge on Wang.

CRITIQUE

The first installment in Takashi Miike's trilogy about Chinese and Japanese gangsters, *Shinjuku Kuro Shakai China Mafia Senso* (Shinjuku Triad Society) was also was also the second of his films to be screened abroad, following *Fudoh: The New Generation* in 1997 at the Brussels International Festival of Fantasy Film. Though the story of two brothers on the opposite sides of the law was hardly original, Miike took it to new extremes—a hallmark of his later work. How many other cop thrillers, then or now, would feature a cop raping a homosexual suspect—not as a punishment but as an incentive? How many would begin a romance with the man slamming a folding chair on a prone

woman, shattering her nose? How many would borrow from *Macbeth* for scenes of a patricidal gangster washing his bloodied hands decades after the event?

That little of this has anything to do with real Chinese gangs in Shinjuku hardly matters. Miike creates an alternative universe with the sort of depraved invention that compels, if not belief, fascination (horrified or otherwise). Though only beginning to scale the heights of outrageousness that he would later reach, Miike is already populating his universe with characters that may embody offensive stereo-types (the Chinese as a vicious and degenerate race, etc., etc.) but seem to exist in a cartoonish dimension of their own, beyond PC critiques. Also, for all the outré violence and sex, Miike is a closet romantic, who believes that lovers can unite and brothers can reconcile, despite every insult and violation. The heart has its reasons, even in Miike's world gone mad.

Shinjuku Yokubo Tantei (1994)

THE HUNGRY SHINJUKU DETECTIVE
Scr.: Yutaka Hirano. *Dir.:* Etsu Totoku. *Prod.:* KSS. *Main cast:* Akira Terao, Hiromitsu Kiho, Takao Osawa, Yukari Morikawa. 90 mins.

The private eye of *Shinjuku Yokubo Tantei* (The Hungry Shinjuku Detective) is a lone wolf, lush, and loser but has kept his integrity in a dirty, dangerous world. As a cop-turned-P.I. named Kusanagi, Akira Terao is hard boiled in the classic Philip Marlowe manner but with a throwaway charm and shaggy stylishness that is somehow 1990s (Shinjuku grunge?). He reminded me of Nick *48 Hours* Nolte, only more cuddly (he's a grinner, not a growler).

The story is typical man-on-a-mission stuff. A retired detective—Kusanagi's father-figure friend—dies of a heart attack in a love hotel. The attack, Kusanagi learns, was caused by a stimulant drug. Also, the cop's companion

Akira Terao plays a down-and-out private investigator in *Shinjuku Yokubo Tantei* (The Hungry Shinjuku Detective, 1994).

at the time was a Taiwanese hostess with a butterfly tattoo on one hand. Kusanagi goes snooping around the bar where the hostess works and gets thrashed by Taiwanese gangsters. Before they can slice and dice him with their switchblades (there are an awful lot of knives flashed in this movie), he is saved by a young punk named Sho (Hiromitsu Kiho) with whom Kusanagi once spent the night in a drunk tank.

Soon after, he has another unexpected encounter, this time with a Taiwanese gang boss named Wang (Takao Osawa). Young, slick, and creepily effete, Wang tells Kusanagi that a rival boss named Yang killed his friend. Kusanagi gets out of the boss's stretch limo, puzzled and curious. Wang may be telling him the truth, but why is he snitching? What really happened in that hotel? When Kusanagi visits the crime scene with his pretty, sharp-tongued assistant (Yukari Morikawa) in tow, he finds a video camera behind a two-way mirror. Who has a tape of that fatal night? Yang, who is the hotel's owner, or someone else?

Working from a script by Yutaka Hirano, director Etsu Totoku fashions a gritty, tightly paced thriller, with occasional baroque flourishes. In the final showdown with the baddies Kusanagi's heroics are so over-the-top they're funny but cool (the thirteen-year-old in us wants to go "wow!"). It is Terao, however, who makes the movie work. A favorite of Akira Kurosawa, who used him—not always to best advantage—in *Ran*, *Yume* (Akira Kurosawa's Dreams) , and *Madadayo* (Not Yet), Terao thoroughly enjoys himself as the sodden hero, a welcome change of pace from playing a Kurosawa stand-in?

Showa Zankyoden: Shinde Moraimasu (1970)

REMNANTS OF CHIVALRY IN THE SHOWA ERA: I WANT YOU TO DIE
Scr.: Morimasa Owaku. *Dir.*: Masahiro Makino. *Prod.*: Toei. *Main cast*: Ken Takakura, Ryo Ikebe, Junko Fuji, Michiko Araki, Takehisa Nakamura, Hiroyuki Nagato, Rin'ichi Yamamoto. 92 mins.

STORY
Hidejiro Hanada (Ken Takakura), a young drifter, commits a breach of etiquette at a gambling den and is beaten senseless by the yakuza who run it. An apprentice geisha (Junko Fuji) discovers him under a tree and, taking pity, revives the young man with sake and shelters him with her umbrella from the falling snow. She runs off to get permission for him to spend the night at the geisha house but when she returns, he is gone, leaving the umbrella. Several years pass and Hanada, now a yakuza himself, gets his revenge on the gambling den's boss. He catches him palming the dice, slices off his hand—and ends up in prison.

When he gets out, after the Great Kanto Earthquake, he returns to Fukagawa—the Tokyo pleasure quarter where he first met the young geisha—and gets a job as a chef at the Kiraku, a Japanese-style restaurant run by a kindly blind woman. The head chef, Kazama (Ryo Ikebe), is an old friend and ally. Then, a man (Takehisa Nakamura) who has been like an uncle to him introduces him to a bevy of geisha—the prettiest of whom happens to be Ikue—the girl he met under the tree so many years before. An excited Ikue begins telling the story of their first encounter to her attentive colleagues in minute detail—until an embarrassed Takakura asks her to stop.

Before romance can properly bloom, however, the boss of the Komei gang finagles the deed to the Kiraku from the old woman's weak-willed son. Reluctantly discarding his plan to go straight, Hanada reunites with an old gangster pal (Hiroyuki Nagato) and plots

The boss would like to see you. Show Aikawa (center) in a poster for the first installment of the Shuraba ga Yuku (The Carnage Comes, 1995) series.

lowing her success in the Hibotan Bakuto (Red Peony Gambler) series. Fuji plays a geisha to twittering perfection—and against her Hibotan Bakuto image as a dominatrix in a kimono. Director Masahiro Makino stages key scenes between her and Takakura in a Japanesque eternity, as though they are both becoming legends before our eyes.

The final clash between Takakura and the Komae gang, though similar to dozens of others in the Takakura oeuvré, is notable for the phrase *"shinde moraimasu"* (I want you to die) that Takakura addresses to the boss just as he is about to run him through (and it is used as the film's subtitle). It's one offer that truly can't be refused.

Shuraba ga Yuku (1995)

THE CARNAGE COMES

Scr./Dir.: Seiji Izumi. *Prod.:* Scorpion. *Main cast:* Show Aikawa, Takeshi Yamato, Masaru Matsuda, Yuko Nito, Nagare Hagiwara, Bunta Sugawara. 91 mins.

STORY

Kishida, the dying boss of the Osaka-based Kowa-kai, names Ryuichi Hongo (Show Aikawa) as his successor, enraging Seiji Ino (Takeshi Yamato), the next in line by seniority. Ino kills Kishida, then tries to pin the blame on Hongo. Hongo narrowly escapes the *oyabun's* house with his men and flees back to his base in Yokohama. Hongo tells his lover Keiko (Yuko Nito) to go to Hokkaido and wait for six months. She reluctantly agrees.

The *kaicho* (chairman) of the Kowa-kai tells Ino that Hongo denies responsibility for Kishida's murder and asks him to avoid doing anything rash. Soon after, however, Ino orders his underling Kura (Masaru Matsuda) to clip Hongo—and tells Kura that he will make him boss of the Ino-gumi in return. Meanwhile, Hongo forms a strategic alliance with the

countermoves. But when he finally walks into the night to attack the Komei headquarters, his only companion is Kazama, who may not be a gangster but is fighting for the thing he loves—the Kiraku.

CRITIQUE

The nine-part Showa Zankyoden series, which ran from 1965 to 1972, depicted the conflict between modern yakuza, who are in it only for the money and power, and the upholders of the gangster's *jingi* code. Though the stories were not continuous, the contentious friendship of the Takakura and Ikebe characters was a staple, as was a star-crossed romance between Takakura and the female lead. The seventh installment, *Showa Zankyoden: Shinde Moraimasu*, featured a memorable pairing of Takakura and Junko Fuji, then at the height of popularity fol-

Mokuyu-kai, a Shinjuku-based gang. He cannot, however, fend off Kura and his crew, who invade Hongo's lair and narrowly miss killing him and Keiko. Kura escapes, leaving several of his crew behind, while Hongo rushes Keiko to a clinic where a gang-connected doctor (Bunta Sugawara) treats her wound.

Ino slashes Kura's face and ejects him from the gang for his failure to kill Hongo. Soon after, another Kowa-kai boss, Kyomoto (Nagare Hagiwara), is released from prison and goes to pray at Kishida's grave. There, he meets Ino—and the two exchange words; Kyomoto suspects Ino of usurping power but has no proof.

Back in Shinjuku, a hot-tempered Hongo-gumi gangster, Ryugaku, and members of a strange gang get into a quarrel at a club. Ryugaku's girlfriend, a hostess at the club, begs him not to start something with Yasukawa, the stimulant-crazed boss of the crew, but Ryugaku refuses to listen. Outside the club, the strange gangsters stomp him. He is saved only by the intervention of his girlfriend. She takes Ryugaku to her apartment to recover—where he confesses his shame for being in the bath when Kowa-kai gangsters attacked his boss—and says he will get them if he has another chance. She in turn tells him that she is pregnant—news he doesn't want to hear now that his gang is at war.

Kyomoto comes to Hongo's office and, flourishing a pistol, demands to know if Hongo killed Kishida. Hongo denies it—and Kyomoto relents, though he is still not quite convinced. The rival gangsters spot Ryugaku on the street and whack him, leaving a gang badge in his hand. Tokumaru, Hongo's burly second-in-command, says that a local gang is responsible, while Hongo adds that, if Kyomoto did it, he will never forgive him.

Ino suspects Kura's loyalty after his failure to whack Hongo. Several of Ino's men, posing as Hongo-gumi members, torture two Kyomoto hoods for information and bury one alive. One escapes, however, and tells his boss that Hongo is to blame. The hot-headed Kyomoto is ready to go to war. After an attack on Hongo's headquarters by Kyomoto's crew, Hongo and Tokumaru find Yasukawa, in the midst of hot sex, and accuse him of killing Ryugaku (while the hapless Yasukawa struggles to disengage). They take him to a warehouse and torture him until he confesses.

The cops, led by detective Onizuka, are disturbed by all the violent goings-on Shinjuku—and are convinced that the Hongo-gumi is responsible. Keiko suddenly returns from Hokkaido and contacts Hongo. When he goes to meet her at a restaurant, he is attacked by Kura, wielding a knife. Hongo has another narrow escape, but a bigger test is about to come. He decides to go to Kyomoto's office and convince him that Ino is pitting them against each other. If he succeeds, he will have an ally. If he fails, he will die.

CRITIQUE

As the first installment in an enduringly popular mid-1990s V Cinema series, *Shuraba ga Yuku* launched Show Aikawa to stardom. In theme and approach, the film is similar to Kinji Fukasaku's Jingi Naki Tatakai series; once again the story revolves around a Byzantine gang succession struggle and once again, the code of *jingi* matters less than the urge to survive.

The divide between black and white, however, is more clear-cut in *Shuraba*, with Takeshi Yamato's Ino being a Machiavellian schemer, who will stop at nothing to achieve his ends. Meanwhile, Show Aikawa's Hongo is clearly the wronged party, who was named gang successor only because his boss thought he was the better man, not because of any machinations on Hongo's part. There are shades of gray as well, however, with Ino rightfully feeling cheated out of a promotion, while Hongo resorts to torture to extract a confession from a rival gangster—a tactic that would never have occurred to the stainless heroes of the *ninkyo eiga*.

Also, Aikawa's performance is more contemporarily cool than traditionally chivalrous; he is the former teenage gangbanger who has evolved into a professional gangster, not a romantic loner who finds himself at the fringes of society. Though his Hongo may be purer at heart than the slithery Ino, he is equally a hood. Bossing a gang is his career—one he has no intention of changing.

The film's most interesting character, however, is Nagare Hagiwara's Kyomoto, who is always on the verge of a meltdown and feels the sort of fierce loyalty to his dead boss that marks him as a throwback. The obvious parallels are the short-fused types that Tomisaburo Wakayama played in the 1960s, but Hagiwara is less an old-fashioned gangster than a punk who got older without ever mellowing out. He also provides one of the film's more memorable images. Imagine a yakuza who, like Ridley Scott's alien, is all but impossible to kill. A good metaphor for the series—and the yakuza genre itself.

Shuraba no Gokudo: Hebi no Michi (1997)

SERPENT'S PATH

Scr.: Hiroshi Takahashi. *Dir.:* Kiyoshi Kurosawa. *Prod.:* Daiei. *Main cast:* Show Aikawa, Teruyuki Kagawa, Yurei Yanagi, Shiro Shitamoto, Kaei Okina. 85 mins.

STORY

Niijima (Show Aikawa) and a former yakuza, Miyashita (Teruyuki Kagawa), kidnap Otsuki (Yurei Yanagi), a gangster that Miyashita believes tortured and murdered his eight-year-old daughter. Taking him in the trunk of a car to an abandoned warehouse, they chain him to a wall. Miyashita then wheels over a television and plays a home video of his daughter, while reading a police report about her murder. Otsuki, defiant, insists on his innocence. But when his kidnappers deny him access to a toilet, force him to eat his food off the floor, and otherwise treat him like an about-be-slaughtered animal, he begins to crack.

Niijima is a teacher of mathematics at a night school, but one who seems to know an uncommon lot about the underworld. When Miyashita asks him why he is so interested in his daughter's case, Niijima simply says that he "felt sorry for her." It is clear, however, that his motives are not entirely disinterested.

Otsuki insists that another gangster, Hiyama (Shiro Shitamoto), is the one responsible for the death of Miyashita's daughter. Deciding to investigate his claim, Niijima and Miyashita go to the golf course where Hiyama is playing with several colleagues—and snatch him as he is searching for a lost ball. A woman with a limp spots them and slashes at them with her cane, tipped with a pop-out blade. They manage to escape, however, and chain Hiyama next to Otsuki. Hiyama is made of sterner stuff than his new companion and insists, almost contemptuously, that he is ready to die. Niijima and Miyashita instead degrade him the same way they did Otsuki.

When Miyashita is away, however, Niijima pulls up a chair to his two prisoners, gives them cigarettes and beer, and confides that he really doesn't care who killed Miyashita's daughter. "If you get your stories together, he'll feel better," he says. Later, Otsuki and Hiyama tell Miyashita that the real killer is Ariga (Kaei Okina), a gang bottom feeder whom they feel is the most disposable. Miyashita agrees to look for Ariga, but Niijima wants to take only one of the gangsters along as a guide. He unchains them, throws a pistol on the floor between them—and walks away as they fight it out. Miyashita and Niijima then take the survivor to Ariga's address—but it turns out to be a vacant lot. Miyashita pulls the trigger and the survivor bites the dust.

They find Ariga's house and shoot their way in. When Niijima finds Ariga cowering in the shower, he warns him not to reveal his true identity to Miyashita. Instead, Niijima tells Miyashita that their new prisoner knows where Ariga is hiding. They take the prisoner back to the warehouse, but he's too fuddled to lie about Ariga's whereabouts. Despite Niijima's warnings to lie low, Miyashita visits Niijima's class and is ID'd by a student—a girl math prodigy who has seen Miyashita's face on a gang-distributed wanted poster. Not long after, the gang is on their trail, as the story moves toward its climax—and disturbing revelations about its principals.

CRITIQUE

Despite its title, Kiyoshi Kurosawa's *Shuraba no Gokudo: Hebi no Michi* (Serpent's Path) is less a gang actioner than a psychological thriller that resembles, in mood and approach, Kurosawa's better known *Cure* and *Kairo* (Pulse). The film unfolds in a strangely depopulated, dehumanized world that exists at a skewed angle to our own, one in which evil walks abroad and little is what it seems.

Kurosawa creates this world through not only the usual device of bizarre characters—the woman with the limp and the lethal cane being one—but by draining characters and actions of their normal affect. Certain lines of dialogue take on the tone of ominous incantation, violence erupts with a stark lack of preliminaries, and colors are eerily desaturated. The yakuza prisoners begin as the most normal of the characters, snarling defiance at their captors, but they descend, in the end, into a horrific otherness.

Also, though the story begins as a simplistic revenge fantasy, Kurosawa and scriptwriter Hiroshi Takahashi (*The Ring*) transform it into a complex, if at times baffling, study of the nature of evil—and the ultimate unknowability of human beings. Show Aikawa, playing against type as a math geek (albeit one with murky motives), impresses, as always, with the economy of his acting, the strength of his presence. He not only effortlessly dominates the film's

yakuza tough guys but connects with them on their level. His air of knowing more than he lets on—and being willing to do whatever is necessary to achieve his ends—deepens the film's atmosphere of unsettling uncertainty. The last scene feels oddly detached from the ones before—as though it were unfolding in another reality. All but the terminally incurious will rewind the video to see what, if anything, they've missed. Not to worry—it's just Kurosawa being Kurosawa, master of enigma.

Shuraba no Ningengaku (1993)

THE ANTHROPOLOGY OF A FIGHT SCENE

Scr.: Takahiro Okabe, Masahiro Kakefuda. *Dir.:* Shun'ichi Kajima. *Prod.:* Tohoku Shinsha, Toei Video, Toei. *Main cast:* Masanobu Takashima, Hirose Fuse, Yoko Minamino, Shinji Yamashita. 109 mins.

Modern yakuza are mainly in it for the money and earn much of it by exploiting Asian women or selling stimulant drugs. Instead of the gangs' unsavory present, however, *Shuraba no Ningengaku* (The Anthropology of a Fight Scene) harkens back to an idealized 1950s. This, the movie tells us, was a freer, more innocent time, when joining a gang could be a thrilling adventure for a naive but reckless youth.

The youth in question is Heikichi (Masanobu Takashima), whom we first see in 1950 as a *tempura gakusei* (phony student) who is pretending to attend classes to please his mother in the countryside, while delivering ice to put money in his pocket. As played by Takashima, a burr-headed Japanese Jerry Lewis, Heikichi is a most unlikely gang recruit. But *Shuraba* is a most improbable movie in which even a clown becomes a wise guy.

While delivering ice to a club, Heikichi becomes embroiled in a street fight between American soldiers and the Ando-gumi, a gang led by the beefy Morishima (Hirose Fuse). The

GIs turn out to be no match for Morishima's wooden sword, but before they retire in ignominious defeat they thrash poor Heikichi. He recovers consciousness in the club, under the ministrations of a pretty hostess named Junko (Yoko Minamino) and the hearty cheers of the gang. He has found a new love and a new life.

Shuraba comically describes the education of this yakuza *Candide*, but it is also in the traditional slash and swagger mold and suffused with a nostalgia for old-time gangsterism, Japanese-style. Imagine Jerry Lewis in a gang movie that expresses a frank longing for the purity of classic Sicilian-American thuggery. The story covers eight years in Heikichi's gang career, from his fumbling beginning to his fumbling end. His misadventures include crashing his motorcycle into the gang boss's car and sleeping with a girl who works at the dance hall of a rival gang. In the first instance, he is let off with a warning (perhaps because he grovels so sincerely). In the second, he is beaten to within an inch of his life by the rival gang. Fortunately, Morishima rushes to the rescue and frees him. Heikichi ends up in the hospital, but Junko forgives him and he recovers to bumble on again.

But Heikichi's luck cannot hold forever: when a businessman who refused to repay a loan to the Ando-gumi is murdered, Heikichi is fingered as the suspect. Although another gang member made the hit, Heikichi and Junko go into hiding. His boss tells him if he is caught, Heikichi must quit the gang and go straight. Desperate, he asks a college-friend, now a journalist, to find him a hideout. The friend agrees, but realizes that if he turns in his old buddy he will get the scoop of the year.

In trying to be all things to all audiences, *Shuraba* ends up being very little indeed. The fight scenes are too phony to be scary: the soldiers all flip out switchblades at the same moment, like dancers in *Grease*. The period cars, clothes, and furnishings are presented for our admiration, like so many collectors' items; instead of sighing with longing for the good old days, I started wondering about prices. I also doubted the credentials of the movie's yakuza. How can these guys be for real when they let a schnook like Heikichi play gangster with them? But the most transparent fake is Heikichi himself; we never see him turn out a hooker, do a drug deal, or otherwise engage in real-life, income-producing yakuza activities. A *tempura gakusei* at the beginning, he remains forever a *tempura yakuza* in a *tempura yakuza* movie.

Shuraba no Okami: Kumo no Hitomi (1997)

EYES OF THE SPIDER

Scr.: Yoichi Nishiyama, Kiyoshi Kurosawa. *Dir.:* Kiyoshi Kurosawa. *Prod.:* Daiei. *Main cast:* Show Aikawa, Ren Osugi, Shun Sugata, Dankan, Moe Sakura, Taro Suwa. 83 mins.

STORY

Niijima (Show Aikawa) is leading a quiet life with his wife (Kumi Nakamura), while keeping alive the memory of his daughter, who was murdered six years ago. When he finds and captures the man (Susumu Terajima) that he thinks is responsible, Niijima tortures him unmercifully for three days—then buries him in the countryside. Returning home, he asks his wife if she would like to leave the country for a month—or a year.

Soon after, he runs into Iwamatsu (Dankan), a high school classmate he has not seen in years. Iwamatsu, who is now president of a small trading company, offers him a job. He accepts and soon discovers that the company is a front: Iwamatsu's real business is murder for hire. His gang includes two *chinpira* and a girl, Miki (Moe Sakura), who helps lure the victims. When they are not whacking strangers, they play in the office, with roller skating being a favorite pastime.

Yoda, a mysterious contractor for the gang, questions Niijima closely and asks him to write a report on Iwamatsu, without explaining why. But Niijima, who has already pulled the trigger himself, is having second thoughts about the whole business—and turns Yoda down. Yoda, however, proves persistent. Niijima is sent to find Hinuma (Shun Sugata), another eccentric underworld boss whose obsession is fossils. He ends up chasing his prey around an abandoned quarry—and helping him sort fossil rocks.

Iwashita asks Niijima to help him pop the boss (Taro Suwa) of the Kinsei-kai. They botch the first attempt, but the next time the gang succeeds in trapping the boss on a country road. Mission accomplished, but soon after Hinuma tells Niijima that the Kinsei-kai boss is, incredibly, still alive. He also commissions a hit—on Iwamatsu. Then, Yoda ends up dead and Miki and Iwamatsu go fishing—but Niijima joins them, with gun in hand.

CRITIQUE

A followup to the 1997 *Shuraba no Gokudo: Hebi no Michi* (Serpent's Path), *Shuraba no Okami: Kumo no Hitomi* (Eyes of the Spider) again has a main character named Niijima, again played by Show Aikawa. However, the story is unrelated to the previous film's, save in its main thread of revenge for the death of a young girl.

In *Hebi no Michi*, the girl is the daughter of Niijima's "client"; in *Kumo no Hitomi* she is the daughter of Niijima himself. Her death shatters his world, upsets all his values. Despite the surface normality of his life, he becomes a monster who can torture without mercy, kill without feeling. Rather than explain this transformation, Kurosawa suggests it by placing Niijima into a new bizarre world that echoes his inner state in its empty amorality. Much of the action, violent and otherwise, seems to unfold in a dream—and points the way to such later Kurosawa films as *Charisma* and *Kairo* (Pulse) in which the disconnect from grass-is-green reality is franker.

In *Kumo no Hitomi*, Kurosawa is still winking at this disconnect, much in the manner of Takeshi Kitano. The Kitano influence extends to the film's minimalist style, with its disdain for camera movements and preference for medium and long shots (one extended chase sequence is filmed from what seems to be the top of a mountain, with pursuer and pursued looking like scurrying ants). The presence of Dankan, a Kitano comic disciple, makes the film feel even more like a Kitano knockoff. Fortunately, Kurosawa would soon shake off the seductive appeal of the Kitano style (or at least better disguise the influence). *Kumo no Hitomi* is a film that, for all its distinctive Kurosawa touches, is only half his own.

Sonatine (1993)

Scr./Dir.: Takeshi Kitano. *Prod.:* Bandai Visual, Shochiku Daiichi Kogyo. *Main cast:* Takeshi Kitano, Aya Kokumai. 94 mins.

Takeshi Kitano's *Sonatine* tries to prove that a yakuza movie can make a statement on the futility and emptiness of the gang life as powerful as that of the *Godfather* films. But the first adjective that sprang to mind as I watched this story of a gangster caught in a war he never wanted was "pretentious." Kitano plays Murakawa, a middle-aged yakuza who wants out. His boss, however, wants Murakawa and his henchmen to go to Okinawa and help an affiliated gang in a turf war. Murakawa reluctantly agrees, but when he arrives he finds himself outmaneuvered and outgunned. After several of his men take fatal hits, Murakawa retreats with the survivors to a hideout in the countryside, where they wait for a chance to counterattack.

The story has a familiar genre arc, but instead of conventional melodramatics Kitano gives us a new version of hard-boiled cool. In one scene, Murakawa has his crew lower a hapless mah-jongg parlor owner into the water

© 1993 Shochiku

Moving the conversation along. Takeshi Kitano (right) as a capo on the losing side of a gang war in *Sonatine* (1993).

with a construction crane, then watches calmly as the minutes pass and the rope twitches, registering the victim's death throes. This is a murder method that would only occur to a film director: the crane could easily be spotted by a passing ship or car. It is also a cruel, cold-blooded act that made me despise the hero. Kitano no doubt wants to establish Murakawa as a tough guy. Then, I suppose, so are boys who seal mice inside jars and watch them suffocate.

The film succeeds in capturing the tension, petty protocols, and the numbing boredom of yakuza life: all those hours of killing time in dumpy offices, cheap bars, and beach houses in the middle of an Okinawan nowhere. Also, his hoods are often cutups when they aren't being killers—a welcome change from macho stereotypes. Murakawa is a cut-up as well, though his jokes are of the practical type. While at the hideout on the beach, he sees two of his young underlings shooting a can off each other's heads with a pistol. He takes the pistol, empties all but one chamber, then has them play a round of scissors-paper-stone with him. He aims the pistol at the loser's chest, pulls the

trigger—and smiles when it doesn't go off. The boys, shaken, wonder if he is crazy. They should have counted the bullets in the sand.

In this scene, as in others, Kitano wants to impress us with his hero's contempt for danger and death. But as the stay at the beach stretches out to weeks (it also begins to feel that long in the theater), I began to see Murakawa less as an existential hero, more as a stand-in for the director, whose TV shows have frequently featured violent slapstick, with the general of the "Takeshi army" controlling the action and the grunts taking the pratfalls.

Some of the film's comic business is funny. Kitano, to give him credit, has a wickedly inventive mind. Much of the movie, however, is self-indulgent, self-congratulatory, and, as Murakawa prepares to meet his end, self-pitying. There is a sultry Okinawan girl (Aya Kokumai) who likes the casual way Murakawa guns down her date-rapist of a boyfriend. There is also a mysterious fisherman who starts knocking off Murakawa's allies and underlings like so many dolls in a shooting gallery. (One of the film's conceits is the immobility of the characters in the bang-bang scenes; they shoot at each other as though their instinct of self-preservation had been surgically removed.)

The focus, however, remains on Murakawa—and his grim and, at times, grimly comic obsession with death. I have seldom seen a film in which death is so drained of drama and emotion. Kitano seems to be saying that, because his characters' lives have no meaning, their deaths can have no charge. So, they go down, one by one, passive victims all. Only Murakawa gets the last laugh and the last bullet. By now, we know how he's going to use it and give *Sonatine* its coup de grâce.

3–4 X Jugatsu (1990)

BOILING POINT

Scr./Dir.: Takeshi Kitano. *Prod.:* Shochiku Fuji, Bandai. *Main cast:* Masahiko Ono, Yuriko Ishida, Takahito Iguchi, Bengal, Minoru Iizuka, Dankan, Beat Takeshi (Takeshi Kitano). 96 mins.

STORY

Masaki (Masahiko Ono) is a gas station attendant who plays on an amateur baseball team, coached by Iguchi (Takahito Iguchi), a hot-tempered bar owner and former yakuza. As a player, Masaki is hopeless—striking out without ever taking the bat off his shoulder or changing his doltish deadpan expression. Nonetheless, Masaki is a favorite of Iguchi, who defends him against his detractors. At the gas station, a yakuza scolds Masaki for servicing his Mercedes too slowly. Masaki takes a swing at the surprised gangster, who complains that Masaki has broken his arm. As phlegmatic as ever, Masaki shrugs off the gangster's threat to make him pay compensation.

Masaki goes to an outdoor cafe with a friend from the team, Kazuo (Minoru Iizuka), who asks him if he has a girlfriend. Masaki says no and rejects Kazuo's offer to set him up with a date, but soon after Kazuo leaves Masaki hits

up a cute waitress, Sayaka (Yuriko Ishida), who agrees to go out with him. Muto (Bengal), a lieutenant from the injured yakuza's gang, comes to the gas station and, taking a liking to Masaki, asks him to join. Hearing of this offer, Iguchi tells Masaki that he would be foolish to accept. Soon after, Iguchi has an altercation with a party of yakuza and hostesses who come into his bar—the former members of Muto's gang. He tries to set things straight with the gang and get Masaki off the hook but ends up getting physical with Muto. Masaki gets a big hit in the game—but passes another base runner, Kazuo, and is called out at the plate. Even so, Masaki now has a purpose in life: marry Sayaka.

Masaki and Sayaka go to the beach with an eccentric stranger and enjoy a brief idyll. Iguchi and Kazuo play pachinko—and Iguchi publicly complains about the take. Iguchi again meets with the gang to calm troubled waters but is beaten up, despite his plea to a former *aniki* (gang brother) who is the gang boss (Hisashi Igawa). "If you don't want to be treated [like a gangster], act like a *katagi* [straight citizen]," the boss warns him. The injured and enraged Iguchi wants to go to Okinawa and buy a gun from a yakuza acquaintance, Uehara (Beat Takeshi), but is in no shape to travel. Masaki and Kazuo volunteer to go in his place.

In Okinawa they encounter Uehara, who is in hot water with his gang for embezzling money. A volatile type, who indulges his appetites for sex and violence at will, Uehara takes his new acquaintances and a gang underling, Tamagi (Katsuo Tokashiki), to a karaoke club. While there, Uehara makes homosexual advances to Kazuo and he and Tamagi beat up two yakuza who make insulting remarks. Later, together with a Japanese and African-American hostess from the club, they go to a room where Tamagi, at Uehara's command, has sex with the Japanese hostess, Fumiyo (Eri Fuse). Then, Uehara pushes Fumiyo aside and proceeds to rape Tamagi. Later, when Tamagi complains,

Uehara orders him to cut off his finger by way of apology.

At the beach the next day, the group has a pleasant time, until Uehara starts abusing Fumiyo. Back in town, Uehara negotiates a deal with a gun dealer. Soon after, a foreigner makes the delivery by bicycle on a deserted road—and Uehara shoots him dead. Uehara takes an automatic weapon, leaving a pistol for Kazuo and Masaki. They go their separate ways—Uehara to get revenge on his own gang, Kazuo and Masaki to return to Tokyo for their own date with destiny.

CRITIQUE

Takeshi Kitano's second feature, *3–4 X Jugatsu* (Boiling Point) is a narratively disjointed film, with the hero of the first act—Masaki the phlegmatic gas station attendant—fading into the background in the second, while the psychotic gangster played by Kitano comes to the fore. Kitano, however, is not trying and failing to script a conventional plot so much as compose a blackly humorous essay on the saying "actions have consequences"—in this case, violent actions and violent consequences.

The film begins and ends with a sandlot baseball game, which for Masaki is not an idyllic escape from society but a distilled expression of its rules and expectations—and the humiliation that follows from not knowing the former and living up to the latter. He is however, more than a hapless loser; his air of quiet determination (or rock-headed stubbornness) appeals to his excitable manager Iguchi and, later, his sweet girlfriend Sayaka. That said, Masahiko Ono's performance as Masaki is too one-note to carry the film, thus the slowness and flatness of the first hour, until Masaki goes to Okinawa and encounters Uehara.

Though not Kitano's first character in a long career of playing violent antiheroes and villains, Uehara is the most madly out of control. This, Kitano seems to be telling us, is the yakuza in his purest sociopathic distillation; not a noble upholder of *ninkyo* virtue or a romantic rebel without a cause, but the id unleashed, violating every rule and norm with grinning impunity. His coolly malevolent gaze, in close-up, is the most frightening image in a movie that rejects decades of yakuza movie myth-making—and recasts the genre in Kitano's unique vision.

Tokyo Gang tai Hong Kong Gang (1964)

TOKYO GANG VERSUS HONG KONG GANG
Scr.: Akira Murao, Teruo Ishii. *Dir.:* Teruo Ishii. *Prod.:* Toei. *Main cast:* Koji Tsuruta, Ken Takakura, Tetsuro Tanba, Ryohei Uchida, Kenjiro Ishiyama, Nobuo Yana, Kyosuke Machida. 86 mins.

STORY

Kitahara (Ken Takakura) arrives in Hong Kong to make a drug buy. Though contacted by Chan (Ryohei Uchida), an envoy of the local drug lord Mao (Toru Abe), Kitahara becomes interested in the sales pitch of a persistent "tour guide," Liu (Kenjiro Ishiyama), and engages him for a tour that leads to an opium den—and an offer. Kitahara, however, balks at Liu's price and breaks off negotiations—too quickly for Liu's satisfaction. Kitahara then closes a deal with Chan, who manages to transfer the goods, evading Liu's gang, but Kitahara is shot before he can board the plane to Japan. Wounded, Kitahara makes his way to the dressing room of a beautiful Beijing opera star (Yoshiko Mita), asking her to deliver a package for him—and dies.

Kitahara's gang, Oka Kogyo, dispatches a top lieutenant, Fujishima (Koji Tsuruta), to Hong Kong. He collects the package from the actress but despite all of his precautions, Liu's gang snatches it—and Fujishima realizes they are Kitahara's killers. Fujishima meets the mysterious Mao (Tetsuro Tanba), who turns out to be an old war buddy—an information officer who decided to stay behind. The joy of this re-union, however, is brief. Fujishima has not only failed in his mission but, on returning home, is discovered to be a drug addict, a disgrace for a yakuza drug dealer. Mao, who has come to Japan to do business with Oka, saves Kitahara from a fatal bullet by offering to make him his "drug slave." Instead, Mao slips him a pistol, having sussed that Oka is really dealing with Liu. But just as Oka's gang is about to receive a big drug shipment from Liu's boat, Kitahara appears in a motor launch, steals the drugs, and makes his getaway to a nearby pier, chased by both Oka's and Liu's men. They follow him to a construction site, where a climactic battle breaks out between the two gangs.

CRITIQUE

Teruo Ishii not only filmed *Tokyo Gang tai Hong Kong Gang* (Tokyo Gang versus Hong Kong Gang) on location in Hong Kong and Macao—an unheard-of extravagance for Toei in the early 1960s—but gave it an unusual two-part narrative structure, with Ken Takakura starring in the first half and Koji Tsuruta in the second (and never the twain did meet). Also, instead of focusing on the expected tourist landmarks, Ishii took audiences on a tour of the Crown Colony's back alleys and *sampans*, immersing them in the sort of low-life detail that Hollywood films of the period scrupulously avoided in their journeys to the Far East. Using hidden cameras, he and cameraman Shichiro Hayashi captured not only candid glimpses of street vendors and mah-jongg players but the mostly indifferent expressions on the faces of passers-by when Takakura collapsed on the street.

The climactic night chase, with Tsuruta and his pursuers blazing away at each other from speed boats in the gloom, added another unusual touch. Unfortunately, the ending, with Kitahara suddenly converting to the anti-drug cause, undercuts Ishii's hard-boiled tale of gangsters loyal less to the gang than to the logic of the deal.

© 1964 Toei Company, Ltd.

New kid in town. Ken Takakura strides down a Hong Kong street in *Tokyo Gang tai Hong Kong Gang* (Tokyo Gang versus Hong Kong Gang, 1964).

Tokyo Mafia: Yakuza Wars (1995)

Scr.: Kazuhiko Murakami. *Dir.:* Seichi Shirai. *Prod.:* Gaga Communications. *Main cast:* Riki Takeuchi, Masayuki Imai, Reiko Yasuhara, Hiroshi Miyauchi, Kojiro Hongo, Ren Osugi. 80 mins.

STORY

Foreign and native gangs have carved up Kabukicho—Tokyo's largest and most dangerous adult playland. A former yakuza, Ginya Yabuki (Riki Takeuchi), heads the Tokyo Mafia, a gang of young bloods who have a new approach to the ancient business of crime in Japan: they have no traditionally defined hierarchy and equitably share the proceeds of their ventures—among the most promising: underground sales of whale meat, with supplies coming from Hong Kong.

As the film begins, the various Kabukicho gangs are scuffling for turf. The Chinese gangsters are particularly vicious, making body parts fly with abandon. Ginya has a long-standing beef with Iwagami (Ren Osugi), the boss of the Yamaryu gang, a man who once bludgeoned him with a marble ashtray. In reply, Ginya shot him in the leg, permanently crippling him. Ginya then announced his resignation from the gang and bit off his little finger to square his obligations—as well as display his defiance and contempt.

Ginya meets with Sho Saimon (Masayuki Imai), a lieutenant with the Yamaryu gang and old friend. After gossiping about a Japanese gangster who donated organs to pay for a drug shipment—at the request of a Hong Kong gang named the Dragon Heads—Ginya asks Sho to work with him on the whale meat business, offering a cut to the Yamaryu gang. Sho later approaches Iwagami, who says he is willing to go along if Ginya slips him a payment under the table. Ginya agrees.

Ginya and Sho have dinner with Eileen (Reiko Yasuhara), who manages a Kabukicho club, and Ryoko, who is fluent in Chinese and wants to be an interpreter. Trouble starts when yakuza thugs walk in and try to make off with the women. The beef ends without fatal consequences, however. Ginya becomes partners with the Dragon Heads, while paying off the police. With the way cleared, he and his Tokyo Mafia crew start raking in the cash from the whale meat business. Then, a rival gang, the Ishiyama-gumi, goes on the attack, hunting down Tokyo Mafia soldiers on the streets. Ginya suspects that Moriwaki (Shohei Yamamoto), the homosexual boss of the powerful Teito-kai with whom the Ishiyama gang is allied, is behind the new offensive.

Ginya counterattacks by ripping the engine out of a Mercedes Benz belonging to the Ishiyama boss. This prompts a raid by Ishiyama forces on the whale meat warehouse. They capture the mastermind behind the operation, Sugiyama, and torture him for information, but he refuses to spill. Ginya and the Tokyo Mafia invade Moriwaki's penthouse apartment by helicopter and arrange for a trade—Moriwaki for Sugiyama. Not long after, a hotblooded Tokyo Mafia gangster whacks Moriwaki—and the underworld bosses meet to decide the fate of the outlaw gang. Realizing that he is in desperate straits, Ginya goes to a gang elder who has helped him in the past. The elder's advice is to apologize or run. Ginya, however, is too proud and stubborn to do either. He'll fight it out with his enemies, even if he is outnumbered ten to one.

CRITIQUE

The first in a three-part series, *Tokyo Mafia* is a basic blood 'n' guts OV, with little claim to artistry or originality. The gore effects—in particular the flying limbs—are ludicrously bad, while Riki Takeuchi's performance as Tokyo Mafia boss Ginya Yabuki is flagrantly over the top. That said, Ginya and his Tokyo Mafia represent a new paradigm for the genre: gangsters who claim to be neither yakuza nor *gurentai*, but a secret society dedicated to crime. (Come to think of it, the Sicilian Mafia once made a similar claim—Ginya's model?) Also different is the gang's organizational structure—profit sharing is in, the old hierarchy and rules are out.

Ginya makes most of his income from the sort of "economic yakuza" business—black market sales of whale meat—that pure-minded heroes of the old *ninkyo* films once deplored. But like the gangster heroes of yore, he never engages in anything truly dirty, such as drug running or extortion—in other words, the main money-making activities of real-life hoods. Ginya also treats the women in his life, including the bright, slinky Eileen, with respect, while dressing smartly in the latest Italian fashions. No mere yakuza thug is he. He is a gangster, in other words, for the more sophisticated and multicultural streets of the post-bubble 1990s, who knows what a flash memory chip is but can still kick butt when he needs to.

And in this film, he satisfies that need to the limit.

Tokyo Nagaremono (1966)

TOKYO DRIFTER

Scr.: Yasunori Kawauchi. *Dir.:* Seijun Suzuki. *Prod.:* Nikkatsu. *Main cast:* Tetsuya Watari, Chieko Matsubara, Hideaki Nitani, Tamio Kawachi, Hideaki Esumi, Ryuji Kita, Hiroshi Cho, Eiji Go, Isao Tamagawa, Michio Hino. 83 mins.

STORY

Tetsu "The Phoenix" Hondo (Tetsuya Watari) is a gangster without a gang now that his boss, Kurata (Ryuji Kita), has gone straight. But Tetsu's old rivals, the Otsuka-gumi, are not about to let him and Kurata go gently into the good night. The boss has borrowed money from Yoshii, a gang-connected loan shark, to buy an office building, but after Otsuka (Hideaki Esumi) gets wind of the plan he has Yoshii whacked and grabs the deed to the building.

Tetsu stakes his life as collateral for Yoshii's loan and thwarts the Otsuka-gumi's plan to kidnap his girlfriend Chiharu (Chieko Matsubara), a slinky club singer. Tetsu is, in other words, a threat that the Otsuka hoods have to eliminate. They lure him to a dance club and trap him in a pit. He escapes, but an Otsuka hitman, Tatsu the Viper (Tamio Kawachi), is on his trail. Meanwhile, the Otsukas put the muscle on Kurata, saying they will pin a murder on him—and get him to hand over the building's seal. To take pressure off his boss, Tetsu leaves town and hits the road alone, with Otsuka goons close behind. Meanwhile, Kurata and Otsuka are reaching an understanding that could have fatal consequences for Tetsu.

CRITIQUE

Tokyo Nagaremono (Tokyo Drifter) might be called Seijun Suzuki's *Guys and Dolls*, i.e., a highly stylized look at Tokyo lowlife, set to music. As Tetsu, Tetsuya Watari wears a powder blue suit and sings or hums the title song at crucial moments. These musical interludes occasionally verge on the bizarre, as when Tetsu—apparently shot dead by Tatsu during a brawl in a Western saloon(!)—starts humming defiantly from the floor—and pulls the trigger. Similarly wacky is the Pop Art look of the night club where Tetsu's girlfriend Chiharu warbles. In the climactic shoot-out, a huge donut-shaped mobile hanging from the ceiling glows blood red as Tetsu dodges bullets on an empty dance floor, against a blazing-white backdrop.

Tetsu triumphs but remains true to his loner code, spurning a tearful Chiharu with the words, "A drifter doesn't need a woman." This is the perfect line for the legions of dateless guys who have helped make *Tokyo Nagaremono* among Suzuki's most popular films. It is a cheeky trampling of genre conventions, whose charms lie more in its Mod stylistics and parodic tone than in narrative coherence—or rather the defiant lack of same. Perhaps a better Hollywood comparison is, not *Guys and Dolls*, but *Austin Powers: International Man of Mystery*.

Unlucky Monkey (1998)

Scr./Dir.: Sabu. *Prod.:* Shochiku. *Main cast:* Shin'ichi Tsutsumi, Hiroshi Shimizu, Akira Yamamoto, Ren Osugi, Ikko Suzuki. 106 mins.

Was Sabu Buster Keaton in a previous incarnation? Like the deadpan master of silent comedy, this actor-turned-director (*Dangan Runner*, *Postman Blues*), builds narrative machinery into his films that, once set in motion, develops a giddy, head-long momentum, according to a crazily logical design. But whereas Keaton's cinematic machines moved in a clean arc, at an increasing rate of speed, Sabu's have tended to start fast, then sputter and slow, with plot complications serving as brakes.

Love on the run. Tetsuya Watari (center) plays a wandering gangster in *Tokyo Nagaremono* (Tokyo Drifter, 1966). Chieko Matsubara is his love interest and Tamio Kawachi is his pursuer.

His third film, *Unlucky Monkey* is Sabu's most ingeniously constructed yet. Like his two previous films, it features a long chase sequence, this time of a bank-robber named Yamazaki (Shin'ichi Tsutsumi) being pursued by the bank's rent-a-cops. Carrying a bag full of cash that has dropped into his arms from the sky, Yamazaki eludes his pursuers but not before a knife he is holding accidentally plunges into a young beautician. Now a possible murderer as well as a thief, he desperately searches for a sanctuary and finds it in the unlikely form of a citizen's group protesting pollution from a local factory. In yet another strange twist of fate, he becomes the group's spokesman.

Meanwhile, on a parallel narrative plane, two yakuza, Kamada (Hiroshi Shimizu) and Matsui (Akira Yamamoto), are conferring in their gang headquarters with Tachibana (Ren Osugi), a high-ranking honcho in a rival gang. With their boss in the slammer on a drug charge, the two are at loose ends and ready to listen to Tachibana's proposal to launch a new overseas joint venture. Then, a third gang member, a drunken practical joker named Kaneda (Ikko Suzuki), bursts in the door wearing Yamazaki's discarded ski mask and, by a freak accident, Tachibana ends up dead. Now, the boys have a body to dispose of and an entire gang of angry yakuza to deal with.

Faced with a dilemma resembling Yamazaki's, they find their lives becoming entangled with his in ways that are madly improbable but in the context of the film's other goings-on make a slapsticky sort of sense. The title, we see, ought to be plural. Like Sabu's other heroes, Yamazaki and his three gangster acquaintances are playthings of fate who refuse (or are simply too scared) to play along. Driven by greed, living in fear, they are not Tarantinoesque icons of cool or Keatonesque masters of slapstick, but harried creations uniquely Sabu. Ikko Suzuki's Kaneda boils with a rage that feels like the genuine, borderline psychotic article, while Shin'ichi Tsutsumi's Yamazaki is possessed of that most unlikely accessory for post-modern cinematic heroes—a tormenting conscience.

The plot is, like those of Sabu's other films, an absurdist contraption whose characters become the butts of cosmic jokes. After three outings, those jokes are wearing thin, but *Unlucky Monkey* is bolder in conception and tighter in execution than its predecessors. Like a stand-up comedian woodshedding his act, Sabu is using the same bits but giving them a different spin and getting more laughs each time out. Yes, he overworks coincidence and, yes, he stretches credibility to the breaking point (especially in a return-from-the-dead scene whose returnee must be a yogi), but his inventiveness and goofball conviction carry us through. One wonders, though, if Sabu will ever make a movie whose hero doesn't have to be a marathoner to survive.

Waga Jinsei Saiaku no Toki (1993)

THE MOST TERRIBLE TIME IN MY LIFE
Scr.: Daisuke Tengan, Kaizo Hayashi. *Dir.:* Kaizo Hayashi. *Prod.:* For Life, Film Detective Office. *Main cast:* Masatoshi Nagase, Yang Haipin, Kiyotaka Nanbara, Jo Shishido. 92 mins.

Filmed in black-and-white, set in corners of Yokohama that still preserve a funky 1960s ambience, Kaizo Hayashi's *Waga Jinsei Saiaku no Toki* (The Most Terrible Time in My Life) is nouveau film noir. It lovingly recreates the look and style of classic gangster flicks while discarding much of the hypertrophied macho romanticism that modern audiences (modern female audiences in particular) find corny and dumb.

Though he sets up *Waga* as a hip takeoff, Hayashi also wants us to respond the way audiences once responded to its models—identifying with the hero, thrilling to the action. But for all of their formulaic tricks, the best of the

A bang from a beret. Masatoshi Nagase as P.I. Maiku Hama in *Waga Jinsei Saiaku no Toki* (The Most Terrible Time in My Life, 1993).

old gang films did reflect the realities of the streets that had inspired them. *Waga* reflects only Hayashi's imagination, whose frame of reference rarely extends beyond the film library. It is a *Paper Moon* for the 1990s: cleverly written, prettily photographed, charmingly retro, essentially empty.

Nagase plays Maiku Hama ("Mike Hammer"), a street-punk-turned-detective whose office is on the second floor of the Nichigeki Theater in Yokohama. Though his clients have to buy a movie ticket to get to his lair, Maiku somehow has the wherewithal to drive a Nash Metropolitan and indulge in frequent games of mah-jongg with his cronies. At one of those games, he gets involved in a quarrel between a yakuza and the parlor's Taiwanese "boy." The yakuza slashes out with his knife, Maiku's little finger goes flying, and the yakuza flees. After Maiku's finger is reattached, the Taiwanese, Yang Haiping (Yang Haiping), presents him with an envelope of money as a token of thanks for saving his life. Maiku refuses at first but takes it when Haiping offers him a job: to find his long-lost older brother.

Enlisting the help of a crooked immigration official and a fast-talking cabby (Kiyotaka Nanbara), Maiku learns that the brother is mixed up with an Asian gang called the Black Dog Society. Also, Haiping tells him that he, his brother, and younger sister were abandoned by their parents when they were children. In their struggle to survive, they became fiercely devoted to each other. Hearing this story, Maiku goes soft inside; he and his younger sister are also orphans (Maiku, noble chap, is working to put her through school). Haiping's case becomes his crusade. Haiping, however, has more in mind than a brotherly reunion. He is a hitman for the Dragon Union, a Taiwanese gang that is fighting a turf battle with the Black Dog Society. It is a gang that his brother once belonged to—and betrayed. Maiku soon has much more on his hands than a missing persons case.

Written by Daisuke Tengan, this story is good, basic genre material, with a few international twists. But Hayashi is not a genre director. He is essentially a fantasist, with a visual imagination unsurpassed among younger Japanese directors for its richness and sophistication. But it's an imagination of surfaces, incessantly calling attention to itself. Nagase, who understands the film's weightlessness all too well, plays Maiku with a tough-guy insouciance that amuses without being quite convincing. Most of the supporting actors go far over the top, including yakuza movie icon Jo Shishido, who hams shamelessly as Maiku's detective mentor.

The Chinese actors give the film whatever emotional weight it possesses. Perhaps they didn't understand that the movie was a goof. Perhaps Hayashi didn't want them to understand. Does it matter to the audience? From the evidence of the box office, not really. After all, they are the same people who drive those fake retro Figaros and Paos—and wonder where Maiku got that funny-looking car.

Waka Oyabun (1965)

YOUNG BOSS

Scr.: Hajime Takaiwa. *Dir.:* Kazuo Ikehiro. *Prod.:* Daiei. *Main cast:* Raizo Ichikawa, Yukiji Asaoka, Shiho Fujimura, Haruo Minami, Mikio Narita, Kei Sato. 86 mins.

STORY

The time: Late Meiji Period, following Japan's victory in its war with Russia (1904–5). Nanjo-gumi *oyabun* is fatally stabbed and, during the funeral, speculation swirls. Who ordered the hit? Suspicion centers on the Takizawa-gumi *oyabun*, whose gang is a fierce rival of the Nanjos. Then, the *oyabun*'s son, Takeshi (Raizo Ichikawa), a handsome young naval officer, appears at the funeral, causing more consternation, especially when he announces that he intends to take over the gang.

When the Takizawa *oyabun* leaves the funeral ceremonies, he is nearly knifed by a maddened Nanjo gangster. "Waka Oyabun" (Young Boss), as Takeshi is now known to his gang un-

derlings, apologizes for the incident. But when he hears from an usually reliable source that the Takizawa boss was indeed responsible for his father's murder, Waka Oyabun decides to confront him and his gang. His *kobun* beg to accompany him, but he decides to go alone. Finding Takizawa and his minions waiting on a bridge, Waka Oyabun more than holds his own in the ensuing battle, slicing off Takizawa's hand before the police arrive.

An idealistic young teacher has fallen in love with the beauteous Chiyoume (Shiho Fujimura), a young geisha, but she is a favorite of Odaguro, another local gang boss. Kyoko (Yukiji Asaoka), the head of the geisha house, consults with Waka Oyabun—for whom she has long carried a flame. He advises patience—though he is opposed to the whole business of buying and selling human flesh.

Kodan reciter Chochuken Kumoemon (Haruo Minami) is scheduled to perform at a Nanjo-run event but is detained at a nearby town by the Odaguro gang for nonpayment of a gambling debt. Waka Oyabun goes to his rescue—and challenges the Odaguro boss to a game of cards, with the winner getting Kumoemon. Odaguro agrees, but when he loses he accuses Waka Oyabun of palming a card—and stabs what he considers to be the guilty hand. Odaguro sees that he is wrong and reluctantly apologizes but is determined to get revenge for this humiliation. Soon after, a suspicious fire burns down the theater, but Kumoemon performs in the ruins. The *kodan* recital attracts Takizawa and his gang—but Takizawa is in a conciliatory mood. He does not blame Waka Oyabun for attacking him, it turns out; instead Takizawa admires his courage. He denies, however, ordering a hit on the old Nanjo-gumi *oyabun*.

While the town celebrates Japan's victory over Russia, Chiyoume runs away from the geisha house to escape Odaguro's clutches and goes to Waka Oyabun for shelter. When Odaguro and his men invade Nanjo's house demanding the geisha, he presents her with her head shaved—yet another insult to Odaguro's pride. He leaves but soon after an attempt is made on Waka Oyabun's life. He captures the would-be assassin—and learns that Odaguro ordered the hit not only on him, but his father. Waka Oyabun borrows a pistol from Takizawa—and goes out alone yet again, this time for revenge.

CRITIQUE

The first of an eight-part series that ran from 1965 to 1967, *Waka Oyabun* (Young Boss) was Daiei's attempt to cash in on the *ninkyo eiga* boom. Samurai drama star Raizo Ichikawa did not fit the standard image of a yakuza boss—part of the series' appeal. In addition to his unusual youth, Ichikawa projected stainless Japanese manhood of a sort more suited to his character's war hero past (and Ichikawa's samurai heroes) than his *oyabun* present. Even so, Ichikawa's Waka Oyabun was, not a colorless stiff, but a forceful, articulate leader who could outwit his opponents, as well as cut them down with his sword.

His love scenes with Yukiji Asaoka have zero sexual charge, however. Even when he proposes marriage, he keeps his distance, not even touching her hand. Asaoka, who has been chafing him throughout the film, tries to look overjoyed; but her smile is slightly tight, as though she is already girding herself for a married life not overflowing with erotic delights.

Kazuo Ikehiro's direction is mostly pedestrian, although in the staging of the final showdown between Waka Oyabun and the Odaguro gang, Ikehiro makes ingenious use of a train yard set at dusk, hiding his fighters in clouds of steam, while the shadows lengthen. The parallel struggle of Kyoko and the Nanjo gang through crowds of merrymakers as they rush to Waka Oyabun's rescue is anticlimactic, as it must be. The film's tweaking of *ninkyo eiga* convention does not extend to its one-against-all ending.

Wakaki Hi no Jirocho (1962)

THE YOUNG DAYS OF JIROCHO

Scr.: Takinosuke Ono. *Dir.:* Masahiro Makino. *Prod.:* Toei. *Main cast:* Kinnosuke Nakamura, Satomi Oka, Michiko Hoshi, Jerry Fujio, Tomoko Watanabe, Kiyoshi Atsumi. 89 mins.

STORY

Shimizu no Jirocho (Kinnosuke Nakamura) and his new bride Ocho (Satomi Oka) are approaching the town of Kofu when they encounter a procession of prisoners. The guards brutally push back the prisoners' sobbing womenfolk, angering Jirocho; his guide, Gon, however, advises him not to do anything rash and to instead circle around the town. A Kofu native, he knows that it is ruled by a yakuza gang acting in the name of the local magistrate and that anyone who crosses the gang ends up in jail—or dead. Soon after, Jirocho comes to the aid of a local man in despair over a gambling debt, giving him one ryo—a sum that effectively saves his life. The man, Sashi, protests that it is too much, but Jirocho only smiles.

Kansuke, the gang *oyabun*, tells a cowering merchant who has run up a large gambling debt, that he will forgive it if the merchant gives him his daughter, Otane. When the girl protests, the merchant slaps her and tells her she has no choice but to obey. Jirocho and Ocho decide to stay in town, but that night Kansuke and his cronies beat and wound Sashi, saying that he must have stolen the money. Gon, Sashi's friend, is outraged and wants to take on the whole gang, but Jirocho advises restraint. Instead, he goes to see Kansuke and introduces himself. The *oyabun* is suitably impressed—Jirocho's reputation has preceded him—but is taken aback when Jirocho pulls out a pistol and tells him to keep his hands off Gon, or else.

A band of Jirocho's men encounters three *chinpira* on the road and soon find themselves in a quarrel. To settle it, the tall, lanky Oishi (Jerry Fujio), whose eye has been slashed by a sword, takes on one of the *chinpira* in a fight. They punch each other silly, call the fight a draw—and become friends. The three *chinpira* join the band on their journey to Kofu. Arriving in town, they meet Jirocho, who apprises them of the situation. The three *chinpira* soon prove their mettle by rescuing the merchant's daughter from the clutches of Kansuke's gang, though two of them throw up their swords and surrender in the melee.

A woman gambler, Oko, is cleaning out Jirocho's men when Ishimatsu, the cool-headed second-in-command, catches her cheating, using sexual wiles to distract the horny gamblers. The pair reach an understanding, however, when they discover they both are of samurai origin.

Sashi dies and his friends want revenge. Jirocho comes up with a plan to rally the common people against Kansuke's gang. He sets it in motion with a showy funeral procession that Kansuke and his men disrupt. They take their quarrel to the *daikan* (magistrate) who decides in favor of Kansuke and has Jirocho and several of his men thrown in jail. There, Jirocho is beaten, but his spirit remains unbroken. Outside, Otake and the other survivors plot countermoves, while Kansuke uses Oko to round up Jirocho's men. A big confrontation is brewing—but to win it Jirocho must prove to the magistrate that, instead of protecting his interests, Kansuke and his gang are robbing him blind.

CRITIQUE

A light entertainment, with several rousing musical numbers, *Wakaki Hi no Jirocho* (The Young Days of Jirocho) is as close as the Japanese gang genre gets to Broadway. Even the fight scenes are staged with comic choreography, as well as with director Masahiro Makino's usual crispness and flair. Samurai swashbuckler star Kinnosuke Nakamura plays Jirocho as a saucy, shining prince of gangsters—more a Robin Hood than a typical gang *oyabun*. Noth-

ing, not even a beating by Kansuke's thugs, can wipe the confident smile off his face.

But though a hero in the storybook mold, with no past sorrows or forebodings of doom furrowing his brow, Nakamura's Jirocho does not hesitate to use bluff and stratagems to get his way. Also, instead of facing off against the evil *oyabun* with a sword, Jirocho confronts him with a pistol—and a mischievous grin. Notable among the by-players is Kiyoshi Atsumi, who would later win fame as Tora-san, the wandering *tekiya* (peddler) with an eye for the ladies but no luck in love. In *Wakaki Hi no Jirocho*, Atsumi plays a comic member of Jirocho's gang, who is hopeless at gambling but succeeds in smuggling a knife to his boss in jail. He is a Tora-san in embryo, in other words, just as the film itself is a template for countless later samurai shows on the small screen.

Watashi no Grandpa (2003)

MY GRANDPA

Scr/Dir: Yoichi Higashi. *Prod:* Toei. *Main cast:* Bunta Sugawara, Yoshiko Miyazaki, Mitsuru Harada, Kiriko Namino, Tadanobu Asano, Masato Ibu. 113 mins.

Some roles demand one actor, period, such as the grandfather in Yoichi Higashi's *Watashi no Grandpa* (My Grandpa). Plenty of Japanese actors can play folksy, warm-hearted granddads, but how many can do one who has recently served a sentence for murder and can still manhandle punks half a century younger? The list quickly narrows to one: Bunta Sugawara.

In movies like *Gendai Yakuza: Hitokiri Yota* (Street Mobster, 1972) and *Jingi Naki Tatakai* (Battles without Honor and Humanity, 1973) Sugawara did for movie yakuza what DeNiro did for Hollywood gangsters—blast away artificial conventions with a force that was just this side of manic (or some cases, psychotic). DeNiro may have had greater craft, but

Sugawara arguably had more raw power: He was a tsunami in a crewcut.

The years may have taken away the wildness, but the charisma and integrity are still intact. *Watashi no Grandpa* may be little more than a Sugawara vehicle, but he holds the screen effortlessly every minute he is on. Perhaps the real parallel is not DeNiro, who is now playing clownish parodies of his greatest roles, but Clint Eastwood, who has eased into old age on the screen with grace, dignity, and self-deprecating humor.

This film, like the one with Clint as an aged astronaut, strains credibility, but entertainingly. As it begins, an aging gangster, Kenzo (Sugawara), has just been released from prison after serving a thirteen-year stretch for killing two yakuza. He arrives, looking as though he has just come from a relaxing soak in the *ofuro* (tub), at the home of his salaryman son (Mitsuru Harada). His perky daughter-in-law (Yoshiko Miyazaki) and cute thirteen-year-old granddaughter, Tamako (Satomi Ishida), are also there to greet him, but not his estranged wife (Kiriko Namino), who knows Kenzo too well to believe that he can stay out of trouble—and would rather not hang around to deal with the results.

Tamako, however, takes an instant liking to the man she is soon calling "grandpa" (or rather, "guranpa") especially when he subdues teenage punks who are harassing her and a sweet-but-nerdy friend. She has also noticed that, far from being regarded as a pariah by the neighborhood, he is welcomed as a returning hero.

Among those giving him a warm reception is Shinichi (Tadanobu Asano), a phlegmatic bar master who is the son of Kenzo's old friend. Among those less enthusiastic is the shiny-domed boss (Masato Ibu) of the Hikita gang, two of whose members Kenzo cut to pieces.

The trouble started in the bubble-economy days, when the gang was in the *jiageya* game, forcing local merchants to sell their property to crooked real estate speculators. When their harassment resulted in the death of Kenzo's friend, he took his revenge—and ended up in the slammer.

Despite his crinkly smile and easygoing ways, Kenzo still has the same strong sense of justice and willingness to mix it up, come what may. He also has his old knack for making friends, adding not only Tamako, but the neighborhood bully boys to a long list. Before he can enjoy his happy Golden Years, however, he must settle a score with Hikita and his gang, with Tamako serving as an unwilling pawn.

Based on an award-winning novel by Yasutaka Tsutsui, *Watashi no Grandpa* is Sugawara's first semi-action role in twelve years, since his turn as a boxing coach in Junji Sakamoto's *Ote* (Checkmate). Now pushing seventy, he can still subdue the bad guys with a throw or a sword, without looking as though he'll need a respirator the moment the camera is turned off. He also plays well opposite newcomer Satomi Ishida as Tamako. Where some actors might turn on the smarmy avuncular charm, Sugawara remains, well, Sugawara—the ideal cool granddad.

Meanwhile, Yoichi Higashi, who won the Silver Bear prize at the 1996 Berlin Film Festival for his childhood drama *E no Naka no Boku no Mura* (Village of Dreams), shows off Sugawara to best advantage, while keeping his own directorial personality in the background. Can you tell, as Howard Hawks famously asked, "who the devil made it"? Perhaps, in the film's understanding portrayal of youth and its depiction of development's impact on traditional communities—both Higashi specialties.

Not that it matters to the audience, who will come to *Watashi no Grandpa*, first and foremost, to see Sugawara in action, the fires banked, but still glowing—a yakuza master for the ages. Who needs Vermeer lighting when you've got a yakuza master for the ages?

Wild Life (1997)

Scr.: Shinji Aoyama, Kumi Sato. *Dir.:* Shinji Aoyama. *Prod.:* Bitters End. *Main cast:* Kosuke Toyohara, Ken Mitsuishi, Mickey Curtis, Yuna Natsuo. 102 mins.

The title of Shinji Aoyama's *Wild Life* is semi-ironic. The hero, Hiroki Sakai (Kosuke Toyohara), is a *kugishi*—a professional adjuster of the pins in pachinko machines—whose life has settled into a dull routine. A phlegmatic, self-deprecating sort, Sakai accepts this existence as a given, until he is roused from his boredom by several blasts from his past. One is Mizoguchi (Ken Mitsuishi), a thin, nervous man who once ran a game center for Sakai's boss but quit after being robbed and brutally beaten by yakuza thugs. Now, Mizoguchi is out for revenge and wants Sakai's help. Another is his boss's daughter, Rie (Yuna Natsuo), grown into slender, sexy womanhood since Sakai last saw her six years ago—and eager to renew her acquaintance with him, despite the objections of a nerdy boyfriend. Without understanding why, Sakai becomes the target of a yakuza boss and his crew, who are convinced that he has a mysterious envelope and, later, an incriminating videotape. Though Sakai tries, sensibly, to stay out of trouble, he is forced into action when his boss, the bearded and pony-tailed Tsumura (Mickey Curtis), is abducted by the yakuza, and the police refuse to help. But while riding to the rescue, Sakai learns that the good guys, including his boss, have spots on their white hats and the truth of this tangled affair is not what it seems.

As Sakai, Kosuke Toyohara underplays with ironic intent: he is diffident with the ladies, polite to the tough guys, and blasé in the face of danger. He also packs a devastating punch and has an unerring aim with a full can of beer. He glides through his part with a comic nonchalance while illuminating his character's motives. When, at the end, Sakai laughs uproariously at the boss's offer to join his gang,

we can laugh with him, understanding not only the joke but why he thinks it is so funny. Breaking his story into eight segments (all have English titles, including such familiar borrowings as *Light in August* and *As Time Goes By*) and using one cut per scene, Aoyama tells Sakai's story with concision, rhythm, and, most of all, humor.

But for all its cartoonish moments, *Wild Life* is less a genre send-up than a meticulously stylized exercise in genre stretching. It delivers the entertainment goods, including fresh takes on yakuza movie conventions, while exploring broader themes, including the unpredictability of life and the elusiveness of truth. It wants to be an existential black comedy, with a thriller punch.

Some of Aoyama's effects are ingenious. In one interrogation scene, the camera circles about, focusing first on the detective, then on the person he is questioning. In one sweep, that person is Tsumura, in the next, Sakai, in the next Tsumura again—around and around, the interrogator's questions and the interrogatee's answers matching perfectly, in a surreal merry-go-round. Though his detective gets nowhere, Aoyama has, in his third feature in two years, come a long way indeed.

Yaju no Seishun (1963)

YOUTH OF THE BEAST

Scr.: Ichiro Ikeda. *Dir.:* Seijun Suzuki. *Prod.:* Nikkatsu. *Main cast:* Jo Shishido, Ichiro Kijima, Misako Suzuki, Shoji Kobayashi, Kizo Shin, Eiji Go. 92 mins.

STORY

A mysterious man in a white hat, Mizuno (Jo Shishido), stomps a yakuza in an argument over a pachinko ball. Later, Mizuno walks into a nightclub, spends a fortune, and calmly tells the gangsters who run the place that he has no money. They take him down the stairs to the boss's lair—a large room with a huge one-way mirror that overlooks the club floor. After a bit of fancy gunplay, however, the stranger reverses the power balance—and the boss offers him a huge salary (far more than his bar bill) to work for the gang.

The real boss of the gang, it turns out, is Nomoto (Shoji Kobayashi), an effeminate type who likes to stroke his pet Persian—and toss knives at newcomers, as Mizuno discovers when he walks into Nomoto's headquarters. There, Mizuno meets his new colleagues, including the bumpkinish Minami (Hideaki Esumi), who later goes with him to his hotel—and is deeply impressed with Mizuno's gun collection. Mizuno makes Minami a friend for life by giving him a snazzy rifle.

Mizuno and Minami shake down a real-estate office that is under the protection of the rival Sanko gang. They defeat the Sanko thugs, with the aid of Minami's new rifle, and deliver 3 million yen in cash to their boss. His investment in Mizuno is already paying off; Nomoto decides to put him on the payroll. Mizuno goes to a memorial service for Takeshita, a deceased police detective, and offers condolences to his widow (Misako Watanabe), but when he sees cops coming, runs. Takeshita committed suicide with his young girlfriend—a huge embarrassment to both the force and his devoted wife. Mizuno visits the woman who runs the call girl ring that Takeshita's girlfriend belonged to. After trying to seduce him, she offers him a job: kill Nomoto and one of his mistresses. "What if I like her better than you?" Mizuno asks.

Mizuno brazens his way into the presence of the Sanko-gumi boss, Onodera (Kizo Shin), and offers to spy on the Nomoto gang, for a fee. The stunned Onodera accepts. Mizuno learns that the power behind the call girl ring is Nomoto's gay half-brother, Hide (Tamio Kawachi). His mother was a *pan-pan* (prostitute), Minami tells him—and Hide becomes homicidal if anyone mentions that fact. Mizuno hunts up Hide, calls his mother a *pan-pan*, and nearly gets knifed—all in an effort to learn the name of Hide's partner. Mizuno hears about a big drug deal the Nomoto gang is about to pull off—and tells Onodera about it. "Just get the money, not the drugs," Mizuno advises, "Otherwise, they'll think Nomoto did it."

Flashback: Mizuno was a cop who was sent to prison on charges of embezzlement and illegal force—charges he stoutly denied. While he was in lockup, Takeshita took care of Mizuno's tubercular wife until her death, a favor Mizuno could never repay. Mizuno is convinced that Takeshita's suicide, like his own bust, was a gang put-up job. Somebody murdered his benefactor—and Mizuno is going to find out who. The money snatch succeeds—and the boss of the ripped-off gang demands a second payment. Nomoto blanches—he doesn't have that kind of money. A Nomoto gangster IDs Mizuno as a cop he saw three years ago in Kobe. To save his skin, Mizuno rats on his Sanko-gumi friends. Playing two sides against the middle is a dangerous game, he is discovering—and there are several more innings to go.

CRITIQUE

Seijun Suzuki's twenty-eighth film, *Yaju no Seishun* (Youth of the Beast) was also the first in which Suzuki gave full vent to the flamboyant style that was to become his trademark—part 1960s, anything-go-goes extravagance; part home-grown *ero-guro-nonsense* (Japanese-English for "eroticism, grotesquery, nonsense"); part Suzuki's own deliriously anarchic and inventive brain. The nightclub with its huge one-way mirror that makes the guests look like the occupants of a giant fish tank. The movie screen in Onodera's office that plays highlights from Nikkatsu films, while similarly lurid action unfolds in front of it. The shot of Jo Shishido getting his puffy cheek plastered against a glass divider, while a hood drives a blade under his fingernails. The bizarre spectacle of Nomoto whipping a drug-addled woman in his garden, as the wind blows up a red sand-storm; and the equally strange sight of Nomoto himself, heaving knives at his victims because guns are "boring."

The usual explanation of these and other outrages against genre conventions and cine-matic rules (particularly the stricture against "taking the audience out of the movie") was Suzuki's own boredom with the repetitive task of cranking out B programers for Nikkatsu. Perhaps, but the gang movie was a relatively new form for him—most of his previous twen-ty-seven films were in other genres. Also, *Yaju no Seishun* was only his second film with the equally flamboyant Jo Shishido as a star. (His first, the action comedy *Tantei Jimusho 23 Kutabare Akutodomo* [Detective Bureau 2–3: Go to Hell Bastards, 1963] laid the groundwork for future excesses.) In any case, the combina-tion of star and story—a disgraced ex-cop takes revenge against two warring gangs for his own frame-up and his colleague's murder—became the catalyst for Suzuki's first masterpiece, a film that rises above its absurdities and clichés into a realm of pure, delirious cool.

Yaju Shisubeshi: Fukushuhen (1997)

THE BEAST MUST DIE: REVENGE
Scr.: Toshiyuki Morioka. *Dir.:* Masato Hironishi. *Prod.:* Daiei. *Main cast:* Kazuya Kimura, Toshiya Nagasawa. 86 mins.

For a film, the right title can spell the differ-ence between box office success or failure. David O. Selznick wanted to call a thriller about postwar intrigue in Austria's capital *A Night in Vienna*. But fellow-producer Alexan-der Korda, and scriptwriter Graham Greene, held out for the original title: *The Third Man*. It's lucky for us they did. Likewise enjoying a long shelf is the main title of *Yaju Shisubeshi: Fukushuhen* (The Beast Must Die: Revenge),

based on a best-selling novel by Haruhiko Oyabu. The novel was first filmed in 1959 as *Yaju Shisubeshi*, with Tatsuya Nakadai starring as a graduate student "beast" who plots the perfect crime. Another version was made in 1980, with Yusaku Matsuda playing a former war photographer who turns to crime in rebel-lion against Japan's straightjacket society.

The third and latest "beast" is Kazuya Kimura, who looks more the pretty-boy gigolo than the cold-blooded killer. But Kimura is ap-propriately affectless playing a man who is a printer by day, a ruthless criminal by night. Watching his cold, dead eyes as he took aim at yet another victim, I saw that his handsome face was the ideal mask for his purpose. Looks may not kill, but they make it easier to get in range.

Directed by Masato Hironishi, from a script by prolific scenarist Toshiyuki Morioka (*Fudo*, *Risutora Daimon*, *Chinpira*), Yaju traces the nefarious career of Kunihiko Date (Kimu-ra), the aforementioned printer. He happens upon a cop staking out a druggie's hideout one rainy night, runs him over with his BMW, shoots him with his own gun, and drives off, barely breaking a sweat. Now equipped with a shooter and a badge, Date targets the boss of a gambling den for the Shanghai Mafia. On the pretext of making an arrest, Date handcuffs the boss to his fancy foreign car and proceeds to beat his shiny-domed bodyguard half to death. He then walks off with a suitcase full of 10,000 yen notes, as casually as though he'd just passed through a supermarket checkout line. Mean-while, the police, led by long-haired detective Katsu Oki (Toshiya Nagasawa), are hot on the trail of the cop killer. Obviously, it was a mob hit or, wonders the intuitive Oki, was it some-thing else?

Not satisfied with his new-found fortune, Date plans to rob an armored truck loaded with 300 million yen in cash. Needing a driver, he recruits a former colleague who is out of work and dying of cancer. The heist is successful, but the cough-wracked driver begs Date to put him out of his misery and take care of his widow and child. Date obliges. What we have here is the dirtiest of dirty heroes, who will do whatever it takes, including murder, to commit the perfect crime. His ultimate object is to become a free agent, beyond the bounds of God and man.

This is a monstrous ambition, and the man who achieves it is a beast who must, of course, die. Date, however, has a wretched past that makes his crimes more understandable, if not excusable. Also, he is kind to his younger sister, laughing and joking with her while taking a stroll on the beach. Finally, he can shoot with consummate skill and tool his Honda motorbike with style. The beast, in short, is a cool dude, whose fashionable gear, including replicas of the guns he uses to snuff his victims, are offered to fans in a drawing by distributor Daiei. Step right up!

All this, as well as the shock ending, may alarm the more tender-minded, but *Yaju* issues a strong, frank appeal to the anti-social loner in all of us. Made quickly and on the cheap, it nonetheless achieves an impact that more carefully crafted films often lack. There is a kind of instructive purity in its absolute amorality. It is not so much a cautionary fable about a human monster as an unapologetic plunge into a male fantasy world. "Sooner murder an infant in its cradle than nurse unacted desires," wrote William Blake. The makers of *Yaju Shisubeshi* must have been listening.

Yakuza, The (1975)

Scr.: Paul Schrader, Robert Towne (from a story by Leonard Schrader). *Dir.:* Sydney Pollack. *Prod.:* Warner Bros. *Main cast:* Robert Mitchum, Ken Takakura, Brian Keith, Herb Edelman, Richard Jordan, Keiko Kishi, Eiji Okada, James Shigeta, Kyosuke Machida, Christine Kokubo. 123 mins. [Japan]; 112 mins. [U.S.]

STORY

Jiro Kato (Kyosuke Machida), an emissary of gang boss Toshiro Tono (Eiji Okada), visits the Los Angeles office of businessman George Tanner (Brian Keith), with the sleeve of a coat belonging to Tanner's daughter Louise. If Tanner doesn't return to Tokyo, says Kato, he will come again—with more than a piece of cloth. Tanner tells his friend Harry Kilmer (Robert Mitchum), a retired P.I., that a yakuza gang has kidnapped Louise and urges him to go to Ken Tanaka (Ken Takakura), a mutual gangster acquaintance, for help. Harry reluctantly agrees and leaves for Tokyo together with Dusty (Richard Jordan), Tanner's young bodyguard. In Tokyo, Harry stays with Oliver Wheat (Herb Edelman), another friend from the Occupation days. Now a college teacher specializing in Japan-America relations, Oliver has a large collection of Japanese swords and guns in his spacious house.

Harry goes to see Eiko (Keiko Kishi), his former lover, at a bar she runs called Harry Kilmer House. Left alone with her baby daughter after the firebombing of Tokyo, Eiko became a black market dealer to survive. Once, when she was sexually assaulted by U.S. soldiers, Harry saved her and spent time in the stockade as a result. They fell in love, but Eiko refused his offer of marriage. Also, her brother Ken, who returned to Japan in 1951 after six years in the Philippine jungles, opposed their union. Ken later became a successful gangster, while Harry left Japan, after giving Eiko money to buy her bar. When he meets her and her daughter Hanako (Christine Kokubo) at the bar Harry realizes that nothing has changed—Eiko is still in love with him, but won't marry him. She does tell him that Ken is running a *kendo* school in Kyoto, however.

When Harry arrives at Ken's school, he gets less than a warm reception though Ken acknowledges his obligation to help him. Harry asks him to intervene with Tono, saying that Tanner intended to deliver the guns to Tono but lost the shipment. Ken says that he hasn't been a yakuza for ten years, but promises to try. Harry, Dusty, and Ken burst into a temple where Tono's men are holding Louise. They rescue the girl, but in the ensuing scuffle Ken kills two of Tono's men. Kato arrives in time to note the damage—and tells Ken that Tono is watching him.

With his daughter safe, Tanner says he will talk to Tono about Ken. Ken says he is not worried; Tono violated the yakuza code by kidnapping Louise and can't move against him without the approval of the other clans—which he is not likely to get. Eiko, however, says that Tono is gunning for Ken and tells Harry that Ken's older brother Goro, a gang advisor, can help. Goro, however, informs Harry that Ken is a lone wolf who broke with the gang against his advice and is thus no longer under any obligation to him. Also, Tono has told the other *oyabun* that Ken is under a sentence of death. If Goro intervenes, he will compromise his position as a neutral advisor—which is what Tono wants. Ken has three alternatives: beg Tono's forgiveness, wait for Tono to kill him, or kill Tono himself. Ken's choice becomes clear after a series of assaults by Tono's men. Harry offers to help him—and together they make a climactic assault on Tono's headquarters.

CRITIQUE

Released shortly after Kinji Fukasaku had thoroughly trashed the myth of the noble gangster in the Jingi Naki Tatakai series, *The Yakuza* is a culturally sensitive, if highly romanticized, take on contemporary gangs. Though Paul and Leonard Schrader had researched the gangs and gang films before the latter wrote the story and the former the script for *The Yakuza*, director Sydney Pollack brought in Hollywood script doctor Robert Towne for a rewrite. And Pollack ended up with what Toei producer Koji Shundo termed a "boring melodrama" (*Ninkyo Eiga-den*, p. 143).

Shundo argued that no wife of a yakuza would be stupid enough to openly carry on an affair with a foreigner, as Keiko Kishi's Eiko did with Robert Mitchum's Harry Kilmer. Also, complained Shundo, Ken Takakura's Ken was entirely too complaisant about these goings-on. "It was so idiotic it made me angry—at one point I shouted that I was through," Shundo later reminisced (ibid.). But though Shundo disliked Pollack ("He looked down on Japanese"), Shundo got along famously with Mitchum, whom he described as "on my side" and "a real gentleman" (ibid., p. 144).

Despite the film's absurdities, as well as all of its earnest, inflated talk about the "spirit of the sword" and the "sacredness of *giri* (duty)" —Mitchum gives one of his best performances as the world-weary but still spry Harry Kilmer. (Mitchum was in his late fifties when he took this physically demanding role.) Most foreign actors look out of place in Japanese settings; Mitchum fits right in, at once respectful of the local niceties and certain of his own identity. Few actors, of any age, look so at home in their own skins. Ken Takakura, by this time nearing the end of his career as a yakuza film star, turns in a competent, if tamped down, performance as the noble ex-gangster Ken Tanaka.

Part of the problem is Takakura's action scenes: Pollack films them with tight shots and fast cuts that blunt the beauty and power of Takakura's sword work. Also, the climactic confrontation is absurdly staged. While the enemy hoods face off against Takakura, both sides armed with nothing but swords, Mitchum advances with guns blazing. Any yakuza in his right mind would flee in the face of this American-style firepower; instead, the bad guys stand and die for the *ninkyo* code. Shundo was right.

Yakuza Keibatsushi: Lynch! (1969)

A HISTORY OF YAKUZA PUNISHMENTS: LYNCH!

Scr.: Yoshihiro Kakefuda, Teruo Ishii. *Dir.:* Teruo Ishii. *Prod.:* Toei. *Main cast:* Ichiro Sugai, Hiroshi Miyauchi, Bunta Sugawara, Yoshiko Fujita, Renji Ishibashi, Shin'ichiro Hayashi, Yoko Koyama, Minoru Oki, Hisaya Ito, Teruo Yoshida. 96 mins.

STORY

The time: the Edo Period (1600–1868). The Kuroiso gang defeats the rival Takeichi clan in a pitched battle. At a banquet celebrating the victory, the Kuroiso *oyabun* (Ichiro Sugai) has his men draw their swords and praises those with the most blood on the blade. He is about to punish Shinkichi (Hiroshi Miyauchi), a young gangster with a clean sword, when Tsune (Bunta Sugawara), one of his best and bravest men, speaks in Shinkichi's defense— and backs up his words by slicing off a finger.

Tsune has a romantic interlude with the *oyabun*'s mistress, Oren (Yoshiko Fujita), who happens to be Shinkichi's elder sister. They are discovered in flagrante delicto by Mamushi no Roku (Renji Ishibashi), one of the *oyabun*'s men and no friend of Tsune's. Then, to compound Tsune's troubles, a young *kobun*, Shohei (Shin'ichiro Hayashi), steals money from a gambling den for his lover, Setsu (Yoko Koyama). Roku, learning about this theft, puts the squeeze on Shohei.

The *oyabun* smells a rat, however, and Roku, to win the old man's favor and save his own skin, turns canary. Roku, his nefariousness knowing no bounds, tries to rape Setsu. Though Shohei gets revenge for this deed, he and Tsune are punished for their crimes by the *oyabun*—with Shohei losing an ear and Tsune, an eye. Revolted by the brutality of these punishments, the gang's *daigashi* (gambling house manager) unleashes his own.

The time: The Meiji Period (1868–1912). Ogata (Minoru Oki) of the Akiba gang cuts down the Sakurai gang's *oyabun* at the order of his *daigashi*, Iwakiri (Hisaya Ito). Instead of getting his expected reward, however, Ogata finds himself caught in a trap devised by the devious Iwakiri—and sent into exile. When Ogata returns, he is subjected to the horrific punishment dictated by gang rules—though he eventually takes his revenge on Iwakiri.

The time: The present day. One hundred million yen is stolen from the Hashiba gang. The gang's *daigashi*, Shimazu (Takashi Fujiki), and his crew subject a suspect to the tortures of the damned, including beating and branding, but he refuses to spill, so they lock him in a car and compact him in a car crusher. The thief, it turns out, was Hirose (Teruo Yoshida), an expert safecracker employed by the rival Omura gang. Shimazu whacks the Hashiba *oyabun*, takes over the gang, and starts a war with the Omuras. Ironically, he is saved from a tight corner by Hirose. When Shimazu finally learns where the money is hidden—in a warehouse guarded by Omura gangsters, he launches a raid that results in slaughter—and a surprise ending.

CRITIQUE

The seventh in Teruo Ishii's series of *ero-guro* films, *Yakuza Keibatsushi: Lynch!* (A History of Yakuza Punishments) represented a shift from the "erotic" to the "grotesque" side of the equation, with the opening credits featuring a tour d'horizon of gangster torture through the centuries, which range from the usual slashings and burnings to an ingenious Edo Era method of slowly drowning a victim by strapping him to a wooden cylinder and whirling him about in a pool of water.

The film aspires to be a yakuza *Mondo Cane*, but Ishii tells fairly conventional stories of gang life in three eras: the Edo, Meiji, and modern day, using leading Toei stars. Though it makes little mention of contemporary headlines, save of the crime-page sort, the film reflects the street violence of the late 1960s, when radicals were bloodying cops in mass demonstrations and each other in sectarian squabbles.

Intended by its producers as sheer exploitation, *Yakuza Keibatsushi: Lynch!* nonetheless defied industry conventional wisdom with its three-part omnibus structure, which was was then thought to be a recipe for box office catastrophe, along with its "educational" explanation of the rules of yakuza society—and the penalties for failing to observe them. Also, by presenting the ugly realities of gang life, however gaudily, the film laid the groundwork for the *jitsuroku rosen* films of the early 1970s. As in much of Ishii's work, a veneer of stylishness and an undercurrent of playfulness make the shock scenes (not to mention the crude makeup and effects) easier to take. Today *Yakuza Keibatsushi: Lynch!* and other of Ishii's *ero-guro* films are regarded abroad as cult classics, while his better, if less flamboyant, gang films have been relegated to obscurity—the unfairest punishment of all.

Yakuza no Hakaba: Kuchinashi no Hana (1976)

YAKUZA BURIAL: JASMINE FLOWER

Scr.: Kazuo Kasahara. *Dir.:* Kinji Fukasaku. *Prod.:* Toei. Cast: Tetsuya Watari, Meiko Kaji, Tatsuo Umemiya, Hideo Murata, Jiro Yabuki, Mikio Narita, Nagisa Oshima, Nobuo Kaneko. 96 mins.

STORY

Osaka police detective Kuroiwa (Tetsuya Watari) is a hard case who may be good at his job but is not above planting evidence on a *chinpira*—bullets identical to ones fired at a recent pro-baseball game—and beating a hapless punk to within an inch of his life to make him confess. His superiors try to rein him in, but Kuroiwa is too stubborn—or simply dysfunctional—to listen.

Kuroiwa and his casually corrupt boss (Nobuo Kaneko) met with leaders of the Nishida-gumi in an effort to head off a war between the gang and the equally powerful Yamashiro-gumi. The gang's Number Two, Sugi, assures the visiting cops that they are gamblers, not warriors—and offers Kuroiwa a packet of money as "carfare." Kuroiwa bluntly rejects it and walks out of the meeting—but on the way to the door gets into an argument with Iwata (Tatsuo Umemiya), a gang subboss who is angry at Kuroiwa for hassling two of his men —including the one he arrested on a phony charge.

Kuroiwa spends the night with his girlfriend, a club hostess whose gangster husband Kuroiwa killed several years ago in the course of a bust. He feels responsible for her—even though she basically sees him as a cash machine. The two *chinpira* Kuroiwa rousted try to get even by attacking him in disguise but he thrashes them; when Kuroiwa threatens to bust them, they promise to do anything for him. He relents—and Iwata later expresses his gratitude to Kuroiwa for his broad-mindedness.

Kuroiwa trails Kanai, a Kusumoto-gumi *shatei*, and threatens to arrest him for carrying a gun. Kuroiwa ends up in the gang office, with yet another gang boss trying to bribe him. Kuroiwa burns the proffered cash with his lighter. Enraged, the boss (Mikio Narita) orders Kanai to find out what Kuroiwa knows about the rival Nishida-gumi. A war breaks out between the Nishida and Yamashiro gangs after Kanai is clipped for refusing to repay a gambling debt. Keiko Matsumoto (Meiko Kaji), the wife of an imprisoned Nishida-gumi boss, warns Kuroiwa that he may be in trouble if investigators find out about his beef with Kanai. She also invites him to go with her to Tottori Prefecture, on the Japan Sea coast, for a much-needed respite. He agrees and, while they are taking a stroll on the beach, they talk about their pasts. She tells him that her father, a Korean, died before he could return to his homeland—then she and Kuroiwa enjoy a passionate pas de deux in the surf.

The police official in charge of quelling the gang war (Nagisa Oshima) announces that a truce may be in sight—but that the Nishida-gumi may break up. Shigeta (Hideo Murota), a police academy classmate of Kuroiwa's, urges Kuroiwa to help dissolve the Nishida gang. "It's your quickest route to promotion," he advises. Shigeta also tells Kuroiwa to marry his hostess girlfriend. Enraged that the police know so much about his affairs, Kuroiwa smells an informing rat. Later, at a party celebrating the merger of the Nishida-gumi with another gang, Kuroiwa gets into a fight with Iwata, who is angered by the cop's attentions to Keiko. By the end, both men are a bloody mess—and become fast friends. As the police pressure on the gang grows more intense, Kuroiwa is faced with a choice: it's either his career or his new lover and the man whom he has come to regard as a brother.

CRITIQUE

Kinji Fukasaku's *Yakuza no Hakaba: Kuchinashi no Hana* (Yakuza Burial: Jasmine Flower) is not, strictly speaking, a yakuza movie—the hero is a cop of the dirtier-than-Dirty-Harry variety—but the film is thematically and stylistically similar to Fukasaku's *Jingi Naki Tatakai* (Battles without Honor and Humanity) series and *Jingi no Hakaba* (Graveyard of Honor). Also, the cop not only bears a strong resemblance to Watari's gangster hero in *Jingi no Hakaba*, particularly in his self-destructive trashing of his career, but becomes a yakuza in all but name, right down to his vow of gang brotherhood with Tatsuo Umemiya's hot-tempered boss.

Yakuza no Hakaba, in fact, is a sort of summation for the entire *jitsuroku rosen* genre, which was already in steep decline at the time of the film's 1976 release and by the end of the decade, all but dead. Though over ambitious—it crams altogether too much plot into its ninety-six-minute running time, while trying to sketch its hero's decline and fall—the film is Fukasaku in top form. Its gritty, explosive, briskly paced exposé shows a world sunk in terminal corruption in which cops and crooks are all but indistinguishable.

Playing a man who can no longer hide his rage at this world, Tetsuya Watari delivers a performance that is beyond edgy, just as watching a fatal car crash is beyond exciting. Not just another rogue cop, his Kuroiwa is a man on the verge of a breakdown, whose nervous tick is slamming his fist into his palm. His salvation turns out to be two of the people he is supposedly fighting—but even they cannot save him from himself. He gives what could have been another over-the-top essay on underworld violence, the resonance of tragedy.

Yakuza Way, The (1998)

Scr./Dir.: Shundo Okawa. *Prod.:* Team Okuyama, S. T. P. International, Inc. *Main cast:* Riki Takeuchi, Eugene Nomura, Maya Hoshino, George Cheung. 82 mins.

STORY

Kanuma (Riki Takeuchi) arrives at L.A. airport where he is greeted by Takada (George Cheung), a smarmy Japanese-American man. Takada drives him to a club in a Hispanic neighborhood, where they meet a scowling hulk of a drug dealer. After the dealer indulges in an outburst of homicidal rage, Kanuma buys two kilos of cocaine, and a shaky Takada drives him back to the airport. Yoko, a flight attendant, has a passionate reunion with Kanuma at Marina Del Ray. It is their first meeting in three years, since he was sent to prison. Kanuma tells Yoko that he wants to quit the yakuza, marry her, and go straight. They spend the night together, but when they come out of the hotel the next morning hitmen shoot at them, killing Yoko, but not before Kanuma gets a good look at them.

Takada tells Kanuma that their contact sold them out. Kanuma is determined to get revenge, no matter what. That, he tells Takada, is the yakuza way. Kanuma has Takada drive him back to the club, but while Kanuma is inside, settling a beef with the punks who work there, Takada is robbed by a Japanese couple. Hauling the briefcase full of coke, they make their getaway in a jeep, with Kanuma in hot pursuit in Takada's car. The police join the chase and trap Kanuma, allowing the thieves to escape.

The thieves, Eiji (Eugene Nomura) and Rika (Maya Hoshino), celebrate their close call, but Rika urges Eiji to stop taking such risks. Meanwhile, the police are interrogating Kanuma. When they are about to arrest him for wasting the punks in the club, he grabs a gun and makes his getaway. "You can't escape American justice," an acne-scarred detective warns, but Kanuma is in no mood to listen. Instead, he make his way to a bail bond office run by an old Japanese acquaintance. The bondsman knows Vincent, the drug dealer who double crossed Kanuma. The bondsman also tells Kanuma that his mother is dead and his sister has gone missing. Kanuma's mother came to Los Angeles when he was a boy, leaving him behind in Japan, and he never saw her again.

After nearly getting ripped off trying to sell the coke, Eiji and Rika ponder their next move. Eiji tells her she'll be safer if they split up. Rika is worried that they'll both be killed. Not long after, Rika is kidnapped by punks working for Vincent. She calls Eiji and tells him to bring the coke to a junkyard. Before Eiji can ride to the rescue, however, he is spotted by Kanuma and a fight ensues. Kanuma is getting the upper hand when Eiji tells him that Vincent has snatched Rika. Kanuma decides to go after Vincent alone, but Eiji insists on joining him— and together they gather an arsenal. After a brush with the cops, Eiji and Kanuma encounter Vincent and his gang at the junkyard. A shootup begins, which ends in victory for Eiji and Kanuma and rescue for Rika. Vincent survives, however—and plots his next move. Meanwhile, Takada is snitching on Kanuma to

Ray, the aforementioned detective, who again vows that Kanuma will not escape justice, American-style.

CRITIQUE
A made-for-export product, *The Yakuza Way* is another in a long line of Japanese films that goes wrong once the characters board the plane at Narita for foreign climes. Out of their element, but determined not to show it, they latch onto the nearest clichés. The results range from the gratingly racist to the risibly clueless. *The Yakuza Way* is more on the clueless side, though director Shundo Okawa has evidently made an intensive study of Hollywood action movies. He knows genre formulas inside out, considerately staging a shoot-out every ten minutes, but seems to have recruited most of his bad guys from jails and homeless shelters and his cops from Central Casting. Meanwhile, he allows his Japanese actors to indulge in every sort of excess, with Riki Takeuchi being the biggest offender. Takeuchi can play a mean action scene, looking the quintessence of cool as he blasts baddies from his Harley, but struts and sneers like a parody of a yakuza tough.

He engages in similar antics in his Japanese films, but in the hands of a Miike or other good director, Takeuchi can also play a character, not merely indulge in mannerisms. In *The Yakuza Way*, particularly in his scenes with foreign actors, he swaggers about clenched and closed off, somewhat like a xenophobic *Terminator* robot. It can be funny, this hyper-macho act, but the joke is on Takeuchi—and the movie.

Yamaguchi Gaiden Kyushu Shinko Sakusen (1974)

THE TATTOOED HITMAN
Scr.: Hiroji Takada (U.S. version: Hiroji Takada, Jack Sholder). *Dir.:* Kosaku Yamashita (called "Ko Yamashita" in U.S. version). *Prod.:* Toei (U.S.

version: New Line). *Main cast:* Bunta Sugawara, Tatsuo Umemiya, Hiroki Matsukata, Tsunehiko Watase. 106 mins. [Japan]; 88 mins. [U.S.]

STORY (U.S. VERSION)

Ishino (Tatsuo Umemiya), a rising young boss, is shot by a hitman at a construction site in Kyushu. His gang brother, Ginji (Bunta Sugawara), vows revenge. But when he wreaks havoc on the office of the Sakaguchi-gumi—the gang Ginji believes responsible—Ishino orders him to get out of town. Ginji ends up working with an Osaka gangster named Blackie, who shakes down store owners for fun and profit. Ginji also reunites with Fusako (Mayumi Nagisa), an old flame who is now working as a counter girl at a pachinko parlor.

While playing pachinko, Ginji observes a beef between a punk, who is using a magnet to direct the balls, and the parlor attendants. They take the discussion outside, where the attendants beat the punk and toss him off the end of a dock. Ginji rescues him, learns that his name in Ken (Tsunehiko Watase), and takes him to Fusako's apartment, where Ginji is staying. That night Ken watches Ginji and Fusako make love—and we learn that she is already carrying Ginji's baby.

After trying to rip off a gambling den—and getting beaten by Blackie's men and stabbed in the hand by Blackie—Ken finds work with Joe, a gang drug dealer. Hearing this news, Ginji bulls his way into Joe's office, tells him that guys who sell that shit are nothing but shit—and forces Ken to dump a packet of white powder out the window. Ginji and Ken break into Blackie's office, snatch money, and, after a dustup with Blackie's crew, depart before the cops come calling. A celebratory session with prostitutes leaves them both with the clap. Ginji cures it with self-administered shots of penicillin—including one for Fusako.

His exile over, Ginji goes to see Ishino, who is now a power in the Syndicate. Together, they go to a club, where Ginji is relegated to the second table. He is introduced to several gangsters, including Sonny (Hiroki Matsukata) of the Bobcat Gang , but abruptly leaves. Ishino later offers him a desk job with an Osaka gang that controls the longshoreman's union. "Guns are all I know," says Ginji, turning down the offer. "Live by the gun, die by the gun," is Ishino's reply.

Ken gets into a street brawl and shoots a member of the Fuji Gang—in front of a gang office. He is dragged inside and beaten. Ginji goes to talk to the boss, who tells him that the matter has been settled, with Ishino's aid. Hating to be obligated to anyone, Ginji shoots Ken as a way of evening the score—and disappears. Hoods from Joe's gang humiliate a Syndicate boss partying at a nightclub. Joe's boss, Tatsu, tries to negotiate with the Syndicate through a gang elder (Takashi Shimura) and manages to save his skin, but a death sentence is passed on Joe and his Skull gang.

Ishii gives Ginji another job: clean up the Skull gang as part of a three-man team. Ginji prefers to work alone but goes along with the plan rather than incur Ishino's wrath. Sonny, a member of Ginji's crew, gets the glory of killing Joe, but Ginji partly redeems himself. Ginji is sent to help another Syndicate boss, Niro, take over the northern territory—but soon gets on the wrong side of a local boss (Rokko Toura) when he tries to steal the boss's woman—a pretty club hostess. Once again, Ginji is in over his head, but this time Ishino can't bail him out.

CRITIQUE

A New Line version of a 1974 Kosaku Yamashita gang film, released in the wake of Stanley Pollack's 1975 *The Yakuza, The Tattooed Hitman* is eighteen minutes shorter than the original, with the credits for the stars somehow stuck somewhere in the last reel. Also, in adapting the script for American audiences, New Line made a hash of Japanese place names, turning Kyushu, where the action unfolds in the original, into Hokkaido, while sticking most of the gangs and gangsters with either English names or altered versions of their Japanese names. Called Shoichi Gunji in the original film, Hiroki Matsukata's character becomes Sonny in the New Line version.

The film itself, however, is not a camp hoot but a straight-ahead *jitsuroku* gang film, with a few inspired moments. Director Kosaku Yamashita, who was responsible for the *ninkyo* masterpiece *Bakuchiuchi Socho Tobaku* (Big Gambling Ceremony, 1968), had little sympathy with or feel for *jitsuroku* realism. Meanwhile, much of the cast, including Bunta Sugawara, Tatsuo Umemiya, and Hiroki Matsukata, had just finished work on the far superior Jingi Naki Tatakai films, and a feeling of déja vu pervades the whole enterprise.

Sugawara plays yet another of his selfdestructive gangsters, who would rather go out in a blaze of glory than sit behind a desk. Despite the hardness in his eyes, he displays little of the fire of his best films. Instead, the younger Tsunehiko Watase supplies most of the eruptions; but compared to Sugawara at his manic height, Watase is little more than a callow punk. Nonetheless, for fans who want to see Sugawara and his fellow Toei stars in their physical primes (if not at their professional peaks), *The Tattooed Hit Man* is the only readily available subtitled choice.

Yoidore Tenshi (1948)

DRUNKEN ANGEL
Scr.: Keinosuke Uegusa. *Dir.:* Akira Kurosawa. *Prod.:* Toho. *Main cast:* Takashi Shimura, Toshiro Mifune, Reisaburo Yamamoto, Chieko Nakakita, Michiyo Kogure, Noriko Sengoku, Eitaro Shindo. 150 mins.

STORY
A gangster, Matsunaga (Toshiro Mifune), goes to a neighborhood clinic run by the irascible Dr. Sanada (Takashi Shimura) to have a bullet removed from his hand. Sanada tells him that he is suffering from tuberculosis and, without treatment, will die. Though he despises gangsters, Sanada wants to help him, but Matsunaga hates both doctors and the thought of his own illness. He gets into a violent quarrel with the doctor and runs off. Sanada is encouraged by this show of temper; it proves that Matsunaga still has the will to live.

The doctor, however, has an illness of his own: alcoholism. Though enraged when he finds a patient drinking at a bar, the doctor quickly gets potted himself. The bar girl (Noriko Sengoku), who has a crush on Matsunaga, quickly susses the fact that Sanada has more than a professional interest in his yakuza patient. A born crusader, living and working in a pestilential slum, Sanada feels compelled to take on the most hardest of hard cases, including a gangster who is more likely to beat him than thank him.

Matsunaga, inevitably, returns, and Sanada urges him to get a chest x-ray, prompting another tantrum and thrashing. Nonetheless, Matsunaga does as the doctor orders, though he returns to the clinic with his x-ray in the middle of the night, dead drunk. When Matsunaga asks, before passing out, if he will get well, Sanada realizes that he has won a victory. It is short lived, however. While meditating on his new life, at a filthy pond that is the neighborhood dump, Matsunaga encounters Okada (Reisaburo Yamamoto), a former boss who has just been released from prison. Under Okada's influence, Matsunaga quickly slips back into his old life—and begins to lose everything, including his club hostess girlfriend (Michiyo Kogure), his position in the gang, and his money. All go to Okada, who lives strictly according to the one true rule of gangsterdom: eat or be eaten.

Meanwhile, Sanada is drawn deeper into not only Matsunaga's problems, but Okada's orbit. Okada and his minions even come to the clinic to claim Sanada's nurse (Chieko Naka-kita), who was once Okada's girlfriend. Sanada resists fiercely, but though he saves his nurse, he cannot save Matsunaga, who continues his downward spiral to death.

CRITIQUE

The first film to depict postwar gangsters, Akira Kurosawa's *Yoidore Tenshi* (Drunken Angel) does not follow any of the yakuza genre rules; it is instead a sui generis film by a director who was less interested in the mythology or sociology of the gangs than the dilemma of individuals living in a society without a moral compass, whose only imperative is survival. Kurosawa, in fact, famously hated gangsters—in *Yoidore Tenshi* he finds them almost too loathsome to contemplate, save in caricature that ranges from the sinisterly lurid to the comically grotesque.

The one exception is Matsunaga, who in Toshiro Mifune's fevered performance springs to life as a swaggering hood and dying consumptive, going to his own doom in helpless adherence to a code that is revealed as a meaningless sham. The pathos of his death has nothing to do with *ninkyodo* romanticism, as presented in hundreds of films before and since, and everything to do with Kurosawa's impassioned humanism. He may see Matsunaga as a representative of postwar malaise, but Kurosawa never loses sight of him as a man who is still in possession of his soul—and deserving of salvation, for all his various sins.

The agent of that salvation is Takashi Shimura's doctor, a self-described "dirty angel"—and Kurosawa's surrogate, who despises the gangs and all their works. This central relationship of gangster and doctor, both sinners who need each other to be saved, also sets *Yoidore Tenshi* apart from the vast majority of yakuza films, whose dramas of redemption or damnation play out within the confines of gangster society. But while defying or ignoring genre conventions, the film documents the postwar world, from its mental climate to its poverty and disease, with impassioned preciseness and inspired symbolism. The film's central image is the filthy pond that stands for what Japan has become—with gangsters being the social equivalent of mosquitoes.

Yurusarezaru Mono (2003)

THE MAN IN WHITE

Scr: Shigenori Takechi. *Dir:* Takashi Miike. *Prod:* Cinema Paradise. *Main cast:* Masaya Kato, Masahiko Tsugawa, Tatsuya Fuji, Ryosuke Miki, Hiroki Matsukata, Kazuki Kitamura, Renji Ishibashi, Jinpachi Nezu. 149 mins.

Takashi Miike's gang film *Yurusarezaru Mono* (The Man in White) has a scale and ambition that belie its low budget. Given its high body count and story of gang intrigue and fraternal rivalry, the inevitable comparison is with *The Godfather*. More pertinent, though, are recent Korean films like *No Way Out*, *Friend*, and *Public Enemy* that reinvigorate tired action formulas with a mixture of dirty realism and extreme violence, while successfully appealing to a mass audience. Miike's film belongs in this company—but given the peculiarities of the Japanese market, it will never reach the same box office summit.

Scripted by Shigenori Takechi, who was also responsible for Miike's *Araburu Tamashii-tachi* (Agitator, 2001), *Yurusarezaru Mono* is, like the previous film, a gang epic with a twisty plot and lengthy (149 minutes) running time. Instead of the usual epic pace and stylistics, however, Miike has opted for a hand-held camera, flash-editing approach that tries to replicate the turbulent inner world of the hero. This is not to say Miike always succeeds. In its third act, *Yurusarezaru Mono* tips over into arcade-game excess, with bodies falling and flying in nearly every scene, but its angle of approach remains consistent. Though hardly a documentary look at gang life, it gets inside its hero's head—and expresses his world view—with a gut-twisting, eye-opening force.

That view, as might be expected, is harshly Darwinian. Gangsters, as director Rokuro Mochizuki once told me, are terrorists who live by intimidation and violence. They move in a highly charged atmosphere in which the will must triumph—or be ruthlessly crushed. *Yurusarezaru Mono* buzzes with a similar juice, as if the camera itself is wired on that yakuza drug of choice: speed.

Azusa (Masaya Kato), a white-suited lieutenant for the Renjo gang, is boarding an elevator with his boss (Masahiko Tsugawa) and the rest of the boss's entourage when a mustachioed hitman blows away everyone but Azusa. The hitman, he sees with shock and anger, is his older brother Gunji (Tatsuya Fuji), who, when he was a teenager, murdered their father with a baseball bat and now, after decades of acting out, is an outcast in both straight and gang society.

Azusa soon feels the heat from Watari (Ryosuke Miki), his hot-headed gang superior, who wonders why he is the only survivor, but after getting a tip from a friendly cop (Hiroki Matsukata), Azusa goes into the streets to avenge his beloved boss's death. Enlisting the aid of Mizutani (Kazuki Kitamura)—a former fellow biker who is now lighting cigarettes for middle-aged women at a host club—he launches an attack against the Sogenkai, a rival gang he believes ordered the hit.

But instead of being a loyal Sogenkai soldier, Gunji is really in cahoots with Sakazaki (Renji Ishibashi), a sleazy opportunist who may be affiliated with the Sogenkai but hopes to profit by stirring up a gang war. The little scheme of this pair is exposed, and they find themselves targets of Sogenkai wrath.

The Sogenkai, in fact, wants peace, and its leaders even step in to settle a potentially explosive internal dispute between Watari and Renjo-gumi second-in-command Shiraishi

(Jinpachi Nezu). But while his gang superiors are playing politics, Azusa is bent on his crusade for rough justice. Inevitably, he and Gunji meet again, with consequences that soon have Miike's effects team working overtime.

A model-turned-actor whose Hollywood career has so far fizzled, Masaya Kato is not Miike's most obvious casting choice for Azusa—he may look terrific in a white suit, but yakuza seldom come with his generically handsome looks. Once he is paired with Kazuki Kitamura—a yakuza movie veteran whose pretty-boy face is suitably dissolute—his presence starts to make sense, however. These two work well together as both friends and partners in a mad, bad rampage, like latter-day Lord Byrons armed with semi-automatic weapons.

Playing the outlaw hitman Gunji, Tatsuya Fuji is, at sixty-two, long in the tooth to be scampering around warehouses spraying bullets. He is Miike's answer to Quentin Tarantino's much-praised casting of Robert Forster in *Jackie Brown*—an actor whose understated but brilliant performance makes you wonder where he has been all these years. Though he may look old enough to be Kato's father, Fuji has the right aura of bitter wisdom and not-so-quiet desperation.

True, the film overdoes the macho romanticism and the mass carnage—Azusa and company wipe out entire divisions of yakuza with weaponry that look as though it belongs in *The Matrix: Reloaded*. Too bad Miike didn't have the budget for 360-degree shots of slo-mo bullets. But if *Yurusarezaru Mono* is any indication, he wants to get there—and one day he just may arrive. Coming soon—the new Miike at a mall near you.

Zankyo (1999)

REMNANTS OF CHIVALRY

Scr.: Yoshiyuki Kuroda, Ichiro Otsu. *Dir.:* Ikuo Sekimoto. *Prod.:* The Zankyo Production Committee.

Main cast: Masahiro Takashima, Masaya Kato, Yuki Amami, Takeshi Kitano, Hiroki Matsukata, Kaori Takahashi. 111 mins.

In the 1990s, Toei's yakuza movies came to resemble Mike Tyson's boxing career: stretches in the box-office slammer, followed by yet another comeback. But like Iron Mike, they couldn't shake their old habits and soon the cell doors were clanging shut again. What was the problem? Toei believed in getting back to the genre basics but the world had moved on since the days when Ken Takakura, Koji Tsuruta, and Junko Fuji were bestriding the Japanese movie business like so many tattooed colossi. Not only were the stars and the studio system that supported the genre gone, but the formulas that once so thrilled audiences had grown stale.

One example of Toei's blast-from-the-past approach is Ikuo Sekimoto's *Zankyo*, a "Best of" boxed collection of yakuza movie clichés. As an assistant director under yakuza specialists—Tai Kato, Norifumi Suzuki, and Sadao Nakajima before making his first contribution to the genre with *Tsukeban Taiman Shobu* in 1974—Sekimoto is the directorial equivalent of the graying lounge singer trying, and failing, to channel Frank Sinatra. The original was better.

Zankyo's hero is Tatsugoro Iwaki (Masahiro Takashima), who begins the film as a young Kyoto brawler, circa 1937. In the opening scene, he defeats a rival, the slithery Toyama (Masaya Kato), in a fight to the death. But instead of driving a knife through his rival's black heart, Iwaki lets him live—a big mistake, as it turns out. Fast forward three years: Iwaki is now a guest of the Hamanaka-gumi in Kyushu. Striding alone into a den of rival gangsters who have been encroaching on Hamanaka turf, he subdues them with his sword, thereby repaying a debt of gratitude to the Hamanaka boss.

Iwaki's next fateful encounter occurs at a card game. A beautiful dealer (Yuki Amami) exposes three cheats and incurs their wrath. Iwaki springs to her defense and, after skewering one cheat and sending the other two packing, learns that one of the survivors (Takeshi Kitano) had murdered her father. The dealer pursues Iwaki with a relentless determination, symbolized by the dragon tattoo on her lovely back. Though tempted by her charms, Iwaki resists them—yet another mistake.

Hit the fast-forward button to 1942: Iwaki returns to Kyoto, where he assembles a band of gang brothers and begins to stake out his own turf. His fledgling Iwaki-gumi, however, soon runs afoul of a gang bossed by his enemy, Toyama. Before the two rivals can settle old scores, a senior boss (Hiroki Matsukata) calls for a truce. Japan is at war and needs the help of every able-bodied gangster, he says. Soon Iwaki, Toyama, and their men are hauling war materials for the army. But Toyama still burns to revenge himself on Iwaki—he can never forgive the man who spared his life.

There is much more. Iwaki falls in love with the pure-hearted Chiyoko (Kaori Takahashi); saves a young Korean from Toyama thugs; and survives a Toyama plot to frame him as a thief of army supplies. Finally, the war ends, and Iwaki is swept up in the chaos of postwar society. While battling nefarious Korean gangsters, fending off Toyama hitmen, and taking care of his *kobun*, Iwaki rises steadily in the Kyoto gang world. But before he can reach the top, he must first prevail in a final confrontation with Toyama. Naturally, Iwaki faces his rival—and all his minions—alone.

Sekimoto has hailed Takashima as the next Ken Takakura. As Iwaki, Takashima is suitably big, buff, and close-cropped, but for all his stoic posing, he is only a Takakura stand-in. Sekimoto does a competent job of choreographing his battle set-pieces, including Iwaki's swordplay heroics, but the director gives his actors license to chew the scenery, with ludicrous results. One scene in which the Korean gangsters expire, grimacing and clawing the air, made my companion laugh so hard he nearly gagged on his mint. Instead of *Zankyo*, this

Getting to the point. Masahiro Takashima (bottom) and Takeshi Kitano (second row right) star in Ikuo Sekimoto's 1999 revival of the *ninkyo eiga* genre in *Zankyo* (Remnants of Chivalry).

lame attempt to revive Toei's signature genre ought to be titled *Zannen* (Regret)—a wasted opportunity.

Zatoichi Monogatari (1962)

THE TALE OF ZATOICHI
Scr: Minoru Inuzuka. *Dir:* Kenji Misumi. *Prod:* Daiei. *Main cast:* Shintaro Katsu, Masayo Banri, Ryuzo Shimada, Gen Mitamura, Shigeru Amachi, Chitose Maki, Eijiro Yanagi. 96 mins.

STORY

Zatoichi (Shintaro Katsu) is a blind former masseur who wanders the countryside, living by gambling and his sword. Coming to Iioka, he visits the headquarters of Sukegoro (Eijiro Yanagi), the boss of a local gang. The boss is not around, but a gambling session is in progress, and Zatoichi asks to roll the dice. Sukegoro's men agree—what is the harm in letting a blind man play?—but Zatoichi proves to be a more formidable gambler than they thought.

When Sukegoro returns he greets Zatoichi like visiting royalty. He is contemplating war with the rival Sasagawa gang, led by the crafty Shigezo (Ryuzo Shimada), and has need of Zatoichi's skill. Sukegoro assigns an underling, Tatekichi (Michio Minami), to wait on Zatoichi hand and foot, but though the boss describes Tatekichi as a "good man," he is in fact an egocentric lout who has abandoned his pregnant lover to her fate, despite the protestations of his sister, Otane (Masayo Banri). When the girl is found dead, floating in a nearby lake, Tatekichi says she got what was coming to her—and Otane suspects him of the foulest of deeds.

While fishing in the lake, Zatoichi meets Miki Hirate (Shigeru Amachi), a gaunt ronin with strangely glittering eyes. Zatoichi quickly senses that Hirate is ill, with tuberculosis as it turns out, and Hirate is in turn amazed by the

blind man's perceptiveness. A beautiful—and tragic—friendship begins.

Zatoichi tells a member of Sukegoro's gang that he was a masseur until three years ago, when he began training himself as a swordsman to get more respect from the sighted. He could have followed other, more traditional paths to achieve status, but this was the one he chose. Now he is a yakuza, but at least he has a profession at which he excels and, more importantly, he has his pride.

Zatoichi protects Otane from her former husband Seisuke (Manabu Morita), a violent gangster, and wins her ever-lasting gratitude. He also stirs other emotions he is not sure he wants to encourage. He has no intention of leaving the yakuza life, and a woman, especially a beautiful one like Otane, can only be a burden.

As a battle shapes up between Sukegoro's and Shigezo's gangs, Sukegoro approaches Zatoichi for his assistance, but the blind man drives a hard bargain. Far from feeling obligated to Sukegoro, he is only in it for the money. Meanwhile, Hirate, who has taken a liking to Zatoichi, is facing death from his illness. Nonetheless, he wants to fight Zatoichi, to test his skills against a man he considers the ultimate swordsman. He will soon have his chance.

CRITIQUE

The first installment in what was to become a twenty-six-part series, as well as a popular TV show, *Zatoichi Monogatari* (The Tale of Zatoichi) is more of a character study than a samurai swashbuckler, albeit one spiced by a turbulent climactic battle. Though the film is based on a short story by Kan Shimozawa, the Zatoichi character also had its genesis in *Shiranui Kengyo* (Agent Shiranui), a 1960 period drama in which Katsu played a blind masseur who murders his master and assumes the dead man's identity to satisfy his own greed and lust.

In *Zatoichi Monogatari* Katsu plays a similarly dirty hero, who cheats and bluffs to put coins in his purse, while owing allegiance to no one. At the same time, Zatoichi adheres strictly to his own code of honor, which obliges him to protect the weak against the strong, no matter what the odds. He has also resigned himself to a lonely fugitive existence, as befits a yakuza, in its original definition as a "good-for-nothing" living outside the society and its laws.

Nearly all of the gangsters Zatoichi encounters in the film are grasping, conniving lowlifes, not the noble outlaws of tradition. Even his patron, Sukegoro, has little regard for the lives of his own men and expends them freely for his own protection and gain. Knowing he lives in a world of wolves, Zatoichi has developed a sharper set of teeth—his mastery of swordsmanship.

The idea of a blind swordsman may be pure hokum, but Katsu embodies it with a bluff panache and conviction. Beginning the film as a stumbling blind man, with an unheroically roly-poly physique, in his action scenes Katsu delivers flashy sword moves with surprising agility (if an eccentric form). Can a mere mortal, let alone a blind man, split a lighted candle in mid-air, with the merest flick of his sword? Perhaps not, but when Katsu performs these and other feats of legerdemain, he seems to enter another, higher dimension. Straining to detect the faintest sound or wisp of air, he twitches his face and flutters his eyes as though he is equipped with more than human senses. Is it Zen in action or showbiz flimflammery? Whichever, only Katsu could bring it off.

In filming Zatoichi's heroics, Kenji Misumi obviously made an intensive study of *Shichinin no Samurai* (Seven Samurai, 1954), *Yojimbo* (1961), and other Akira Kurosawa samurai classics, striving, in the finale, for their chaotic intensity as well as for their nuanced character development, adding dark, realistic touches of the sort that most period dramas of the time avoided. Ironically, Zatoichi proved to be a more enduring character than Kurosawa's most popular creation, Yojimbo, but only by evolving into a superhero locked forever in the same situations and attitudes. In his first outing, however, he is still quite human—and compellingly watchable.

GLOSSARY

BIBLIOGRAPHY

VIDEO & DVD SOURCES

FINDING GUIDES

GLOSSARY

aniki, anikibun: Gang "older brother." When used in direct address, it indicates that the *aniki* is senior to and of higher rank than the speaker.

ashi o arau: Literally, "to wash the feet." To quit the gang life.

baishakunin: The senior gangster who officiates at a *sakazuki.*

bakuchi: Gambling. A professional gambler is often called a *bakuchi'uchi.*

bakuto: Professional gambler—the traditional occupation for a yakuza.

banto: Leader of a juvenile gang or *gurentai.*

boryokudan: Literally, "violence group." A police term for the gangs, not used by gangsters to refer to themselves.

bosozoku: Literally, "speed tribe." Refers mainly to biker gangs, which have become prime recruiting grounds for the yakuza.

buta-bako: Jail cell, lockup.

butsu: Drugs.

chinpira: Apprentice gangsters, who act as servants and factotums for their seniors.

daigashi: Gambling house manager, who works for the *kashimoto,* or boss gambler.

deiri: Gang warfare.

dosu: Sword.

furyo: Delinquent, undesirable. Also has the meaning of bad, inferior, and damaged. Common expressions include *furyo shonen* (delinquent youth) and *furyo gaijin* (undesirable alien). Furyo are often said to *gureru* or "go bad." Thus *gurentai* or "street gangs" literally means "gang-of-those-who-have-gone-bad."

giri-ninjo: Literally, "duty and human feelings." *Giri-ninjo ni katai* means to strictly fulfill one's obligations, whatever the personal sacrifice. In yakuza films, *giri-ninjo* often serves as a plot engine, with the hero torn between his duty as a gangster and feelings as a man.

gokudo: Literally, "the extreme way." Refers to gangsters and the gangs, as in the series title *Gokudo no Onnatachi* (Gang Wives).

gurentai: Juvenile gang. *Gurentai* sprang up everywhere in the social chaos after World War Two and became a prime breeding ground for the yakuza.

hajiki: Pistol. Also called a *chaka.*

hamon: To be expelled from the gang, either permanently or for a fixed period.

hangoroshi: To beat severely or, literally, "half to death."

irezumi: Tattoo. Traditional, Japanese-style tattoos devoted to such subjects as dragons or the goddess Kannon are considered a symbol of gang affiliation (though not all their wearers are gangsters). Movie gangsters frequently display such tattoos, by suddenly exposing a shoulder or back, to intimate rivals.

jingi: Literally, "honor and humanity." In the yakuza world, it refers to the gangster code of honoring seniors and caring for juniors. In short, doing one's duty in the Confucian sense. The theme of Kinji Fukasaku's *Jingi Naki Tatakai* (Battles without Honor and Humanity) is the breakdown of this code under the pressures of Westernization and modernization.

kai: Usually a suffix meaning gang, group, or association. See also *Rengo.* The Inugawa-kai is a major gang in the Tokyo-Yokohama region.

kaicho: Chairman. Usually refers to the titular head of a major gang with a corporate organizational structure.

kamisan: The *oyabun*'s wife, who in films sometimes takes over the gang after her husband's death. More informally known as *anego* or *ane.*

kashimoto: Boss gambler who runs a gambling house and lends money to gamblers.

katagi: A member of straight society.

keizai yakuza: Yakuza who are more concerned with modern means of money making, both legal and illegal, than traditional gangster activities. In films, they are often depicted as effete, corrupt types who flout the *ninkyo* code.

kesu: Kill. Similar expressions are *tatamu* (fold) and *yaru* (do).

kobun: Underling, subordinate. Less a rank than an indicator of a gangster's relationship to his *oyabun* (boss).

kumi or, with a name preceding, *gumi:* Gang or crew, though it is also used in straight society to indicate a group or corporation. The Yamaguchi-gumi is Japan's largest gang, while Obayashi-gumi is a legitimate construction company.

kumicho: Gang boss—a formal title.

kyakubun: A yakuza "visitor" to a gang. In films, he is often a noble loner who incurs a possibly fatal obligation by accepting the hospitality of the host gang.

kyodaibun: A gang "brother," who is of equal rank, usually by virtue of having joined the gang at the same time.

matatabimono: Stories, plays, and films about wandering gangsters in premodern times, who usually follow the gambler's trade.

minbo: A contraction of *minji kainyu boryoku; minbo* is cop talk for gangsters ripping off nongangsters through various scams.

mizu shobai: Literally, "water world." Refers to the world of clubs, cabarets, bars, and other nightlife spots, gang-run or not.

musho: The joint. An abbreviation of *keimusho* (prison).

nagurikomi: To invade the headquarters of an enemy gang. In *ninkyo eiga,* the *nagurikomi,* with the hero striding into battle with a sword, occasionally accompanied by one or two allies, is almost always the climactic scene, though there may be preliminary *nagurikomi.*

nawabari: Gang territory or turf. *Nawabari arasoi* is a "turf war."

ninkyo: Literally, "chivalry." *Ninkyodo* refers to the gangster code of righteous behavior, which includes obeying one's seniors and honoring one's obligations, whatever the personal sacrifice.

oyabun: Gang boss—an informal title. His *kobun* often address him as *oyaji* (father).

rappa: Untruth, lie.

rengo: Association. Also used in the legitimate business world.

sakazuki: Literally, "wine cup." Refers to a ceremony in which sake is ritually consumed to celebrate a gang alliance or promotion. Gangsters keep the sake cup used in this ceremony as a token of their fealty. Breaking the cup is considered equivalent to breaking the bond pledged at the *sakazuki* ceremony.

sangokujin: Literally, "people of three countries." Refers to the Koreans, Taiwanese, and Chinese who were brought to Japan during World War Two to work in mines, factories, and other war-related jobs. In the postwar period, many *sangokujin* formed gangs that fought pitched battles with the yakuza. Now the word is widely considered a pejorative term.

satsu: Cop. An abbreviation of *keisatsu* (police). Police are also known as *poriko* or *inu* (dogs).

shaba: World outside prison.

shabu: Stimulant drugs.

shatei: Literally, "younger brother," though in the gang hierarchy it often refers to subbosses who have their own gangs under the authority of a *kyodai* (brother) or *shatei-gashira.*

shatei-gashira: The gang third-in-command, after the *wakamono-gashira.* Has subgangs under his direct control. Often shortened to *kashira.*

shima: Literally, "island." A gang's territory.

socho: Usually translated as president or chancellor of an institution, though sometimes used as a title for a gang boss of bosses.

sopurando: "Soapland." Often shortened to *sopu* in katakana. Massage parlors that are fronts for prostitution. Formerly called *toruko*—shortened form of Turkish bath—until Turkish protests forced owners to change the name. The women who work in them are called *sopujo* (soap girls).

tekiya: A street-stall seller, who traditionally plies his trade at festivals and other places where people gather for relaxation and amusement.

tosei: The gang world. Can also means one's business or trade in straight society.

toseinin: Gangster.

utau: To "sing" or confess.

wakamono-gashira (also *wakashu-gashira*): The gang second-in-command, who carries out the boss's orders and has gangs under his direct control. Often shortened to *kashira.*

yakuza: Gangster. Originated from a losing hand of eight (*ya*), nine (*ku*), and three (*za*) in a traditional card game. Starting as a gambler slang term for "useless," *yakuza* came to refer to the gamblers themselves and finally to all gangsters of whatever occupation.

yubitsume: A ritual act in which a gangster cuts off a finger to atone for a misdeed. The initial cut is usually made to the first joint of the left little finger, though if the offense is a major one, an entire finger may be removed. In premodern times it was thought that, by cutting off his little finger, the miscreant would not be able to grip a sword as tightly—and would thus become more dependent on the protection of his *oyabun.*

zenka: Criminal record.

BIBLIOGRAPHY

Aikawa, Show. *Ore, Furyohin*. Tokyo: Toho Shuppan, 2001.

—— and Masaki Tanioka. *Aikawa Sho Teppodama Densetsu*. Tokyo: Otta Shuppan, 2001.

Ando, Noboru. *Jiden Ando Noboru*. Tokyo: Bunkasha, 2001.

Black and Blue, eds. *Japanese Film 1955–64: Showa 30-Dai no Hit Series Jo*. Tokyo: Neko Publishing Co., 1999.

Buruma, Ian. *A Japanese Mirror: Heroes and Villains of Japanese Culture*. London: Penguin Books, 1985.

Fukuma, Kenji, and Mikio Yamazaki, eds. *Dai Yakuza Eiga Yomihon*. Tokyo: Yosensha, 1993.

Inomata, Katsuhito, and Rikiya Tayama. *Nihon Eiga Haiyu Zenshi: Danyu-hen*. Tokyo: Shakai Shisosha, 1977.

——. *Nihon Eiga Haiyu Zenshi: Joyu-hen*. Tokyo: Shakai Shisosha, 1977.

Ishii, Shinji, ed. *Yakuza to Iu Ikikata*. Tokyo: JICC Shuppan, 1986.

Ishii, Teruo, and Kenji Fukuma. *Ishii Teruo Eigakon*. Tokyo: Wides Shuppan, 1992.

"Japan's Most Wanted." *Japanzine* (October 2002), pp. 4–9.

Johnson, William. "Ichikawa and the Wanderers." In *Kon Ichikawa*. Edited by James Quandt. Toronto: Cinematheque Ontario, 2001.

Kaplan, David, and Alec Dubro. *Yakuza: The Explosive Account of Japan's Criminal Underworld*. Reading, Mass.: Addison-Wesley Publishing Co., 1986.

Kato, Tai, Sadao Yamane, and Yoshio Yasui. *Kato Tai, Eiga o Kataru*. Tokyo: Chikuma Shobo, 1994.

McDonald, Keiko. "The Yakuza Film: An Introduction." In *Reframing Japanese Cinema*. Edited by Arthur Noletti, Jr., and David Desser. Bloomington: Indiana University Press, 1992.

Macias, Patrick. *Tokyoscope: The Japanese Cult Film Companion*. San Francisco: Cadence Books, 2001.

Mogami, Toshinobu, and Toshiro Maruo, eds. *Ninkyo Star Retsuden: Toei Ninkyo Ogon Jidai*. Tokyo: Wides Shuppan, 1999.

Mellen, Joan. *The Waves at Genji's Door: Japan Through Its Cinema*. New York: Pantheon Books, 1976.

Miyamoto, Haruo. *Sengo Hero Heroine Densetsu*. Tokyo: Asahi Shimbunsha, 1995.

Nozawa, Kazuma. *Nikkatsu 1954–1971: Eizo o Sozo Suru Samurai-tachi*. Tokyo: Wides Shuppan, 2000.

Okada, Shigeru. *Kuinaki Waga Eiga Jinsei*. Tokyo: Zaikai Kenkyujo, 2001.

Richie, Donald. *A Hundred Years of Japanese Film*. Tokyo: Kodansha International, 2001.

—— and Joseph Anderson. *The Japanese Film: Art and Industry*. Expanded edition. Princeton: Princeton University Press, 1982.

Sato, Tadao. *Currents in Japanese Cinema*. Tokyo: Kodansha International, 1987.

——. *Nihon Eiga no Kyoshotachi III*. Tokyo: Gakuyo Shobo, 1997.

Schilling, Mark. *Contemporary Japanese Film*. New York: Weatherhill, 1999.

——. *The Encyclopedia of Japanese Pop Culture*. New York: Weatherhill, 1997.

Schrader, Paul. "Yakuza Eiga: A Primer." *Film Comment* 10:1 (January 1974).

Shiba, Tsukasa, and Sakae Aoyama. *Yakuza Eiga to Sono Jidai*. Tokyo: Chikuma Shinsho, 1998.

Shundo, Koji, and Sadao Yamane. *Ninkyo Eiga-den*. Tokyo: Kodansha, 1999.

Tanioka, Masaki. *V Cinema-kon: Nisenbon Doshaburi o Tsukushimi*. Tokyo: Yotsuya Round, 1999.

Tansman, Alan. "Where's Mama? The Sobbing Yakuza of Hasegawa Shin." In *Word and Image in Japanese Cinema*. Edited by Dennis Washburn and Carole Cavanaugh. Cambridge: Cambridge University Press, 2001.

Taro, Sugisaku J., and Takeshi Uechi. *Jingi Naki Tatakai: Roman Album*. Tokyo: Tokuma Shoten, 1998.

Tomita, Riichi, ed. *Illustrated Who's Who of Japanese Cinema: Directors*. Tokyo: Kinema Junposha, 1997.

VIDEO & DVD SOURCES

Nearly all the films mentioned in this book have been released on DVD or video and in either Japanese- or foreign-language versions. How to buy them, not to mention perusing the thousands of other Japanese films on disk and tape? The easy solution would be to provide a list of online sellers and let the reader take it from there.

Unfortunately, no one seller carries everything that's available, though some come close for the DVDs made for their particular region. Also, prices vary, as do shipping costs and conditions. Here are some of my own quick-and-dirty tactics for finding what I want:

(1) For films by a popular director or actor, try Epinions at http://www.epinions.com/; PriceGrabber at http://www.pricegrabber.com/; DVD Price Search at http://www.dvdpricesearch.com/; Best Price UK at http://www.bestpricedvd.co.uk/; or other price-comparison sites. Who knows? There may be a better deal out there than you can find on Amazon.

(2) Try Ebay. Chances are, if a title exists on DVD or video, someone, somewhere, is trying to sell it. Ebay is especially good for obscure titles that are out of stock at most online stores.

(3) Try Google. If you can't find a DVD review or an on-line seller of your film within the first two or three pages of results, you are in trouble.

(4) Search the Asian film section of the Mobius Home Video Forum: http://www.mhvf.net/. The members of this forum are Asian film fans who obsess over every subbed or dubbed DVD release. If they don't know whether the film you want is available, probably no one does.

(5) Don't know the official English or Japanese title? Try the Internet Movie Database (IMDB) at http://us.imdb.com/. Though patchy in terms of accuracy and completeness, IMDB is among the easiest ways to bridge the title gap.

(6) Members of the KineJapan mailing list, mainly scholars and fans, frequently post about new DVD releases, as well as any and all topics related to Japanese films. For information on joining, visit the Kinema Club site at http://pears.lib.ohio-state.edu/Markus/Welcome.html.

(7) Check out the Asian DVD Guide at http://www.asiandvdguide.com, which lists Japanese DVDs released by distributors in Japan, Taiwan, and Hong Kong. Also, the site has a forum whose members sell, trade, and exchange information about Asian DVDs.

Perhaps you feel more comfortable buying from Amazon or another big online seller. Fine. But specialty sellers often have a far broader selection of Japanese films, while offering competitive prices and services. Also, many distributors sell directly from their own web sites. Midnight Eye http:// www.midnighteye.com/ is a must-see web site for anyone interested in Japanese film and provides an extensive list of video and DVD sources, as well as frequent updates on new releases.

Here is my own list of favorite sources, categorized by country or territory:

NORTH AMERICA
Poker Industries
http://www.pokerindustries.com/
Import DVD and video specialist, with a strong Asian section.

DVD Asian
http://www.dvdasian.com/
Asian film specialist with an impressive Japanese film selection.

HKFlix.com
http://www.hkflix.com/home.asp/
Asian specialist with large Japanese action lineup.

Diabolik
http://www.diabolikdvd.com/
Cult specialist that offers many Japanese titles.

1 World Films
http://www.1worldfilms.com/index.htm/
Extensive lineup of world cinema, including films from Japan.

UNITED KINGDOM
Blackstar
http://www.blackstar.co.uk/
A general DVD and video site, but with a strong Asian selection.

Movie Mail
http://www.moviem.co.uk/
A specialist in World Cinema and cult films, including those from Japan.

Bensonsworld
http://www.bensonsworld.co.uk/
General DVD and video seller with a fairly extensive Japanese lineup.

FRANCE
FNAC
http://www.fnac.com/
A general on-line retailer with a large Japanese film section.

AUSTRIA
Sazuma Trading
http://www.sazuma.com/
Import specialist with an extensive Asian selection.

HONG KONG
DDD House
http://www.dddhouse.com/
Hong Kong movie specialist with a basic lineup of Japanese films.

Yes Asia
http://us.yesasia.com/ (North America)
http://global.yesasia.com/ (Global)
Offers a large Japanese film lineup but relatively few titles in the action genre.

JAPAN
CD Japan
http://www.cdjapan.co.jp/
Good selection of new Japanese films but few with subtitles.

Neowing
http://www.neowing.co.jp/movie/
General site with large lineup of Japanese films but no English-language site.

HMV Japan
http://www.hmv.co.jp/
Large selection of recent Japanese films, on both Japanese and English sites.

Amazon Japan
http://www.amazon.co.jp/
DVD section has an advanced search feature that allows you to search for all films with English, Japanese, or other subtitles. English-language site with lineup of subbed Japanese films.

Amotokyo
http://www.amotokyo.com/.
Anime specialist that is rapidly expanding its Japanese movie section.

FINDING GUIDES

DIRECTOR GUIDE

Aoyama, Shinji: *Chinpira* (1996), *Wild Life* (1997)

Cappello, Frank: *American Yakuza* (1994), *No Way Back: Toso Yugi* (No Way Back, 1995)

Fukasaku, Kinji: *Bakuto Gaijin Butai* (Sympathy for the Underdog, 1971), *Bakuto Kaisanshiki* (Gambler's Dispersion, 1968), *Gang tai G-men* (Gang versus G-men, 1962), *Gendai Yakuza: Hitokiri Yota* (Street Mobster, 1972), *Jingi Naki Tatakai* (Battles without Honor and Humanity, 1973), *Jingi Naki Tatakai: Hiroshima Shitohen* (Battles without Honor and Humanity 2: Fight to the Death at Hiroshima, 1973), *Jingi Naki Tatakai: Dairi Senso* (Battles without Honor and Humanity 3: Proxy War, 1973), *Jingi Naki Tatakai: Chojo Sakusen* (Battles without Honor and Humanity 4: High Tactics, 1974), *Jingi Naki Tatakai: Kanketsuhen* (Battles without Honor and Humanity 5: The Final Episode, 1974), *Jingi no Hakaba* (Graveyard of Honor, 1975), *Kaoyaku* (Boss, 1965), *Nihon Boryokudan: Kumicho* (Japan Organized Crime Boss, 1969), *Yakuza no Hakaba: Kuchinashi no Hana* (Yakuza Burial: Jasmine Flower, 1976)

Gosha, Hideo: *Gokudo no Onnatachi* (Gang Wives, 1986), *Gokudo no Onnatachi: Kejime* (Gang Wives: Decision, 1998)

Harada, Masato: *Kamikaze Taxi* (1995)

Hashimoto, Hajime: *Shin Jingi Naki Tatakai: Bosatsu* (Another Battle: Conspiracy, 2003)

Hayashi, Kaizo: *Harukana Jidai no Kaidan o* (The Stairway to the Distant Past, 1994), *Waga Jinsei Saiaku no Toki* (The Most Terrible Time in My Life, 1993)

Higashi, Yoichi: *Watashi no Grandpa* (My Grandpa, 2003)

Hironishi, Masato: *Yaju Shisubeshi: Fukushuhen* (The Beast Must Die: Revenge, 1997)

Horiuchi, Yasuhiro: *Gorotsuki* (Tough Guys, 1992)

Ichikawa, Kon: *Matatabi* (The Wanderers, 1973)

Ikehiro, Kazuo: *Waka Oyabun* (Young Boss, 1965)

Ishii, Takashi: *Freeze Me* (2000), *Gonin* (1995), *Kuro no Tenshi, Vol. 1* (Black Angel, Vol. 1, 1998)

Ishii, Teruo: *Abashiri Bangaichi* (A Man from Abashiri Prison, 1965), *Abashiri Bangaichi: Bokyohen* (A Man from Abashiri Prison: Going Home, 1965), *Hana to Arashi to Gang* (Flower and Storm and Gang, 1961), *Juichinin no Gang* (Eleven Gangsters, 1963), *Kaoyaku* (Boss, 1965), *Narazumono* (The Untamed, 1964), *Tokyo Gang tai Hong Kong Gang* (Tokyo Gang versus Hong Kong Gang, 1964), *Yakuza Keibatsushi: Lynch!* (A History of Yakuza Punishments: Lynch!, 1969)

Ishihara, Shigeru: *Don e no Michi* (The Road to Bossdom, 2003)

Itami, Juzo: *Minbo no Onna* (The Gentle Art of Japanese Extortion, 1992)

Ito, Daisuke: *Chuji Tabi Nikki* (Diary of Chuji's Travels, 1927), *Oedo Gonin Otoko* (Five Men from Edo, 1951).

Ito, Hidehiro: *Otokotachi no Kaita E* (The Man with Two Hearts, 1996)

Izumi, Seiji: *Shuraba ga Yuku* (The Carnage Comes, 1995)

Izutsu, Kazuyuki: *Kishiwada Shonen Gurentai* (Boys, Be Ambitious, 1996)

Kajima, Shun'ichi: *Jitsuroku Ando Gumi Gaiden: Garo no Okite* (The True History of the Ando Gang: Rules of the Starving Wolf, 2002), *Shuraba no Ningengaku* (The Anthropology of a Fight Scene, 1993)

Kato, Tai: *Choeki Juhachinen* (Sentence: Eighteen Years, 1967), *Hibotan Bakuto: Hanafuda Shobu* (Red Peony Gambler: Flower Cards Match, 1969), *Hibotan Bakuto: Oinochi Itadakimasu* (Red Peony Gambler: Death to the Wicked, 1971), *Meiji Kyokakuden: Sandai Shumei* (Blood of Revenge, 1965)

Kawashima, Hide: *Ryuji* (1983)

Kawashima, Naomi: *Gokudo no Ane: Reiko* (Gang Lady: Reiko, 1994)

Kitano, Takeshi: *Brother* (2000), *Kids Return* (1996), *Sonatine* (1993), *3-4 X Jugatsu* (Boiling Point, 1990). As an actor: *Brother* (2000), *Sonatine* (1993), *3-4 X Jugatsu* (Boiling Point, 1990), *Zankyo* (Remnants of Chivalry, 1999)

Kiuchi, Kazuhiro: *Kyohansha* (Partners in Crime, 1999)

Komizu, Kazuo: *Gokudo no Ane: Reiko* (Gang Lady: Reiko, 1994)

Kumashiro, Tatsumi: *Bo no Kanashimi* (Hard-Head Fool, 1994)

Kurosawa, Akira: *Yoidore Tenshi* (Drunken Angel, 1948)

Kurosawa, Kiyoshi: *Fukushu: Kienai Kizu Ato* (The Revenge: The Scar that Never Fades, 1997), *Katte ni Shiyagare!! Godatsu Keikaku* (Suit Yourself or Shoot Yourself: Extortion Plot 1, 1995), *Shuraba no Gokudo: Hebi no Michi* (Serpent's Path, 1997)

Lee, Chi Ngai: *Fuyajo* (Sleepless Town, 1998)

Makino, Masahiro: *Nihon Kyokakuden: Naniwahen* (1965), *Nihon Kyokakuden: Shiraha no Sakazuki* (1967), *Showa Zankyoden: Shinde Moraimasu* (Remnants of Chivalry in the Showa Era: I Want You to Die, 1970), *Wakaki Hi no Jirocho* (The Young Days of Jirocho, 1962)

Masuda, Toshio: *Burai Yori Daikanbu* (Gangster VIP, 1968), *Kurenai no Nagareboshi* (The Velvet Hustler, 1967)

Masumura, Yasuzo: *Heitai Yakuza* (Hoodlum Soldier, 1965), *Karakkaza Yaro* (Afraid to Die, 1960)

Matsuda, Yusaku: *A Homansu* (1986). Also as an actor: *A Homansu* (1986)

Matsuo, Akinori: *Otoko no Monsho* (Symbol of a Man, 1963)

Matsushima, Tetsuya: *Level* (1994)

Miike, Takashi: *Dead or Alive: Hanzaisha* (Dead or Alive, 1999), *Full Metal Gokudo* (Full Metal Yakuza , 1997), *Gokudo Kuro Shakai Rainy Dog* (Rainy Dog, 1997), *Gokudo Sengokushi Fudo* (Fudoh: The New Generation, 1996), *Jitsuroku Ando Noboru Outlaw-den: Rekka* (Deadly Outlaw: Rekka, 2002), *Koroshiya Ichi* (Ichi the Killer, 2001), *Nihon Kuroshakai Ley Lines* (Ley Lines, 1999), *Shin Jingi no Hakaba* (Graveyard of Honor, 2002), *Shinjuku Kuro Shakai China Mafia Senso* (Shinjuku Triad Society, 1995), *Yurusarezaru Mono* (The Man in White, 2003)

Misumi, Kenji: *Zatoichi Monogatari* (The Tale of Zatoichi, 1962)

Mochizuki, Rokuro: *Chinpira* (Chinpira/Two Punks, 2000), Gedo (The Outer Way, 1998), *Minazuki* (Everyone's a Moon, 1999), *Mukokuseki no Otoko: Chi no Shukaku* (Pinocchio: A Man without Nationality, 1997), *Onibi* (The Fire Within, 1997), *Shin Kanashiki Hitman* (Another Lonely Hitman, 1995)

Murahashi, Akio: *Shiawase ni Naro ne* (Let's Get Happy, 1998)

Nakashima, Sadao: *Don o Totta Otoko* (The Man Who Shot the Don, 1994)

Negishi, Kichitaro: *Kizuna* (Ties, 1998)

Okamoto, Kihachi: *Ankokugai no Kaoyaku* (The Big Boss, 1959)

Okawa, Tochimichi: *Nobody* (1994). As Okawa, Shundo: *Yakuza Way, The* (1998)

Omori, Kazuki: *Keisho Sakazuki* (Succession Ceremony, 1992)

Ozawa, Shigehiro: *Kunisada Chuji* (1958)

Pollack, Sydney: *Yakuza, The* (1975)

Sabu: *Unlucky Monkey* (1998)

Sakamoto, Junji: *Shin Jingi Naki Tatakai* (Another Battle, 2000)

Sawashima, Tadashi: *Jinsei Gekijo: Hishakaku* (Theater of Life: Hishakaku, 1963)

Sekimoto, Ikuo: *Zankyo* (Remnants of Chivalry, 1999)

Shinoda, Masahiro: *Kawaita Hana* (Pale Flower, 1964)

Shirai, Seichi: *Tokyo Mafia: Yakuza Wars* (1995)

Suzuki, Kosuke: *Blood* (1998)

Suzuki, Seijun: *Hana to Doto* (Flower and the Angry Waves, 1964), *Irezumi Ichidai* (One Generation of Tattoos, 1965), *Kanto Mushuku* (Kanto Wanderer, 1963), *Tokyo Nagaremono* (Tokyo Drifter, 1966), *Yaju no Seishun* (Youth of the Beast, 1963). As an actor: *Shiawase ni Naro ne* (Let's Get Happy, 1998)

Tanaka, Tokuzo: *Akumyo* (Tough Guy, 1961)

Totoku, Etsu: *Shinjuku Yokubo Tantei* (The Hungry Shinjuku Detective, 1994)

Toyoda, Toshiaki: *PornoStar* (1999)

Tsuji, Kichiro: *Kutsukake Tokijiro* (1929)

Wakamatsu, Koji: *Asu Naki Machikado* (End of Our Own Real, 1997)

Yaguchi, Shinobu: *Adrenaline Drive* (1999)

Uchida, Tomu: *Jinsei Gekijo: Hishakaku to Kiratsune* (Theater of Life: Hishakaku and Kiratsune, 1968)

Yamashita, Kosaku: *Bakuchiuchi Socho Tobaku* (Big Gambling Ceremony, 1968), *Yamaguchi Gaiden Kyushu Shinko Sakusen* (The Tattooed Hitman, 1974)

ACTOR GUIDE

Aikawa, Show: *Dead or Alive: Hanzaisha* (Dead or Alive, 1999), *Fukushu: Kienai Kizu Ato* (The Revenge: The Scar that Never Fades, 1997), *Gokudo Kuro Shakai Rainy Dog* (Rainy Dog, 1997), *Jitsuroku Ando Gumi Gaiden: Garo no Okite* (The True History of the Ando Gang: Rules of the Starving Wolf, 2002), *Katte ni Shiyagare!! Godatsu Keikaku* (Suit Yourself or Shoot Yourself: Extortion Plot 1, 1995),

Nihon Kuroshakai Ley Lines (Ley Lines, 1999), *Onibi* (The Fire Within, 1997), *Shiawase ni Naro ne* (Let's Get Happy, 1998), *Shuraba ga Yuku* (The Carnage Comes, 1995), *Shuraba no Gokudo: Hebi no Michi* (Serpent's Path, 1997), *Shuraba no Okami: Kumo no Hitomi* (Eyes of the Spider, 1997)

Ando, Noboru: *Bakuto Gaijin Butai* (Sympathy for the Underdog, 1971), *Choeki Juhachinen* (Sentence: Eighteen Years, 1967), *Gendai Yakuza: Hitokiri Yota* (Street Mobster, 1972), *Jingi no Hakaba* (Graveyard of Honor, 1975), *Jitsuroku Ando Gumi Gaiden: Garo no Okite* (The True History of the Ando Gang: Rules of the Starving Wolf, 2002), *Nihon Boryokudan: Kumicho* (Japan Organized Crime Boss, 1969)

Arashi, Kanjuro: *Abashiri Bangaichi* (A Man from Abashiri Prison, 1965), *Hibotan Bakuto: Hanafuda Shobu* (Red Peony Gambler: Flower Cards Match, 1969), *Hibotan Bakuto: Oinochi Itadakimasu* (Red Peony Gambler: Death to the Wicked, 1971), *Meiji Kyokakuden: Sandai Shumei* (Blood of Revenge, 1965)

Arimori, Narimi: *Shiawase ni Naro ne* (Let's Get Happy, 1998), *Shin Jingi no Hakaba* (Graveyard of Honor, 2002)

Asano, Tadanobu: *Koroshiya Ichi* (Ichi the Killer, 2001), *Watashi no Grandpa* (My Grandpa, 2003)

Asaoka, Ruriko: *Kurenai no Nagareboshi* (The Velvet Hustler, 1967)

Atsumi, Kiyoshi: *Wakaki Hi no Jirocho* (The Young Days of Jirocho, 1962)

Bando, Tsumasaburo: *Oedo Gonin Otoko* (Five Men from Edo, 1951)

Chiba, Shin'ichi "Sonny": *Gang tai G-men* (Gang versus G-men, 1962), *Jingi Naki Tatakai: Hiroshima Shitohen* (Battles without Honor and Humanity 2: Fight to the Death at Hiroshima, 1973), *Jingi Naki Tatakai: Chojo Sakusen* (Battles without Honor and Humanity 4: High Tactics, 1974), *Jitsuroku Ando Noboru Outlaw-den: Rekka* (Deadly Outlaw: Rekka, 2002)

Crowe, Russell: *No Way Back: Toso Yugi* (No Way Back, 1995)

Forster, Robert: *American Yakuza* (1994)

Fuji, Junko: *Bakuchiuchi Socho Tobaku* (Big Gambling Ceremony, 1968), *Hibotan Bakuto: Hanafuda Shobu* (Red Peony Gambler: Flower Cards Match, 1969), *Hibotan Bakuto: Oinochi Itadakimasu* (Red Peony Gambler: Death to the Wicked, 1971), *Jinsei Gekijo: Hishakaku to Kiratsune* (Theater of Life: Hishakaku and Kiratsune, 1968), Kao-yaku (Boss, 1965), *Meiji Kyokakuden: Sandai Shumei* (Blood of Revenge, 1965), *Nihon Kyokakuden: Shiraha no Sakazuki* (1967), *Showa Zankyoden: Shinde Moraimasu* (Remnants of Chivalry in the Showa Era: I Want You to Die, 1970)

Hakuryu: *Bo no Kanashimi* (Hard-Head Fool, 1994), *Don e*

no Michi (The Road to Bossdom, 2003), *Gedo* (The Outer Way, 1998), *Kishiwada Shonen Gurentai* (Boys, Be Ambitious, 1996), *Blood* (1998)

Harada, Yoshio: *Onibi* (The Fire Within, 1997)

Hazuki, Riona: *Kuro no Tenshi, Vol. 1* (Black Angel, Vol. 1, 1998)

Ichikawa, Raizo: *Waka Oyabun* (Young Boss, 1965)

Ikebe, Ryo: *Kawaita Hana* (Pale Flower, 1964), *Showa Zankyoden: Shinde Moraimasu* (Remnants of Chivalry in the Showa Era: I Want You to Die, 1970)

Inoue, Harumi: *Freeze Me* (2000)

Ishibashi, Renji: *A Homansu* (1986), *Jingi Naki Tatakai: Chojo Sakusen* (Battles without Honor and Humanity 4: High Tactics, 1974), *Jitsuroku Ando Noboru Outlaw-den: Rekka* (Deadly Outlaw: Rekka, 2002), *Shin Jingi Naki Tatakai: Bosatsu* (Another Battle: Conspiracy, 2003), *Yakuza Keibatsushi: Lynch!* (A History of Yakuza Punishments: Lynch!, 1969), *Yurusarezaru Mono* (The Man in White, 2003)

Ishibashi, Ryo: *A Homansu* (1986), *American Yakuza* (1994), *Chinpira* (1996), *Level* (1994), *Mukokuseki no Otoko: Chi no Shukaku* (Pinocchio: A Man without Nationality, 1997), *Shin Kanashiki Hitman* (Another Lonely Hitman, 1995)

Iwashita, Shima: *Gokudo no Onnatachi* (Gang Wives, 1986), *Gokudo no Onnatachi: Kejime* (Gang Wives: Decision, 1998)

Kaga, Mariko: *Kawaita Hana* (Pale Flower, 1964), *Narazumono* (The Untamed, 1964)

Kaneko, Masaji: *Ryuji* (1983)

Kataoka, Reiko: *Onibi* (The Fire Within, 1997)

Katase, Rina: *Gokudo no Onnatachi* (Gang Wives, 1986), *Gokudo no Onnatachi: Kejime* (Gang Wives: Decision, 1998)

Kato, Masaya: *Brother* (2000), *Nobody* (1994), *Yurusarezaru Mono* (The Man in White, 2003), *Zankyo* (Remnants of Chivalry, 1999)

Katsu, Shintaro: *Akumyo* (Tough Guy, 1961), *Heitai Yakuza* (Hoodlum Soldier, 1965), *Zatoichi Monogatari* (The Tale of Zatoichi, 1962)

Kitamura, Kazuki: *Chinpira* (Chinpira/Two Punks, 2000), *Freeze Me* (2000), *Minazuki* (Everyone's a Moon, 1999), *Mukokuseki no Otoko: Chi no Shukaku* (Pinocchio: A Man without Nationality, 1997), *Nihon Kuroshakai Ley Lines* (Ley Lines, 1999), *Yurusarezaru Mono* (The Man in White, 2003)

Kitano, Takeshi (credited as "Beat Takeshi"): *Brother* (2000), *Gonin* (1995), *Sonatine* (1993), *3-4 X Jugatsu* (Boiling Point, 1990), *Zankyo* (Remnants of Chivalry, 1999)

Kobayashi, Akira: *Don e no Michi* (The Road to Bossdom, 2003), *Hana to Doto* (Flower and the Angry Waves, 1964),

Jingi Naki Tatakai: Chojo Sakusen (Battles without Honor and Humanity 4: High Tactics, 1974), *Kanto Mushuku* (Kanto Wanderer, 1963)

Machida, Kyosuke: *Burai Yori Daikanbu* (Gangster VIP, 1968), *Hibotan Bakuto: Hanafuda Shobu* (Red Peony Gambler: Flower Cards Match, 1969), *Hibotan Bakuto: Oinochi Itadakimasu* (Red Peony Gambler: Death to the Wicked, 1971), *Juichinin no Gang* (Eleven Gangsters, 1963), *Kaoyaku* (Boss, 1965), *Tokyo Gang tai Hong Kong Gang* (Tokyo Gang versus Hong Kong Gang, 1964), *Yakuza, The* (1975)

Matsuda, Yusaku: *A Homansu* (1986)

Matsukata, Hiroki: *Don o Totta Otoko* (The Man Who Shot the Don, 1994), *Jingi Naki Tatakai* (Battles without Honor and Humanity, 1973), *Jingi Naki Tatakai: Chojo Sakusen* (Battles without Honor and Humanity 4: High Tactics, 1974), *Jingi Naki Tatakai: Kanketsuhen* (Battles without Honor and Humanity 5: The Final Episode, 1974), *Jinsei Gekijo: Hishakaku to Kiratsune* (Theater of Life: Hishakaku and Kiratsune, 1968), *Yamaguchi Gaiden Kyushu Shinko Sakusen* (The Tattooed Hitman, 1974), *Yurusarezaru Mono* (The Man in White, 2003), *Zankyo* (Remnants of Chivalry, 1999)

Mifune, Toshiro: *Ankokugai no Kaoyaku* (The Big Boss, 1959), *Yoidore Tenshi* (Drunken Angel, 1948)

Mihara, Yoko: *Juichinin no Gang* (Eleven Gangsters, 1963), *Narazumono* (The Untamed, 1964)

Mishima, Yukio: *Karakkaza Yaro* (Afraid to Die, 1960)

Mitchum, Robert: *Yakuza, The* (1975)

Miyamoto, Nobuko: *Minbo no Onna* (The Gentle Art of Japanese Extortion, 1992)

Mortensen, Viggo: *American Yakuza* (1994)

Nagase, Masatoshi: *Harukana Jidai no Kaidan o* (The Stairway to the Distant Past, 1994), *Waga Jinsei Saiaku no Toki* (The Most Terrible Time in My Life, 1993)

Nagisa, Mayumi: *Gendai Yakuza: Hitokiri Yota* (Street Mobster, 1971)

Nezu, Jinpachi: *Gonin* (1995), *Kuro no Tenshi, Vol. 1* (Black Angel, Vol. 1, 1998), *Nobody* (1994), *Yurusarezaru Mono* (The Man in White, 2003)

Oki, Minoru: *Kaoyaku* (Boss, 1965), *Meiji Kyokakuden: Sandai Shumei* (Blood of Revenge, 1965), *Nihon Kyokaku-den: Shiraha no Sakazuki* (1967), *Yakuza Keibatsushi: Lynch!* (A History of Yakuza Punishments: Lynch!, 1969)

Okochi, Denjiro: *Chuji Tabi Nikki* (Diary of Chuji's Travels, 1927), *Kutsukake Tokijiro* (Kutsukake Tokijiro, 1929).

Okuda, Eiji: *Bo no Kanashimi* (Hard-Head Fool, 1994), *Minazuki* (Everyone's a Moon, 1999), *Onibi* (The Fire Within, 1997)

Sakuma, Yoshiko: *Jinsei Gekijo: Hishakaku* (Theater of Life: Hishakaku, 1963), *Kaoyaku* (Boss, 1965), *Gang tai G-men* (Gang versus G-men, 1962)

Sawaki, Asami: *Shin Kanashiki Hitman* (Another Lonely Hitman, 1995)

Shishido, Jo: *Jingi Naki Tatakai: Kanketsuhen* (Battles without Honor and Humanity 5: The Final Episode, 1974), *Kurenai no Nagareboshi* (The Velvet Hustler, 1967), *Waga Jinsei Saiaku no Toki* (The Most Terrible Time in My Life, 1993), *Yaju no Seishun* (Youth of the Beast, 1963)

Sugawara, Bunta: *Gendai Yakuza: Hitokiri Yota* (Street Mobster, 1972), *Jingi Naki Tatakai* (Battles without Honor and Humanity, 1973), *Jingi Naki Tatakai: Hiroshima Shito-hen* (Battles without Honor and Humanity 2: Fight to the Death at Hiroshima, 1973), *Jingi Naki Tatakai: Dairi Senso* (Battles without Honor and Humanity 3: Proxy War, 1973), *Jingi Naki Tatakai: Chojo Sakusen* (Battles without Honor and Humanity 4: High Tactics, 1974), *Jingi Naki Tatakai: Kanketsuhen* (Battles without Honor and Humanity 5: The Final Episode, 1974), *Nihon Kyokakuden: Shiraha no Sakazuki* (1967), *Nihon Boryokudan: Kumicho* (Japan Organized Crime Boss, 1969), *Shuraba ga Yuku* (The Carnage Comes, 1995), *Watashi no Grandpa* (My Grandpa, 2003), *Yakuza Keibatsushi: Lynch!* (A History of Yakuza Punishments: Lynch!, 1969), *Yamaguchi Gaiden Kyushu Shinko Sakusen* (The Tattooed Hitman, 1974)

Takahashi, Hideki: *Irezumi Ichidai* (One Generation of Tattoos, 1965), *Otoko no Monsho* (Symbol of a Man, 1963)

Takakura, Ken: *Abashiri Bangaichi* (A Man from Abashiri Prison, 1965), *Abashiri Bangaichi: Bokyohen* (A Man from Abashiri Prison: Going Home, 1965), *Hana to Arashi to Gang* (Flower and Storm and Gang, 1961), *Hibotan Bakuto: Hanafuda Shobu* (Red Peony Gambler: Flower Cards Match, 1969), *Jinsei Gekijo: Hishakaku* (Theater of Life: Hishakaku, 1963), *Jinsei Gekijo: Hishakaku to Kiratsune* (Theater of Life: Hishakaku and Kiratsune, 1968), *Juichinin no Gang* (Eleven Gangsters, 1963), *Kaoyaku* (Boss, 1965), *Narazumono* (The Untamed, 1964), *Nihon Kyokaku-den: Naniwahen* (1965), *Nihon Kyokakuden: Shiraha no Sakazuki* (1967), *Showa Zankyoden: Shinde Moraimasu* (Remnants of Chivalry in the Showa Era: I Want You to Die, 1970), *Tokyo Gang tai Hong Kong Gang* (Tokyo Gang versus Hong Kong Gang, 1964), *Yakuza, The* (1975)

Takenaka, Naoto: *Chinpira* (Chinpira/Two Punks, 2000), *Freeze Me* (2000), *Gonin* (1995), *Kyohansha* (Partners in Crime, 1999)

Takeuchi, Riki: *Blood* (1998), *Dead or Alive: Hanzaisha* (Dead or Alive, 1999), *Gokudo no Onnatachi: Kejime* (Gang Wives: Decision, 1998), *Gokudo Sengokushi Fudo* (Fudoh: The New Generation, 1996), *Jitsuroku Ando Noboru Outlaw-den: Rekka* (Deadly Outlaw: Rekka, 2002), *Nobody* (1994), *Tokyo Mafia: Yakuza Wars* (1995), *Yakuza Way, The* (1998)

Takigawa, Yumi: *Jingi no Hakaba* (Graveyard of Honor, 1975)

Tanba, Tetsuro: *Abashiri Bangaichi* (A Man from Abashiri Prison, 1965), *Bakuto Kaisanshiki* (Gambler's Dispersion, 1968), *Gang tai G-men* (Gang versus G-men, 1962), *Jingi Naki Tatakai: Dairi Senso* (Battles without Honor and Humanity 3: Proxy War, 1973), *Jitsuroku Ando Noboru Outlaw-den: Rekka* (Deadly Outlaw: Rekka, 2002), *Narazumono* (The Untamed, 1964), *Shin Jingi no Hakaba* (Graveyard of Honor, 2002), *Tokyo Gang tai Hong Kong Gang* (Tokyo Gang versus Hong Kong Gang, 1964)

Tsuruta, Koji: *Ankokugai no Kaoyaku* (The Big Boss, 1959), *Bakuchiuchi Socho Tobaku* (Big Gambling Ceremony, 1968), *Bakuto Gaijin Butai* (Sympathy for the Underdog, 1971), *Bakuto Kaisanshiki* (Gambler's Dispersion, 1968), *Gang tai G-men* (Gang versus G-men, 1962), *Hana to Arashi to Gang* (Flower and Storm and Gang, 1961), *Hibotan Bakuto: Oinochi Itadakimasu* (Red Peony Gambler: Death to the Wicked, 1971), *Jinsei Gekijo: Hishakaku* (Theater of Life: Hishakaku, 1963), *Jinsei Gekijo: Hishakaku to Kiratsune* (Theater of Life: Hishakaku and Kiratsune, 1968), *Juichinin no Gang* (Eleven Gangsters, 1963), *Kaoyaku* (Boss, 1965), *Meiji Kyokakuden: Sandai Shumei* (Blood of Revenge, 1965), *Nihon Kyokakuden: Naniwahen* (1965), *Nihon Boryokudan: Kumicho* (Japan Organized Crime Boss, 1969), *Tokyo Gang tai Hong Kong Gang* (Tokyo Gang versus Hong Kong Gang, 1964)

Toyokawa, Etsushi: *No Way Back: Toso Yugi* (No Way Back, 1995), *Otokotachi no Kaita E* (The Man with Two Hearts, 1996), *Shin Jingi Naki Tatakai* (Another Battle, 2000)

Umemiya, Tatsuo: *Gang tai G-men* (Gang versus G-men, 1962), *Jingi Naki Tatakai* (Battles without Honor and Humanity, 1973), *Jingi Naki Tatakai: Dairi Senso* (Battles without Honor and Humanity 3: Proxy War, 1973), *Jingi Naki Tatakai: Chojo Sakusen* (Battles without Honor and Humanity 4: High Tactics, 1974), *Jingi no Hakaba* (Graveyard of Honor, 1975), *Jinsei Gekijo: Hishakaku* (Theater of Life: Hishakaku, 1963), *Juichinin no Gang* (Eleven Gangsters, 1963), *Yakuza no Hakaba: Kuchinashi no Hana* (Yakuza Burial: Jasmine Flower, 1976), *Yamaguchi Gaiden Kyushu Shinko Sakusen* (The Tattooed Hitman, 1974)

Wakao, Ayako: *Karakkaza Yaro* (Afraid to Die, 1960)

Wakayama, Tomisaburo: *Bakuchiuchi Socho Tobaku* (Big Gambling Ceremony, 1968), *Bakuto Gaijin Butai* (Sympathy for the Underdog, 1971), *Choeki Juhachinen* (Sentence: Eighteen Years, 1967), *Hibotan Bakuto: Hanafuda Shobu* (Red Peony Gambler: Flower Cards Match, 1969), *Hibotan Bakuto: Oinochi Itadakimasu* (Red Peony Gambler: Death to the Wicked, 1971), *Nihon Boryokudan: Kumicho* (Japan Organized Crime Boss, 1969)

Watari, Tetsuya: *Burai Yori Daikanbu* (Gangster VIP, 1968), *Jingi no Hakaba* (Graveyard of Honor, 1975),

Kurenai no Nagareboshi (The Velvet Hustler, 1967), *Tokyo Nagaremono* (Tokyo Drifter, 1966), *Yakuza no Hakaba: Kuchinashi no Hana* (Yakuza Burial: Jasmine Flower, 1976)

Watase, Tsunehiko: *Jingi Naki Tatakai: Dairi Senso* (Battles without Honor and Humanity 3: Proxy War, 1973), *Shiawase ni Naro ne* (Let's Get Happy, 1998), *Yamaguchi Gaiden Kyushu Shinko Sakusen* (The Tattooed Hitman, 1974)

Yakusho, Koji: *Kamikaze Taxi* (1995), *Kizuna* (Ties, 1998)

SUBJECT GUIDE

Edo Era (pre-1868)

Chuji Tabi Nikki (Diary of Chuji's Travels, 1927)

Kunisada Chuji (1958)

Kutsukake Tokijiro (1929)

Matatabi (The Wanderers, 1973)

Oedo Gonin Otoko (Five Men from Edo, 1951)

Wakaki Hi no Jirocho (The Young Days of Jirocho, 1962)

Zatoichi Monogatari (The Tale of Zatoichi, 1962)

Meiji Era to Early Showa Era (1868–1945)

Akumyo (Tough Guy, 1961)

Bakuchiuchi Socho Tobaku (Big Gambling Ceremony, 1968)

Bakuto Kaisanshiki (Gambler's Dispersion, 1968)

Hana to Doto (Flower and the Angry Waves, 1964)

Heitai Yakuza (Hoodlum Soldier, 1965)

Hibotan Bakuto: Hanafuda Shobu (Red Peony Gambler: Flower Cards Match, 1969)

Hibotan Bakuto: Oinochi Itadakimasu (Red Peony Gambler: Death to the Wicked, 1971)

Irezumi Ichidai (One Generation of Tattoos, 1965)

Jinsei Gekijo: Hishakaku (Theater of Life: Hishakaku, 1963)

Jinsei Gekijo: Hishakaku to Kiratsune (Theater of Life: Hishakaku and Kiratsune, 1968)

Kanto Mushuku (Kanto Wanderer, 1963)

Meiji Kyokakuden: Sandai Shumei (Blood of Revenge, 1965)

Nihon Kyokakuden: Naniwahen (1965)

Nihon Kyokakuden: Shiraha no Sakazuki (1967)

Otoko no Monsho (Symbol of a Man, 1963)

Showa Zankyoden: Shinde Moraimasu (Remnants of Chivalry in the Showa Era: I Want You to Die, 1970)

Waka Oyabun (Young Boss, 1965)

Zankyo (Remnants of Chivalry, 1999)

Postwar Period (1945–1975)

Abashiri Bangaichi (A Man from Abashiri Prison, 1965)

Abashiri Bangaichi: Bokyohen (A Man from Abashiri Prison: Going Home, 1965)

Ankokugai no Kaoyaku (The Big Boss, 1959)

Bakuto Gaijin Butai (Sympathy for the Underdog, 1971)

Burai Yori Daikanbu (Gangster VIP, 1968)

Choeki Juhachinen (Sentence: Eighteen Years, 1967)

Gang tai G-men (Gang versus G-men, 1962)

Gendai Yakuza: Hitokiri Yota (Street Mobster, 1972)

Hana to Arashi to Gang (Flower and Storm and Gang, 1961)

Jingi Naki Tatakai (Battles without Honor and Humanity, 1973)

Jingi Naki Tatakai: Hiroshima Shitohen (Battles without Honor and Humanity 2: Fight to the Death at Hiroshima, 1973)

Jingi Naki Tatakai: Dairi Senso (Battles without Honor and Humanity 3: Proxy War, 1973)

Jingi Naki Tatakai: Chojo Sakusen (Battles without Honor and Humanity 4: High Tactics, 1974)

Jingi Naki Tatakai: Kanketsuhen (Battles without Honor and Humanity 5: The Final Episode, 1974)

Jingi no Hakaba (Graveyard of Honor, 1975)

Jitsuroku Ando Gumi Gaiden: Garo no Okite (The True History of the Ando Gang: Rules of the Starving Wolf, 2002)

Juichinin no Gang (Eleven Gangsters, 1963)

Kaoyaku (Boss, 1965)

Karakkaza Yaro (Afraid to Die, 1960)

Kawaita Hana (Pale Flower, 1964)

Kurenai no Nagareboshi (The Velvet Hustler, 1967)

Narazumono (The Untamed, 1964)

Nihon Boryokudan: Kumicho (Japan Organized Crime Boss, 1969)

Shuraba no Ningengaku (The Anthropology of a Fight Scene, 1993)

Tokyo Gang tai Hong Kong Gang (Tokyo Gang versus Hong Kong Gang, 1964)

Tokyo Nagaremono (Tokyo Drifter, 1966)

Yaju no Seishun (Youth of the Beast, 1963)

Yakuza no Hakaba: Kuchinashi no Hana (Yakuza Burial: Jasmine Flower, 1976)

Yamaguchi Gaiden Kyushu Shinko Sakusen (The Tattooed Hitman, 1974)

Yoidore Tenshi (Drunken Angel, 1948)

Women and the Gangs

Asu Naki Machikado (End of Our Own Real, 1997)

Bo no Kanashimi (Hard-Head Fool, 1994)

Freeze Me (2000)

Gendai Yakuza: Hitokiri Yota (Street Mobster, 1972)

Gokudo Kuro Shakai Rainy Dog (Rainy Dog, 1997)

Gokudo no Ane: Reiko (Gang Lady: Reiko, 1994)

Gokudo no Onnatachi (Gang Wives, 1986)

Gokudo no Onnatachi: Kejime (Gang Wives: Decision, 1998)

Hibotan Bakuto: Hanafuda Shobu (Red Peony Gambler: Flower Cards Match, 1969)

Hibotan Bakuto: Oinochi Itadakimasu (Red Peony Gambler: Death to the Wicked, 1971)

Jingi no Hakaba (Graveyard of Honor, 1975)

Jinsei Gekijo: Hishakaku (Theater of Life: Hishakaku, 1963)

Juichinin no Gang (Eleven Gangsters, 1963)

Karakkaza Yaro (Afraid to Die, 1960)

Kawaita Hana (Pale Flower, 1964)

Kurenai no Nagareboshi (The Velvet Hustler, 1967)

Kuro no Tenshi, Vol. 1 (Black Angel, Vol. 1, 1998)

Kutsukake Tokijiro (1929)

Level (1994)

Meiji Kyokakuden: Sandai Shumei (Blood of Revenge, 1965)

Minazuki (Everyone's a Moon, 1999)

Minbo no Onna (The Gentle Art of Japanese Extortion, 1992)

Onibi (The Fire Within, 1997)

Ryuji (1983)

Shiawase ni Naro ne (Let's Get Happy, 1998)

Shin Jingi no Hakaba (Graveyard of Honor, 2002)

Shin Kanashiki Hitman (Another Lonely Hitman, 1995)

Showa Zankyoden: Shinde Moraimasu (Remnants of Chivalry in the Showa Era: I Want You to Die, 1970)

Comic Takes

Adrenaline Drive (1999)

Hana to Arashi to Gang (Flower and Storm and Gang, 1961)

Katte ni Shiyagare!! Godatsu Keikaku (Suit Yourself or Shoot Yourself: Extortion Plot 1, 1995)

Keisho Sakazuki (Succession Ceremony, 1992)

Kishiwada Shonen Gurentai (Boys, Be Ambitious, 1996)

Koroshiya Ichi (Ichi the Killer, 2001)

Matatabi (The Wanderers, 1973)

Minbo no Onna (The Gentle Art of Japanese Extortion, 1992)

Shiawase ni Naro ne (Let's Get Happy, 1998)

Tokyo Nagaremono (Tokyo Drifter, 1966)

Unlucky Monkey (1998)

Wild Life (1997)

Yaju no Seishun (Youth of the Beast, 1963)

Punks

Asu Naki Machikado (End of Our Own Real, 1997)

Chinpira (1996)

Chinpira (Chinpira/Two Punks, 2000)

Gorotsuki (Tough Guys, 1992)

Kids Return (1996)

Kishiwada Shonen Gurentai (Boys, Be Ambitious, 1996)

PornoStar (1999)

International Connections

American Yakuza (1994)

Bakuto Gaijin Butai (Sympathy for the Underdog, 1971)

Blood (1998)

Brother (2000)

Fuyajo (Sleepless Town, 1998)

Gokudo Kuro Shakai Rainy Dog (Rainy Dog, 1997)

Jingi Naki Tatakai (Battles without Honor and Humanity, 1973)

Kamikaze Taxi (1995)

Kuro no Tenshi, Vol. 1 (Black Angel, Vol. 1, 1998)

Kyohansha (Partners in Crime, 1999)

Mukokuseki no Otoko: Chi no Shukaku (Pinocchio: A Man without Nationality, 1997)

Narazumono (The Untamed, 1964)

Nihon Kuroshakai Ley Lines (Ley Lines, 1999)

No Way Back: Toso Yugi (No Way Back, 1995)

Shin Jingi Naki Tatakai (Another Battle, 2000)

Shinjuku Kuro Shakai China Mafia Senso (Shinjuku Triad Society, 1995)

Tokyo Gang tai Hong Kong Gang (Tokyo Gang versus Hong Kong Gang, 1964)

Yakuza, The (1975)

Yakuza Way, The (1998)

Crossing Genres (Horror, SF)

A Homansu (1986)

Dead or Alive: Hanzaisha (Dead or Alive, 1999)

Freeze Me (2000)

Fukushu: Kienai Kizu Ato (The Revenge: The Scar that Never Fades, 1997)

Full Metal Gokudo (Full Metal Yakuza , 1997)

Gokudo Sengokushi Fudo (Fudoh: The New Generation, 1996)

Koroshiya Ichi (Ichi the Killer, 2001)

Otokotachi no Kaita E (The Man with Two Hearts, 1996)

Tokyo Nagaremono (Tokyo Drifter, 1966)

Yakuza Keibatsushi: Lynch! (A History of Yakuza Punishments: Lynch!, 1969)

Loners and Outsiders

A Homansu (1986)

Akumyo (Tough Guy, 1961)

Abashiri Bangaichi: Bokyohen (A Man from Abashiri Prison: Going Home, 1965)

Bo no Kanashimi (Hard-Head Fool, 1994)

Brother (2000)

Gedo (The Outer Way, 1998)

Gendai Yakuza: Hitokiri Yota (Street Mobster, 1972)

Gokudo Kuro Shakai Rainy Dog (Rainy Dog, 1997)

Gonin (1995)

Heitai Yakuza (Hoodlum Soldier, 1965)

Jingi no Hakaba (Graveyard of Honor, 1975)

Jitsuroku Ando Gumi Gaiden: Garo no Okite (The True History of the Ando Gang: Rules of the Starving Wolf, 2002)

Karakkaza Yaro (Afraid to Die, 1960)

Kizuna (Ties, 1998)

Koroshiya Ichi (Ichi the Killer, 2001)

Kutsukake Tokijiro (Kutsukake Tokijiro, 1929)

Minazuki (Everyone's a Moon, 1999)

No Way Back: Toso Yugi (No Way Back, 1995)

Onibi (The Fire Within, 1997)

Ryuji (1983)

Shin Kanashiki Hitman (Another Lonely Hitman, 1995)

Shinjuku Yokubo Tantei (The Hungry Shinjuku Detective, 1994)

3-4 X Jugatsu (Boiling Point, 1990)

Tokyo Nagaremono (Tokyo Drifter, 1966)

Yaju Shisubeshi: Fukushuhen (The Beast Must Die: Revenge, 1997)

Yoidore Tenshi (Drunken Angel, 1948)

Yakuza no Hakaba: Kuchinashi no Hana (Yakuza Burial: Jasmine Flower, 1976)

Zatoichi Monogatari (The Tale of Zatoichi, 1962)

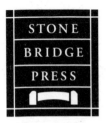

The Anime Encyclopedia

A Guide to Japanese Animation Since 1917

BY JONATHAN CLEMENTS AND HELEN MCCARTHY

This richly detailed guide is required reading for every fan, collector, and moviegoer. Covering more than 80 years of anime history and over 2,000 titles with critical finesse and authority, it is the most comprehensive guide in any language to the entertainment universe that is rapidly winning new audiences and influencing creative cultures far beyond its native shores. With titles in English and Japanese, lists of key creatives (directors, writers, composers, studios), and parental advisories. Fully indexed and cross-referenced.

576 pp, 7 x 9", paper, 100+ b/w photos
ISBN 1-880656-64-7, $24.95

Animation on DVD

The Ultimate Guide

ANDY MANGELS

This is the first authoritative guide to animated films on DVD. It reviews 1,600+ films, everything from early-20th-century works to Disney, Warner Bros., and cutting-edge digital CGI. Included are foreign films, major hits like *Batman* and *Shrek*, and hundreds of Japanese anime releases, plus a separate section on mature-themed material like *Fritz the Cat* and *Heavy Metal*. Entries include storylines, reviews, history, key personnel, and ratings, plus details on DVD-only materials like storyboards, Easter eggs, and production shorts. An invaluable resource for film buffs, parents, and libraries. Illustrated with DVD covers; fully indexed.

600 pp, 7 x 9", paper, 1,600+ b/w photos
ISBN 1-880656-68-X, $24.95

Anime Explosion!

*The What? Why? & Wow!
of Japanese Animation*

PATRICK DRAZEN

Written for fans, culture watchers, and perplexed outsiders, this is an engaging tour of the anime megaverse, from older arts and manga traditions to the works of modern directors like Miyazaki and Otomo. At the end of the book are essays on 15 of fandom's favorite anime, including *Evangelion, Escaflowne, Sailor Moon*, and *Patlabor*.

385 pp, 6 x 9", paper, 100+ b/w images
ISBN 1-880656-72-8, $18.95

Dreamland Japan

Writings on Modern Manga

FREDERIK L. SCHODT

A collection of insightful essays on the current state of the manga universe, the best artists, the major themes and magazines, plus what it means for the future of international visual culture. By the author of the acclaimed *Manga! Manga! The World of Japanese Comics*.

360 pp, 6 x 9", paper, 8 pp in color, 100+ b/w illustrations
ISBN 1-880656-23-X, $19.95